William Penn

William Penn

A Life

ANDREW R. MURPHY

OXFORD
UNIVERSITY PRESS

OXFORD
UNIVERSITY PRESS

Oxford University Press is a department of the University of Oxford. It furthers the University's objective of excellence in research, scholarship, and education by publishing worldwide. Oxford is a registered trade mark of Oxford University Press in the UK and certain other countries.

Published in the United States of America by Oxford University Press
198 Madison Avenue, New York, NY 10016, United States of America.

Library of Congress Cataloging-in-Publication Data
Names: Murphy, Andrew R., 1967– author.
Title: William Penn : a life / Andrew R. Murphy.
Description: New York : Oxford University Press, 2018. |
Includes bibliographical references and index.
Identifiers: LCCN 2018016591 (print) | LCCN 2018017065 (ebook) |
ISBN 9780190234256 (updf) | ISBN 9780190234263 (epub) |
ISBN 9780190234249 (hardback)
Subjects: LCSH: Penn, William, 1644–1718. |
Pioneers—Pennsylvania—Biography. | Quakers—Pennsylvania—Biography. |
Pennsylvania—History—Colonial period, ca. 1600–1775. |
Great Britain—Politics and government—1660–1688. |
BISAC: BIOGRAPHY & AUTOBIOGRAPHY / Religious. |
BIOGRAPHY & AUTOBIOGRAPHY / Historical. |
HISTORY / Europe / Great Britain.
Classification: LCC F152.2 (ebook) | LCC F152.2 .M875 2018 (print) |
DDC 974.802092 [B]—dc23
LC record available at https://lccn.loc.gov/2018016591

1 3 4 5 7 9 8 6 4 2

Printed by Sheridan Books, Inc., United States of America

For Pete and Sam, who love Philadelphia

CONTENTS

ACKNOWLEDGMENTS

As a young boy making my way through the public school system in Bucks County, Pennsylvania, I grew up surrounded by William Penn. He cast a long shadow, both literally and figuratively: in the statue atop Philadelphia City Hall, and more broadly in the culture of the place. As time went on and my interest in the history of religious liberty in England and America deepened, I became further convinced that Penn was a figure whose life and political career deserved far more study than historians of political thought, like myself, had thus far given them. In publishing *Liberty, Conscience, and Toleration: The Political Thought of William Penn* several years ago, I aimed to rectify that lacuna, at least in part. But I had also long been convinced about the need for a new biography of Penn that incorporated the entirety of Penn's numerous publications as well as his private papers and correspondence. I hope now to have provided that work.

William Penn has been in the making for many years, and over the course of those years—as my family, friends, and colleagues will readily attest—I have talked about William Penn with anyone who would listen (and many who wouldn't). Some of these conversations were brief one-offs, while others stretched over months and years. But each one helped me better understand, in some way, Penn's importance in both historical and contemporary terms. Trying to come up with a list that is anywhere near comprehensive has been daunting, and no doubt I will omit someone(s). That said, I am grateful for insights offered in conversations or correspondence (or both) with a host of colleagues: Steve Angell, Teresa Bejan, Alastair Bellany, Jane Calvert, John Coffey, Ben Pink Dandelion, Jim Farr, Suzanne Forbes, Jason Frank, Mark Goldie, David Gutterman, Evan Haefeli, Mark Hall, Anna Hellier, Ben Kaplan, Susan Liebell, Mike Lienesch, Howard Lubert, Diego Lucci, Maxine Lurie, Christie Maloyed, Emily Mann, John Marshall, Rob Martin, Lisa Miller, Lily Milroy, Hiram Morgan, Luke Pecoraro, Dan Richter, Jessica Roney, Peter Silver, Quentin Skinner,

Manfred Svensson, John Smolenski, Scott Sowerby, Abram van Engen, Adrian Weimer, David Williams, Joanne Wright, and Karin Wulf. Chris Beneke read an earlier draft of the entire manuscript and offered a stunning combination of overarching comments and specific stylistic suggestions, and the final product has benefited from his careful and thorough feedback.

Over the years, audiences at a wide range of institutions have offered helpful comments and questions about various aspects of Penn's life and my study of it. In addition to the supportive intellectual atmosphere provided by my colleagues in the Department of Political Science and at the Eagleton Institute of Politics at Rutgers, conferences and symposia sponsored by Grove City College, the McNeil Center for Early American Studies, the Omohundro Institute of Early American History and Culture, Pennsbury Manor, Yale University, the Rothermere American Institute (University of Oxford), Rutgers University, the University of Southampton, the University of Navarro, the University of Utah, George Fox University, the Newport (RI) Historical Society, the University of Cambridge, Texas A & M University, Roger Williams University, and the Universidad de los Andes have provided venues for thoughtful conversation about Penn and his world. An invitation to speak at "The World of William Penn: Toleration and Migration," a wonderful conference on Penn's time in Ireland organized in September 2016 by Hiram Morgan and Ruth Canning at University College Cork, brought home to me the critical importance of Ireland and County Cork in the genesis of Penn's political thought; and preparing the Quaker Studies Research Association's George Richardson Lecture during spring 2018, as this book went to press, helped crystallize many of the thoughts I offer in the Epilogue about Penn's overarching historical importance.

I also benefited from queries offered by commentators and audience members at meetings of the Association for Political Theory, the American Political Science Association, the International Society for Intellectual History, and the Society of Early Americanists. And I was the beneficiary of the collegial atmosphere provided by my colleagues in the 2015–2016 "Ethical Subjects" seminar cohort at the Rutgers Center for Historical Analysis, directed by Seth Koven and Judith Surkis; and at numerous events sponsored by the Rutgers British Studies Center, particularly its generous sponsorship of "The Worlds of William Penn," a November 2015 conference held at Rutgers and devoted to Penn's multifaceted career.

One of the most gratifying aspects of this project has been discovering that interest in the life and times of William Penn is hardly confined to academic audiences. Speaking at Friends Meetings—in both New Jersey (Princeton, New Brunswick) and England (Jordans, Woodbroke)—and community programs at institutions like the Princeton Public Library have been particularly meaningful. I've also benefited greatly from my association with Pennsbury Manor, whose director, Doug Miller, possesses a zeal for all things Penn that rivals my own, and who oversees a dedicated team of staff and volunteers who keep Penn's memory alive for future generations.

Current and former graduate students have patiently endured my Penn obsession, and helped move the project toward completion in a number of ways. Thanks go especially to Greg Zucker, who read and commented on the entire manuscript, and who traipsed around Greater London with me, camera in hand, during July 2016; as well as to Michael Richards and Sarah Morgan Smith, whose work on *Liberty, Conscience, and Toleration* also assisted a great deal on this book. The Aresty Research Center at Rutgers has provided generous support for a number of undergraduate research assistants over the years, including Kristen Hamilton, Jack Landry, Steven Mercadente, Jeff Niesz, Lahari Sangitha, Justin Schulberg, and Chir Wei Stephanie Yuen.

Although *The Papers of William Penn* is available on microfilm—and the full, fourteen-reel collection is owned by Rutgers University Libraries, thanks to the efforts of the indefatigable Tom Glynn, history and political science librarian at Rutgers's Alexander Library—numerous other archives and archivists have been extraordinarily helpful in granting me access to consult Penn-related materials among their collections. Without the kind assistance of all of these individuals and institutions, the account of Penn's life offered in this book would be deeply impoverished. Thanks to Frances Bellis at Lincoln's Inn; Adey Grummet at All Hallows by the Tower, London; Jennifer Milligan and Tabitha Driver at the Library of the Religious Society of Friends (Friends House, London); Anna Petre of the Oxford University Archives; Judith Curthoys at Christ Church College, Oxford; and Christopher Moriarty at Friends Historical Library, Dublin. More generally, research staff at the Bodleian Library, the Cork City and County Archives, the Cambridge University Library, the Historical Society of Pennsylvania, and the Library Company of Philadelphia were unfailingly helpful. I was welcomed to Jordans Friends Meeting by John and Sue Smithson, and shown around the Chigwell School by Gillian Punt. Everyone, without exception, gave generously of their time and expertise and I am profoundly grateful.

William Penn is my third book with Oxford University Press, and my second with editor extraordinaire Theo Calderara. I remain amazed at Theo's ability to combine big-picture advice about the craft of writing with sentence-level attention to syntax and punctuation, and to communicate it all in ways that are simultaneously critical and supportive. (That said, I fear there are still far too many semicolons and parentheses in the book. They are my responsibility, not his.) Drew Anderla at OUP also helped smooth the complicated process from manuscript to book in more ways than I can remember, and the entire Oxford team has been, once again, a joy to work with.

As mentioned above, I was born and raised in Pennsylvania, and I retain a warm affection for Penn's capital city and the vibrant story of American diversity that is part and parcel of its history. That story also reaches to my own family: Mom, Betsy, Matt, Jim, Dale, Veronica, Rachael, Caroline, Emma, Nick, Cassidy, and all the rest of the Murphys, Wislers, Angells, and McLeods. I continue to owe a debt of gratitude beyond words to Beth Angell for the daily gift of her presence. Thirty years now. We were so young.

Finally, I dedicate this book to my two sons, Peter and Sam. They have grown up with William Penn as a constant presence in their father's life (and thus, whether they liked it or not, in their own lives), and have borne that presence with good cheer and, I must admit, slightly bemused tolerance. They were boys when I began studying William Penn; they are now grown into wonderful young men. I'm afraid that I can't improve on Penn's own words, written more than 300 years ago to his own son: "I cannot love you better than I do."

Andrew Murphy
April 2018

GUIDE TO NOTES AND ABBREVIATIONS

The volume of primary source material cited in this book is extensive, and I have attempted to provide both complete bibliographic information on each source used as well as information allowing readers to locate those sources in the most accessible form possible.

The foundation of all direct information regarding Penn's life is the fourteen-reel microfilm edition of *The Papers of William Penn*, which was published in 1975 by the Historical Society of Pennsylvania. The microfilm Papers brought together and chronologically organized the Historical Society's extensive holdings of Penn material, and remains the most comprehensive resource for the study of Penn's life. I cite documents from this collection as *PWP* reel: frame, using standard Arabic numbers for the reel. Thus William Penn's letter to the Commissioners of the Navy is cited as:

> To the Commissioners of the Navy, December 31, 1670, *PWP* 1: 283.

And his letter from Logan:

> From James Logan, May 12, 1702, *PWP* 10: 202.

From that voluminous collection, an editorial team headed by Richard S. and Mary Maples Dunn selected and assembled a subset of documents, which were published in four print volumes (along with a fifth listing each edition of every published work authored by Penn) during the 1980s. These volumes represent the most accessible format in which most readers looking for a firsthand exposure to Penn's original documents are likely to find them. (They are also lavishly edited and extensively footnoted.) I cite them using Roman numerals for volume number, followed by page numbers. For example, Sir William Penn's last will is cited as:

Will of Sir William Penn, January 20, 1670, *PWP* I: 149.

And his letter to Robert Turner:

To Robert Turner, March 5, 1681, *PWP* II: 83.

Correspondence to or from William Penn is cited as To [name] or From [name]. For all other correspondence I indicate the name of both the correspondent and the recipient. Insofar as the five-volume print edition of Penn's *Papers* is held by most major libraries and still available for purchase, I refer to them whenever possible. Readers looking for a complete listing of the documents in the microfilm Papers can consult the "Calendar of Microfilmed WP Documents" found at the back of Volumes I–IV of the print *Papers*. The Notes contain abbreviated bibliographic information, and the Bibliography provides full information, on all works cited.

The two-volume *Collection of the Works of William Penn*, compiled by Joseph Besse and published in 1726, is cited in the Notes as *Works*.

Finally, the voluminous correspondence between Penn and his Pennsylvania secretary, James Logan, will be cited in the notes as *Penn-Logan*, volume: page. The full bibliographic information appears in the Bibliography under the title *Correspondence Between William Penn and James Logan*.

William Penn

Prologue

Fleet Prison, January 1708

By the time William Penn passed through its gates in January 1708, London's Fleet Prison had been housing prisoners—primarily debtors, like Penn himself—for more than half a millennium. The Fleet had been leveled by rebellious peasants who stormed London under the leadership of Wat Tyler during the Peasant Revolt of 1381, and again when it succumbed to London's Great Fire in 1666. Yet it was rebuilt each time, most recently welcoming prisoners again in January 1671 after a multiyear rebuilding effort following the fire.

Penn's arrest in 1708 provided the Fleet with only the most recent of its many high-profile residents. The prison's origins dated back to the twelfth century, and over the years it had hosted some of England's most celebrated prisoners. Prior to being burned at the stake, sixteenth-century Anglican bishop John Hooper spent eighteen months in the Fleet for opposing "Bloody" Queen Mary. The poet John Donne spent a brief time in the Fleet in early 1602, after marrying against the wishes of his powerful employer, Lord Keeper of the Great Seal Sir Thomas Egerton. (That Donne's bride was none other than Egerton's niece Anne no doubt made matters worse.) The irascible Puritan agitator William Prynne's *Histrio-mastix*, a thousand-page 1633 attack on stage plays, actresses, the magistrates who permitted them, and the spectators who viewed them, earned royal displeasure from a King who had enjoyed watching his queen perform at Court. Prynne was sent to the Fleet and later lost both his ears at the pillory. "Freeborn John" Lilburne, agitator for religious and political liberty, was imprisoned in 1638 for distributing unlicensed publications—not coincidentally, perhaps, one of Prynne's own—and whipped while being dragged behind an oxcart from the Fleet to the pillory at Westminster. He later thanked God (in verse) for sustaining him through his ordeal:

When from *Fleet-bridge* to *Westminster*, at *Carts Arsse* I was whipt,
Then thou with joy my soul upheldst, so that I never wept.

1

> Likewise when I on Pillory, in *Palace-yard* did stand,
> Then by thy help against my foes, I had the upper-hand.

After Parliament abolished the Court of Star Chamber, which had evolved under the Stuarts into a tool for prosecuting the monarchy's critics, in 1641, the Fleet became almost exclusively a facility for the confinement of debtors.[1]

Since the prison sat in a neighborhood outside the jurisdiction of the Bishop of London, it became home to a great deal of clandestine activity. "Fleet marriages," for example, provided couples with the opportunity to wed outside the purview of the church, without the required "banns" (declarations of intent read publicly in the local parish church before the marriage took place). Not all of these marriages were scandalous, but they did allow the parties to avoid excessive publicity around their nuptials. The Fleet became "the most popular and famous centre of clandestine marriage" in London— responsible for somewhere between 200,000 and 300,000 such marriages between 1694 and 1754—and "dominated the clandestine marriage market in London in the first half of the eighteenth century." The clandestine marriages persisted until the passage of the Marriage Act of 1753, which took effect the following year and targeted both the marriages themselves and the clergy who performed them.[2]

Over the course of its centuries-long history, not surprisingly, the Fleet (as well as the broader practice of confining debtors) had evoked its fair share of controversy. Many of these complaints, also not surprisingly, were raised by prisoners themselves. The common practice of delegating oversight of the prison's operations to the highest bidder created a situation rife with opportunities for corruption and abuse. In 1621, an anonymous author laid out nineteen charges against warden Alexander Harris, citing "extortions, oppressions, tyrannies, and excesses toward the lives, bodies, and goods of prisoners." Twenty-five years later, in his *Liberty vindicated against slavery*, Lilburne cited Magna Carta's guarantees of jury trial as evidence of the illegitimacy of imprisonment for debt. And two years after England's 1688 Revolution, London printer Moses Pitt opened his *Cry of the oppressed* with a rhetorical flourish by insisting that

> the ten first persecutions under Nero . . . the massacre at Paris, the persecutions of the poor Protestants of the valleys of the Piedmont, the rebellion of Ireland, and the tyranny and cruelties at this time exercised by that monster of France [Louis XIV], against his poor innocent Huguenot subjects, do not exceed the barbarities practiced at this day in our own nation, against poor imprisoned debtors.

Not only was imprisonment for debt cruel and corrupt, Pitt argued, but it was counterproductive. Debtors were far more valuable, to their creditors as well as to society, when they were free to resolve their financial difficulties. Eventually James Oglethorpe, who went on to found Georgia in 1732—the first British colony chartered in North America since William Penn's own, five decades earlier—would lead a 1729 parliamentary inquiry into conditions at the Fleet after a friend who had been imprisoned there died of smallpox.[3]

* * *

William Penn was a prime candidate for the Fleet. Despite his prominence as the son of a famed naval hero, a public spokesman for the Society of Friends (Quakers), an activist on behalf of religious toleration for Dissenters, and the founder of Pennsylvania, his chronic money problems stretched back for decades. He had been involved in American colonization for more than thirty years, beginning with his role mediating a dispute over the proprietorship of New Jersey in the mid-1670s and continuing through the attainment of his own colony in the early 1680s and two voyages to America (1682–1684 and 1699–1701). Despite recruiting hundreds of investors into the enterprise and undertaking an impressive promotional and sales campaign over the ensuing decades, he never realized the financial promise that American colonization dangled before his eyes. As one of the editors of Penn's *Papers* has put it, "the selling of Pennsylvania was a grand success all around—except for William Penn." Twenty years after his first voyage to America, Penn found himself deeper in debt than ever, this time to Bridget Ford, the widow of his longtime associate (and fellow Quaker) Philip Ford. Ford and Penn had worked closely together since the late 1660s, with Ford managing Penn's finances, handling land sales in Pennsylvania, and defending Penn against his enemies. During that time, Penn had signed a number of documents acknowledging his indebtedness to Ford, documents that he later admitted reading only cursorily, if at all.[4]

The legal battles had begun in earnest after Philip Ford's death in January 1702. Bridget Ford and her children claimed that, over the course of the 1680s and 1690s, Penn had transferred ownership of his American colony to Ford— and thus, as his heirs, to them—as collateral in lieu of repayment of his considerable debts, and had agreed to pay rent in exchange for retaining possession of the colony. Subsequently, they insisted, Penn had neither repaid them nor made the agreed-upon rent payments. They offered to sell him back his colony for the sum they deemed themselves owed by him: more than £11,000. Already deeply in debt to others, Penn possessed nothing remotely approaching this sum. Fortunately, he was able to persuade Bridget Ford not to probate the will (i.e., present it in court) as long as he worked toward payment, an arrangement that held for several years. But by late 1705, her patience had run out. She probated her husband's will and filed suit against Penn, claiming that she and her children were the rightful proprietors of Pennsylvania. In doing so she not only inflicted a public humiliation on Penn, but also evoked the wrath of Quakers, who disapproved of Friends using the civil courts for intra-Society disputes.

For his part, Penn claimed fraud and malfeasance, and insisted that he was the victim of unscrupulous associates who had taken advantage of both his kind and generous nature and his propensity for signing documents without carefully reading them. That the Fords were fellow Quakers only made the dispute more bitter. The case stretched on for several years, and hinged on a number of highly disputed amounts and accounting practices that Penn vigorously contested and the Fords just as vigorously defended. Finally, in November 1707, the Fords obtained a jury verdict against Penn on the rent payments, which set his debt at nearly £3,000. He had nowhere near that amount in ready money. When apprehended in early 1708 in front of London's Gracechurch Street Meetinghouse—one of the central hubs of London Quakerism, and the precise location where, nearly four decades earlier, a much younger William Penn had been arrested for preaching in the street, setting him on his path as a public advocate for liberty of conscience and propelling him to national fame—Penn refused to pay and instead surrendered. He was sent to the Fleet.

Confinement in the Fleet was not pleasant for Penn, although the situation could have been much worse. He was granted permission to lodge a block away, in rented rooms at the Old Bailey, near the famous courthouse of the same name. Having visited Penn in March 1708, Pennsylvania Quaker merchant and public officeholder Isaac Norris wrote to James Logan, Penn's secretary and representative in Pennsylvania, that Penn had "good lodgings" and "has meetings there, is often visited, and lives comfortably enough for the circumstances." (Norris then added, almost as an afterthought, "Their daughter Hannah is dead at Bristol.") Negotiations with the Fords continued while Penn remained under confinement at the Fleet, and a number of his fellow Quakers—eager to avoid the extended public embarrassment that the episode was causing—contributed funds to pay the Fords a settlement, which was finalized in October 1708. Released from the Fleet and with possession of Pennsylvania once again under his control, Penn nonetheless continued to face a very difficult financial future: he had been forced to borrow all but £1,000 of the £7,600 paid to the Fords. That his creditors were no longer the antagonistic Fords but a friendlier group of Quakers, who became trustees of his colony, was likely somewhat cold comfort. After all, according to the terms of their agreement, if Penn did not repay their money within two years, the trustees would assume possession of Pennsylvania. When it came to William Penn's finances, the more things changed, the more they stayed the same.[5]

* * *

How had William Penn's life come to this? How could the governor and proprietor of a major American colony, a former confidant and advisor to kings, and a spokesman for religious and political liberty known throughout Europe and America have fallen so far from the halls of power he once roamed? Penn's mythic status in the founding lore of his colony, to say nothing of the United States, which was declared into existence in his capital city more than fifty years after his death, has often obscured the tumultuous life he lived and the high hopes and crushing disappointments that accompanied his efforts. Furthermore, his profound Quaker commitments and his description of Pennsylvania as a "holy experiment" have tended to monopolize interpretations of the colony's early history. But as will become clear in the pages to come, the founder of Pennsylvania was a complex and multifaceted individual. Quakerism surely provided the bedrock of his identity from the moment he joined the Society of Friends in 1667, but William Penn's life is too complex to be viewed through only one lens.

To grasp the significance of the Fleet in William Penn's career requires us to look anew at the totality of his life in all its complexity. William Penn pursued political and religious liberty indefatigably, in ways that benefited thousands of Dissenters in England and America and across Europe. He passionately defended Quakers from the attacks of their many critics. He invested years of his life in pursuit of a utopian settlement in America where "sober people of all sorts" might build a common society across religious, ethnic, and social differences. He also engaged in petty feuds, displayed an inordinate capacity for self-pity, and nursed bitter grudges against those he deemed to have wronged him. He routinely mismanaged money and proved unwilling or unable to bring his expenses in line with his income. And in a final indignity, Penn was struck down by illness just as his efforts to give up control of his colony, which he blamed for his chronic financial difficulties and considered vilely ungrateful for all that he had done for it, promised to at last allow him to put his finances in order.[6]

A full telling of William Penn's life, then, will bring out the significance of a number of key developments: his momentous conversion experience at the age of twenty-three, which set his life on an entirely new trajectory; his intense involvement in the Quaker movement as well as the broader political struggle for religious toleration in early modern England; his securing of the charter for Pennsylvania and his two-year sojourn in America; his close relationship with King James II and the disastrous consequences of that relationship after the Revolution of 1688; his increasing alienation from his colony's government and eventual return to Pennsylvania after a sixteen-year absence; and his growing financial distress and physical infirmity during the early eighteenth century. For the final six years of William Penn's life, he was severely incapacitated as a result of a series of strokes, and his affairs were ably managed by his wife Hannah. Prior to that time, however, he played an outsized role in the religious and political controversies of his time. His eight months in the Fleet represent, on the one hand, the culmination of years of financial mismanagement and an inability to live within his means. On the other hand, however, they are just one small episode in a rich and eventful life.

1

Origins

In late 1670, a grieving twenty-five-year-old William Penn set out, along with his mother Margaret, to compose an epitaph for his father. Admiral Sir William Penn had passed away in mid-September of that year at age forty-nine, his body racked with gout and worn down from years at sea. The epitaph, inscribed on a monument that also featured the elder Penn's armor along with pennants that he had captured from Dutch warships, describes "Sir William Penn Knight, and sometimes General" as hailing from "the Penns of Penns-Lodge, in the County of Wilts, and those Penns of Penn, in the County of Bucks, and by his mother from the Gilberts in the county of Somerset, originally of Yorkshire." Although the pennants have been replaced with replicas, the monument remains to this day, mounted high on a wall in the west end of St. Mary Redcliffe, the Anglican parish church in Bristol where Sir William's body lies beneath the south aisle.[1]

By 1670, St. Mary Redcliffe had played a significant role in Penn family history. Sir William's parents, Giles Penn and Joan Gilbert, were married there in November 1600. Although Sir William had called London and the Essex village of Wanstead home for more than a decade before his death—and before that had spent time in Ireland and held a variety of naval commands—his body was laid to rest at St. Mary in honor of his request "to be buried . . . as near unto the body of my dear mother . . . as the same may conveniently be."[2]

Other than the fact that, as indicated in her son's epitaph, she hailed from the Gilberts of Somerset, little is known about Sir William's mother. We know far more about his father's family, though for an individual who would play such an outsized role in British and American public life, William Penn's ancestry remains tantalizingly unclear. The relationship between the two sets of Penns referenced in Sir William's memorial has never been conclusively established, but based on the language of the epitaph Sir William surely considered himself descended from both lines.

Buckinghamshire and the surrounding area, from which one group of Penns hailed, would play a significant role in the life of our William Penn, the admiral's son and founder of Pennsylvania. His first wedding took place in Chorleywood, just across the county line in neighboring Hertfordshire, and he lived for five years in nearby Rickmansworth. He visited the village of Penn Street, in the Buckinghamshire parish of Penn, with his future wife Gulielma Springett before leaving for Ireland in 1669. Jordans, where William, his two wives, and a number of his children would find their final resting place, lies in southeast Buckinghamshire, and during the eighteenth century his son Thomas would lay several of his own children to rest just a few miles away in the parish church of Penn. These three villages, so rich with Penn resonances, lie within a dozen miles of each other.[3]

The Penns of Buckinghamshire have been called "the most ancient and illustrious family of that name," and their roots reached back to 1066, when a "de la Penne" accompanied William the Conqueror to England and received a Buckinghamshire estate in return for services rendered. The Penns remained lords of that manor for centuries, and the French connection continued, with one John Penn receiving a knighthood from Edward III in recognition of his service in France. Such a connection with the Crown might explain why, during the sixteenth century, David Penn's wife Sibyl was reportedly summoned to Court to care for Henry VIII's children, the future monarchs Edward, Mary, and Elizabeth. But the connection to either William Penn or his father, Sir William, is less clear, and it is possible that they were simply mistaken about the relationship with these particular Penns.[4]

The connection with the Wiltshire Penns of Penn's Lodge, on the other hand, has been established beyond question. A direct line of descent links the William Penn buried in Minety parish church in 1591, his grandson Giles, and Giles's son William, the father of the founder. Named for its mint plants, Minety lay near the edge of Braden Forest in Wiltshire, just a few miles north of Penn's Lodge. Of this first William Penn, the man whom Penn's biographers call "William Penn of Minety," there is no shortage of mystery. According to some reports, he took holy orders as a young man and embarked upon the life of a monk at Glastonbury Abbey, only to find himself forced to start anew when Henry VIII dissolved the monasteries during the late 1530s. He has been described variously as a "small yeoman"; as warden of Braden Forest; as keeper of Penn's Lodge; or, more expansively, as "a person of social distinction," given his burial under the floor in front of the altar in the parish church. William Penn of Minety laid to rest at least one wife and a son before his own passing, as his will makes no mention of a wife but does make provisions for his grandchildren. He left £20 to each of them, and funds for their education to their mother Margaret, widow of his son (also named William).[5]

Tracing the Wiltshire Penn line back beyond William Penn of Minety, or ascertaining how the Wiltshire Penns got to Wiltshire, is nearly impossible. Perhaps some member of the family came east from Buckinghamshire. There may have been a Welsh connection, and William Penn himself is reported to have hinted at Welsh roots to some of his colonists. On board the *Canterbury* in 1699, on his second journey to Pennsylvania, he is said to have told a fellow passenger that "I am a Welshman myself." And twenty years before that purported conversation took place, he told Irish Quaker Robert Turner that, when initially asked what he would name his new colony, "I chose New Wales," before being rebuffed by the King's secretary, "a Welshman," and acquiescing to the King's professed desire to name the colony for Sir William. Or perhaps, as others have suggested, both the Buckinghamshire and the Wiltshire Penns hailed originally from Wales. But very little concrete evidence supports any of these speculations.[6]

* * *

Giles Penn, one of those grandchildren to whom William Penn of Minety left funds in 1591, quickly made his way west to Bristol and entered into an apprenticeship under the linen draper John Horte. In 1600, the same year that he married Joan Gilbert at St. Mary Redcliffe church, Giles completed his apprenticeship and was admitted to the "liberties of the city" as a cloth and textile merchant. Over the next two decades, Giles and Joan would have at least four children, and perhaps as many as seven. The youngest, the future Sir William, was born in 1621.[7]

Settling in Bristol would have made a great deal of sense for Giles, as that city was becoming an increasingly important center of English trade. By the end of the seventeenth century, as his grandson's American colony came to play an increasingly central role in the early British empire, Bristol had become, after London, "the preeminent Atlantic port in England . . . [whose] trade touched nearly every important international market." But even a century earlier, the city had developed into a thriving center for imports and exports, owing much of its prosperity to the rise of a merchant class composed of "traders who lived exclusively by their large-scale dealings in foreign commerce."[8] Into this growing network of traders and merchants came Giles Penn.

Although Sir William's memorial referred to his father as "Captain" Giles Penn—and although a legend has grown up, repeated by Sir William's biographer Granville Penn, that Giles served in the Royal Navy—no evidence exists to substantiate claims of a military career on Giles's part. He did, however, play an important part in the growth of English trade with the Mediterranean, North Africa, and the Levant during the 1630s. By the third decade of the seventeenth century, Giles Penn had plainly made a name for himself in Bristol and beyond. Records of a 1631 dispute over a shipment of iron to Tetuan, in present-day northern Morocco, bring to light the intriguing fact that Giles had brought back hawks from that city as a gift to King Charles I. Five years later, Giles attempted to get himself placed in charge of an expedition to combat "Moorish pirates" near Sallee (also in present-day Morocco). Disappointed at the slow pace of preparations for the expedition, and at having to watch others obtain command of a voyage for which he had laid out his own funds, Giles stressed his "knowledge of the people, their language, to read or answer their letters, or acquaintance with them," and urged that if he were not appointed to command the fleet that he at least be employed as a messenger or ambassador. That plea was apparently not successful either, as Giles later reminded royal officials that he had "expected some good place [with the expedition], but was omitted without any reward," and still later requested that he be appointed "agent or consul of Sallee and the kingdom of Fez." And in fact, in 1637, after two dozen merchants wrote to the King, calling Giles "a man well experienced in the language and customs of the said country," Charles appointed him to that post. Giles's death in 1656 (perhaps in Fez) makes it highly unlikely that his grandson would have had a personal relationship with him, though surely stories of his exploits would have circulated in the family.[9]

Both of Giles's sons would also pursue maritime careers: George, the elder, as a merchant in Spain, and William (our William Penn's father) in the Royal Navy. Over the course of the 1630s George settled in Spain, married a Catholic woman, and amassed a significant fortune. His fortunes took a dramatic turn for the worse in 1643, however, when he was arrested by officers of the Spanish Inquisition. George was excommunicated and taken to Seville, where he was imprisoned and tortured for more than three years. He was eventually publicly branded a heretic and accused of planning to abscond to England ("a land which of all others in the world overfloweth with all sorts of most damnable heresies and disobedience to the see of Rome"). His sentence included the confiscation of his fortune, in excess of £10,000, banishment from Spain, and divorce from his wife, who was then to be married to a Spaniard, "securing of her soul from my heretical suggestions," as he later wrote.[10]

George Penn would pursue his revenge against the Spaniards for the rest of his life. Despite the testimony of twelve London merchants, who offered "both eye and ear-witnesses of my misery" and who attested to his "honest dealing," George was unsuccessful in a later appeal to the Lord Protector, Oliver Cromwell's son Richard, for some recourse for his mistreatment and for a position that would allow him to put his knowledge and experience of Spain to the use of his home country. He renewed this request to King Charles II and was granted a position as envoy to Spain, only to die in 1664 before he could take up the post. But he was present to some extent in his brother's life. The Penns' neighbor and Sir William's colleague at the Navy Office, famed diarist Samuel Pepys, reported sharing a meal with George Penn in late September 1661, and described him as "a merry man," who, not surprisingly, "sp[oke] Spanish very well." It seems to have been a very merry night, with Pepys recounting that "at dinner and supper I [drank] . . . so much wine, that . . . I was almost foxed, and my head ached all night." The admiral's son, too, kept alive the memory of his uncle's treatment at the hands of the Spanish, unsuccessfully petitioning the Crown for compensation from the Spanish during negotiations to end the War of Spanish Succession, nearly seventy years after George's expulsion from Spain.[11]

* * *

Giles and Joan's youngest son, William, the father of our William Penn, was, as a young boy, "educated under [Giles's] own eye, for the sea-service," and "serv[ed] with his father . . . in various mercantile voyages to the northern seas and to the Mediterranean." William would not have grown up with the expectation of a significant inheritance, that being reserved for his older brother, and thus the navy would have represented a natural path for him to pursue. He began his naval service in the late 1630s under William Batten, who would serve the parliamentary cause during the early years of the Civil Wars, go over to the King's side by the end of the 1640s, and be named Surveyor of the Navy after the Restoration. Batten and Penn would remain close for the next three decades. Despite Giles's entreaties that his son pursue a mercantile career, William wrote to his father in 1644, with the country in the grip of a civil war, that "If God ever send a peace, an honourable peace, peace and truth on this our nation, I may then, if I continue the sea, think of a Levant voyage." In the meantime, the navy would be his route to both personal advancement and national service, and his naval career would reward him—and ultimately his son—handsomely.[12]

Sir William Penn's epitaph claims that he attained the rank of captain, his first recorded commission, at twenty-one. Other sources suggest that Captain Penn began his steady rise through the ranks of the navy at the age of twenty-three, when he was appointed to the command of the *Fellowship*, seized from royalist forces a year earlier. Like all the major institutions of English society, the navy had been swept up in the growing conflict between king and Parliament during the 1630s and early 1640s. Though it seems an overstatement to claim, as Granville Penn did, that "the great vital questions, of domestic peace or civil war, were brought at length to turn upon the single hinge, of the appointment to the chief command of the navy of England," naval command was surely one of the significant points of contention between the two sides. Parliament deeply distrusted Sir John Penington, the King's choice to command the fleet, and agitated for the Earl of Warwick to be named Lord High Admiral instead.[13]

Captain Penn's wife Margaret—our William's mother—did not achieve her husband's renown, but what we know of her life before the birth of her eldest son makes clear that she, too, lived through extraordinary times and encountered first-hand the combustible mix of religion, politics, and violence at the heart of early modern European history. Granville Penn refers to Margaret simply as the "daughter of John Jasper, of Rotterdam." Pepys, with characteristic cattiness, described her as "a well-looked, fat, short, old Dutchwoman . . . that hath been heretofore pretty handsome." Never one to miss a chance to undercut his rival, he also noted that Margaret "hath more wit than her husband." (She has also been described, even more implausibly, as an "unworldly, speculative, dreamy German.") Further inquiry reveals a far more interesting story. Margaret's parents, John Jasper and his wife Alet (or Marie), were indeed Dutch, but had been naturalized in Ballycase, County Clare, Ireland, sometime during the mid-1630s. So although Dutch in one sense—her birth surely predated her parents' Irish naturalization—Margaret had also spent a number of years, possibly as much as a decade, in Ireland, marrying Nicholas (or Nicasius) van der Schuren, a Dutch émigré.[14]

Margaret's first marriage was to end tragically. Nicholas apparently traveled to Ireland to escape one religio-political conflict, the Thirty Years' War, only to meet his end in another: the Ulster uprising of 1641, in which Catholic Irish gentry rose against the English administration in an attempted coup that soon devolved into a far bloodier conflict. Graphic reports of atrocities committed by Irish Catholics began to reach London almost immediately. Many Irish Protestants fled to the protection of city walls in Cork, Dublin, or Derry, but others, like the Jaspers, set out for London instead. Tales of Catholic savagery in Ireland fanned the flames of virulent English anti-Catholicism and added to the growing strain between king and Parliament. By 1642 Margaret had left Ireland for England with her parents, and shortly thereafter she met the young naval officer William Penn. They were married on June 6, 1643, at St. Martin's Church in Ludgate, London. The date of the marriage has occasioned some controversy among Penn's biographers, as Pepys reported attending an anniversary party at the Penn home on January 6, 1662, at which "eighteen mince pies" were consumed, "the number of years that he hath been married." But the June date is by now firmly established.[15]

The young couple resided on Tower Hill, just northwest of the Tower of London, within the jurisdiction known as Tower Liberty. They lived in a small house "built with brick," consisting of a "parlor and kitchen with a divided [cellar] underneath." Upstairs were "two fair chambers," and "in the second story two more chambers and two garrets over the same." The house had a small yard as well. It was to be the first home of William Penn.[16]

According to the ship's journal, the *Fellowship* set sail from the Royal Navy Yard at Deptford, London at 6 a.m. on October 12, 1644. But other reports have the captain joining his ship a month later, after the *Fellowship* joined the rest of the fleet in the Downs, off the Kent coast, where the English fleet often gathered before setting sail. Doing so would have allowed him to be present for the birth and baptism of his first child, born on October 14, named for his father and those many William Penns before him.[17]

* * *

Nine days after his birth on Tower Hill in London's St. Katherine's Parish—his friend and first biographer, Restoration polymath John Aubrey, reported that "Twas upon a Monday, he thinks . . . about 7 o'clock in the morning"—William Penn was brought by his parents to the Church of All Hallows Barking (also known as All Hallows by the Tower) to be baptized. All Hallows was the oldest church in the City of London, predating even the Tower of London itself. It had borne witness to a number of important events in English religious and political history. The headless bodies of Sir Thomas More and Bishop John Fisher, executed at the Tower in 1535 for refusing to acknowledge Henry VIII as supreme head of the English Church, had passed through its doors; in a fitting coda, Henry's chief minister Thomas Cromwell, who had engineered those executions, was himself beheaded on Tower Hill in 1540. And just three months after young William Penn's baptism, another headless corpse—that of Archbishop of Canterbury William Laud, also beheaded at the Tower—would make its way to All Hallows before eventually reaching its final resting place at Laud's college, St. John's, Oxford.[18]

The register at All Hallows records the baptism of "William son of William Penn and his wife Margaret, of the Tower Liberties" on October 23, 1644. It does not specify who administered the sacrament, but the rector at the time was Thomas Clendon, appointed by Parliament after it removed the previous rector, Laud's nephew Edward Layfield. Like Laud, Layfield valued Anglican ceremonialism and detested the growing influence of Puritanism, which brought him into no small amount of conflict with his congregation. At one point, he was dragged from the church while saying Mass, with a prayer book tied around his neck, and taken to prison. (Layfield had the last laugh: after the Restoration he was reinstated as vicar and served until his death in 1680.)[19]

By virtue of his birth at this particular moment in English history, William Penn entered a world racked by religious and political discord, civil war, and social unrest. Parliamentary forces battled royalists as England's Civil War entered its third year, and the effects of these events were felt across England, Scotland, Ireland, and Europe, as well as in the nascent English colonies in America. Parliament and its Puritan supporters agitated for a meaningful role in the governance of church and kingdom, against what they perceived as an increasingly autocratic political atmosphere and a rising tide of Catholics or Catholic sympathizers in positions of power. The dynamics that underlay these conflicts would convulse the kingdom for years to come, and set the parameters within which William Penn would navigate his own religious and political challenges during the second half of the century.

* * *

At this point, with the infant baptized and his father having rejoined the English fleet and taken command of the *Fellowship*, the documentary trail of young

William Penn goes cold for much of the rest of the decade. The "Author's Life" that Joseph Besse included in the first comprehensive edition of Penn's *Works*, in 1726, says nothing about any events in Penn's life between his birth and his entrance to Oxford University at age fifteen. With the exception of the family's relocation from London to Essex, sometime during William's first decade, we know almost nothing about young William Penn's experiences (and even, at times, his whereabouts) during the first ten years of his life. Penn's biographers have generally assumed that he continued to live with his mother in the house on Tower Hill while his father patrolled the Irish coast and rose through the ranks of the navy: to Rear Admiral in 1646, and in 1649 to Vice Admiral of Ireland. Naval operations, primarily in the Irish Sea and Ireland's west coast—Admiral Penn saw action at Youghal, Bunratty, Galway, Limerick, and Waterford—would keep him away for most of the decade.[20]

Of course he did get back to London on occasion, returning briefly in the summer of 1646, while his ship was in port for repairs. And he made occasional visits to inform his parliamentary masters of the status of operations. On one such occasion, after being ordered to assist in suppressing a royalist revolt in Wales during early 1648, Parliament summoned the admiral back to London and ordered him confined on suspicion of corresponding with royalists. The case was dropped for lack of evidence, and by early May he had received new orders and was back in command. In 1650 Parliament sent him to the Mediterranean in pursuit of Prince Rupert, the king's nephew. The search would prove fruitless, as Rupert evaded Parliament's ships, but the choice of Admiral Penn for this command indicates the high regard in which Parliament held him, despite persistent rumors that his commitment to the cause was less than steadfast.[21]

Ever-present fears of plague in "disease-ridden, raucous, and conspiring London," along with a bout of smallpox suffered by a three-year-old William, which may have "burned every remnant of hair from his head," apparently contributed to Margaret's desire to move to healthier and less-crowded surroundings. Penn's loss of hair would constitute a lifelong source of conversation and no small amount of controversy, as his attachment to wearing a wig would at times conflict with his fellow Quakers' objections to luxury and finery. If Penn did contract smallpox at the age of three, and if this illness took place prior to his move out of the city, then he and his mother remained in London at least until his fourth year.[22]

Penn's biographers disagree about whether the relocation was to Wanstead or Chigwell. Wanstead was, at the time, a sparsely populated town; a 1670 census counted just forty houses. But it offered convenient access to London as well as to Admiral Penn's navy mentor, Sir William Batten, who lived just three miles to the northwest in Walthamstow. Batten would remain a patron of Penn, and an ally in the tangled personal politics of the Navy Office after the Restoration.

Chigwell, just to the north, was rather larger than Wanstead, and young William Penn would be schooled there.[23]

For a young, impressionable, and religiously sensitive boy like William, the move was surely significant, and he had several important religious experiences while in Essex, which was well known as a Puritan stronghold. "Puritanism"— a contested and amorphous term, then as much as now—refers generally to a movement that sought a thoroughgoing reformation of the English church during the late sixteenth and seventeenth centuries. Not satisfied with merely breaking from the authority of the Roman Catholic church, Puritans sought to purge the Church of England of its "popish" remnants, such as ornate clerical vestments, the practice of bowing to altars and making the sign of the cross, the emphasis on beautiful worship over sound preaching, and a hierarchical structure that allowed distant bishops and archbishops to exercise authority over local congregations. Puritans emphasized personal piety as well, often keeping detailed diaries of their inner spiritual lives and embracing "a demanding regime of personal devotion, including godly reading, psalm-singing, prayer, fasting, and spiritual meditation," along with strict observance of the Sabbath.[24]

Fervor for religious reformation ran high in Essex. Historians have described it as "particularly godly" and as "steeped in Puritanism." John Hampden, one of the leading parliamentary opponents of Charles I, who would later die fighting for Parliament in the English Civil War, referred to it as the place with "the most life of religion in the land." Emmanuel College, Cambridge, founded in 1584, soon became a training ground for Puritan clergy, and connections between the college and the Essex region ran deep. The great Puritan divine and founder of Connecticut colony Thomas Hooker led a monthly conference of Essex ministers prior to his 1633 emigration to New England.[25]

Chigwell, more specifically, housed a vigilant and vigorous laity suspicious of "popish and superstitious ceremonies, corrupt and dangerous opinions ... [and] scandalous and blasphemous words." Just a few years before William Penn's birth, Chigwell's parishioners had petitioned the House of Commons to remove their vicar, Emmanuel Utey. The petitioners objected to Utey's high-church leanings—thinly veiled "popery," in their view—citing a host of objectionable practices ranging from "frequent and offensive bowing and cringing" toward, and kissing of, an altar he had erected in the church; advocacy of prayer to saints; and apparent support of divine right episcopacy, which claimed that the church's bishops, and not the king, were the true heads of the church. What's more, the petitioners claimed, "he hath said, that the Houses of Parliament hath nothing to do in matters of religion." According to other sources, Utey had called Parliament "mechanics and illiterate." (Utey's frequent drunkenness and his apparent bullying of his wife in an attempt to get her to bow to a crucifix did not improve his image with the locals either.) Although the petition was taken up by

the House of Commons's Committee on Scandalous Ministers within a month
of its receipt in 1641, Utey retained his position and salary for another two years.
Once Parliament did remove him, however, the Chigwell pulpit remained vacant until at least 1650.[26]

Young William Penn, of course, would have known little about any of this
political and religious ferment. He was, after all, a mere schoolboy. Penn was
enrolled at the Chigwell School when he was nine—prior to that, he probably received lessons at home from his mother or private tutors. The original Chigwell
building still stands, has named one of its Senior School Houses after its most famous former student, and even features a "Penn window" from which the young
student may have gazed onto the grounds below. Despite the paucity of information about Penn's time as a student at Chigwell, "all Chigwellians . . . accept as
an Article of their Creed, that William Penn . . . was educated" at the school, and
his is the only name mentioned in the Chigwell *Register's* list of students for the
entire seventeenth century.[27]

We know very little about Penn's experiences there, though we can make
some inferences based on the school's history. The school had been founded in
1629 by Samuel Harsnett, Archbishop of York, who fondly recalled his time in
Chigwell, where he had served as vicar during his early years in the ministry.
Harsnett left an endowment as his "mite of thankfulness to God, who from a
poor vicar of this parish hath called me to my so high a dignity in his church," and
also remembered Chigwell in his will, providing funds for a church bell and the
wages of a clerk to ring it, along with bread for the poor.[28]

The school—actually two: one English and one Latin—likely offered
curricula typical of the time. The English school, which instructed the boys of
Chigwell town along with several from each of the surrounding villages, taught
reading, writing, grammar, and basic mathematics ("casting accounts and arithmetic"). For the Latin school, Harsnett emphasized the importance of the
classics, instructing the use of the most common Greek and Latin grammars
of the time, with "no novelties or conceited modern writers." The archbishop
also left specific instructions governing the selection of the schools' Latin headmaster, from his minimum age and education (twenty-seven, and a university
graduate) and religion ("of a sound religion; neither papist nor puritan") to his
lifestyle ("sober, honest, and grave"; "no tippler nor haunter of alehouses, no
puffer of tobacco"). Above all, Harsnett desired a schoolmaster "apt to teach and
severe in his government." Students at Chigwell put in long hours: an eight-hour
day during the winter months increased to ten in the summer, with one hour on
Thursdays and Saturdays set aside "for play."[29]

Penn's facility with Latin and Greek language and literature likely dates
to his time at Chigwell, where he would have studied with the Latin school's
master, Edward Cotton. Given Cotton's long tenure (he served as master for two

decades), he must have cast a long shadow over many students' experiences. We know that he buried two wives and a number of his young children in Chigwell's graveyard, and that he was not, in Aubrey's words, "of [Penn's religious] persuasion," though what that persuasion was, at the boy's young age, is not entirely clear. And of course there is far more to a young boy's life than school. The Essex region was known for its sports and recreations, and a boy as introspective as Penn would no doubt have enjoyed roaming in the nearby Epping Forest.[30]

As he entered his second decade, William Penn was, he later recalled, a particularly sensitive boy with a rich and active inner spiritual life. Intensely pious, with a vivid sense of the divine presence in his life, Penn was, in his own words, "solitary and spiritual . . . a child alone." In *Brief Lives,* his collection of biographical sketches, Aubrey described the young Penn as "mighty lively, but with innocence; and extremely tender under rebuke," and added that he "delighted in retirement [i.e., solitude] and reading and meditating of [*sic*] the scriptures." Even before his schooling at Chigwell, Aubrey claims, Penn "had marked over the Bible" and "oftentimes . . . in his meditations ravished with joy, and dissolved into tears." Years later Penn referred to Christ's having "visited my soul in my young years," and "spread my sins before me, reproved me, and brought godly sorrow upon me, making me often to weep in solitary places." Aubrey also recounts the "first sense [Penn] had of God," which came "when he was eleven years old at Chigwell." Alone in his room, Penn was "suddenly surprized with an inward comfort and (as he thought) an external glory," which from that time on convinced him that he "had the seal of divinity and immortality, that there was a God and that the soul of man was capable of enjoying his divine communications." His account of Penn was likely based on conversations with the man himself; they were both Fellows of the Royal Society, and Penn later provided Aubrey with a glowing account of his early months in Pennsylvania.[31]

The mystical experience at Chigwell would turn out to be the first in a life filled with spiritual "ravishings" and an intense sense of direct connection with God's Spirit. During his 1677 travels through Holland and Germany, Penn mentioned that "the Lord first appeared to me . . . about the twelfth year of my age, anno 1656," and added, without offering any more details, that "at times betwixt [age twelve] and fifteen the Lord visited me." Ultimately, of course, Penn's pivotal Quaker convincement would set his life on a new and unexpected path. But that dramatic turn of events was still more than a decade in the future.[32]

* * *

Whatever the precise nature of William Penn's schooling and his experiences as a young boy in Wanstead or Chigwell, things changed dramatically in 1655, when Oliver Cromwell imprisoned his father in the Tower of London. It was a stunning reversal of fortune, and to understand Admiral Penn's fall from grace requires understanding the importance of Cromwell's ambitious "Western Design," which aimed at "nothing less than the complete conquest of Spain's Atlantic empire."[33]

In August 1653 Admiral Penn had been with the fleet during the First Anglo-Dutch War, at the Battle of Scheveningen, and received a gold chain and medal from Cromwell in recognition of his part in the victory. (The medal would remain in the Penn family for generations.) A year later, Cromwell placed Penn in command of the naval portion of a massive force being assembled to conquer Spain's territories in the West Indies. Prior to the fleet's departure, the Protector granted Admiral Penn lands in Ireland in recognition of his valuable service and of his wife's lost estate there. The force departed in late December 1654, stopped to add troops and supplies at Barbados a month later, and quickly began to unravel. In April 1655, hampered by illness, exposure to the tropical sun, and lack of water, English soldiers failed in their attempt to take Hispaniola (present-day Haiti and the Dominican Republic), which was intended as the first step in a steady English conquest of Spanish America. Spanish authorities on Jamaica did surrender to the English in May, but a guerilla campaign kept the invaders off balance. And then, just a month later, Admiral Penn—followed shortly thereafter by Edward Venables, who had commanded the expedition's land forces—sailed for England, ostensibly to update English leaders on developments. The departure of the force's two commanders, however, leaving a portion of the naval contingent and the entire army behind, aroused Cromwell's ire and demoralized those who remained.[34]

Although Cromwell famously meditated on the reasons for the expedition's failure—it sent him into a deep spiritual crisis, wondering for which sins God was punishing him in particular or England more generally—such theological ruminations did not prevent him from venting his wrath on his commanders. On September 20, 1655, he sent Penn and Venables to the Tower. They were released a month later, at which time Admiral Penn resigned his commission as General of the Fleet. He also, probably wisely, thought it best to remove himself from London (and eventually from England altogether). In August 1656 the admiral took his wife and family (which by now included, in addition to young William, a daughter, Margaret, born in 1651; another son, Richard, born in 1655; a slave named Jack; and a parrot) to Ireland, settling on their lands in Macroom, County Cork.[35]

* * *

Macroom, to which the Penns came in 1656, had grown substantially over the preceding half-century. The imposing façade of Macroom Castle—held by the MacCarthy Clan since the fourteenth century—sat on the east bank of the River Sullane. (The castle's gatehouse still stands, though the rest of the castle was burned to the ground in 1922 following the War of Irish Independence.) The MacCarthys had sought to populate the town and its surroundings with settlers from England and from the city of Cork, and with the influx of inhabitants it soon acquired a church, a wooden bridge fording the Sullane, a prison, a market house, two gristmills, a malthouse, a brewhouse, orchards, and pastures. The more affluent inhabitants of Macroom—primarily English and Protestant— lined the north side of the town square, with the poorer residents, mostly native Irish Catholics, to the south. By the time the Penns arrived, the town's population stood at approximately three hundred people, with homes stretching east from the castle, away from the river.[36]

William Penn was presumably taught by private tutors in or near the castle, and he remained in Macroom until he left to matriculate at Christ Church College, Oxford, in the summer of 1660. Macroom must have seemed an incredibly remote place to the young boy, not only physically, as it was more than twenty miles from Cork, but also culturally, as the Penns were part of an occupying force that had wreaked devastation on the land and its inhabitants. His time in Macroom represented William's first exposure, however little he understood it at such a young age, to the broader systems of colonization and imperialism that were so essential to early modern British politics, and in which he would later play such an important role. It also provided his first exposure to Quakerism.[37]

* * *

When the eleven-year-old William Penn arrived in Macroom, he became a part of an English colonial project more than a century old. Cromwell's scheme to redistribute land to the English officers and soldiers who had conquered and occupied Ireland, which provided Sir William Penn with his extensive Irish landholdings, was just the latest in a long-running attempt, in the words of historian Nicholas Canny, to "make Ireland British." "What ensued in Ireland during the Cromwellian conquest was a product of the policies favoured by English settlers and officials in Ireland, and their children, since the closing decade of the sixteenth century." English policy in Ireland aimed to "civilize" a backward race; secure English social, political, economic, and religious hegemony; and provide a bulwark against "popish" predation both by the Irish themselves and by their Catholic allies across Europe.[38]

Although the English conquest of Ireland under Cromwell was driven largely by the events of the 1640s—the Ulster uprising of 1641 and the stories of atrocities committed against Protestants, the intense anti-Catholic sentiment within Parliament and Cromwell's New Model Army—notions of an English mission to conquer and civilize Ireland long predated Admiral Penn's arrival. They were "not the product of any one mind or any short-term decision but rather the fulfillment of a programme that had been delineated several decades previously." By the 1580s nearly eight thousand English soldiers were based in Ireland, and English authorities were planning a large-scale colonization of Munster, the south-easternmost Irish province. Poet and social critic Edmund Spenser, himself a colonial official, envisioned a brutal military pacification of the island in his 1596 *View of the present state of Ireland*, with English communities settling on lands confiscated from native Irish. Fierce opposition from Irish Catholics culminated in a devastating revolt against English rule in 1598, part of the broader Nine Years' War, in which Irish Catholics fought English rule with support from Spain.[39]

Plans for further English settlements in Ireland, fueled by deep-seated English anti-Catholicism, continued into the seventeenth century, and Ireland fell increasingly under English domination. When Charles I (whose queen, Henrietta Maria, was herself Catholic) ascended the throne in 1625, Irish Catholics hoped that he might restrain the most harmful tendencies of aggressive English anti-Catholic prejudice, and perhaps even grant them freedom of worship.

But tensions between king and Parliament continued to grow. When a weakened Charles capitulated to the Scots in a conflict over control of the Scottish church, the Irish could not help but be inspired. One key difference, of course, was that the Scots were Protestants, and thus they garnered support from Puritans in Parliament. It is difficult to conceive of royal concessions to Irish Catholics being acceptable to English political elites, but that did not prevent the Irish from pushing back. The outbreak of unrest in Ulster in October 1641, which so affected William Penn's mother Margaret and her family, began as an effort by a small number of discontented landowners to air their grievances, and quickly developed into a widespread popular uprising against English rule. Graphic reports circulated of the "expulsion of Protestants from within the Catholic community and the destruction of objects and places associated with Protestants and Protestantism." Many, including the young widow Margaret van der Schuren and her parents, fled the violence. One wonders what that widow, now Margaret Penn, felt upon her return to Ireland, fifteen years after burying her first husband there.[40]

The 1641 uprising reinforced, in the minds of many English Protestants, the perfidy of Irish Catholics and the threat that Ireland posed as a potential gateway for subversive influences from the Continent. After their final victory over the king and the execution of Charles I in 1649, parliamentary forces sought to extinguish any remaining pockets of opposition once and for all, setting their sights on the wholesale conquest and pacification of Ireland. The fighting was brutal and laid the foundation for an Act of Settlement in which confiscated lands were given to those who had served Parliament during the previous decade. In 1652 Macroom Castle and the surrounding lands (approximately three thousand acres) were seized. Cromwell bestowed them on Admiral Penn as the latter prepared to set out for Hispaniola three years later.[41]

* * *

We know virtually nothing about the day-to-day activities of the Penn family during the Macroom years. But one event did stand out in William Penn's mind: his first encounter with the Society of Friends, in the person of Thomas Loe, an itinerant Quaker minister then preaching in Munster. Sometime during the Penn family's time at Macroom, Sir William invited Loe to the castle. The visit remained vivid in Penn's memory for the rest of his life. He would later remember:

> While he was but a child living at Cork with his father Thomas Low
> [Loe] coming thither, his father proposed to some others (when it was
> rumored a Quaker was to come from England) to be like the noble
> Bereans to hear them before they judged em and sent to TL to come
> to his house where he had a meeting in the family, and though WP was
> very young yet observed what effect TL's doctrine had on the hearers
> so that a black of his father's could not contain himself from weeping
> aloud. He looking on his father saw the tears running down his cheek
> also; he thought in himself what if they should all be Quakers.[42]

Penn did not mention any more details about Loe's brief visit to the Penns in Macroom, but his first encounter with Quakerism had made a profound impression on him. When placed alongside his mystical experience of God's presence while at Chigwell School, Penn's own descriptions of his spirituality as a young boy, and Aubrey's reports about Penn's emotional religious life and sense of his own sinfulness, we get a picture of the young William Penn as an extremely pious and introspective boy with an active religious imagination and a strict conscience. Defending himself against the attacks of an Anglican clergyman in the mid-1670s, Penn insisted, apparently referring to his encounter with Loe and its effect on his spiritual development, that "from 13 years of age I have been a sedulous pursuer after religion, and of a retired temper." His Quaker convincement lay well in the future, but the encounter with Loe reflected Penn's continuing spiritual sensitivity.[43]

* * *

While the Penns were in Ireland, events in England had been moving toward yet another regime change. With the 1658 death of Oliver Cromwell and the crumbling of his son Richard's rule, sentiment grew for restoring the king. Admiral Penn, by then Sir William Penn thanks to a knighthood granted by Richard Cromwell (an honor that was later reconfirmed by King Charles II), kept a keen eye on these developments. He was also elected to the House of Commons as a member of Parliament from the coastal town of Weymouth, a seat he would hold until his death ten years later. And Admiral Penn was on board the *Naseby*, which brought Charles II back to England from his exile in the Netherlands. Thus began a long association with the royal family that would yield a number of benefits to him and his family, and provide a vast American colony to his eldest son.

2

A Young Man on the Move

The first half of the 1660s was a time of movement, conflict, adventure, and turmoil—both inner and outer—in the life of young William Penn. In the summer of 1660, a fifteen-year-old Penn left Macroom Castle bound for Christ Church, Oxford. He matriculated in late October of that year, inaugurating a deeply unhappy two-year period at the most prestigious college in the land. As the eldest son of a prominent naval commander, a host of opportunities lay before him. But his path would be far from smooth.

***

"The grandest of all Oxford colleges," Christ Church was a training ground not only for the Anglican clergy but for those who would go on to fill positions in law and government. University education was central to the preparation for such careers: "Those who were well born were sent to the university with the intention that they should acquire sufficient knowledge to allow them to play their expected roles in national and local affairs and be able to converse in a learned and informed manner." Christ Church had stood for more than a century by the time of William Penn's admission. A bastion of Anglican loyalism during the Civil War, it had preserved the Church of England during the lean years of disestablishment and persecution under Cromwell and, when Penn entered, was preparing to resume its leading role under the restored Stuart monarchy. For an ambitious father like Sir William Penn, eager to facilitate his son's entry into the corridors of power and privilege, Christ Church must have seemed a perfect place to continue his son's education. From the son's perspective, however, given what little we know about William at this age—the mystical tendencies, the intense spirituality, the pious and somewhat sheltered childhood, the emotional memory of Thomas Loe's visit to Macroom—Christ Church likely seemed, to say the least, less than ideal.[1]

Located on the site of the former St. Frideswide's priory, which had been suppressed by Henry VIII in 1524, Christ Church had its origins in a royal license for "Cardinal College" granted by the king to his trusted advisor, Lord Chancellor and Archbishop of York Cardinal Thomas Wolsey. Wolsey poured resources into the grand undertaking over the next five years, and Cardinal College survived its namesake's fall from royal favor in 1529 (though it was renamed for King Henry VIII). Henry established Christ Church as both the cathedral of the bishopric of Oxford and an academic institution in 1546, and granted it a revenue far greater than any of Oxford's other colleges. With a robust financial foundation and a full complement of academic and ecclesiastical staff in place, "it was only a matter of a few years before a fee-paying undergraduate body was well-established." The college (and cathedral) would go on to become one of the university's largest, "a powerhouse of Edwardian Protestantism" during the 1540s and 1550s, a strong supporter of the Calvinist theology championed by the Anglican church.[2]

During the seventeenth century, "a golden age of academic endeavor" in Oxford, Christ Church maintained its leading role among Oxford colleges, hosting Parliament while the plague ravaged London during the early 1620s and welcoming the king and queen on a lavish royal visit in 1636. Charles I appointed his close confidant, Bishop of London William Laud, Chancellor of the university in 1630. Laud was elevated to Archbishop of Canterbury three years later, and became a lightning rod in the clashes that led to civil war in 1642. During the war years, Oxford provided a safe haven for the king and his supporters, and nowhere in Oxford was Charles more welcome than at Christ Church. The university raised £10,000 in a week after the king requested a loan to help him confront Parliament, and Christ Church alone likely provided nearly half of that amount. When the king's forces took the city, Christ Church became their base. (The queen lodged at neighboring Merton College, and the small door built into the wall between the two colleges to allow Charles to reach her, for business official and unofficial, remains to this day.) With the eventual triumph of parliamentary forces, Christ Church Dean Samuel Fell and his family were expelled from the college, with his wife and children famously carried out in their chairs, which they refused to vacate, in April 1648.[3]

For most of the next decade, while Oliver Cromwell dominated English politics and the realm was refashioned first as a Commonwealth and later as a Protectorate, the college operated under the deanship of John Owen, Cromwell's chaplain and advisor. Owen, who assumed the position of dean in March 1651 and became vice-chancellor of the university the following year, remains one of the towering figures of English religious history. Notwithstanding Oxford's (and Christ Church's) well-known sympathy for the former regime, Owen proved himself to be "a remarkable dean who valued tranquility, possessed the art of turning a blind eye, but who also knew when to put his head over the parapet." Seven months before Penn's arrival, Owen was removed from the deanship and, with increasing evidence of the imminent reestablishment of the Church of England, retired to his home in Stadhampton, roughly ten miles outside of Oxford. There, he continued to hold informal lectures, attracting students and Dissenters alienated from the Church of England (including, much to his father's chagrin, young William Penn). Freed from responsibilities at Christ Church, Owen became a prolific writer on behalf of the toleration of Protestant Dissenters. Owen was, to be sure, no friend to Quakers; he disliked their theology and deplored their disruptive behavior. In 1654 he approved the torture of two Quaker women who attempted to preach in Oxford, a fact later lamented in print by Quakers, including Penn himself. In the Oxford of the early Restoration, however, the two were "fellow sufferers in terms of embracing a punishable nonconformity." By the end of the decade, Penn would find himself joined with Owen in a loose alliance of tolerationists, and he spoke fondly of him for the rest of his life.[4]

* * *

"Guil Penn, equitis fil. nat. max"—in other words, William Penn, the knight's eldest son—appears in the Christ Church admissions register for Michaelmas term, on October 26, 1660, and in the University's matriculation register for that same day, which also indicates that Penn paid the standard university matriculation fee of £1. Three months earlier, he or his father had paid Christ Church £10 in "caution money," a sum assessed to incoming students to cover breakage or charges left unpaid upon their departure from Oxford. Having just turned sixteen, Penn signed his own name in the register and, betraying none of his eventual Quaker antipathy to Anglicanism or to oaths, subscribed allegiance to the Anglican Thirty-Nine Articles of Religion (the theological foundations of the Church of England) and the Oath of Supremacy like all entering students. He entered the college as a "gentleman commoner," a slightly ambiguous term indicating the elevated social standing of "sons of the social elite." Gentlemen commoners were educated separately from the general undergraduate body, due less to their social prestige and more to their general youth and lack of preparation.[5]

Less than a month after Penn's arrival at Christ Church, a new dean of the college was appointed, one who would have an enormous impact on young William's brief and unhappy stay in Oxford. John Fell was an "intransigent episcopalian of the most dogmatic kind" who combined a pious zeal for the Church of England with a personal sense of responsibility for Christ Church's role in the defense of church and monarchy, and thus took it upon himself to recruit the sons of the British elite to the college. Fell was a Christ Church man from birth—his father had served as dean until he was deprived of his position and the entire family was ejected from the college in 1648. He was also something of a child prodigy, receiving his BA from Christ Church at age fifteen. During the Cromwellian years, Fell had remained in Oxford, keeping the Anglican royalist faith and serving as the "linchpin of . . . [an] emerging network of [royalist] clients, patrons, and friends." Fell's staunch Anglicanism and intense loyalty to the monarchy would enable him to hold the deanery for more than a quarter-century, even after becoming Bishop of Oxford in 1675. Fell's greatest ambition was to produce a learned Anglican ministry, and the list of other projects he took on as dean, such as securing the donation of objects that would become the Ashmolean Museum and rejuvenating the Oxford University Press, is astonishing. Under Fell's leadership Christ Church "became the ideological champion of the restored regime, dedicated to preserving the *status quo* in church and state."[6]

* * *

To say that Penn's time at Oxford is opaque to those interested in better under-standing his life is to understate the paucity of concrete information we have about the time he spent there. About John Vincent, his likely tutor, we know very little, except that he matriculated at Christ Church in 1648, receiving his BA in 1650 and his MA two years later. The average Oxford undergraduate was educated toward "the acquisition of a mastery of language and literature," and the ideal of the erudite general scholar held sway for much of the seventeenth century. The undergraduate course of study included logic, natural and moral philosophy, classical authors, mathematics, and religion. Shortly after arriving at Christ Church, Penn composed some Latin verses on the death of Henry, Duke of Gloucester, the king's younger brother, who had succumbed to smallpox in September 1660. The composition was included in a memorial volume of poetry authored by a variety of Oxford academics and clergy. We can infer from Penn's frequent invocation of the classics throughout his career that his education in-cluded exposure to classical rhetoric, literature, and logic, and that he attended, and perhaps participated in, the oral disputations that were the hallmarks of an Oxford education.[7]

    We do know that about six months after his entrance into Christ Church, in the spring of 1661—April 22, to be exact—Penn journeyed to London to watch Charles II's procession to Whitehall Palace to be crowned king. Pepys recorded in his diary that it was "impossible to relate the glory of this day." Charles, "in a most rich embroidered suit and cloak, looked most noble." The king's brother James, Duke of York, saw Sir William and his son, along with other colleagues from the Navy Office, watching from a window and pointed the party out to Charles.[8]

    William Penn's two years at Oxford were deeply unhappy ones. The young student's intense piety was clearly out of place in Restoration Oxford, and his al-ienation from the established church solidified during his time at Christ Church. In a 1673 letter to Mary Pennyman, a fellow Quaker with whom Penn disputed in print throughout the 1670s, he described himself as "a great sufferer" for his faith "from [age] 16 . . . at the university." In September 1677, while visiting the Labadist religious community in Wieuwert, north of Amsterdam, Penn described his time at Oxford as "my persecution," recounting that "the Lord sustained me in the midst of that hellish darkness and debauchery." Nor was it only the student who harbored doubts about Christ Church: his father seems eventually to have realized that the college and his son were a poor match. Pepys reported an early 1662 conversation with Sir William in which the admiral broached the possibility of removing his son from Oxford, possibly to Cambridge.[9]

If his entrance to the university was recorded in official matriculation documents, Penn's departure from Oxford is shrouded in mystery. He later claimed to have been "expelled for writing a book the priests did not like," though it is not clear what that book might have been. He told the Labadists that he had been "banished [from] the college." Other accounts have Penn joining with like-minded critics of the established church in Oxford to hold their own meetings for worship, accounts given some credence by Penn's later admission, in his response to an interlocutor, the Presbyterian John Faldo, that he had originally found sympathetic company among Dissenters early in the Restoration. (Penn also reported, in his response to Faldo, that "many of you grew dry again"—in other words, lost their spiritual fervor—while he continued his spiritual journey until his eventual convincement as a member of the Society of Friends.) The fact that Penn received his caution money back upon his departure from Christ Church suggests that, at least, he did not leave debts to the college unpaid. There is no hard evidence to support widespread reports of Penn refusing to wear the required Anglican surplices, or attempting to forcibly remove surplices from fellow students. But correspondence between his son and Owen, the former Dean of Christ Church, discovered in his son's possession by an increasingly uneasy Sir William, provides the clearest evidence that young William had taken up with Oxford's Nonconformists in some capacity.[10]

Regardless of the specifics of his departure from the university, it seems clear that William Penn's introspective spirituality, intense personal piety, and tendency toward self-interrogation and self-examination were bound to clash with both the ritualistic Anglican ceremonialism that dominated Christ Church (and Oxford more generally) and the widespread Restoration libertinism that prevailed at the university. It is also not surprising that the institution emerged intact while the student was sent on his way. According to Pepys, by March 1662 William was home and "not well." He added, about the Penns, that "all things . . . do not go well with them; they look discontentedly, but I know not what ails them." He would soon find out. In late April of that year, Sir William showed his neighbor some letters his son had received from Owen, whom, his father confided to Pepys, had "much perverted [William's] opinion." It was certainly not the last time that his son's religious sensibilities would cause Penn's father great distress.[11]

* * *

While William Penn suffered at Oxford, his father had been busy. In 1660 the admiral's knighthood was reaffirmed by the restored king, and he was named a commissioner on the Navy Board, along with Pepys and his old ally William Batten. Although personal and professional rivalries would lead to jealousy and, particularly from Pepys's side, increasing bitterness as time went on, the three men were "sociable and hospitable neighbors" on Seething Lane near Tower Hill, and Pepys and Penn worked together in drafting the Naval Discipline Act, which Parliament passed in 1661. He continued to sit in Parliament as a member from Weymouth, a port town on England's southern coast. It was a busy year for Sir William's Irish affairs as well; he was appointed governor and captain of the Kinsale fort, near Cork, commander of a company of foot soldiers there, and member of the Munster Provincial Council. Aside from a brief sojourn to Ireland with the Duke of Ormond in summer 1662, duties at the Navy Office kept Sir William busy for much of this time. Tensions with the Dutch were growing once again and would soon boil over into war.[12]

* * *

Although William Penn reported later that his exit from Oxford brought down his father's wrath—"whipping, and beating, and turning out of doors"—by the summer of 1662 the two had patched up their differences, perhaps due to the intervention of his mother. Rather than attempting to argue, or hector, or beat, his son's religious scruples out of him, Sir William seems to have decided on a more indirect route. He decided to send William to Europe, an emerging rite of passage for young men of his social class. The prospect of getting William away from undesirable influences like Owen undoubtedly played some part in Sir William's thinking. And what better place to coax his pious son to embrace the wider world than the opulent French court, with its ambitious and extravagant young monarch, Louis XIV, who had recently assumed personal control over the French government?[13]

   Although it would only emerge as a full-blown cultural experience during the eighteenth century, the "Grand Tour" was quickly becoming a standard component of the training of young English gentlemen, introducing them to the Continent's great cities and to the classical ruins that linked Europe's heritage to the glories of Greece and Rome. During the late 1630s, John Milton toured France and Italy, meeting such luminaries as Hugo Grotius, Galileo, and a host of poets, playwrights, and theologians. Thomas Hobbes also made a grand tour, accompanying his young charge William Cavendish in 1610. And years earlier, Francis Bacon had traveled through France, Italy, and Spain studying law and languages and observing political systems along the way. The Grand Tour generally began with a journey to Paris and included visits to a number of Italian cities, including Rome, Venice, Florence, or Naples. Over the course of the seventeenth century the tour became "a fully established social convention and educational institution," combining study, tourism, and "social finishing."[14]

The Grand Tour aimed to broaden young men's horizons and give them a more capacious understanding of the world beyond England's borders. Although the Grand Tour is generally considered a coming-of-age experience, with young Englishmen eager to embrace the licit and illicit pleasures available in the wider world, William Penn would have cut a somewhat unique figure: sent by his father, likely against his wishes, to experience a world that he surely viewed as corrupt and sinful, filled with temptations to waylay the godly. The details of his experiences on the tour are unknown, and no correspondence from him during these years survives. We do not know, for example, whether Penn took advantage of the "great opportunity for sexual adventure," particularly in Paris, which also offered diversions like gambling, the theater, and all sorts of other entertainments.[15]

Penn embarked on his tour of Europe in late spring 1662, accompanied by a few companions and servants. Robert Spencer, who had held the title of Earl of Sunderland since his infancy and whom Penn likely met at Christ Church, was one of his fellow travelers, as was William Lindsay, who would become Earl of Crawford in 1678. The tour represented the beginning of a lifelong relationship between Penn and Sunderland, three years his senior. If they followed the most common route taken by travelers, the company would have journeyed from London southwest to Dover—a distance of approximately seventy-five miles—and made the Channel crossing to Calais. From there they would have traveled south to Paris. Like other aristocratic travelers from England, they were introduced at Louis XIV's court at the Palace of Fontainebleau, just south of the capital—Versailles would not be completed for another twenty years—which offered Penn a glimpse of the elaborate spectacle and foppery he would so come to detest after his Quaker convincement.[16]

* * *

Unlike most English travelers on the Grand Tour—and unlike Sunderland and Crawford, apparently—Penn left Paris before too long, and by early 1663 he had moved on to the Protestant Academy of Saumur, roughly two hundred miles southwest of the French capital. Perhaps he had soured on the excesses of the French court. Perhaps he had been aiming for the Academy all along. In either case, he would remain there for more than a year, and though he rarely spoke explicitly about his time in Saumur, it seems to have left its mark on him.

Saumur was a thriving and prosperous town of approximately 10,000, and an important center of French Protestantism. Although the Edict of Nantes had ensured a range of legal protections for Huguenots, as French Protestants were known, since 1598, these guarantees had become increasingly precarious in the intervening years. As a result, like Protestant Dissenters in England, whose Dissenting academies were founded as a result of their exclusion from

Oxford and Cambridge, French Protestants formed their own network of educational institutions, and none was more important than the Academy at Saumur. Founded in the 1590s by the celebrated French theologian (and governor of Saumur) Philippe Duplessis-Mornay, it was perhaps best known for its most noteworthy scholar, Moses Amyraut, who was "without contest the most influential Reformed theologian of the seventeenth century." Amyraut, in his mid-sixties and in increasingly ill health by the time Penn arrived, had held positions in both the church and the Academy at Saumur since the early 1630s. He had likely retired from active involvement in the academy by the early 1660s, and was referred to in a 1660 publication as "late" professor of divinity at Saumur ("late" here meaning no longer active, not dead). But he made quite an impression on Penn.[17]

An outspoken proponent of conciliation and tolerance between rival Christian factions, Amyraut had long maintained warm relations with French nobles and an irenic approach to contentious issues. From Amyraut, Penn likely imbibed an emphasis on and confidence in the power of human reason in religious matters. It was a commitment that he would later bring to Quakerism: Penn stood apart from many of his fellow Quakers not only because of his educational and class background, but because of his willingness to embrace a role for reason alongside the Inner Light so central to Quakerism, although what exactly he meant by "reason" was not always clear.[18]

Theologically speaking, Amyraut constructed an understanding of human salvation—known as "hypothetical universalism"—that placed him at odds with many of his fellow French Calvinists. In Amyraut's understanding, "God wanted all men to be saved and gave them the potential for faith." But alongside his universalism lay a clearly Calvinist understanding of predestination in which God granted faith to those who are decreed to be saved, and faith is the "gratuitous gift of God." Amyraut's softening of Calvinist notions of predestination, and the enhanced role he thus saw for some form of free will, was one of his more contentious theological innovations. He narrowly escaped condemnation at the Synod of Alençon in 1637 and again at the Synod of Charenton seven years later. Yet Amyraut saw himself as working firmly within the Calvinist tradition. In the words of Stephen Angell, "What Amyraut found in Calvin's writings was a covenant that carried dual characteristics, a universal grace that was available to everyone and a more limited grace that was efficacious only for the elect." Whether Amyraut's strand of Calvinism was what Penn had in mind ten years later when he condemned "J. Calvin's horrendum decretum of predestination" we do not know, but his time at Saumur surely exposed him to the broad legacy of Calvin in seventeenth-century European Protestantism.[19]

The standard curriculum leading to the master's degree at Saumur generally took two years, the first for logic and ethics, the second for physics and metaphysics, in addition to instruction in Greek, Hebrew, theology, rhetoric, and mathematics. Theology students tended to spend an additional year and to focus further on Scripture and rhetoric. Since Penn spent just over a year at Saumur, arriving midway through one academic year (which ran from October to September) and leaving midway through the next one, it is not clear what sort of program of study he undertook. But his time at Saumur would likely have been similar, in many ways, to the life he had left behind in Oxford: attending worship, hearing sermons, and engaging in disputations on philosophical and theological topics. In late April 1664, an acquaintance of Sir William related that he had "heard a very good character of your son . . . at Saumur," where he was "outdoing most of his countrymen," although this was secondhand information and by the time the letter was even written Penn was probably already home and with his father.[20]

Amyraut died in January 1664, and Penn left the academy later that year. Perhaps with the master gone, the student had less interest in remaining. From Saumur Penn continued on his tour in the company, once again, of Sunderland, with whom he likely passed through Lyon and crossed the Alps into Italy at Savoy or Grenoble. He got as far as Turin before receiving a letter from his father summoning him home. Tensions with the Dutch were rising, and Sir William wanted his son by his side.

By August Penn was back in London, and very much acting the part of the young gentleman his father had hoped he would become. Pepys reported that young William came to see him, having just returned from Europe, and "stayed an hour talking with me." "I perceive something of learning he hath got, but a great deal, if not too much, of the vanity of the French garb and affected manner of speech and gait." (Pepys also perceived William to be paying a bit too much attention to his wife Elizabeth.) Penn seemingly referred to this phase of his life when he later insisted that his relentless pursuit of religious truth "from 13 years of age" had "suffered but one intermission to please my relations, and that was no farther than finery, and gaiety." Yet even in the midst of his apparent reconciliation with the ways of the world—the "French garb," the "affected manner"—Penn continued to struggle with the conflict between his intense spirituality and a world he considered sinful and temptation-filled. In a piece of unpublished verse written at about this time, he denounced "tyrant lust" and condemned "Delilahs" with their "witchcrafts," against which "Heaven's power is the soul's coat of mail." Despite his inner torment, Penn expressed his yearning to "silently converse with those/That in a faithful God their trust repose."[21]

Later in life, as he prepared to sail for America, William Penn would look back on his time in France and recall one particularly memorable incident. In the chapter on pride from the 1682 edition of *No cross, no crown*, Penn related that

I was once myself in France set upon about eleven at night, as I was walking to my lodging, by a person that waylaid me, with his naked sword in his hand, who demanded satisfaction of me for taking no notice of him, at a time when he civilly saluted me with his hat; though the truth was, I saw him not when he did it. I will suppose he had killed me, for he made several passes at me, or I, in my defence, had killed him, when I disarmed him, as the earl of Crawford's servant saw, that was by; I ask any man of understanding or conscience, if the whole ceremony was worth the life of a man, considering the dignity of the nature, and the importance of the life of man, both with respect to God his Creator, himself, and the benefit of civil society.

This brief anecdote offers a number of insights into both the young William Penn and the European world through which he was traveling during these years. Of course Penn highlights the absurdity of the early modern honor culture that led human beings to threaten each other with grave harm, and engage in often-fatal duels, over perceived slights like the failure to doff one's hat in respect to another person. But the story also makes clear the near-constant violence that was a part of everyday life in early modern cities. Even though Paris was one of the first European cities to institute professional night watches and street lighting, walking alone at night incurred a great deal of risk. To the biographer, all sorts of additional questions cry out for more details. To which lodging was Penn returning when the attack took place? Did this incident take place in Paris, or Saumur, or somewhere else entirely? How did Penn disarm his attacker? How did the episode end? Who was the Earl of Crawford's servant, and did he involve himself in the fracas? Like so many of Penn's experiences during his first two decades, the answers to these questions will likely never be known.[22]

* * *

After his time in Oxford, his sojourns in Europe, and his study at Saumur, it is not surprising that upon his return William Penn enrolled at Lincoln's Inn, one of the four "Inns of Court" and perhaps the most prestigious law school in the land. Enrolling at Lincoln's Inn, sometimes referred to as "the third university of England," did not mean that Penn intended to pursue the law as a profession; the study of law represented "a valuable foundation for anyone embarking on a life involving business, not least in pressing his father's Irish claims." The study of law, particularly English law, which was not taught at either Oxford or Cambridge, would certainly have been useful for a young English gentleman like William Penn, whose father had extensive landholdings in Ireland and who stood to inherit them one day. From his previous courses of study at Oxford and Saumur, Penn likely had a solid foundation on which to build in developing a deeper understanding of English law.[23]

And so on February 7, 1665, William Penn, "son and heir of Sir William Penn of the City of London, knight," was admitted to Lincoln's Inn. Having trained the sons of many prominent Puritan families—to say nothing of such luminaries of the English legal tradition as John Fortescue, Thomas More, and Matthew Hale, and political and literary figures like William Prynne and John Donne—Lincoln's Inn likely seemed a place where Penn could thrive in ways that he had not at Oxford. He certainly began with promising connections. William Batten, son of Sir William's naval mentor of the same name, served as one of Penn's manucaptors (members of the Inn who vouched for applicants, guaranteed payment of their dues and fees, and often took on responsibility for the students' well-being more generally). Batten's role as manucaptor provides evidence that young Penn's exit from Oxford and absence from England had not harmed his prospects in English society, and that he retained a comfortable place within a wide patronage network stemming from his father's position.[24]

Whether, given his religious leanings, Penn ever worshipped in the Lincoln's Inn chapel, designed by the famed architect Inigo Jones and consecrated by John Donne in 1623, we do not know. What we do know is that his stay at the Inn was short-lived. Not long after Penn was enrolled, war with the Dutch broke out, and it seemed increasingly likely that his father would require his services. But by then an even greater threat had emerged in London.[25]

* * *

It all began with a flea bite. *Xenopsylla cheopis*, the rat-flea, passed on the *Yersinia pestis* bacilli from its rodent host to humans. Symptoms would begin to appear within several days. First came headaches, fever, chills, and perhaps vomiting; then swollen lymph nodes in the groin, armpits, or neck, sometimes called "buboes," and hence the name, *bubonic plague*. Nearly a third of those infected died within two weeks, with mortality rates often approaching 90 percent. And it was a particularly unpleasant death, featuring "gangrenous inflammation of the throat and lungs, violent pains in the chest, vomiting and spitting of blood, pestilential odor from bodies and breath, tumors in the groin . . . and on the neck, constipation or diarrhea, and purple spots (caused by subcutaneous hemorrhages)."[26]

Bubonic plague had wreaked havoc on European societies for more than three centuries. The Black Death—so named for the discolorations that afflicted victims' skin—had first arrived in England in late summer 1348 and would afflict the realm intermittently for more than three hundred years. Between 1500 and 1665, for example, London was plague-free for only about twelve years total. In addition to being medical or public health catastrophes of the first order, plague outbreaks upended relationships, devastated families and communities, undermined social trust and neighborliness, reshaped political and religious life, wreaked havoc on local and national economies, and hampered war efforts.

The Tudors had made significant efforts to coordinate responses to the plague, with decidedly mixed results: early in Elizabeth's reign, plague wiped out perhaps 20 percent of London's population. In 1593, there were 23,000 dead out of a London population of 150,000. In 1603, as England welcomed its new king, James I, roughly 15 percent of Londoners and nearly a third of the inhabitants of York were taken by the plague. Nor were politics and plague ever far from each other: over the course of the sixteenth and seventeenth centuries royal officials had become more involved in enforcing measures to stop the spread of plague, and the king moved Parliament to Oxford in 1625 partly in response to an outbreak of plague. In 1665 skeptics suggested that Charles II used "the excuse of the prevalence of plague to free himself temporarily from the shackles of parliamentary control."[27]

The plague of 1665–1666—which later scholars would dub "London's Last Dreadful Visitation," but which was at the time just another "great national outburst of the disease"—coincided with the outbreak of the Dutch war, and unsettled and decimated an already anxious populace. Rumors traced this latest outbreak to merchandise from Holland, which only further linked the devastation of plague with the devastation of war in the popular mind. In reality London's out-parishes, with their slumlike and unhygienic conditions, overcrowding, and poverty, provided ideal conditions for the disease to thrive. From scattered deaths attributed to the plague outside the city walls in late 1664, the outbreak was well under way by spring 1665. Those with means, including many doctors and clergy, fled the city. (Among the many who fled was John Milton, then working on *Paradise Lost*. On the recommendation of Thomas Ellwood, who would later become one of William Penn's closest friends, Milton took a cottage about twenty miles outside the capital, in Chalfont St. Giles.) The king and court followed in July, leaving a political vacuum in the capital at a particularly inopportune time. At its peak, in mid-September, the plague took more than seven thousand victims in a single week. In late October, Sir William Penn and his navy colleague Peter Pett wrote to the Navy Commissioners that "plague [was] rife among the seamen." In his *Journal of the plague year*, Daniel Defoe claimed that "notwithstanding the violence of the plague in London and in other places . . . it was never on board the fleet," but Pett and Sir William were actually with the fleet and presumably knew better. Such a depleted navy raised fears of a Dutch invasion. Nearly 10,000 people took refuge in ships on the Thames in an attempt to avoid infection, and those left in the city often turned to foul-smelling disinfectants or tobacco in the belief that such substances would ward off plague. Schoolboys even reported being whipped for not smoking![28]

By early 1666 the king considered conditions safe enough for him to return to London. Other indicators of "normal" city life slowly followed. All told, the great outbreak had taken the lives of nearly 100,000 Londoners, roughly a quarter of

the population, to say nothing of the 40,000 dogs and 200,000 cats that were reportedly slaughtered in an attempt to prevent them from spreading the plague.
As Defoe versified at the conclusion of his *Journal of the Plague Year,*

> A dreadful plague in London was
> In the year Sixty-Five.
> Which swept an hundred thousand souls
> Away; yet I alive![29]

* * *

Between the outbreak of the Second Anglo-Dutch War in March 1665 and the first
signs of plague in London at roughly the same time, William Penn's legal education
ended almost before it began. He left Lincoln's Inn to join his father sometime in
March. By mid-April he was with Sir William and the fleet, which was assembling
at Gunfleet Bar off the coast east of London. He may have attempted to return to
the Inn after carrying his father's messages to the king and navy officials in London,
but it closed its doors in June as the plague gathered intensity.

The Second Dutch War would cement the bond between the Penn family
and the Stuarts, both King Charles II and his brother James, who was then
Duke of York but would later rule as King James II. In the fall of 1664, the
Duke of York appointed Sir William as "captain great commander" on his
ship, the *Royal Charles,* while the fleet was undergoing preparation for battle.
The relationship would bear fruit in many ways and redound to the benefit
of the admiral's son when he turned his attention to American colonization
in the early 1680s.[30]

While Sir William worked alongside James, preparing to engage the Dutch,
he employed his son to make a special trip to see the king at Whitehall Palace,
the chief residence of the English monarch for most of the fifteenth and sixteenth
centuries. The warm tone of the correspondence sent by Penn to his father
hints at a thaw in their formerly rocky relationship, and perhaps the approach
of war served to mute the long-simmering conflict between father and son over
William's religious sensibilities. In any event, the son's concern for Sir William's
safety as war loomed was plainly evident. "I pray God, after all the foul weather
and dangers you are exposed to . . . that you come home as secure," he wrote in
late April. Penn further expressed his firm belief that "if God has called you out
to battle, he will cover your head in that smoky day." "I never knew what a father
was," he continued, "till I had wisdom enough to prize him," and he referred to
Sir William as "both a father and a friend."[31]

Two weeks later, he wrote with more detail of his mission to the king. He had
arrived at Whitehall early in the morning, before the king had awoken. Upon
hearing of the message from the duke, the king himself appeared, "earnestly

[leaping] out of his bed," clad "only in his gown and slippers." Recognizing
the younger Penn, the king asked, "how does Sir William"; and William, surely
knowing his father would relish hearing of the king's esteem, added that "he
asked how you did at three several times." Penn delivered news about the fleet's
preparations to the king and Lord Arlington, the Secretary of State, and also
spoke to Duchess Anne Hyde, James's wife.[32]

Even during the extended preparation for war, Sir William did not forget his
affairs in Ireland. William's errand to London also included attending to legal
wrangling over Sir William's Irish lands. Penn had the ear of Robert Southwell,
clerk of the Privy Council, who was well positioned to provide the Penns with
information about their dispute and promised to advocate for Sir William's claim
if it became necessary.

And of course there was always more to life than business. William's sister
Margaret had recently met Anthony Lowther, one of the original Fellows of
the Royal Society and the son of a London alderman, whom Sir William hoped
would prove a suitable match for his daughter. William made clear to his father
that "since he saw her," Lowther "was very much taken" with Margaret.[33]

* * *

As 1665 came to an end, then, William Penn could look back on an eventful five
years. He had entered, and been ejected from, Christ Church; embarked on a
tour of Europe; and studied at Saumur. Along the way he had encountered John
Owen and Moses Amyraut, "two theological giants in the Reformed Protestant
camp." By early 1665, Penn had returned to London, entered Lincoln's Inn to
begin the study of law, and was called into service as his father's messenger,
carrying missives between the English fleet and the king.[34]

After William's report to his father in May 1665, we know little about his
movements for the remainder of the year. The plague raged on. By the end of
1665, Sir William had decided to send his son to Ireland to negotiate new leases
with his tenants and to advocate for his land claims at the Court of Claims in
Dublin, and by early the next year the twenty-one-year-old was on his way to
Ireland. It was to be a fateful mission. On the one hand, William successfully
fended off challenges to his father's claims and secured title to nearly 12,000
acres of Irish land. On the other hand, much to Sir William's chagrin, his son's
journey to Ireland would set his life on a radically new trajectory and dash many
of his father's hopes for his son's future rise in English society. He became a
Quaker, and his life would never be the same.

3

Cork, and Convincement

It had been Admiral William Penn's good fortune to receive Macroom Castle and its surrounding lands in County Cork from Oliver Cromwell, in recognition for his service to Parliament, the Commonwealth, and the Protectorate. It was his particular misfortune that Cromwell had seized those lands and that castle from Donough MacCarthy, a staunch supporter of the king on whom Charles had bestowed the title Earl of Clancarty while the monarch was still in exile. Thus it surprised no one when the restored monarch decided to return the Macroom lands to the earl. Then again, Sir William had served the king too, and Charles was not one to leave his supporters empty-handed. And so began the search for other Irish lands with which to compensate the Penns for the loss of Macroom. It then became, in turn, the misfortune of Colonel Peter Wallis, a onetime officer in Cromwell's army, to have received lands in and around Shanagarry, in east County Cork, when the king went looking for new acreage to bestow upon Sir William. Wallis was not one to go quietly, and the legal disputes over Shanagarry dragged on for several years. During his spring 1665 mission to London on his father's behalf, Penn wrote to Sir William that "Mrs. Wallis presented another petition," which he expected would prove "uneffectual enough," given his father's proximity to those in power, both in England and in Ireland. But uncertainty prevailed.[1]

The confused nature of land titles in Ireland generally, which were in disarray after multiple regime changes over the course of the previous decade, only exacerbated the problem. An Act of Settlement passed at the Restoration had attempted to bring some order to this chaos, laying out procedures for adjudicating conflicts and setting up a Court of Claims in Dublin to oversee the process. And so in early 1666 Sir William Penn, preoccupied with the Dutch war and his service in Parliament, and increasingly hobbled by gout, wrote apologetically to Sir George Lane, secretary to the Duke of Ormond, the Lord-Lieutenant of Ireland, that he simply could not leave the king's service to attend to his Irish affairs. He asked Lane to look after his eldest son, whom he was dispatching to Ireland to secure his Shanagarry titles and to negotiate new leases with his tenants. William's time in Ireland would include a great deal of the mundane and monotonous. It would also include high drama.[2]

* * *

We know rather little about the details of William's trip. Unlike the Irish journey he would undertake in the fall of 1669, on this visit Penn kept no journal. Most of those with whom he did business would have been living on expropriated land and paying rent to Sir William to the tune of approximately £1,000 per year. (Sir William, in turn, paid the Crown £113 annually.) Penn was granted fairly wide latitude to make agreements with his father's tenants. Not long after his arrival, for example, he met with John Rowse, a Cromwellian soldier who leased 150 acres in Imokilly, County Cork, and whom Sir William asked his son to "afford . . . all the Irish favor in your power, and . . . continue him my tenant at as easy terms for him as conveniently you may." The surviving correspondence between William and his father is rather straightforward, businesslike, and filled with advice and instructions on how to deal with tenants and Irish officials. He urged William to represent his interests with diligence and care, and reminded him that "my frame of mind" inclined him to seek "peace with all so far as possible." Nonetheless, he responded sharply to personal slights or to perceptions that he was being denied what was rightfully his: "You well know that I yield to no men," Sir William wrote on one occasion, and "cannot be hectored out of anything." Technically speaking, the negotiation of new leases had to await full confirmation of Sir William's lands in the form of letters patent from the Court of Claims in Dublin, but William pressed forward anyway.[3]

One of the chief obstacles he faced was the continued presence of Colonel Wallis. To Mabel Brailsford, one of Penn's biographers, Wallis was "a serpent" in the Penns' "Irish Eden." To Wallis and his family, no doubt, he was simply a man trying to maintain his claim to property that had been granted to him. Sir William specifically mentioned his desire for an agreement with Wallis in a letter to his son in early 1667, though in the same letter he also told William to await the Earl of Ossory, who had been specifically instructed by the king to favor the Penns' claims. (Ossory, son of Ormond, the Lord-Lieutenant of Ireland, had served with Sir William at the Battle of Lowestoft in June 1665.) William obtained the letters patent in spring 1667, bringing the conflict with Wallis to a close. The Penns' relationship with Wallis seems to have survived more or less intact; Penn met him two years later during his next visit to Ireland, and in 1693 Wallis's daughter married Charles Gookin, who would later be named Lieutenant Governor of Pennsylvania by this same William Penn.[4]

Sir William Penn surely hoped that his son's engagement in Irish affairs would further his preparation for life as an English gentleman. From his position in the Navy Office, he did what he could to smooth William's entry into the halls of power. His aspirations for his son, dealt a blow by the Oxford debacle, had been given new life by Penn's European tour, as well as his brief stay at Lincoln's Inn and service as messenger to the king. Clearly, representing family interests in Ireland would be the next step in William's training. We have already noted Sir George Lane. The Duke of Ormond's two sons, the Earls of Ossory and Arran, also figured prominently in Sir William's attempts to secure his land titles and to facilitate his son's social connections. William also met Roger Boyle, the Earl of Orrery and Lord President of Munster, the province in which County Cork was located. The acquaintance between Penn's father and Orrery dated back more than twenty years, to when Orrery was Baron of Broghill and governor of the besieged Irish town of Youghal, in County Cork. The two men conferred frequently about military matters over the ensuing years, and socialized on a number of occasions in and around Cork. When Broghill was named Lord President in 1660, he named Sir William a member of his council. Young William's association with Orrery's brother Francis, Lord Shannon, also demonstrated his ability to build bridges to those members of the governing elite who wielded power in Ireland.[5]

* * *

Like many soldiers garrisoned across Ireland, those at Carrickfergus, just north of Belfast, had been "unpaid for months and reduced almost to starvation." On May 22, 1666, they mutinied. Rejecting offers of clemency, the mutineers issued a series of demands intended to rally other garrisons to follow their example. It didn't happen. Instead, they found themselves facing troops led by the Earl of Arran and the Duke of Ormond. (Complicating matters was the fact that the soldiers whose job it would be to suppress the mutiny were themselves owed months of back pay. Unfortunately for the mutineers, these troops followed orders.) The uprising was quickly put down, and more than a hundred soldiers faced courts-martial. Among those assisting in the suppression of the Carrickfergus mutiny was William Penn, who had had been in Ireland for just a few months at that point. What he thought of the sentences imposed by those courts-martial— nine executed and the rest sent to Dublin for impressment into naval service or deportation—we do not know. But his performance was impressive enough that the lord-lieutenant wanted to offer Penn a position commanding troops, and wrote to Sir William, advising him to resign command of the Kinsale fort so that his son might be granted the position.[6]

It would be wonderful to know just what William Penn did to gain the fulsome praise lavished upon him by Arran and Ormond. His actions must have been substantial. We only know that he assisted Arran in some important capacity, "to his no small reputation," according to his cousin, Captain Richard Rooth. Perhaps not surprisingly, the proposal to grant the twenty-one-year-old William his father's position at Kinsale was not well received, and a terse letter from Sir William advised his son not to let his "youthful desires . . . outrun your discretion." That the proffered appointment would have required Sir William to step down from the position surely had something to do with his lack of enthusiasm for the scheme, since at this point he still nursed hopes of retiring to his Irish estates. "God sending an end to this present war (which I hope will not long continue)," Sir William told Ormond, he would "endeavor to follow the great inclination which I have, to fix in Ireland." Besides the question of retiring to Ireland, as he pointed out to his son in July 1666, the post yielded him £400 a year, a significant sum with which he was loath to part. He did enthusiastically offer his son advice about the office of royal victualer at Kinsale, which was granted either to William or his cousin of the same name (the records are unclear; the name is identical). Victualing was a potentially lucrative position that promised profits if managed skillfully; a savvy victualer could, for example, inflate the number of soldiers for whom he claimed to be providing rations, and thus increase the amounts billed to the Crown. Sir William himself would gain a share of the victualing accounts for the Royal Navy in January 1669, and the debts due him from the Crown would prove useful in his son's negotiations with the Crown for his American colony in early 1681.[7]

* * *

While his son was in Ireland, Sir William Penn had his hands full with the English fleet and the Dutch war. Between his service alongside Pepys and the other commissioners at the Navy Office in London, and his role inspecting the fleet in port at Harwich, Sir William was a busy man. Despite a promising beginning, with a resounding English victory in June 1665 at the Battle of Lowestoft, English fortunes took a decidedly discouraging turn as the war unfolded. In the immediate aftermath of Lowestoft, the English neglected to pursue the retreating Dutch fleet and thus squandered their military advantage and ushered in a period of finger-pointing that divided those in command. Though the outcome of the Four Days' Battle in early June 1666 was initially communicated to anxious Londoners as a victory, further reporting soon revealed that the Dutch had actually inflicted enormous damage. England lost twenty-three ships (compared to just four Dutch), suffered 1,500 fatalities, and saw nearly two thousand sailors captured. In a letter from late June 1666, Sir William told his son that he had been away from home for several weeks, dealing with "a shattered fleet" in the wake of that confrontation. On at least two occasions over the next several months, the Duke of York sent him to Harwich, with orders to oversee the repair and dispatch of naval vessels. Nor did things improve the following year. But Sir William and the English war effort would soon face yet another, even greater, challenge.[8]

* * *

Seventeenth-century London was a tinderbox. Wooden houses with thatched roofs or tar-covered walls crowded together in narrow lanes, and upper floors jutted out over lower ones, in some cases nearly touching the buildings across the street from them. An ineffective and disorganized system of municipal fire-fighting attempted to make do with frequently inoperative pumping systems. Indeed, during late summer 1666 "the Thames water-house was out of order, so that the conduits and pipes were almost all dry." Firebreaks were a key com-ponent of firefighting strategies of the time, but their effectiveness depended on firefighters' ability to pull down or demolish large buildings on short notice, in a timely and thorough manner, while fires were burning nearby. Add in a long dry summer like that of 1666 had been, and all was in place for a calamity to ensue. And thus was sparked what became known as the Great Fire of London.[9]

When he closed his bakery on the night of September 1, 1666, Thomas Farrinor, whose bakery in Pudding Lane provided bread for the Royal Navy and who held the office of "Conduct of the King's Bakehouse," neglected to douse his oven completely. Whether or not Lord Mayor Thomas Bludworth, surveying the fire in its early hours, really did exclaim "Pish! A woman could piss it out!," as critics later claimed, his inaction and initial reluctance to authorize the pulling down of neighboring houses to create a firewall allowed the flames to spread rap-idly. Windy conditions over the following days facilitated the fire's spread, and residents rich and poor worked tirelessly to get their goods out of harm's way. Some chose to place their possessions on barges in the Thames, and Restoration diarist John Evelyn reported seeing "the Thames covered with goods floating." Like a number of his colleagues, Sir William Penn moved his valuables to Kirby Castle, home of Sir William Rider, a merchant who played a major part in supplying the navy. But Penn and his neighbor Pepys also chose more cre-ative ways to secure their prized possessions: on the evening of September 4, according to Pepys, the two men "did dig [a pit in the garden], and put our wine in it; and I my Parmazan cheese, as well as my wine and some other things." The next day Pepys climbed the steeple at All Hallows church, where Sir William had baptized his namesake, and reported "the saddest sight of desolation that I ever saw; everywhere great fires, oil cellars, and brimstone, and other things burning." The two men also worked indefatigably in the face of the mayor's indecision, authorizing workmen to blow up and otherwise remove buildings for firewalls.[10]

The fire continued for days. The king, along with the Duke of York, person-ally took part in firefighting efforts, as Evelyn put it, "even laboring in person, and being present, to command, order, reward, and encourage workmen; by which he showed his affection to his people, and gained theirs." In addition to the wholesale destruction of homes, churches, and public buildings, the capital suffered a catastrophic breakdown in public order, an explosion in the number of homeless (nearly 200,000, by Evelyn's account), and the predictable search for scapegoats. The ongoing war with the Dutch, and ever-present anti-French and anti-Catholic sentiment, provided two potent targets, but foreigners of almost any stripe were fair game. Robert Hubert, a French watchmaker, claimed to have started the fire on orders from the pope. Hubert was likely insane, and his story certainly untrue, but he was convicted (by a jury including three members of the Farrinor family) and hanged, and his body dismembered by the assembled crowd. As time went on, the notion that Catholics were behind the Great Fire became more firmly entrenched in English political debate, particularly as the political winds twisted in the early 1670s and Charles's alliance with France faced growing opposition.[11]

The reasons for the fire and its rapid spread were painfully obvious, even in its immediate aftermath:

> The negligence of the master of his servants, in whose house the fire did first begin; the solitariness of the night, the narrowness of the place, the weakness of the buildings, the quantity of combustible and bituminous matters gathered thereabout, the preceding summer which was extraordinarily hot and dry, the east wind that blew violently all that while, and the want of engines and water to quench the fire.

Of course, these factors were also understood within a providential framework. Those who looked at the events with a clear eye would see "the heavy hand of God on us, for our sins, showing us the terror of his judgements in thus raising the fire; and immediately after, his . . . mercy, in putting a stop to it when we were in the last despair." The plague of 1665 joined in the public mind with the fire of 1666 to cement the idea of a wrathful God turning his judgment on a sinful land.[12]

By the time the fire was extinguished, a week after it started, Evelyn would recount that he "went again to the ruins, for it was now no longer a city." "London was," he wrote during the fire, "but is no more." When William Penn returned to London the next year, he would find the city transformed, both in the massive destruction it had suffered and the quick plans for rebuilding that prominent citizens began proposing even while the embers were still smoldering. On September 11, 1666, for example, less than a week after the fires had finally been put out, Evelyn "presented His Majesty with a survey of the ruins, and a plot for a new city." Other plans for rebuilding were submitted by well-known architect and royal favorite Sir Christopher Wren, natural scientist and philosopher Robert Hooke, and cartographer Richard Newcourt. Although none of these plans were adopted in their entirety, William Penn would draw on insights gleaned from the rebuilding of London when he designed his own capital city of Philadelphia fifteen years later.[13]

* * *

Having survived plague in 1665 and fire in 1666, William's parents had cause for celebration in early 1667. Their daughter Margaret was getting married.

The marriage license for Anthony Lowther and Margaret Penn was issued on February 12, and in his diary entry for February 15, Pepys reported hearing that "Peg Penn is married this day privately; no friends, but two or three relations on his side and hers." Never one to miss an opportunity to tweak Sir William, Pepys added that the Penns had "borrowed many things of my kitchen for dressing their dinner." Several months seem to have passed before Sir William informed his eldest son, who was still in Ireland when the wedding took place, that his sister had married, and by that time he was writing of his hopes that Margaret would soon provide him with a grandchild, and—ever the pragmatist—giving young William updates on Lowther's financial situation.[14]

Sir William was also becoming increasingly eager to see his son. In part his eagerness might have been due to the performance of the navy, which reached its nadir with the infamous "Raid on the Medway" of June 1667, in which Dutch ships sailed up the Thames River all the way to Gravesend, just twenty-five miles from the capital, and inflicted a devastating loss on the English fleet. Thankfully, Sir William wrote, he was nowhere near these events when they happened, but the cumulative effect of plague, fire, and war had clearly taken its toll on the national mood, as well as his spirits.[15]

At the same time, Sir William was clearly torn between his desire to see his son, who had now been away for more than a year, and his concern to obtain, at long last, clear and undisputed title to his Shanagarry lands. He initially expressed concern that William's romantic attachment to a young lady in England might tempt him to cut his Irish business short ("I have reason to believe you have kindness for a person on this side of the water"), and so reiterated that William should wait until he had obtained possession of the letters patent before returning to England. Once William had accomplished his primary task—the letters patent were finally issued in April—Sir William expected his son back home post haste, and wondered why William did not return at once. He recommended signing short leases with his tenants until the two of them had an opportunity to calculate the expenses involved in maintaining Irish properties, and assured his son, "I think I shall be the gladdest person to see you notwithstanding any expectations you might have from flattering women." In the meantime, he added tersely, "I know not what should keep you there."[16]

And yet William remained in Ireland. He was clearly still working on matters related to the running of the Penn estate, and he spent time that spring with Sir William Petty, one of the most important figures in the English colonizing project in Ireland, with whom he would form a lifelong friendship. Petty, two decades Penn's senior, had first come to Ireland as Physician-General to the parliamentary army in 1652, and by 1655 was overseeing the most ambitious land survey in Irish history. Completed in just a few months, Petty's Down Survey—which has been described as "the rock upon which successive Acts of Settlement founded two centuries of 'Protestant Ascendancy' in Ireland"—surveyed more than two million acres, facilitating the mass expropriation of land from Irish to English settlers. His work for Cromwell notwithstanding, Petty was knighted by Charles II in April 1661 and would, like Penn, become a Fellow of the Royal Society. William Penn was no doubt eager to hear Petty's thoughts on improvements that could render Irish lands profitable, something that bedeviled his father as it had English landlords for years.[17]

Sir William's letters to his son during October 1667 give voice to a father's growing concern about his son's actions, and indeed even his whereabouts. Two separate letters in October—one of which referred to "several" others that were apparently written and have been lost—went unanswered by a son plainly in the midst of a major life crisis. Finally, on October 22, Sir William commanded his son to "repair to me with all possible speed," adding that he was not to "make any stay [in Bristol] or any place upon the road . . . unless for necessary rest and refreshment." Sir William clearly knew that something was up. And something was, indeed, up.

By the time his father's letter reached him, William Penn had in all likelihood already been imprisoned, along with eighteen other Quakers, in the Cork city prison. His son had joined the Society of Friends, aligning himself with one of the most despised and persecuted sects of the day, targeted since their emergence and subject to fines, jailings, seizures of goods, and public whippings. It was the first of what would be many confrontations between Penn and the legal system resulting from his membership in the Society of Friends.[18] But who exactly were the Quakers, and why were they so controversial? In order to understand why Penn might have found Quakerism so appealing, and what made his decision to associate with them so momentous, we need to take a step back and look at the emergence of the Society of Friends, in both England and Ireland, out of the turmoil of the 1640s.

* * *

George Fox, son of a Leicestershire weaver, turned twenty the year William Penn was born. Penn would later eulogize Fox as "a new and heavenly-minded man . . . an original, no copy," and their alliance would transform the religious and political landscape of the Atlantic world. From an early age, Fox's contemplative nature and relentless pursuit of spiritual peace drove him to seek authentic spiritual experience and true religion wherever he might find it. But he was repeatedly disappointed, lamenting that "there was none among them all that could speak to my condition." At last, however, "When all my hopes . . . in all men were gone, so that I had nothing outwardly to help me, nor could I tell what to do . . . then, I heard a voice which said, 'There is one, even Christ Jesus, that can speak to thy condition'; and when I heard it," Fox wrote in his *Journal*, "my heart did leap for joy."[19]

Fox's inner spiritual turmoil mirrored his country's roiling political, religious, and social unrest. The breakdown of existing structures of authority during the Civil War years paved the way for an explosive growth in religious activity. Names familiar to twenty-first-century audiences (Baptists, Presbyterians, Congregationalists) as well as those that have passed into history (Familists, Ranters, Muggletonians) filled the vacuum produced by the overthrow of the Church of England along with the monarchy that had supported it. Part of Quakerism's power lay in its capacity to speak to individuals in the midst of enormous political and spiritual upheaval, and its egalitarian insistence on the divine spark, "that of God in every man," often referred to as the Inner Light or Light Within, articulated by Friends from their earliest days.[20]

This transformative spiritual experience drove home to Fox the utter unsuitability of all the religious options available in his society. He embarked on a traveling ministry, preaching repentance, worshipping in silence while waiting for the Spirit to move within the believer, and insisting on the fundamental importance of the Inner Light. Along the way, a number of practices grew up within these congregations, practices that would come to define the Quaker movement: a refusal to doff hats in the presence of social "superiors" and to swear oaths, an insistence on plain speech (thee and thou), and an eagerness to proselytize in often confrontational ways. Early Quakers were eager to preach the doctrine of the Inner Light whenever and wherever they could, and took particular pleasure in "declaring truth" at local parish churches during regular worship, a practice that often led to their imprisonment or physical abuse (or both) at the hands of worshippers or clergy (or both). These commitments violated conventional standards of behavior, to say nothing of the law of the land, in numerous ways, and Fox was repeatedly imprisoned during his travels.[21]

The Quaker movement quickly gathered momentum, and the early 1650s brought a number of crucial developments in its growth into a large-scale movement. The "creative moment in the history of Quakerism," according to Quaker historian William C. Braithwaite, came on Pendle Hill in east Lancashire in May 1652, when Fox had a vision of a great company of people dressed in white. The Pendle Hill vision was followed the next month by Fox's visit to the family of Judge Thomas Fell at Swarthmoor Hall in Cumbria, where the judge's wife Margaret was "convinced" by Fox's preaching. (Early Quakers tended to use the word "convincement" instead of "conversion," a practice that continues to this day.) Margaret Fell quickly became a pillar of the movement, justifying the prominent role of women in the Society and using her social prominence to advance the cause. Though her husband did not formally join the Quakers, he "was more than usually loving . . . to our Friends," Margaret later explained, and "sought after God in the best way that was made known to him." Judge Fell was known to sit in the next room, with the door ajar, when a Meeting was taking place. More importantly, he used his position to shield Friends from persecution whenever possible and to defend them from the full force of the law.[22]

The early 1650s also saw the convincement of James Nayler and Richard Farnsworth, two of the most influential early Quaker converts. Braithwaite calls Nayler "the most brilliant of the Quaker preachers," and he was second in importance only to Fox in the development of early Quakerism. By 1652, the Quaker movement had gained a base at Swarthmoor, with "Fox as general organizer, then Fell as administrator in charge of finance, and thirdly Nayler as chief publicist with Farnsworth in support." Friends also began to maintain a more regular presence in London, and a growing number of itinerant preachers—often referred to as "the Valiant Sixty"—took the Quaker message to the rest of England, Scotland, and Wales.[23]

From England, Quakers quickly fanned out across the British Atlantic. Friends arrived in the American colonies as early as 1655, traveling along a route from Barbados to Massachusetts and back again. Rhode Island and Maryland served as bases for their work. As they had in England, Quakers in America encountered a great deal of unwelcome attention and hostility; Massachusetts Bay authorities began legislating against them in the mid-1650s, with three Quakers suffering ear-croppings in late 1657 and four hung on Boston Common between 1659 and 1661. In late 1657 New Netherland authorized a £50 fine for those who hosted Quakers, which led some residents of Long Island to draft a petition, known to later generations as the Flushing Remonstrance, asking for leniency toward Quakers. Further south, Quakers in Anglican-controlled Virginia were initially prosecuted according to a 1643 law against Nonconformist preachers; in the early 1660s, Governor William Berkeley's government legislated directly against Quakers, and Friends were imprisoned, whipped, banished, and fined.[24]

But it is the story of Quakerism in Ireland that is most relevant to William Penn at this point in his life. Many of the English who received land in Ireland after the Civil Wars were parliamentary soldiers who had served under Cromwell, and religious radicalism was a hallmark of Cromwell's New Model Army. William Edmundson, generally considered the father of Irish Quakerism, was just such an individual. He had served in the army during the Civil War years, after which he and his wife settled in County Antrim. On a visit to England in 1653, Edmundson heard Nayler preach and became a convinced Quaker. Upon his return, Edmundson founded the first Irish Quaker Meeting, at Lurgan in County Armagh. From this tiny group of seven Friends, meeting in silence in Edmundson's home, the movement spread rapidly, with Edmundson in traveling ministry and Friends from England like Edward Burrough and Francis Howgill visiting Ireland during the second half of the 1650s. Concentrated in the larger towns and port cities—Dublin and Cork, where English Quakers like Elizabeth Fletcher and Elizabeth Smith, along with Burrough and Howgill, reinforced what Edmundson had begun; and Kinsale, where a sympathetic governor shielded Howgill from a warrant for his arrest—Irish Quakerism weathered persecution and grew steadily. Quaker Thomas Loe, as we have seen, preached to the Penn family at Macroom Castle some time during the mid-1650s, and by the time William Penn returned to Cork a decade later Friends had put down roots there. Fox himself would not visit Ireland until early 1669, but he formed a lasting bond with Edmundson, who accompanied him to America in 1672.[25]

From the Society of Friends' earliest days, the movement struggled with a tension between the incipient anarchic tendencies of its emphasis on the Inner Light or Light Within on the one hand, and Fox's desire for an organizational structure that would enable Quakers to speak authoritatively to broader audiences and coordinate the activities of its members on the other. Quakerism's emphasis on immediate revelation tended to produce internecine struggles, since Spirit-filled individuals did not always readily submit to the judgment of others. Fox attempted to rein in erratic behaviors, but—to provide just one example—Nayler's reenactment of Christ's entry into Jerusalem, in Bristol in 1656, proved a public relations disaster of the first order as well as a vivid illustration of the rivalry between these two leading Friends (and their followers). Nayler received a gruesome punishment after being convicted of blasphemy by Parliament—branded with a "B" for blasphemer, his tongue bored through with a hot iron, and two years of hard labor—and although the Bristol episode was gleefully recited by anti-Quaker critics, it also solidified Fox's position as, in his biographer H. Larry Ingle's words, "first among Friends." Over the ensuing years, Fox's supremacy would produce conflict with other leading figures, particularly due to his aspiration for a disciplinary structure to maintain cohesion, rein in wayward Friends, and provide support for those suffering. The structures simultaneously, and not coincidentally, cemented Fox's own position as "first Friend" and, to critics, restrained the exercise of conscience among those Spirit-filled individuals who had flocked to Quakerism seeking something other than the ecclesiastical hierarchies of Anglicans and Presbyterians.[26]

* * *

Given the extraordinary magnitude of William Penn's Quaker convincement and the impact it would have on developments on both sides of the Atlantic, it is surprising how few of its details were passed down by Penn or his fellow Friends. The closest thing we have to a contemporaneous account appears in the "Harvey manuscript," a secondhand account "delivered by [Penn] to Thomas Harvey" (whose identity remains a mystery), roughly thirty years later, which Harvey then related to an anonymous author, who in turn wrote it down "in a brief manner as well as his memory would serve him after such a distance of time." The document itself is dated 1729, thus more than sixty years after the events that it describes took place. Further complicating matters, we know neither who Thomas Harvey was, nor to whom he recounted the story of Penn's convincement.[27]

The precise timing of Penn's convincement has never been definitively established. Most likely, he began attending Friends Meetings at some point during the summer of 1667. Late in August, Penn received a letter from Lord Shannon (Orrery's brother), which indicates nothing out of the ordinary and in fact reads like a rather jovial recounting of social visits from one member of the Cork elite to another. Shannon mentions having recently seen Penn "in a young lady's company," and concluded by stating, "I hope to see you in two or three days at Cork." In mid-October, Shannon wrote to Penn again, and at this point something was clearly amiss. He assures Penn that "the malice of no ill-bred persons (which this country swarms [with]) shall in the least decline the real esteem I have for you, nor my civility to you," which suggests that he had, at least, heard rumors that cast aspersions on Penn's character. But what were those rumors?[28]

By October 1667, too, Sir William was openly complaining about his son's failure to respond to his letters and explain his continuing absence. Did William, in fact, "have kindness for a person on this [English] side of the water," as Sir William had hinted earlier? Were the "flattering women" mentioned by his father in Ireland, or England? We simply do not know, although Shannon's letter did mention having seen Penn "in a young lady's company." Fifteen years later, in 1682, an anonymous attack on Penn claimed that his Quaker convincement in Cork was in fact an elaborate subterfuge to escape a duel over a married woman with whom he had been carrying on an affair. The anonymous author described Penn in Ireland as "a pretty young gentleman" who deviously befriended his lover's husband so that he might "have free access to the admirable object of his passionate desires." Unfortunately for Penn, however, he had a rival for his beloved's affections, and in the ensuing confrontation the rival challenged Penn "to give the satisfaction . . . of a gentleman." According to this account Penn accepted, but subsequently "marched quite off," and "immediately turned Quaker . . . and left his love and honor behind him." Penn's departure from Ireland, then, was less about a summons home by his father and more about cravenly avoiding the possibility of fatal injury. It is a salacious and enticing story, though one utterly without corroborating details (namely, names). And the publication was clearly timed to embarrass Penn just after he had set out for America: the tract's subtitle dates it as "the 15th day of the month of Abib, in the first hegira or flight of the Prophet Penn to his Sylvania."[29]

Whatever the specifics of its timing, Penn's convincement would likely never have happened if not for the ministry of Thomas Loe. Loe had, to be sure, made an impression on the entire Penn family when he preached to them in Macroom during the mid-1650s. Young William had been particularly moved, and recalled observing his family's response to Loe's words and thinking, "What if they should all be Quakers?" In the intervening years, unbeknownst to Penn, Loe had become a leading Quaker minister, preaching in his hometown of Oxford as well as across England and Ireland. While buying clothes in Cork in 1667, William Penn related his memory of Loe's preaching to a Quaker shopkeeper, telling her that "if he knew where the person was if 'tware an hundred miles he would go to hear him again." He was in luck, she told him: Loe had recently arrived back in Ireland, and would be preaching at the local Friends Meeting the very next day.[30]

Penn arrived at the Meeting eager to hear Loe preach. Another Friend spoke first, and Penn reported that he "was not effected with his testimony." When Loe began to speak, however, Penn was overcome with emotion, "exceedingly reached so that he wept much," and immediately rose to his feet, since it had "seemed to him as if a voice said stand on thy feet, How dost thou know but somebody may be reached by your tears." After the Meeting, Penn spoke with Loe at length, and from this point on he seems to have attended Meetings regularly. But he still had something to learn about the Quaker peace testimony, which renounced "all outward wars and strife, and fighting with outward weapons." This was, after all, the same William Penn who just a year earlier had assisted in putting down the mutiny at Carrickfergus; and who had recently had the command of the Kinsale fort dangled in front of his eyes. A portrait of him during this period—one of the few painted during his lifetime—depicts him wearing an armor breastplate. And so when a "soldier came into the meeting making a great disturbance," William "[went] to him, [took] him by the collar, and would have thrown him down stairs" had he not been stopped by a Friend who asked Penn to let the man go, "for they was a peaceable people and would not have him make a disturbance there."[31]

Although Penn's use of force against the soldiers showed how far he had to go to fully embrace Quaker principles, the incident proved to be crucial to Penn's emerging sense of himself as one of them. Following the confrontation, the soldier whom Penn had accosted "went to the magistrates and brought the officers which broke up the meeting and made several of them prisoners, and [Penn] among the rest." Thus came to pass the first great crisis of Penn's life as a Quaker. Not surprisingly, given the length of time William had spent in the area over the past year and the prominence of the Penn name, "the magistrate . . . knowing [Penn] told him he did not think him a Quaker so would not send him to jail." This attempt to draw a distinction between Penn and his newfound coreligionists drew a rebuke from the defendant, who took the opportunity, perhaps for the first time publicly, to cast his lot with the Friends. He "told [the magistrate] whether he thought him [a Quaker] or not . . . he was one and if he sent his friends to prison he was willing to go with them."[32]

Whether he thought him a Quaker or not . . . he was one and if he sent his friends to prison he was willing to go with them. In a sense, setting aside the details of

his convincement and its timing, William Penn became a Quaker at just this
moment, making a public profession—"he was one"—and rejecting an opportunity to draw on family connections to obtain his release. The magistrate proved
only too willing to accede to Penn's request, and committed him to jail with the
rest. Penn and his fellow Quakers, nineteen in all, were charged with "being present at a riotous and tumultuary assembly," violating a 1661 royal proclamation
banning Quaker Meetings, as well as the 1664 Conventicles Act. They were confined in the city jail.[33]

The Cork imprisonment was important to William Penn for a number of
reasons. It provided him with his first opportunity to identify with the Society
of Friends, not only to himself and to Friends, but before the wider world,
and at significant personal cost. His refusal to accept a release further enabled
him to express his solidarity with persecuted Friends, an identification made
more powerful, one suspects, by the ill treatment and collective experience of
"suffering" that accompanied it. More broadly, his Cork imprisonment must
have laid bare to Penn the dual nature of his existence in Ireland. On the one
hand, as his father's agent, he represented an occupying colonial elite and
enjoyed easy access to the corridors of power. On the other, as a Quaker, he
identified with a persecuted and widely reviled sect and found himself punished
by the same political and legal order within which he had been working for the
past year and a half.

His confinement in the Cork jail also resulted in William Penn's first written
denunciation of persecution and defense of liberty of conscience, inaugurating a
long public career that would stretch over more than four decades. On November
4, 1667, Penn composed an indignant letter to the Earl of Orrery, Lord President
of Munster, on behalf of himself and the Quakers arrested along with him.
Although this brief appeal does not break any new conceptual ground in the development of arguments for religious liberty (it was intended to convince Orrery
to release the prisoners, not to engage in extended philosophical debate over the
merits of toleration) it does provide the first documentary evidence of Penn's
embrace of them. Appealing to the earl for the "speedy releasement to all for
attending their honest callings," Penn argued for the compatibility of religious
dissent with economic prosperity and civil peace. He urged Orrery, who was of
course a key colonial administrator, to realize that persecution would constitute
"a bad argument to invite English hither" (i.e., to Ireland). The earl must surely
know, based on "the acquaintance you have had with other countries . . . [that]
diversities of faith and worship contribute not to the disturbance of any place,
where moral uniformity is barely requisite to preserve the peace." In brief, Penn
saw "no way so effectual to improve, or advantage, this country as to dispense
with freedom in things relating to conscience." These brief references to moral
uniformity as mitigating the potential discord brought on by religious diversity,

and toleration as the key to prosperity, were the kernels of the far more elaborate theory of toleration that Penn would develop over the course of the next four— not to mention forty—years.[34]

William Penn was no stranger to the Earl of Orrery, who had assisted him in securing Sir William's title to his Irish lands and formed part of the Irish elite with whom he had associated so closely during his sojourn there. In this case, the personal connection did him little good, and the earl swiftly replied that he had been "surprised and sorry" to see Penn associating with Quakers. He reiterated his intention to enforce the law, and reminded Penn that the king was the ultimate arbiter: "The liberty which it seems you would have cannot be allowed by me, unless it first be allowed by his majesty's authority." He further informed Penn that before he even received his letter, he had directed the mayor to release the prisoners with a stern warning. "Tis the law which I shall make my rule," Orrery wrote, "and I advise you to do the like, but if your conscience be against the law . . . you cannot expect that I will hinder the magistrates from doing their duty." But perhaps most unfortunately, from William Penn's perspective, Orrery wrote that "I sent this day by post to your father" news about his son's imprisonment.[35]

And so the proverbial cat was out of the bag. Sir William's suspicions of something awry in Ireland were confirmed. William could delay no longer, and he set out for London.

* * *

To say that his son's casting his lot with Quakers was not part of Sir William Penn's grand plan for his son, and that he was displeased by the events of the fall of 1667, would be rather an understatement. No doubt all the bitterness of the Oxford expulsion came flooding back into the father–son relationship. William surely knew how his father would feel, so on his way home, despite Sir William's explicit instructions, he stopped in Bristol—"strengthen[ing] himself know[ing] his father would not be very pleasant upon him"—visiting with his father's old navy colleague George Bishop. Bishop, a brewer and convinced Friend whose 1661 *New England judged* had excoriated Massachusetts Puritans for their persecution of Quakers, wrote a heartfelt letter for William to carry to his father, in which he urged Sir William to receive his son "into your arms, and love," and not to "by any kind of estrangedness, put sadness on him." The two men—Bishop, the longstanding Friend, and William, the new convert— clearly spoke at some length about William's recent experiences, and Bishop wrote to Sir William that his son had at last experienced "the true sense and conviction of that which all along since his childhood he hath sought to understand." He urged his old navy colleague to acknowledge that William's Quaker convincement rested "in his conscience to God, which is out of the power of man . . . and is to be cherished."[36]

And so, armed with Bishop's letter (and little else), William Penn arrived in London to face his father by early December. (Pepys reported hearing of his return on December 5, 1667.) Accompanying him to this day of reckoning was Josiah Coale, a powerful Quaker preacher about a dozen years William's senior who, like him, had been raised in a prosperous family and became a convinced Quaker in his twenties. By the time he accompanied William Penn to London, offering support in (as Penn would later put it) "the gloomy and dark day of my early and deep exercises," Coale had already traveled to Holland, Barbados, and North America, and had authored a widely circulated account of the aid that Native Americans had rendered to itinerant Friends in the American wilderness. While Coale was present in the Penn household, Sir William "kept his temper," but after he departed the reality of young William's religious transformation, and the totality of his rejection of his father's hopes and plans, seems to have taken hold. It would have been impossible for a father and son to have even the most cursory of conversations without the enormity of Penn's religious turn becoming plainly evident, since the son's use of "thee" and "thou" toward his father—the Quaker practice of plain speech—was in direct contravention of the deferential customs expected when addressing one's elders or social superiors.[37]

The issue of plain speech shows clearly how, in joining with the Society of Friends, William Penn was not merely adopting a new set of religious "beliefs." He was doing nothing less than taking on a new identity, emphatically and openly turning his back on his father's world and on its guiding assumptions: that social rank deserved a certain type of deference; that worship ought to take place in established religious institutions; or even, remembering his encounter in France, that insults to personal honor, and disputes more generally, ought to be settled by force. Penn explained to his father that "twas in obedience to God and not in any disrespect to him" that he insisted on plain speech and address. But his father surely *did* see it as disrespect, and offered his son a compromise, telling William that "he might thee and thou those who he pleased" so long as he used respectful address to the king, the Duke of York, and his own father. William's unwillingness to accept even this compromise infuriated Sir William, who ended the conversation and went to bed.[38]

William feared that his father might take him in person to the king or the Duke of York to place the issue of his thee-ing and thou-ing directly before the royals and forcing him into a public confrontation he desperately wanted to avoid, but this concern turned out to be unfounded. Instead, the next morning Sir William took his son out for a ride in his coach and poured out his deep disappointment and grief over this recent turn of events in his son's life. Reflecting on what William's decision said about his own parenting, he told William that "he could not tell what he could think of himself after he had trained [William] up in learning and other accomplishments for a courtier—as for an ambassador or other minister that he should become a Quaker." Not surprisingly, William did not think his religious decisions in any way worthy of disapproval; after all, he had finally found a spiritual home after twenty years of seeking and spiritual turmoil. He attempted to divert his father from focusing on what his son was giving up (fame, wealth, influence) and instead emphasized that his convincement represented "obedience to the manifestation of God in his own conscience." He also reminded his father of Thomas Loe's visit to Macroom, and how he had "observed his father in tears at that time"—adding, perhaps inadvisedly, that he had believed Sir William "to be convinced of the truth of the doctrine of the Quakers as well himself only the grandeur of the world was too great for him to give up."[39]

Following this conversation, the pair went next to a tavern, where William "expected he was to be caned." Instead, his father intended only to beseech his son one more time—"he would kneel down and pray to God that [William] might not be a Quaker nor go to any more of their meetings." Rejecting his father's plea in the most dramatic way available to him, William threatened to throw himself out of the window to avoid hearing any more of his father's pleas. Fortunately for William, just then a nobleman who had been passing by and seen the Penns' coach at the tavern stopped in to speak to the pair. More fortunately for William, this unnamed nobleman proceeded to praise the young man to his father, saying that "he might think himself happy in a son that could despise the grandeur of the world and refrain from the many vices they were running after."[40]

"After some time," Penn's convincement narrative continues, William journeyed with an unnamed friend to an unspecified destination. On the way he discarded his wig; recall that a childhood bout of smallpox had led to the loss of much of his hair. Quaker renunciation of worldly pleasures notwithstanding, his throwing away of the wig would not last long, and he would continue to wear one on occasion for years to come. Yet at this early point of his Quaker convincement, Penn reported that the wig became "burdensome to him," so he "took off his hat, turned his wig off his head behind him, not looking back to see what became of it." It was on this journey, too, that "William's mouth was first opened" and he preached for the first time to a gathered congregation, indicating his entry into the Quaker ministry. But he was no ordinary Quaker; he was the oldest son and heir of a famous father, and his preaching did not go unnoticed. Local magistrates made sure that Sir William received word that his son was "causing tumults by preaching the Quaker's doctrine." Once again, just as he had been in Ireland, William was summoned home by his father. And once again— as he had upon returning from Ireland—William took his time in complying with his father's wishes.

Unlike the delay in Bristol on his way home to face his father, which merely delayed the inevitable, this delay would change William Penn's life in a more fundamental way. Returning to London, he attended a Meeting before facing his father, no doubt to steel himself for what was to come. "After [the] meeting," Penn reported, he "went up into the room where a Friend brought Guli Springett which was the first time he saw her who was afterward his wife." We know nothing about this first encounter between the two other than that he "saw her." Did many words pass between them? Was it love at first sight? Penn reports only that "he saw her" and that afterward he returned home to face his father's wrath.[41]

The passage of time had not softened Sir William's attitude toward his son, and the news of William's Quaker proselytizing surely did not help matters. He was finished with pleading and bargaining, Sir William said, and ordered his son to "take his clothes and be gone from his house," adding that "he should dispos[e] of his estate to them that pleased him better." This last salvo was bound to miss the mark in a young man so devoted to rejection of the world and its riches, and William voiced his sorrow, not at losing his inheritance, but at having lost his father's affection. He gathered up his things and bid farewell to his mother and sisters. As he was leaving he insisted to his father that he would continue to pray for him; and with that, to the great sorrow of the rest of the family, he departed. Just before the account of Penn's convincement concludes, however, the story takes one final turn. "He was not got far before a servant was sent for him to return . . . when he returned his father was gone out of the way so he soon got to his room till his father's displeasure was something abated."[42]

Virtually all accounts of Penn's life assume that he was summarily dismissed from the household and reduced to poverty, a view propounded by Penn's first biographer, Joseph Besse. Pepys reported in late December that William "is a Quaker again, or some very melancholy thing," and that "he cares for no company." The Harvey manuscript calls this claim into question, or at least makes a clear chronology more difficult to nail down. The editor of the Harvey manuscript suggests that perhaps the "banishment [lasted] less than a day, though possibly the estrangement [between father and son] lasted longer." But whether he was summarily dismissed from his father's house, or whether his father's "displeasure was something abated" after a briefer period, as the Harvey manuscript suggests, what is not in dispute is that a great deal of animosity continued to poison the air between father and son.[43]

* * *

And so began a period of exile, perhaps from his father's house but certainly from his father's favor. William attempted to lower the heat of the disagreements by plainly laying out his newfound faith in a document intended for his father, "who at that time was in high wrath against me, because of my separation from the world," as he put it sometime later. In the work, which he titled "The Two

Kingdoms of Darkness and Light," the newly convinced Quaker selected and arranged scriptural passages in two columns, vindicating his newfound faith by contrasting worldly practices with those of the true Spirit of Christ. Since his Quaker convincement, Penn wrote to his father, "I [have] been made daily desirous of dying to all the sin, pomp, and vain fashion of this world." No response from Sir William survives. He may well not even have read it.[44]

The departure from his father's pleasure, if not his house, was simultaneously William Penn's full-blown entrance into the life of a Quaker controversialist: Penn "rushed into the scrimmage" of Restoration religious debate, taking part in two public confrontations with critics of Quakerism during 1668 and drawing sustenance from the London Quaker community, which may have sheltered him if, in fact, he was ejected by his father from the family home. It was a perilous existence; Parliament had specifically targeted Quakers for punishment and Friends experienced almost universal hostility in society more generally. By the end of the year he would be languishing in the Tower of London on a blasphemy charge. But for the first half of the year, his whereabouts are unknown.[45]

We do know, however, where Penn was in October 1668. He was in High Wycombe, Buckinghamshire, along with Thomas Loe and George Whitehead. Whitehead, a leading Quaker polemicist and one of the Valiant Sixty, had been convinced by Fox in the early 1650s and would become one of Penn's closest companions in the Quaker ministry. Whitehead had endured whipping and imprisonment while preaching across England, and in the process had amassed a wealth of legal knowledge. The three Quakers—Penn, Loe, and Whitehead—were visiting the Duke of Buckingham, appealing to him to use his influence to ease persecution on Dissenters, when Loe fell ill. He was moved to the home of Edward Mann, a London Friend who frequently offered his residence as a Quaker gathering place. There Loe remained in a weakened state for more than a week, during which time Penn too fell ill. Knowing the severity of Loe's illness, Penn insisted on leaving his own bed to be with his friend, whom he described as "in a sweet readiness to be gone." After exhorting Friends to remain faithful, Loe offered a benediction for the young man whom he had brought to the faith: "Taking my hand, he spake thus, Dear heart, bear thy cross, stand faithful for God, and bear thy testimony in thy day and generation, and God will give thee an eternal crown of glory that none shall ever take from thee."

Loe passed away on October 6, and was buried a day later: "We laid the vessel in the ground," Penn wrote to Isaac Penington, a leading London Friend and Gulielma Springett's stepfather, "as having done its master's work and well." Passing along the sad news, he lamented the loss of one "whom my soul loved, whilst alive; and bemoans, now dead, yet have pure fellowship with that which lives forever."[46]

* * *

But there was little time to mourn Thomas Loe: the enemies of Quakerism were all around and denunciations of Friends came from all sides. Midway through the seventh chapter of his 1668 *Guide to the true religion*, Anglican priest Jonathan Clapham, of Wramplingham in Norfolk, listed Quakers among "those that overthrow the foundations of Christianity." In fact, Clapham insisted, Quakerism "cannot properly be called a sect of Christians, but rather . . . a total apostasy from Christianity." Clapham distinguished between the variety of Protestant sects in England at the time—which he called "different forms of the same religion"—and Friends, whom he placed in the category of "damnable heresies," alongside Catholicism and Socinianism (the latter a forerunner, of sorts, of modern-day Unitarianism). "Christians," he wrote, "can have no communion with them." Clapham was no newcomer to the world of anti-Quakerism. His 1656 *Full discovery and confutation of the wicked and damnable doctrines of the Quakers* had not only denounced their denial of the Trinity and other basic Christian doctrines, but called them "enemies to all civility and good manners."[47]

Penn showed himself to be a quick study in the thrust and parry of early modern religious debate, in which authors traded personal insults alongside substantive theological points. He was adept at both the extended point-by-point rebuttals (which often stretched on for page after page) and the ad hominem attacks that were part and parcel of early modern public controversy. Penn went on the offensive, publishing *The guide mistaken* and pointing out how Clapham had temporized and equivocated during the tumultuous years of the English Civil Wars and Interregnum. (He had, after all, dedicated his *Full discovery* to Oliver Cromwell.) After criticizing Clapham's religious views, Penn moved on to accuse his "peevish adversary" of hypocrisy in arguing for adherence to the Anglican church when he had shifted his allegiances during the 1640s and 1650s. The only constant he could see in Clapham's career, Penn insisted, "has been the keeping of his Parish through his very great *inconstancy,* in his perswasions."[48]

And yet in the midst of this heated back-and-forth, Penn also found a way to make a substantive political point. In outlining the boundaries of legitimate government, he reminded civil magistrates that

> their authority cannot reasonably extend beyond the end for which it was appointed, which being not to enthrone themselves sovereign moderators in causes purely conscientious . . . but only to maintain the impartial execution of justice, in regulating civil matters with most advantage to the tranquility, enrichment and reputation of their territories, they should not bend their forces, nor employ their strength, to gratify the self-seeking spirit of the priests, or any private interest whatsoever.

Politics as "the impartial execution of justice," concerned with the regulation of civil matters; the sanctity of "causes purely conscientious"; legitimate government as endangered by "self-seeking" priests who use the power of the state for their own ends: the core components of William Penn's mature theory of religious toleration appears in these few sentences, written when he was a twenty-four-year-old controversialist entering one of his first public debates.[49]

Clapham did not reply to Penn's critique, and no doubt Penn considered himself to have vanquished his foe. No doubt, too, the Anglican considered his Quaker foe not worth responding to. Not long thereafter, though, Penn would be drawn into yet another public debate.

* * *

Up next in Penn's burgeoning career as Quaker controversialist were the Presbyterians Thomas Vincent and Thomas Danson. Like many Nonconforming clergy, Vincent had performed heroic service during the 1665 plague, remaining in London and ministering to those in need after so many Anglican priests had fled the city and left their congregants bereft of spiritual, to say nothing of material, comfort. Unlike Clapham, Vincent did not have a track record of anti-Quaker activities or writing, and his confrontation with Penn and Whitehead seems to have been sparked by something much more personal: two of his congregants visited a Friends Meeting and ended up convinced Quakers. Danson, on the other hand, a minister in Sandwich, Kent, was a longstanding and vociferous critic of Friends. The contentious exchange that passed between Penn and Whitehead on the one hand, and Vincent and Danson on the other, provides a window into the raucous religious and political atmosphere of Restoration London.[50]

According to Penn, the controversy began when two members of Vincent's Spitalfield congregation decided to fulfill St. Paul's injunction to "prove all things; hold fast that which is good": "Two persons lately of Thomas Vincent's auditory in Spittle-Yard . . . being desirous to prove all things, and hold fast the best, visited our Meetings, to understand if we were as really deserving blame, as represented by our Enemies."[51] In Penn's telling, these discerning Christians decided to visit a Quaker Meeting to see for themselves whether Friends were as vile as their critics claimed. (In his published response to Penn, *The foundation of God standeth sure*, Vincent presented a darker view of these two congregants, describing one of them as having "a perverse will."[52]) When they visited the Meeting, Penn wrote, "it then pleased Divine Goodness to visit them with the call of his Light, from the inventions, carnal observations, will-worship, and vain conversation of those to whom they formerly were related, that they might be made children of the day." These earnest Presbyterian seekers, in short, were convinced of the truth of Friends' principles and the inadequacy of their former religious attachments. But of course in the boisterous religious marketplace that was Restoration London, the Quakers' gain was the Presbyterians' loss. When, despite his earnest entreaties, Vincent's followers left his congregation, Penn claimed, Vincent's

> peevish zeal transported him beyond, not only the moderation of Christianity, but the civility of education, venting his folly and prejudice much to this purpose, That he had as [leave] they should go to a bawdy-house, as to frequent the Quakers Meeting, because of their erroneous and damnable doctrines: And pointing to the window, said, If there should stand a cup of poison, I would rather drink it, than suck in their damnable doctrines. He further exprest himself in this manner to one of them; If ever you go again, I will give you up, and God will give you up, that you may believe a lie, and be damn'd.

In Penn's view, Vincent's persecuting spirit epitomized the shortcomings of so much of the orthodox Christianity of his day. Unwilling to honor the consciences of his parishioners, Vincent elevated doctrinal differences above basic morality (claiming that he would rather have his congregants visit a brothel than a Quaker Meeting). That Vincent viewed his actions as "zealous endeavor to keep a poor soul out of the dark path" did not make his conduct any less objectionable to Penn. To him, Presbyterians like Vincent had no problem claiming that *they* ought to be tolerated, but vigorously interfered with the liberty of others whose consciences dictated a different religious path. Presbyterians were only interested in their own sufferance, something many sectarians had been claiming for years. John Milton himself had insisted, in his 1646 sonnet "On the New Forcers of Conscience," that "new presbyter is old priest writ large."[53]

To Penn's delight, Vincent's appeals to poison and bawdy houses did not convince these new Friends to forsake their newfound Quaker brethren. As a result of Vincent's abuse, Penn and Whitehead asked for a public meeting, "in which we might have liberty to answer on the behalf both of ourselves and Principles." Vincent agreed, but he "rigged the meeting for maximum dramatic effect," setting the time for debate at two in the afternoon, but telling his supporters to arrive an hour early:

> As a result, rather than a serious and civil debate, the Presbyterians engaged in laughing, hissing, shoving, striking, and stigmatizing us with the opprobrious terms of confident fellow, impudent villain, blasphemer, &c. And, as the usual refuge of shallow persons . . . he questioned much whether I was not some Jesuit.[54]

Vincent cut the debate short by extinguishing the candles and dismissing the audience, abruptly departing the scene. The Quakers remained even after Vincent had left, attempting to vindicate themselves, and Vincent eventually reappeared, coming "very palely" down the stairs (in Penn's telling) and commanding the people to be gone. According to Penn, Vincent agreed to another meeting to continue the debate, an agreement on which he later backtracked, offering only to meet Penn and Whitehead in private. If Vincent thought that he could avoid further meetings with the Quakers that easily, he underestimated the resolve of Penn and Whitehead, who visited his parish in person attempting to secure a public engagement, whereupon, according to Penn, Vincent "slunk most shamefully away."

Vincent, of course, claimed that he vanquished the Quakers, and insisted that Penn had rambled and had not presented clear arguments. A public debate proposed by Penn and Whitehead never took place, and Danson instead published his *Synopsis of Quakerism*, which attacked Penn, and charged the Quakers with blasphemy. Penn prepared detailed replies to each of Danson's main points—concerning the nature and sufficiency of the Light Within for salvation, the possibility of attaining freedom from sin in this earthly life, the relationship between sanctification and justification, and the nature of the Trinity—but never made them public. Whitehead's defense of Quaker principles, *The divinity of Christ*, responded to Vincent and Danson and even took aim at Penn's old mentor John Owen.[55]

The disputes with Clapham, Vincent, and Danson provide some sense of Penn's whereabouts and his doings during the months after he left his father's house in early 1668. Following the unsuccessful attempts by Penn and Whitehead to arrange another debate with the Presbyterians, events set in motion by the controversy took on a life of their own. Penn's *The sandy foundation shaken* presented, in addition to a narrative of the controversies with the Presbyterians, a justification of Quakers' conduct and a defense of their theological positions on the Trinity, atonement theory, and the divinity of Christ. Pepys had his wife read the book to him, and displaying once again his dismissive attitude toward the Penns, pronounced it "so well writ as, I think, it is too good for him ever to have writ it." He also, though, called it "a serious sort of book, and not fit for everybody to read." The book soon became the primary exhibit in a blasphemy charge against William Penn and his printer, John Darby.[56]

* * *

If Penn's first imprisonment—a day or two in the Cork jail—was over almost as soon as it began, his second lasted much longer. He was confined in the Tower of London for nearly eight months, from December 1668 to July 1669, as a result of the publication of *The sandy foundation shaken*. Darby, who had frequently found

himself in trouble with the authorities for publishing unauthorized works, was
sent to the Gatehouse prison, near Westminster Abbey. The Gatehouse had
seen its share of famous prisoners as well, including Sir Walter Raleigh; three
decades later, Pepys would find himself briefly confined there. While in the
Tower, Penn was held "close prisoner": in other words, he was denied exercise,
fresh air, and most visitors, except for his father, a family servant, and Anglican
clergymen specifically charged with convincing William to recant his theological positions. Given the prisoner's social prominence, royal chaplain Edward
Stillingfleet received permission to visit him and attempt to persuade him out of
his "blasphemous and heretical opinions." Years later, Penn recalled Stillingfleet's
"humanity" toward him as well as his "moderation, learning, and kindness." Less
fondly remembered, surely, would be Humphrey Henchman, Bishop of London,
who threatened Penn with life imprisonment if he would not publicly recant his
views.[57]

But William Penn had clearly learned something from his time with Quakers
in England and Ireland, and wholeheartedly embraced the role of martyr for
conscience. "Tell my father," he told his servant, "that my prison shall be my
grave before I will budge a jot, for I owe my conscience to no mortal man," and
he offered similar assurances to London Quakers, some of whom may have
expressed some uncertainty about the strength of their prominent new convert's
resolve. Meanwhile, his father was petitioning the king for his son's release,
insisting that William's "departure from the Protestant religion hath been, and
still is his very great affliction."[58]

Six months or so into his confinement, Penn wrote a remarkable letter to Lord
Arlington, the Secretary of State. Although the ostensible purpose of the letter
was to plead his innocence and seek an audience with the king, Penn used the
occasion to rehearse a number of substantive arguments against persecution, all
of which would become part of his emerging thinking on liberty of conscience.
A year in the company of leading London Quakers had clearly had an effect, and
the letter to Arlington provided an extensive elaboration of the points advanced
in skeletal form in his letter to Orrery from the Cork jail.

In the letter to Arlington, Penn lamented the notion, which he saw undergirding
his imprisonment and the persecutory framework of Restoration Anglicanism,
that individuals must conform to established religious understandings in order
to "eat, drink, walk, trade, confer, or enjoy their liberties or lives." "What if I differ
from some religious apprehensions publicly imposed? Am I therefore incompatible with the well-being of human societies?" He insisted, in an echo of his earlier
reference to Orrery about "moral uniformity," that it did not take a great deal
of scholastic subtlety to understand that "whoredom, perjury, lying, cozening,
intemperance, injustice, etc. are unlawful, or destructive of good order." Civil
government should focus its efforts on punishing those who violate principles

of good neighborliness and civil order, and govern by a "balancing of parties." This argument about civil interest and moral uniformity often carried a singularly economic aspect, given Quakers' frequent invocation of their own sober industriousness: as Penn put it, "No man is wont to come and ask at any shop of what religion the master is, in order to a bargain, but rather what's the price of this or that commodity."[59]

Penn also drew on scriptural passages, including the distinction between things owed to Caesar and those owed to God (Matthew 22:21), and Paul's reference to faith as the gift of God (Ephesians 2:8). He cited numerous historical examples from Jewish Scriptures, classical history, and the early church to provide compelling evidence of "with what success kingdoms and commonwealths have lived by the discreet balancing of parties" and the toleration of multiple religious communities in one polity. Penn also drew on the well-known epistemological argument for toleration, asserting that "the understanding can never be convinced by other arguments then what are adequate to her own nature . . . he is always in the wrong, who by . . . corporal extremities thinks to illuminate and convince the understanding." Such physical punishments "may indeed make hypocrites, not converts." Drawing on English law, Penn insisted that his imprisonment was "contrary . . . to the natural privilege of an Englishman."[60]

Although the letter to Arlington presented a number of positions in favor of a policy of toleration, to which Penn would return repeatedly in the years to come, he also kept busy with other things while in the Tower. He continued to participate in religious debate with critics of Quakerism, penning a scathing letter to Lodowick Muggleton, founder of the eponymous "Muggletonians," who claimed to have brought about the death of Josiah Coale by putting a curse on him. Penn denounced Muggleton in extremely personal terms, ridiculing the idea that Coale's death "was the effect of thy silly curse" and calling Muggleton a "confederate with the unclean croaking spirits reserved under the chains of eternal darkness." Put a curse on me, Penn dared him, and see whether it does me any harm. As one scholar has put it, "Although Muggleton was perfectly happy to curse Penn and warn him of the fate of other Quakers who had opposed him, he cautiously avoided predicting Penn's immediate death."[61]

While in the Tower, Penn also began work on a substantial work of social critique and Quaker apologetics that laid out objections to such practices as hat-honor, honorific titles, and luxurious apparel, which would be published the following year as *No cross, no crown*. If the letter to Arlington, with its nascent arguments for religious toleration, sketched out the kernel of his political theory, *No cross, no crown* sought to justify Quaker approaches to social conventions more generally. It offered Penn's first systematic articulation of the social practices that distinguished Quakers from many of their contemporaries, such as their refusal to swear oaths and remove hats in the presence of their social superiors, as well as plain speech and opposition to finery and ornate apparel. In just over a hundred pages, Penn laid out dozens of reasons for Quaker positions and buttressed those arguments with testimonies from ancient and modern statesmen and philosophers, church fathers, and Reformers.[62]

* * *

Much like his missive to Orrery, Penn's letter to Arlington seems not to have achieved its desired effect. He remained in the Tower for another five weeks. Despite his appeal to the secretary for "the favor of an access to the King" to clear his name, the official order for his release relied on Stillingfleet's claims that Penn was "sensible of the impiety and blasphemy of his said heretical opinions, and . . . doth recant and retract the same," and that he had retracted his heretical opinions in print. Although he did publish *Innocency with her open face*, which secured his release from the Tower by publicly affirming his belief in the divinity of Christ, Penn insisted that *The sandy foundation* had been misunderstood and that he had never held the views attributed to him. Penn was released into the custody of his father, and six weeks later he was on his way back to Ireland.[63]

4

Celebrity

Sir William hoped to accomplish two things by sending William back to Ireland. First, and probably more importantly, he wanted to get his son out of England and thus, hopefully, keep him out of trouble. William had already been imprisoned once in Ireland and once in England, which was two times too many from his father's perspective. Second, conscious of his own declining health and notwithstanding his grave disappointment at his son's religious transformation, he hoped to further groom William into the life of an English gentleman and landholder in Ireland. Perhaps he hoped that the outcome of another Irish trip would be something like the outcome of his earlier Grand Tour of Europe, which had produced a Penn (at least outwardly) at ease with the world and its values.

One thing Sir William was surely not interested in doing was encouraging his son's Quakerism. By this point he seems to have become somewhat resigned, though still heartily opposed, to his son's religious scruples. Perhaps he had even read the "The Two Kingdoms of Darkness and Light." But the disharmony between the two had not fully dissipated. In a letter to his son a month after his departure, Sir William wrote that "If you are ordained to be another cross to me, God's will must be done, and I shall arm myself against it."[1]

As it turned out, William Penn did spend a great deal of time during his nine-month stay in Ireland visiting imprisoned Friends, attending and preaching at Quaker Meetings, disputing with representatives of other religious communities, and appealing to officials in Cork, Dublin, and elsewhere for gentler treatment of Quakers. That his efforts were largely unsuccessful, despite generally courteous treatment befitting the son of an English nobleman, is perhaps not surprising. After all, his father's fame notwithstanding, William Penn still represented a despised and outlawed sect, and was asking for what many officials considered both a dangerous policy and a legal impossibility: a direct contravention of the king's wishes and settled law.

The trip came at a crucial time in William Penn's life. He had been a convinced Quaker for nearly two years, had twice suffered imprisonment for his faith, and had become active in publicly defending English Quakers against their critics.

The tension between the two aspects of William Penn's identity—Quaker and English—would grow more pronounced during this second trip to Ireland. As a Friend, he traveled far and wide, in a broad circuit between Cork and Dublin, as a member of a persecuted sect, subject to arrest or fines at any time. As a Penn, on the other hand, he traversed the land as representative of a colonizing elite that had expropriated vast amounts of Irish land and dispossessed countless native inhabitants in a centuries-long, exceedingly violent conquest, of which Oliver Cromwell's devastation was only the most recent example. His tasks on his father's behalf included negotiating new leases with tenants as well as overseeing the transfer of authority at the Kinsale fort (which his father had decided to relinquish, due to his increasing health problems) and mingling with the ruling elite. One wonders how events might have turned out differently if Sir William had resigned the Kinsale command in 1666, when the Duke of Ormond had wanted to bestow it upon his son. Would William have been in Cork to hear Loe's preaching? Would he have come to Quakerism by some other route, or not at all?

During his previous trip to Ireland, William had shown himself more than capable of looking after his father's business. Notwithstanding his Quaker convincement and subsequent imprisonment, he had successfully secured the letters patent confirming the Penn claims in Shanagarry, cementing his father's land titles and setting the family's finances on firmer footing by removing their main rival claimant, Colonel Wallis, from the picture. Sir William no doubt saw sending his son on this journey as a win–win proposition—making himself useful in Ireland, and staying out of trouble in England—and William left London in mid-September 1669, just six weeks after his release from the Tower. He was getting out of the country for his own good—and for his father's.

* * *

As he made his way west from London to Bristol, where he would take passage to Ireland, William Penn visited English Friends, including some of the most "weighty" Quakers in the land. First, he stopped at the home of Isaac Penington, then living at Amersham in Buckinghamshire, about twenty miles northwest of the capital. Penington came from a prominent family—his father had served as Lord Mayor of London in 1642—and had become a convinced Quaker upon hearing Fox preach in 1658. His prolific writings on political affairs as well as his defenses of Quaker principles, along with his numerous imprisonments, had earned him a place of honor among Friends. Before its seizure by the Crown, Penington's estate, the Grange in Chalfont St. Giles, had served as a hub for Quaker activity, but by 1669 he and his family—his wife was Gulielma Springett's mother Mary—had relocated to Amersham. Friends held Meetings at Penington's home as well as in nearby Jordans, where William Russell's farm served as a frequent Quaker gathering place. (Nearly two decades later, Friends would build a Meetinghouse on the site, and William, Gulielma, his second wife Hannah, and several of his children would eventually be laid to rest there.)

William Penn of course had his father's business to attend to, but he also tended to affairs of the heart, since a visit to Isaac Penington was also a visit to Gulielma. He remained in Amersham long enough to spend time with Gulielma, including a day trip to Penn-Street, a village several miles away.[2]

Joining Penn at Amersham was Philip Ford, who arrived on September 20 from his home in Aylesbury, just to the north. Ford, a shopkeeper who had shared a prison cell with Isaac Penington four years earlier, would spend much of the next three decades as Penn's land agent, business manager, and traveling companion. After decades of working closely together, Penn would find himself in significant debt to Ford, and that debt would become the source of much trouble later in his life, ultimately—as we saw in the Prologue—landing him in the Fleet prison in 1708.

Also joining the company was Thomas Ellwood, son of a Puritan parliamentarian whose journey to Quakerism mirrored Penn's. Ellwood, who would go on to achieve lasting fame as John Milton's amanuensis (a position that Isaac Penington helped secure for him), had come to Quakerism in 1659 after hearing the words of Edward Burrough and James Nayler. Like Penn, Ellwood's convincement provoked the wrath of his father, and he was thrown out of his family's house and forced to depend on the supportive network of London Quakers—in this case the Peningtons, with whom he went to live, tutoring the children in Latin. Ellwood would remain lifelong friends with Gulielma and the Peningtons, and would ultimately be buried with his wife alongside the Penns at Jordans.[3]

Penn, Ford, and Ellwood visited Friends in the Reading jail on September 21, and continued on to Bristol. In Bristol, home to a thriving Quaker community that persisted despite periods of intense persecution, Penn lodged with Dennis Hollister, a prominent Friend and former member of Parliament whose granddaughter Hannah would become his second wife a quarter-century later. He was soon joined by Whitehead. In all, Penn spent more than a month in Bristol.

Perhaps most importantly, while there he visited with George Fox, who had just returned from Ireland, and Margaret Fell. Fox and Fell were planning to marry that month. They had worked together on Friends' business for many years, and had been imprisoned together in Lancaster after a celebrated 1664 trial. Although the two were advanced in years and there was little suggestion of physical passion at the root of their relationship, the pair had been discussing marriage for some time, and the match represented a fusing of Quakerism's singular voice (Fox) with perhaps its most influential and important supporter (Fell). Larry Ingle describes it as "a dynastic union with God as an involved third party," which Fox "approached . . . with all the excitement of someone completing a business deal." With the exception of one of Margaret's sons, who opposed the plans, the Fell children "had expected and wished for the marriage" and were fully supportive.[4]

Though he had departed for Ireland by the time the wedding took place, Penn offered a stirring testimony at the Bristol Men's Meeting, describing the union of Fox and Fell as

> the true character, resemblance, and express image of that ancient marriage of the Lamb . . . that was before the fall . . . for all marriage hath been in the fallen and apostate state from the pure, heavenly marriage of the lamb; but as the [church, and seed], is come out of the wilderness state, and that in-strumentally by our dear friend [George Fox]; so is this marriage likely to be betwixt our dear friends; that pure marriage, white with the church and the seed, has been in the wilderness. It is now come out from thence.[5]

Not only did the Fox–Fell marriage augur well for the unity and coherence of the Quaker movement, in Penn's view it would also aid in ushering in the Kingdom of God.

In his remarks, Penn echoed sentiments voiced by Fell and Fox themselves, who saw in their marriage not merely the joining of two people but a mystical union that held transcendent meaning for the redemption of humankind. Little is known about the physical relationship between these two leading Friends, and they spent very little time together during their long marriage, though their correspondence reveals "their mutual aim to usher in the Kingdom of God on earth as they under-stood it." These high hopes for the marriage were no doubt behind Margaret's in-sistence that she was pregnant during her imprisonment in Lancaster the following year. Middlesex Quaker Elizabeth Bowman wrote to Penn in Ireland with the sur-prising news of Margaret's "being with child and . . . her time being out almost," a situation made the more dire due to George's imprisonment at the time. Margaret was then in her fifties, and distraught over her separation from her husband. But she was apparently not pregnant after all, and at fifty-five years old was unlikely to become pregnant (though one of her biographers has suggested the possibility of a "menopausal miscarriage"). Nonetheless, the episode provided fodder for critics of Quakerism who saw in it the overheated enthusiasm of individuals excessively certain of their own role as conduits of God's Spirit.[6]

By late October William Penn was ready to make the crossing to Ireland.

* * *

Penn was a busy man during his nine months in Ireland. He was "almost con-tinuously on the move, and covered many hundreds of miles on horseback," from prisons to the Privy Council and almost everywhere in between. Between October 1669 and July 1670 he would interact with a veritable "Who's Who" of Irish Quakerism and the governing elite in Ireland. He worked at a frantic pace. The ostensible purpose of this trip, of course, was to do business with his father's tenants, but Penn's "journey was primarily a spiritual one," and even a cursory reading of the journal he kept shows that Penn spent the majority of his time on Quaker business.[7]

He and his companions—including Thomas Lower, who was married to Margaret Fox's daughter Mary, and the Rogers brothers, Francis and William, Bristol Friends with Irish commercial interests—sailed for Cork on October 24. Penn spent his first three days in the city almost entirely in the company of Friends. His first meal was at the home of Thomas and Susanna Mitchell; Thomas, a Quaker merchant, had shared the Cork jail cell with William two years earlier. Penn visited Friends imprisoned in the city jail, dining with them twice and holding a Meeting in the prison itself. The next day he and fellow Quaker William Morris (who would accompany him through much of his Irish journey) gained an audience with Mayor Matthew Deane, seeking relief from Friends' persecution, "but to no purpose." He did not entirely neglect Sir William's business, though, writing to his father's tenants to give them notice of his arrival. Even during his first week in Ireland, then, Penn the Quaker vied with Penn the landlord for William's attention.[8]

After several days in Cork, Penn and his traveling companions departed for Dublin. They set a brisk pace, making the 160-mile journey in just four days. Again, the cursory entries in his journal provide only brief glimpses into the complex world Penn was navigating. His anti-Catholicism was in full view when Penn noted passing through "Holy Cross (so called) from a superstitious conceit that a piece of Christ's cross was brought thither from Jerusalem." The next day the company arrived at the home of William Edmundson, just in time for the General Meeting for Leinster province. Edmundson presided at the Meeting, Penn reported, "and heavenly it was."[9]

Arriving in Dublin, where he would spend the next month, on November 2, Penn lodged with John Gay, a prominent Friend who had served as a land commissioner during the 1650s and who held an influential position in the legal system. As had been the case in Cork, Penn devoted the lion's share of his time to activities on behalf of Friends. Six weeks after leaving London, it seems, he had still not written to his father (or if he did, he did not record it in his journal). The National Meeting of Irish Friends was held at Penn's lodgings on November 5, and over the course of the month he took part in at least half a dozen additional Meetings, which were attended by some of the most influential Quakers in Ireland. Not all of these Meetings proceeded smoothly. On the 21st, for example, "many people came, amongst them the rude and boisterous gallants to gaze on me, which they did for almost an hour." After the Meeting had concluded, Penn went on, "I spoke to them very sharply, and so we parted."[10]

Like their English brethren, Friends in Ireland collected accounts of sufferings, using them to build solidarity in the midst of persecution and to frame appeals for relief from the authorities. Penn worked with Friends to build reports of Quaker suffering into an address to John (Lord) Robartes, who had replaced the Earl of Ossory as Lord Lieutenant of Ireland in May 1669. In Dublin, as they had in Cork, Penn and William Morris visited the local mayor. Once again they appealed for an easing of the punishments being meted out on Quakers. Once again they were rebuffed, this time with even more vigor than they had encountered in Cork: "most abusively called rogues, rascals, inhuman rogues, whelps, deserving to be lashed out of the town, and sent to Barbados." Needless to say, their address was refused, "with scorn, and with the greatest detestation flung to the ground." The Friends ought not to have been surprised: 1669 would turn out to be the high point of Quaker persecution in Ireland during the final four decades of the seventeenth century.[11]

At a Meeting a few days later Penn met Anthony Sharp, who had recently resettled in Dublin from Gloucestershire, England, and would quickly become one of the most prominent Friends in all of Ireland. Along with Edmundson, Sharp played a central role in the history of Irish Quakerism. A well-connected merchant who served as a Dublin alderman and master of the Weaver's Guild over the course of a long public career, Sharp later served as one of the original proprietors of West Jersey. He would be one of the first people to whom Penn would write when he received his charter for Pennsylvania and, although Sharp never emigrated to America, Penn considered him "one of his key contacts in Ireland for the dissemination of promotional material about Pennsylvania and possibly for the recruitment of settlers."[12]

During his travels in Ireland, Penn met with anyone in authority who would grant him an audience in his ongoing attempt to mitigate persecution of Friends. Although Friends did get a bit of good news on November 29, when eight Quakers were released from prison after a grand jury declined to charge them, more often than not Penn was treated "with all civility" but left with very little material success to report. On one occasion, his journal explained, the Privy Council did not meet due to the Lord Lieutenant's illness; on another, he noted without comment, "the Address was not read." In late November, despite his entreaties to individuals on the Privy Council, one of them a friend of his father, "Nothing was done, nor is likely to be done at Council." He was, though, able to distribute a number of Quaker writings, including works by Fox, Burrough, Whitehead, and himself.[13]

But of course there was other work to be done. Penn had to attend to the ostensible reason for his trip: negotiating leases with Sir William's tenants and continuing the defense of Penn's titles against rival claimants. By the end of November he had reached agreement with Wallis on some final outstanding matters pertaining to the disputed lands in Shanagarry, but only in December did Penn make any serious effort to begin direct negotiations with his father's tenants. He also had work to do on behalf of Gulielma, whose great-uncle had left land in County Meath, just northwest of Dublin, to her father, and which she had inherited after his death. Unfortunately, as Penn reported to his journal on November 20, "the estate being neglected is gone, all but a third." Penn seems to have set aside one day per week for correspondence to England, writing on November 13, 20, and 27. He wrote to Gulielma each time, but not until November 20, more than two months after he had left London, did Penn write to his father. He also visited several times with Sir William Petty while in Dublin. The two friends no doubt discussed schemes for turning a profit on their Irish lands and other questions of political economy.[14]

After spending nearly a month in Dublin, Penn began to make his way back toward Cork in December to begin dealings with his father's tenants in earnest. A small and unexpected bit of excitement along the way was provided by John Penington, Gulielma's half-brother, who was accompanying Penn as his assistant. John's skittish horse knocked him off the ferry while the group was crossing the turbulent Blackwater River south of Clonmel, and he had to be rescued by Penn and the ferryman. In fact, John Penington seems to have complicated Penn's journey on several occasions. In addition to his inadvertent swim in the Blackwater, he also tumbled into a trench on Wallis's land in late December. And, without casting aspersions, it is worth noting that Penington was also with Penn when he got lost in the Knockmealdown Mountains between Tallow and Clogheen in January 1670. A month later he had to be left behind at Shanagarry, "ill of a stoppage in his throat."[15]

Arriving back in Cork in early December, Penn went immediately to the prison to visit and comfort Friends confined there. But his other business was calling, and much of the next two months was spent in negotiations in and around Cork. Having reached agreement with Wallis, Penn and Ford visited many other properties, measured and surveyed land where disputes and discrepancies had arisen, and inspected the degree to which tenants had "improved" their lands ("improving" the land being a central element of the English plan to civilize the Irish people). He expressed satisfaction at Wallis's improvements, including a system of trenches and ditches, "by which it may become profitable land," and pronounced John Boles's farm "well improved." At times Penn offered generous terms: "I abated [6 shillings] per acre," he described one such interaction, "and [we] agreed on all sides." But not all negotiations went so smoothly, and his Irish journal contains numerous references to cases in which Penn and the tenants "could not agree." He reported on January 26 that "Captain Richard

Smith's wife, and Hull's wife came to me . . . about Captain Smith's farm; they
earnestly solicited for an abatement of the [rent], but I could not be moved from
my commission and judgment." Notwithstanding his sympathies for suffering
Friends, Penn was also the agent of a colonial landowner, and knew that his father expected results.[16]

Although his father's business clearly occupied much more of William Penn's
time and attention in December and January than it had at any time since he
arrived in Ireland, his work on behalf of Friends continued as well. He appealed
to sheriffs in Cork, seeking relief for imprisoned Quakers, and visited them
in prison at least three times in December alone. During the final week of
December, Penn returned to his father's home in Shanagarry, about twenty miles
from Cork, where their tenant Wallis was living in the manor house.

While there, Penn began preparing a response to Christopher Davenport's *An
explanation of Roman-Catholick belief*, a brief tract that had just been published in
a fourth edition, and which aimed not only to establish the validity of Catholic
beliefs but also to insist on Catholics' political loyalty. Penn's response would
appear later that spring as *A seasonable caveat against popery*, and although no
copies of that initial printing have survived, Penn returned to it after his release
from Newgate in 1670 and published a second edition early in 1671. *A seasonable caveat* took aim at the entire panoply of Catholic doctrine and practice: its
views on Scripture, the Trinity, prayer to saints and angels, faith and works, transubstantiation and the administration of the Eucharist, praying in Latin, prayer
for the dead, and "of the moral law, of obedience to civil magistrates." For each
of these points of contention he offered both his own critique and selected
passages from Catholic authors themselves, cautioning Protestants to maintain a
deep suspicion of Catholic protestations of loyalty and peacefulness. Protestants
should remember the "sea of blood" loosed by Catholics across Europe against
those whose consciences prevented them from conforming to the church's
teachings. And yet, he insisted, "it is not our purpose to bring them under persecution, but to present the people with such an information, as may prevent
them from ever having power to persecute others." Work on his "answer to the
Jesuits" went quickly, and he sent the first sheet to the printers less than a week
after taking up his pen.[17]

As with much of Penn's writing, a critique of Catholicism was only ever partly
about Catholicism. "Popery" was never simply a description of Catholic religious doctrines, but a more general set of claims about the power-hungry, violent, and persecuting tendencies that lead one group of people to inflict harm on
others due to religious differences. After his effusive denunciations of Catholics,
Penn concluded his work by acknowledging that even "some Protestants . . . are
mostly busied in persecuting Dissenters," which foreshadowed his further claim
that persecution represented a betrayal of Protestant principles of conscience.

He would elaborate on these claims later the same year in his first major work of political theory, *The great case of liberty of conscience*.[18]

Penn's attention during January was occupied largely by discussions of leases and rents, but over the next few months he returned more frequently to Friends' business. He reports attending no fewer than ten Meetings in February alone, including the Six Weeks' Meeting at Cork, another in that city on February 27, "a precious Meeting as I was ever in," and a Youghal Meeting the next month at which "the mayor himself said, had he not been mayor he would have come." Despite such glowing reports, all was not well. Priests and constables frequently interrupted worship, and on February 28 "many of the dirtiest people of the town" nearly broke up a Meeting. In Penn's telling, he confronted the officers to great effect, guaranteeing that the Meeting could go on: "I spoke much to the [constable], at last the man was smit and departed."[19]

But the difficulties at these February Meetings proved to foreshadow more serious and sustained trouble to come the next month. Penn's first mention of a fresh outbreak of persecution in Cork appears in a terse journal entry on March 11: "Philip Ford came from Cork . . . Friends imprisoned, great severity expressed." Three days later: "Friends barbarously dealt with." He decried the fact that "the judge went out of town and left the prisons full," and pronounced that "a wickeder mayor or judge has not been in the city of Cork since truth came."[20]

Two days after thus deriding the mayor and judge, while staying at the home of Captain Richard Bent in Castle Mary, near Cloyne, William Penn wrote in his journal that "I set about a book against persecution, called the Great Case of Liberty of Conscience debated and defended." This is the first mention of a treatise that would lay the foundation for his many years of advocacy for religious liberty in England and America. *The great case* would turn out to be something unique in Penn's fledgling career as Quaker controversialist: not merely a defense of Friends against their critics or a diatribe against the theological errors of others, but a preface and six substantive chapters laying out a systematic examination of the foundations of liberty of conscience, and a vigorous, principled defense of freedom of worship. The Cork persecutions provided the immediate impetus for the work's composition, but Penn also made clear reference to the English Parliament's passage of the Second Conventicle Act, which had forbidden unauthorized religious gatherings, in the spring of 1670. He would have been aware of the contention over the Act in London before he departed in the summer of 1669, and surely would have heard news about the legislation from Friends during his Irish journey. The first edition of *The great case*, which appeared in Dublin early in 1670, referred explicitly to "the late Act" in its full title, and Penn wrote in the dedication that he was driven to present his work to the king "before the late Act has made too great a progress in [Ireland]."[21]

Although the work of a young man, a twenty-five-year-old who still had a long career ahead of him, all of the arguments that Penn advanced in *The great case* would remain central to his theory of toleration, which he continued to refine throughout the 1670s, attempted to implement in Pennsylvania, and, later, alongside James II, would work tirelessly (and unsuccessfully) to bring to fruition in England during the second half of the 1680s. He wrote at a brisk pace; in addition to all the other tasks before him, the text seems to have been substantially finished within a few weeks. He "proceeded and almost finished my discourse against persecution" just four days after he beginning the work, and he "sent one sheet" to the printer less than a week later. He continued to tinker with the text through early April, and it was published in late spring 1670.[22]

Yet the persecution continued. In mid-May Penn met with Mayor Deane after some of his books—likely *A seasonable caveat* and *The great case*—were seized by the authorities, whereupon, Penn reported, "he abused me with names." Penn was threatened with arrest, and "they missed me, though they saw me, and came for me." Here again William the Penn vied with William the Quaker. Penn wrote to Lord O'Brien, the Earl of Orrery's son-in-law, and to Orrery himself (son of the Earl of Orrery to whom Penn had written during his first imprisonment in 1667), seeking the return of the seized books and the release of jailed Friends. Although O'Brien told Penn that "I shall never encourage [the Mayor of Cork] to be uncivil to a person of your quality," he immediately followed this admission with a defense of the mayor's action in administering the law and added a blistering denunciation of Quakers:

> I cannot agree to the state of the case as you represent it . . . I fear all this trouble you undergo is because you don't believe, not what you can't but what you won't believe, and as it is certainly possible for you to believe our faith, for it is reasonable, we must punish them that can't because they may and will not have it.

In other words, Penn *could* have conformed to the established religion if he wanted to, but he instead obstinately refused to endorse a "reasonable" faith, and thus had brought the force of the law upon himself. This forthright denial of one of the core tenets of the tolerationist movement—that belief is a matter of understanding and not of will, and thus it cannot be forced—illustrates the depth of opposition to toleration faced by thinkers like Penn during the early Restoration years.[23]

* * *

In the midst of this turmoil and persecution, of course, Penn family business continued to press on him. His father chided him for not writing and expressed his wishes for his son to return home quickly, "for I find myself to decline." Penn assisted with the transfer of the governorship of the Kinsale fort—the same post that the Duke of Ormond had once thought to bestow upon William himself—to Sir William's fellow naval commander Captain Richard Rooth. At Kinsale, in addition to his cousin of the same name (often referred to as "Ensign" William Penn), Penn stayed one night with William Crispin, who was married to Penn's cousin Rebecca Bradshaw and who would later be commissioned as chief justice for the fledgling settlement of Pennsylvania. The transfer of Kinsale involved a number of complicated financial arrangements among Rooth, Ensign Penn (who was being retained as clerk of the cheque), and Sir William's old friend Robert Southwell, the governor of Kinsale.[24]

Penn the landlord still had work to do during the spring, and he was not above taking strict measures in pursuit of his father's interests. "For all his obvious and sincere piety, he was a cool-headed businessman who knew how to conclude an advantageous bargain with prospective tenants." At the end of March, just after sending the first sheet of *The great case* to the printers, Penn seized the cattle of one of those tenants, Abel Guilliamson, for nonpayment of rent, though a day after that he agreed to a "great bargain" to another tenant "in consideration of old friendship, and great service done my father." Late May was taken up with negotiations, with making agreements with tenants who came to see him in Cork, and with visiting Friends who remained in prison, before Penn headed back to Dublin at the end of the month to advocate for Friends in prison there.[25]

In addition to attempting to mitigate persecution and obtain Friends from prison, Penn defended them from the attacks of their critics. Attacking Catholicism while in Ireland, as he did in *A seasonable caveat*, would have made obvious sense to Penn—it was all around him, and he debated "a popish colonel" in Cork in late May, and with more "papists" a month later, and "manifested their great folly." But he recorded other disputes as well, including one with merchant John Mead that touched on original sin, the nature of Jesus's death, and "the moral religion and water baptism." Penn also had numerous interactions with Christopher Vowell, the Earl of Orrery's chaplain. Orrery considered Vowell a "lazy, drunken braggart," and Vowell was later deprived of some of his parishes for drunkenness.[26]

And yet William remained a Penn, well known to political elites despite his unorthodox religious leanings. He met Lord Berkeley, the recently named Lord Lieutenant, as well as Chancellor of Ireland Michael Boyle and the Earl of Arran. While advocating for imprisoned Friends Penn also found time to dine with members of the elite. Occasionally these connections paid dividends. The Lord Lieutenant ordered Friends released from the jails in early June, the same week that "my father's business was also done"; and a week later an order of the Privy Council freed the remaining prisoners.[27]

In addition to these important matters of faith and business—which frequently pulled him in two different directions—Penn's journal also contains a number of glimpses into his private life. On December 19 he received a letter from his younger brother Richard, about whom we know virtually nothing, except that he died young. (Penn recorded nothing about its contents in the journal.) Early the next month he bought cloth for his sister Margaret. And once again he attended to his hair: while in Dublin in November, he "caused my hair to be cut off and put into a wig because of baldness since my imprisonment." (In February he again "shaved my head.") Penn told Fox that his baldness was the result of both childhood smallpox and his later confinement in the Tower of London, where his "his hair shed away." Either way, Penn's lack of hair clearly vexed him, Quaker opposition to worldly luxuries notwithstanding. The matter of Penn's wig—and the criticism it raised from some in Quaker circles—would continue to dog him. It even led Fox himself to speak up in defense of Penn's wig as "a short civil thing," which he wore "to keep his head and ears warm and not for pride." (In any event, Fox added, it was "so thin, plain and short, that one cannot well know it from his own hair.")[28]

* * *

Penn's Irish journal breaks off on July 1, 1670, apparently for a rather simple reason: he had run out of pages in the book he was using. He also fell quite ill with a fever at about this time. He returned to England sometime around August 1, leaving Ford to manage some remaining business. Penn's prominent social position ensured a level of scrutiny and surveillance of which he might have been unaware, and a number of letters written to him during the summer of 1670 were intercepted by royal censors and thus never reached their intended recipient. Had he received them, he would have known about a number of important developments back in England: his father's increasingly frail health; his mother's continuing devastation over his Quaker convincement; Margaret Fox's phantom pregnancy; and the imprisonment of both Fell and Isaac Penington, which imposed severe hardships on their families and the community of Friends.

Most of the confiscated letters dealt with personal matters. Gulielma—who opened her letter reporting their joy at receiving a letter from him and her half-brother John, "but yourselves would have been much more acceptable"—wrote with news of George Fox's visits to their Meetings, and of her stepfather's imprisonment at Reading. Isaac Penington had gone to the jail to visit imprisoned Friends, where he was apprehended by Sir William Armorer, and imprisoned for refusing to swear the oath. (Armorer was such a prodigious persecutor of Friends in and around Reading that, several years earlier, his exploits had been collected into a volume and published under the title *Persecution appearing with its open face*.) The separation had been particularly hard on her mother, a sentiment echoed by Mary herself, who added a postscript to the letter that "we would rather if we might choose that he had been in almost any other place," a point reiterated by John Gay, who reported that Penington "had been cruelly used by an evil-minded justice." Penington would remain in prison until May 1672, when the king issued a general pardon in the wake of his Declaration of Indulgence.[29]

Perhaps the most poignant of these intercepted letters came from John Gay, relating details of a visit he had made to William's parents at Wanstead. Sir William was ill and unable to receive visitors, but Gay met with Penn's mother and conveyed her son's respects. In tears, Margaret Penn recounted her dismay at her son's continued attachment to Quakerism ("full of tears she was concerning you that you should continue of that judgment still"). Gay attempted, without much apparent success, to reassure Lady Penn of her son's devotion to his parents, even citing Penn's *Letter of love to the young convinced*, which exhorted newly convinced Friends to treat their family members with "all due respect." Margaret further criticized the Quaker refusal to give hat-honor—"what a strange thing was it to speak to a King with the hat on"—which afforded Gay an opportunity to praise another of Penn's writings, the recently published *No cross, no crown*. Gay clearly wanted to set his mother's mind at ease, and told her about the influential members of the English elite with whom William continued to mingle, particularly the Lord Lieutenant, who treated the Quakers with civility. Perhaps most pointedly, Gay reported to Penn, Margaret lamented that "your father had intended to make you a great man, but you would not hearken to him."[30]

Gay was able to get some family news for William: his sister, Margaret Lowther, had recently delivered a baby girl, and his brother Richard was in Italy, "well but a little wild," in his mother's words. Most seriously, though, Gay recounted the precarious health of Sir William, who longed for his son to return, suffering as he was with a range of maladies including "a dropsy, scurvey, and jaundice and . . . a very great belly and full of water." He was confined to the home, and his doctors had said he was not likely to survive the "the fall of the leaf." His doctors would turn out to be prescient.[31]

But all this news was unknown to William Penn as his time in Ireland wound down. Had he received Gay's letter, and known his father's condition, would he have hastened to Wanstead to be at Sir William's side? If he had done so, he might not have been in London in mid-August. And had he not been in London in mid-August, he certainly would not have been preaching outside the Quaker Meetinghouse in Gracechurch Street. And that might have set Penn's life and public career on a very different course.

* * *

If the precise timing of William Penn's return to England in the summer of 1670 remain unclear, we do know exactly where he was on August 14: with William Mead, a London linen draper, on the street outside the Quaker Meetinghouse

on London's Gracechurch Street, preaching to a crowd of several hundred
people. Mead, fifteen years older than Penn but a more recently convinced
Quaker, had joined the Friends earlier that year; he would later marry Margaret
Fox's daughter Sarah. Why were they preaching in the street? The government
had closed the Meetinghouse: "We were by force of arms kept out of our lawful
house," in Penn's words, "and met as near it in the street, as the soldiers would
give us leave." The two Friends were apprehended and sent to Newgate Prison,
facing charges that they "unlawfully and tumultuously did assemble and congre-
gate themselves together, to the disturbance of the Peace." Their trial at the Old
Bailey began on September 1.[32]

The Penn–Mead trial is probably the single most important event in the
emergence of William Penn as a celebrated and controversial public figure. The
trial pitted the Lord Mayor of London, Sir Samuel Starling, who had held the
office of sheriff since just after the Restoration and embodied the forces of political and religious orthodoxy, and Court Recorder John Howel on the one hand,
against Penn and Mead and ultimately a sympathetic jury on the other. Each
side produced its own "transcript," which sold hundreds of copies in short order.
The first to appear, likely authored at least in part by Penn himself, was titled *The
peoples ancient and just liberties asserted*, and it appeared almost immediately after
the trial's conclusion.[33]

In addition to Starling's zealous animus against Dissenters in general, he
seems also to have harbored a particular grudge against William Penn, telling
him "that he would see me whipped, and that I should have my hat pulled off,
for all I was Admiral Penn's son . . . that starved the seamen."[34] (Starling here referred to accusations that Sir William had been involved in the embezzlement
of seized goods from the Dutch in 1665, a flagrant violation of the naval laws of
seizure. In fact, the charges would derail the king's attempt to give Sir William
a command in 1668, and lead to impeachment proceedings against him in the
House of Commons in the spring of that year.) By William's account, he rebuked
the mayor for his uncharitable words: "I told him I could very well bear his severe expressions to me concerning myself, but was sorry to hear him speak those
abuses of my father, that was not present." Following their appearance in Court,
Penn and Mead were sent to the Black Dog Inn near Newgate Prison to await trial.
Whether out of a misunderstanding of the serious legal predicament he faced, or
a desire to set his father's mind at ease, Penn told Sir William that he expected to
be set at liberty in a few days. Whether or not Sir William had a few days, however, was very much in question. While the son took part in what was portrayed
in the Dissenting press as a heroic resistance to the forces of persecuting orthodoxy, the father lay near death just ten miles away in Wanstead.[35]

The arrest and jailing of Penn and Mead was not an isolated incident, but
formed part of a larger set of public confrontations in and around London, in

which Dissenters did battle with the Restoration church-state. The trial set in motion a legal and political drama that would catapult Penn into the public eye, and into the ongoing agitation over the Conventicle Act and its aftermath. If his Irish experiences—from his 1667 Cork imprisonment to the publication of *The great case of liberty of conscience* in the spring of 1670—had nurtured Penn's fledgling career as Quaker controversialist and theorist of religious toleration, and his eight-month confinement in the Tower of London had impressed upon English Quakers the depth of his commitment, the trial and its aftermath would establish him firmly on the public stage.[36]

At the outset of the proceedings, when instructed to enter his plea, Penn requested a written copy of the indictment against him, proclaiming his ignorance of the law ("I am unacquainted with the formality of the law"): this claim was technically true, given his ill-fated and short-lived career at Lincoln's Inn five years earlier. Then again, he had successfully navigated the Dublin Court of Appeals and secured his father's title to Irish lands, a notoriously complex and convoluted process studded with legal obstacles. Mead made a similar request, and although the judge promised not to take advantage of their inexperience in legal matters, he refused to let them see the indictment: "You must first plead to the indictment, before you can have a copy of it." Both promptly entered pleas of not guilty.[37]

After an adjournment lasting a few days, the trial resumed, but not without another skirmish in the courtroom. Penn and Mead appeared before the bench with their hats off—the expected sign of deference for those entering the royal presence (or in this case, a royal court). What happened to the Quaker refusal to doff their hats in the presence of social superiors or political authorities? After all, Penn had laid out Quaker objections to hat-honor in *No cross, no crown*, which he had published the year before, and the refusal to doff hats—and therefore to show humans the sort of respect they considered due only to God—was one of Friends' key practices. Why then did Penn and Mead confront the judge with their hats off? Apparently they had removed their hats, or found a way to have them removed, before entering the courtroom, so that they didn't have to make the gesture—"capping," or removing the hat as a sign of honor—in the judge's presence. They had not, technically speaking, removed their hats as a sign of respect, and had he wanted to, Starling could surely have looked the other way, since the defendants had, in fact, approached the bench with their hats removed. But Starling clearly saw an opportunity to tweak Penn and Mead by insisting that they doff their hats to demonstrate their submission to his authority in the courtroom. Thus he instructed the court officers to put their hats back on their heads, so that he might order the defendants to remove them. When they refused to do so, Starling imposed a fine on them "for your contempt of the court."[38]

The court clearly saw, from the beginning of the trial, that there might be problems with the case. One member of the jury, Edward Bushel, was made to swear the juror's oath twice, with the authorities claiming that he had not kissed the Bible while swearing the first time. (Bushel's name would forever be associated with the Penn–Mead trial, after he successfully petitioned for relief from fines imposed upon him as a result of his jury service, in a case that established the principle of jury independence.) A number of witnesses testified that Penn and Mead had been preaching in the street, although the evidence offered left a great deal to be desired. Two informants admitted that "I saw Mr. Penn speaking to the people, but I could not hear what he said, because of the noise"; "There was such a great noise, that I could not tell what he said"; "Mr. Penn I suppose was speaking; I saw him make a motion with his hands, and heard some noise, but could not understand what he said." The defendants were primed for battle, however, with Mead addressing the jury directly: "Observe this evidence, he saith, He heard him preach, and yet saith, he doth not know what he said."[39]

After the government's witnesses had testified, Penn raised the stakes considerably, and set about turning a trial about unauthorized preaching into a full-fledged assault on the Restoration state-church and its persecutory foundations. In effect, the defendants "elevat[ed] a misdemeanor accusation into a critical dissection of the entire common law tradition and a case on which depended the lives, liberties, estates, and families of all Englishmen." This undertaking involved, first of all, casting doubt on one of the most widely held components of the British legal tradition: the sanctity of common law. Penn demanded that the court provide him and Mead with a clear accounting of which laws they had broken, and insisted that a vague reply like "the common law" was unacceptable, "for if it be common, it should not be so hard to produce . . . [and] unless you shew me, and the people, the law you ground your indictment upon, I shall take it for granted, your proceedings are merely arbitrary."[40]

Unless you show me, and the people . . . Penn had just made the trial not merely about the specific charges against Mead and himself, but about the rights and liberties of all Englishmen. "I have asked but one question," he said—to be told what law I've broken—"and you have not answered me; though the rights and privileges of every Englishman be concerned in it." In the preface to the published version of the trial's "transcript," Penn voiced his view that in "this ensuing trial . . . not only the prisoners, but the fundamental laws of England have been most arbitrarily arraigned." All these objections to the court's proceedings, and to the use of common law to prosecute peaceful, conscientious religious exercise, boiled down to the question Penn posed to the Court in dramatic fashion: "The Question is not whether I am guilty of this indictment, but whether this indictment be legal."[41]

Finally, Starling had had enough. He ordered Penn removed from the court-room and sent to the bail-dock—a cage in which prisoners sat while waiting for their cases to be called—leaving Mead to face his accusers alone. But Mead proved more than adequate to the task, addressing the jury directly, invoking the Quaker peace testimony to deny claims of riotous behavior, and reiterating the defendants' demand for a clear account of the law they were accused of having broken. Mead cited Coke's *Institutes*, the definitive handbook of the English common law, on the definition of riot, to which the court recorder responded, "you are a troublesome fellow." The mayor told Mead, "You deserve to have your tongue cut out" and sent him, too, to the bail-dock. But even from outside the courtroom the defendants continued to insist on their right to be present when the jury received their charge. Penn insisted that he had "at least ten or twelve material points to offer, in order to invalidate their indictment."[42] (These material points were appended to the printed version of the trial.)

And now the truly suspenseful part of the trial began. Juries in early modern England were hardly the independent deliberative bodies that citizens of twenty-first-century democracies have come to expect. The early modern courtroom hardly resembled its present-day counterpart, and it lacked the presumption of innocence, exclusion of hearsay evidence, guarantees of defense counsel, burden of proof on the prosecution, and the right to silence. As Penn and Mead were soon to find out, judges expected juries to comply with their instructions and were frequently incensed when they failed to do so.[43]

The first reported result—a jury divided, with eight on one side and four on the other—produced threats from the bench, with particular abuse directed at Bushel, whom the court clearly saw as the ringleader in an obstructionist campaign to undermine the prosecution and secure a verdict of not guilty. The mayor sent them back to reconsider, whereupon the jury announced a verdict of "guilty of speaking in Gracechurch street"—not the charge against the defendants, and arguably not a crime at all. The jury returned once more with the same verdict: "We the jurors, hereafter named, do find William Penn to be guilty of speaking or preaching to an assembly, met together in Gracious [Gracechurch]-Street, the 14th of August last, 1670, and that William Mead is not guilty of the said indictment."

In response, the court recorder made clear how early modern court proceedings were supposed to work, telling the jury that "you shall not be dismist, till we have a verdict that the court will accept; and you shall be lock'd up, without meat, drink, fire, and tobacco: You shall not think thus to abuse the court; we will have a verdict by the help of God, or you shall starve for it." Meanwhile, Penn insisted that the integrity of a jury's verdict lay at the heart of fundamental English law, and appealed to the jury to remain strong in their verdict. "The freedom of jurors to follow their consciences," writes de Krey, "was thus added to the issue of freedom of conscience for religious worship."[44]

At this point Starling, following up on the recorder's threat, commanded that the jury be confined overnight without food or drink (and, Penn claimed, not even a chamber pot, a charge Starling flatly denied). The next morning an obviously weary jury nonetheless repeated, twice, their earlier verdict—"Guilty of speaking"—prompting the court recorder to again tell the jury that "I will have a positive verdict, or you shall starve for it."[45]

At this point in the drama, the judge and recorder were clearly near their wits' end, facing a recalcitrant jury, obstreperous defendants, and an emerging public relations nightmare. The jury was instructed once again to reconsider their verdict. Another day passed, and finally the jury returned an unambiguous verdict: not guilty.

* * *

Starling was not amused. He fined the jury and sent the defendants back to jail, citing the contempt ruling he had imposed at the trial's outset for refusing to remove their hats. Penn wrote three letters to his father within the span of three days, filling Sir William in on the court's behavior and expressing his concern about Sir William's "distemper, and the pains that attend it." He begged his father not to pay the fines that had been assessed on him. Someone must have sent word to his son regarding the severity of his father's health concerns, because William opened his third letter by telling his father that he was "truly grieved to hear of thy present illness," before going on to voice his worry that allowing his fines to be paid would give a veneer of legitimacy to the court's "arbitrary and base proceedings" and "satiate their revengeful, avaricious appetites."[46]

Despite his protestations, someone paid the fines, and William appeared at his father's side as Sir William neared death. He passed away on September 16. Years later, Penn recounted his final visit to his father, describing a tearful reconciliation between father and son. By this account, Sir William urged three things on his son: to be true to his conscience, to consider his course in life carefully and then pursue it steadfastly, and to persevere through disappointments. Sir William also lamented the degeneracy of England, though a skeptic might note that the condemnations Penn records his father hurling at the world around him—"Woe to thee, O England! God will judge thee, O England! Great plagues are at thy door . . . God has forsaken us . . . we shall be destroyed!"—sound rather more like those that the enthusiastic young Quaker was likely to issue than like the words of the pragmatic and ambitious admiral. Finally, and most remarkably, Penn reports his father's offering of a kind of dying benediction in which he makes peace with William's Quakerism: "Son William, if you and your friends will keep to your plain way of preaching, and keep to your plain way of living, you will make an end of the priests to the end of the world."[47]

By early the next month Sir William had been buried at St. Mary Redcliffe, in Bristol, and his widow and son had arranged for the memorial to his memory to be erected there. The memorial celebrated Sir William as a naval commander, Member of Parliament, and hero of the Anglo-Dutch Wars. Not surprisingly, it made no specific mention of his service to Cromwell, the failed Western Design expedition, his imprisonment in the Tower, or the parliamentary impeachment proceedings. The admiral had named William as executor of his estate, and left him the gold chain and medal that Cromwell had bestowed upon him for service in the First Anglo-Dutch War. To his son Richard, and not the peaceful Quaker William, he left "all my swords, guns, and pistols."[48]

In the months following Sir William's death, his son remained busy. He made several trips to London in order to settle his father's affairs, in particular to look for a copy of a map of the River Medway that the naval commissioners had inquired about. He continued to speak out on behalf of Friends, composing a blistering letter to Peter Mews, president of St. John's College, Oxford, and vice-chancellor of the university. He condemned Mews's persecution of Quakers, calling him a "poor mushroom" and insisting that "better were it for thee, that thou hadst never been born." No doubt recalling his own unhappy years at the university a decade earlier, Penn accused Mews of "proud, peevish, and bitter actings" that targeted the conscientious children of God while allowing the "vain, prodigal, lascivious to go unpunished."[49] He wrote a thundering and vivid jeremiad, "God's Controversy Proclaimed," that called the nation to repentance and threatened divine judgment on persecutors, though he ultimately decided against publishing it.[50]

He also took part in a public debate on the Quaker doctrine of the Light with Baptist Jeremy Ives, continuing his role as spokesperson for Friends. As Ellwood told the story, the public debate was occasioned by "some bickerings . . . between some Baptists and some . . . Quakers," in which not only Friends in general, but Penn in particular, were targeted by their adversaries. As a result, a public meeting was arranged and (again in Ellwood's words) the outcome proved "better than I expected." Ives, encountering some resistance from the audience, left the stage and departed the room along with a few of his supporters after he had finished his remarks, "with purpose to have broken up the assembly." But "the people generally stayed" and listened carefully to Penn—which, not surprisingly, brought Ives back into the hall to castigate the crowd for paying attention to Penn's nonsense. Ellwood claimed a Quaker victory. Ellwood sent Isaac Penington a pithy verse in Latin at the conclusion of the meeting, which, translated, read "Truth hath prevailed; the enemies did fly: We are in safety; Praise to God on high."[51]

* * *

But all this public activity was bound to catch up with him sooner or later, and it turned out that the English legal system was not finished with William Penn. In February 1671 he was arrested again, this time for preaching at a Quaker Meeting at the Wheeler Street Meetinghouse, in Spitalfields, which lay just outside the City of London. According to Penn, soldiers observed the Meeting and allowed him to speak for half an hour, at which point "the sergeant came and pulled him down, and led him through the throng of the Meeting into the street, where the constable and his watchmen joined the soldiers, and . . . brought him to the Tower." He refused to take the oath when pressed—not out of a lack of allegiance, he insisted, but on account of his objection to oaths in general—"scrupling any oath." Unlike Starling, who had taken aim at Penn and his father in print, Sir John Robinson, lieutenant of the Tower of London who oversaw this second trial, professed that "your father was my friend." But, since Penn had chosen to associate with troublesome Quakers, "you stir up the people to sedition."[52]

Penn's second confinement in Newgate lacked the public spectacle of his first; the private trial before judges instead of a jury, made possible by charging him under the Five Mile Act (which forbade dissenting clergy from coming within five miles of any incorporated English town) rather than common law, ensured that there would be no grandstanding or pleas for public sympathy from heroic Dissenters. Unfortunately for Penn, persons accused under the Five Mile Act were not guaranteed a jury trial and thus, after some sharp exchanges with the judges in the case, he was sent back to Newgate for six months.

Denying all disloyalty, Penn denounced Robinson and his fellow magistrates as betraying the principles of the Protestant Reformation—"Twas then plea good enough, my conscience won't let me go to Mass, and my conscience wills that I should have an English testament"—and identified the nub of the issue between them: "Thy religion persecutes, and mine forgives."[53]

Given the success of *The Peoples ancient and just liberties*, it is probably not surprising that Penn considered publishing a "transcript" of this second trial as well. But though he composed it, he did not publish it. The editors of his papers suggest, convincingly, that Penn likely did not want to further antagonize the authorities, who were empowered to extend his sentence at their discretion. But once again Penn put his time in confinement to good use, composing some verses against persecution, which he sent to Gulielma, and drafting an appeal to Parliament criticizing efforts at passing a new law against Dissenters, which he signed along with four other Quakers also imprisoned in Newgate. At Fox's urging, he worked with Whitehead on a reply to Thomas Jenner, a Puritan minister who had settled in Ireland and whose *Quakerism anatomized* had appeared in Dublin the previous year, bemoaning the "spreading gangrene of Quakerism" in Ireland. Jenner hit on all the major points of anti-Quaker polemic, including the purported incompatibility of the Light with the authority of Scripture, Quakers' undermining of hierarchies in church and state, and their rejection of basic elements of Christian orthodoxy. To Jenner, Quakers were merely the latest in a long line of heretics that had bedeviled the church since its earliest days. Penn and Whitehead's *Serious apology*, their response to Jenner, appeared at the end of June 1671, while Penn was still confined at Newgate. Penn also composed *Truth rescued from imposture*, a rebuttal of Starling's account of the trial—again, the public back-and-forth of early modern political debate—and took a leading role in composing a letter to the sheriffs of London protesting Friends' treatment at the hands of their jailors.[54]

But the most significant work Penn undertook while imprisoned was to revise and expand his *The great case of liberty of conscience*. Penn had published the first edition in Dublin during his Irish journey; now he added a new preface and elaborated on a number of his main arguments. The second edition no longer linked the work with a specific piece of legislation (the Conventicle Act), but rather set itself a much broader agenda, describing the work on its title page as "a general reply to such late discourses, as have opposed a toleration." And there were many such discourses, none perhaps more prominent than *A discourse of ecclesiastical polity* by Samuel Parker, then Archdeacon of Canterbury. Parker's ferocious polemic was a bitter and often ad hominem attack on toleration that framed the religious, political, and philosophical case for religious orthodoxy and political uniformity in its most uncompromising form.[55]

Penn began this second edition of *The great case* by laying out a concise definition of his key term:

> [T]hat plain English, of liberty of conscience is this; namely, the free and uninterrupted exercise of our consciences, in that way of worship, we are most clearly persuaded, God requires us to serve Him in (without endangering our undoubted birthright of English freedoms) which being matter of faith; we sin if we omit.

Quoting at slightly greater length will make clear the radical nature of this definition:

> By liberty of conscience, we understand not only a meer liberty of the mind, in believing or disbelieving this or that principle or doctrine, but the exercise of ourselves in a visible way of worship, upon our believing it to be indispensibly required at our hands . . . Yet we would be so

understood . . . not to contrive, or abet any contrivance destructive of
the government and laws of the land, tending to matters of an external
nature . . . but so far only, as it may refer to religious matters, and a life
to come, and consequently wholly independent of . . . secular affairs.

A definition of liberty also implies a definition of restraint, in this case one aimed
at reframing what it meant to interfere with the free exercise of religion:

By imposition, restraint, and persecution, we don't only mean, the strict
requiring of us to believe this to be true, or that to be false; and upon
refusal, to incur the penalties enacted in such cases; but by those terms
we mean thus much, any coercive let or hindrance to us, from meeting
together to perform those religious exercises which are according to
our faith and persuasion.

In other words, liberty of conscience includes protection not only of the rights
to belief, but also to worship and assembly. Penn also redefined the term "imposition" to include not merely political and legal sanctions for religious exercise,
but any obstacles set in the way of individuals meeting for religious worship.
Communicating and meeting with others, in other words, served an integral
purpose to the exercise of individual conscience.[56]

Penn built his notion of liberty of conscience upon a bifurcation between "religious matters" and things "of an external nature," about which civil magistrates
may (indeed must) concern themselves. Christianity, he insisted, "entreats all,
but compels none," employing spiritual weapons in the pursuit of spiritual goals.
Forcing Dissenters to conform was not only unlawful; it was unchristian.[57]

The great case collected all the standard arguments against persecution in one
place. Persecution represented an affront to God because it interposed human
authority between individuals and the Deity, and attempted to decree how God
was to be worshipped. Such efforts "directly invade divine prerogative, and di-
vest the almighty of a due, proper to none besides himself . . . [and] enthrones
man as king over conscience." Penn offered a range of scriptural examples, from
Jesus' parables and the Golden Rule to Paul's exhortations to bear meekly with
others. Not only was persecution impious and antiscriptural: it was also anti-
Protestant. Calling those who view their religious obligations differently than
oneself "heretics" is a "story . . . as old as the Reformation," Penn argued, and
Protestants' persecution of other Protestants renders their own denunciations
of persecuting Catholics far less convincing.[58]

Other arguments against persecution and in favor of toleration were less
overtly religious, though since God created humans, we should not overstate the

division between "religious" and "nonreligious" reasons in support of toleration. Penn's emphasis on understanding and judgment, and the necessity of both for true belief, represents an ongoing commitment of advocates for religious liberty down through the seventeenth century, made most famously by John Locke later in the seventeenth century. Because it misunderstood the workings of the human mind, persecution was bound to fail: physical punishments are power-less to effect the real inner change at the heart of true religion.[59]

Of course toleration was ultimately a question of governmental policy, and thus Penn presented elements of a political theory of toleration, defining gov-ernment as "an external order of justice, or the right and prudent disciplining of any society, by just laws." In making this argument Penn advanced a distinc-tion between "fundamental" and "superficial" law. Fundamental law, most no-tably Magna Carta, protected subjects from the exercise of arbitrary power. Superficial laws, passed by particular Parliaments for particular purposes, might be adjusted due to specific contingencies and circumstances. But in all cases, fundamental law trumped superficial law, since "the superstructure can not quarrel or invalid its own foundation," Penn argued, "without manifestly endangering its security." Parliamentary passage of legislation did not guarantee its legitimacy; as Penn had told the court during his trial: "The question is not whether I am guilty of this indictment, but whether this indictment be legal."[60]

Finally, Penn noted, persecution harms peace and prosperity. Like other tolerationists of his day, Penn cited the Netherlands as a neighboring example of prosperity and religious liberty going hand in hand. Persecution undermines the common good and the smooth operation of the economy, especially when considering how crucial Dissenters are to the nation's trade. Penal laws "are so far from benefiting the country, that the execution of them will be the assured ruin of it, in the revenues . . . For where there is a decay of families, there will be of trade; so of wealth, and in the end of strength and power." The importance of such prudential judgments, Penn insisted, had been grasped by tolerating rulers from Cato and Hannibal down to English Kings James and Charles I.[61]

All in all, even if religious dissent were a fault on the part of Dissenters, "yet the infliction of a corporal or external punishment, for a mere mental error . . . is unrea-sonable and inadequate, as well as against particular directions of the Scriptures."[62]

* * *

By August 1671, when he was finally released from Newgate, William Penn had successfully navigated (twice) the complexities of his father's Irish affairs, emerged from numerous scrapes with English and Irish authorities, established himself as a rising young figure in the Society of Friends, and begun to articu-late all the fundamental arguments about toleration and liberty of conscience that would constitute his mature theory of toleration over the next four decades. His relationship with Gulielma Springett continued to flourish, and he had carried out his father's last wishes by arranging for his burial in Bristol and the commemoration of Sir William's life and career with a monument in St. Mary Redcliffe. But attacks on Quakers from across the religious and political spectrum would continue in the years to come, and someone had to answer them. Increasingly, that someone would be William Penn.

5

"The Great Opinionist"

In the late 1660s, William Penn emerged as an exuberant and highly visible convert to the Society of Friends as well as a sufferer for the cause. The next decade would solidify his position as one of the foremost spokespersons for Quakerism in the public arena: George Fox's biographer H. Larry Ingle claims that Penn even "rivaled Fox as the most well-known Quaker," and Richard Baxter—one of the leading English Dissenters of Penn's day, and no friend to Quakers—commented that "of late one William Penn has become their leader." In the first half of the 1670s alone, Penn took on more than a dozen interlocutors in defense of Quaker doctrines and practices. He also embarked on his first trip to the Continent as a Friend.[1]

During the early 1670s, attacks came at Quakers from a wide range of critics, who denounced Friends' notion of the "Light Within" and questioned its compatibility with orthodox Christian doctrines and principles. But criticism also came from within Quakerism itself, as the unity that Friends so frequently professed continued to represent a distant aspiration. Such internal agitation raised questions about the degree to which the Quaker faith, with its emphasis on the sanctity of the individual conscience and the leadings of the Holy Spirit within each individual, could coexist with the organizational structure that Fox was attempting to put in place to ensure the movement's long-term survival. Penn grew increasingly into the role of Fox's defender, one of the First Friend's most trusted lieutenants. His role in the Quaker community also grew to include membership on a number of important Meetings, including the Second Day's Morning Meeting, which oversaw defenses of Friends in print and worked to create a unified outward-facing front that could speak to external critics with one voice. Penn's growing involvement in Friends' business would also provide the opening for his first foray into American colonization.

The early 1670s were also a time of personal transformation for William Penn. He buried his father shortly after his release from prison in September 1670. In April 1672, after a lengthy courtship, he married Gulielma Springett. The couple

moved into their new home, Basing House in Rickmansworth, and by the end of
the year, they were expecting their first child.

* * *

In August 1671, Penn and Gulielma, along with a number of other Friends, saw
George Fox off on his voyage to North America and the West Indies. Penn and
Thomas Rudyard then headed across the North Sea to Amsterdam. Rudyard, a
London lawyer, had surely been known to Penn before their journey, since he
frequently assisted Friends in their legal struggles against persecuting magistrates.
Rudyard may have had a hand in writing *The peoples ancient and just liberties* the
previous year; at around the same time, he also compiled and published a work
entitled *The second part of the peoples ancient and just liberties asserted*, which
recounted his own trial and those of a number of other Quakers. *The Second
part*, like its predecessor, denounced the tyrannical tendencies of judges and provided copious examples of violations of English law in the trials of Quakers. It
also included a fictional dialogue defending the rights of juries to render verdicts
according to their consciences. He and Penn would work together closely during
the 1670s, and both would become involved with American colonization in the
1680s, Penn in New Jersey and Pennsylvania and Rudyard serving a rocky tenure
as Deputy Governor of East Jersey and, briefly, Attorney-General of New York.[2]

In Amsterdam, Penn and Rudyard met with Benjamin Furly, a leading Quaker
merchant. Originally from England, Furly had settled in Rotterdam in the late
1650s, frequently hosting visiting Friends and translating for them when they
traveled in the Netherlands. In the 1680s Furly would form a crucial link in the
European promotional network that recruited settlers to Pennsylvania. (Furly is
often better known for his close association with John Locke, who stayed at his
house during the latter's Dutch exile during the 1680s.)[3]

Although Penn had lauded Dutch toleration in *The great case*—"Holland ... so
improved in wealth, trade, and power, chiefly owes it to her indulgence in
matters of faith and worship"—he was far less positive about what he saw
when he encountered the place up close. Amsterdam's worldliness clearly offended Penn's pious sensibilities, and he responded with a vigorous warning to
the Dutch people. Penn's "A trumpet Sounded" contained all the hallmarks of
Quaker prophesying, including calls for repentance, denunciations of hypocrisy
and worldliness, and warnings of impending divine judgment. Penn invoked the
Quaker doctrine of the Inner Light in assuring the Dutch people that all that was
required of them was to "turn to the Light of Christ in your conscience which
God hath caused to shine there, that it may give man a true discerning of his condition, and how it stands betwixt God and his soul."[4]

At the conclusion of his appeal Penn proclaimed that regardless of his
audience's reaction, "I have cleared my conscience before the Lord." Perhaps he

had, but Penn clearly still had things to say to the Dutch. Nine months later, after returning to England, he would once again denounce the Dutch "glory, pride, earthly-mindedness, oppression, and forgetfulness of God," calling on them to "sweep the streets of all lewdness . . . and bow unto God's righteous appearance." Not all his communications with Dutch Friends were critical; he also sent missives encouraging them to unity, and offering solace and comfort in their afflictions.[5]

By early October 1671, Penn, Rudyard, and Furly had traveled several hundred miles east to Heerwerden (present-day Herford, Germany), where Penn had long hoped to visit a religious community gathered under the leadership of John de Labadie, a French Protestant cleric. De Labadie's theology, like the Quakers', emphasized the power of the Spirit working in and through regenerated individuals and fostered a deeply communal ethic. Also like Quakers, the Labadists had aroused the intense hostility of many of their neighbors. The group had originally come together in Amsterdam, but after encountering resistance and hostility had relocated to Herford, accepting an invitation from Princess Elizabeth of the Palatine to settle on her lands there.

The visit, to put it mildly, did not go well. Penn had high hopes for the Labadists, and was particularly eager to meet Anna Maria van Schurman, one of the most famous women in Europe (and possibly the first female to attend a European university). He was disappointed, however, at the less-than-enthusiastic reception he and his fellow travelers received, which he attributed either to the Labadists being "void of common civility and humanity" or fearing that Quakers would make converts from among their ranks. What really seemed to rankle Penn, however, was their apparent insincerity, which he detected when he later encountered Labadists' denunciations of Quakers in print. Penn criticized de Labadie for arrogating the term "father" to himself and voiced his view that the group was characterized by "an exalted spirit," which led them to the dangerous extremes of "looseness and Ranterism."[6]

* * *

Although Penn had begun his career as a Quaker controversialist well before his journey to Holland and Germany, it was only upon his return to England in October 1671 that he took on the leading role he would occupy for the remainder of the decade. He returned at Harwich, the same port from which, six years earlier, he had carried a message from his father to King Charles II. The authorities were watching. The keeper of naval stores in Harwich reported that "On Tuesday, out of a packet-boat from Holland, arrived here Sir William Penn's eldest son, the great opinionist; he went presently and associated himself with the Quakers of this town."[7]

Having made contact with local Friends, Penn subsequently traveled through Essex and Suffolk. A letter to Friends in Suffolk and Cambridgeshire addressed an ongoing dispute within the Society about the proper Quaker attitude toward oaths, or rather—since an opposition to swearing oaths had been part and parcel of Quakerism since its earliest days—the more particular question of how Friends ought to articulate the grounds of their opposition to swearing. This was no small matter: oaths of a variety of kinds were ubiquitous in the early modern world, and were required for all sorts of undertakings, from courtroom proceedings to economic contracts to political officeholding. "Quakers might appeal to the Word of God and to their conscience," one scholar has explained, "but for the state, the oath was the measure of conscience." Quakers were not the only sect that refused to swear, but they quickly became the most prominent. Parliament had passed the Quaker Act in 1662, which made it illegal to refuse the Oath of Allegiance. Some Friends suggested pursuing legal challenges to the specific wording of oaths—some of which, at that point, were still sworn in the name of King James, who had died in 1625—while others emphasized the Quaker practice of not swearing at all, on principle. Penn pointed to the flaws of the former approach and insisted on the latter, arguing that "the ground of one not taking the oaths is not these two words [King James] but our not swearing . . . not swearing is the only reason." Of course, Penn had firsthand experience with the consequences of such refusal, as his imprisonment at Newgate in February 1671 had come about due in part to his refusal to swear before the Lieutenant of the Tower of London.[8]

Penn's November 1671 missive to Friends would be followed by a far more extensive defense of the Quaker position just a few years later. In 1675 Penn, along with a dozen other leading English Quakers, published *A treatise of oaths*, which laid out Friends' reasons for refusing to swear and offered more than a hundred examples of statesmen, church fathers, Reformers, philosophers, and contemporaries in support of their position. Although Penn shared billing with the other Friends on the *Treatise*'s dedication page, the style of the writing, as well as the format (a blend of Scripture, logic, and extensive historical examples), bore all the hallmarks of his authorship.[9]

By weighing in on the matter of oaths, Penn had resumed his dual roles as a defender of Quakers from outside critics and an increasingly prominent figure within the Society itself. In these capacities he also spent a great deal of time and energy denouncing Friends' persecutors. For example, Quakers in Ely had suffered at the hands of Edward Partridge and Thomas Richman, two Justices of the Peace there. Penn visited the area during the fall of 1671 and composed a blistering attack on Partridge's and Richman's conduct, which was accompanied by a wide-ranging exploration and condemnation of persecution. Though persecutors—who either force individuals to conform to a manner of faith and worship that they don't believe, or prevent them from practicing the faith they *do* believe—"think they . . . do God service as well as themselves," persecution in fact was nothing more than "the Devil's offspring." It made a travesty of English liberties and represented an affront to the English "ancient constitution," which said nothing about "the necessity of our conforming to any kind of religion, in order to enjoy the benefit" of the laws. (This argument was, of course, the same one that Penn and Mead had made during their trial at the Old Bailey fourteen months earlier.) True prophets had met with opposition and violence for ages, and Friends' struggles were merely the latest chapter in the long history of the struggle between light and darkness. Furthermore, persecution was false to the traditions of Protestantism and its embrace of individual conscience, insisting on a "moral impossibility": that an individual profess a religion that he or she does not believe. Penn attributed persecution to base motives like hatred, revenge, and self-interest, and pointed out its destructive consequences for the economy, the community, and individual integrity.[10]

Having laid out the case against persecution in its many dimensions, Penn proceeded to condemn the justices of the peace for their actions, which included physical assaults (even against elderly and infirm Friends), fines, destruction of Friends' property, and seizure of goods. Most gratuitously, on January 5, 1671, Partridge and Richman "caused their horses to be brought into the Meeting, where they made a turd, and sent for drink to make merry." (One assumes that the magistrates, and not the horses, were the ones sending for drink to "make merry"; and that the horses, not the magistrates, made the "turd.")[11]

Although Penn was well connected at the royal court and used those connections when necessary, he also realized that local authorities often had leeway in the enforcement of laws like the Conventicle Act, and so directed his efforts at justices of the peace, sheriffs, and other magistrates. After all, as historian John Miller has written, "It was one thing to pass a law and quite another to enforce it: most of the battery of laws against Catholics went unenforced most of the time." At times, these targeted letters to individual magistrates introduced concepts or themes that Penn would later develop at length in published polemics. For example, in a 1673 letter to Cumberland sheriff Daniel Fleming, Penn invoked the notion of "civil uniformity," which echoed his 1667 letter to the Earl of Orrery and previewed his more extensive elaboration of the idea of "civil interest" in years to come. There is "such a thing as civil uniformity, where a religious one may be inobtainable," he insisted.[12]

* * *

Despite the best efforts of Penn and his fellow Quakers, to say nothing of other leading Dissenters, Parliament proved resolutely unwilling to ease the burdens on religious exercise. The Cavalier Parliament was, after all, an intensely Anglican body that had passed the legislation known as the Clarendon Code, which reestablished the Church of England and cracked down on Dissenters. With the monarch himself, however, Dissenters had more success. On March 15,

1672, just two days before he declared war against the Dutch, Charles II issued a Declaration of Indulgence expressing the king's desire that "the execution of . . . all manner of penal laws in matters ecclesiastical, against whatsoever sort of nonconformists or recusants, be immediately suspended." Friends enjoyed a brief respite from persecution and were able to hold Meetings relatively undisturbed. Hundreds were pardoned and released from prison in the following months. Ironically, perhaps, the end of persecution and the freedom to worship openly actually *increased* attacks on Quakers, as their critics' opposition and hostility now had a more concrete target: Friends openly practicing in their midst. To make matters worse, the parliamentary backlash was not long in coming.[13]

As important as these developments no doubt were for William Penn, and as pleased as he must have been for the respite from state persecution, Penn had other things on his mind. A week before the king made his declaration, the Upper Buckinghamshire Monthly Meeting had given its consent to Penn's marriage to Gulielma Springett. The marriage itself followed in early April.

* * *

Gulielma Springett was the daughter of Sir William Springett and his wife Mary. Springett died in 1644 while commanding parliamentary forces at the siege of Arundel Castle, leaving behind a pregnant wife who soon gave birth to a daughter and provided her with a distinctive name: Gulielma is a Latinized combination of her father's and mother's names. Her middle name, Posthuma, commemorated her birth after her father's death. Mary Springett married Isaac Penington in 1654 and by the end of the decade had, along with her husband and daughters, become a convinced Quaker. By the early 1670s the Peningtons were living in Buckinghamshire and had become pillars of the Quaker community.[14]

Gulielma was both wealthy and beautiful, described by Thomas Ellwood as "in all respects a very desirable woman (whether regard was had to her outward person . . . or to the endowments of her mind . . . or to her outward fortune, which was fair)." William Penn and his future wife came from broadly similar social backgrounds and were roughly the same age. Her kindness, Ellwood wrote, was "expressed in an innocent, open, free, and familiar conversation, springing from the abundant affability, courtesy, and sweetness of her natural temper." In fact, Ellwood himself confessed to some "sparklings of desire" toward her (and promptly added that those sparklings had gone unrequited). She remained unmarried until the comparatively late age of twenty-eight, "openly and secretly sought and solicited by many, and some of them almost of every rank and condition," according to Ellwood, "till at length he came, he for whom she was reserved."[15]

William Penn and Gulielma Springett had been well acquainted by the time they announced their intention to marry, though we know very little of their courtship. Only a few letters between the two have survived, and most are filled with reports of Friends' activities and persecutions. Penn led an itinerant life during his early years as a Quaker (which were also the early years of their courtship)—in and out of jail, traveling in Ireland, England, Germany, and Holland—but he did look after her interests and estates in Ireland, and wrote to her in October 1668 with the sad news of Thomas Loe's death. She and her mother wrote to William in July 1670, telling him of Isaac Penington's imprisonment in Reading Jail and their visit to Friends in prison there. In August 1671, shortly before his departure to Holland and Germany, William went along with Gulielma and their mothers to see George Fox off to America. So by the time they announced their intention to marry, it was no surprise to any member of the Meeting.

According to the minutes of the Monthly Meeting for the Upperside of Buckinghamshire, the initial declaration of intent took place at a Meeting held at Ellwood's house on February 7, 1672. In accordance with Quaker custom, several Friends, in this case Thomas Zachary and Ellwood himself, were appointed to investigate the parties' "clearness of their proceedings" and discern whether any impediments existed to their being united in marriage. (One wonders if the "sparklings of desire" had been entirely extinguished in Ellwood's heart by this time. He had, after all, married Mary Ellis three years earlier.) No impediments being found, the couple received the "consent and approbation" of Friends at the next Monthly Meeting in early March.[16]

The wedding itself took place at King John's Farm in Chorleywood, in Hertfordshire, where the two "solemnly and expressly [took] each other in marriage, mutually promising to be loving, true, and faithful to each other in that relation, so long as it shall please the Lord to continue their natural lives." Their marriage certificate is dated April 4, 1672, and a pair of non-Quakers appear at the top of the list of witnesses: Penn's mother Margaret and his brother Richard. His sister and her husband apparently did not attend. If his Irish journal reads like a "Who's Who" of Irish Quakerism, then the list of witnesses on the marriage certificate of William Penn and Gulielma Springett reads like a "Who's Who" of English Quakerism: Isaac and Mary Penington, Gulielma's mother and step-father, along with her half-siblings, Mary and John; Alexander Parker; George Whitehead; Thomas Rudyard; Thomas Ellwood and his wife Mary; and James Claypoole, who would serve on the Pennsylvania Provincial Council during the 1680s. And this is only a partial list.[17]

The marriage of William and Gulielma took place at an important time in the development of Quaker approaches to marriage. Fox's attempts to establish a coherent structure of Meetings had a number of goals, but among them was more effective oversight of the Society's marriages. Fox had repeatedly written to Friends about marriage procedures, and he issued no fewer than sixty epistles on the subject during his lifetime. Worries about marriage outside the sect were as common among Friends as in any other community concerned about preserving its distinctive character. Suspicions about people attending Meetings "who seemed drawn to a Quaker girl rather than the inward light" animated the idea that the Meeting had a role to play in clearing proposed matches; and evaluating proposed matches developed as one of the important roles of Women's Meetings. Fox and other leading Quakers had long counseled consultation with more senior Friends, as well as parents and family members, before young couples entered into conversations about marriage. Such a process promoted, if not necessarily the consent, at least the involvement, of parents as well as of the Meeting. Penn, too, had written on the topic, and although he insisted on parental and Meeting involvement, he also reminded Friends that the promptings toward marriage should "arise purely and simply from within the parties themselves." The requirement that the couple publicly announce their intentions to their Meeting, and that time be allowed so that representatives from the Meetings could ascertain the couple's "clearness," aimed to guard against unwholesome or hasty choices. Because Friends took each other in marriage, before witnesses, without the services of a priest, Quaker marriages always faced the risk of delegitimation (e.g., goods forfeited, children declared illegitimate). For this reason, Margaret Fell had proposed as early as 1656 that newly married Friends "appear before the Justice of the Peace the next day or as soon as possible to have [the marriage certificate] included in the civil record."[18]

Although marriage in early modern England was not always concerned with physical attraction or mutual affection, such factors were becoming increasingly significant among Quakers during the 1660s and 1670s. Even more particular to Quakerism was an emerging view, advanced by Fox and echoed by Penn, that the married couple existed in a relationship akin to Adam and Eve before the Fall. Recall Penn's words just prior to the Fox–Fell wedding:

> As by [Fox] God in these last days first brought forth the knowledge of his pure light and food of life, which had been in the wilderness for many generations, so is this marriage by him proposed to be accomplished, the true character, resemblance, and express image of that ancient marriage of the Lamb, the food that was before the fall.

Penn seems to have endorsed this view of Friends' marriages in general, describing marriage as that "which gives to every man his own rib; of twain makes one again . . . where the lust of the eye rules not."[19]

The young couple's entrance into marriage and subsequent move to Basing House, Rickmansworth, just a few miles from Chorleywood and roughly twenty miles northwest of London, occasioned a considerable increase in William Penn's expenditures, and we might view it as the beginning of his lifelong struggles with money. Just three months after their wedding, the couple sold three pieces of land, which Gulielma had inherited from her father, to cover expenses incurred in setting up their new home. The sale of these parcels of land made the purchase of Basing House possible, but once sold they of course no longer produced rental income for the couple. All told, Penn's properties in England and Ireland should have produced nearly £2,000 per year, but continuing difficulty collecting rents from tenants in Ireland, to say nothing of a penchant for borrowing to pay off debts and an inability or unwillingness to curtail expenses, contributed to his financial challenges.[20]

Married life certainly did not diminish Penn's zeal for the cause. During the fall of 1672 he combined preaching with travel through Kent, Sussex, and Surrey collecting rent from tenants on Gulielma's lands there. The four-week journey reunited Penn with his former traveling companion John Penington as well as with Alexander Parker, a prominent Public Friend (Quakers who traveled in a preaching ministry) and close associate of Fox who had also signed the Penns' marriage certificate. The company set out from London on September 11— Gulielma, pregnant with her first child, stayed with Friends in Watford, just a few miles to the east of Rickmansworth—and Penn reports the next day holding a "large, living, and open meeting" in Rochester. They moved on to Canterbury and to another large Meeting "with all sorts of people." Of course Quaker Meetings, especially open and public ones, often attracted unwelcome attention, and Penn encountered "a young ruffian" in Canterbury who expressed "wicked epithets" at Friends. "But," Penn concluded, "God's power was over him, and . . . he came creeping in at night, confessing to what had been said to him at noon."[21]

In just under a month, Penn and his companions had covered roughly three hundred miles and taken part in nearly two dozen Meetings, many of which he described as drawing significant crowds. At Deal, a week after their departure from London, they held a "convincing, open, powerful, and exceeding tender Meeting"; in Ashford, outside Wye, on September 24, "the parlor, kitchen, entry, garden, etc. were crammed." Not only were Friends moved and encouraged by these Meetings, but "many confessed that never were at Meetings before." By early October Penn had reunited with Gulielma, who gave birth to a daughter in January. This first child, named for her mother, survived less than two months before dying in mid-March, the first in a number of heartbreaking developments during the early years of their marriage. William's brother Richard also died, at Rickmansworth, having only reached the age of eighteen, in April 1673. Twins born in late February 1674 would suffer the same fate: a boy, William Jr., survived only three months, while his twin sister Margaret would die in just under a year.[22]

* * *

The first year of William and Gulielma's marriage coincided with the king's Declaration of Indulgence, which provided liberty for Friends to meet openly without fear of persecution. But the Declaration, which was followed six months later by a pardon of nearly five hundred imprisoned Quakers, set the stage for even more vitriolic and vigorous criticism of Dissenters. After all, if Dissent was more visible, then it was more open to critique and denunciation. Attacks came not only from Anglicans who defended established structures of church and state as well as orthodox Christian doctrine, but also from other Dissenters, who saw Friends as theologically misguided, politically subversive, and socially divisive. Worse yet, all this happened while Fox was away in America. And thus Penn's budding career as leading Quaker controversialist accelerated, including a number of bitter confrontations (in both print and person) with Baptists, Independents, Anglicans, Presbyterians, and even Muggletonians. This increasingly frenetic activity resulted in Penn's publishing nearly two dozen defenses of Quakerism—to say nothing of other writings, like pleas to Parliament and the king for religious toleration—during the first half of the decade alone.[23]

The king's Declaration of Indulgence was fated to last only about a year. It was deeply unpopular with Parliament, which perceived it as infringing on its own prerogatives; they ultimately forced the king to withdraw it. Worse still, Parliament also forced him to accept further restrictions on Dissenters in the form of the Test Act of 1673, which mandated that all civil and military officeholders subscribe oaths affirming allegiance to the monarch and affirming him as head of the Church of England—known as the Oaths of Allegiance and Supremacy—as well as another disavowing transubstantiation. It also stipulated that all officeholders take Holy Communion in the Church of England within three months of the Act's passage. Quakers, of course, did not believe in transubstantiation, but neither did they believe in swearing oaths, and thus they feared—in a concern voiced by Penn in a petition to Parliament shortly after the Act's passage—that they would be punished under laws intended for Catholics. Penn's petition protested Quaker loyalty but reminded the House of Commons that "for pure conscience we cannot swear at all" and asked instead that they be allowed to "promise, verify, or attest" their loyalty, and be held to the same penalties "as if" they had sworn an oath. Unfortunately for Penn and the Quakers, there is no evidence that Parliament ever considered the petition.[24]

Even after the king withdrew his Declaration, Penn continued his efforts to mitigate the persecution of Friends, insisting to John Bowles of Wiltshire, who had been involved in the seizure of goods from a Quaker in 1674, that "we have been plundered and pillaged enough already." Parliament would soon produce legislation to ease the persecution of Dissenters, Penn claimed, and continued harassment of Friends would incur the king's wrath. (As it happened, such a bill did pass the House of Commons, but was held up in the House of Lords and prevented from becoming law by the king's dismissal of Parliament.) Penn sent copies of his *Seasonable caveat* and *The great case of liberty of conscience* to Middlesex magistrates in 1674, both to ensure that they understood that Quakers were not Catholics and to insist that their Meetings were not seditious. As a practical matter, Penn insisted that magistrates always had options other than jailing or fining Quakers: they could simply look the other way, or perhaps offer "some gentle caution for the future." Perhaps most fundamentally, though, Penn told the Middlesex magistrates that "you have work enough to employ yourselves about, in . . . executing all laws, that recover and preserve morality, mercy, justice, sobriety, and godly living." Here again, drawing on a distinction that he had broached in *The great case* and would further develop the following year in *England's present interest*, Penn contrasted the ancient and fundamental law of England with superficial or circumstantial ones aimed at addressing specific issues, and insisted, echoing his defense in the Penn–Mead trial, that Quakers did not forfeit their English rights when they followed their consciences outside the established church.[25]

* * *

But targeted directives to specific magistrates, though perhaps useful in aiding individuals or specific groups of Friends, did not offer the public stage that Penn's published defenses of Quakers and Quakerism did. Many of the criticisms Quakers faced voiced a deep distrust of the doctrine of the Inner Light, and asked whether Quakers believed that the Light Within was, in itself, sufficient to the salvation of the believer's soul. The logical consequence of such a doctrine, to their critics at least, was to undermine the central role of Scripture and Christian doctrine, to say nothing of sacraments like baptism and the role of ecclesiastical authorities. It also undermined social hierarchies and corroded deference to "superiors" and political authority, linking Quakers to a long line of libertines and false prophets. Quakers were just like their anarchic predecessors in Munzer, argued Thomas Jenner in his 1670 *Quakerism anatomized*, who "pretended an immediate mission to act from the spirit, and by virtue of an immediate command, above the trial of the scriptures." Critics also lodged objections to Quaker denials of doctrines such as justification and sanctification, key elements of the Protestant separation from Rome. All in all, critics charged Friends with an arrogant and unwarranted confidence in their ability to "live without sin," or perfectionism, and insisted that the result of such a theology was far more likely to be libertinism than humble discipleship.[26]

Although Quakers considered themselves true Protestants, traditional elements of Christian orthodoxy held little water for them. To one critic, Penn insisted on "the universality, divinity, and sufficiency of that Light within to salvation" and that "predestination, and sacraments, are generally . . . without any foundation in Scripture or reason." To another, he expressed the Quaker view that Scripture represented "an excellent transcript or copy of the mind and will of God"; and he assured yet another correspondent that "the Scriptures and the

spirit bear a mutual testimony to each other. . . . They jar not, they interfere not."
To the Presbyterian John Collinges, Penn defended his criticism of the doctrine
of the Trinity, calling it a "popish school-personality" not found in Scripture.
Many of these contentious exchanges took place in private correspondence, but
Penn's most extended, vituperative remarks were reserved for the public realm.[27]

* * *

Not surprisingly, Quakers found themselves on the receiving end of a great deal
of criticism from representatives of the Church of England. In 1673, Henry
Hallywell, an Anglican vicar from Sussex, weighed in with a bitter attack on
Friends, equating them with the controversial Family of Love. The Familists, as
they were often called, were a radical sixteenth-century movement long accused
of sexual improprieties and of teaching that humans were, or could become, free
from sin. Hallywell canvassed the broad range of criticisms of "Quakery," claiming
that Quakers were "the refuse of the world, persons of the meanest quality and
lowest parts and education," and that their doctrines were "not only destructive of
all civil polity and government, but of religion itself and the worship of Almighty
God established amongst us." Penn's swift response, *Wisdom justified of her children*,
presented a point-by-point, chapter-by-chapter rebuttal of Hallywell's "ignorance
and calumny." He concluded by describing himself as "a Friend to all men, who
would have vice punished, conscience tolerated, and righteousness established."[28]

Where Hallywell presented a broad-brush and totalizing denunciation of
Quakerism, other Anglicans undertook more focused attacks on specific Quaker
teachings. Samuel Grevill, an Anglican priest from Banbury in Oxfordshire,
criticized Quakers for an insufficient devotion to the Scriptures at the expense of
the Inner Light. More specifically, Grevill's 1674 *Discourse* targeted *A Testimony
of the Light within*, published more than fifteen years earlier by Penn's good
friend and prominent Quaker Alexander Parker. Penn's defense of Parker was
also, of course, a defense of the broader Quaker teaching, and stressed the transformative experience of accepting the Light's guidance in the believer's life. Penn
pointed to the foundational text from John's gospel: "This was the true Light that
lighteth every man that cometh into the world."[29]

Several years later Penn found himself in a public dispute with another
Anglican clergyman, John Cheyney from Warrington in Cheshire. Cheyney was
tireless in his assault on Friends, and published at least four anti-Quaker works
in 1676 alone. Penn could not respond to each one, but Cheyney's charge that
Quakers elevated individual conscience above Scripture drew his particular notice. Penn's further entanglements with Cheyney illustrate the intertwining of
multiple strands of Restoration religious and political debate. Cheyney's *A skirmish made upon Quakerism* was actually a critique of Penn's 1672 response to
the Presbyterian John Faldo (whom we shall meet shortly); thus, in responding

to Cheyney, Penn was also rekindling his running dispute with Faldo. Penn's dismissive reply, *The skirmisher defeated*, mocked Cheyney for extracting a few sentences from a four-year-old work and using it as the basis for an extended rant over issues that had already been well covered. Penn insisted on the essentially Protestant nature of Quakers' understanding of conscience, invoking Luther, Calvin, and English Reformers in support of his claims.[30]

These public disputes notwithstanding, not every interaction between Quakers and Anglicans threw off such rhetorical sparks. In the spring of 1675, Penn received a long and detailed letter from Anglican scholar Henry More, noted "Cambridge Platonist," poet, and theologian, whose patron, Lady Anne Conway, would later convert to Quakerism. More's letter eschewed invective and instead engaged in a searching and substantive engagement with Quaker principles and doctrines. While lamenting that Protestants should be so disputatious with each other, More praised the "wit and seriousness" and "several excellent passages" of Penn's writings and expressed his pleasure that the Friends had "two such able and faithful guides [Penn and George Keith, a Scottish Quaker with whom Penn worked closely during these years] to keep them within the main verge of Christianity." More went so far as to disavow the equation of Quakers and Familists. Early Quakers might have been guilty of such beliefs, but More rejoiced that "the Quakers have emerged above that low beginning of . . . Familism." This is not to say that More agreed with Quaker doctrines: he offered an extensive discussion of the scriptural roots of baptism and Holy Communion, and an elaborate exegesis of verses from John's gospel regarding the Light. He was straightforward in his criticism of Quaker objections to hat-honor, and claimed that "there is no ground in Scripture . . . for this scrupulosity in the Quakers." But the tenor of the exchange, and its complimentary tone, differed radically from Penn's interactions with many non-Quakers.[31]

Quakers had often been accused of Socinianism, a strand of Christianity that criticized the doctrine of the Trinity and the notion that Jesus died to atone for the sins of the world. Recall that Penn had been sent to the Tower for such views when he published *The sandy foundation shaken*; Vincent's *Foundation of God standeth sure* had charged Quakers with being "Rank Socinians, who more grossly err in the fundamentals of religion, than the papists themselves." But in 1672 Penn had found himself debating an actual Socinian, Henry Hedworth. Hedworth's *The spirit of the Quakers tried* was an attack on Friends and more particularly on Fox, whom Hedworth declared "a false prophet, liar, or imposter." Hedworth—sometimes referred to as the first Unitarian—particularly took aim at Fox's use of Scripture, bringing up no fewer than fifty scriptural references that he claimed Fox misquoted or mangled. In fact, he went further and insisted that what Quakers called "the Light" was really just the Protestant principle of "the light of common and certain principles written in every man's heart," and that

Friends needlessly complicated things by giving it a new name and making ex-cessive claims for its efficacy. Furthermore, he accused Fox and other prominent Quakers of arrogating authority to themselves and imposing "ceremonies," such as the removal of hats in worship.[32]

Penn took up Hedworth's challenge in *The spirit of truth vindicated*, beginning with the timing of Hedworth's attack. For one thing, Fox was in America and thus unable to defend himself. For another, Dissenters were enjoying a long-awaited respite from persecution under the auspices of the king's Declaration:

> Why . . . does the man choose the present season, to shower down his
> displeasure against us; just when we should make the best of an unex-
> pected toleration, to the refreshment of our afflicted minds and bodies,
> by the late persecutions that have been? . . . Is he angry that we have
> liberty, or does he think that none deserve it but himself?

Penn used his response to Hedworth not only to defend Fox's use of Scripture, but also to develop a more elaborate understanding of the Light Within and its relation to Scripture as a guide for Christian life. Referring to the Light as "uni-versal, supernatural, and infallible," he defended a number of Quaker principles in depth and detail.[33]

Once again, one dispute led to another. It was not long before Penn's contre-temps with Hedworth led him into a bitter dispute with the Baptist John Morse of Watford, just a few miles from Rickmansworth. Morse had been invited to a Quaker Meeting by a young servant, who claimed that "the Light in her" had in-spired her to extend the invitation. Their subsequent discussions of the Quaker doctrine of Inner Light—and the young woman's apparently inadequate and unsophisticated answers to Morse's theological questions—led to a protracted interaction with Penn himself, since she had presented Morse with a copy of Penn's *The spirit of truth*. Upon perusing it, Morse found that Penn's book was filled with "error if not blasphemy," a claim that initiated a series of letters be-tween the two men, which Penn published under the title *Plain-dealing with a traducing Anabaptist*. He noted, once again, how unfortunate it was that just when Dissenters had finally achieved the toleration they had sought for so long, they should occupy themselves by attacking each other. It is "a strange use that these men make of toleration . . . to persecute by revilings those that have the most suffered for want of it . . . for whilst that persecuted, they seemed to pity us; but now that [the government] tolerates, they appear to envy us."[34]

In the dispute with Morse, once again, questions about the Light and its re-lation to the Scriptures formed the core of the argument. Penn used his discus-sion of the Light to attack the Calvinist doctrine of predestination, which he considered an affront to the notion of a loving God who desired that all should be saved. "O barbarous cruelty, and most aggravated injustice!" Penn wrote. "It renders the most merciful and just God most cruel and unjust." He did not deny that Morse's servant may have held an overly simplistic understanding of theological matters, but he condemned Morse's "un-Christian and uncharitable spirit." In private correspondence, Morse complained that Penn had published his letter without his permission, but got no pity from the Quaker, who called him "a creeping slanderer of a man thou knewest not."[35]

* * *

These controversies, however, pale before those between Penn and his chief adversaries during these years, the Baptist Thomas Hicks and the Congregationalist John Faldo. Each of these disputes stretched on for several years. Faldo, a Congregationalist from near Barnet, north of London, found his congregants forsaking his preaching for nearby Quaker Meetings, and in an attempt to stanch the flow, produced *Quakerism no Christianity*, a two-hundred-plus-page attack on Friends. In addition to detailed and scorching critiques of Quaker doctrines—he called the Light Within "a false God"—Faldo included a targeted critique of Penn's *The spirit of truth* and the "false, anti-Christian and anti-Scriptural tenets" that Quakers cloak in "Scripture-words and phrases." Lamenting the "great shoals that have been taken in by the net of Quakerism" and charging Friends with "know[ing] no God above that they call the Light in their consciences," Faldo appealed directly to Friends to return to orthodox Christian churches. Quakerism was not Christianity, he argued, and Quakers should "no more call themselves Christians."[36]

Penn's lengthy response, published in March 1673, insisted that Quakerism was, as his title claimed, "a new nick-name for old Christianity," and pronounced Faldo's arguments "lame . . . fictitious and forged." In addition to justifying the Quaker doctrine of the Light and Friends' understanding of Scripture, Penn's reply lamented the ways in which Dissenters of all stripes were piling on Quakers just when they should all be celebrating their newfound liberty. He targeted Faldo in particular, claiming that "No adversary has treated me with more incivility, and less learning" and calling him a "wretched scribbler."[37]

Penn's other nemesis during these years was the Baptist Thomas Hicks, who attacked Quakers in his 1673 *Dialogue between a Christian and a Quaker* in which, not surprisingly, "Christian" thoroughly bested "Quaker" in a debate over faith and doctrine. In a postscript to the reader, Hicks voiced his hope that his dialogue would assist "towards the discovery and detecting the opinions, hypocrisy, and deceit of the Quakers." Penn collaborated with George Whitehead on a response, *The Christian-Quaker*, which presented a systematic theological defense of the Quaker doctrine of the Light. It may also have been for this purpose that Penn wrote his "Description of a true Quaker," a private document he circulated during this time. Since so much criticism of Friends revolved around the question of the Light Within, Penn sought to clarify and explain, in clear and pithy terms, the workings of the Light in the believer's life. Far from an erratic, troublesome, and destabilizing influence on behavior, as many of their critics claimed, Penn insisted that the Light actually compels the believer to moral behavior, and drew on his own experience in making the point, saying that he was "not without some knowledge experimental of what I say . . . [that] the Light shows that it's inconsistent with a man fearing God to be wanton, passionate, proud, covetous, backbiting, envious, wrathful, unmerciful, revengeful, profane, drunken, voluptuous, [and] unclean." In other words, "He that obeys the light is thereby taught to deny ungodliness and worldly lusts, to be sober, righteous, patient, humble, meek, merciful, forbearing, forgiving, peaceable, gentle, self-denying, constant, faithful, and holy because the Lord his God is holy." Acknowledging the Light is part of the process by which "God has begotten better desires" within individuals, who are in turn transformed by that experience.[38]

Hicks, however, was not deterred, and produced a kind of sequel, *A continuation of the dialogue*, in which, once again, Quaker errors were skillfully presented in dialogue format. This new version of Hicks's attack particularly alarmed Penn, as the dialogue format gave the impression that Hicks was actually quoting Quakers' own words, when in fact he was (in Penn's view at least) deliberately presenting Friends' views in an unflattering light and allowing their fictional interlocutor to have the last word. And so Penn sprang back into action, publishing *Reason against railing*, which once again rehearsed Quaker positions. Hicks also came through Penn's neighborhood at this time; in a letter to his neighbors, Penn reported hearing that Hicks had been to Watford, and proclaimed himself willing to defend Quakerism publicly and in person "from his forgeries, perversions, slanders, and false consequences." Additional charges and countercharges flew in other writings.[39]

Debate in print could only go so far and was bound to lead to debate in person. In fact, Penn's dual disputes with Faldo and Hicks came together in the summer and fall of 1674. Penn had called on Baptist leaders to disavow Hicks—calling his interlocutor a "counterfeit Christian"—and in early August he provided Baptist leaders with copies of his works criticizing Hicks. Later that month, a number of London Baptists called for a public meeting with Quakers, with Penn and Whitehead as the primary Quaker participants. The Baptists' invitation failed to reach the two Friends in time for them to attend, however, as both men were away from London at the time. The Baptists taunted the Friends for not appearing to defend their claims in public, implying that Quakers were afraid of meeting in an open debate. Thomas Rudyard saw a more calculating process at work, claiming that the Baptists waited until they knew that Penn and Whitehead would not be able to participate—"till they might be sufficiently assured of the Absence of W. P. & G. W. either of them being far distant, and on before-designed Journeys"—before issuing their challenge.[40]

Penn and Whitehead missed the debate, but Faldo showed up, adding his own criticisms of Quakers and hoping for a chance to engage Penn in person. Faldo had repeatedly challenged Penn to debate publicly, and in October 1674 Penn replied with a note of weariness, pointing to "how furiously a sort of men crowd in print upon me" and insisting that he was busy responding to a slew of attacks already. Penn suggested, instead, that Faldo attend the debate scheduled for later that month at the Quaker Meetinghouse on Wheeler Street, London, but Faldo declined. The Wheeler Street debate went forward as scheduled: in fact Baptists and Quakers debated twice during October, once at Wheeler Street and once at the Congregationalist meetinghouse at the Barbican in London. From all accounts they were raucous affairs, with years' worth of bitterness and acrimony discharged—and, one suspects, few minds changed.[41]

While relations between "caviling Baptists" and Quakers remained raw, the Penn–Faldo dispute had largely petered out by 1675, when Faldo stoked its embers again by reissuing his *Quakerism no Christianity*, this time featuring the endorsement of twenty-one clergy, including one of the most famous Dissenters in the land: Presbyterian Richard Baxter, who had been ejected from his position as a clergyman in the Church of England as a result of the Act of Uniformity in 1662 but who remained perhaps the most influential English Dissenter during the Restoration. Faldo compared Penn's writing to Pandora's box, "which when opened, filled the world with many plagues," and accused him of engaging in personal, ad hominem attacks on his character. Faldo made much of his unsuccessful efforts to secure a public debate with Penn, which he claimed that Penn "industriously avoided, as if the day were a terror to him." Though Penn refused to reengage with Faldo—his *A just rebuke to the one and twenty . . . divines* reminded readers of just how much ink he had spilled over Faldo's attacks over the past two years—Baxter's appearance in the mix was a new development, one Penn took as a direct attack on him by an adversary with a national reputation.[42]

* * *

The debate with Baxter would turn out to be one of the most high-profile public disputations of Penn's career. Baxter visited Rickmansworth and preached in parish churches there; he challenged Penn to a debate and rehearsed all the standard criticisms of Friends' doctrine. Penn's overriding concern, by contrast, was political, and he endorsed toleration (or, as it was often styled, "indulgence") while criticizing moves for "comprehension," an alternative approach to the politics of religious diversity that expanded the parameters of acceptable theology within the established church while maintaining a hard line against Dissent outside it. Quakers had long considered comprehension a particularly dangerous prospect, since it offered the appearance of moderation—allowing Presbyterians, for example, a place within the Church of England—while providing a political and ideological justification for continuing to persecute those sects whose views fell farther outside the mainstream. Quakers feared that Presbyterians like Baxter, if successful in attaining their own inclusion in the Church of England, would quickly turn around and suppress many of their fellow Dissenters. Penn later denounced comprehension in a letter to Baxter, calling him a persecutor who, along with his Presbyterian brethren, "are for casting us and others to the dogs by a comprehension, leaving us under the clutches of merciless men" and "hath preached up the use of civil power to restrain consciences."[43]

Like many such public disputations, the debate between Penn and Baxter, which stretched for seven hours without interruption on October 5, 1675, shed far more heat than light. The two men were, after all, arguing at cross purposes. Penn wanted a debate about Baxter's endorsement of Faldo's anti-Quaker diatribes, while Baxter wanted a more general dispute about the merits (or lack thereof) of Quakerism. "Let [Penn] in plain discourse . . . give them the reasons why they should be Quakers," Baxter offered, "and I would give them the reasons why they should not, and leave it to their consciences to discern who spake the truth." Penn later complained of Baxter's "tedious harangues, and almost unpardonable evasions and perversions," and immediately proposed another meeting with firmly established rules of procedure. Baxter, for his part—who also knew something about suffering for one's faith, having been imprisoned several times since the Restoration—claimed that Penn had displayed a "designing, persecuting spirit" and invoked the specter of James Nayler to tar Quakers with blasphemy. In a dig at Penn's social background, he noted the irony of Penn's denunciation of paid clergy "while he swims himself in wealth." Baxter, sixty years old and never in the best of health, having endured tuberculosis as a young man, claimed that he was able to speak no more than an hour or two. Penn mocked Baxter's purported infirmity as a convenient way of evading another confrontation and, as a crowning insult, pronounced Baxter "neither a good man, a charitable man, nor a fair disputant." Not surprisingly, the proposed second meeting never took place.[44]

* * *

Much of Penn's time during the 1670s was taken up in defending Friends against criticisms from across the religious and political spectrum. But not all the slings and arrows aimed at Quakers came from outside the Society: there had always been tension within Quakerism itself. An individualistic, Spirit-filled movement of individuals animated by the direct experience of "that of God within" could be hard to organize in ways that would ensure its survival amidst difficult circumstances. Fox had long aroused the ire of some Friends by his leadership style: gathering authority to himself, exerting control over wayward Friends, attempting to build an organizational structure, and denouncing his critics in harsh terms. All this sat uneasily, to some, alongside a movement premised on the Inner Light and the movings of the Spirit within the believer. William Penn, however, experienced no such doubts, and proved to be an eager, energetic, and loyal lieutenant.

The history of Quakerism is replete with instances where individuals or groups expressed objections to Fox's dominance. We have already seen how James Nayler's 1656 ride into Bristol on the back of a donkey brought the full force of law down upon him, occasioned a deep rift between Nayler and Fox, and cast Quakers in a harshly unfavorable light for years to come. John Perrot, an Irish Quaker who had traveled to Rome in an attempt to convert the pope, criticized the Quaker practice of men removing their hats during prayer, which he viewed as an unacceptable ritual imposition. Although Perrot died in the mid-1660s, traces of his influence remained. After having received what he described as an "idle, envious, and deceitful letter" from one Henry Clark, William Penn responded—nearly a decade after Perrot's death—that having looked into Clark's background he was unsurprised to find that Clark had supported Perrot. For that matter, Fox spent some time during his American journey in the early 1670s attempting to quell any remnants of Perrotian sympathies among Friends in the Americas.[45]

During the first half of the 1670s, the most sustained criticism of Fox came from William Mucklow and John and Mary Pennyman. Like many of those who voiced opposition to Fox, these were not newcomers but rather long-established members of the Society who had suffered for the faith: both Mucklow and Mary Pennyman had been imprisoned during the early 1660s. Although Penn told Mucklow that he would "endeavour to heal that breach" between him and the Quakers, his correspondence was anything but conciliatory. Mucklow's specific complaint evoked Perrot's: the Quaker practice of removing the hat to pray, as a sign of deference and honor to God, looked to him dangerously similar to an imposed religious ceremony. Although Penn shared Mucklow's aversion to ceremonialism, he insisted that just as the soul participated in worship, so too did the body, and therefore worship practices that embodied believers' subservience to God should not be discouraged. The Quaker removal of hats in worship was really simply the logical consequence of their refusal to doff their hats to humans: "We pull off our hats to almighty God to express that honor, homage, and reverent respect to the immortal King of glory, which we cannot and dare not give to any mortal man." Given "the trivialness of the thing," he considered those who insisted on keeping their hats on during prayer guilty of a "conceited, singular, self-separating, self-exalting spirit." Penn rebuked the Pennymans for undermining the Society's unity, and argued that such actions reinforced criticisms from outside the community, "thereby strengthening the hand of the common adversary to lay waste God's heritage."

Though internal criticism was different from external, Penn insisted, in a letter to Mary Pennyman, that those Quakers who opposed Fox's leadership were "one in the ground, though not in appearance, with the spirit of John Faldo, Thomas Hicks, [and] Henry Hedworth."[46]

Given the harsh tone of Penn's letter to Mucklow, it is probably not surprising that his exhortation to "come in, come home" fell on deaf ears. But the dispute had not run its course. Soon after their exchange of letters, the dispute between Mucklow and "Foxonians"—his term for mainstream Quakers—burst into view with Mucklow's publication of *The spirit of the hat*, in which he criticized Fox and Quaker leadership, accusing them of attempting to "introduce an arbitrary and tyrannical government over the conscience, over the flock of God." In other words, Mucklow claimed that Quakers put the judgment of the Society above the promptings of the individual conscience. Penn's response, *The spirit of Alexander the coppersmith*, asserted that religious bodies had a right to manage their own affairs, and that Mucklow's criticisms essentially boiled down to a fit of pique. His failure to convince Quakers of his views on hat-honor had made Mucklow "a man enraged beyond all bounds of not only Christianity, but manhood [and] with folly, madness, and desperate revenge . . . endeavored our ruin among men." Penn focused on Mucklow's contentiousness and his alliance with the wealthy and ostentatious Pennymans rather than simple, God-fearing Friends.[47]

Not surprisingly, Mucklow did not allow these claims to go unanswered. In *Tyranny and hypocrisy detected*, Mucklow hurled increasingly bitter criticisms at Fox, and brought forward additional charges against the Friends, essentially accusing them of running a bait-and-switch operation. Although Quakers claimed to celebrate the Light Within and the absolute sanctity of the individual conscience, such talk was "but a shooing-horn to draw people in, and . . . when they are brought over to them . . . then they must be ruled and guided by the judgment of G. Fox and the ruling elders." Penn replied once more, in *Judas against the Jews*, denying these charges, of course, and lamenting that an alliance of Dissenters and dissatisfied Friends had come together to attack Quakers. To Penn's defense of Fox were added testimonies of a number of Friends who defended the Penn–Fox position on church government and "Gospel Order."[48]

* * *

One of the central points of internal dissention among Friends related to Fox's efforts to bolster Quakerism's organizational structure. Fox had endeavored for some time to establish regular Monthly and Quarterly Meetings to preserve "Gospel Order"; organize poor relief; discipline wayward believers; and register births, marriages, and deaths. By 1668 "a nation-wide system of local and regional meetings, linked by correspondents with London, had been set up," and Fox used his journey to Ireland in May 1669 to set up similar structures there. But the real organizational advances came with the establishment of the Six Weeks' Meeting (1671), which advised local Meetings; the Second Day's Morning Meeting (1672), which oversaw the Quaker press; and the Meeting for Sufferings (1675), which gathered evidence of persecution and advocated against it.[49]

In addition to these national-level Meetings based in the capital, a parallel system of Women's Meetings also dates to the late 1660s, and grew over the course of the next decade. Like the Men's Meetings they, too, distributed poor relief and assessed couples' suitability for marriage. Not surprisingly, the require-ment that Men's Meetings submit to the judgment of Women's Meetings with regard to clearing marriages did not sit well with some men. The Box Meeting, made up entirely of Quaker women, supported Friends in need, provided funds for traveling women Friends, and corresponded with other Women's Meetings throughout the colonies. Perhaps not surprisingly, in the gathering storm that became the Wilkinson–Story schism, "the greatest source of contention was the introduction of women's business meetings," since, as Phyllis Mack has observed, the establishment of the Women's Meeting "involve[d] the authority to instruct and discipline male relatives and neighbors."[50]

The origins of the Yearly Meeting date to the late 1660s when, after a series of false starts interrupted by organizational difficulties and intermittent persecu-tion, leading Friends met in London. The Yearly Meeting was not quite yearly at this point, but did convene at least a half-dozen times during the 1670s, to as-semble accounts of Quaker sufferings, collect funds supporting itinerant minis-ters, and oversee the publication of books and pamphlets defending the Society from its many critics. A 1673 epistle from the Yearly Meeting exhorted Friends to unity and urged them to settle their differences within the Society, without going to civil courts. In May 1675, the Yearly Meeting's epistle to English Friends laid out a number of decisions on issues as varied as the regulation of marriages and the settlement of disputes within the community. It also defended the for-mation of Women's Meetings, an issue that had been swept up into the growing opposition to Fox that was coalescing around two Westmoreland Friends, John Wilkinson and John Story. For many, the Yearly Meeting was "a novelty . . . and roused much adverse criticism."[51]

But some of the most significant and substantive opposition came about be-cause of other Meetings pioneered by Fox. The Second Day's Morning Meeting, which consisted primarily of Public Friends and was charged with managing the work of Quaker preachers around Britain and with organizing Quaker responses to their critics, first met in September 1673 at the home of Gerrard Roberts, a London wine cooper and leading Quaker spokesman. Of course to respond to critics one needs to know who those critics are, and what they say, so George Whitehead and William Penn were directed to obtain copies of all books written against Friends. Much of the Morning Meeting's work during the middle to late 1670s consisted of assigning members to read and report on proposed responses to anti-Quaker tracts, and given Penn's prominence as a controversialist, he played an important role in these discussions. The Morning Meeting was, from the beginning, a key body in crystallizing and articulating Friends' doctrine for a wider (often hostile) public. Although London Friends clearly predominated, Quakers from other parts of the realm also attended, often when other business brought them to the capital. As time went on and the Quaker presence in North America and the Caribbean grew, the Morning Meeting increasingly took on responsibility for providing colonial Quakers with Friends' writings. Still, many Friends around the country viewed the Morning Meeting with particular suspicion.[52]

The increasing power of the Morning Meeting aroused intense and prolonged opposition over the course of the 1670s. Many of these discontents had coalesced around "the two Johns," Wilkinson and Story, farmers from Westmoreland in northwest England and members of the Preston Patrick Meeting. Story and Wilkinson, Friends since the 1660s, grew increasingly disenchanted with Fox's leadership and were in turn attacked by Fox for supposedly fleeing from the authorities (attempting to avoid detection by holding Meetings in the woods) rather than embracing martyrdom in the face of persecution. By the middle of the decade, while Fox lay in Worcester jail, the Preston Patrick Meeting faced a schism over resistance to the newly erected Meeting structures and Fox's claims of authority. In May 1675, Penn was instrumental in putting together an epistle from the Yearly Meeting calling for Friends to maintain open Meetings "and not decline, forsake, or remove their public assemblies, because of times of suffering," and defending the institution of Women's Meetings. Penn was also among a group tasked by the Morning Meeting in late October 1677—a busy month for him, what with his growing family, other responsibilities, and his extended debate with Baxter—with attempting to arrange a conference with the Story–Wilkinson dissidents.[53]

Finally, and perhaps most significantly, these years saw the founding of the Meeting for Sufferings, which was first convened in October 1675 and quickly grew to encompass a wide range of tasks relating to the recording of persecution suffered by Friends and attempts to mitigate it wherever possible. The growth of Quakerism and the convincement of a number of Friends versed in legal matters brought into the Society "pragmatists who realized that organization, lobbying, and legal tactics were imperatives to any strategy of survival in a hostile political and religious environment." The initial charge of the Meeting for Sufferings avoided pronouncing definitely on whether Friends ought to endure suffering or might seek to contest their treatment in courts of law—in its words, "the Meeting doth not enjoin, impose upon, or advise any Friends . . . to take course at law for a remedy, neither . . . can we impose on them not to use the law." It included Penn and other important members of the Society such as Rudyard, Mead, and Whitehead. The scope of its work was not restricted to England alone, and it directed its attention to the mistreatment and persecution of Friends as far away as Barbados, Jamaica, Ireland, Germany, Maryland, and New England.[54]

By later in the decade the Meeting for Sufferings had taken responsibility for organizing appeals to the king or Parliament, as well as advocating with colonial proprietors who controlled territories in which Quakers faced hostility or persecution. A session of the Meeting for Sufferings in November 1677, for example, discussed "the business . . . between the Lord Baltimore and Friends" and "referred . . . William Penn to attend the said Lord Baltimore and to give an account the next meeting." (At the Meeting's next session he reported a successful outcome of two conferences with Baltimore.) Penn was also one of a group sent to intervene with the governor of Jamaica on behalf of Friends there, to the king to advocate for better treatment of Friends in Barbados, and to agents of New England about their persecution of Friends. He worked during 1677 and 1678 to ease the frequent prosecution of Friends under penal laws aimed at Catholics. And along with James Claypoole, who would later emigrate to Pennsylvania and serve as treasurer of the Free Society of Traders, Penn corresponded with Irish Friends regarding the Meeting's business.[55]

At the same time that he was arguing for religious liberty across English society, then, Penn was participating in Fox's project to control the face that Quakerism presented to the outside world and to set up a mechanism for disciplining Friends who displayed potentially embarrassing or disruptive behaviors. The effort would continue to convulse the Society. Fox's allies, of course, viewed the emerging Meeting structure as "Gospel Order," a set of institutions to streamline procedures for the growing movement and ensure its survival. Their critics, not surprisingly, saw the introduction of a dangerous hierarchy that eviscerated the spiritual core of Quakerism and cemented into place a system of bureaucratic and patriarchal censorship. Even as early as the 1660s, but certainly growing over the course of the next decade, Rosemary Moore argues, "The charismatic Quaker movement had gone, and was being replaced by the Religious Society of Friends."[56]

* * *

What made defending Fox and Quakerism more difficult was the First Friend's extended absences: first in America, where he traveled from August 1671 through June 1673, and later, after his return, in Worcester jail (off and on between December 1673 and February 1675). In *The spirit of truth vindicated*, Penn pointed out that if Henry Hedworth had such a negative view of Fox, he should have visited him in person, "and not (at a juncture, when he might understand him to be at so great a distance as America) to exhibit an angry charge against him in England."[57]

Fox having gone to America was one thing; Fox in prison in England was quite another. About six months after his return from America in spring 1673, Fox was returning to Swarthmoor from London when he and Margaret stopped at Rickmansworth to visit William and Gulielma Penn. After they had left the Penns and continued northward, Fox was arrested after preaching at a Meeting in a barn near Armscote, Warwickshire, and sent to Worcester to await trial. His case attracted some sympathy from the judges there, who saw little evidence that a law had been broken, and were able to slow the process down considerably. The case bounced back and forth between Worcester and the King's Bench in London, and ultimately, sensing a conviction on the original charges unlikely, the local justices tendered Fox the Oath of Allegiance. He of course refused to swear, and thus in July 1675 received a sentence of "praeminure"—essentially a life sentence unless lifted by the king.[58]

Thomas Lower, Fox's son-in-law (he was married to Margaret's daughter Mary), remained with him during much of his imprisonment, which brought both physical and emotional suffering. Fox's aged mother, whom he had hoped to visit on his northward journey, died shortly after his arrest. In August 1674, Lower reported that Fox was "weakly and sick; rather worse than better; and wants air very much to refresh him, but cannot get down stairs and up, he is so weak." Margaret and numerous other Friends went to London and pleaded with the king on his behalf, but to little avail. For their part, Friends tried to put the best face on Fox's continuing imprisonment. Early in 1675 Penn wrote an open letter to Friends, telling them that "dear George Fox is prisoner," but that "Truth increases, [and] the hearts of thousands are enlarged and love is begotten in many."[59]

Penn and his old ally William Mead, assisted by the Earl of Middlesex, called on the king and the Duke of York in an attempt to secure Fox's release. The duke pronounced himself "against all persecution for the sake of religion" and promised to take Fox's case up with his brother. The king's attempt to grant Fox's release got caught up in a dispute with Sir Heneage Finch, the Lord Keeper, a situation that clearly left Fox mystified: if the king wanted him released, he wondered, how was it that he still languished in jail?[60]

While Fox was confined, Friends tried several strategies to effect his release. A royal pardon would have granted Fox his freedom immediately, but would also have required him to admit guilt, which Fox refused to do. "If thou canst affect my release without the title of a pardon." Fox wrote to Penn in October 1674, "though mayest." Penn thought it best not to tell the king that Fox had refused a pardon. Craig Horle points out that "Fox's principled refusal to accept a pardon . . . had placed Friends in the untenable position of turning down offers from the crown predicated either on sureties [funds posted to secure good behavior] or on willingness to be pardoned."[61]

Another strategy—which eventually did prove successful—was to find errors in the indictment and to use those to secure a dismissal of the charges. In these efforts, Penn consulted with Rudyard and other Friends well versed in the law, searching for legal grounds for Fox's release. Ultimately, Fox's supporters secured a writ of habeas corpus granting him an audience before the King's Bench in London. But the process continued to drag on. In January 1675, Fox offered a sample text spelling out "what I can say instead of the oath." He was ultimately released in February 1675 as the King's Bench in London identified numerous errors with the indictment. In mid-March Penn wrote to Margaret that her husband was finally free, and in London.[62]

Fox's extended imprisonment proved to be a galvanizing event in the development of the Quaker movement. The efforts of so many Friends to secure his release produced, at times, a disorganized series of poorly coordinated efforts that, while ultimately successful, "indicated the necessity for a centralized and coordinated approach to prosecutions." Not coincidentally, it was during the year after Fox's release that the Meeting for Sufferings was finally placed on a firm footing with the clear support of the London Yearly Meeting.[63]

* * *

While Fox was in prison, he had assigned a number of important tasks to Penn. At Fox's request, Penn appealed to Lord Baltimore on behalf of Friends in Maryland, who had sought the proprietor's approval to affirm rather than swear oaths. He spoke with Whitehead about Fox's desire for the printing of a Book of Sufferings. (This latter task turned out to be a daunting one and, despite the formation of the Meeting for Sufferings in 1675, did not reach fruition until the eighteenth century). Penn also kept Fox informed about the public dispute with the Baptists—"We think to challenge out the Baptists that have cleared Thomas Hicks," he wrote in September 1674—and attempted to bring about a reconciliation with those Friends sympathetic to Wilkinson and Story.[64]

But not all of Penn's work as a leading Quaker occurred on such a national scale. The heart of Quaker life, of course, lay in the local Meeting, where worship and business took place and support for Friends in need was organized. He was an active member of the Upper Buckinghamshire Meeting between 1672 and 1676, when he and Gulielma moved from Rickmansworth to Walthamstow in Sussex. Penn and fellow Quaker Nicholas Noy were sent to meet with Friends from nearby Amersham and encourage them to keep up their Meeting, which was showing signs of faltering. He was one of eighteen Quakers who wrote to the London Men's Meeting granting their approbation of the proposed marriage of his agent Philip Ford to Bridget Goshell in September 1672. (Had he known of

his future entanglements with Bridget, might he have given a different report?)
In June 1673 he was again part of a small group of Friends directed to visit two
first cousins who "continue and cherish an unlawful affection to each other."
Later that summer, Penn was listed as contributing £5 to help John Gigger (or
Giggour), a Friend who had signed the Penns' marriage certificate and whose
son was Gulielma's servant, pay off some of his debts.[65]

* * *

It seems, at times, that during the mid-1670s William Penn was simply everywhere: key member of the Morning Meeting and the Meeting for Sufferings;
petitioner to Parliament, the king, and local magistrates; traveling preacher in
Europe and around England; public debater and spokesman for the Society of
Friends against such adversaries as Baxter, Faldo, and Hicks; author of dozens
of controversial tracts; and defender of George Fox from the likes of Story,
Wilkinson, Mucklow, and the Pennymans. He was by no means above using his
connections at court, writing directly to the king in 1674 alleging a wide variety
of official misconduct (e.g., the use of perjured informers, the imposition of fines
without warrants, and the collection of two or three times the amount of fines
allowed) and naming specific individuals who had been reduced to beggary as
a result.[66]

The overlapping and simultaneous nature of many of these different aspects
of Penn's activism complicates any attempt to provide a clean narrative of Penn's
life during the 1670s. For example, during January 1675, Penn was involved in
the ongoing efforts to secure Fox's freedom, continued to parry attacks from
John Faldo, and—in an undertaking that would launch him on his career as an
American colonizer—was brought into a dispute between Friends John Fenwick
and Edward Byllinge over their joint interest in the proprietorship of New Jersey.
Thus did William Penn become, in the words of his editors, "a colonizer quite
by accident" more than a decade before receiving his charter for Pennsylvania.
Though he would not travel to America until 1682, from this point onward
Penn's political vision was not confined strictly to England or Europe, but looked
westward across the Atlantic.[67]

6

American Affairs and Popish Plots

If William Penn emerged as a bold new voice in the world of English Quakerism during the first half of the 1670s, the second half of that decade saw him solidify that status and play an increasingly important role in the Society of Friends' multifaceted and transatlantic operations. He stepped into the role of mediator in several divisive conflicts, and once more journeyed to spread the word outside England, traveling with leading Friends to Holland and Germany. He relocated from Rickmansworth, Hertfordshire, to a much larger manor house in Warminghurst, West Sussex. His family was growing, with two surviving children, a son and a daughter, by the end of the decade. But events would conspire to push him even further afield. England would soon find itself in the throes of a social, political, and constitutional crisis, and as a result Penn would begin to plan a way out of the seemingly intractable conflicts that had thus far doomed his attempts to secure toleration for Dissenters: an American province with liberty of conscience at its core.

* * *

Although William Penn is most commonly associated with the colony that bears his (or his father's) name, Pennsylvania was not his first foray into American affairs. In early 1675, he was asked to mediate an intra-Quaker dispute between John Fenwick and Edward Byllinge, which involved a share of the proprietorship of New Jersey. That experience added a new and unexpected dimension to his political activism: despite Penn's claims, twenty years after the fact, of "an opening of joy" toward America during his time at Oxford, the editors of his *Papers* note that "there is no evidence that he had any interest in America before he was suddenly drawn into the settling of a dispute between two Quakers over land in West New Jersey."[1]

New Jersey historian Maxine Lurie has called that state "the most complex and diverse of [the Middle Colonies]," and its background is convoluted and arcane even by the convoluted and arcane standards of seventeenth-century imperial politics. As we have seen, tension between the English and the Dutch had broken out into armed conflict on several occasions, conflicts in which James, the Duke of York, along with individuals familiar to our story like Sir William Penn and Samuel Pepys, had played key roles. In August and September 1664, while Penn was on his way back to London from his European tour, an English naval expedition had blockaded the colony of New Amsterdam and secured a quick and bloodless surrender from its Dutch governor, Peter Stuyvesant. This conquest helped launch the Second Anglo-Dutch War in which Sir William Penn would see action alongside the Duke of York, further cementing the connection between the Stuarts and the Penn family.[2]

After the English conquest of New Netherland, Charles granted the lands to his brother: hence, New York. Shortly thereafter, James bestowed roughly five million acres of the territory (approximately 7,500 square miles) on two of his associates, Sir John Berkeley and Sir George Carteret. The following spring saw the adoption of the Duke's Laws, an extensive legal code that, among other things, granted towns limited self-government and ensured broad toleration for Protestants within their borders. (James had not yet, at this point, publicly confessed his Catholicism.)

Longstanding supporters of the Stuarts during and after the Civil Wars, Carteret and Berkeley received from James a territory already inhabited by Dutch, Finns, Swedes, and even some transplanted Puritans from New England. It had a temperate climate good for agriculture, and abundant supplies of fish and game. In February 1665, Berkeley and Carteret issued the "Concession and Agreement of . . . New Jersey," which promised that "no person . . . shall be any ways molested, punished, disquieted or called in question for any difference in opinion or practice in matter of religious concernments," and guaranteed all residents the right to "freely and fully . . . enjoy . . . their judgments and consciences in matters of religion." (It also contained incentives for settlers to bring slaves with them when they settled in New Jersey. This simultaneous protection of religious liberty and slavery—guaranteeing one species of liberty while at the same time rewarding the deprivation of another—illustrates with stark clarity the enduring paradoxes of American colonization and American history more generally.) The early settlement of New Jersey was further facilitated by the appointment of a governor: Philip Carteret, Sir George's cousin. Towns like Elizabethtown (now Elizabeth), Woodbridge, Piscataway, Navesink (now Monmouth), and Newark sprang up during the mid-1660s. None of this happened smoothly or without conflict: political turmoil over taxes and quitrents—a form of payment for land use derived from earlier feudal arrangements—and a brief Dutch reconquest of the territory between July 1673 and November 1674 further complicated New Jersey's prospects.[3]

Most relevant to William Penn, however, was Berkeley's March 1674 sale of his portion of the New Jersey proprietorship to two Quakers, Edward Byllinge and John Fenwick. Byllinge, a London brewer who had been convinced in 1657 by the preaching of George Fox himself, was deeply in debt, and the purchase was actually made by Fenwick, another longstanding Friend who had served in Cromwell's army. The ensuing quarrel provided Penn's introduction to American colonization.

Byllinge had a checkered financial past, having been accused of embezzling funds from the Society of Friends several years previously, and was nearly bankrupt. Facing numerous creditors, he was no doubt thrilled by the prospect of selling land in America to restore his financial health. Then again, these were complicated relationships: Fenwick actually put up the money used to purchase Berkeley's New Jersey interest. The two men soon quarreled, and at this point— with Quaker leaders fearing that the intra-Society feud would go public, and that Fenwick might (as he was threatening) pursue relief from the court of chancery, thus airing Quaker dirty laundry for the outside world to see—the need for a mediator from within the Society became readily apparent. Given William Penn's background, education, social standing, and bona fides as a prominent representative of Quakerism across England, he must have seemed an obvious choice.

Fenwick refused to accept Penn's original proposal for settling the dispute, making Penn just one of many individuals who would fail to meet Fenwick's approval. Further complicating matters was the fact that Fenwick kept the deeds to the New Jersey territories in his own possession, and insisted on receiving sole ownership of a portion of New Jersey in any settlement. Penn wrote to Fenwick in January 1675 that the strife between him and Byllinge "fills the hearts of Friends with grief" and in the hope of arriving at some settlement acceptable to both sides, "as oppressed as I am with business," offered to revisit his original proposal to "prevent the mischief that would certainly follow divulging it in Westminster Hall." Penn pleaded with Fenwick to accept the proposed settlement, defending both his proposals and his character. "I am an impartial man," he insisted.[4]

As time went on, Penn's frustration with Fenwick would grow. "I am sorry, that a toy, a trifle, should thus rob men of time, quiet, and a more profitable employ," he wrote a month later. "I entreat thee . . . thy days spend on, and make the best of what thou hast, thy great grandchildren may be in the other world before what land thou hast allotted will be employed." He did, however, adjust his proposed settlement in Fenwick's favor. The February 1675 settlement to which both parties eventually agreed offered Fenwick more generous terms, which Byllinge grudgingly accepted: Fenwick received one-tenth of the New Jersey territory and a partial repayment of his money. The other 90 percent of the land was put into a trust, and the trustees (Penn, along with fellow Quakers Gavin Lawrie, a London merchant, and Nicholas Lucas, a Hertford malt dealer) were empowered to sell land in order to pay off Byllinge's debts.[5]

The rest of 1675 was spent working out the concrete details of dividing Byllinge's and Fenwick's shares of New Jersey, a complex process that Fenwick, ever the troublemaker, almost immediately undermined. Intent on making his mark on the colonial settlement of North America—in the words of one historian, "consumed by a single purpose, to found a colony of his own"—Fenwick recruited a shipload of settlers to the colony during the summer and sailed for America. Fenwick's company arrived in November 1675 and founded Salem, the first English settlement on the Delaware River's eastern shore. It was to be a tumultuous time for Fenwick, who clashed with almost everyone he met: the New Jersey trustees, who disapproved of his hasty exit from England; the commissioners they deputized to work on their behalf in America; his own settlers; and, most fatally—in just the opening salvo of what would become a long-running campaign by New York officials to discredit, weaken, and undermine New Jersey—New York governor Edmund Andros, who claimed the right to govern the New Jersey territory and who would throw Fenwick in jail twice over the ensuing years. (Andros had a contentious and combative streak of his own, eventually finding himself imprisoned by Boston resisters in the wake of the 1688 Revolution.[6]) As Andros repeatedly pointed out, Fenwick had neglected to survey land for his settlers, and he possessed no legal right to govern the territory.

To summarize a complicated set of legal doctrines: although James had transferred the right to the territory ("the soil"), the king retained the right to govern ("the government") until he specifically granted that authority to a designated individual. This same distinction would later bedevil Penn's efforts to gain full authority over the "Lower Counties" during the next decade. Back in England, the trustees continued their efforts to have the duke confirm their rights to govern the territory, but it was a laborious and complicated process, made more so by rising controversies over James's place in the line of succession to the throne, which would culminate in the Exclusion Crisis of 1679–1681.[7]

By the middle of 1676 the New Jersey triumvirate of Penn, Lawrie, and Lucas, along with their former partner Byllinge, had negotiated the formal division of New Jersey into two provinces, with Carteret retaining control over East Jersey and the four Friends receiving West Jersey. As with most early modern boundaries, the line was almost immediately disputed. All colonial settlements in America faced precarious border questions, of course, with inaccurate maps and a legacy of conquests and "purchases" of land from natives producing conflicting and overlapping claims.[8] But even against such a backdrop, New Jersey was particularly unsettled, with English surveys and titles overlain on preexisting Dutch ones, the governor of New York claiming jurisdiction over much of the territory, and the division between East and West Jersey adding yet another layer of complexity.

The separation of the two provinces did, however, allow the West Jersey colonizing project to get under way. In the summer of 1676, Penn and about 150 others signed the West Jersey Concessions, which in forty-four chapters laid out a structure of government and the fundamental laws of the colony. Though he was not the sole author, Penn certainly played an important part of the process: he appears as a signatory to the Concessions, along with 30 others who signed in London, to which were added an additional 120 who signed the following spring in America.[9]

Among the important features of the Concessions was the fundamental principle that legitimate government was based in the consent of the people and embodied in representative institutions. The trustees wrote to their commissioners that "they may not be brought into bondage but by their own consent . . . we put power in the people . . . to meet, and choose one honest man for each propriety . . . all these men to meet as an assembly there, to make and repeal laws." Trial by jury was also included as a fundamental right, ratifying a commitment that Penn had held at least since his 1670 trial with Mead. The Concessions provided the inhabitants with the right of access to their legislature, granting that "it shall be lawful for any person or persons during the session of [the General Assembly] to address, remonstrate, or declare any suffering, danger, or grievance" to the Assembly. And of course the provisions for liberty of conscience invoked the sort of language that Friends had been developing for years:

> That no men, nor number of men upon earth, hath power or authority to rule over men's consciences in religious matters; therefore . . . no person or persons . . . shall be any ways, upon any pretence whatsoever, called in question, or in the least punished or hurt, either in person, estate or privilege, for the sake of his opinion, judgment, faith or worship towards God, in matters of religion.

There were other Quaker influences in the document as well, such as the power of forgiveness in court proceedings. Plaintiffs, the Concessions stated, "have full power to forgive and remit the person or persons offending against him or herself . . . and pardon and remit the sentence, fine, and punishment of the person or persons offending."[10]

Despite the fact that it was never fully enacted, the West Jersey Concessions was a remarkable document, and it has been described by one historian of New Jersey as "one of the most innovative political documents of the seventeenth century" and, even more ambitiously, "easily the most radical document about politics accepted by any American colony before the Revolution." A number of its elements would appear again in Pennsylvania's founding documents, and would remain as core features of the US Constitution and Bill of Rights.[11]

The Concessions were followed in relatively short order by several important decisions. In August 1676, not long after Fenwick had sailed for America with his band of settlers, the trustees appointed three commissioners: James Wasse, a London doctor who had purchased 5,000 acres from Fenwick a year earlier; Richard Hartshorn, who had hosted George Fox at his New Jersey home in 1672; and Richard Guy, a cheesemonger who purchased 10,000 acres from Fenwick and was part of the company who had sailed with him. The trustees directed the commissioners to begin the process of laying out towns. One of their first concerns was Fenwick, who, to the consternation of both New York's governor and the New Jersey trustees, continued to act as if he were sole proprietor in New Jersey. Penn and his colleagues instructed their commissioners to meet with Fenwick's company and to work with them if possible. If Fenwick refused to cooperate, however, the commissioners were to "let the country know . . . that [Fenwick] hath no power over the persons or estates of any man or women more than any other person." That same month, Penn and his partners wrote separately to Hartshorne, giving news of the province's division— "ours is called New West-Jersey"—and describing the various elements of the Concessions as "being such as Friends here and there (we question not) will approve of." The trustees directed Hartshorne to purchase land from the natives and to begin laying out a town on the other side of the Delaware River from New Castle in modern-day Delaware, originally settled by the Dutch but now in English hands, "it being in the minds of many Friends to prepare for their going" the following spring. The town eventually founded, roughly fifty miles north of New Castle, would become Burlington, New Jersey.[12]

New Jersey, and particularly West Jersey, was widely seen as a Quaker colony from the start, especially since Penn and associates pointed out that they did "in real tenderness and regard as friends, and especially to the poor and necessitous, make friends the first offer." They also promoted their undertaking publicly in a September 1676 letter to those proposing to settle in West Jersey. For a group that had made reflection on suffering part of its collective identity, as Friends had, promoting this American opportunity had to be done carefully, so as not to encourage believers to view emigration as an easy way to evade persecution. The trustees sought to discourage anyone who might have viewed emigration to New Jersey as a means of avoiding persecution, "lest any of them . . . should go out of a curious and unsettled mind, and others to shun the testimony of the blessed cross of Jesus."[13]

Penn's role in New Jersey was significant, but limited. He was one proprietor and trustee among several, and none of the New Jersey–related correspondence during these years was sent over his name alone. That said, West Jersey was heavily influenced by several fundamental political concepts that had long been key to Penn's thinking and that formed part of the milieu in which he operated during the 1670s. The substantive commitments at the heart of the New Jersey experiment—juries, consent, representative institutions, liberty of conscience—reflect what Jane Calvert has called "Quaker constitutionalism," which grew out of Friends' experience in England and first took root in America in colonial New Jersey.[14]

Over the next few years, nearly eight hundred settlers made their way to West Jersey. Settlers sent back glowing reports, praising its "wholesome air, and general and great increase of all things planted" and pronouncing the "rye and peas, much better than any [ever seen] in England or Ireland." The colony largely drops out of Penn's correspondence, however, after the introductory letters to the commissioners and prospective settlers. Political tension continued to bedevil the settlement, and as late as June 1678 West Jersey Quaker George Hutchinson was writing anxiously to Penn, pointing out that contentious disputes over governmental jurisdiction with the governor of New York continued to cast a shadow over the colony. But although he would maintain an interest in New Jersey's prosperity—later authoring *The case of New Jersey stated*, which appealed to the Duke of York to release New Jersey from the requirement to pay customs duties to New York on goods imported by settlers—by 1678 William Penn had his hands full in England, and was being pulled back into religious and political controversy.[15]

* * *

While Fenwick, Byllinge, and his fellow trustees were getting the settlement in New Jersey under way, William Penn remained busy with his work for the Society of Friends. Chief among these tasks was his role as Fox's close ally, a role that he embraced in his continuing efforts to reconcile the sides in the Wilkinson–Story schism. The separating Friends boycotted a fall 1675 arbitration meeting, and in their absence, not surprisingly, the judges ruled against the separatists. Penn wrote to Fox that "much blame is laid upon the procedure . . . and many untoward objections are stated against the inequitableness and haste of the judgment." Despite Penn's entreaties, Fox did not attend a second meeting about the matter, a four-day gathering in April 1676 at Draw-well, Yorkshire. There, Wilkinson and Story signed an obliquely phrased statement that expressed their deep regret for their role in the divisions, and it appeared that Quaker harmony and consensus had been restored.[16]

But even after the two principals had expressed their regret, divisions continued. Alexander Parker and George Whitehead wrote up a report of the proceedings, stating that Wilkinson and Story had repented of their schismatic behavior, a characterization that their supporters took as uncharitable blame-casting. And so the animosity continued. In May, thirty leading Friends condemned the schism and urged Wilkinson and Story to publicly disavow it once again. By summer, all semblance of a reunification had vanished, and mistrust between the two sides was stronger than ever. In September 1676, while Fox remained at Swarthmoor, Penn wrote a blistering letter to Buckinghamshire Quaker John Raunce and his son-in-law Charles Harris, two prominent Buckinghamshire Friends. "The Lord stop you by his power," he wrote, describing the separatists as "loose and libertine spirits . . . [afflicted with] poisonous and infectious jealousies" who attempted to "tread down our hedge, under the specious pretense of being left to the light within." Insisting that "blood will lie at your door in the day of account . . . if ye persist," he signed his letter, "Your mourning Friend."[17]

Dealing with the ongoing fallout from the schism took up a great deal of Penn's time and energy. But he had other tasks as well, including his work with the Meeting for Sufferings and the Morning Meeting. The Meeting for Sufferings continued to appeal to Friends to keep accurate accounts "of those that first brought the message of glad tidings among them" and the persecutions they suffered. The Meeting suggested appealing to moderate men of influence to discourage local magistrates from persecuting Friends. Penn was responsible for the publication of two editions of *The continued cry of the oppressed*, the first in 1675 and the second a year later, which presented long and detailed lists of the persecutions to which Friends were being subjected.[18]

Working with Friends in London, or dealing with the Wilkinson–Story separatists in the north, provided Penn with a national perspective on the challenges Friends faced. But there was also a great deal of important work to be done, day in and day out, in coordinating the activities of his local Meeting, especially helping Friends who had suffered misfortune of one kind or another, from the serious (imprisonment, the death of a spouse) to the mundane (a broken leg).[19]

* * *

While his public profile was growing, Penn's personal life was also being transformed. Late in 1676, he and Gulielma and their young son Springett, the first of their children to survive infancy, moved to Warminghurst, West Sussex. Their new home was a "larger and far costlier establishment," and included a manor house complete with gardens and servants. Not surprisingly, it placed additional strain on the household's finances. Once again, in a repeat of the earlier pattern, the couple sold several parcels of (Gulielma's) land, and William took on several additional loans to finance the move. Such decisions provided cash in hand and allowed the Penns to live the sort of life to which they were both accustomed, but also meant that those lands no longer yielded rental income—and this at a time when the rents received from William's Irish tenants were consistently falling below his expectations. Warminghurst was also considerably farther from London than Rickmansworth had been, and thus made for costlier travel to and from the capital.[20]

During these years the Penns' friendship with the Foxes, George and Margaret, grew increasingly close. Gulielma and William had seen George Fox off at Land's End when he departed for America in 1671, and welcomed him home upon his return in 1673. The bond between the two couples was further forged by Penn's work on Fox's behalf during his 1674 imprisonment and his tireless efforts against the Wilkinson–Story separatists. The relationship was not without complications: Gulielma's family had close friends among Wilkinson and Story's chief sympathizers, and William endured a great deal of criticism for his single-minded defense of Fox. But the relationship would remain strong for the remainder of their lives. Years later, one of the last letters Penn wrote before sailing to Pennsylvania in 1682 would go to Margaret, as would one of the first he wrote when he returned two years later. He was tasked, as well, to write to Margaret with news of her husband's death in January 1691. And Penn was one of the Friends designated to write a Preface to Fox's *Journal* when it was published in 1694, although opposition from Mead, with whom Penn had fallen out in the intervening years, complicated that task.[21]

Margaret and Gulielma also shared a close and affectionate relationship. Margaret's letter of October 1677 showed the friendship that had grown up between her and Gulielma; "thy dear wife," Margaret called her, "whom I honor in the Lord for her faithfulness, and constancy, and innocency." Both George and Margaret kept in close contact with Gulielma while her husband was in America; Margaret sent gifts from Swarthmoor, and corresponded with Gulielma about domestic matters. Bonnelyn Young Kunze, Margaret's biographer, explains that to the Penns, Margaret "was a mother superior of Quakerism and an intimate adopted mother who showed them special affection and understanding."[22]

* * *

Penn had not been outside England since his travels to Holland and Germany in 1671. In September 1676, however, as he was dealing with the fallout of the Wilkinson–Story schism and working on the settlement of New Jersey, he received a letter from Robert Barclay, then in Edinburgh. Penn and Barclay, whose 1676 Latin *Theologiae vere Christianae apologia*, translated into English as *An apology for the true Christian divinity*, two years later, has been called "the first systematic defense of the Quaker faith and a work that did much to make Quakerism respectable in scholarly and intellectual circles," had met in the early 1670s. The two Friends shared a great deal in common—educated sons of military men, convinced of the truth of Quakerism about a year apart—and would develop a close personal and working relationship spanning both Quaker concerns and colonial interests over the coming years.[23]

Barclay expressed his desire that Penn "could make a step for Holland to put a stop to any unhappy differences [which] may be stirring among them which hinders the general progress of truth." Although Penn would not make the trip until the following summer—Barclay himself was arrested at Aberdeen that November, and held in prison until the spring—a return to Europe to tend to Friends' business in those territories was on Penn's agenda. Preparations began in earnest after the 1677 Yearly Meeting resolved to send leading Friends to Holland and Germany, and after Penn, Fox, and John Burnyeat had huddled together at Warminghurst, completing the text of *A New England firebrand quenched*, their reply to Roger Williams's anti-Quaker polemic *George Fox digged out of his burrows*.[24]

And so on July 22, 1677, William Penn left a pregnant Gulielma and their young son Springett at Warminghurst, and journeyed to London. The next day he visited his mother, then living at Walthamstow in Essex. Now part of Greater London, Walthamstow was about a half-dozen miles north of the Tower Hill home where the Penns had lived when William was a young boy. As he prepared to sail for Holland, Penn joined a number of important Quakers, including Fox; Isabel Yeamans, Margaret Fox's daughter; George Keith and his wife Elizabeth; Barclay; and Colchester merchants John Furly (Benjamin's brother) and William Talecote. After a Meeting at Harwich "where the Lord gave us a blessed earnest of his love and presence," the company boarded a ship to Brill, the seaport about fifteen miles west of Rotterdam. To Penn's surprise, the ship's master had served under his father, and thus gave the Friends access to the best accommodations on board. By midday on July 28, the company had arrived in Rotterdam. Over the next few days they held Meetings ("a great company of people," Penn recorded, "some of them being of the considerable note of that city") and visited Friends individually. By August 1 Penn, along with Fox, John Furly, Talecote, and Yeamans, had set out for Amsterdam, where a General Meeting of Dutch Friends was held at the home of Gertrude Diriks, a prominent Friend whose home served as the main Amsterdam Meetinghouse. Fox preached, and "all things ended, with great concord and comfort."[25]

This Dutch Meeting adopted a number of the elements of "Gospel Order" that Fox had been formalizing in England: the institution of Men's, Women's, Quarterly, and Yearly Meetings, as well as rules about procedures for the admonishment of Friends and the adjudication of disputes, with the strong exhortation to "let [controversies] not be told out of your meeting; because such speeches tend to the defaming of such persons and meetings, and to the hurt of the common unity." Another Meeting the following day adopted additional guidelines regarding marriage procedures. As had English Friends before them, Dutch Friends reiterated that marriage was the work of God and ought not to be performed by priests or clergy: "For we marry none; tis the Lord's work, and we are but witnesses." Also like English Friends, however, allowances were made for Friends to notify magistrates of their marriages if they were so inclined. And in a Dutch analogue to the London Friends' Morning Meeting, they agreed that some members of the Meeting should take up the task of supervising publications "to the end, no book may be published, but in the unity." These Meetings represented a significant step in the organization of Dutch Friends along the lines of the English, and as in England, they would no small amount of division and contention.[26]

Also while in Amsterdam, in response to a request from suffering Friends in the Polish city of Danzig, Penn wrote to the King of Poland. His letter asserted Friends' essential peacefulness and stressed their endorsement of basic Christian principles. Despite the fact that "we cannot join in the common and public worship of these parts," yet Friends "with a meek and quiet spirit . . . come together after the manner of the ancient Christians . . . and with godly fear, and a retired mind . . . wait upon God." He also briefly presented the scriptural, epistemological, and prudential arguments in favor of toleration, and invoked the tolerationist example of King Stephen of Poland, the sixteenth-century ruler whom Penn had also cited as an exemplar in *The great case.*[27]

By August 9 Penn, Keith, Benjamin Furly, and Barclay had separated from Fox and traveled two hundred miles east to Herford, to the court of Princess Elizabeth of the Palatine. The princess was a deeply pious and learned Protestant who famously corresponded with Descartes and had rejected a marriage proposal from the king of Poland due to his Roman Catholicism. Penn would later memorialize Elizabeth in the 1682 edition of *No cross, no crown*:

> Her meekness and humility appeared to me extraordinary; she
> never considered the quality, but the merit of the people she
> entertained . . . though she kept no sumptuous table in her own court,
> she spread the tables of the poor in their solitary cells; breaking bread to
> virtuous pilgrims, according to their want, and her ability. Abstemious
> in herself, and in apparel void of all vain ornaments.

The company was eager to meet the princess and her companion, Anna Maria, Countess van Hoorn, who served as Canoness of the Abbey and who had translated Isaac Penington's works into Dutch. Although Penn had harbored suspicions about the Labadite community in Herford—recall that his 1671 visit to the group had not gone especially well—he praised the princess for her willingness "to favor . . . those who separate themselves from the world for the sake of righteousness." The Quakers stayed at Herford three days and engaged in deep and heartfelt spiritual conversations, holding many Meetings, including one with the servants of the household during which "the same blessed power, that had appeared to visit them of high, appeared to visit them of low degree also." The princess and countess prevailed upon Penn to provide the group with "an account . . . of my first convincement, and of those tribulations and consolations." He held forth for several hours, and reported that "they heard me with an earnest and tender attention."[28]

Setting back out from the princess's estate on August 13, the company traveled south to Paderborn. A fairly regular pattern repeated itself at many of the towns they visited. As they neared a town, they would inquire as to "who was worthy in the city" (i.e., who were the religious seekers who might be receptive to Friends' message). In other words, they sought out like-minded believers who emphasized the Spirit's movings within the believer and not external rituals or set liturgies. They would then seek a meeting or lodging, or both, with those believers. Upon their departure from town, the company always left behind some books of Quaker doctrine. Despite considering Paderborn "a dark popish town," the Quakers found lodgings with an "ancient, grave, and serious" woman as well as a Lutheran with whom Penn conversed over supper. Braving torrential rains, the group made its way southeast to Kassel and by August 20 had arrived at Frankfurt, where they held productive discussions with Lutherans and Calvinists. By the time they reached Mannheim on August 25, they had traveled more than 250 miles from Amsterdam in just over two weeks.[29]

The Friends arrived in Mannheim with hopes of speaking to the Elector of Palatine Karl Ludwig, Princess Elizabeth's brother. Unfortunately he was away in Heidelberg. In lieu of a personal audience, Penn wrote an effusive letter to the prince, praising him for his indulgence toward "all people professing religion, dissenting from the national communion" and calling such toleration "a most natural, Christian, and prudent thing." Perhaps the most intriguing part of Penn's letter to Karl Ludwig, however, in light of the future trajectory of Penn's career, was his asking "what encouragement a colony of industrious families might hope to receive from thee, in case they should transplant themselves into this country?" and his particular praise of Karl Ludwig's rule as "very excellent respecting taxes, arms, oaths, etc." The West Jersey undertaking was well under way, but Penn was clearly continuing to think about issues of emigration and re-settlement in a variety of settings.[30]

Returning to Frankfurt via the Rhine, to Mainz, by the end of August the company had reached Cologne, which Penn described as "a great popish city." By early September they had arrived in Duysberg, where they (unsuccessfully) attempted to make contact with Countess Charlotte von Dhaun-Falkenstein, whose intense piety had inspired her father, Count Wilhelm of Dhaun-Falkenstein, to hold "a strict hand" over her. A chance meeting with the count himself, who was embarking on a walk just as the Quakers were passing by, did not go well. Upon querying the Friends about their business in his country, and noting that they did not remove their hats in his presence, "the Graf called us Quakers, saying unto us, we have no need of Quakers here; get you out of my dominions; you shall not go to my town," after which "he commanded some of his soldiers to see us out of his territory." Reaching Duysberg that night, they found the city gates already shut, and "laid us down together in a field, receiving both natural and spiritual refreshment."[31]

The next day, Penn wrote to the countess. He of course knew something about parental opposition to their children's religious impulses, and reached out to her as a kindred spirit, "because of that suffering and tribulation thou has begun to endure for the sake of thy zeal towards God, myself having from my childhood been both a seeker after the Lord, and a great sufferer for that cause from parents, relations, companions, and the magistrates of this world." He recounted his own youthful striving after holiness and his convincement, and urged her to remain faithful to the light in her own conscience; concluding by reporting that "my parents, that once disowned me for this blessed testimony's sake . . . have come to love me above all." To the countess's father, on the other hand, Penn composed a much different letter, denouncing him for his uncharitable and persecuting behavior. "And as for thy saying, We want no Quakers here, I say . . . you do. For a true Quaker is one, that trembleth at the word of the Lord: that worketh out his salvation with fear and trembling. . . . And oh! That thou wert such a Quaker!"[32]

Having been warned in a return letter from the countess to avoid further contact with her father, who was known to set dogs or soldiers on trespassers, the Friends moved on—via Wesel, Rees, Emmerick, Cleves, Utrecht, and Rotterdam—returning to Amsterdam on September 7, about a month after they had left. Two days later, at Haarlingen, Penn reunited with the others. Fox returned to Amsterdam while Penn continued on toward Wiewort to visit the Labadists and Anna Maria van Schurmann, who had taken over leadership of the community after its leader's death. There he also met the Sommelsdyke sisters, daughters of a Dutch nobleman, who had followed Labadie and who were sympathetic to the Quaker message. Penn's description of the Labadists was far more charitable on this visit than it had been in the past: he referred to them as "a serious, plain people . . . coming nearer to Friends as to silence in meetings, women speaking, preaching by the spirit, plainness of garb, and furniture in their houses, than . . . any other people I know." Each offered a brief testimony of his or her conversion, and Penn offered one of the most elaborate descriptions of his childhood that he ever committed to writing, from the time that "the Lord first appeared unto me, which was about the 12th year of my age," through his unhappy years at Oxford, the expulsion from his father's house, and "the deep sense [the Lord] gave me of the vanity of this world [and] of the irreligiousness of the religions in it." Just as Penn was despairing of ever finding true religion, he told his listeners, "the Lord visited me with a . . . testimony of his eternal world through one of those the world called a Quaker," and despite opposition, "the Lord had preserved me to this day, and had given me . . . the assurance of life everlasting."[33]

By mid-September Penn was again on a ship, crossing from Delfzijl to Embden. Embden was, Penn recorded, a city "where Friends have been so bitterly and barbarously used . . . they having been banished some 30 and some 40 times, and above" and to whose Senate Penn had written several years previously, in December 1674, condemning persecution. While there, Penn met with the president of the council. Although he was "reported to have been the author of this cruelty to our Friends," Penn found that "he comported himself with more kindness, than we expected at his hand."[34]

After a brief stop in Bremen, they returned once again to Herford, and Princess Elizabeth, on September 21. It was a joyous reunion, and the travelers brought the princess and countess up to date on all that had transpired since their last meeting. Over the next few days, they shared meals, held Meetings, informed their hosts about the conditions faced by Friends in England, and even held a cordial debate with the Graf of Donau over Friends' refusal of hat-honor. Penn wrote that "the truth had passage, and the hungry were satisfied and the simple hearted deeply affected." His conversation with the Graf enabled Penn to provide a testimony "of my retreat from the world, and the inducements I had thereto." By September 25 they had bid the princess farewell, and were heading back through Lipstadt, Hamm, and finally to Wesel.[35]

It was an arduous journey. "We rid 3 nights and days without lying down on a bed, or sleeping, otherways than in the wagon, which was only covered with an old ragged sheet." The princess and her family weighed heavily on Penn, and he unburdened himself in a long letter to Elizabeth when he arrived in Wesel, expressing his concern with the spiritual consequences of her dual role as civil and ecclesiastical leader, which required her to appoint ministers of the gospel. "My soul is deeply affected with thy condition," he wrote, expressing his view that the position of abbess "is a complex of civil and ecclesiastical power not to be found in Scripture," but rather "the offspring of a dark apostasy." Having ministers appointed by the civil magistrate was objectionable in its own right ("what a persecution thy conscience lyeth under, since thou art forced to choose and place priests at all"), and in addition Penn noted the fact that some of those priests "thou canst not hear, or have fellowship with yet install them in their positions to preach to the people." He exhorted her to use the position of abbess "Christianly" and to appoint only "true Christian priests," thus exercising "the righteousness of true magistracy."[36]

The company finally reached Dusseldorf on October 2. There they met the famous Reformed theologian, hymnist, and teacher Joachim Neander, whom

Penn considered to have "a zeal for God." Yet Penn feared that Neander's many duties threatened to force him off the path of righteousness: he was required "to perform set duties at fixed times; pray, preach, and sing, and that in the way of the world's appointments." "His office is very Babylonish," Penn wrote, "namely, a chaplain; for tis a popish invention." "How can a minister of the gospel be at the beck of any mortal living," he wondered. "The thing in itself is utterly wrong." Moving on to Wesel again, Penn reported several glorious Meetings, including one in which those present "were extremely affected and overcome by the power of the Lord; twas like one of our [Herford] meetings. . . . Let me say this, that more kindness and openness we have scarcely found in all our travels." From Wesel they made their way back to Amsterdam, where the Friends engaged in several debates with Galenus Abrahams, leader of the Anabaptist sect known as the Collegiants, whose company were, in Penn's view, "the most virulent and obstinate opposers of truth in this land." Having made their way back to Brill via the Hague—"the lust and pride of that place!" Penn remarked—and Rotterdam, they returned to England at the end of October.[37]

It had been an exhilarating trip for Penn, and many of the people whom he met along the way would later become part of his Pennsylvania enterprise. By 1677, he had observed firsthand, or nearly firsthand, the complexities of colonization and resettlement in a number of different settings. First, of course, was Ireland, where he had spent five years during his youth and to which he had later returned to manage his father's estates. His acquaintance with Sir William Petty had also brought him into the orbit of those with more involved and intricate expertise in English colonization. He had taken part, admittedly at some distance, in the New Jersey project, lending his name and skills to a North American undertaking. And his travels through Karl Ludwig's Palatinate domains and his knowledge of the travails of the Labadists taught him that migration might take place to the east rather than west. When the time eventually came for him to take on his own settlement, then, he had been thinking about the complexities of moving goods and people for more than a decade. From the most local Meeting to working at the intersections of English and Dutch Quakerism, William Penn had clearly arrived as a leading English Quaker and, increasingly, a figure known across Europe as well.

* * *

Returning to England in late October, William Penn quickly discovered that the troubles he had left behind had not disappeared.

Immediately upon his return, Penn had written to Dutch and German Friends expressing his joy over the time they had spent together: "Nor sea nor land, nor time nor place can ever separate our joy, divide our communion, or wipe out the remembrance that I have of you." Just a few weeks later, however, he wrote in a much less charitable tone, having heard about new contention among Dutch Friends surrounding questions of marriage. The General Meeting held in Amsterdam had confirmed that, in line with English practice, Dutch Friends were to be married without clergy, and that if any desired to notify local magistrates of their marriages, such a decision was to be left to the discretion of the couple. Some Dutch Friends, including Benjamin Furly, sought to have *all* marriages reported to the authorities, as required by Dutch law. To further complicate matters, other Dutch Friends wanted a prohibition on Friends reporting *any* marriages to magistrates. "My soul has been made sad" to hear of these divisions, Penn wrote to Pieter Hendricks, a leading Dutch Quaker, and urged Friends to unity.[38]

Meanwhile, for many English Quakers, persecution remained the norm, and it also hit Penn close to home. Shortly after his return Penn found himself on the receiving end of unwelcome attention from a pair of (over) zealous Justices of the Peace in Sussex, who "endeavor to make my living there uneasy." Penn reached out to Charles Sackville, the Earl of Middlesex, who had assisted him when George Fox was imprisoned, in hopes that the earl would use his influence "to allay their heat" and scuttle their attempts to prosecute William and Gulielma as Catholics (or, more accurately, "popish recusants" [i.e., Catholics who refused to attend the Church of England]).[39]

As important as such personal outreach must have been, it was hardly the only way in which Friends made their concerns known to public officials. In January 1678 Penn and several other Quakers addressed the king and the Privy Council on the issue of Friends being prosecuted under legislation aimed at Catholics. Charles was sympathetic but directed them to seek their relief from Parliament. And so to Parliament they went, with Penn presenting a petition asking "that our word may be taken instead of an oath" and for relief from prosecution under laws against popery. In March 1678 he testified again, making a careful attempt to deflect the claim that Quakers were "a sort of concealed papists" while maintaining that Catholics too deserved the liberty to follow their consciences; as he put it, "we have good will to all men, and would have none suffer for a truly sober and conscientious dissent." Or, as Penn put it even more clearly: "I am far from thinking that papists should be whipped for their conscience, because I declaim against the injustice of whipping Quakers for papists." He proposed two toleration bills, which went nowhere, and the king dissolved Parliament in January 1679; Penn's lack of success may have pushed him to more direct involvement in political affairs, including his close work with Algernon Sidney in the parliamentary elections of 1679.[40]

But these forays into political life and his continuing contact with Dutch Friends notwithstanding, most of Penn's time following his return to England was taken up with internal Friends' business. A letter from Margaret Fox received soon after his return brought Penn news of the continuing

Wilkinson–Story schism. The language Fox used to describe the separatists sounded distinctly reminiscent of that used by early "publishers of Truth" in their combat with the established churches. The separate meetings, she wrote, "will hardly suffer any Friend to come amongst them," and one Scottish Friend was "moved to go amongst them, as to a priest in the steeplehouse." (In other words, the separatist Friends should be treated as if they were not Friends at all.) Penn exhorted Friends in Sussex and Hampshire to unity and denounced those who would foment division, and early in 1678 attempted once again to bring the Wilkinson–Story schism to an end by convening a meeting with William Rogers, who had emerged as one of the leaders of the separatists in Bristol. Rogers and Penn had known each other for years; Rogers was a prosperous Bristol merchant with whom Penn had visited before sailing for Cork in 1669.[41]

To call the February 1678 meetings with Rogers and other separatists unsuccessful would be too generous, for what the meeting established was just how far the bitterness and animosity had progressed, and how dim the prospects for unity had become. The dissenters opened their list of "dissatisfactions" with a straightforward assault on George Fox's status as leader of the Quaker movement: "We are not satisfied that George Fox hath of late been guided by the spirit of truth in all such matters relating to the truth wherein of late he hath concerned himself." Rogers criticized the Meeting structure Fox had set up over the course of the 1670s as incompatible with the Quaker exaltation of the Spirit-filled believer. "How comes it to pass," he asked, "that an outward hierarchy and order comes to be laid down as the order of the government of the church of Christ?" They again dissented from the requirement that marriages be cleared by Women's Meetings, and pointed out that Fox's own marriage had not been proposed to the Women's Meeting in Bristol. Even Story's October 1679 apology for his role in the schism, signed before the Morning Meeting in October 1679, in which he "confess[ed] that it was not well done of me . . . and I am sorry for it" did not end the conflict, particularly since his collaborator, John Wilkinson, had made no such apology.[42]

But while Penn was busy advocating for Quakers, appealing to Parliament for toleration, and attempting to heal the Society of Friends' internal divisions, something much larger was about to make its presence felt: the three-year agglomeration of rumor, innuendo, lies, half-truths, perjury, and violence known as the Popish Plot, and an associated political and constitutional uproar, the Exclusion Crisis.

* * *

Charles II had no legitimate male heir, and thus his brother James was next in the line of succession. (James, of course, was Sir William's former naval colleague, who had pledged to Penn that "whenever I had any business . . . he would order that I should have access.") James was also an open Catholic, who had resigned his position as Lord High Admiral in the Royal Navy after the passage of the 1673 Test Act. The Act, as we have seen, required public officeholders to receive the Anglican sacraments, and James chose to resign his command rather than compromise his Catholic faith. Thus when Titus Oates, a former Anglican priest recently arrived in England from France, alleged a Jesuit plot to kill the king, the charges shook the English political system. According to Oates, English Catholics with the backing of Rome had hatched the scheme at a secret meeting at London's White Horse Tavern. The king and his advisors were skeptical of Oates's reports, as they relied on suspect documents and unreliable witnesses. Oates's tale, however, fit neatly into existing prejudices about scheming Catholics and the threat they posed to the kingdom, from the Reformation to the Spanish Armada, from the Gunpowder Plot to the Fire of London. That the king surrounded himself with known or suspected Catholics only made the rumors more worrisome. Parliamentary leaders saw an opportunity to undermine Catholics and their sympathizers at the royal court, and took Oates's claims as further evidence of a Catholic threat.[43]

The rumors sparked not only a divisive social conflict but a genuine political and constitutional crisis over the succession. During the fall of 1678, parliamentary investigations heard testimony about purported Catholic subversion at the highest levels of English society and government. On November 1, the House of Commons declared that "This House is of opinion that there hath been and still is a damnable and hellish plot contrived and carried out by the popish recusants for assigning and murdering the King."[44]

Five Catholic members of the House of Lords were imprisoned in October 1678, and a second Test Act was passed at year's end, this one extending the Act's jurisdiction even to members of Parliament. Given the widespread suspicion that Quakers were closet Catholics, it is perhaps not surprising that aspersions were being cast on Penn. Derbyshire Quaker John Gratton wrote that "they say thou art turned to be a Jesuit, and doth hide thyself or art fled the country." Accusations of Jesuit sympathies were not idle banter; they potentially placed their target in considerable danger. In fact Penn's own lawyer, the Catholic Richard Langhorne, was arrested in October and would be hanged at the Tyburn gallows the following summer.[45]

Even in the midst of the confusion brought on by the plot, and the suspicion cast on Friends for their refusal to swear allegiance, Penn sought to keep up Quaker spirits. He published an open letter to Friends, which acknowledged the dark clouds over the nation but voiced hope that a faithful remnant could save England from God's wrath. "My soul," Penn wrote, has been "unusually sad for the sake of this nation," and "for some time I have had a deep sense that the overflowing scourge of God's wrath . . . [was] ready to break out upon the people." If Friends remained faithful and stood forth as a holy example to their neighbors, Penn insisted, "Then shall God lift up the light of his countenance upon us . . . and we shall be yet called, The Island Saved by the Lord." Fox wrote to Penn shortly thereafter, lamenting "all this work that is abroad among the plotters," and prayed "the Lord God Almighty preserve all Friends."[46]

Still, the nation's politics continued on a perilous path. Facing an evidently insoluble deadlock over finances and the disbanding of the army, Charles finally dissolved the Cavalier Parliament in January 1679. Preparations began for the first general election in nearly two decades. In the coming months, William Penn would enter the political realm in new and, for him, unprecedented ways.

* * *

Penn's friend Algernon Sidney had spent much of the Restoration in exile, only returning to England in 1677. Politically, Sidney was far more radical than Penn; he was a true republican, hostile to monarchy itself and not merely the policies or excesses of particular kings. He had opposed King Charles I during the Civil Wars and later served in the parliamentary army as well as in the Commonwealth. In the elections of February 1679, Sidney (unsuccessfully) stood for election to Parliament in Guildford, Surrey, roughly thirty miles southwest of London, and Penn strongly supported his candidacy. Not surprisingly, given the raucous way seventeenth-century English elections were conducted—with groups of prospective voters "made free" or granted the right to vote just weeks before the election, nonresidents often allowed to cast ballots, time and place of polling subject to change, the threat of violence and intimidation often explicit, and bribery of various sorts widespread—Penn and Sidney found fault with the procedures. Penn encouraged his friend to contest the results, offering to draw on his connections in Parliament to help the cause, "for to me it looks like an unfair election . . . to be put aside, by such base ways, is really a suffering for righteousness." But Sidney demurred.[47]

Although the authorities had sought to keep the plot allegations, which they considered pure fabrications, secret, rumors and gossip circulated widely, and during 1679 the first published accounts of the plot began to bring the details to the broader public. The resulting anti-Catholic hysteria spread rapidly. The summer of 1679, during which Penn was occupied with the campaign, turned out to be particularly gruesome. More than a dozen Catholics were executed between late June and late August, and of course the rumors only exacerbated tensions in Ireland, where the Catholic archbishops of Dublin and Armagh were imprisoned. As summer turned to fall, the pope was burned in effigy at anti-Catholic processions, including a particularly noted one that purportedly drew 200,000 spectators in London. Penn wrote to a group of Dutch Friends that "[t]he discovery of the plot and plotters goes on notwithstanding all arts to smother it. . . . The bells ring, the fires burn, and the people are extremely agitated."[48]

As it turned out, the first Exclusion Parliament—so named for Shaftesbury's introduction of a bill excluding James from the succession to the crown—lasted only a month before it too was dissolved. In the next elections, which took place during July 1679, Sidney stood for a seat from Bramber, Sussex, not far from Warminghurst. Shortly before the election, Penn heard distressing news: Sidney's estranged brother Henry was being put forward as a candidate for the same seat. Despite Penn's imploring Algernon to visit Bramber personally, he declined, and this election too went against him, with his brother eventually emerging victorious. (Then again, winning a seat might have been a hollow victory for Sidney, since the king did not summon this Parliament to meet for more than a year.)[49]

The furor over Oates's accusations and the increasing suspicion of James—who, if he was not part of the plot, nonetheless stood to benefit from its success—emboldened parliamentary leaders to attempt to remove him from the succession. Exclusion bills, championed by Shaftesbury, were introduced in each Parliament between 1679 and 1681 and dominated English politics during these years, though none became law. Much of the furor was built upon hearsay and prejudice, accusations, allegations, and rumors. Ultimately, historian Peter Hinds argues that the plot years represent "a fascinating, yet an ultimately tragic, lesson in the historical importance not of what happened, but of what people believed to have happened."[50]

Throughout all of the unrest, William Penn attempted to defend Quakers from accusations of disloyalty and to refute the implication that they held Catholic sympathies. Although he had endorsed the liberty of Catholic conscience along with Protestant Dissenters in his spring 1678 testimony before Parliament, those remarks predate the furor over the plot. Penn's rhetoric was markedly less anti-Catholic than that of most of his Whig contemporaries, but his most pressing concern was always to safeguard Quakers from the danger that came from association with Catholics. He was the primary author of an appeal to the king and Parliament, which was published in 1680 on behalf of the Society of Friends. The appeal pointed to "two acts of Parliament, directly made against us, by the name Quakers" and lamented that "many of us are now daily exposed to utter ruin in our estates, upon the prosecution of the statutes . . . made against popish recusants . . . which we really are not." Another work, written by Whitehead, specifically objected to Quakers' continuing mistreatment under the nearly decade-old Conventicle Act.[51]

* * *

Despite his lack of success in securing Sidney's election, William Penn produced a number of important pieces of political writing during 1679. Since the publication of *The great case of liberty of conscience*, he had been developing a robust theory of religious liberty. Penn located the essence of true Christianity in the protection of individual conscience from political or ecclesiastical elites. Such a view led Penn to denounce persecution against Dissenters in England as a betrayal of the very principles of the Reformation and a travesty of English justice, and to see in Anglican efforts to enforce uniformity a troubling resemblance to Catholic persecutors of old. "You are afraid of popery," he wrote, "and yet many of you practice it; For why do you fear it, but for it's compulsion and persecution? And will you compel or persecute . . . ? If you will, pray let me say, You hate the papists, but not popery." In raising the alarm against popish plotters, Penn warned English voters that the "principle which introduces implicit faith and blind obedience in religion, will also introduce implicit faith and blind obedience in government."[52]

With tales of popish plotters circulating wildly, Penn issued an *Address to Protestants upon the present conjuncture*, which referred to the "(reputed) Reformed world" and lamented the refusal to tolerate Dissenters as "our great declension from primitive Protestancy," early in 1679. At its core, Protestantism offers "a restoring to every man his just right of inquiry and choice," and thus it is far worse for Protestants to persecute than it is for Catholics to do so. "We have the better religion, but . . . we also are more condemnable." But Penn also sought, in the midst of a social and political crisis, to bring the nation to a realization of its own sinfulness and need for repentance. He denounced the sin and impiety evident in the realm's widespread "drunkenness, whoredoms and fornication; excess, in apparel, in furniture, and in living; profuse gaming . . . [and] oaths, prophaneness, and blasphemy." These practices threatened to bring God's judgment upon the land, and Penn called on the civil magistrate to exterminate them.[53]

As the above passages make abundantly clear, Penn's radical argument for liberty of conscience always sat alongside a conventional, even austere, notion of personal morality. Denunciations of sin and vice went hand in hand with calls for the toleration of conscientious dissent, and the two campaigns mutually reinforced each other. To act against immorality, he insisted, "is not troubling men for faith, nor perplexing people for tenderness of conscience." "There can be no pretense of conscience to be drunk, to whore, to be voluptuous, to game, swear, curse, blaspheme, and profane," since such behaviors "lay the ax to the root of human society, and are the common enemies of mankind."[54]

The *Address* also took on what Penn called "church evils," namely the propensity of people to persecute those with whom they disagreed on matters of faith. Drawing on the Christian distinction between things belonging to Caesar and things belonging to God, Penn described the former as "to love justice, do judgment, relieve the oppressed, right the fatherless, be a terror unto evil-doers, and a praise to them that do well." Unfortunately, Penn insisted, authorities too often targeted those who dissented in religious matters, when they should have taken action instead against "thieves, murderers, adulterers, traitors, plotters, drunkards, cheats, vagabonds, and the like mischievous and dissolute persons."[55]

That same year, Penn published *England's great interest in the choice of this new Parliament*, which has been described as the "manifesto [of] the first Sidney/Penn campaign." The pamphlet asserted the House of Commons' fundamental rights of property, legislation, and juries, and defended the right of Parliament to a share of the governance of the realm. "No law can be made or abrogated in England without you . . . not a penny legally demanded (not even to defray the charges of the government) without your own consent," he insisted, adding that "no man according to the ancient laws of this realm, can be adjudged in matter either of life, liberty, or estate, but it must be by the judgment of his peers . . . commonly called a jury." Representative institutions, be they juries or Parliament, served as potential bulwarks against would-be tyrants, and guarantors of popular rights.[56]

Of course elections to House of Commons, and a Parliament that would relieve persecution of Dissenters, formed just one aspect of Penn's vision of a good society. Penn argued that although one might hope for a religiously unified society, given the liability of humans to error, rulers would be well served to acknowledge the fact of religious diversity. In *One project for the good of England*, Penn introduced the notion of civil interest, "the foundation and end of civil government." He emphasized the civil bonds uniting English Protestants of all stripes:

> [A]ll English Protestants, whether conformists or nonconformists agree . . . that they only owe allegiance and subjection unto the civil government of England . . . and . . . they do not only consequentially disclaim the pope's supremacy . . . but therewith deny and oppose the Romish religion, as it stands degenerated from Scripture . . . which makes up a great negative union. . . . [I]t is the interest of the ruling, or church-Protestants of England, that the pope should have no claim or power in England. It is also the interest of the Dissenting Protestants, that the pope should have no claim or power here in England.

One project linked civil interest with territorial integrity and national security, and more broadly with a generic Protestantism encompassing the broadest swath of the English population. A legitimate government safeguarding civil interest poses no threat to religion properly understood, he argued. Since religion in the true sense is about loving God above all, and one's neighbor as oneself, then the claim that the pope possesses political authority over English Catholics represents a potent political threat to the liberties of the entire English nation.

(Whether English Catholics themselves believed this, by this point in the history of Catholicism, is not entirely clear, and perhaps rather doubtful.) Even though real theological differences divided English Protestants, Penn argued, these differences should not blind them to their shared interest in the preservation of English liberties and the defense of Protestantism at home and abroad.[57] Penn would go on to emphasize this vision of common civil interest throughout his career. An excessive focus on the things that divided the nation along religious lines played directly into the hands of those who sought to undermine the common good (Catholics, perhaps, but also the French and Spanish).[57]

Of course, politically speaking, Penn's view of civil interest was hardly an easy sell. It had to contend with forces of orthodoxy and absolutism in both church and state, especially in the midst of fears of popish plotting. His *One project* brought forth *A seasonable corrective to the one project*, which attacked Dissenters as prone to "a phantasie to new opinions" and objected to his attempt to remove religious concerns from the purview of civil government: "Government, as it derives from heaven, so doubtless is it obliged to make heaven its last and highest end." If humans have souls, then the care of those souls must be a chief concern of the government, as had long been the case.[58]

* * *

Penn's notion that civil interest lay at the root of civil society did not rid him of his deep and abiding Protestant mistrust of Catholicism. Despite this longstanding hostility to Catholic religious teachings and his suspicions of their political loyalty, however, Penn did not take an active role in either the plot agitation or the exclusion controversy. During the late 1670s, he divided his time between London, the hub of English Quakerism, and Sussex, where he had a growing family. There were surely other reasons for his relative silence on the plot and James's precarious political position. Penn's father, after all, had been part of the contingent that traveled to Breda to fetch Charles II back to England at the Restoration, and had served with James during the Second Anglo-Dutch War. When Penn had been attempting to secure Fox's release from Worcester jail, James had declared himself "against all persecution for the sake of religion." The relationship between the two men would only grow stronger after Penn's return from America in 1684 and James's accession as king a year later. Furthermore, Penn needed the royal family, as he was increasingly involved in pursuing a royal grant of land in America. He needed royal assent and cooperation—not only the king's approval of a colonial charter, but James's agreement to cede his interest in the surrounding lands—if his emerging American colony were ever to bear fruit.[59]

Charles's dissolution of the Oxford Parliament—the third Parliament convened during the Exclusion Crisis—in late March 1681, after it had met for just one week, effectively ended the Exclusion Crisis. The aftershocks of the crisis would produce more radical Whig plans to resist the Stuart monarchy, and would ultimately lead to Algernon Sidney being tried for treason and beheaded on Tower Hill in December 1683. But by then he and William Penn had fallen out, and Penn had been in America for more than a year.

7

Penn's Woods

Mine eye is to a blessed government, and a virtuous, ingenious, and
industrious society, so as people may live well, and have more time to
serve the Lord, than in this crowded land.
William Penn to Thomas Janney, August 21, 1681

On board the *Welcome*, anchored off the English coast, William Penn awaited the
propitious winds that would send him to his new province in America. It was late
August 1682. Earlier that month he had conducted a flurry of last-minute business
in London before setting out toward Deal to meet the ships. London newspapers
noted his departure, "along with . . . many families and others who are gone to
settle themselves in that colony." A farewell epistle to Friends expressed his "love
that many waters cannot quench, nor time, nor distance wear away." To Stephen
Crisp, a leading Dutch Quaker, Penn confided that "many are my trials," but he
also expressed his assurance that "there is work enough to be done, and room to
work in." "Surely," he wrote, "God will come in for a share in this planting-work."[1]

On the final day of August, the winds picked up, and the *Welcome* set sail.

* * *

The sole remaining copy of William Penn's May 1680 petition to Charles I for
land in America survives only in fragmentary form, "one half of it being worn
away." It is clear, however, that the king had reacted favorably toward Penn's request. Charles, "being graciously disposed to gratify the petitioner in his humble
suit," referred Penn's petition to the Lords of Trade and Foreign Plantations (also
known as the Committee of Trade, or Lords of Trade), which oversaw English
colonial settlements. As Penn's request made its way through the labyrinthine
bureaucracy of the English government, a number of interested parties watched
closely: Charles Calvert, Lord Baltimore, proprietor of Maryland who controlled
the territories to Penn's south; the Duke of York, who controlled New York to the
north; and Henry Compton, the Bishop of London, who looked after the interests
of the Church of England. Thus began a ten-month process of commentary,

bargaining, negotiation, and not a little subterfuge, in which Penn faced, as he put it, the "great opposition of envious great men."[2]

On June 14, 1680, William Penn made his first appearance before the Committee of Trade to discuss his proposed province's boundaries. In addition to Baltimore's concerns about the precise location of Penn's southern border, it soon became apparent that Penn would need the active support of James, since "part of the territory desired by [Penn] is already possessed by the Duke of York." Penn and James, of course, knew each other well, though their relationship had cooled somewhat during the Exclusion Crisis. Penn had not supported excluding James from the throne, but the duke felt that he had not defended him vocally enough and told Barclay that "he had not seen [Penn] in these times of his troubles." But by the middle of October, after a finding by the Attorney General that the proposed grant did not infringe on Maryland, the duke was "very willing Mr. Penn's request may meet with success."[3]

Even after Penn received James's support, however, Baltimore continued to raise concerns. The two men had directly conflicting interests, and one proprietor's victory would be the other's loss. Baltimore worried about Penn's colony impinging on his northern border, while Penn wanted access to a deepwater port to ensure his colony's commercial viability. Complicating these tense discussions was the fact that the "precise location of the 40th degree of latitude—the boundary specified in both the charters [i.e., Pennsylvania and Maryland]—was still unknown" as late as spring 1682. The Duke of York's secretary, Sir John Werden, pointed out that "description by lines of longitude . . . and of latitude, are very uncertain," and added that "under what meridian the head of the Delaware River lies . . . I do believe hath never yet been observed, by any careful artist." Considering this lack of clear knowledge, he suggested, "it were most proper to have the advice of counsel learned in the laws, for settling the boundaries of any new patent, which may be liable to encroach on those of another's possession."[4]

Over the course of late 1680 and early 1681, a number of additional interested parties weighed in on the specific terms of Penn's charter. Final revisions insisted upon by the Bishop of London, for example, required Penn to allow an Anglican chaplain if settlers requested one. Another provision required Penn to fully enforce the Navigation Acts, which controlled trade between England and the colonies, and provided for Crown review of all colonial legislation. And so, little by little, Penn's request inched forward.[5]

After months of negotiations—and "many waitings, watchings, solicitings, and disputes"—William Penn received a royal charter granting him proprietorship of his American colony in March 1681. As he explained to Robert Turner, a Dublin cloth merchant and leading Irish Friend, the process was not without some last-minute drama over the territory's name. Penn proposed "New Wales," for reasons that have never been entirely clear, though as we saw in Chapter 1, he later claimed Welsh ancestry. He did mention that both places (Pennsylvania and Wales) were hilly, though his claim that "Penn in Buckinghamshire" was "the highest land in England" was surely incorrect. Secretary of State Leoline Jenkins, himself a Welshman, objected to the name, whereupon Penn suggested "Sylvania." Jenkins and his undersecretaries then added "Penn" to "Sylvania," to which Penn objected, fearing that he might be thought vain. Even an attempt to bribe the undersecretaries would not get "Penn" removed from the name, especially since the king insisted it stay. And so Pennsylvania it was, "a name the King would give it in honor to my father . . . whom the King often mentions with praise." Penn concluded his letter to Turner by expressing his hope that God would make Pennsylvania "the seed of a nation."[6]

* * *

But why did William Penn want an American colony in the first place? It was not, or at least not explicitly, a refuge from persecution, since as we have seen, Quakers generally embraced their status as persecuted martyrs, and frowned on attempts to evade punishment. One of the issues that drove the Wilkinson–Story schism, after all, had been Fox's criticism of those Friends who had attempted to flee punishment and avoid detection by the authorities.

A number of scholars over the years have argued that Penn's colony was motivated quite simply by his commitment to religious liberty and Quaker principles. Nineteenth-century Quaker historian Samuel Janney epitomized this position, describing Penn's object as "not only to provide a peaceful home for the persecuted members of his own society, but to afford an asylum for the good and oppressed of every nation, and to found an empire where the pure and peaceable principles of Christianity might be carried out in practice." A Quaker colony would, of course, by definition be a settlement founded on principles of religious liberty.[7]

More skeptical observers, however, have taken issue with this view as naïve about the benefits that Penn expected to reap from his colony, and the strategic choices he made in order to obtain it. Mary Geiter has argued that, in pursuing and accepting his colonial charter, Penn sold out his Whig allies and showed his true colors: those of a courtier, more interested in access to the corridors of power and in making a profit than in standing up to the powerful.[8]

Neither Janney's nor Geiter's account is entirely satisfactory, and each one oversimplifies a complex reality. Quaker commitments and Whig sympathies reinforced each other in Penn's political thinking. In addition to his tireless work on behalf of Dissenters, William Penn had vigorously defended Parliament and the jury system as guarantors of English liberties (in theory, if not always in practice). He assured settlers already living in Pennsylvania's lands, soon after receiving his charter, that "you shall be governed by laws of your own making, and live a free and, if you will, a sober and industrious people." The Preamble to Penn's Frame of Government would later claim, "Any government is free to the people under it . . . where the laws rule, and the people are a party to those laws, and more than this is tyranny, oligarchy, or confusion."[9]

Of course an American colony offered significant economic opportunities for someone like Penn, in desperate need of an infusion of cash. Richard S. Dunn has pointed out that "one of [Penn's] prime reasons for wanting to start an American colony was to salvage his fortune." Since one of his arguments in favor of religious toleration had always been the economic prosperity it would bring about, there was not necessarily any tension between material and spiritual motivations. "I desire to extend religious freedom," he wrote in July 1681, "yet I want some recompense for my trouble." And Penn described his aspirations succinctly shortly after he arrived in America: "The service of God first, the honor and advantage of the King, with our own profit, shall I hope be all of our endeavours."[10]

But regardless of Penn's motives, what did the king have to gain by granting Penn his charter? The ostensible reason—cited by Penn in his initial petition and repeatedly thereafter—was that the grant of land repaid a debt that the Crown owed to Sir William for providing supplies to the navy during the 1660s. That debt, which was originally in the neighborhood of £11,000, had purportedly grown to nearly £16,000 by the early 1680s. Yet the king certainly did not have to repay the money, and more than a decade had gone by when Penn submitted his petition. The grant to Penn certainly served the Crown's imperial aims by cementing English control over the eastern seaboard of North America. That said, it also cut against the more recent trend toward reining in the colonies and reasserting Crown control over the realm's increasingly far-flung colonies. In July 1683, for example, the Crown would move to withdraw the Massachusetts Bay Colony's charter, and Penn's Deputy Governor, William Markham, reported in March 1684 that there was much talk at the royal court of "bring[ing] back the governments to the King." Penn's successful petition suggests that his "personal connections were stronger than the government's imperial policy." So the king's motivations are not entirely clear either.[11]

* * *

"[T]his day my country was confirmed to me under the great seal of England, with large powers and privileges, by the name of Pennsylvania," Penn wrote to Turner in March 1681. "It is a clear and just thing, and my God that has given it me through many difficulties will, I believe, make it the seed of a nation." The receipt of the charter for Pennsylvania represented both the culmination of nearly ten months of persistent negotiation and the beginning of another frenzy of activity, a blizzard of promotional correspondence that began almost as soon as the ink on the parchment had dried. This promotional effort would take up the lion's share of William Penn's attention over the next eighteen months.

"Founding a successful proprietary colony in late seventeenth-century America was hard work," the editors of Penn's papers explain. "A proprietor had to be an aggressive, pragmatic businessman who could publicize his colony widely; offer land, trading rights, and powers of government to a broad variety of settlers on attractive terms; and compete effectively with other proprietors who had the same basic objective—making their colonies pay." William Penn threw himself into this task with gusto, all the while continuing his work with the Meeting for Sufferings and the Morning Meeting (though his attendance became less frequent as his Pennsylvania business accelerated), composing a petition to Parliament rehearsing arguments for toleration, and attending parliamentary sessions during the fall of 1680. All the while, he was managing the complex task of providing for his growing young family.[12]

To start off the promotional process, both the king and the new proprietor wrote to inhabitants already living in the newly created province of Pennsylvania, which Sir John Werden had earlier described as "being planted promiscuously by Swedes, Finlanders, Dutch, and English." Penn commissioned a Deputy Governor, his first cousin William Markham, and sent him to America to begin overseeing settlement and negotiating land purchases with natives and settlers "till I myself shall arrive." He wrote to his new southern neighbor, Lord Baltimore, making an "offer of friendship" and expressing his hope for "a just and friendly intercourse" between the two. He wrote to Irish Quakers, admitting the irony of a critic of government establishing a colony, noting that "as my understanding and inclinations have been so much directed to observe and reprove mischiefs in government, so it is now put into my power to settle one." He wrote to Barclay, whom he hoped would assist him in selling land to Scots as well as obtaining clear title to lands adjacent to Pennsylvania that were controlled by the Duke of York. Though he and Penn had become close during the 1670s, Barclay was clearly pulled in several directions: Pennsylvania's prospects were complicated by the presence of East and West Jersey, territories where land was cheap and where Friends were also welcome. Barclay, who would later be appointed Governor of East Jersey, told Penn point-blank late in 1681 that his prices were too high: "Thou has land enough so need not be a churl if thou intend to advance thy plantation"—although he later offered a more upbeat assessment of the prospects of Penn selling land to "several sober persons of the Presbyterian way."[13]

And, of course, Penn began promoting more publicly. Before the end of March 1681, he had published *Some account of the province of Pennsylvania in America*, which was soon translated, probably by Benjamin Furly, into German and Dutch. In order to realize the advantages Penn hoped to reap from his American undertaking, he had to address a widespread view, epitomized by thinkers like Roger Coke—political economist and grandson of the great English jurist Edward

Coke—that colonies were detrimental to the overall health of the mother country. In his 1670 *A discourse of trade*, Coke had argued that "Ireland and our plantations have exhausted our men, whereby our trade and strength is abated and diminished." Penn disagreed, referring to colonies as "seeds of nations"—the very formulation he had used to describe Pennsylvania in his letter to Turner—and insisting that they were a boon for both population and commerce. *Some Account* insisted that Pennsylvania's political legitimacy would rest upon representative institutions. "The people and governor have a legislative power, so that no law can be made, nor money raised, but by the people's consent," and he assured those considering settling in the province that "the rights and freedoms of England" would be honored there. The colony's political framework would be the product of an open-ended and consultative process, aiming to "encourage planters, and settle a free, just, and industrious colony." Those "most fitted" to this new settlement, in Penn's view, included workers and artisans encountering difficulty making a living in their native land, as well as others with an interest in promoting the public good.[14]

Copies of *Some account* were distributed widely. In an accompanying explanatory letter, Penn wrote "that it hath pleased the Lord to dispose the mind of the King . . . to grant a country to me, in America," and pledged that he would "secure all in their civil and religious rights." A second promotional work, *A brief account of . . . Pennsylvania*, reprinted Charles's letter to the inhabitants of Pennsylvania and reiterated the terms upon which land could be obtained. At this point in his career as colonizer, barely thirty-seven years old, Penn clearly viewed himself as a visionary reformer and saw his own undertaking against a broader historical backdrop that included virtuous founders like Moses, Lycurgus, Theseus, and Romulus.[15] Pennsylvania, too, would be a distinct homeland for a distinctive people.

The process of recruiting settlers to Pennsylvania was facilitated by Penn's extensive networks among European Dissenters. He was well known, of course, from his several trips to Europe on behalf of Quakers and other suffering Dissenters, as well as his high-profile interventions in English politics for more than a decade. Later that same summer, Penn wrote to James Harrison, a Lancashire Quaker who would later become his steward at Pennsbury, his American estate, and offered what would become the most enduring description of his aspirations for the colony. "I desire . . . that an example may be set up to the nations. There may be room there, though not here, for such a holy experiment." (In the same letter, Penn admitted that his journey to America unfortunately "is not like to be so quick as I had hoped.")[16] The notion of Pennsylvania as a "holy experiment" has played an outsized role in attempts to understand both the colony and its founder, and what Penn meant by the term has perplexed historians and biographers ever since. (In the Epilogue,

I offer some reflections on what Penn might have meant and why it is significant for Pennsylvania's historical legacy.)

In the meantime, aided by the mediation of Barclay, Penn continued to appeal to
the Duke of York for a patent granting him the right to govern the Lower Counties.
Like New Jersey, the three counties to the south of Pennsylvania and to the north
and east of Maryland had a checkered history of European settlement, with the
Dutch and Swedish governments exercising control for much of the first half of the
seventeenth century. As part of Charles II's 1664 grant to his brother, the counties of
Kent, Sussex, and New Castle—with the town of New Castle assuming increasing
commercial importance—represented invaluable access to the Atlantic, without
which the development of Pennsylvania would be sharply curtailed. But in the early
days of Penn's proprietorship, Werden routinely turned a deaf ear to Penn's pleas.[17]

* * *

William Penn was obviously not the first English colonizer in America. He
was, in fact, a latecomer to the whole enterprise. Compared to the West Indies
(Caribbean), New England, and the Chesapeake settlements, the mid-Atlantic
coast had received relatively little attention from English colonizers during the
early seventeenth century. The charter Penn received in 1681 served the aims
of the Crown by continuing the Restoration push for English imperial control between New England and the Chesapeake, beginning with Jamestown in
1607 and continuing through Massachusetts and Maryland during the 1630s,
Carolina in the 1660s, and New Netherland, which the English had taken back
from the Dutch once and for all in 1674.[18]

Nor was this activity limited to North America. A variety of religious, economic, and political motivations drove Europeans across the Atlantic to the
Caribbean islands and North America during the seventeenth century. The
large-scale migration of people, ideas, and goods profoundly shaped the settlers,
the native peoples they encountered, the land itself, and the world they left behind. Jamaica and Barbados formed essential cogs in the imperial economy, with
Barbados's sugar and rum complemented by Jamaica's agricultural products and
profits generated by smuggling and piracy. In fact, "during the mid-seventeenth
century, the West Indies became the great magnet for English transatlantic migration," focused largely on Barbados, which by the time of the Restoration was
providing nearly all the sugar consumed in England, and had also become the
first English colony with an enslaved, black majority.[19]

All this colonial expansion facilitated the spread of Quakerism, and Quakers,
who had arrived in North America as early as 1655, eagerly exploited those networks in their proselytization efforts. The first Quakers were missionaries aiming
to convince settlers and Native Americans of the Light of God within every human
being. These itinerant "publishers of Truth" traveled along a route from Barbados

to Massachusetts and back again, with Rhode Island and Maryland serving as bases for their work. When Fox visited Rhode Island in the summer of 1672, he discovered that nearly all of that colony's public officials were Friends.[20]

Although Friends would eventually become leaders in the abolitionist movement, in these early days most Friends did not take such a position, and in the West Indies Quakerism existed side by side with slavery. By 1672, Barbados Friends had five meetinghouses and were the second largest religious group in the colony.[21] Fox visited Barbados during his American journey, and his Meetings on Barbados and Jamaica in 1671 and 1672 drew significant crowds. William Edmundson had condemned slavery during his preaching tour of Antigua and Nevis in 1671, but during his trip to America in the early 1670s Fox said little about the topic. In fact, he disavowed the charge "that we . . . teach the negroes to rebel," insisting that Friends only "exhort and admonish them to be sober, to fear God, to love their masters and mistresses, and to be faithful and diligent in their service and business, and then their masters and overseers would love them, and deal kindly and gently with them."[22]

Unlike in New England or Virginia, as we have seen, much of the territory that would become Pennsylvania was already inhabited by Europeans—a mélange of Swedish, Finnish, Dutch, and English settlers who had settled on the land over the years and who remained there even as control seesawed back and forth between Dutch and English governments. Relying on erroneous maps and, in the words of his editors, "particularly confused and misinformed," Penn wrote to settlers in Maryland in April 1681 instructing them to stop paying taxes to Baltimore, an action sure to poison the already-tense relations with his southern neighbor. And sure enough, the following spring, when Baltimore became aware of Penn's letter, he dashed off one of his own, to Markham, denouncing Penn's meddling in his province as "a thing not kindly taken and . . . not according to the Golden Rule mentioned in Mr. Penn's letter to me." Not only were the two provinces religiously and ethnically distinct, but each proprietor saw the other as a direct threat.[23]

And of course Europeans were only part of this story. As Daniel Richter has observed, "Throughout the period before the United States declared its independence, the vast majority of eastern North America was neither English nor French nor Spanish territory. It was, clearly, Indian country." The Lenapes, also known as the Delaware, were no strangers to European settlers, having created a hybrid society with them, anchored in perceptions of mutually beneficial trading relationships, in the decades before Penn's arrival. In May 1672, and again in September of that year, Lenape guides led Fox safely through the region they called Lenapewihittuck (now central and southern New Jersey, eastern Pennsylvania, and Delaware). Penn's friend Josiah Coale had even written to

Fox, as far back as 1660, suggesting the possibility of purchasing a piece of land from the natives, although such a plan never came to fruition.[24]

The Lenape had welcomed trade with Europeans since the arrival of Henry Hudson. Although they destroyed a Dutch settlement at Swanendael, near Cape Henlopen, and killed its residents, in 1631, the region had been spared the kind of large-scale violence that characterized native–settler relations in New England and Virginia. The Lenapes regularly granted the Swedes, Dutch, and English permission to build trading posts and forts in the area, and allied increasingly with Swedes and Finns against Dutch authority, while retaining their Dutch trading connections. The English conquest in 1664 further complicated this already complex situation, though the Lenapes continued to engage with European settlers in strategic ways, creating, in the words of Jean Soderlund, "a polyglot society . . . one in which the Lenapes held the upper hand and remained flexible to win allies and accommodate trade." In other words, by the time Charles II granted William Penn his charter and ships began taking Quaker families and other settlers to this new province, a diverse society had been in the making for some time, incorporating a range of European and native populations whose interactions benefited each side in distinctive ways. Upon his arrival in August 1681, Markham had quickly taken several Swedes familiar with Lenape ways as advisors, and allowed local courts to continue functioning as they had previously. In this regard, from the natives' perspective, James Merrell's description of Penn may well be the most apt: he was "only the latest in a long line of uninvited guests from faraway lands to show up on the banks of the Delaware."[25]

From his experiences with New Jersey and through his negotiations with the Duke of York, Penn would certainly have understood the general backdrop to his colony's founding. But it is unclear how many of the details of this history he knew. He certainly understood that dealing with tribes in ways that fostered their cooperation offered economic and diplomatic advantages to him and his settlers. Although Pennsylvanians interacted extensively with the Lenapes, there remained a great deal about that tribe that they did not know, nor did they always grasp the complex relationships that obtained between tribes, and early Pennsylvania would provide many examples of the mutual misunderstanding, failures of communication, and resentment. Penn's colony, in other words, provided the backdrop for complex interactions between European Americans as well as between those settlers and Native Americans. And if Pennsylvania would later develop a reputation as a colony that avoided the bloody precedents established by English settlers to their north and south, we should not overlook the fact that Penn's Quaker means were always employed in the service of his own advantage. For that matter, the Lenapes may have brought their own peaceful precedents to their dealings with Penn, as much as the other way around.[26]

In his first letter to the Lenapes, Penn invoked "one great God and Power that hath made the world and all things therein," stating that he hoped to enjoy his territory "with your love and consent, that we may always live together as neighbors and friends." Of the myriad examples of Europeans treating the natives unjustly, Penn offered a curt comment: "I am not such a man." He promised them fair treatment in any disputes with settlers, and ended his letter by stating simply, "I am your friend. William Penn." Two months before he set sail, Penn wrote to "the Emperor of Canada"—likely a native chief somewhere in upstate New York—professing his people's "just, plain, and honest" character, and introducing the Free Society of Traders, "to traffic with thee and thy people for your commodities, that you may be furnished with that which is good at reasonable rates." A month later Markham completed the first purchase of land from the Lenapes—land they had previously sold to New York Governor Andros, but now made over to Penn—obtaining the site on which Penn would build Pennsbury Manor, in present-day lower Bucks County, Pennsylvania.[27]

The notion of Pennsylvania as a singular example of peaceful relations between settlers and natives, and of Penn as the benevolent Quaker patriarch overseeing that idyll, quickly became part of the colony's founding mythos, later memorialized in Benjamin West's 1772 painting *Treaty of Penn with the Indians* and Edward Hicks's 1847 painting of the same name. To be sure, the colony did not endure the sorts of brutal conflicts that had recently afflicted New England during King Philip's War, or Bacon's Rebellion in Virginia, during the previous decade. That said—no doubt motivated by his deep indebtedness—Penn began selling land to investors well before he had secured title to it from the Lenapes. Nor is it even clear what, if anything, transpired beneath the famed "Treaty Elm" at Shackamaxon, subject of the long-established tradition that Penn exchanged promises of perpetual amity with Lenapes there not long after his arrival in 1682. As would become apparent with the passage of time, the parties' notions of "owning" land differed dramatically; and although Penn attempted to outlaw the sale of liquor to the natives, his settlers, including many Quaker merchants, routinely ignored such prohibitions. Griffith Jones, a member of the Free Society of Traders who would later serve as Philadelphia's mayor, was among six individuals indicted for providing liquor without a license in March 1683. The remarkable growth of Pennsylvania over its first few decades of existence would push the Lenapes west, while settlers eager for land moved into the territory that had once been the Lenapewihittuck, in a pattern of settlement that we might describe as dispossession by purchase.[28]

* * *

The whole point of promoting the colony, of course, was to sell land. As spring 1681 went on, Penn began to realize that his original plan—selling five-thousand-acre shares for £100 each—was overly ambitious and required resources that many potential investors simply did not have. So he announced his willingness to allow groups of ten purchasers to pool their resources and purchase five-thousand-acre parcels. (He would eventually sell lots as small as 125 acres, and most purchasers bought a thousand acres or less.) By July 1681, Penn had finalized the terms for sale of land to his "First Purchasers," providing choice lots in a "large town or city" to be laid out "in the most convenient place upon the [Delaware] River for health and navigation," with incentives for those who would bring over families and servants and settle on and cultivate their land. Penn's motivations in this regard were both economic and cultural: a population like New England's, made up of families, was likely to be far more stable than one composed chiefly of single men, such as Virginia. Alan Taylor has described the Virginia settlers as "an unstable and fractious mix of gentlemen-adventurers in command and poor vagrants rounded up from the streets of London and forcibly sent to Virginia." Such a society would likely bear little resemblance to Penn's vision of the "sober and industrious people" he lauded in his first letter to the inhabitants of Pennsylvania.[29]

Penn offered a series of "Concessions" to his First Purchasers, both to entice them to invest and to set clear procedures for minimizing conflict between settlers and natives. The Concessions provided for public markets and identical liability for harming natives and settlers, and reiterated that English laws involving slander, trespass, weights and measures, cursing, apparel, and the like would remain in force, at least "till altered by law in this province." With the Concessions in place, land sales began to pick up. His first sale, not surprisingly, was a five-thousand-acre parcel to his agent, Philip Ford. Several dozen more followed in the next few months, including five hundred acres to Bristol merchant Thomas Callowhill, whose daughter Hannah would become Penn's wife twenty-five years later. By October, more than 250 individuals had purchased land in Pennsylvania.[30]

Land sales occupied a great deal of Penn's time during 1681 and early 1682, and more than half of his first two hundred purchasers, no doubt eager to gain access to lots in the "great town," bought their lots during the first six months that land was available. His First Purchasers were "recruited . . . from districts where Quakerism was strong and where he had personally spent much time and was well known," though the depth of their attachment to Quakerism has long been a matter of debate. Penn's investors hailed from a wide range of occupational backgrounds: more than eighty different occupations appear in a list of the first 350 purchasers, and the urban centers of European Quakerism—London, Dublin, Bristol, Rotterdam, Cork—were heavily represented. Penn also provided land to a number of relatives and friends; some received their lots as gifts, while others paid only partially, or not at all. He soon had a network of agents in place to facilitate sales. In addition to Ford, who was based in London, those interested in purchasing land in Pennsylvania also worked through Barclay in Scotland, Turner in Dublin, Furly in Rotterdam, and Harrison in Lancashire. The First Purchasers would not only occupy significant portions of Pennsylvania land, but would go on to play prominent roles in the Provincial Council and Assembly.[31]

Shortly after signing the Concessions, Penn sent commissioners to begin laying out "a great town," at a place along the Delaware River "where it is most navigable, high, dry, and healthy" and suitable "for navigation, healthy situation, and good soil for provision." He initially conceived of this town as a series of lots spaced along a fifteen-mile stretch of the Delaware River, in the middle of which his own house would sit. "Conscious of the destruction wrought by the Great Fire of London of 1666 as it swept through London's narrow and twisting streets," Elizabeth Milroy explains, Penn "stipulated that houses be erected at the center of each tract so as to leave a generous space for gardens and orchards." In Penn's own words, he sought "a green country town, which will never be burnt and the spirit be wholesome." A month later, in a brief set of instructions to Markham, he declared that "I do call the city . . . by the name of Philadelphia."[32]

Unfortunately, Penn had little knowledge of actual conditions on the ground, having never seen the territory with his own eyes. (Unfortunately for William Crispin, one of Penn's commissioners, he would die without ever seeing Pennsylvania: the ship bearing him was blown off course and arrived instead in Barbados, where he died shortly thereafter.) When the commissioners arrived in Pennsylvania, they discovered that the only suitable place for Penn's "green country town" was not, as the proprietor had assumed, near the well-established settlement of Upland (present-day Chester, Pennsylvania), but some fifteen miles upriver near the mouth of the Schuylkill River. Finding the proper site for Penn's capital city was just one of the commissioners' challenges. By this point, colonists were arriving by the shipload, eager to be settled onto their properties, which increased pressure on the commissioners to lay out an urban center rather than Penn's original "green country town." The pressure would continue into the next year: one recently arrived settler wrote home in August 1682 that "a crowd of people striving for the country land" was now at Upland, and that "we are short of our expectations." Penn attempted to relieve his commissioners by appointing Thomas Holme, a Friend who had fought in Cromwell's army during the Civil Wars and later received land in Ireland, as Pennsylvania's first Surveyor General in April 1682, although Holme and his family would not arrive in America until just a few months before Penn himself.[33]

* * *

Despite all these preparations, without a workable political framework to govern settlers' political relations and interactions with each other—and with the natives—investing in Pennsylvania would remain a risky proposition.

Penn made his first attempt at formulating the colony's political foundations, the Fundamental Constitutions of Pennsylvania, shortly after he received the charter. Though it was never made public, it does give a glimpse into his thinking as he prepared to make the transition from critic and theorist to proprietor and hands-on governor. The document's Preamble defined good government as "a constitution of just laws, wisely set together for the well ordering of men in society, to prevent all corruption or justly to correct it." It stressed the importance of popular consent for legitimate government and emphasized that the proper goal of government was the common good, "the virtue, peace, and prosperity of the people."[34]

Not surprisingly, the Fundamental Constitutions guaranteed each inhabitant

> the free possession of his or her faith and exercise of worship towards God, in such way and manner as every person shall in conscience believe is most acceptable to God, and so long as every such person uses not this Christian liberty to licentiousness (that is to say, to speak loosely and profanely of God, Christ, or religion, or to commit any evil in their conversation), he or she shall be protected in the enjoyment of the aforesaid Christian liberty by the civil magistrate.

The Fundamental Constitutions envisioned an annually elected lower house, from which a smaller Council with broader governing and oversight responsibilities would be chosen. The Assembly's members were to receive written instructions from their electors and to consult with them on the passage of laws, "that they may always remember they are but deputies and men entrusted to the good of others and responsible for that trust." Penn also mandated a jury system and restricted the practice of imprisonment for debt. The governor and Council played a limited role in the legislative process, while elections, and the Assembly's votes, were to be conducted by secret ballot. Provisions that no oaths be sworn in legal proceedings reflected Quaker beliefs, and, given his own personal austerity, Penn also insisted that Pennsylvania was to have no taverns or alehouses, "nor any playhouses, nor morris dances, nor games as dice, cards, board tables, lotteries, bowling greens, horse races, bear baitings, bull baitings, and such like sports, which only tend to idleness and looseness." By empowering the legislature and guaranteeing liberty of conscience, the Fundamental Constitutions harkened back to the West Jersey Concessions. It was an ambitious plan of government with robust public involvement at all levels. Yet like the Concessions, it would remain largely theoretical.[35]

Over the next six months or so, Penn received suggestions and commentary from a range of colleagues, and a new governing framework for the colony gradually took shape. Advice came from many corners: John Darnall, who had played an important role in drafting the colonial charter; Rudyard, with whom Penn had worked closely for more than a decade; Sidney, Penn's erstwhile Whig ally; and Furly, who provided a detailed comparison of Penn's final draft with his first.[36]

By the time that the Frame of Government appeared in May 1682, accompanied by more than three dozen "Laws Agreed upon in England," Penn was nearing his time to depart for America. In the intervening months, he had made some fairly significant changes from his earlier model. The Frame's preamble, like that of the Fundamental Constitutions, argued that government is necessary because of human sin, endorsed the principle of popular consent, and argued that "any government is free to the people under it (whatever be the frame) where the laws rule, and the people are a party to those laws, and more than this is tyranny, oligarchy, or confusion." Penn emphasized the importance of placing morally upright individuals in positions of political power, and pronounced the "great end of all government" to be "to support power in reverence with the people, and to secure the people from the abuse of power."[37]

Compared to the Fundamental Constitutions, the Frame's governing structure granted greater power to the governor and a small, directly elected Council of seventy-two members. The governor received a triple vote in the Council, while the Assembly (which he initially envisioned as containing two hundred members) was relegated to affirming or negating laws proposed by the governor or Council.

But not everything had changed. Among the laws appended to the Frame, liberty of conscience remained, although now more explicitly limited to those who publicly confessed belief in God and behaved peacefully:

> That all persons living in this province, who confess and acknowledge the one Almighty and eternal God, to be the Creator, Upholder and Ruler of the world; and that hold themselves obliged in conscience to live peaceably and justly in civil society, shall, in no ways, be molested or prejudiced for their religious persuasion, or practice, in matters of faith and worship, nor shall they be compelled, at any time, to frequent or maintain any religious worship, place or ministry whatever.

The franchise and officeholding were restricted by the Frame to professing Christian, or in the words of the Frame those who "possess faith in Jesus Christ, and that are not convicted of ill fame, or unsober and dishonest conversation."[38]

A number of Penn's friends viewed his retreat from the ambitious republicanism and popular sovereignty of the Fundamental Constitutions with alarm. Algernon Sidney accused Penn of having "a good country but the basest laws in the world, not to be endured or lived under," making the rupture between the two former friends complete, with Penn pronouncing himself "sorry we were ever so well acquainted." Furly "far prefer[red] thy first draft to this last," and wondered "who should put thee upon altering them for these, and as much how thou could ever yield to such a thing." Other than a brief defensive letter in response to Sidney, though, we know very little about Penn's thought processes while he was drafting these various documents. He was playing three roles simultaneously: proprietor, with an enormous amount of leeway to structure Pennsylvania as he saw fit; subject of the Crown, which retained veto power over his laws and could withdraw his charter at any time; and businessman who needed investors, who in turn wanted practical guarantees of political stability. These competing imperatives further complicated planning for the colony. Then again, Penn's Whig sympathies and Quaker egalitarianism had always coexisted with a degree of social conservatism and a longstanding commitment to social order.[39]

Though the shift in governmental authority from the 1681 Fundamental Constitutions to the 1682 Frame was unmistakable, the differences between the two documents should not be overstated. Significant areas of commonality remained, including punishments for bribery, as well as provisions for trials by jury and affirmations instead of oaths in legal proceedings. The Frame also contained a litany of moral outrages that were to be forbidden in the colony, which expanded those laid out in the Fundamental Constitutions:

> All such offences against God, as swearing, cursing, lying, prophane talking, drunkenness, drinking of healths, obscene words, incest, sodomy, rapes, whoredom, fornication, and other uncleanness . . . all treasons, misprisions, murders, duels, felony, seditions, maims, forcible entries, and other violences, to the persons and estates of the inhabitants within this province; all prizes, stage-plays, cards, dice, May-games, gamesters, masques, revels, bull-battings, cock-fightings, bear-battings, and the like, which excite the people to rudeness, cruelty, looseness, and irreligion, shall be respectively discouraged, and severely punished.

Liberty of conscience, of course, had been one of Penn's firm principles since the earliest days of his political activism. But insisting on toleration did not extend to things he considered morally corrupt. Such a complex mix of liberty and restriction was not unique to Penn—John Locke's *Second treatise of government* famously distinguished between liberty and license—but it was certainly on public display in the Frame of government.[40]

Just one piece of the Pennsylvania puzzle remained to be fit into place: the colony's economic and commercial foundation. Penn reported to Turner in August 1681 that he had recently turned down an offer of £6,000 for a monopoly on the Indian trade, but he fully intended to benefit from Pennsylvania's enormous financial promise. In March 1682, Penn chartered the Free Society of Traders in Pennsylvania, a joint-stock company designed to control and manage the colony's agriculture, mining, manufacturing, fishing, and fur trade. If the Concessions to First Purchasers sought to manage settlers' migration, then the Charter of the Free Society of Traders represented Penn's attempt to make the most of his colony's economic promise. In the words of Gary Nash, the "lessons of nearly one hundred years of English colonization were clear: success was unthinkable without the steady infusion of capital during the early years of settlement. Even a man of Penn's resources could not hope to underwrite single-handedly the manifold expenses of planting a colony." (Not to mention the fact that Penn's resources were never as extensive as he often let on, and were getting less so with each passing year.) More than two hundred individuals invested in the Free Society, pledging more than £12,000, £6,000 of which had actually been paid by the time Penn departed.[41]

The Free Society was dominated by London Quakers and Penn's close associates, and the important role that he provided for it—his willingness to carve out special privileges for those who would shoulder the economic burden needed to launch Pennsylvania as a viable commercial undertaking—illustrates the close association between economic prosperity and the success of a colonial enterprise. The charter granted the Society a manor of 20,000 acres in the colony, and empowered the Society to administer justice, collect taxes, and manage its own affairs. Penn also granted the Society the right to appoint three members to the Provincial Council. The Society published an account of its aspirations in London in April 1682, insisting that "this society is calculated both to promote the public good, and to encourage the private."[42] Prosperity and salvation would go hand in hand in Penn's woods.

* * *

The first half of 1682 was a whirlwind of activity for William Penn, and must have been exhilarating as well as physically and emotionally taxing. He exulted that "Pennsylvania prospers daily, and people [are] preparing" to emigrate in a January letter to James Harrison, and counseled a young Friend considering emigration to "be cool, and patient, and contented with God's will" and "to have a tender regard to thy father and mother," while telling her parents that "I purpose to go this summer the Lord willing." Despite a number of important milestones during his preparation for the journey—the Free Society's charter in March; the promulgation of the Frame of Government and Laws in May; the publication in August of a much expanded (now weighing in at nearly six hundred pages) *No cross, no crown*, which had evolved from a head-on denunciation of worldly practices to a more contemplative, devotional text about the virtues of self-denial and "the daily bearing of Christ's Cross"—personal grief and trials hit him hard. In March, his mother died at Walthamstow. Mary Penington, Gulielma's mother, continued to decline, and would pass away just after Penn departed. The prospect of separation from his three young children and Gulielma weighed heavily on him. Eldest son Springett was then seven years old, daughter Letitia four, and William Jr. just seventeen months. He had initially hoped to take his family with him to America, but Gulielma's health had never been robust, and she was pregnant once again. And though he had expected that land sales in America would have restored him to solvency, his financial situation was still precarious.[43]

Regardless of these personal challenges, though, August 1682 was a month for farewells, final arrangements, and leave-taking. While at Warminghurst early in the month, Penn wrote a farewell letter to Gulielma and the children. In it, he spoke tenderly about his affection for his wife, and with poignancy about the uncertainty of his ever seeing her again. "Remember," he told Gulielma, "thou wast the love of my youth, and much the joy of my life, the most beloved as well as most worthy of all my earthly comforts." He urged her to hold steadfast in the faith, to maintain attendance at Meetings, and in a rare moment of candor about his financial difficulties, implored her to "live low and sparingly, till my debts are paid." (It was, to say the least, an awkward bit of moralizing from one who had never shown any ability to "live low and sparingly.") He even quoted a saying of her stepfather, Isaac Penington, that "I desire not riches, but to owe nothing." In addition to offering Gulielma a detailed set of recommendations about the education of their children—"abundantly beloved of me as the Lord's blessings, and the sweet pledges of our mutual and endeared affection"—he addressed the children directly, urging them to "remember your creator in the days of your youth," "be obedient to the Light within," "help the poor and needy," and to honor their mother, "whose virtue and good name, is an honor to you." He further implored them to comport themselves in an upright and temperate manner and to devote themselves to some "honest industrious course of life, and that not of sordid covetousness."[44]

By the next week he was in London, having had "a precious meeting with the Friends of this city" and bidding George Fox farewell at Enfield, a village ten miles north of the capital. While in London he received some final advice from his old friend Sir William Petty, who had purchased land from Penn and was contemplating settling in Pennsylvania. Petty cautioned the proprietor about overselling his colony, and emphasized the value of holding land back for later development and the importance of gaining an accurate survey of the whole territory, along with the flora, fauna, and resources of the place. And finally, on August 24, just before he sailed, Penn secured the title to the Lower Counties from the Duke of York, an enormously important achievement toward which he had been working for nearly two years. The cumulative effect of the previous

half-dozen years of Quaker involvement with American colonization was significant, and "by the end of 1682 Quaker proprietors held all the lands from
New York to Maryland."[45]

In mid-August he wrote one final time to each of his children. The letters are
brief and touching. To Springett, his eldest son: "Be good, learn to fear God, avoid
evil, love thy book, be kind to thy brother and sister and God will bless thee and
I will exceedingly love thee. Farewell dear child." To daughter Letitia: "I dearly
love thee, and would have thee sober, learn thy book, and love thy brothers. I will
send thee a pretty book to learn in. The Lord bless thee and make a good woman
of thee. Farewell." And to little Billy: "I love thee much, therefore be sober and
quiet, and learn his book, I will send him one, so the Lord bless thee. Amen."[46]

But not all the final arrangements went smoothly. On August 23, Penn had
received an accounting of his financial affairs from Philip Ford. Ford informed
Penn that, despite having raised more than £6,000 in Pennsylvania land sales, his
account also included significant debts. Since many of the First Purchasers were
either relatives or friends, to whom Penn gave land as gifts, his considerable land
sales had not significantly improved his financial condition. Penn was heavily engaged with final preparations and, as he often did, signed Ford's accounting and
the papers he presented (including a mortgage on 300,000 acres of Pennsylvania
land as collateral) without closely inspecting them. It was an action he would
come to bitterly regret.[47]

Most of Penn's biographers have viewed Ford as unscrupulous, preying on
Penn's trusting nature by virtue of their longstanding relationship. John Pomfret
claims that Penn was "relentlessly mulcted of his substance" by Ford, and
Marion Balderston calls him a "dishonest character." But from Ford's perspective, no doubt, two incontrovertible facts presented themselves in the summer
of 1682: Penn's expenses had outrun his income for years, and he was about to
undertake a risky journey from which he might well never return.[48]

And so, having taken care of business, William Penn sailed in the *Welcome* for
America.

8

To America ... and Back Again

The average ocean crossing during the second half of the seventeenth century took about eight weeks, and William Penn's journey on board the *Welcome* was relatively average in this regard, as well as in the challenges posed by weather and disease; smallpox claimed about thirty passengers and crew on the passage. He landed at New Castle on October 28, 1682, bearing the deeds granted him by the Duke of York, and was presented with "quiet and peaceable possession" of the Lower Counties by John Moll, who administered the territories as justice of New Castle court. (The official ceremony of transfer included a handful of turf and a basin filled with river water.) Penn gathered the inhabitants at the court there, "assuring them of their spiritual and temporal rights," including "liberty of conscience and civil freedoms." The next month saw a flurry of activity and movement on Penn's part. Within a few days he had inspected the site of his proposed capital city and, "impatient to secure a quick confirmation of his authority" (and, no doubt, to secure the loyalty of those already living there), issued election writs for an Assembly to convene soon at Upland, which he renamed Chester. On November 9 he was in New York, attempting to mediate political disputes raging there. He also visited East New Jersey, where his old associate Thomas Rudyard had recently been named Deputy Governor, and attended Friends' Meetings on Long Island, before returning to Pennsylvania. In early December, he convened his first Assembly.[1]

The Chester Assembly lasted just a few days, from December 4 to 7, but they were important days. Little is known about the assembly's membership, and only an incomplete set of minutes survives. We do know that the members chose Nicholas More, an influential London Anglican and president of the Free Society of Traders, as the Assembly's chair, clear evidence that not all Pennsylvania offices would be held by Friends. Penn's "Quaker colony" also had to contend with a sizable population of non-Quakers, concentrated in the Lower Counties, whose residence predated Penn's charter. Accordingly, one of the Assembly's most important actions was passage of an Act of Union between Pennsylvania and the three Lower Counties, whose representatives had presented a petition requesting "that as one united province, they may be endowed with the same privileges of law and government." The Assembly also passed an act offering naturalization to the non-English inhabitants of the colony, "mak[ing] them as free as other members of this province" upon professions of allegiance. For a proprietor who had argued that "civil interest" represented the civic glue that could bind together a community of individuals with differing religious commitments, it must have been a particularly gratifying development, a step toward his oft-stated goal of a society made up of "sober people of all sorts."[2]

The Chester Assembly approved the "Great Law," which was made up of approximately seventy of the ninety laws that Penn had proposed. The Great Law enshrined liberty of conscience as fundamental, of course, and addressed a wide array of civil and criminal matters. The Great Law also contained, in its first article, a prohibition on religious insult and invective. After ensuring freedom of conscience to all who professed belief in God, it further proclaimed that "if any person shall abuse or deride any other for his or her different persuasion and practice in matters of religion such shall be looked upon as a disturber of the peace and be punished accordingly." Such a provision reflected Penn's frank acknowledgment of the fundamental importance of mutual restraint in the project of living together peacefully with one's neighbors in this multireligious, multiethnic American experiment.[3]

During this brief Assembly session, though, the first cracks in Penn's carefully constructed network of governing institutions began to show. For example, the Assembly declined to confirm the Free Society of Traders' charter. The reasons for this step are not clear, but resentment of the Society's commercial monopoly or of its chief officer are likely candidates. Nicholas More was irascible and bad-tempered, and James Claypoole, the Society's treasurer, had told Penn to set More aside as president of the Society if he proved to be "perverse and stubborn." (More later resigned the presidency of the Society, and in March 1683 he would be called before the Council for making contemptuous remarks about the government. Ultimately, he was expelled from the Assembly for judicial misconduct and impeached while serving as Pennsylvania's chief justice in 1685.) Or perhaps the Assembly's actions were motivated by concerns about the "extensive feudal privileges" granted to the Society under its charter. Either way, when the news reached the Society's treasurer, James Claypoole, who would soon join Penn in Pennsylvania, he wrote sharply to Penn:

> We are like to suffer, both in our stock and reputation. When it comes among the people I am afraid they will say they are all cheated, for the charter or patent which thou signed was a great inducement to many to subscribe and others to pay in their money . . . and we did not doubt but

that according to our desire and thy promise, the first Assembly would confirm the charter and choose assistants to manage the business.

Given the importance of the Free Society of Traders to Penn's plans for the province, and his own prosperity, this was an ominous beginning. Indeed, it turned out to be a harbinger of things to come. The Society never achieved the sort of preeminence envisioned by Penn and his associates. Pennsylvania's economic flourishing came about in spite of, rather than because of, the top-down model of economic control that Penn and his associates envisioned in chartering the Free Society. By the mid-1680s the Free Society was, in Gary Nash's words, "all but defunct except as a land company."[4]

After adjourning the Assembly on December 7, Penn headed to Maryland to meet with Baltimore, while the process of clearing streets and laying out lots in Philadelphia proceeded, with special consideration given to those purchasers who were present and ready to build on their lots or who had sent agents ahead of them to prepare. Settlers had been arriving for months and were waiting with increasing impatience; some even began clearing their lots before official surveys were completed. Those who had invested sizable sums were understandably upset when they arrived to find a reality on the ground that differed markedly from Penn's lofty promises, and much of Penn's attention during these early months involved compensating disappointed settlers with additional land elsewhere if they would allow him to move their plots to another part of the city.[5]

Responsibility for dealing with conflicts over land generally fell to Surveyor General Holme, whose biographer Irma Corcoran describes as quickly realizing that "this small wedge-shaped tract . . . would not allow the generous proportions of the city and liberty land that William Penn envisioned." Another scholar of early Pennsylvania estimates that Penn "had oversold by some 13,000 acres." By late 1683 Holme, who sat on the Provincial Council and whose relationship with the proprietor had grown increasingly close, was advising Penn to shrink the size of city lots as a result of the unexpected number of new arrivals. Land disputes would continue to bedevil Penn for the entirety of his first American visit.[6]

* * *

William Penn threw himself enthusiastically into the time-consuming and contentious business of founding. His challenge was to harmonize the political theorizing he had articulated in England with practical conditions on the ~
in America. He continued the laborious process of laying ou
and erecting functioning courts and worked closely with Hol
of warrants for surveys in both Pennsylvania, which now comp
of Philadelphia, Bucks, and Chester, and the Lower Counti
Kent, and Sussex. Penn's presence in the colony, along with h

resolving differences and the high regard in which settlers of both Pennsylvania and the Lower Counties apparently held him—settler Thomas Paschall, a Bristol native, called Penn "well approved of," and reported that on his recent trip to New York he had been "extraordinarily entertained, and . . . behaved himself as noble"—enabled him to manage many of these initial tensions. "The Governor's own energy, authority, and charisma, especially among his fellow Quakers, played a vital role in persuading his colonists to cooperate with one another, and with him."[7]

With each arriving ship, "colonists . . . poured in faster than acres could be surveyed." But gradually, as lots were laid out and inhabitants began clearing and building on them, the city of Philadelphia slowly took shape. New York merchant William Frampton planned a brewery and bakehouse; an Irish cooper named Archibald Mickle arrived in hopes of plying his trade; George Guest, a smith from West Jersey, expanded into the brickmaking business; Philip England, a recent arrival from Dublin, planned a tavern and ferry on the less developed Schuylkill side of the city. A Meetinghouse and burial ground was proposed for the Center Square, located midway between the Delaware and Schuylkill Rivers. Francis Daniel Pastorius, who represented the Frankfurt Company, a group of German and Dutch investors, arrived in Philadelphia on August 20, 1683, and by mid-October had obtained a warrant from Penn for a six-thousand-acre parcel that would become known as Germantown. Despite telling Penn in the summer of 1684 that "we are resolved to send over a party of people even before this winter," no other members of the Frankfurt Company would come to America. In his more than thirty years in Pennsylvania, however, Pastorius himself would serve a number of civic functions. By the end of 1683, Philadelphia was increasingly crowded with log houses, and some residents constructed dwellings set into caves along the Delaware River bank.[8]

Penn's promotional efforts did not end with his arrival in Pennsylvania. He attempted to keep his province in the public eye, to stress how successfully things were going, and to undermine unflattering rumors. Rumors of his death—often adding, gratuitously "that thou was dead a Jesuit"—circulated after his departure. Philip Ford traced some of these back to Penn's old adversary Thomas Hicks, and published *A vindication of William Penn* to lay the rumors to rest. Penn also battled gossip, much of it coming from West Jersey, about conditions in the province: "Whatever men may say, our wilderness flourishes as a garden, and our desert springs like a green field." And with settlers like Paschall writing back that "I never wished myself at Bristol again since my departure," Penn's promotional efforts proved immensely successful.[9]

From the beginning, Pennsylvania consistently attracted settlers, such that the time he had been there for a year, Penn reported that a hundred houses had been built in Philadelphia, housing six hundred residents, with roughly three thousand settlers in the territory as a whole. Throughout his first visit to America, Penn sent back reports about Pennsylvania's natural bounty, its thriving Meetings, and its growing city and towns. "I like the land, air, and food very well," he wrote soon after his arrival. "I never ate better at Lamb's or Lockett's [two noted London taverns]." He pronounced that "the air proveth sweet and good, the land fertile, and the springs many and pleasant" in a letter to Chief Justice Lord North. "The weather often changeth [without] notice and is constant almost in its inconstancy," he wrote, and listed the abundant resources in the colony, including "sassafrass, cypress, cedar, black walnut, chestnut, oak . . . diverse wild fruits as plum, peach, and grape . . . [and] mineral of copper and iron." To Robert Spencer, the Earl of Sunderland, Penn's former traveling companion on his European tour, Penn extolled the fragrances produced by American trees: "all send forth a most fragrant smell, which every breeze carries with it to the inhabitants where it goes." As for the animals, "I have had better venison, bigger, more tender, and as fat as in England." Although the natives "are savage to us, in their persons, and furniture: all that is rude," nonetheless "they observe property and government," and "they are an extraordinary people." And Penn managed to combine a plea for toleration with a report on conditions in America in a letter to his old friend in Ireland, the Earl of Arran, under whom he had served with such distinction at Carrickfergus.[10]

One of the most important pieces of business, of course, was to establish a system of Quaker Meetings throughout the province. The Philadelphia Monthly Meeting first met in January 1683, immediately gave its approval to Pennsylvania's first Quaker marriage, and began investigating the proper site for a meetinghouse. By the spring of 1683, Pennsylvania Friends had formed nine Meetings, and each of the three counties had its own Men's and Women's Monthly Meeting. The first Philadelphia Yearly Meeting took place in 1683, and the following year saw two Yearly Meetings—one in Burlington and one in Philadelphia—after which Yearly Meetings alternated between the two locations. In a letter to English Friends, Pennsylvania Friends compared their growth in America to the creation of woman out of man, saying that "we . . . are as flesh of your flesh and bone of your bone." Correspondence with Friends in England emphasized the thriving Meeting structure, which apparently attracted even those from outside the Society: Penn reported that "blessings flow amongst us . . . heavenly are our assemblies and large, and the people flock in that are not Friends." Even the governor of New York, "though a papist," attended a Meeting. All of these developments encouraged him in his aspirations for the colony: "Truth's authority is [raising] I hope an example to the nations." He also corresponded with Friends in Barbados, although a planned Barbadian Quaker settlement in Pennsylvania never came to fruition, due in large part to Penn's failure to secure access to land at the mouth of the Susquehanna River where they had planned to settle.[11]

And yet even among Friends, all was not easy. Jasper Batt, an English Friend with whom Penn had shared a London jail cell in 1671, apparently criticized the proprietor's failure to ensure Quaker control of Pennsylvania politics. But how, Penn argued, would a Quaker power grab in America play in England?

> We should look selfish, and do that, which we have cried out upon others for, namely, letting no body touch with government but those of their own way. And this hath often been flung at us . . . If you Quakers had the power, none should have a part in the government but those of your own way.

Penn pronounced Batt's letter "meddling, intruding, and presumptuous," but the next year Batt wrote again, claiming Penn had misunderstood his intent. His concern, he insisted, was that Penn himself was exercising too much political power. Batt pointed to the governor's veto power over all legislation and the high bar for amending the Frame of Government, as evidence of an unseemly power grab, particularly for a Quaker. Other Friends, too, raised cautionary concerns to Penn about his rise in worldly prominence. Stephen Crisp wrote to Penn that "I have had a great exercise of spirit concerning thee. . . . My prayer to God is . . . that you may be kept in the Lord's pure and holy way." "Prefer the Lord's interest, and he will make thy way prosperous." Like Batt, these Friends seemed to be warning Penn about the potential for the pursuit of worldly influence to distract Friends from a single-minded focus on the Inner Light. "I know it is always best with us when we are kept low, for the Lord beautifies the meek with salvation," Claypoole wrote in April 1683.[12]

* * *

The first Pennsylvania General Assembly sat from March 10 to April 4, 1683, in the new capital city of Philadelphia. As Penn prepared for that body's first meeting, he had become aware of the necessity of rethinking some of the details in his Frame of Government. The freeholders of New Castle had written in February that "we have chosen twelve persons for delegates to Provincial Council," but that there were very few people in their county, and of those, fewer still were "fit for public business." They sent twelve names and suggested that Penn choose three for the Council and place nine in the Assembly, "leaving your honor to increase the number as you shall see cause hereafter." Similar sentiments were expressed by the freeholders of the other two Lower Counties, and Penn agreed that "it may do best as the case stands, and our infancy considered."[13]

The immediate consequence of these developments was a radically smaller government. Rather than the seventy-two-member Council and two-hundred-member Assembly laid out in the Frame, Pennsylvania and the Lower Counties ended up with a Provincial Council of eighteen and an Assembly of fifty-four, which the governor pronounced "a good number at present." The Act of Settlement, which the General Assembly passed a week into its meeting, explained that "the fewness of people, their inability in estate, and unskillfulness in matters of government, will not permit them to serve in so large a Council and Assembly, as by the charter is expressed." But diminished numbers did not guarantee institutional passivity. The Assembly almost immediately petitioned the governor for the right to initiate legislation. As Jane Calvert notes, this dynamic would persist: "[T]he popular Assembly [sought] to co-opt the legislative powers of both Penn . . . and the Provincial Council, while Penn and his supporters tried to curb the Assembly in its grasping for power." Penn claimed that spring, in correspondence with English Friends, that the General Assembly "passed 83 laws, and all but 3 and those trivial without any nay—the living word in testimony and prayer opening and closing our assemblies in a most heavenly manner, like to our general meetings." In this claim, Penn was clearly expressing his continuing hopes for Quakerly harmony, and offering a rosy version of events, akin to other promotional literature that "assumed a civic identity that had not been achieved." Dissension was never absent, and the Assembly's early records report that some of its members were suspected of casting "undeserving reflections and aspersions upon the governor."[14]

This first General Assembly was a productive affair. It passed the Act of Settlement, a body of laws, and a revised Frame of Government. The alterations to Penn's original Frame—including the reduced number of legislators and slight revisions to the dates of election and meeting of the Assembly and Council, to accommodate the Pennsylvania weather—were codified into a revised Frame, which also explicitly clarified its applicability to the Lower Counties. This second Frame differed from Penn's original in some rather minor respects, but the structure of government did not differ radically from the Frame published the previous year. In Richard Ryerson's words,

> All in all, William Penn had reason to be pleased as he signed the second Frame of Government on April 2, 1683. . . . [His] colonists gained a streamlined, workable government. William Penn gained a government which, because of his suggested alterations, and the reduced size of the Council, he could dominate more easily.

Despite the apparent conservativism of the Frame of Government when compared with the earlier Fundamental Constitutions, which had occasioned such criticism from Furly and Sidney, Pennsylvania was governed from its inception by elected representative bodies. The political culture of early Pennsylvania was characterized from the beginning by attachment to popular rights and the empowerment of representative institutions to manage political change and pursue reform in an orderly fashion.[15]

* * *

Penn's status as a Fellow of the Royal Society enabled him to keep his colony fresh in the minds of an influential segment of English society. He had been elected in November 1681, although his involvement was never extensive and his signature does not appear in the charter book, whether because doing so involved subscribing an oath, or simply because of the press of business surrounding his colonial undertaking during that time. Although his sponsor, the London apothecary and merchant John Houghton, presented the society with a map of Pennsylvania on his behalf, it is unclear how many of the Society's meetings Penn actually attended. The Society likely considered Penn an ideal "resident correspondent" in the new territory that lay between New York and Virginia, though his close friendship with Society Fellows William Petty, John Aubrey, and Robert Boyle surely helped as well.[16]

In spring 1683 he wrote to Aubrey, "The air, heat, and cold resemble the heart of France; the soil good, the springs many and delightful. The fruits, roots, corn and flesh, as good as I have commonly eaten in Europe, I may say of most of them better." He reeled off a list of fruits and vegetables—strawberries, peas, beans, cherries, mulberries, walnuts, chestnuts—and noted that the "fish in these parts are excellent and numerous" and that he had begun a vineyard. (Despite his intention to prohibit taverns in the Fundamental Constitutions, Penn had opted for a series of strict regulations instead.) He provided an even more expansive account of life in Pennsylvania in *A letter ... to the Committee of the Free Society of Traders*. He could not resist opening the letter by assuring his readers that "I am still alive, and no Jesuit, and I thank God, very well." In evocative language—he described the air in winter as "dry, cold, piercing, and hungry"—Penn vividly recounted, in extraordinary detail and with great care, Pennsylvania's features, including the soil, air, waters, weather, fruits and vegetables, and wildlife, to say nothing of medicinal plants. The land was populated with "elk, as big as a small ox, deer bigger than ours ... and some eat young bear, and commend it," while the beauty of the native flowers in America outshone the gardens of London. He also described the natives in great detail: their physical characteristics and bearing, language, marriage and childrearing customs, and government. "In liberality they excel," he wrote, "nothing is too good for their friend," and "if they are ignorant of our pleasures, they are also free from our pains." Although in religion they are "under a dark night ... to be sure ... yet they believe in a God and immortality." Penn suspected them to be a lost tribe of Israel, a somewhat common (if misinformed) view at the time. Included with this letter was the famous *Portraiture of the City of Philadelphia*, Thomas Holme's map of the emerging city that presented a series of ordered grids bounded by the Delaware and Schuylkill Rivers and interspersed with public squares. Holme's 1683 map was hardly the first map of the territory that Penn had used to promote his colonial undertaking—the 1681 *Map of some of the south and eastbounds of Pennsylvania* predated it and figured prominently in Penn's pre-voyage promotional efforts—but it crystallized Penn's ambitious plans for his capital as a place in which virtue, commerce, and community might walk hand in hand.[17]

Although letters between England and America were often lost or misdirected, Penn's correspondents in England attempted to keep him informed of developments in his homeland. Philip Ford passed along news of increasing persecution of Quakers in Sussex. From John Tucker, who represented the Bermuda Company in London, Penn received news of Lord Shaftesbury's flight to Amsterdam in late 1682; from his sister, Margaret Lowther, news of Algernon Sidney's arrest and conviction along with others accused in the Rye House Plot against Charles II in the spring of 1683. Captain John Purvis, whose ship *The Duke of York* sailed frequently between London and America and whose brother-in-law, Alexander Parker, had witnessed William and Gulielma's wedding, wrote from Virginia in the spring of 1684—months after the fact—that "it is said that the warrant was signed for the execution of Col. Sydney, who is to be beheaded on Tower Hill." (Sidney had actually been executed the previous December.)[18]

He also, of course, received information of a more personal nature. In one of the first letters directed to him, written just weeks after his departure, Ford reported the death of Gulielma's mother Mary Penington, who had died in the company of her daughter. She was buried at Jordans, where Penn and Gulielma would later be laid to rest, along with Hannah and a number of his children. James Claypoole wrote in April 1683 that he, along with George Fox and Ford's wife Bridget, had recently visited Gulielma and the children, including an infant daughter born after her father's departure. (The child died shortly after Claypoole's visit: "It was near dead when it was born, which I think it never got over," Gulielma confided to Margaret Fox.) Penn's brother-in-law Anthony Lowther wrote him a warm and affectionate letter that admitted, given his "unactive" temperament, that he would likely not be coming to Pennsylvania, although he dearly wished to see Penn. With disarming honesty, Lowther admitted that "I am altogether unfit for any undertaking that shows the least of difficulty in it."[19]

In February 1683, insisting that "our hearts are good, and our hands are strong," Penn had told Virginia governor Lord Culpeper that

> I am mightily taken with this part of the world; here is a great deal of nature, which is to be preferred to base art and methinks simplicity with enough, is gold to lacker, compared to European cunning. I like it so well, that a plentiful estate and a great acquaintance on the other side

have no charms to remove, my family being once fixt with me; and if no other thing occur, I am like to be an adopted American.[20]

"If no other thing occur . . . " Of course something else *did* occur, which impelled him back to England rather than bringing Gulielma and the children to Pennsylvania: his escalating feud with Baltimore.

* * *

It is impossible to overstate the significance of Penn's contentious relationship with his southern neighbor. Built upon a zero–sum competition that turned on which of the two gained control over the Lower Counties, tensions between the two proprietors had begun well before Penn even set foot in America. Attempts by Baltimore and Markham to settle the boundary before Penn's arrival argu-ably worsened prospects for a peaceful settlement. Baltimore was understand-ably sensitive about threats to his authority, and Penn's inexperience on the ground in colonial affairs contributed to the rapid degeneration of relations. If the Penn–Baltimore dispute, as it developed over the coming years, would deal largely in mundane arguments invoking American landmarks and degrees of lat-itude, much more was potentially at stake, since the boundary questions evoked related disputes over royal authority to distribute new lands in America. That said, Penn was not the only proprietor with whom Baltimore quarreled; Baltimore also found himself in frequent contention with Virginia authorities over control of the Potomac River.[21]

Despite Penn's hopes that "a little time, by fair and friendly conferences (with God's blessing) will quiet and fix all to the common benefit of us all," relations with Baltimore became increasingly acrimonious in 1683. In brief, "Penn wanted ocean access, and Calvert did not want any of his land being granted away to William Penn." In late 1682, Quaker merchant George Heathcote, who would later settle in Pennsylvania, pointed out, in a letter to Penn, that the very process of surveying the line was fraught with difficulty: "In winter time it is hard and tedious observing, by land, both by reason of the uncertainty of the weather and the sun shining forth be-sides the many observations they must make before they bring it exactly to the true latitude." In terse letters written during March and April 1683, just five months after his arrival, Penn insisted that while he was "extremely desirous to yield in all points not essentially destructive to my right," nonetheless he was "not often deceived and will not easily be abused." (Perhaps the apple had not fallen too far from the tree after all. Recall Sir William's words to his son in 1666: "I yield to no men, and cannot be hectored out of anything.") The two men met in person at the end of May, again without coming to any agreement, and Penn told Baltimore that he had "upon serious thoughts, determined with myself, to embark for England by the first convenience" if a quick agreement was not forthcoming.[22]

In June 1683, Baltimore laid out his many grievances against Penn in a lengthy letter. Penn, for his part, began gathering depositions from settlers in the Lower Counties, chronicling more than a decade of Baltimore's abusive behavior toward them. Correspondents in the Lower Counties reported that Baltimore had encouraged people to refuse to recognize Penn's authority, and had derided him in harsh and personal terms. The next month Penn sent commissioners from his Provincial Council to negotiate once more with Baltimore. By late July, he had decided to send Markham to London to represent his interests before the Committee of Trade, with detailed instructions about how to argue his case and letters of introduction to influential officials, and offering lumber, otter skins, and snakeroot water for the king, duke, and others whose favor he hoped to curry. In August 1683, after hearing that Baltimore had informed the Lords of Trade of his side of the dispute, Penn submitted an extended and detailed narrative of his own. He continued to receive updates from loyal inhabitants of the Lower Counties. Baltimore's actions continued into the fall: undertaking unilateral surveys, laying claim to territories also claimed by Penn, and harassing or threatening settlers who refused to acknowledge his authority.[23]

* * *

By early 1684, the situation had deteriorated still further. Several Delaware colonists rejected Penn's authority, and Baltimore's cousin and Councilor, Colonel George Talbot, constructed a fort near New Castle. At Penn's request, Governor Dongan of New York attempted to convince Baltimore to demolish the fort and resolve the dispute peacefully. Penn apprised the Duke of York of his difficulties with Baltimore in February and again in June. Markham wrote to Penn from England, urging him to appear in person when the Lords of Trade heard Baltimore's complaint. Dongan agreed; Baltimore "is going for England," he wrote in early May, "and I believe if you could go over it would not be to your disadvantage."[24]

By late spring the prospect of armed conflict between deputies of the two men seemed increasingly likely. William Welch, Penn's commissioner, asked whether "we might not seize [Talbot or other supporters of Baltimore] and convey them to Philadelphia." Both proprietors sent agents to New York to scour the records of Dutch settlements along the Delaware River and interview longstanding residents about the conditions under which they had received their land, since the extent of Baltimore's patent depended on when and where the Dutch had settled earlier in the century. Penn enlisted New York merchant Nicholas Bayard to search the Dutch records there, and gathered affidavits from elderly settlers who testified that the Dutch had settled the west bank of the Delaware River before the arrival of the English. These plans were put on hold, however, by news of Baltimore's departure for England in late May 1684, at which point the die was surely cast. Penn would return as well, and the two proprietors would argue their cases in person before the Committee of Trade.[25]

* * *

The bitterness of the dispute notwithstanding, Baltimore was hardly the only colonial figure with whom Penn found himself at odds during his first visit to America. He was soon embroiled in difficulties with his eastern neighbors in the Jerseys, an outcome made all the more painful by the fact that nearly all the principals in the dispute were Quakers, and that Penn had been involved with New Jersey affairs since the mid-1670s. Shortly after arriving in America, he visited Elizabeth, East Jersey's capital, where Thomas Rudyard had recently been appointed Deputy Governor and where the political situation remained highly unsettled. In a January 1683 letter to Penn, Rudyard detailed his ongoing conflict with Samuel Groome, his Surveyor General, lamenting Groome's "angry, pettish humor." He also requested that Penn attend the upcoming meeting of the East Jersey Provincial Council in his capacity as proprietor. Rudyard hoped to use Penn's popularity with the people of East Jersey to calm ongoing disputes between the people and their government, not to mention between him and Groome. Penn obliged, hoping that his presence there might settle differences, but the contention continued unabated.[26]

Later that summer Penn was still attempting to mediate grievances between East Jersey settlers and the colony's proprietors in England, as well as to find a way to settle numerous disputes over land titles. To the proprietors, Penn suggested, as a gesture toward easing tensions, that more of them take up residence in the colony. At the time of his writing only four had done so, and Penn himself was unable to devote his full attention to East Jersey affairs. He recommended a conciliatory approach aimed at settling the land disputes then raging in the colony, even if it meant allowing some settlers to remain on land for which they lacked clear title. The editors of Penn's *Papers* point out, correctly, that "[Penn] tried to act as peacemaker in these disputes, but he never devoted the time or effort to the colony's tangled affairs that peacemaking required." In mid-July the proprietors appointed Barclay governor of East Jersey, replacing Rudyard, and named London Quaker Gawen Lawrie Deputy Governor, in an attempt to further soothe tensions. Lawrie, who was well known to Penn, set out for America armed with a long list of instructions regarding land titles, the East Jersey–West Jersey line, and the collection of rents.[27]

Notwithstanding their long association, trouble between Penn and Rudyard arose during the summer of 1683, when Penn, most likely aiming to solidify his own political influence in East Jersey, purchased an interest in the town of Elizabeth from resident Luke Watson. New York Governor Dongan reported to Penn, in October, that he had recently spent time with Rudyard, who "seems not to be well pleased with you, because he has heard you designed to buy one of his patentee's interests." Popular discontent with Rudyard simmered, and George Heathcote reported to Penn in November 1683 that many in East Jersey had applied to the New York government for protection. With Lawrie's arrival in the province in February 1684, Rudyard returned to Pennsylvania and sought his old job (Master of the Rolls) back, an attempt Penn rebuffed forcefully in June of that year. Rudyard eventually left America for Barbados, where he died in 1692.[28]

* * *

In his dealings with his East Jersey neighbors, Penn attempted to mediate between the interests of distant proprietors and the realities of political life in the colonies, using what personal influence he had to seek a resolution acceptable to all concerned. His relations with West Jersey, by contrast, soon became much more embittered and personal.

While Penn was on board the *Welcome*, his lawyer John Darnall, on Penn's instructions, purchased a major share of John Fenwick's interest in Salem, West Jersey. A letter from Darnall arrived from England shortly after Penn did, with instructions for claiming his ownership. Penn's agent James Nevill visited Salem early in 1683 to take formal possession, but encountered opposition from the inhabitants, who seem to have mistrusted Penn's intentions. He wrote to Penn in early March 1683, "Some said if the government belonged to thee, thou might assume it without our petitioning . . . thee thereto." Nevill informed the West Jerseyans that Penn "wouldst rather have it by consent of the people also" and called a second meeting, at which nearly sixty residents of Salem signed an agreement acknowledging Penn's authority. Conspicuously absent from these discussions was Fenwick himself, who, Nevill reported, refused to recognize Penn's legitimacy. "I do foresee," Nevill wrote, "that he and his tribe will be so arrogant, that the peace of the people will be much disquieted thereby if not prudentially prevented." Nevill suggested offering Fenwick land in Pennsylvania as a way to mute his influence in West Jersey; Penn ultimately bought out the rest of Fenwick's interest in Salem at the end of March.[29]

As 1683 wore on, Penn became aware of continuing rumors circulating in England about him and his colony: that he was a Jesuit, that he had died, that Pennsylvania and Maryland were engaged in armed conflict, that Penn had lost his port access and thus Pennsylvania faced crippling obstacles to developing its economy. Penn saw these rumors (rightly, it seems) as attempts to scare settlers away from Pennsylvania in favor of West Jersey, in the same way that Baltimore's discounted land sales in Maryland offered incentives to settle under Penn's southern neighbor. (To be fair to the West Jerseyans, they no doubt knew how Pennsylvania had sapped the numbers of migrants interested in settling in their colony, which had been in existence well before Penn's.) In response, Penn sent commissioners to present his grievances to the government of West Jersey, citing "great and . . . irreparable injuries by some members of your colony . . . a wrong and cruelty [if true] transcending what I have met with in the world from the worst of men." "England is filled with a noise of wars in Pennsylvania." He identified one resident of West Jersey—Thomas Matthews, a fellow Quaker, who admitted to sending reports to England but denied any malicious intent—as one of the chief culprits, and asked the authorities to fine or publicly rebuke Matthews. Further infuriating Penn, Matthews had described hostile actions taken by Baltimore a decade earlier as current events: "It is hard for me . . . to conceive, what other reason he could have to mention that affrightening cruelty . . . if not to terrify people from settling in [Pennsylvania]." In April of the following year, Penn was still complaining to authorities about "untrue and unkind reflections" about him emanating from West Jersey.[30]

West Jersey trouble would follow Penn back to England, and he wrote to Thomas Lloyd, President of the Provincial Council, in October 1684 that East Jersey governor Lawrie "has writ a most wicked letter about West Jersey business against me. What shall I say of such men."[31]

* * *

Penn's relations with his northern neighbor, New York, were not free from conflict either. Although much of his attention during his first year in America was devoted to settling the Pennsylvania government and the dispute with Baltimore, in the summer of 1683 Penn turned his attention to the Susquehanna River Valley, which "not only watered a vast region highly suitable for agricultural development, but also held the key to the coveted Iroquois fur trade." Having ownership of the land by royal patent was one thing; having clear title and possession was another, and depended on purchasing the lands from Iroquois tribes that controlled it and maintaining friendly relations with the government of New York. He sent commissioners to Albany to negotiate purchases with the Mohawks and Senecas, an undertaking that was interrupted by the long-awaited arrival of the new governor, Thomas Dongan, in August 1683.[32]

Whatever his eventual fate, in the shadow of his predecessor Andros's stormy tenure, Dongan understood the strategic importance of New York's retaining control of the fur trade. Upon first meeting Dongan, Penn's commissioner William Haig wrote that Dongan had "a slight opinion of thy affairs" and that "he proclaims himself Lord Baltimore's friend and I understand at second hand that he says thou has wronged him." Despite Penn's personal visit to New York in late September 1683, Dongan put a stop to all negotiations with the natives until the Pennsylvania–Maryland boundary issues were settled, and told Penn that the natives "find they cannot agree amongst themselves" about the Susquehanna lands. He recommended that Penn shelve his plans for a settlement there for the time being.[33]

In his dealings with Penn, Dongan showed himself to be deeply concerned about the implications of Penn's Susquehanna plans for New York's trade. As Gary

Nash has put it, "If Penn purchased the huge tract along the upper Susquehanna River from the Indians, he would immediately threaten New York's control of the Five Nation fur trade . . . Any such loss of the fur trade would have a devastating economic effect on New York as well as Albany." The relationship between the two men soured over Dongan's suspicions of Penn's pretensions to horn in on the fur trade. By early the next year, Penn's plans for western settlements had largely fallen apart; by March 1684 Dongan was writing defensively to Penn denying that he had bad-mouthed Penn behind his back, and insisting that "when I have anything to say against anyone, I do it always to their face." He also admonished Penn about his extreme sensitivity to criticism, telling him that "if you take notice of all people say you will be very uneasy."[34]

Notwithstanding this inauspicious beginning, Penn and Dongan shared a patron, the Duke of York, and by October 1683 Dongan wrote to Penn that "as for your affair with Lord Baltimore, it is my opinion that you should keep possession." Despite the cooling of their relationship, Dongan seems to have supported Penn in his deepening conflict with Baltimore: "I have always written to the Duke about you, as I would have done for my own brother, had he been in your place."[35]

* * *

During the first year or so of Pennsylvania settlement, Penn "encountered little overt criticism from his Pennsylvania colonists." But tensions, particularly with First Purchasers and merchants in the capital city, were never absent. The slow pace at which lots were surveyed and the adjustments Penn made as he faced the challenge of distributing them led to growing discontent. Penn's ongoing financial woes were exacerbated by his decision in July 1683—which he clearly viewed as a magnanimous gesture—to forego customs duties voted by his first General Assembly. But by the end of the year he was pressuring his tenants for payment of their quitrents, pointing out that "I receive neither custom, nor taxes, but maintain my own table and government at my own cost and charges." At the end of May 1684, twelve prominent merchants wrote to the governor requesting that he permit a sum to be raised by voluntary subscription rather than by enforcement of the excise tax on liquor that the Provincial Council had passed. (The governor agreed, though the sum seems never to have been raised in its entirety, evidence of, at the least, a lack of enthusiasm.)[36]

Just as he was realizing that he would have to return to England to pursue the dispute with Baltimore, Penn was presented with a remonstrance from a number of the leading residents of Philadelphia. These "adventurers and purchasers"— perhaps advised by Rudyard—pointed out that they had "of their own charge transported themselves and families into this city and province, and by their own expense in building and improvements . . . have turned a wilderness into a town of value," while the proprietor had failed to live up to the terms upon which he promised land to those who would make the journey to America. The petition mentioned the distribution of waterfront lots and the failure to guarantee mineral royalties to his settlers, the fact that Philadelphia still lacked a city charter, and Penn's continuing inability to provide them with land titles "free of Indian titles and encumbrance" as he had promised. Penn's terse reply, which concluded with his pointing out that "I have made the most purchases and been at the greatest charge of any proprietor and governor in America," did little to assuage his aggrieved settlers. The remonstrance provides a preview of the steadily deteriorating relationship with Pennsylvanians that would characterize much of the rest of Penn's life.[37]

Other issues requiring Penn's attention displayed undercurrents of tension as well. Notwithstanding the Act of Union and the naturalization bill passed by the Chester Assembly, Quaker-dominated Pennsylvania continued to coexist uneasily with the far more ethnically and religiously diverse Lower Counties. Such tensions often emerged in unexpected ways, such as the witchcraft trial of Margaret Mattson, a Swedish settler and longtime resident who had lived in the region since the mid-1650s. Charged with witchcraft and threatening her neighbors, Mattson's jury trial was presided over by Penn himself, in early 1684. The jury found her "guilty of having the common fame of a witch, but not guilty . . . as she stands indicted"—in other words, guilty of being thought a witch, but not guilty of being a witch. What Penn, who had years earlier been the beneficiary of a jury suggesting that he was guilty of "speaking" in the street but refusing to find him guilty of riot and unlawful assembly, thought of the verdict, we do not know, as he is not quoted in the Council's minutes. Mattson left Pennsylvania for West Jersey after her acquittal, and her co-defendant departed the area as well, relocating to New Castle. But the tensions that had become evident in the colony's early years—within the Quaker community, between Quaker and non-Quaker, and between Pennsylvania and the Lower Counties—would continue to bedevil Penn's efforts to cement all the residents of his territory under the umbrella of civil interest.[38]

* * *

As William Penn prepared to return to England to press his case against Baltimore, he could see, all around him, the beginnings of a major urban settlement in the making. More than 250 lots had been surveyed, and more than 350 houses stood, in the capital city. Upriver, work on his country manor, Pennsbury, located just below the Falls of the Delaware, continued under the oversight of his friend James Harrison and Harrison's wife Anne, though not without incident. The property had been purchased from one Thomas King, who, according to Harrison, committed "great and unsufferable trespasses and abuses" by hauling away sections of fence and building materials from the site without authorization. Little is known about the progress of the estate's construction, though it seems to have been largely completed by the summer of 1684, and a session of the Bucks County court was held there that March. Pennsbury was also listed in a letter of March 1684 as the location of the Falls Quaker Meeting. The proprietor left detailed instructions for Pennsbury's gardener, Ralph Smith, including which vegetables and fruit trees to plant and which walks to cover with gravel.[39]

Whether or not Pennsylvania was, at this point, a "holy experiment," as Penn had once suggested, is less certain. The early years of Pennsylvania had been a time of great promise and accomplishment, as well as of tension and conflict. William Penn had sharpened his argumentative skills in his years defending Friends against their adversaries in England, and he undertook his colonizing enterprise with the same sort of intensity and determination. There had certainly been no shortage of tensions. Penn had struggled with his neighbors in East New Jersey over land titles and control of islands in the Delaware River; with West New Jerseyans, some of whom attempted to discourage settlers from going to Pennsylvania by spreading rumors about conditions in the colony; and of course with Lord Baltimore. The conflict with Baltimore also complicated Penn's relations with his neighbors in New York as well as his attempts to purchase lands along the Susquehanna River. And of course he had plenty to keep him busy with his own colonists: in its first two years the Provincial Council heard cases involving public drunkenness, fornication, contract and wage disputes, runaway apprentices, tavern regulations, counterfeiting, and selling rum to the natives.[40]

If Penn envisioned Quaker harmony on the banks of the Delaware in the months leading up to his arrival in the fall of 1682, by the time he set sail back to London less than two years later, on August 18, 1684—in what one scholar has called "the greatest mistake of his life"—the colony had diverged in key ways from those earlier, and headier, moments. "What had begun as the first step in a holy experiment," another historian argues, "had become, in essence, a broadly conceived real estate development."[41]

Leaving the Provincial Council in charge of the colony, Penn sailed for England, having spent just a few months short of two years in America.[42] But not before offering his famous prayer for Philadelphia:

> And Thou, Philadelphia, the virgin settlement of this province—named before thou wert born. What love, what care, what service and what travail there have been to bring thee forth and to preserve thee from such as would abuse and defile thee. Oh that thou mayest be kept from the evil that would overwhelm thee; that faithful to the God of the Mercies, in the life of righteousness, thou mayest be preserved to the end. My soul prays to God for thee that thou mayest stand in the day of trial, that thy children may be blest and thy people saved by His power.[43]

9

Trouble on Both Sides of the Atlantic

Once the shock wore off, the fury must have followed almost immediately. Arriving in England on October 3, 1684, after a relatively quick ocean crossing, and having "got safe to my dear family and found them well," William Penn discovered that the most important papers in his case against Baltimore had been left behind in Pennsylvania. He blamed his secretary, Philip Lehnmann, who had served him for more than a decade and was responsible for packing the necessary documents. Lehnmann "has most carelessly left behind the York papers . . . the ground and very strength of my coming," he lamented bitterly in a letter to James Harrison, steward of his Pennsbury estate, just days after his arrival. "I am now here with my finger in my mouth. He could not have done me a worse injury nor Baltimore a greater service, if he had had the bribe of 10,000 [pounds] to do it." He implored Harrison to move with all possible speed to get copies of the relevant papers on their way to him on the next available ship, and to label them "to me, for his Royal Highness' service speed speed and care."[1]

The "York papers" included key affidavits taken from elderly settlers in New York, as well as transcripts of Dutch documents from the archives there, essential to his case against Baltimore. In a letter to Thomas Lloyd, president of the Provincial Council, and thus Pennsylvania's chief executive during Penn's absence, Penn was even more scathing. "Philip Lehnmann can never while he lives repair me this wrong by his supine neglect. So often did I speak . . . to him, be sure I have the York papers . . . he said they were [packed] and not a scrap of them to be found. This is a trouble beyond measure to me and an injury to the whole." Penn was beside himself with anger at Lehnmann, and also mortified and humiliated at his predicament. (Unable or unwilling to forgive the disservice done him by Lehnmann, Penn sent Markham back to Pennsylvania the next year and gave him Lehnmann's position as secretary.)[2]

Thomas Lloyd did not need Penn's urging to set out for New York, as he was already courting Patience Story, the widow of a prominent New York merchant. The two would wed by the end of December 1685, after which time Lloyd's absences from the colony would become lengthier and more frequent. But even at this point, his travels had an impact on the function of Pennsylvania's government. The Provincial Council, Pennsylvania's chief governing body, did not meet at all between late October 1684 and the end of January 1685. Robert Turner, who had served in several public offices in Pennsylvania and was one of the West New Jersey proprietors, recommended that Penn "expect not Thomas Lloyd to live [here]. His wife finds not this place sufficient for gain," and as late as September 1686 the proprietor would still be asking Lloyd if Patience might be willing to "give thee up sometimes" for the good of Pennsylvania and its government.[3]

In addition to rushing letters off to Pennsylvania as soon as he could, Penn also, not surprisingly, spent time with his family and began reconnecting with his closest friends. He wrote to Margaret Fox, thanking her for her kindness to Gulielma during his long absence. "My love to thee is beyond expression." He extolled the vibrancy of Pennsylvania's Meetings and the prosperity of the place, dismissing the "many stories" about problems in the colony as "the effects of envy." His favor with the royal family still seemed intact, which augured well for his attempts to relieve Friends of persecution and for the pursuit of his case against Baltimore. He had seen the king and the Duke of York at the Newmarket Heath horse races in October shortly after his return, he told Margaret, and "they . . . were kind to me." He also resumed his role as Quaker spokesman, and his close relationship with James facilitated the pardon of Richard Vickris, a London Quaker facing a death sentence under the penal laws. At Penn's urging, James convinced his brother to issue Vickris a pardon.[4]

Penn's legal struggle against Baltimore could only be settled in London, so the paperwork that had been left behind in Pennsylvania was of the utmost importance. Fortunately, his connections at Court enabled Penn to have the case postponed. The delay in his hearing before the Lords of Trade would turn out to be just the first of several developments that conspired to keep Penn in England far longer than he had intended. And it was essential to the success of Pennsylvania that its proprietor prevail. If Baltimore emerged victorious, it was entirely possible that Penn would lose his own capital city.[5]

Penn's mood toward Lehnmann could certainly not have been improved by his receipt of a letter from the secretary reporting the spoilage of a great deal of cargo on a ship largely owned by Penn. (The ship was commanded on this ill-fated voyage by Benjamin East, a well-known London Friend who earlier in the decade had, in a true East-meets-West story, married Hannah, the daughter of London merchant John West.) Although a good deal of the wine was spoiled due to its being "ill-packed" and "badly corked," apparently by Penn's indolent brother-in-law Anthony Lowther, Penn had hoped that the beer might "be sold for as much profit as is reasonable." Unfortunately, Lehnmann reported, half of it was ruined in transit.[6]

But in the early days after his return, Penn knew little about any of this, and he had other things to worry about. He was quickly reminded of the difference between being a Quaker in Pennsylvania and in England, when he was apprehended at a Meeting in Westminster, charged under the Conventicle Act, and fined £20. He would face similar difficulties at least two more times over the next year. His prospects in regard to future difficulties with the law would be greatly improved by a royal pardon granted to him and his family in early March 1686. Citing the service to the Crown rendered by Sir William, and his son's loyalty, the pardon halted all legal proceedings against Penn or members of his family for nonattendance at Anglican services.[7]

* * *

On February 2, 1685, King Charles II suffered a massive stroke. As Penn described it, in rather graphic terms, to Thomas Lloyd, the king had just sat down to shave when "his head twitched both ways or sides, and gave a screech, and fell as dead, and so remained for some hours." Four days later, despite a variety of interventions, including bleeding, cupping, and "ply[ing] his head with red hot frying pans," Charles, whom Penn described as "an able man for a divided and troubled kingdom," was dead.[8]

The king's passing not only changed the landscape of English politics but also altered William Penn's prospects in profound ways. The accession of Charles's brother James paved the way for Penn to wield influence at the highest levels of English politics and held out the prospect of attaining the goal for which he had worked so hard for so long: toleration for England's Quakers, and for all the realm's Dissenters. James told Penn just weeks into his reign that "he desired not that peaceable people should be disturbed for their religion." In accordance with the Privy Council's order Penn instructed the Pennsylvania Provincial Council to proclaim James as king immediately upon receipt of the news. Over the longer term, Penn's association with James would have disastrous consequences, as he quickly became identified (by the public, by other members of the political elite, and within the Quaker community) with James's increasingly unpopular policies. In these early days, however, Penn was hopeful that the new king, whom he had known for years and who had favored his Pennsylvania undertaking by granting him possession of the Lower Counties, would play an important role in the ongoing quest for political and religious liberty.[9]

Just a handful of years removed from a movement to exclude him from the succession amid rumors of plotting Jesuits, James II ascended to the throne with remarkably little disturbance. He took great care in the early days of his reign to avoid major alterations to his brother's policies, and went out of his way to voice his respect for the Church of England. "I shall make it my endeavor to preserve this government both in church and state as it is by law established," he assured

Anglicans. "I know the principles of the Church of England are for monarchy and the members of it have shown themselves good and loyal subjects; therefore I shall always take care to defend and support it." Left unspoken, but no doubt implied, was the question of the king's attitude toward the Church of England if its members ceased, in his opinion, to comport themselves as "good and loyal subjects."[10]

These early efforts at conciliation, however, did not fully mollify the governing elite, and James engaged in some impolitic behavior of his own. His promises to the church notwithstanding, many English Protestants expressed uncertainty about the intentions of their openly Catholic monarch, especially as he began to pressure his ministers to attend Mass with him. Rebellions broke out, headed by the Scottish Earl of Argyll and the Duke of Monmouth, Charles's illegitimate son who claimed to be his rightful heir. They were decisively defeated by early July and Chief Justice George Jeffreys, with the king's blessing, imposed draconian punishments. Both leaders were beheaded, and several hundred rebels lost their lives, with hundreds more sent to the West Indies in a series of trials that became known as the "Bloody Assizes." In the wake of these rebellions, Parliament provided the king with generous financial support, and James took the triumph over his enemies as evidence of divine blessing on his rule.[11]

But signs of trouble were present as well. Scholars have long pointed to character traits that hastened James's downfall, including political naïveté, a narrow-minded insistence on his way, and a tin ear to the perceptions of English Protestants. James also held unrealistic political ambitions: an Anglican Tory Parliament would clearly never repeal penal laws, which ensured the dominance of the Church of England in English society, or the Test Acts, which secured its monopoly on officeholding. Penn reported "great preaching here in town against popery, even at Whitehall, in the royal chapel," and that "the King goes to open Mass with his queen." James clearly took anti-Catholic preaching by Anglican clergy personally. While he assured them that "I will keep my word and undertake nothing against the religion which is established by law," James added ominously, "unless you first break your word to me. But if you do not do your duty towards me . . . I shall find means to do my business without you." Indeed, a year later, having seen Anglicans' unwillingness to support his tolerationist program, James would turn to Dissenters for support, and William Penn would play an integral role in that (ultimately unsuccessful) campaign.[12]

Further complicating the prospects for James's reign was the fact that the Protestant–Catholic tensions with which he had to contend were not merely domestic in nature. James's reign was caught up in events outside his borders, most significantly Louis XIV's revocation of the Edict of Nantes in October 1685. Louis's actions, which closed Protestant churches and schools and removed the legal protections for Huguenots (French Protestants) to exercise their religion, not only exacerbated English Protestant fears of a Catholic ruler, but, not unlike 1641, produced a stream of refugees to England with tales of Catholic violence and persecution. Fears that James aimed at French-style absolutism were widespread and, after the revocation, took on a new urgency, giving the overt anti-Catholicism that had long held sway in English public life a specific contemporary target.[13]

Though Penn surely exaggerated when he wrote that there was "in France, not a meeting of Protestants left," the popular reaction to Louis's action did not bode well for a Catholic king in England, much less for one so open in his devotional practices. Nor should it have encouraged a high-profile Dissenter, like Penn, who allied with such a king. Rumors claiming that Penn was Catholic had, as we have seen, been circulating for many years. He publicly disavowed them again, not long after Charles's death, when pro-Catholic verses appeared over the initials "WP." Denying that he was the author (or, for that matter, a poet), Penn pointed out the obvious fact that "the two letters begin five hundred names besides mine." He insisted again, in early 1686 correspondence with John Tillotson, Dean of Canterbury Cathedral, that "I am no Roman Catholic, but a Christian, whose creed is the Scripture." But the rumors would not be put to rest by mere denials, certainly not in a country that had so recently been gripped with anti-Catholic hysteria.[14]

The allegations would continue to dog him. Two years later, Penn's friend William Popple, who later became secretary to the Board of Trade and would translate Locke's *Letter concerning toleration* into English, reported hearing that Penn had "taken orders at Rome, and there obtained a dispensation to marry; and that you have, since then, frequently officiated as a priest, in the celebration of the Mass" with James and the royal family. Penn denied these charges as well. Accusations of Catholicism, or worse yet Jesuitism, were not merely a slander on one's name, but could easily lead to violence. During the summer of 1688, a mob of butchers smashed windows near Covent Garden, with cries of "No Toleration No Declaration No Baxter No Penn." (That Penn had been lumped together with his old nemesis Richard Baxter is no small irony, but one suspects that he took no great pleasure in it.)[15]

The increasingly close relationship between James and Penn has often perplexed observers. Scholars have long assumed that James did not really endorse toleration as a principle, but only as a means of empowering English Catholics. What could an autocratic Catholic have in common with the author of *A seasonable caveat against popery*? How could the champion of religious liberty make common cause with the *bête noire* of liberty-loving English Protestants? Yet the two men shared a great deal. James was just ten years older than Penn, and had served with his father in the Royal Navy against the Dutch. Penn and James were each members of marginalized religious communities that had been excoriated, savaged, and persecuted by the English government, encouraged by the Church of England. They were both intensely pious and devout, practicing their religion with the zeal of the convert. The presence of Penn's old Oxford friend and European traveling companion Robert Spencer, the Earl of Sunderland, who had regained James's favor after supporting exclusion in the late 1670s to become Secretary of State and president of the Privy Council, surely helped cement their relationship. Penn's ultimate goal was always the achievement of liberty of conscience, which he considered a fundamental right of all English subjects, and he was less concerned with the mechanisms by which that goal was achieved.[16]

* * *

Back in Pennsylvania, a successful 1685 Yearly Meeting attracted more than a thousand Friends to Philadelphia. Samuel Carpenter reported to the proprietor that things were "well and quiet and people industrious and pretty cheerful upon good and honest grounds," but went on to add, "I hope the Lord in mercy to us will restore thee to us again." Other accounts, however, suggested that after Penn's departure, the colony had begun a slow descent into recrimination, mistrust, and political infighting. One of the first extended reports Penn received after arriving back in England came from Nicholas More, who reported that "there is here much robbery in city and country, breaking of houses, and stealing of hogs" as well as tensions with the natives. More feared that "vices creep in like the old serpent." Thomas Lloyd virtually abandoned the colony while wooing the woman who would become his wife. The Assembly continued its campaign for real legislative power, a goal prohibited by the Frame of Government and denounced by Penn himself. To the south, turmoil had enveloped the Maryland government when Colonel George Talbot murdered the royal collector of customs, Christopher Rousby. And all parties awaited the judgment in the Penn versus Baltimore case.[17]

As had often been the case, disputes over land lay at the heart of much of the turmoil. Penn had laid out enthusiastic plans for an additional settlement in the Susquehanna Valley, to the north and west of Philadelphia. Ralph Fretwell, a wealthy sugar planter and one of the leading Quakers on Barbados, had arrived in Philadelphia in 1684 to explore the possibility of planting a Barbadian settlement there. Penn had suggested that "somebody be deputed, deliberately to see and understand things in these parts" before making any decisions. Initially, Fretwell was welcomed by the Philadelphia Meeting, and shortly before Penn left for England he issued Fretwell a warrant for land along the Schuylkill. But in the proprietor's absence, complications arose. The appropriately named Fretwell was, by all accounts, an argumentative and disputatious individual—Nicholas More wrote to Penn late in 1684 that "I wish him in Barbados again"—who made himself increasingly unpopular by his insistence on receiving the full allotment of twelve square miles along the Schuylkill River that Penn had promised. The Council put him off repeatedly, well aware of the compromises and substitutions that so many other settlers and First Purchasers had been forced to accept when the realities of the land's limitations had become clear. Perhaps most seriously, the mouth of the Susquehanna River turned out to lie within the borders of Maryland. A settlement was ultimately reached whereby Fretwell accepted six square miles along the Schuylkill, but he continued to complain to Penn and to anyone in Pennsylvania who would listen: about Holme, whom Fretwell claimed "wants abilities or honesty for the true interest of the country"; about Lloyd, whose "absence at New York" he deemed "considerable"; about the distribution of city lots; about Penn's own naïveté and gullibility in dealing with people ("thou knowest not men so well as thou may"); about the location of the Philadelphia Meeting, which Penn wanted in the Center Square but Philadelphia's Friends preferred nearer to the Delaware. The planned Barbadian settlement ultimately came to naught, and Robert Turner reported to Penn at the end of October 1685 that "as to Ralph Fretwell's great tract of land, it's at an end." Later that year, Fretwell returned to Barbados, where he died in 1702.[18]

The Free Society of Traders also continued to struggle, despite the fact that the proprietor had appointed many of its officers to positions of public authority. Samuel Carpenter, who had relocated to Pennsylvania after a prosperous career as a merchant in Barbados, brought suit in fall 1684, alleging that the Society was refusing to pay debts owed to him. Even though a number of the judges in the provincial court were Society officers, Carpenter prevailed. He cautioned Penn that the Free Society was deeply unpopular, and that "I am heartily sorry thou and so many good Friends should be concerned" in a Society whose actions "cannot but cast unkind reflections and have bad effects." His victory against such a well-connected body of merchants and close associates of the governor prefigured the eventual demise of the Free Society, which gradually dwindled over the course of the 1680s. Nor was Carpenter the only one complaining about the Society: James Graham, who served as Recorder of New York City and who would go on to become that province's Attorney-General, wrote to Penn late in 1684 that "the Society are still in arrears to me and take no course to give me satisfaction."[19]

By 1685, when More resigned as its president, the Society was short of cash, had poorly maintained its records, and had failed to communicate regularly with its English investors. Penn was already considering moving the Society's base from Philadelphia to England and bringing in new investors, especially given the dissatisfactions voiced in increasingly assertive ways by the Society's London subscribers, who petitioned that "we have had no account . . . [which] greatly dissatisfies us," and requesting a careful inspection of the Society's finances. A year later, More brought suit against the Society over the buyout of his shares. The suit, which polarized and divided the Philadelphia elite, further inflamed the feud between More and Pennsylvania Friends. Penn entreated Lloyd, in private correspondence, to heal the breach: "Try what is possible to quiet them; endeavor, by your private visits and admonitions to sweeten them; much good may come of it." But he also complained bitterly to the Council about the Society's poorly kept records, calling it "a great reproach to the province."[20] By the end of the 1680s the Free Society of Traders was, in the words of one historian, "all but defunct."[21]

* * *

The case against Baltimore was the reason why Penn had returned to England, and eventually he received the information he needed to pursue it, and (to his mind) establish that the Dutch had settled in the Lower Counties before the Calverts received their patent for Maryland from Charles I. In early September 1685, Baltimore and Penn personally attended the Lords of Trade, and Penn presented his evidence, which the Lords ordered copied and made available to Baltimore so that he might prepare his defense. Although Baltimore attempted to challenge the affidavits from elderly settlers, by late October the Lords had ruled in Penn's favor. On November 13, 1685, the king affirmed their judgment "that the land intended to be granted by the Lord Baltimore's patent was only land uncultivated and inhabited by savages, and that this tract of land now in dispute was inhabited and planted by Christians at and before the date of the Lord Baltimore's patent." Ideally, the decision would have resolved the controversy, but the tensions continued to simmer. Maryland officials persisted in their attempts to dissuade residents of the Lower Counties from acknowledging Penn's authority, often using heavy-handed methods.[22]

In the wake of his victory in court, Penn redoubled his promotional efforts, publishing *A further account of . . . Pennsylvania and its improvements* in December 1685. In it, he gave no hint of his private concerns about the conduct of his government and the colony's settlers, instead celebrating Pennsylvania as a land populated with "a collection of divers nations in Europe," who nonetheless "under one allegiance . . . live like people of one country, which civil union has had a considerable influence towards the prosperity of that place." An enormous bounty of produce thrived in the Pennsylvania climate: "wheat, barley, rye, oats, buckwheat, peas, beans, cabbages, turnips, carrots, parsnips, cauliflowers, asparagus, onions, shallots, garlic, and Irish potatoes," to say nothing of peaches, muskmelons, watermelons, and grapes. Fish and game were plentiful, the colony provided itself with beer and punch, and a brewhouse was under construction. *A further account* also included several letters from prominent Pennsylvanians praising the colony's development, including one from Turner that put the number of houses in Philadelphia at six hundred, many of them constructed of brick, and mentioned other noteworthy developments like an emerging fish and whaling trade. "Next summer," Penn concluded, "God willing, I intend to go back, and carry my family, and the best part of my personal estate with me."[23]

Penn could have returned to Pennsylvania in the wake of the ruling. He wrote joyfully to the Provincial Council shortly after the decision, adding that since he had emerged victorious in this all-important dispute, "I hasten to you when I can." He would repeatedly express his intentions to return, even as the horizon continually receded: "this fall" (March 1685), "not long" (July 1685), "next season" or "spring" (October 1685), "when I can" (October 1685), "with all the speed I can" (November 1686), and "this summer" (April 1687). Penn later claimed that he had actually begun preparations for a return to Pennsylvania immediately after the Baltimore decision, but when news arrived of events in America, "packet upon packet of the abuses of [Baltimore's] people" in intimidating settlers in the Lower Counties, contesting land titles and surveys there, and the continuing provocation of Talbot's fort at Christiana, he was forced to reconsider. Although by September 1686 Penn had apparently convinced Gulielma to make the journey to Pennsylvania with him—and mentioned, at one point, "Americanizing my family"—until he could be sure that Baltimore was complying with the king's order (and thus that he would not have to return to England yet again) he felt he had to remain in England.[24]

Ultimately, Penn was "willingly sucked into the whirlpool of English politics." He clearly saw his continued presence in England as serving a number of important purposes: for liberty of conscience, which he later called "my old post and province"; for better treatment of English Friends; and for sheltering Pennsylvania from the Crown's increasing attempts to revoke proprietary colonial charters. The movement to call in colonial charters had begun under Charles II and was accelerating under James, who had already brought Bermuda and New England under direct Crown control. In April 1688 the proprietors of East Jersey would surrender their government to the Crown. But with a powerful ally like Sunderland, Pennsylvania remained safe. "My being here," Penn wrote to Thomas Lloyd in the fall of 1686, "has not only advanced the reputation of the province, and gained many great persons into our interest, but prevented a storm as to us, that is falling upon other colonies." And of course he was only human: the attention lavished on him by the new king was surely flattering.[25]

Penn's victory over Baltimore paved the way for his increasingly prominent role in English politics. Liberty of conscience for Dissenters, for which Penn had worked his entire life, appeared closer than ever, with a sympathetic king who cultivated Penn's presence at Court. "I have been an instrument to open the prison doors for our brethren all over the nation." In the same month that the king confirmed the Lords' ruling in Penn's favor, James announced his intention to pursue repeal of the Test Acts and to employ Roman Catholics in public offices and the army. It was the first salvo in the political struggle that would consume the nation for the next three years. Parliament responded by refusing to vote the king funds, whereupon James suspended Parliament. It would not meet again for the remainder of his reign. Penn's proximity to the levers of power enabled him to press the king for particular leniency to Friends, who soon benefited from a suspension of almost all forms of persecution. Meetings, he wrote in the fall of 1686, were "open, large, and sweet," and the jails were being emptied.[26]

* * *

His victory over Baltimore notwithstanding, Penn remained troubled by a number of things. He was concerned by what he heard about Pennsylvania from others, both Friends and their critics. He strenuously denied rumors, passed along by Dutch Quaker Gertrude Diricks, whom he had met during his visit to the Netherlands in 1677, that Pennsylvania Quakers were engaging in military service and bearing arms. Penn was also forced to deny rumors about purported "retrospects" (claims that he had reneged on agreements to First Purchasers and others) in his dealings with Pennsylvania settlers. He flatly denied these charges: the April 1683 revision of the Frame of Government, after all, had been insisted upon by the General Assembly, not the proprietor. And reports of guns and violence likely referred to the decaying supplies at New Castle's Fort Casimir, and Talbot's and Baltimore's aggression upon residents of the Lower Counties, not to Pennsylvania Quakers.[27]

The proprietor repeatedly insisted to Pennsylvania Quakers that their enemies, in England and elsewhere, were eagerly watching their every move, and would love nothing more than to discredit them by pointing to division, contention, and strife in their province. Specifically, he cautioned against disrespect of royal officers, who continued to suspect Pennsylvania authorities of turning a blind eye to smuggling, privateering, and violations of the Navigation Acts. The colony is "sufficiently watched by friends and foes," and West Jersey residents were all too eager to hear news of factious behavior in Pennsylvania, which they assiduously spread to attract settlers to their own colony. "Cannot more friendly and private courses be taken to set matters to rights in an infant province, whose steps are numbered and watched? For the love of God, me, and the poor, country," he implored them, "be not so governmentish, so noisy and open in your dissatisfactions." He urged the Council to "punish vice" and to "accommodate differences quietly and quickly . . . If faults are committed, let them be mended without noise and animosity."[28] (In other words, embody Friends' principles in your practices.) In mid-June 1686 he urged the government to set an example for the people: "Remember that your station obliges you to be the lights and salt of the province; to direct and season those that are under you, by your good example . . . Keep down all contentions that may arise as much as you can," because "many eyes are upon you of all sorts." And later the same year he exhorted them, quite simply: "Be you peacemakers." But rumors and reports of strife continued to make their way back to England. As his second year in England drew to a close, Penn was still excoriating the leaders of the colonial government: "I am extremely sorry to hear that Pennsylvania is so litigious, and brutish." Between what was really happening in Pennsylvania and the malicious rumors spread by those who wish it ill, "we have much ado to keep our heads above water here."[29]

Penn was also deeply troubled by his colony's unwillingness to provide him with funds. His sense of personal honor was easily offended, and he would relate to anyone who would listen, and many who would prefer not to, how many thousands of pounds he had invested in Pennsylvania without any return. The amounts Penn cited were substantial, and ranged widely, from £1,500 up to £6,000. These figures may well have been accurate—the province did, repeatedly, decline to provide him with funds—but it no doubt sounded excessively tetchy and defensive to others who had also invested in the enterprise, especially coming from one who retained ownership of tens of thousands of acres in his own name and those of his children. Penn's professions of penury constitute a running theme in his increasingly bitter correspondence with Pennsylvania's Quakers, and his resentment of Pennsylvanians' ingratitude toward him grew increasingly intense as time went on.[30]

Some of his allies did attempt to secure funds for the governor. Markham reported in late August 1686 that he had urged the Council "many times the great charge and vast expense you have been and daily are at," without any success, and later acknowledged that Penn's orders were often received and read, and then "no other notice taken of it." Nor was this problem confined to Pennsylvania. The Lower Counties too gave "cold entertainment" to officials' attempt to collect revenue, and ongoing efforts by Baltimore to contest the boundary discouraged residents from paying rents that Penn was sure were rightfully his. On more than one occasion Penn directly tied his indebtedness to his ongoing inability to return.[31]

At least some of these financial woes were of Penn's own making. In 1683, during the enthusiastic and visionary early days of the colony's founding moment, the proprietor had agreed to accept rent payments in the form of produce, a crucial concession to the realities of a young and cash-strapped society. Three years later, he instructed his commissioners to begin collecting rents in specie, insisting that "my new rents are to be paid in money or silver, not in produce." His order had little effect, and Samuel Carpenter's ambitious attempt to create a comprehensive inventory of all rents owed to the proprietor came to nothing. What made this refusal to provide Penn with funds even more frustrating were the reports he received about the colony's thriving economy. After recounting the ships taking wheat and corn between Pennsylvania, Barbados, and New England, David Lloyd, newly arrived in the colony as agent for the New Mediterranean Sea Company, a London venture, wrote to Penn that before long "the province will certainly be the grainary of America." He praised the governor's vineyard at Pennsbury as well. And yet not a penny was provided to Penn himself, as he continued to fume in England—not even a sample of his own wine. "I could have been glad of a taste last year," he wrote to Harrison late in 1686.[32]

As had been the case since the colony's earliest days, land distribution and social conflict went hand in hand. While he had been physically present, Penn's personal touch had enabled him to minimize the fallout of many potential conflicts over land surveys and titles. But with the proprietor gone, the situation quickly worsened. The Fretwell case ended in acrimony, with the potential Barbadian settlement collapsing before it began and Penn receiving no money for his trouble. Since so much depended on accurate and reliable surveys of land and its assignment to the appropriate parties, the growing tension between Surveyor General Thomas Holme and his deputies had enormous consequences. Most seriously, relations between Holme and Charles Ashcom, deputy surveyor for Chester County, steadily worsened, with Holme accusing Ashcom ("that vile C.A.") of corruption, sloppy surveying, and a refusal to turn over copies of maps to the Surveyor General's office. Worse yet, Ashcom apparently surveyed a tract for a group of London Quakers that encroached on "the Welsh tract," a parcel of land promised to a group of Welsh settlers whom Penn had recruited personally and to whom he had promised extensive autonomy in organizing their affairs.[33]

Accommodating Penn's promises and surveying the Welsh tract gave Holme and his deputy surveyors no shortage of difficulty. By spring 1688 the Welsh settlers had sent Penn a petition with more than twenty signatures, claiming that he had reneged on his promises to them, that they were being summoned to serve on juries in both Philadelphia and Chester counties since their tract spanned that border, and that they feared being assessed taxes by both counties as well. Joseph Growden, a First Purchaser from Cornwall who was instrumental in settling Bucks County, became entangled in a dispute with John Gray, an ambitious Catholic gentleman who would go on to play a prominent role in West Jersey. Penn's Bucks County neighbor and good friend, Phineas Pemberton, described the Growden–Gray conflict as "the most railing and reviling business that I ever saw." Penn had granted Gray some land that Growden considered his own, and the dispute went on for years. The zero–sum nature of many of these land disputes made satisfactory resolutions elusive. "[T]o knock one in the head to make way for another I think is none of the best way to settle countries," Growden wrote bitterly to Penn in March 1688.[34]

Other, more personal, worries crept in on Penn as his absence from the colony dragged on. Reports of Thomas Holme's drinking, and accusations that Holme and Philip Lehnmann solicited bribes (they "move slowly in their offices, without bottles of wine and treats") caused him grave concern for both personal and political reasons. Holme had served Penn faithfully for years, a fact acknowledged by the proprietor even while he contemplated removing him from his position because of his "infirmity." "He is a man I love, and wish well, and I believe he loves me and my interest, but his infirmities and follies have cost me dear, in trouble of spirit, and reputation." Penn wrote privately to Thomas Lloyd, asking him to "speak earnestly" to Holme about the dishonor done to the province by reports of his "drinking collations." At the same time, Holme's bitter dispute with Ashcom threatened to snatch defeat from the jaws of Penn's victory by throwing the integrity of Pennsylvania land titles into disarray in the wake of his legal victory over Baltimore. And in February 1687 Penn was particularly galled to hear that "the great oak" (located either on his son's or his own land) "is felled, that I so often and solemnly warned people not to fell." From the fate of a single tree to something as important as the distribution of land, Penn was proving increasingly unable to shape events in his own province.[35]

* * *

He was further troubled by the sporadic information he received about progress on construction of his country manor, Pennsbury, located roughly thirty miles up the Delaware River in Bucks County. He did not receive any news about the estate— or any news at all, for that matter—from James Harrison, steward at Pennsbury, for nearly seven months after his departure. Responding to a letter from Harrison in September 1686, Penn complained that "I should have been glad of a partic- ular account of the improvements, in the fields, house, and gardens, but thou hast omitted it." Harrison was clearly a busy man, having served on the Council and as a judge in the Bucks County Court, and never managed to provide the proprietor with the level of detail he so craved. "Let me hear all," he implored Harrison as his absence from Pennsylvania entered its third year, in a plea that incorporated his specific concerns about Pennsbury as well as his broader dissatisfaction with news from Pennsylvania. But details remained hard to come by.[36]

Yet the lack of specifics from America did not dampen Penn's enthusiasm for the project. He took every available opportunity to send servants and supplies— including several slaves—as well as detailed instructions to Harrison about his wishes for the property. One ship arriving in Philadelphia in December 1685 alone contained more than 250 trees as well as bags of seeds, garden knives, spades, shovels, and hammers. He specified details about the various outbuildings on the estate: "I would have a kitchen, two larders, a wash house and room to iron in, a brewhouse and in it an oven for baking, and a stable for twelve horses." His correspondence regularly included detailed requests about walkways, courtyards, steps, and trees on the property (including, for example, specific instructions to plant a line of poplars along the walk from the house down to the river, the type of banister he wanted around the garden, the spacing of fence rails, and the shingling of Pennsbury's roof). He displayed special concern about the barge that transported him between Philadelphia and Pennsbury, instructing Harrison to be sure to put it in dry dock. He sent additional carpenters, smiths, joiners, and gardeners to assist the staff—whom he often called "my family." And in 1687, he instructed Harrison with a request surely familiar to anyone who has ever entertained guests: "Pray don't let the fronts of the house be common places to go in and out for their shoes will spoil the steps and boards, and their hands soil the doors and walls."[37]

Despite Penn's impatience, things at Pennsbury seemed to be proceeding well enough. Harrison's report to Penn about the 1686 harvest evoked an enormous bounty: peach trees groaning under the weight of the fruit on their branches; pears, plums, apples, berries, figs, and apricots in abundance; and sheds full of corn put up for winter. In fact, Penn's gardener James Reid suggested that he make an agreement with English gardeners, with whom he could exchange trees, herbs, and flowers, some of which were unknown in England, for a steady stream of English plants to supply Pennsbury.[38]

In all this talk of workmen and servants and Penn's "family" at Pennsbury, one thing becomes clear: William Penn owned slaves, and displayed no sign of a troubled conscience over it. In this sense he was not unique, neither among Pennsylvania Quakers nor among Quakers more generally. Many of the most prominent Friends in Pennsylvania—Carpenter, Norris, Claypoole— participated in the slave trade, abetted by the interconnections between the Pennsylvania and Caribbean economies, which provided most of the slaves in Pennsylvania. Claypoole, the Free Society's treasurer, wrote his brother in Barbados, late in 1683, to "send me four blacks." The nascent Quaker movement against slavery in Meetings seems not to have had a significant impact on their involvement. If anything, the "bother and expense" of dealing with sick and in- firm slaves seems as likely as principled objections to the practice to have dis- couraged Pennsylvania Friends from dealing in slaves, and a tax on importing slaves aimed as much at raising revenue as making a stand against the practice.[39]

For his part, Penn seems neither to have been troubled by slavery nor, frankly, to have given it much thought. In Ira Brown's catalogue of "Pennsylvania's antislavery pioneers" from 1688 through the Revolution, William Penn does not play a central role.[40] At some point, Penn seems to have acquired an African American fisherman, whom he instructed Harrison to sell in 1685. Having sent over a gardener, Penn recommended to Harrison that he should train up some others in the art. "It were better they were blacks," he wrote, "for then a man has them while they live." Near the end of 1685 he told Harrison that he had "as good as bought . . . the blacks of Captain Allen." In a letter to his Bucks County neighbor Phineas Pemberton, Penn communicated his distress about the loss of "my black" in a shipwreck: "I would not have lost him for 50 pounds sterling." In the same letter, he broached the idea of a building a house on one of his children's lands, "intending to buy blacks to put upon the place with a white overseer."[41] (We can be thankful that this project, like so many of Penn's plans for his colony, went nowhere.)

Although Pennsylvania Friends developed a strong antislavery tradition in the eighteenth century, such views were far less prevalent in the colony's early years. The 1688 Germantown Friends petition is rightly celebrated as a pioneering statement against slavery, yet no formal action on it was taken by the Monthly, Quarterly, or Yearly Meetings to which it was forwarded. "Even Quakers who began to feel that the enslavement of other human beings was wrong," Jordan Landes has written, "did not always see how they could extricate themselves from the practice on which they had grown economically dependent." The most extended denunciation of slavery was actually advanced by the schismatic "Keithian Quakers" in 1693. And the first mention of slavery in a transatlantic Quaker epistle came in the Philadelphia Yearly Meeting, which raised the issue in a 1712 letter to the Morning Meeting. During the eighteenth and nineteenth centuries, of course, Friends would develop a more consistent and coherent witness against the slave trade, and the history of abolition in the United States can hardly be written without an acknowledgment of their important role. But seventeenth-century Quakerism was another matter. Even for devout Quakers, the economic gain and luxury derived from the labor of slaves took precedence over any incipient moral scruples about the practice.[42]

The proprietor's painstaking attention to Pennsbury suggests that Penn intended to return soon, and to bring Gulielma and the children with him. Of course this had been his intention for some time, and he had written to her as he prepared to return to England in August 1684 that "I should think well of thy coming and living here, where a sweet place and retired is provided for thee and thine." But his wife had never been in robust health, and had suffered a serious illness after giving birth in March 1683. Her child survived only a few weeks, and Gulielma was herself laid up for a time after giving birth, writing to Margaret Fox that "I was very weak a long time after my lying in." Gulielma had considered making the journey to Pennsylvania after the birth of her daughter, perhaps in late 1683, but her health posed more of an obstacle than she foresaw, and before long news of her husband's impending return to England began to reach her. After she gave birth to a girl (the second daughter named for her mother) in November 1685, moving to America with the family became even less likely. In the best of circumstances, it would have been a herculean undertaking. Given his wife's frail health, his increasing importance to the king, and his worsening financial situation, Penn's return was well-nigh impossible.[43]

* * *

Although reports of discord and division troubled the proprietor, he may have been troubled most by what he did *not* hear: months went by with no news at all. "I wonder I have not heard from President Lloyd and my cousin Markham," Penn wrote in April 1686. To the president of his Council, his Surveyor General, and one of his closest friends, in the same month, Penn wrote in an exasperated tone that "I have writ to you several times . . . to which I never had any answer, nor the least respect or salute." Letters from individuals in government were appreciated, he acknowledged, but they lacked the authoritative nature of official communications.[44]

One of Penn's keenest frustrations was his inability to obtain a complete and updated set of the province's laws. The colonial charter had granted Penn and his legislature the right to make laws for the good of the colony, so long as those laws were consistent with the laws of England, and provided a five-year period for review of all colonial legislation by the Privy Council. Pennsylvania's laws, however, had never been formally submitted to English authorities, and as the five-year window approached for the earliest laws to be submitted, the proprietor pleaded over and over, to no avail, for a complete set of the laws. Without a clear sense of political and legal affairs, it would be difficult for Penn to defend Pennsylvania against the various criticisms leveled against it. It would also open the door to renewed efforts to bring Pennsylvania under royal control.[45]

All of these concerns, on top of his increasing involvement with the king's tolerationist program, left Penn oscillating between helpless anger and despondency. In a letter to Thomas Lloyd in November 1686, Penn lamented that hearing nothing in response to his requests for a copy of the laws, receiving no money from his colonists, and being constantly forced to deal with rumors about conflict and faction in Pennsylvania "almost tempts me to deliver up to the King and let a mercenary governor have the taming of them. Oh where is fear of God and common decency?" He thus raised the possibility of selling his colony back to the Crown, to be rid of the entire undertaking, the first mention of a plan that he would pursue intermittently for the rest of his life.[46]

And so as time went on, Penn's correspondence with Pennsylvania Quakers came to be characterized less and less by expressions of benevolence, and more and more by commands. Or, put another way, the professions of Quakerly love that open each of his missives seemed increasingly pro forma, quickly set aside in place of recitations of grievances and complaints. He himself admitted this, telling James Harrison in January 1687 that since his letters seemed "so slightly regarded," he would take another approach, "by proclamations under my hand and seal." Three such proclamations—about caves along the Delaware, land surveys, and cutting timber—followed within the space of a week, though it is not clear how closely, if at all, they were followed. From such a distance, with such uncertainties of communication, he was simply unable to effect change on the ground. Declarative commands about surveys to Thomas Holme (lay out 10,000 acres for Philip Ford, in this location; or 5,000 acres for someone else, at another) took months in transit and often arrived only after decisions had long since been made by actors on the ground.[47]

Furthermore, perceptions of Quaker favoritism, fanned by rivalries between Pennsylvania and the Lower Counties, seem to have been widespread. "There are grudges in some," Holme wrote to Penn late in 1686, "that none are put in places of power but Friends," and Pennsylvania politics blurred the boundaries of church and state. These disputes not only divided Pennsylvanians from those in the Lower Counties, but also cut through the Quaker community as well, with Holme observing to Penn that "many disorders and confusions ensue, all fellows in a church way, makes not so in civil government." Holme reported his failed attempts to convince those around him that Penn was due an income from the colony, reporting on one occasion "no hope of any supplies of money for public use," and that "our Friends like thee well to be their governor, if thou put them not to a penny charge."[48]

In an attempt to bolster his government, and due in no small part to his worries about the impending threat of royal intervention in Pennsylvania's affairs, in April 1686 Penn sent David Lloyd to the colony, naming him Attorney General. Lloyd arrived in Pennsylvania in mid-July and presented his credentials to the Provincial Council in early August. He came with Penn's hearty endorsement, described by the proprietor as "sober and ingenious." In his early months in the province, he attempted to chart a moderate course between the various factions in Pennsylvania and the Lower Counties, but Lloyd would ultimately become the proprietor's nemesis, a skilled and effective Assembly speaker who spearheaded opposition to Penn's interests. In the words of his biographer, Lloyd became "more a colonist with interests of his own and less a proprietary agent devoted to the interest of his employer." The story of Penn's deteriorating and increasingly bitter relationship with Lloyd would track the history of Pennsylvania for the next three decades.[49]

* * *

In addition to his growing influence at Court and constant worries about affairs in Pennsylvania, Penn maintained his ties to East and West Jersey. The East Jersey proprietors had a difficult job on their hands, attempting to settle land disputes in their own territory, resist attempts by the New York government to annex the colony, and ensure the orderly laying out of townships in the province. They were not helped by the actions of their Deputy Governors: the proprietors rebuked Lawrie and Rudyard on several occasions for reserving the best lands for themselves and failing to keep the proprietors informed of developments in the province. Their dissatisfaction never abated, and they replaced Lawrie with Lord Neill Campbell in September 1686. In the meantime, as the Crown realized that its revenue from New York was declining as ships began docking in New Jersey and the Lower Counties, James began the process of bringing East

Jersey under direct Crown rule. Ultimately, the proprietors would surrender their charter to the Crown in April 1688.[50]

And, of course, Penn remained a well-known member of, and spokesman for, the Society of Friends. As a prominent member of the Meeting for Sufferings, he continued to seek relief from penal legislation for Friends who found themselves under attack by local magistrates, many of whom were reluctant to follow the king's announced policies of leniency toward Dissenters. In late 1686, Penn toured northern and western England, visiting Quaker Meetings at Yorkshire, Manchester, Oxfordshire, and Cheshire. "Meetings never larger, or better," he wrote back to Pennsylvania. And his involvement with the king seemed to bear fruit: with the king's pardon of Friends and the publication of his Declaration of Indulgence in 1687, conditions improved dramatically for Dissenters. He retained a number of important connections with Dutch Quakers as well, none more so than William Sewel, the prolific Quaker historian and translator. Sewel wrote to Penn frequently regarding the translation of Penn's works into Dutch, often laboring over particular passages or citations from classical sources or criticizing the quality of others' translations. Sewel's letters to Penn, which he usually wrote in Latin, are warm and affectionate. Even as Penn's political and personal fortunes hit a low point in the years to come, Sewel would consistently defend him against critics. "I never doubted the sincerity of your heart," he opined, and unfortunately "there are many who have rejoiced in secret over your ill fortune." Sewel used his position at the *Amsterdam Courant* to "suppress or refute distorted rumors about you" when such circulated in the Netherlands.[51]

And even in the busy days of June 1688, as the political situation roiled with uncertainty and opposition to James reached a fever pitch, Penn took the time to speak at the funeral of Rebecca Travers, who had spent more than thirty years as a leading Quaker, a "fearless and powerful preacher," and a confidante of early Quaker leader James Nayler. In his remarks, which said little about Travers herself but rather emphasized the importance of perseverance and faithfulness "in the midst of all our trials and exercises," Penn no doubt expressed his own sense of unease about the rapidly changing world in which he was operating.[52]

* * *

And yet as his control over Pennsylvania slipped away from him, Penn found his influence in England growing. James's repeal campaign would not begin in earnest until the spring of 1687, but the king's efforts to dismantle the persecutory apparatus of the English state through the use of pardons and the dispensing and suspending powers (the authority of the king to excuse individuals or groups from the punishments incurred by particular laws) were already under way. Facing continued resistance by Anglicans to his calls for toleration, James cast off his Tory allies and turned to Dissenters over the course of 1686. This change in strategy, not surprisingly, led Penn into deeper and deeper involvement in the movement for toleration. In support of the king's policy, he engaged, as he had so many times before, in the polemical and pamphlet wars over toleration. He defended the Duke of Buckingham's 1685 *Short discourse upon the reasonableness of men's having a religion*, a plea for the toleration of Dissenters, against a variety of its critics, including an unnamed interlocutor who claimed that Buckingham had been seduced by "the Pennsylvanian" into Quaker errors. (Buckingham was, to say the least, no Quaker.) Penn also visited the Duke in person while touring the north of England late in 1686, attempting to convince him to reenter public life in support of toleration. Despite warm and affectionate words for Penn himself, Buckingham demurred, citing his declining health. He died the next year.[53]

In his defenses of the Duke, Penn insisted that England's penal legislation and Test Acts represented governmental overreach, when an individual "pays twenty pounds monthly, and has two-thirds of his real estate exposed to sequestration" simply for refusing to attend the established church. He lamented the uncharitable and persecuting spirit with which the Church of England conducted itself in its treatment of Dissenters: "There's not one word of winning one poor Dissenter to the church, no more than of tolerating them out of the church. But how peaceable soever he be, he is cast out for a vessel of wrath, good for nothing but to be hanged here, and damned hereafter."[54]

Penn's involvement in the debate over Buckingham's *Short discourse* culminated in his *Perswasive to moderation*, an extended work that combined a plea for liberty of conscience with a clear sense of its limits. As before, Penn defined liberty of conscience as the "free and open profession and exercise of . . . the apprehension and persuasion a man has of his duty to God." Since intense debate persisted on these questions, Penn insisted on setting aside, politically speaking, the question of whether one religion was "true." He also insisted that claims of conscience could not justify criminal or uncivil behaviors. In other words, Penn hedged in the conscience he had just liberated with moral limitations: "I always premise, this conscience to keep within the bounds of morality, and that it be neither frantic nor mischievous, but a good subject, a good child, a good servant: As exact to yield to Caesar the things that are Caesar's, as jealous of withholding from God the thing that is God's."[55]

A good subject, a good child, a good servant: this was an ideal of citizenship to which anyone, of any religious persuasion, could aspire. To the degree that they comported themselves peacefully and observed basic norms of civility, individuals deserved the liberty to seek God in the way they felt was best.

A Perswasive to moderation advanced a wide range of political and religious arguments in favor of toleration. Studiously avoiding any explicit reference to his own colony, Penn mentioned "the down-right toleration in most of his Majesties plantations abroad" as proof that toleration could coexist with monarchy. At the heart of his argument was a pragmatic notion of balanced governance. "Interest will not lie," Penn wrote on more than one occasion. Repealing penal laws would reconcile Dissenters to the government and ensure that "no man suffer[s] in his civil right for the sake of . . . dissent." He also included the standard arguments about prosperity, arguing that "as men, in times of danger, draw in their stock, and . . . transmit it to other banks . . . so this mildness entreated, setting every man's heart at rest, every man will be at work, and the stock of the kingdom employed."[56]

Rulers also benefited from toleration: "severity . . . is [injurious] to the interest of the prince" and "the interest of prince and people . . . conspire in the repeal" of penal legislation. Persecution presented Dissenters with the options of "be ruined, fly, or conform": forfeit one's goods, leave for other countries or colonies, or hypocritically conform to the established church without believing in its doctrines. Granting liberty to Dissenters secures the government both at home and abroad, since "to be loved at home, is to be feared abroad."[57]

The *Perswasive* also offered the standard religious and epistemological defenses of toleration that had been part of Penn's (and the larger tolerationist movement's) rhetorical arsenal since the late 1660s: that conscience could not be forced; that Christ taught forbearance; that as the Church of England eschewed claims of infallibility, to persecute its critics was unreasonable. The essence of the Christian religion, he claimed, was "admitted of all in the text, and by all acknowledged, in the Apostle's Creed." (This claim was, to say the least, a highly optimistic gloss of the differences that divided Protestants in England, but it made a more basic political point about shared Protestantism overshadowing doctrinal differences.) Dissenters were not seditious sectaries but decent people who contributed to the welfare of their communities.[58]

And yet Penn aimed to be realistic. He never called for disestablishing the Church of England, nor did he attack the church's privileged position in society or the government:

> That the Church of England is preferred, and has the fat of the earth, the authority of the magistrate, and the power of the sword in her son's hands, which comprehends all the honors, places, profits, and powers of the kingdom, must not be repined at: Let her have it, and keep it all . . . But to ruin Dissenters to complete her happiness, is Calvinism in the worst sense.

The bottom line for Penn during these debates, harkening back to his view of the legitimate functions of government, was that English law provided plenty of resources for authorities to punish criminal behavior and actual political subversion without resorting to punishments for conscientious worship. "We have other laws enough to catch and punish the offenders."[59]

* * *

Penn's relationship with James strengthened as the king's pursuit of toleration deepened. In the summer of 1686, James sent Penn to consult with William of Orange, the Dutch Stadtholder (who was married to James's daughter Mary), a mission that Penn disguised by attending the Amsterdam Yearly Meeting and visiting Friends in Germany. Penn met William several times, attempting to persuade him to support James's plans to repeal the English penal laws and the Test Acts. The attempt failed, though the trip did allow Penn to see his old friend Henry Sidney, then serving as English envoy to The Hague. Sidney would play the role of go-between for Penn and William again in September 1687, when he reported the prince's continued unwillingness to endorse James's repeal program.[60]

William of Orange's skepticism of James's intentions—especially given the widespread concern about Louis XIV and the plight of Protestants in France— was shared by many English Protestants as well. In July 1686, James revived a system of ecclesiastical commissioners to suppress anti-Catholic preaching in London and to ensure royal oversight of a range of church-related institutions. The Crown sponsored the publication of Henry Care's *A vindication of the proceedings of His Majesties ecclesiastical commissioners*, which provided an historical and legal justification for the king's actions, but debates over the Ecclesiastical Commission had more to do with political questions than historical ones. "Those who defended the Commission tended . . . to emphasize the personal supremacy of the king. Many who opposed it offered a constitutional case stressing parliamentary limitations on the royal prerogative," Jacqueline Rose explains. In the absence of a sitting Parliament, the success of James's attempts at toleration depended upon his use of royal proclamations as well as the dispensing and suspending powers. The scale of James's use of those powers alarmed many observers already primed to worry about Catholics' tyrannical pretensions.[61]

At the heart of James's determination to pursue toleration by royal decree was an expansive understanding of the monarch's authority. James's confidence in his practice of dispensing with the requirements of the Test Acts was bolstered by the June 1686 ruling in *Godden v. Hales*, which upheld his claims to extensive dispensing powers. Parliament, for its part, worried about power-hungry kings seeking to rule arbitrarily. Penn and others like him, who supported the king's program, viewed the penal laws and Test Acts as fundamental infringements on English liberties, and thus had fewer scruples about the mechanisms by which persecution was eased. Henry Care's defense of James focused on "the resolution of this single question, Whether persecution in itself be lawful? . . . They, and they only, that will undertake to justify the affirmative, may reasonably appear for the continuance of the penal laws and Tests." This was certainly Penn's view and, in his own mind at least, it balanced his longstanding commitment to consent-based politics and fundamental law with his defenses of James's sweeping use of the suspending and dispensing powers. If liberty of conscience was a fundamental or natural right, anything the king did to promote or ensure it might be justified.[62]

Ultimately, James decided to pursue liberty of conscience in a two-step fashion: first, by proclamation and declaration; and second, by calling for the election of a new Parliament that would enshrine the terms of the Declaration into law. His first Declaration, issued in February 1687, applied only to Scotland. That April, James issued a Declaration of Indulgence for England, and placed Penn in charge of securing Dissenters' addresses of thanks. Nearly two hundred were forthcoming, although historians have long debated how genuine such addresses really were. The London Yearly Meeting endorsed an address of thanks to the king, and Penn led a delegation of Friends to Windsor Castle to deliver it in person. Although Penn's close association with an increasingly unpopular king had produced benefits for Friends and other Dissenters, his presence among the ranks of courtiers caused controversy among Quakers, some of whom feared a backlash. (His old co-defendant William Mead was one of them.) As the king became more firmly committed to the repeal of penal laws and the Test Acts, and as Penn became more central to that effort, Penn informed his colonists that his work on behalf of Friends in England required him to remain there: "Friends unwilling and the King and some of his ministers not very inclinable to part with me till this liberty of conscience be established by a repeal of all those laws the King has so tenderly suspended." Once again, a return to Pennsylvania would have to wait.[63]

* * *

August 1687 saw the publication of *A letter to a Dissenter*, penned by George Savile, the Marquis of Halifax. The *Letter* acknowledged that Dissenters surely must welcome the relief from persecution granted by James's Declaration, but it warned them about the consequences of James's aggrandizement of the monarch's powers and sought to sow doubt about the king's motives. Had the Catholic church really suddenly come to embrace the interests of Protestant Dissenters? Did the king really believe in liberty of conscience as a principle? Surely not, Halifax insisted; rather, Dissenters "are . . . to be hugged now, only that you may be the better squeezed at another time." Dissenters should note the dangerous precedent that the king's actions were setting, and although acknowledging "the benefit of the end," Halifax insisted that Dissenters should "look into the danger of the means." Admitting that the Church of England had treated Dissenters badly in the past, Halifax assured them that "all the former haughtiness towards you is forever extinguished." The real threat to Dissenters' liberty was not the church but a king who ruled by proclamation and declaration rather than by settled law.[64]

William Penn's contribution to this dispute, which embraced both the procedural and the substantive dimensions of the issue of toleration, took the form of three *Letters from a gentleman in the country*, published in spring 1687, and a subsequent larger tract entitled *Good advice to the Church of England*. In his *Letters*, Penn insisted, repeatedly, that repeal of the penal laws and Test Acts was in the country's civil interest. After all, by the late 1680s, the realm had endured more than a century of strife over religion with no end in sight, and it was simply acknowledging the obvious to admit that "we cannot agree to meet in one profession of religion." The government's time, effort, and power was better spent on projects benefiting the whole. In this view, hysteria over Catholics "hav[ing] a few offices with us" was wildly overblown, since Protestants and Catholics had been "hunting, hawking, gaming, and marrying" side by side for years.[65]

In the *Second letter*, Penn suggested that the common aphorism "Let every tub stand on its own bottom" provided a fruitful illustration of the appropriate arenas of church and state: "The government should stand on its own legs, and the church upon hers. The legs of the civil government, is the civil interest of the government, which is that of all the people under it, so that the government is obliged to secure all, because all are for their own interest bound to secure it." Penn repeated this imagery of seating things on their proper "bottom" several times during these years. Defending himself against charges of Catholicism, he opined that "if we could not all meet upon a religious bottom, at least we might meet upon a civil one . . . the common interest of King and people." A devotion to civil interest would allow for the accurate assessment of individuals' skills and their potential to contribute to the common good, he claimed in the *Third letter*: "Should a man's being of any religion, hinder him from serving the country of his birth? Does his . . . believing transubstantiation, render him uncapable of being a good clerk? It were as reasonable to say, that tis impossible for a phanatic to be a good shoemaker, or a papist a good tailor. The very notion is comical."[66]

Penn firmly believed that the primary obstacle to pursuing civil interest was the Church of England, which monopolized public offices and benefited from property seizures and fines inflicted on Dissenters. The church represented not "England" but merely a portion of it, and its dominance was maintained in place by the coercive authority of the state. The real reason that the church opposed toleration, he insisted, was its lack of confidence in its own ability to attract members if it were deprived of the authority to force people into its churches. He also blasted the blatant inconsistency between the church's long profession of passive obedience and its current role in opposing James. Was this really the same church that had steadfastly defended King Charles I during the

Civil Wars? It seemed to him to have "quit those high principles of loyalty and Christianity she valued herself once upon . . . [and] divid[ed] in judgment from him that she has acknowledged to be her ecclesiastical head."[67]

* * *

In summer 1687 James finally dissolved Parliament, and his repeal campaign began in earnest. Coordinated and funded by Crown officials, it was helped along by a network of Dissenters who worked to ensure the election of a sympathetic Parliament and the removal of uncooperative local officials. Penn was instrumental in this effort, the "intellectual architect of the king's toleration project and one of its leading exponents." He was involved in pragmatic details like overseeing the regulation of English towns, and he accompanied the king on his progresses through the country as he sought to drum up support for the policy of repeal.[68]

James hoped that by securing parliamentary ratification of the repeal of persecutory legislation, and a "new Magna Charta," he could "settle [liberty of conscience], so that it shall not be in the power of after ages to alter it." Penn had proposed to "have . . . constraint upon conscience prevented by a glorious Magna Charta for the liberty of it." In other words, he sought "another Great Charter, to bury all our prejudices, and establish a lasting civil union among the inhabitants of this ancient and famous kingdom." His fellow royal propagandist Henry Care, with whom Penn worked closely in support of the king, sought to "establis[h] liberty of conscience on so firm a legal basis, that it shall not be in the power . . . of any one party to invade the immunities of the rest." Fundamental law had played a central role in Penn's political thinking since his earliest entry onto the public scene, and his support of James's efforts reflected this emphasis: a new "Magna Charta for liberty of conscience, established . . . by the wisdom of a Parliament," would enshrine liberty of conscience as a fundamental right. He wrote to the Commissioners of State in Pennsylvania that "we hope here for a Parliament to settle a great charter for liberty of conscience," and added, rather optimistically, that "things here are well disposed toward it."[69]

But events would show the depth of skepticism toward James's plans, skepticism that the king would ultimately be unable to overcome. As one critic pointed out, any king who would set aside parliamentary legislation could surely find a way to evade a "new Magna Charta." Another voiced skepticism about whether a king who had trampled on the old Magna Carta would really honor a new one. Of course much of this hostility and opposition was rooted in the rich soil of English anti-popery, and the repeal campaign faced an uphill battle from the beginning. The reasons for James's failure are manifold, but the visceral nature of English anti-Catholicism surely played a large part. "James and the repealers faced a difficult challenge," writes Scott Sowerby, "how to deal with an opposition so wedded to a conspiratorial narrative that any attempt to counter the narrative was taken as further evidence of a conspiracy." The repeal movement was, in other words, a movement against conspiratorial paranoia, an attempt to envision a multiconfessional British future.[70]

Furthermore, accomplishing this legislative task would require quite a different Parliament than the one that had sat for the past three decades, and thus the king's repeal program involved a concerted effort to remove unsympathetic officeholders and replace them with more agreeable candidates. In support of his agenda, the king embarked on a trip through western England in August and September 1687. Penn accompanied him, and large crowds turned out to hear Penn speak on behalf of toleration. Many, although surely not all, of these crowds were friendly; he spoke to thousands in Bristol and Marlborough, but was shouted down by a crowd in Shrewsbury. He certainly attracted the ire of those members of Parliament ejected by James's attempt to secure a compliant Parliament. But the king's overtures to Dissenters and former Whigs were not entirely without success, as many voiced a willingness to vote for repeal in the upcoming Parliament. (Nor were Anglicans uniformly opposed; Sir William Petty had offered several proposals earlier in James's reign and endorsed the idea of a toleration scheme that included Catholics.) But the depth of resistance to James's program became clear to Penn by early 1688, as he and others involved in the repeal movement gathered answers to questions posed to more than two thousand officeholders across England and Wales. The results were, to put it mildly, not encouraging, and even without the Dutch invasion of 1688, it is far from clear that James's plan had any chance for success.[71]

What William Penn thought about the king's persistence in his muscular and frontal assault on the Church of England, we do not know. Much of the documentary evidence from the period has been lost or, more likely, destroyed. Penn seems to have become convinced that repealing the penal laws might be possible, but that Parliament would never agree to undo the Test Acts, and that pushing too hard for that goal could backfire. In this regard, he allied himself with his old friend Sunderland, who was quickly falling out of favor with James and would be dismissed from the king's service in October 1688. (Not even a rather desperate conversion to Catholicism in June of that year could salvage Sunderland's position.) But James would not be deterred, and had clearly misread the Anglican doctrine of nonresistance, which he had pushed to its breaking point.[72]

James continued to appoint Catholics to positions in the army and in England's universities. In none of these cases did the struggle gain more notoriety than that of Magdalen College, Oxford, where the conflict stretched on for more than seven months, with Penn attempting (unsuccessfully) to mediate the dispute and to convince the Magdalen Fellows that continued resistance to the king's wishes would invite a royal takeover of the entire college. James ultimately prevailed, but the loss of trust brought about by his heavy-handed imposition of royal favorites was significant. The Magdalen affair not only involved anti-Catholic sentiment but also raised fears that James was about to begin seizing his subjects' property, since college fellowships were considered the property of their holders.[73]

In April 1688, James reissued his Declaration, and repeated his intention to have his actions confirmed by Parliament. In enacting the provisions of the Declaration into law, the king claimed, liberty of conscience could be put on "such just and equal foundations as will render it unalterable, and secure to all people the free exercise of their religion forever." He also insisted that the Declaration be distributed to all the parish churches by the bishops so that it could be read from every Anglican pulpit. When seven bishops appealed to the king to withdraw his order—hoping to avoid having to read the Declaration, though not contesting the Declaration itself—James had them arrested, sent to the Tower, and tried on charges of seditious libel. It was a move that divided even his closest advisors. A London jury found the bishops not guilty in June 1688, and a public celebration ensued, illustrating just how far James had fallen out of public favor. Soon the bishops' prosecution became intertwined with political rebellion: on June 30, 1688—the very day of the bishops' acquittal—the "Immortal Seven" set the Revolution in motion by drafting their invitation to William to intervene in defense of English laws and liberties.[74]

Another event during June 1688 sealed James's political fate: the birth of a son. While the Catholic king lacked a legitimate male heir, many English Protestants were content to endure his policies, trusting Providence that his (Protestant) daughter Mary, next in line for the throne and married to the staunchly Protestant Prince of Orange, would succeed her father. But the birth of a prince upset all such calculations, presenting the kingdom with the prospect of not only a Catholic sovereign, but a Catholic heir and successor. In August, James issued writs for a parliamentary election, but events would soon overtake his plans. As credible accounts of William's preparations for invasion reached him, James offered concessions to his critics. But despite this desperate attempt to salvage his reign, the repeal effort came crashing down all around James—and Penn. By the end of 1688, William would be in England with his army, James would be in France, and William Penn would be under suspicion of treason.

* * *

1688 is remembered in England, of course, for the Glorious Revolution and the events that led to the establishment of the Protestant succession, parliamentary sovereignty, and the Toleration Act. It was a tumultuous time in Pennsylvania as well. While Penn was knee-deep in his efforts to procure a Parliament supportive of the king's program, his frustration with those governing his colony reached a breaking point. In July, exasperated with continuing reports of discord, the proprietor took the extreme step of appointing a non-Quaker as his Deputy (or Lieutenant) Governor—and not only a non-Quaker (since after all Penn's cousin William Markham, in whom he placed great confidence, was an Anglican), but a New England Puritan. John Blackwell had fought in the parliamentary army during the English Civil Wars, served in Parliament during the mid-1650s, and settled in Boston, where he served as a Justice of the Peace. Given the outsized symbolic role played by New England Puritans' persecution of Quakers—epitomized by the hanging of four Quakers in Boston between 1659 and 1661—one can only imagine the affront that Blackwell's appointment offered to Pennsylvania Friends. Penn described Blackwell to the Council as a "grave, sober, and wise man" and emphasized his service to the Commonwealth, voicing his hope to "use his not being a Friend, to Friends' advantage." Penn further hoped that Blackwell's administration might improve the prospects of receiving, at long last, some relief from his difficult financial circumstances in England, "it being his talent to regulate and set things in method, easy and just."[75]

Penn had clearly reached a breaking point with his factious colonial government. Empowering the Provincial Council had not worked. Appointing five commissioners of state had not worked. Thomas Lloyd had turned down Penn's offer of the position of Deputy Governor. Perhaps it was truly time for drastic action, though the appointment of Blackwell seemed rather clearly to signal, at the very least, the end of the Quaker colony as Penn had always understood it. Then again, seemingly unwilling to jettison his aspirations for the colony's Quaker foundations, Penn told colonial authorities to "let him see what he can do a while . . . If he do not please you, he shall be laid aside." This particular experiment would last less than two years, as Blackwell was indeed "laid aside," but not before Penn had permanently poisoned his relationship with leading Pennsylvania Friends, and driven both Lloyds—Thomas and David—into open opposition to his interests. David's bitterness, in particular, would become the single greatest obstacle to Penn's control over Pennsylvania for the rest of his life.[76]

The Blackwell episode also illustrates with exceptional clarity the unpredictability of transatlantic communication. Penn extended his offer of the lieutenant governorship to Blackwell in a letter of July 12, 1688, though he did not inform his commissioners of state of Blackwell's appointment until a letter of September 18, which they surely did not receive for at least another month. By this point James had already issued writs for the upcoming parliamentary election, though by October he would cancel them as reports of preparations for the Dutch invasion began to reach him. The summer and fall of 1688 in England were almost entirely consumed with the specter of a Dutch invasion. Meanwhile, unaware of Penn's plans to appoint Blackwell (an appointment that had surely not yet reached Blackwell), William Markham wrote to Penn in July, reporting "much dissatisfaction . . . in the Assembly" during its May 1688 session. The Assembly continued, as it had since its first meeting, to agitate for a more substantial role in governing the territories, rather than simply affirming or denying laws proposed by the Council. Markham attributed some of the Assembly's restiveness to the mistaken "belief that they are the chief court of record in the province" and traced some of the problems back to Penn's indulgence during the initial Chester Assembly, when he had permitted the Assembly to elect a speaker and a clerk. Markham also reported continuing disputes about the caves along the Delaware River, and his particular frustration with the case of Benjamin Chambers, a Friend whom Markham could not persuade the Council to move against in court, despite the fact that he refused to either vacate his cave or pay rent for it. Imploring the Council to act against Chambers, Markham was told that "they must proceed on a religious account."[77]

Blackwell wrote to Thomas Lloyd on November 11, informing him of his appointment as Penn's deputy, and to the proprietor himself, accepting the commission, on November 20. By this point, though neither Blackwell nor the Pennsylvanians knew it, William had landed at Torbay with nearly 15,000 troops—the beginning of the end of James's reign, and with it Penn's position of influence in the English government. Blackwell's letter to Lloyd, though somewhat prolix, was nonetheless conciliatory, and he expressed his view that "your sole continuance would have been to much more advantage of the honorable proprietor & province, than can be expected from me, who am much a stranger to the government and laws established amongst you." Despite having informed Lloyd of his plan to journey to Pennsylvania by way of New York, no one in the Pennsylvania government met Blackwell when he arrived in Philadelphia on December 17, leaving him to assume that his letters had not arrived. Attempting to find Markham, Blackwell went to Penn's house, where he was met neither by Markham nor by a welcoming committee of the colony's government, but only "a great number of boys laughing" at him in the street. Obtaining a key to the Council's meeting room, Blackwell "found the place . . . full of dust and papers scattered about."[78]

This awkward and foreboding introduction of the Pennsylvania government to its new Deputy Governor provided a preview of a protracted and bitterly divisive year to come. Thomas Lloyd and the Council sought to obstruct Blackwell's exercise of authority by any and all means at their disposal. As President of the Council, Lloyd held the Great Seal, which was required to make pronouncements and laws official, and he refused to set the seal to many of Blackwell's actions, kept official papers from him, and delayed carrying out his orders. Lloyd and the other members of the Council, to varying degrees, embarked on a policy of "harassment, delay, and enmity." In this impasse Blackwell deemed it necessary to seek the advice of his Council, "but here he ran into more trouble, for he was unable to procure their attendance until nearly a month after his arrival." But while Lloyd and Blackwell engaged in combat over the levers of power in Pennsylvania, unbeknownst to them, James had fled England and Penn was under arrest.[79]

10

Seclusion and Solitude

William of Orange invaded England in November 1688. James II fled a month later, but not on his first try: after throwing the Great Seal, the key symbol of sovereign authority, into the Thames on December 11, the king made it as far as the coast before being apprehended on the Isle of Sheppey. He was returned to London and placed under Dutch guard. But William had little appetite for keeping James around, and even less for making him a martyr. He ordered James to leave London, ostensibly for his own safety, and proceeded to turn a blind eye so that the erstwhile monarch, then at Rochester, could flee a second time. James made it safely to France, crossing the Channel and arriving at Ambleteuse on Christmas morning 1688. By year's end he was ensconced in the palace of St. Germain, Louis XIV's birthplace just west of Paris, and the recipient of a 50,000-franc monthly pension from the French king. From his new base, James began to plan a campaign to retake his throne.[1]

James's flight left supporters like William Penn to fend for themselves in a time of great social and political upheaval. And in the Revolution's immediate aftermath, Penn's own situation was indeed precarious. He was arrested before December was out and released after posting a significant amount of bail. But no matter how difficult things might have seemed in late 1688, the next few years would be even more trying. As war between England and France escalated, Penn's background as a confidant of James and vocal spokesperson for extending toleration to Catholics continued to cast suspicion on him. Penn also had to deal with continuing criticism from within Quaker circles, as many Friends felt that his close association with James's unpopular policies had brought the Society into disrepute. In early 1691, facing several treason charges stemming from allegations of contact with James, Penn decided that the most prudent course of action was to go into hiding until he could clear his name. That process would take several years. His withdrawal from public life, along with the unreliability of communication between England and America during wartime, exacerbated the difficulty of overseeing Pennsylvania and contributed to tensions between Penn and his colonists. Those governing the colony increasingly dropped their deferential pretenses and treated Penn as he no doubt appeared to them: as an absentee landlord with no understanding of American political realities.

As a result of these myriad difficulties, Penn turned his attention away from Pennsylvania politics and back to defending Friends in England against their critics, as he had done so energetically during the 1670s. He used his time in seclusion to write a number of pieces, most notably his 1693 *Some fruits of solitude*, a collection of maxims on a variety of topics that were assembled and arranged during Penn's own enforced solitude. It became, and remains, one of his most popular and enduring works. And yet he never took his mind off larger questions, and in that same year published *An essay toward the present and future peace of Europe*, which proposed a European Parliament to settle conflicts without recourse to war and violence. And, of course, he continued to hope for a return to Pennsylvania.[2]

* * *

With James's departure and the arrival of William and Mary, the political situation in England remained volatile and often even violent, far from the "Bloodless Revolution" so often trumpeted by historians. Anti-Catholic riots and violence had sporadically broken out since the fall of 1688, but with James's flight they assumed new intensity, as Catholic chapels and Dissenting meetinghouses were targeted for destruction. In the immediate aftermath of his flight to France, James actively planned his return to the throne, and many of his supporters in England remained faithful to his cause. (Despite the important role played by Anglican bishops in undermining James's rule, for example, only eight of twenty-seven English and Welsh bishops swore allegiance to the new monarchs, and more than four hundred other clergy refused to subscribe the new Oath of Allegiance.) Hopes for James's restoration were almost entirely dashed after the Battle of the Boyne, in which William's forces decisively routed James's troops, but that battle would not take place until the end of June 1690, more than eighteen months after William's invasion. And even after that defeat, fears of a French invasion persisted, in light of French rout of English and Dutch naval forces at Beachy Head off the Sussex coast just days later. Louis was ultimately forced to abort plans for an invasion of England, as France itself faced a potential invasion by the Duke of Savoy, but rumors of ongoing activity by James's supporters (known as Jacobites) would persist into the 1690s, and would continue to complicate William Penn's efforts to clear his name and return to America.[3]

Elections to the Convention Parliament, which would decide the fate of the monarchy, took place in January 1689. Though William had earlier insisted that he did not seek the throne, Parliament proclaimed William and Mary King and Queen of England in February. They were crowned in April. Of particular significance to the career of William Penn and the nearly century-long campaign for liberty of conscience was Parliament's passage of the Toleration Act the next month. Eschewing the extensive justificatory preamble that James had attached to his Declaration of Indulgence in 1687, the Act announced its minimalist intentions from the start, asserting that "some ease to scrupulous consciences in the exercise of religion may be an effectual means to unite their Majesties Protestant subjects in interest and affection." The act applied only to Protestant Dissenters who denied transubstantiation, who swore or affirmed the Oaths of Supremacy and Allegiance, and who registered their meetinghouses with the government and kept their doors unlocked during worship. Its provisions did not apply to Catholics, or to those Dissenters who denied the Trinity, and the Test Acts remained in full force. That said, the Act was a major step forward in the history of religious liberty in England. John Locke thought the Act was a beginning: "Toleration has now been established by law . . . Not perhaps so wide in scope as might be wished for . . . Still, it is something to have progressed so far." Nonetheless, the rights protected by the Act fell far short of what James had offered, and what William Penn had sought to implement in America.[4]

Shortly thereafter, William took England into the alliance fighting the Nine Years' War, or War of the League of Augsburg, initiating an extended period of armed conflict with France that took the monarch away from his new subjects for months at a time. And in December, William and Mary accepted the Bill of Rights, which established the supremacy of Parliament and codified subjects' rights.[5]

As one of the highest-profile supporters of the disgraced king, William Penn immediately incurred the enmity of the new regime. In December 1688 Penn had been questioned and required to post bail. On February 27, 1689, however, a warrant was issued for his arrest on suspicion of high treason. In an attempt to retain his freedom, Penn wrote to the Earl of Shrewsbury, a member of the group that had invited William to intervene in English affairs and who would soon become Secretary of State. Penn hoped to secure permission to remain in seclusion rather than face confinement. "I do profess solemnly in the presence of Almighty God," he insisted, "I have no hand or share in any conspiracy against the King or government, nor do I know any that have." Penn requested that he be allowed to remain at large "at my house in the country." The letter seems to have had its desired effect, as the king allowed Penn to remain at Warminghurst with his family.[6]

Late June saw the issuance of yet another warrant, however, this one directing the king's messenger to "make strict and diligent search for William Penn Esqr, and . . . apprehend [him] for suspicion of high treason or treasonable practices." Despite their past differences, Penn sought to enlist the Marquis of Halifax's intervention on his behalf, and assured him that "I am no fighter, caballer, nor plotter." Enumerating his many disappointments, Penn added that "I have lost my estate in Ireland" and was now "torn from my children and my bread." Prior to the warrant being issued, he protested, he had been quietly retired at his home, "out of all conversation, in Sussex." But this time, he was not so fortunate. James, the exiled king, had landed in Ireland in March, at the very same Kinsale port at which young William Penn had gone about his father's business during the 1660s, and the English government was on edge. Penn was imprisoned in June and once again from late September through November 1689.[7]

Political figures were not the only audiences at which Penn directed his attempts to clear his name. Late in 1689, in a general letter to Friends, he proclaimed his innocence of the charges that were being raised against him, particularly "Jesuitism, popery, and plots." "The Lord God almighty knows," he wrote, "that I have universally sought the liberty and peace of [this nation]." He continued to defend James's pursuit of toleration, denying that it was "a trick or snare as some have represented it," and insisting that it was merely an attempt to restore to English Dissenters "our just and Christian privilege." And he wrote to the London Yearly Meeting in May 1691, from seclusion, that his hiding was "not because men have sworn truly, but falsely against me . . . who have never sought *myself,* but the good of all, [and who] always desired that truth and right-eousness, mercy and peace might take place amongst us."[8]

Twice more—in July 1690 and January 1691—proclamations for Penn's ap-prehension would be issued. The first, in which Penn's name appeared as one of nineteen accused conspirators, resulted in him spending a month in jail. By mid-September he was writing to the Pennsylvania Provincial Council that "I am well, and at liberty," although he would not be formally cleared of the charges until November. Despite these protestations of innocence, Penn was clearly con-cerned about potentially incriminating evidence connecting him to James's re-gime. He attempted to ensure the destruction of his correspondence with the Duke of Buckingham, which had been found in the duke's possessions following his death. Let my letters "follow him they were writ to" (i.e., to the grave), he asked the Earl of Arran, who had been with the duke when he died in April 1687.[9]

The second of these proclamations posed a much more serious threat. It resulted from the discovery of correspondence between James and his English supporters under the direction of Richard Graham, Viscount Preston, who had served as president of James's Privy Council and had been receiving funds from Louis XIV to work for James's restoration. On January 1, 1691, Preston was apprehended with a packet of letters, two of which were showed evidence of having been written by Penn himself. A warrant for Penn's arrest was issued in January, and a royal proclamation calling for his apprehension was published early the next month. In late February, Penn sent his brother-in-law Anthony Lowther to arrange a private conference with his old friend Henry Sidney. Unbeknownst to Penn, Sidney suspected his friend's involvement in the affair and had told the king a month earlier that "Mr. Penn is as much in this business as anybody." At their meeting, Penn begged Sidney to tell the king that "he was a true and a faithful servant to King William and Queen Mary, and . . . he knew of no plot." Sidney passed along an account of his meeting with Penn to the king, who was then at The Hague in discussions with allies. Penn wrote to Sidney several more times that year, appealing to the king's "justice and goodness," and again asserting that "I know of no invasions, or insurrections, men, money, or arms for them . . . nor have ever met with those named as the members of this conspiracy, or prepared any measures with them." Unfortunately, Sidney reported to Penn late in 1691 that "when I speak to the King about you, his answer to me is, that you have been one of his greatest enemies, that you have done him all the harm you could." He thus continued to labor under a cloud of suspicion.[10]

By this time Penn had made the decision, likely a wise one, to go into hiding. He did attend George Fox's burial in late January 1691, along with several thousand Friends. Although he was already being sought by the authorities, it is difficult to imagine any circumstances keeping him from paying his final respects to Fox, who had held such a high place in his affections for so many years and with whom he had worked so closely. He reported to Thomas Lloyd that he spoke at Fox's funeral, and "that night, very providentially, as ever since, I escaped the messenger's hands." How diligently the authorities searched for him we do not know, although much of his surviving correspondence from 1691 to 1694 does not list his location, as had been his customary practice before then. A letter to Thomas Lloyd on June 14, 1691, for example, is headed only with "Eng[land]" and the date. He may have stayed relatively close to London—his editors suggest Hoddesdon, Hertfordshire, on the main road from London to Cambridge, as one possible location. Noting the pardons that the king had offered to Irish rebels—to say nothing of that granted to Preston, ringleader of a Jacobite plot—Penn lamented that he continued to be viewed with suspicion, asking his old acquaintance John Tillotson, who by then had become Archbishop of Canterbury, to "speak to the king and press him to let me live safely and easily, and I do promise, by the help of God, to live very peaceably." To Lord Nottingham, he promised that "I shall never misuse the liberty I humbly crave"; he once again entreated Nottingham, in the fall of 1692, for a word to the king. All I ask, he wrote, is for the king to say, "Let him go about his own affairs." Somewhat later, still seeking to clear his name, Penn complained that he had "been above . . . three years hunted up and down, and [never] allowed to live quietly in City or County, even then when there was hardly a pretence against me."[11]

Another indictment on a charge of treason—this one by a Dublin grand jury in early 1691—further complicated Penn's legal situation and encouraged him to remain in hiding. These charges were based on testimony by William Fuller, who had served in James's royal household and more recently lodged with Titus Oates, whose fame (or infamy) dated back to the Popish Plot allegations. Penn denounced the charge as "a bill found upon the oaths of three scandalous men," and insisted that he had not been in Ireland for twenty years. He announced that he was "ready to appear," but pointing to the "corrupt evidence" sworn against him in Dublin, "I cannot without an unjustifiable presumption put myself into the power of my enemies." Penn insistently denied all charges—"whatever are my faults, falsehood and revenge are none," he wrote in 1692—but the damage to his already tenuous reputation with the king and queen was done.[12]

Fuller was later declared an impostor by the House of Commons, yet, Penn pointed out, "my estate in Ireland is . . . lately put up among the estates of outlaws to be leased for the Crown, and the Collector . . . ordered to seize my rents and lease it in the name of the government, and yet though I am not convicted or outlawed." As part of his efforts to secure his power in Ireland, James had agreed to repeal the 1662 Act of Settlement, which threatened to throw Irish land titles like Penn's—inherited from his father, who had received land from Charles II and, prior to that, from Cromwell—into disarray yet once again.[13]

* * *

What made the proclamation for his arrest, and his ensuing need to go into hiding, so painful to Penn was that it came just as he was preparing to return to America. Of course he had promised Pennsylvanians on numerous occasions that he would be returning, but this time seems to have been different. He told a Friend in England that "I was going [April 1691] at the farthest, all things preparing . . . when this trouble broke out on me." His return had been timed to coincide with the launch of a major new settlement in the colony. In 1690 Penn published *Some proposals for a second settlement in the province of Pennsylvania*, which laid out his intention to sponsor "another city . . . upon the river Susquehannah," roughly a hundred miles west of Philadelphia, and sought London investors for this new undertaking. He was also, apparently, considering this return permanent. In this brief promotional pamphlet he also announced his intention to go to Pennsylvania "with what speed I can, and my family with me, in order to our future residence." In preparation for that journey, he wrote to several potential investors, "I have begun to open my shop again, as I may call it, and expose to sale my ware." He asked Thomas Holme to encourage colonists holding lots on the Schuylkill side to swap them for lots on the Delaware, so that he might find "a way for me to pleasure the Susquehannah Company." And he informed a number of potential investors on January 8, 1691, that he intended "to go for America as soon as the Lord opens my way."[14]

The discovery of the Jacobite plot in January 1691, and the allegations about Penn's role in it, scuttled all these plans. Precisely who Penn meant by "the Susquehannah Company" is not clear: he may have planned to oversee the new enterprise himself, or he may have referred to Daniel Coxe's New Mediterranean

Sea Company, which had raised more than £10,000 in London and had ambitious plans to purchase 100,000 acres in northern Pennsylvania to gain entry to the fur trade near Lake Erie. Coxe, a doctor and scientist who purchased the right to govern West Jersey from Edward Byllinge's heirs in 1687 and who had briefly governed West Jersey before moving on to other colonial undertakings, has been described as "one of the most active of the schemers who dreamed of wealth and empire in the New World." He had purchased 10,000 acres from Penn in 1686 and that same year sent David Lloyd to Pennsylvania as the New Mediterranean Sea Company's agent. In June 1686 Penn had drawn up deeds, which were never executed, for an additional 100,000 acres to the New Mediterranean Sea Company. Despite grandiose aspirations, however, neither Penn's Susquehannah Company nor Coxe's New Mediterranean Sea Company ultimately came to fruition.[15]

* * *

Had Penn actually been able to journey to Pennsylvania in early 1691, he would have found the colony in turmoil, with the Lower Counties nearly ready to secede. To fully understand how things had gotten this bad requires revisiting the disastrous Blackwell episode. Placing Blackwell in charge of the colony was probably an experiment doomed from the start, but it had unraveled in spectacular fashion over the course of 1689. By the time Penn told the Provincial Council, in August of that year, that he had decided to remove Blackwell from office and "to throw all into your hands" so that the Council might "pu[t] your common shoulder to the public work," tensions in the province had risen to unprecedented heights and the grand failure of the Blackwell appointment had become plain for all to see. The "wound" that Blackwell had inflicted on the colony's government, Penn's close friend Phineas Pemberton suggested, held the potential to "ulcerate and run to utter ruin" if the proprietor did not act swiftly. But from a distance of three thousand miles, facing the ever-present threat of imprisonment for treason, Penn's options were severely limited.[16]

The Quaker elite that had been governing Pennsylvania in Penn's absence understood that Blackwell represented an existential threat not only to their own personal and political influence, but to the Quaker character of the colony itself. Blackwell was not simply a non-Quaker: he was a New England Puritan, and Jane Calvert has commented that "it is hard to imagine [Penn's] lack of foresight as to the animosity this would cause," bringing in "a Quaker arch-enemy to govern a self-consciously Quaker colony." Pemberton compared Blackwell to that inveterate foe of Quakers and nemesis of a much younger William Penn, John Faldo, but then noted that Blackwell posed a far greater danger than Faldo ever had, since "he hath lived some years in New England to strengthen him in prejudices and to ripen him in cruelty towards us." Provincial Councilors denounced Blackwell's "want of true love to us and our principle" and begged Penn not to allow his colony "to be overwhelmed by a person of no interest amongst us." For his part, Blackwell returned the favor, telling Penn that his coreligionists were "unsuitable to civil government and polity" and branding them "a people who have not the principles of government amongst them."[17]

The Thomas Lloyd–Blackwell conflict pitted Philadelphia Quakers against the proprietor's handpicked deputy. Lloyd's early and unyielding opposition to Blackwell manifested itself in a number of ways: refusal to mark pronouncements and judicial appointments with the Great Seal of the province, of which he was officially the keeper; rallying the opposition of other leading figures in the government; and making it nearly impossible to assemble a Council quorum and transact business. (In May 1689, Blackwell complained to Penn, "I can get no Councils.") In just a few months, Blackwell had encountered the long reach of Lloyd's influence. Blackwell refused to admit Lloyd to the Council even after he had been elected as a member to represent Bucks County, and the April 1689 Council meetings exploded into a storm of recrimination and bickering after Lloyd refused to leave the Council room, insisting on his right to take his seat. Eight Councilors wrote to Penn to complain about Blackwell's conduct and defend Lloyd; grievances included declining to seat duly elected Council members, taking Council minutes in an illegible shorthand, changing the wording on provincial commissions, and, more generally, conducting himself in a "harsh, unkind, and arbitrary" manner.[18]

Blackwell, not surprisingly, saw things differently. He blamed a "faction made in Council against me," and cautioned Penn against assuming that just because Thomas Lloyd and his allies shared a religious bond with the proprietor, they had his best interests at heart. "I pray God deliver you, for they threaten you," he wrote. "It has been your great unhappiness to be overtaken with mere glossing pretences of friendship." Lloyd, "a serpent of your own cherishing," had steadily aggrandized power to himself—"he knows no superiors"—and his refusal to mark judicial appointments with the Great Seal had made a functioning system of justice impossible. Lloyd's frequent absences from Philadelphia, and the accompanying uncertainty about the whereabouts of the Great Seal, only exacerbated the conflict. What's more, Quakers shielded other Quakers from prosecution, Blackwell insisted, and such nefarious behavior was abetted by the Quaker practice of attesting rather than swearing oaths. Lamenting the failure of a Pennsylvania grand jury to indict the fomenters of a riot, Blackwell observed that "such is the virtue of the attestations that passed here, for oaths; Especially when the parties concerned or any of them are Friends."[19]

Not surprisingly, when Blackwell received a letter in October from Shrewsbury, the Secretary of State, ordering preparations for war against the French, the stage was set for yet another conflict between the Puritan army veteran and the pacifistic Quaker Pennsylvanians. Again, the Council was paralyzed by internal divisions. The issue of colonial defense would continue to bedevil Pennsylvania Quakers for years, pitting the Quaker peace testimony against the colony's place in an imperial system in which each colony was expected to fulfil quotas for militia troops and supplies in support of their common defense.

Penn's letter relieving Blackwell of his commission and returning the government to the Council reached Pennsylvania in December 1689, a year after Blackwell's arrival in the colony. The Puritan was happy to be rid of his burdensome responsibility. He had given Penn and his colony a year of his life with little to show for it, and "I now only wait for the hour of my deliverance for I see tis impossible to serve you in this place . . . Besides, sir, the Climate is over-hot for my Constitution and age; and the hosts of mosquitos are worse than of armed men."

In a final coup de grace, in the January 1, 1690, Council meeting at which Blackwell surrendered his commission as governor, the Council immediately elected Thomas Lloyd as its president and once again installed him as chief executive officer. In attempting to bring his obstreperous province to heel, Gary Nash notes, Penn had "succeeded only in giving the colonists new cause to resist what they now concluded was an unsympathetic and estranged proprietor."[20]

In yet another puzzling move, however, while relieving Blackwell of his deputy governorship, Penn simultaneously appointed him Receiver General, charged with collecting rents and supervising Pennsbury. Anyone Penn nominated as Receiver General was bound to have a hard lot; why Penn thought Blackwell might have success is even more difficult to fathom. Nor did the proprietor make things any easier for his new tax collector. Along with the notice appointing him Receiver General arrived a list of no fewer than fourteen tasks that Penn wanted Blackwell to perform in his new post, ranging from the unlikely to the impossible. For example, having heard of how bitter and divided the colony was under Blackwell's rule, Penn nonetheless instructed him to "call all persons to account . . . that have had anything to do with my goods or estate . . . and set in a time to pay what is due," to "build two . . . granaries in Kent and Sussex counties," and "bring my mill [on Chester Creek] to some certainty and profit." In a bitter response to Penn, Blackwell poured out a year's worth of accumulated frustrations, denouncing Pennsylvania's Quaker elite as "such a people as neither regard yourself or me," "whom neither God nor man can prevail with by entreaties" and who "despise all dominion and dignity that is not in themselves." Later he would claim to a correspondent in England that "the wild beasts that fill [Penn's] forests can better govern than the witless zealots who make a monkey-house of his assembly."[21]

As to the question of "taking up some other station" and serving as Receiver General, Blackwell observed that it would surely "be attended with the same evil circumstances as the government, with the addition of more contempt" from Friends, whom he described as "satanical spirits." Blackwell promised Penn that he would do what he could while he remained in Pennsylvania awaiting improved spring weather to make his way back to New England, but no doubt "I shall have little assistance or encouragement" from the residents. Given the degree to which Blackwell had alienated a large segment of Pennsylvania's population, and Penn's complaints that "I have not received one tittle or farthing" from Pennsylvania, it is hard to imagine Blackwell having much success in his new position, despite the fact that Penn had named Blackwell as his Deputy Governor largely due to his purported skill at managing practical affairs. (Blackwell had earlier, in New England, proposed one of the earliest schemes for issuing paper money in the American colonies, though it ultimately came to nothing.) Then again, Blackwell had still not received the salary that Penn had promised him, since that sum was to have been taken out of the colony's rents and tax revenues, so perhaps he figured it was worth at least an attempt.[22]

Sure enough, Blackwell was never able to collect his salary, or much of anything else. Despite his creation of a comprehensive rent roll—an extraordinarily ambitious undertaking, considering Pennsylvania's history of complex land sales and spotty recordkeeping, to say nothing of the general hostility to Blackwell throughout the colony—it soon became clear that objections, complaints, and the resignation of his chief collector, John McComb, would doom Blackwell's efforts. By the end of March 1690, having appointed Turner his deputy, Blackwell was back in Boston and asking his wife (then in England) to press Penn personally for payment of his salary. He wrote to Penn one final time in May of that year, warning him of the growing resentment harbored by residents of the Lower Counties, detailing his inability to get Pennsylvanians to pay Penn's rents, and asking once again that Penn pay his salary to Blackwell's wife, lest he be "a loser by your favor."[23]

Blackwell had not been entirely without supporters during his time in Pennsylvania, however. Many in the Lower Counties saw his arrival as heralding a frontal assault on the entrenched power of Philadelphia Quakers, who in their view had run roughshod over the interests of non-Friends. Conflict between the province (Pennsylvania) and the territories (Lower Counties) had been growing in Penn's absence. Many Dutch settlers in the Lower Counties, for example, resented the tardiness of Pennsylvania's proclamation of William and Mary as monarchs—William had, after all, been Dutch Stadtholder before he was King of England. Residents of the Lower Counties were more likely to endorse Blackwell's attempts to support a militia to defend against potential French and Indian incursions, as they perceived themselves more exposed to those threats than the Philadelphians and lacked the Quakers' skittishness toward bearing arms. Blackwell also threatened the economic power of Philadelphia Quaker merchants, whom he accused of oppressing the colony's poorer residents by charging exorbitant rates for imported goods.[24]

After the strife had died down, Penn attempted to justify his actions in appointing Blackwell:

> Since no Friend would undertake the governor's place, I took one that was not, and a stranger that he might be impartial and more reverenced. He is in England and Ireland of great repute, for ability and integrity and virtue. I thought I did well; it was for good . . . and no end of my own. You see what I have done, on your complaints.[25]

Most of those charged with governing Pennsylvania in his absence did not see things this way, to say the least.

* * *

In the wake of Blackwell's dismissal, the previous pattern of spotty correspondence and frustration resumed. Nine months after Blackwell's replacement Penn chastised the Council: "I have not heard a word from you"; two months later, "I hoped to have heard from you by every opportunity," and "More letters arrive by Maryland ships but to my astonishment not one word from the government." "I know not who is in government, how I am represented, or what you do, what officers are in the government," he further complained. Late in 1690 he had still not received any record of the colonial laws or a comprehensive census of the province's freemen. Nor did any funds come the proprietor's way, despite Penn's appointment of Commissioners of Property and of Samuel Jennings, who had previously served in the government of West Jersey, as Receiver General.[26]

Then again, the wartime years after 1689 rendered the shipping upon which communication depended even more unreliable than normal. To take just one example, the *Trial*, carrying letters and goods from Pennsylvania, was seized by the French in 1689. Some of the materials on board, including Penn's long-sought copy of the province's laws, eventually made their way to their addressees, but not until September 1691. Such interruptions—ships not sailing, or waiting for convoys so as to travel more safely, or being taken by enemy forces—were frequent and wreaked havoc on already tenuous networks of communication.

* * *

Despite Penn's difficulty in acquiring information about colonial affairs, reports of tensions between the Upper and Lower Counties had been reaching him for years. Such tensions were deeply rooted in the inhabitants' ethnic and religious differences as well as Baltimore's continuing contestation of Penn's legal claim to the Lower Counties. Many of the residents of New Castle, Kent, and Sussex resented Pennsylvania Quakers' dominance of government and the judiciary, as well as the displacement of New Castle's important commercial role by the growth of Philadelphia. Things came to a head at the spring 1691 Council meetings. By empowering the Council to decide how the colony would be governed—collectively, by any five of its members, or by a Deputy Governor of its choosing, which turned out to be Thomas Lloyd—Penn had made a conflict between the Council and the Lower Counties almost inevitable. Calling rule by a Deputy Governor, particularly one as partial to Philadelphia Friends as Lloyd, "most disagreeable and grievous," the Council members from the Lower Counties withdrew from attendance on April 1, 1691. When the Council chose Lloyd as Deputy Governor a day later, the Lower Counties' Councilors left Philadelphia and returned to New Castle, where (by their own account, at least) they were welcomed enthusiastically by the people. The "Declaration" justifying their actions drew a clear distinction between "[Council] members of the Province" and "us the representatives of Council of the three Lower counties." They also accused Lloyd of wanting to concentrate power in himself, a point echoed by Robert Turner, who described the Deputy Governor as "laboring to ingratiate himself unto the people, by offering great favors . . . that it might redound the honor to him and slighting to thee." They wrote directly to Penn as well, enumerating their many grievances with the Philadelphia government, including the distance between many of their homes and the seat of government ("some of us at a 140 miles distance," or three days' journey, from the capital); the Council's refusal to ensure that judges made biannual circuits to the Lower Counties; and Thomas Lloyd's reluctance to set the Great Seal on judicial commissions, which threw the justice system into disarray and produced numerous miscarriages of justice. Turner wrote to Penn in late May 1691 that "we are in great distraction and disorder."[27]

The animosity between Pennsylvania leaders and leading figures in the Lower Counties was mutual, and the Council members from Pennsylvania had their own account of what had transpired. They praised Lloyd for steadily guiding the colony through the aftermath of the Revolution, which left many of their neighboring colonies suffering under unrest and tumults, and for defending Friends' principles under the Blackwell regime. They blamed Markham for the lack of a book of laws and accused him of frequenting "loose clubs" at "unseasonable hours." But some Quakers offered deeper diagnoses of the problems dividing the two territories. Joseph Growden traced the roots of the current difficulties to the earliest days of Pennsylvania's settlement, and laid responsibility at Penn's own feet. According to Growden, Penn had "not been so kind unto us as was our expectation, our due, and thy promise," and offered as evidence the Act of Union, which brought the Lower Counties into the colony, a "Pandora's box" that had produced "innumerable miseries" upon its opening. "Had it not been for this," he went on, Penn would never have had to return to England, "the rebel Blackwell" would not have been imposed on the province, and "we had been blessed still with thy company." Growden also pointed out that Penn had been absent from the colony for going on seven years now, and those in America had far more accurate and up-to-date knowledge of the character of various individuals and their suitability to serve in the government. A joint letter from the Council and Assembly the following month lamented that "we are forsaken by all our stepbrethren of the Lower Counties . . . so that we are at present by reason of their absenting themselves incapable of making laws" and referred to inhabitants of the Lower Counties as "both strangers to ourselves and [principles]."[28]

* * *

As the Blackwell episode receded and the rupture with the Lower Counties grew, the correspondence between Penn and his government took on an increasingly sharp edge. In justifying their actions with regard to the Lower Counties, the Council professed their love for Penn, "for whose sake many of us left our native country and have since been . . . exposed to divers inconveniences." That said, such allegiance was neither unconditional nor without limits. The Council and Assembly told him straightaway that their "fidelity to thee is not native but dative, not universal but local," and insisted that their rights as "free born English" were not forfeited by removing from the mother country to a colony across the sea. Earlier, several members of the Council had emphasized "[a]ll the hardships that we have gone through in settling this wilderness country and all that we have spent and wasted therein for the promotion and improvement thereof, almost to the utter ruin of some of us and our families." Penn had, of course, complained for years about all of the expenses he had incurred in the settlement of the colony, and words like these echo his own, but the colonists clearly did not include the proprietor in their "we." The divergence between his interests and their own, expressed in the remonstrance presented just prior to Penn's departure from Pennsylvania in 1684, widened with the passage of time, and his extended absence allowed those emerging conflicts and divisions to fester. Penn's close friend Phineas Pemberton also emphasized the fact that "we have labored and spent ourselves, estates, and some their lives to get for themselves and families a livelihood and to raise thee and thine an estate." "We" and "thee and thine" are subtly, though not entirely, disentangled in Pemberton's description of Pennsylvania's history. Longstanding allies like Turner attempted to defend Penn's interests against an increasingly emboldened faction led by the two Lloyds, David and Thomas. But it was an uphill battle, waged with few allies and many adversaries.[29]

The political manifestation of this growing divide between the province and the proprietor was put succinctly by Growden, who told Penn that he disapproved of the Council governing the colony. He was "unwilling that the people's representative should be the governor's deputy; lest we should too nearly espouse the cause of one to the injury of the other; the interest of the governor and people in my thoughts sometimes being opposite to the other." In all his planning for Pennsylvania, Penn likely never contemplated the notion that his own interests and those of his colonists could diverge in such a way.[30]

Acrimony persisted. Penn called out Thomas Lloyd by name (or more accurately, in seventeenth-century fashion, by initials: T.LL.) in a September 1693 letter that drew a stinging rebuke from Lloyd in which all pretense to deference was dropped. "I am not the man thou takest me to be," he insisted. "Thou understandest me not." (For his part, Penn responded in an identical, tit-for-tat manner: "I have not been the man you have taken me.") Lloyd blamed Penn's "credulity to ill affected persons," and closed his letter with the hope that "the Lord [will] preserve thee from false friends, as well as from thy open adversaries." In a separate letter, Lloyd's supporters defended his conduct, and told Penn bluntly that "we know him better." He has "wasted his estate in thy service." The misinformation that had soured the proprietor on his Deputy Governor, they claimed, was the work of "the faction against him."[31]

Perhaps most vexing to Penn, however, was the behavior of the Assembly, which continued to seek greater authority and to aggressively assert a claim to active involvement in the legislative process, in direct contradiction of the Frame of Government. When he found out about the Assembly's actions Penn condemned them in no uncertain terms as "an absolute overthrowing of the constitution." Blackwell had precipitated some of these conflicts, as when he instructed the Philadelphia sheriff to arrest John White, former Attorney General and Speaker of the Assembly, on a misdemeanor charge, in May 1689. Some members of the Assembly voted to censure those who had issued the warrant for White's arrest. The Assembly also continued to seek audiences with the Council to present grievances, a practice that Penn denounced repeatedly: "Surely you do not consider how great a violation of the charter that is." From the great distance separating Penn from his colony, things no doubt seemed simple, and he told the Council to "reduc[e] the Assembly to the Charter . . . aye or no." On the ground, in the province, however, things were hardly so straightforward.[32]

Other divisions persisted as well. Conflict over the Welsh tract, which had occasioned sharp disputes between Surveyor General Holme and his deputy Ashcom as well as between Penn and his Welsh settlers, remained vibrant. The Welsh petitioned Penn again in May 1691, citing their continuing dissatisfaction. Like the Germans at Germantown, the Welsh had sought (and thought Penn had given them) a territory that they could organize in such a way as to maintain their distinctive religious, linguistic, and cultural practices. Penn had promised the Welsh settlers their own manor free from county taxes, but Chester County was attempting to tax them and annex their lands. When some Welsh voted in the 1689 Council elections, and elected one of their own, merchant John Eckley, as a Councilor from Philadelphia County, the Council, at Blackwell's urging, voided the election. Lloyd reinstated Eckley to his seat on the

Council immediately after Blackwell's dismissal, but a far more serious and far-reaching rupture was just around the corner. Superimposed upon these struggles over Blackwell's authority were the continuing tensions between Penn's interest and that of his colonists, and between the Lower Counties and Pennsylvania's Quaker-dominated government. And those tensions were about to boil over.

* * *

The tumultuous disunion of Pennsylvania and the Lower Counties distressed Penn. "Your division has torn me to pieces," he wrote to the Council, "you can not imagine what use is made by all sorts . . . of your divisions." Echoing his earlier articulation of civil interest as a solution to England's religious divisions, which he had advanced in support of James's tolerationist efforts, he urged the Council to remember that "though you are not of one judgment in religion, you are of one family *in civilis*, and should aim at the public good." He also attempted to contest Growden's complaints about the Act of Union by offering his own narrative of founding unity. "You of the lower counties call to mind how you desired to be joined to the upper, and you of the upper counties how much you were pleased at the union of the lower." Then again, his letter of September 11, 1691, did not arrive in Pennsylvania until seven months later, by which time the colonists had accepted a separate proposal Penn had made, for two separate Deputy Governors to preside over the two separate territories. Thomas Lloyd became deputy for Pennsylvania, and William Markham for the Lower Counties. With this division in place, the Council was able to reunite, at least for a time, "to act as one general governor in legislation." Though Penn himself had countenanced such a solution, he deeply regretted the inability of the Council to work out the differences between the two territories.[33]

Ultimately, though, there was little Penn could do from his precarious political position thousands of miles away. He requested that the Assembly meet in the Lower Counties once every three years. He even appealed to George Whitehead to intervene with Pennsylvania Quakers, hoping that Whitehead's impeccable Quaker credentials might help smooth over this latest unpleasantness. The tensions present in Pennsylvania were hardly limited to that place, but were in fact part of a larger colonial dynamic, especially strong in the Middle Colonies, by which representative institutions in America displayed an increasing assertiveness vis-à-vis officials in England. But no doubt Penn would have taken little comfort in knowing these facts.[34]

* * *

As Penn had feared, divisions in America gave encouragement to those in England who aimed to bring the colonies under firmer Crown control. In addition, his period of enforced hiding made advocating for Pennsylvania impossible and emboldened his American rivals. "My concerns" in America "suffer beyond imagination," he told Rochester. Indeed, just a month after he warned Pennsylvania Friends that "you can not imagine what use is made by all sorts . . . of your divisions," the Lords of Trade recommended that Penn's proprietorship be revoked, and the colony ruled directly by the Crown.[35]

In October 1691, amid concerns about the Quaker government's neglect of colonial defenses in light of rising tensions with the French and Indians, the Crown stripped control of Pennsylvania from Penn, adding Pennsylvania to the portfolio of New York governor Benjamin Fletcher. It was a grievous blow to Penn, who had invested so much—financially, to be sure, but also emotionally, socially, and religiously—into his American undertaking. Though his own situation was severely compromised, Penn wrote directly to Fletcher in early December 1692, "to give thee this caution, that I am an Englishman and that country and government of [Pennsylvania] inseparably my property, dearly purchased every way." Penn imputed the seizure of his colony to "misinformation" received by the Crown about the dangers posed by French and Indian attacks. In separate correspondence, he encouraged Pennsylvanians to resist any attempts by Fletcher to alter the Quaker nature of the province. "Insist upon your patent with wisdom and moderation but steady integrity," he instructed, and urged colonists to take up their pens in defense of the colony and Friends' management of it. Letters could be sent to Friends in England, who will "deliver your representations to the Lords of Trade or the King in Council if you protest against any proceeding of the Governor of New York upon this arbitrary commission." (Fletcher obtained a copy of Penn's letter and submitted it to the Board of Trade, which then laid the matter before the king.) Penn's concerns about Fletcher were surely not eased when he learned that, upon his arrival in Philadelphia, the governor had removed seven leading Friends from the Provincial Council. Nor could he have been pleased to learn that more than a hundred citizens of Philadelphia presented Fletcher with a grateful and welcoming *Address* upon his taking up the reins of government.[36]

* * *

Given his seclusion from public life and the continuing difficulty of getting reliable information about goings-on in Pennsylvania, by the time Penn found out about the schism that had torn through the Pennsylvania Quaker community, the affair was more than a year old. Then again, it soon became impossible for him to avoid, as it moved on from Philadelphia right into the heart of the London Yearly Meeting.

What would become known as the "Keithian schism" coalesced around the figure of George Keith, Scottish Presbyterian turned Quaker, who was well known to Penn. Keith had traveled with Penn, Barclay, and Fox during their 1677 tour of the Netherlands and Germany, suffered numerous imprisonments for his faith, and been singled out by Henry More as one of the most theologically sophisticated Friends. In 1685, thanks to his connections with Barclay, Keith arrived in America as Surveyor General for East Jersey. He was an eager and ardent defender of Friends against their critics, and had even attempted to debate leading New England Puritans while in Boston in the spring of 1688. In 1689 he was named headmaster of the Quaker school in Philadelphia. But during his time in Pennsylvania, Keith became increasingly troubled by what he saw as theological ignorance among the colony's Quakers. He proposed a catechism for use in the instruction of Quaker youth, and a system of elders that he hoped would increase the orderliness and discipline of Pennsylvania Quaker Meetings.[37]

Unfortunately for Keith, the province's leading Quakers did not see things his way, and in 1690 the Yearly Meeting rejected his proposals. By this point, the bitterness between Keith and the leading Friends in Philadelphia had reached new heights, and he and his followers were soon holding separate Meetings. Not surprisingly, his growing resentment of religious authority in the colony fired political and social conflict. But Keith not only ruptured Quaker unity by gathering a group of supporters and holding separate Meetings; he also formed an alliance with printer William Bradford, and took his criticisms public. In *Some Reasons and Causes of the Late Separation*, published in June 1692, Keith denounced the toleration of theological error among Pennsylvania's Quakers and criticized the colony's Public Friends. His critique went to the basics of the Quaker faith, and thus differed from those of previous internal Quaker critics like Wilkinson and Story, who had objected primarily to church organization and the institution of particular procedures.[38]

Disruptive and bitter though these disputes were, they were about to get even more heated. In October Keith published *An appeal from the twenty-eight judges*, his response to the Pennsylvania Public Friends who had cast him out earlier that year. The *Appeal* compared Public Friends to "the Roman-Hierarchy," and urged the next Philadelphia Yearly Meeting to consider "whether there is any example or precedent [in] Scripture, or in all Christendom, that ministers should engross the worldly government, as they do here?" The notion that Quakers ought not hold public office would, of course, have effectively ended the idea of Pennsylvania as a Quaker colony, and Pennsylvania would, in one sense, cease to be Pennsylvania if Friends ceased to "engross the worldly government."[39]

In December 1692, after they were disowned by the Philadelphia Yearly Meeting, Keith and several of his followers were convicted in the colony's civil courts of sedition and slandering magistrates. The judges in those courts, of course, were themselves leading members of the Philadelphia Quaker community. This intertwining of church and state in a colony that proclaimed itself a beacon of religious liberty was not lost on Keith or his supporters, and they viewed themselves as persecuted for the sake of conscience just as surely as Friends had been under the Conventicle Act, and in New England, in years past.

But Keith's most strident and cutting contribution to the whole affair came in early 1693, with the publication of a pamphlet entitled *New England's spirit of persecution transmitted to Pennsylvania*. *New England's spirit* presented a "transcript" of the trials of Keith and his associates the previous December, with Keith featured as persecuted Dissenter. Given the importance of William Penn's famed turn as a defendant, more than twenty years earlier, in a highly celebrated trial, and Penn's publication of a "transcript" of that trial, Keith's claims were clear. Quakers in Pennsylvania had become no different than Puritans in New England (the recent example of Blackwell no doubt helped cement his accusation), or Anglicans in England, while Keith defended the sanctity of Quaker conscience against persecuting judges. And it was an effective piece of political rhetoric: anti-Quaker polemicists would continue to revive memories of the Keithian trials for years to come.[40]

Given his increasing disaffection with Lloyd and the Pennsylvanians and his long acquaintance with Keith, it is not surprising that Penn initially defended the dissident. He suggested that "T[homas] L[loyd]'s height, has administered occasion for a difference in spirit between [Keith] and him from the first. For as to doctrines, they cannot but agree." They were both leading Friends, after all. Penn did admit that Keith's approach to scriptural interpretation "may be a little too philosophical." But Keith's insistence on faith in the basics of Christian doctrine as the heart of Christianity raised once again the relationship between the Inner Light and Christian doctrine that had occasioned earlier disputes between Friends and their critics. Penn initially affirmed Keith's theological point by affirming that "believing in Christ's manhood, it is Friends' principle." He also criticized Keith's "separation from communion" as a "weak and a wrong step," especially by one who had denounced separatists in England, and called on Keith to "let fall his separate meeting" in hopes that "peace would follow."[41]

Those who were present in Pennsylvania and had been watching the conflict unfold over the course of several contentious years, however, were aghast that Penn sided, even gently, with Keith. "Thee canst hardly believe that [Keith] is gone as bad as he is," wrote Pennsylvania Friend Hugh Roberts. "I can truly affirm thee . . . that I never saw a man (under any profession) in more passion and bitterness of spirit and more ready to catch and to discover the weakness of Friends, than he is." Roberts reported that Keith's was "not only a tearing, devouring spirit but a cursed, lying spirit" and expressed his dismay that Penn and English Friends seemed not to realize the severity of the separatists' divisiveness. "He is a man that is gone from the truth," who "[ran] Friends down . . . because they refused to subscribe his creed" and called Thomas Lloyd "a pope, a hypocrite, an impudent man." And indeed, the more Penn learned about the conflict, the more inclined he was to lay blame for the affair at Keith's feet.[42]

To make matters even more complicated, the first news of the Keithian strife reached Penn just as he learned that his colony's government was being turned over to Fletcher. He wrote in December 1693 that "the trial of [George Keith] has been industriously spread all about the nation, especially at London, at the Court, Westminster Hall, and the Parliament house" (in other words, in all the halls of power populated by people with the authority to decide Pennsylvania's fate). "The odium it has contracted in some [and] stirred up in others . . . against . . . Friends having power, against me, and you in particular are great and lamentable."[43] As he was then preparing to petition the Crown to restore his control of Pennsylvania as proprietor and for the revocation of Fletcher's commission, the news of Keith's dissent and the prosecutions could hardly have come at a worse time.

But the true extent of Keith's disaffection from Friends would only become fully evident the following year. When Fletcher arrived in Philadelphia, Keith requested and received a certificate of good behavior and sailed for England to pursue his dispute with Pennsylvania Friends before the London Yearly Meeting. From that point on, the schism was no longer a distant irritant but rather a clear and present danger to William Penn. Keith defended himself in front of the 1694 London Yearly Meeting, which declared that he ought not to have published his criticisms of fellow Friends. The following year's Meeting disowned Keith for continuing his public disparagement of Pennsylvania Quakers, whereupon Keith complained that the Second Day Meeting "may be fairly compared to the conclave of cardinals in Rome." (The effects of Keith's campaign to discredit Friends were felt for years, and Keith eventually became an Anglican priest and returned to America.)[44]

The Keithian affair cut across a variety of dimensions of early Pennsylvania society: economic, political, theological, and geographical (i.e., Lower Counties vs. Pennsylvania). It involved not only leading Public Friends but also everyday Quakers. The schism had clear theological roots—Keith's pointed description of his group as "Christian Quakers" illustrates this aspect of the dispute clearly enough—yet it also implicated the whole range of social, political, and economic cleavages in the colony and between the colony and the Lower Counties. As Gary Nash has put it, "A whole stratum of lesser merchants, shopkeepers, and master artisans . . . found that Keith's program provided a means of challenging the Lloydian 'greats,' who were resented for their aggrandizement of their own positions of authority and their narrow control of provincial life."[45] Keith attracted support from the Lower Counties, many of whose residents saw his critique of the Philadelphia elite as a useful way to further their own agendas. In fact, the bitterness of the disputes had a great deal to do with Penn's vision for Pennsylvania: despite his longstanding desire to attract "sober people of all sorts," from the very beginning of the undertaking Penn envisioned his settlement as firmly under the control of Friends. And with a critical mass of Friends in positions of political, social, and economic influence, dissent and division within the Meeting were bound to bubble over into social and political conflict.[46]

* * *

But not all the news from Pennsylvania was grim. Penn seized on the glowing reports he received for his ongoing promotional efforts, publishing a collection of them as *Some letters . . . from Pennsylvania* in 1691. Richard Morris wrote that he had "found the government in good order; the people generally in good health, only some few visited with smallpox, but no many died." What really impressed Morris, however, was the development of Philadelphia, and the improvements to the economy, agriculture, and construction. He praised the corn, hemp, and flax; the horses, oxen, cows, and hogs; pelts from beavers, otters, mink, deer, bears, fox, and cats; the manufactures of oil and whalebone, as well as wool; and the arrival of colonists from other territories relocating to Pennsylvania. And he noted the continuing rapid growth of the capital city. "The bank and river-street is so filled with houses, that it makes an enclosed street with the front in many places." There were, he reported, at least 1,400 houses, many of them large and constructed of brick. John Goodson insisted that "matters relating to Truth and the government are well amongst us" (perhaps due to the recent deliverance from Blackwell's regime). If he and his family were there, he assured Penn, "your hearts would be greatly comforted to behold this wilderness land, how it is becoming a fruitful field and pleasant garden."[47]

* * *

Even after passage of the Toleration Act, Friends continued to attract a great deal of hostility and, insofar as he was able from his enforced seclusion, Penn attempted to weigh in on issues relating to Quaker doctrine and practice. On three separate occasions during June 1692, Penn defended Quakers against criticisms that appeared in *The Athenian Mercury*, a London magazine. These brief columns, along with *A key opening the way*, a longer pamphlet that sought to convince his audience that Quakers were sincere Christians worthy of the protections offered by the Toleration Act. *A key* listed the various aspects of Quaker doctrine and practice that had attracted so much criticism for so long— the Light Within, the importance of Scripture, the divinity and manhood of Christ, political allegiance, to name just four of more than a dozen topics—and denounced the "perversions, misrepresentations and calumnies of their several adversaries, both upon their principles and practices."[48]

Just measures also appeared in 1692, and addressed the continuing divisions within the Society of Friends, which had persisted even after the deaths of "the two Johns" (Story and Wilkinson), whose dissent had given rise to separate Meetings and such bitter disputes during the 1670s. While reiterating his longstanding commitment to liberty of conscience, Penn argued that the issues raised by critics, particularly the Friends' requirement that prospective marriages be cleared by both Men's and Women's Meetings, did not reach the level of fundamental questions of faith. Such practices, Penn argued, were "chiefly concerned in the good order and service of the church," so insistence on them did not violate of individuals' consciences. He also defended the institution of Women's Meetings by pointing out that women were as fully a part of the church as men, and that separate meetings allowed women to "exercise their gifts, of wisdom and understanding" in settings free from the potentially overbearing and intimidating presence of men.[49]

Some fruits of solitude, which collected aphorisms and reflections on life's vicissitudes, and which Penn assembled during his time in seclusion, was published in 1693. It consisted of several hundred brief anecdotes on a wide variety of public and private topics such as government, religion, patience, industry, marriage, friendship, love, and personal conduct. Despite the factors that conspired to impose his solitude on him, Penn wrote that he "blesseth god for his retirement," for the opportunity it gave him to consider his life and to examine his conduct. The advice offered in the pages of *Some fruits* stressed the importance of self-control and reliance on God, and of avoiding ostentation and a host of other vices in one's personal affairs.[50]

* * *

Working in support of Friends was of course one key element of Penn's lifelong career as Quaker publicist and polemicist. But he had also, always, spoken to broader audiences. Penn's *An essay toward the present and future peace of Europe* appeared in 1693. Louis XIV's assistance to James as he attempted to regain the English throne had given King William III a justification for taking England into war against France in May 1689. The nation's entry into the war marked a stark reversal in its foreign policy: Charles II had maintained a French alliance for much of his reign, twice taking England into war against the (Protestant) Dutch. Charles and James had each benefited from Louis XIV's financial support at various times during their reigns, and had gained the backing of Anglican Tories mistrustful of Dutch republican politics, commercial pretensions, and shelter for English political exiles. Many Whigs, on the other hand, sympathized with the Protestant Dutch and instead viewed Catholic France, and Louis, as their chief foe. As a result, William's anti-French foreign policy found many supporters, and England joined the Grand Alliance against France in 1689. Whether defended as a war for Protestantism against a dangerous Catholic tyrant, a war bent on securing European states more generally against French expansionism, or a war against a foreign power seeking to return England's deposed king to the throne, the new monarchs vigorously prosecuted the conflict with France from the beginning of their reign.[51]

By 1693, when Penn published his *Essay*, the European war had been raging for four years. It would continue for another four, bringing with it the customary fruits of war: human carnage; high taxes; interrupted commerce; and increasing domestic disputes over foreign policy, the prosecution of the war effort, and England's role in the world. (It would also lead to the creation of the Bank of England, which was chartered in 1694 as a way to facilitate financing of the war effort.)[52] On the title page of his *Essay*, Penn beckoned to both Christian and classical sources by citing both the Beatitudes and Cicero's *De officiis*. He pointed to the "bloody tragedies . . . in Hungary, Germany, Flanders, Ireland, and at sea," and the "mortality of sickly and languishing camps and navies, and the mighty prey the devouring winds and waves have made upon ships and men since [16]88." He bluntly contrasted peace and war:

> Peace preserves our possessions; we are in no danger of invasions: Our trade is free and safe, we rise and lie down without anxiety. . . . It excites industry, which brings wealth, as that gives the means of hospitality. . . . But war . . . seizes all these comforts at once, and stops the civil channel of society. The rich draw in their stock, the poor turn soldiers, or thieves, or starve; No industry, no building, no manufactury, little hospitality or charity; but what the peace gave, the war devours.

Although all of these denunciations of war and celebrations of peace reflect recurrent themes in Penn's thought, it is also worth noting that, in private correspondence, he pointed out to Pennsylvanians that the European war might improve the prospects for colonial trade.[53]

Moving from a condemnation of the current war to a plan for avoiding future wars, Penn proposed a Diet, or Parliament, of European states. Such a body would be consultative in nature, and would ensure the representation of a broad range of European interests and constituencies. It included a number of features aimed at minimizing the opportunity for bribery and corruption and soothing the easily offended honor of early modern princes, including a round meeting table "to avoid quarrel for precedency" and Venetian balloting. Each state would be granted a number of delegates proportional to "an estimate of the yearly value" of that country's production; as a partial and rough estimate, "the Empire of Germany to send twelve; France, ten; Spain, ten; Italy, which comes to France, eight; England, six; Portugal, three; Sweedland, four; Denmark, three; Poland, four; Venice, three . . . And if the Turks and Muscovites are taken in, as seems but fit and just, they will make ten a piece more." As is evident, Penn took an expansive notion of "Europe," and included not only Turkey but also Russia as potential members. In this regard, his *Essay* departed from other early modern schemes of this sort, most of which understood Europe as a federation of Christian states.

And ever the pragmatist, Penn did acknowledge that such a European Diet would help rehabilitate Christianity's reputation "in the sight of the infidels."[54]

Although it does not mention Friends' principles specifically, Penn's *Essay* is a quintessentially Quaker tract; it clearly grounds itself in the Quaker peace testimony and other works that sought an end to the violent prosecution of human designs. The publication of the *Essay* was also part of a larger process by which Penn, during these difficult years and his time of seclusion, was turning his thoughts to political units larger than the colonial and the national levels.

* * *

At long last, at the end of November 1693, after more than two years in hiding and thanks to the intervention of well-placed associates like Henry Sidney (now Lord Romney), William Penn was cleared of all charges against him. Being told by the Secretary of State, Sir John Trenchard, an old acquaintance of Penn's, that he was "as free as ever" brought an end to this most humiliating and dangerous period of Penn's career and renewed his hopes of returning to America. Penn's sense of relief was palpable, and he preached in public at London's Wheeler Street Meetinghouse in mid-April. His fellow Quaker John Gratton wrote that "I am glad my eyes see the time of thy return out of this captivity." But tension between the Lloyds and Penn continued to poison his relations with his colony, Fletcher remained in control of Pennsylvania's government, and the news about the Keithian affair undermined Penn's claims that Quakers could govern themselves peacefully and that his colony should be restored to him.[55]

Furthermore, the removal of the cloud over his legal status did not erase all of Penn's difficulties. He had been living beyond his means for some time, and his financial situation did not improve during the early 1690s. In addition to his continued inability to secure funds from the Pennsylvania government—his frequent complaints about an unfulfilled £500 subscription that Philadelphia merchants had promised him in 1684 achieved nothing—Penn also faced the final collapse of his rents from his Irish properties. Instead of the £1,000 that he expected to reap annually from his Irish tenants, Penn claimed that he had received nothing for nearly two years. The central role played by Ireland in James's attempt to retake his throne, and the political uncertainty swirling around land titles and the consequent inability to collect rents, disadvantaged Irish landholders like Penn substantially, and in 1692 he described his Irish estate as "almost ruined." Penn's calculations of the economic hardships that Pennsylvania had inflicted on him continued to grow, and he claimed a "loss of above 30,000 pounds"—though on another occasion he cited merely £20,000. Early in 1693 he proposed that the inhabitants of Philadelphia extend him an interest-free loan of £10,000 to finance his return to America.[56] They declined.

To Penn's legal, political, and financial problems were added domestic grief and a series of physical ailments. He complained of a six-week spell of fever in July 1690, to which was added, in November 1692, a five-week bout of fever along with rheumatism and an abscess. A year later Penn suffered an extreme toothache that impeded his ability to accomplish everyday tasks like writing. In November 1689 Penn's daughter Gulielma, the second child named for her mother, died. The child had been, he said, a "delight and diversion in my troubles." Though Springett, Letitia, and William Jr. survived, little Guli was the fourth of William and Gulielma's children to die before the age of five.[57]

But death had further shaken Penn's world during these difficult years. Three lions of the Quaker faith passed from the scene within four months early in the 1690s: John Burnyeat in September 1690; Penn's dear friend and fellow theologian Robert Barclay in October 1690; and George Fox in January 1691. Penn described Burnyeat, who had been convinced by Fox in 1653 and spent nearly four decades playing a leading role in Friends' affairs, as "a choice and seasoned vessel of Christ," a "fixed and bright star in the firmament of God's heavenly power and kingdom." Penn described Barclay, the most theologically sophisticated Friend of his generation, as "bold and able in maintaining Truth, sound in judgment, strong in argument, cheerful in travails and sufferings, of a pleasant disposition, yet solid, plain, and exemplary in his conversation." "He was a learned man," Penn noted, as well as "a good Christian, an able minister, a dutiful son, a loving husband, a tender and careful father, an easy master, and a good and kind neighbor and friend."[58]

But surely the most grievous blow among these three, not only to Penn himself but to the Society of Friends more generally, was the loss of Fox, who had occupied the role of "First Friend" for decades, outlasting (and outliving) his rivals for that position, and had served as a kind of surrogate father to Penn. He died at the London home of Quaker Henry Goldney, near the same Gracechurch Street Meetinghouse at which a younger William Penn had been arrested in 1670. As a sign of Penn's importance, even in these difficult times, he was charged with writing to Fox's widow Margaret and telling her the news. "I am to be the teller . . . of sorrowful tidings . . . that thy dear husband, and my beloved and dear Friend George Fox, has finished his glorious testimony this night." "He died as he lived, a lamb, minding the things of God and his church to the last in an universal spirit." Penn provided additional details to Friends in the colony, informing them that Fox had particularly remembered them even as he approached death. "He earnestly recommended to me, his love to you all, and said, 'William, mind poor Friends in America.'" In his memorial to Fox, Penn praised Fox's "plainness, zeal, steadiness, humility, gravity, punctuality, charity, and circumspect care in the government of church affairs," describing him as "no busy-body, nor self-seeker, neither touchy nor critical." He was "meek, contented, modest, easy, steady, tender, [and] it was a pleasure to be in his company," "a man that God endowed with a clear and wonderful depth, a discerner of others' spirits, and very much a master of his own." In short, Penn concluded, "he was an original, being no man's copy." Penn concluded with the following words: "Many sons have done virtuously in this day, but, dear George, thou excellest them all."[59]

And death would hit even closer to home in early 1694. Gulielma had been ill with an undisclosed malady for nine weeks in early autumn 1692, and "dangerously relapsed" that November, during which time the couple were apparently separated from each other. John Gratton had "heard . . . of her weakness and exercise," and Penn reported that Gulielma "has run a weak course" the following fall. Her increasingly frail condition persisted until finally, on February 23, 1694, in the presence of her husband and children, Gulielma Springett Penn died. Grieving with "extreme great affliction for the decease of my dear wife," William pronounced himself "though afflicted, not forsaken." He took comfort in the fact that "in great peace and sweetness she departed," having had the opportunity to bid farewell to her husband, children, and friends in the days before her passing.[60]

Penn's grief was deep and intense. His relationship with Gulielma tracked, in a way, his life as a convinced Quaker. The two had met shortly after his convincement. Her family, including the formidable presence of Isaac Penington and Gulielma's mother Mary, had provided him with a solid Quaker influence that the Penns, as non-Friends, could not and did not offer. Testimonies to Gulielma's generous spirit and keen intelligence came from many sources, and Penn later wrote in her memory, quite simply: "She was an excelling person . . . as child, wife, mother, mistress, friend, and neighbor." In a letter written late in April, Penn, still grieving, described Gulielma as "one of the most excellent women that the age or I believe the world has had." He was "very ill" in the months following his wife's death.[61]

* * *

Amidst his grief over Gulielma's death, Penn continued his attempts to regain his colony. He formally petitioned Queen Mary for the return of his proprietorship, emphasizing the peacefulness that had obtained in Pennsylvania in the wake of the 1688 Revolution and the unlikelihood of French or Indian incursion due to its location "in the center of the English colonies." Penn also dismissed complaints about Quaker pacifism, pointing to the population of non-Quakers available to defend the territory, and ended his plea by emphasizing that although his name had been cleared and "the King is pleased to let him enjoy his liberty," nonetheless that liberty was "imperfect, whilst he cannot enjoy and improve his property" (i.e., his colony). The queen's legal advisors, Attorney General Sir Edward Ward and Solicitor General Thomas Trevor, weighed in during the following two weeks. On August 3, the Lords of Trade recommended to the

Queen that Penn's colony be restored to him and that Fletcher's commission be revoked. Less than a week later, the queen announced the monarchs' decision to her Council. Finally, on August 20, the proclamation from William and Mary restoring Penn to his proprietorship was published at Westminster. It was one of the few pieces of good news Penn received that year. [62]

It was not an unqualified victory, however: Penn was forced to make painful concessions in order to regain Pennsylvania. The royal proclamation stated that Penn "has given us good assurance, that he will . . . provide for the safety and security of [the province and territories]." The report of the Lords of Trade had spelled out more clearly what such a phrase meant, and had reported Penn's agreement to "the supplying such quota of men or the defraying of their part of such charges as their majesties shall think necessary for the safety and pres- ervation" of the country. (Pennsylvania's quota at that time was eighty men.) In other words, Penn had committed the Quaker government of Pennsylvania to either provide or pay for militiamen. If he did not deliver on that promise, Penn agreed that "he will then submit the direction of military affairs to their majesties pleasure." He had also agreed to maintain Markham, the non-Quaker, as his Deputy Governor, and to return in person to Pennsylvania as soon as was feasible. Despite his pleas to the Provincial Council that he had made the best deal he could, and that "we must creep where we cannot go," the Quaker govern- ment was no more willing to fund a militia contribution when the request came from Penn himself than when it came from Blackwell or Fletcher.[63]

In his account of the events of 1688, Steve Pincus has argued that "the pe- riod 1689–1697 is best understood as an era of revolutionary warfare." William Penn's career was one of the casualties of that warfare. But as 1694 drew to a close, having emerged from hiding, buried his wife, and regained control of his colony, Penn had reason to hope that his fortunes were changing for the better.[64]

1. Admiral Sir William Penn (1621–1670), portrait by Sir Peter Lely, c. 1665/ 1666. © National Maritime Museum, Greenwich, London, Greenwich Hospital Collection, used by permission.

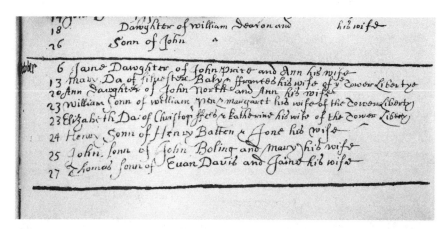

2. Register entry showing the baptism of "William, sonn of William Penn and Margaret his wife of the Tower Liberty," at All Hallows by the Tower, London, October 23, 1644. Photograph by Angelo Hornak, and used courtesy of All Hallows by the Tower, London.

3. The "Penn window" at Chigwell School, through which a young William Penn may have looked during his time as a student. Photo courtesy of The Chigwell School.

4. The original building and entrance of the Chigwell School, seen here, remain in everyday use as part of the school's campus. Photo courtesy of The Chigwell School.

5. The Castle Arch at Macroom Castle. Virtually all that remains of the castle in which the Penns lived during the second half of the 1650s is this entrance, which faces the town square away from the River Sullane. Teresa Mucha/Pixels.com.

6. Ruins of Macroom Castle. Photograph by the author.

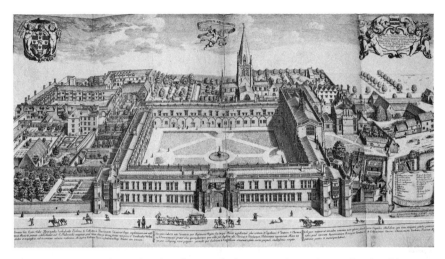

7. David Loggan, *Christ Church College, Oxford*, c. 1673, shows the north side of the Great Quad (now known as Tom Quad), completed in 1665, which would have been under construction during Penn's time at Oxford.

8. Sir William Petty (1623–1687), political economist, overseer of the Down Survey of Ireland, and sometime advisor to William Penn. Portrait by Isaac Fuller, c. 1651. © National Portrait Gallery, London, used with permission.

9. William Penn, artist unknown, c. 1666. Courtesy of the Philadelphia History Museum at the Atwater Kent, The Historical Society of Pennsylvania Collection.

10. Gulielma Springett Penn (1644–1694), artist unknown. © Religious Society of Friends (Quakers) in Britain.

11. Benjamin West (1738–1820), *Penn's Treaty with the Indians*, 1771/1772. Courtesy of the Pennsylvania Academy of the Fine Arts, Philadelphia. Gift of Mrs. Sarah Harrison (The Joseph Harrison, Jr. Collection).

12. Edward Hicks (1780–1849), *Penn's Treaty with the Indians*, c. 1840/1844. Courtesy National Gallery of Art, Washington.

13. Pennsbury Manor, Penn's estate on the banks of the Delaware River in Bucks County, Pennsylvania, as reconstructed and rebuilt during the 1930s. Courtesy of Pennsbury Manor, Pennsylvania Historical and Museum Commission, and the Pennsbury Society.

14. William Penn, pastel portrait by Francis Place, c. 1696. Courtesy of the Historical Society of Pennsylvania.

15. Hannah Callowhill Penn (1671–1726), pastel portrait by Francis Place, c. 1696. Courtesy of the Historical Society of Pennsylvania.

16. William Penn, engraving by John Posselwhite, after John Hall. Hall's 1775 engraving of a reversed image of Penn as depicted in Benjamin West's *Penn's Treaty with the Indians* provided Posselwhite with his image of the founder. © National Portrait Gallery, London, used with permission.

17. Hannah Callowhill Penn (1671–1726), painting by Joseph Hesselius. Courtesy of the Philadelphia History Museum at the Atwater Kent, The Historical Society of Pennsylvania Collection.

18. James Logan (1674–1751), portrait by Thomas Sully, 1831. Logan accompanied Penn to Pennsylvania in 1698 and served as his secretary for the rest of Penn's life. After Penn's death he assisted Hannah and held a number of other public offices, including Mayor of Philadelphia. Courtesy of The Library Company of Philadelphia.

19. Jordans Meetinghouse, Buckinghamshire, England. Visible here are both the meetinghouse, which was built in 1688, and the headstones marking the graves of William, Gulielma, and Hannah Penn, along with five Penn children. Photo by Gregory Zucker.

20. The Penn graves in the burial ground of Jordans Meetinghouse. Photo by Gregory Zucker.

21. Alexander Milne Calder's 37-foot bronze statue of William Penn was cast in 1892 and raised to its current location atop Philadelphia City Hall in 1894. K.L. Kohn/ Shutterstock.

11

Return to Public Life

Although by the end of 1694 he had regained control of Pennsylvania, William Penn was still no closer to making his long-delayed return to his colony. Financial woes continued to plague him. The war continued, though at long last prospects for the alliance arrayed against Louis were improving, and English military fortunes began looking up. In part the resurgence of military success was due to the stabilizing influence of the Bank of England, which "helped to boost the war effort by salvaging confidence in government short-term credit." By 1695 French forces were on the defensive. Still, communication with his colonial government—and shipping in general—continued to be extremely difficult. Even the announcement of his recovery of Pennsylvania in August 1694 was delayed in reaching the colonists, when the ship bearing the queen's revocation of Fletcher's commission was "unhappily taken by the French" and the correspondence "carried into France." The news likely did not even reach Pennsylvania until early 1695, and Penn had to pay for a second copy of the Queen's proclamation out of his own pocket. The war would finally end, driven less by a decisive victory than by financial exhaustion on all sides, with the Treaty of Ryswick in September 1697. Requiring all parties to cede territory conquered since 1688, and including a pledge from Louis XIV to end his support for Jacobites, nonetheless "no amount of [English] rejoicing could altogether obscure the fact that a massive expenditure of blood and treasure had produced precious little wool for England."[1]

During these years, Penn divided his time between Warminghurst, Sussex, where he had made his home with Gulielma and his children since the mid-1670s and where, after his son's marriage in January 1699, William Jr. and his new wife Mary would take up residence; London, where Friends' business and proprietary affairs continually required his presence; and Bristol, his new center of gravity after his remarriage in spring 1696. His marriage to Hannah Callowhill brought together one of the pillars of London Quakerism and a leading family in the Bristol Quaker community. Bristol was fast becoming the second center of English Quakerism, rivaling London; Penn attended the 1696 Yearly Meeting in both Bristol and London. By the fall of 1696 Hannah was pregnant with their first child and the newly married couple were busy setting up their home and thus hardly eager to undertake an arduous and intense transatlantic voyage.[2]

* * *

After emerging from his legal difficulties and his years in hiding, and having secured return of his colony, William Penn decided to undertake an extended preaching tour of southwestern England. And so began a feverish journey of the kind he had not undertaken since his younger days. Accompanied by his eldest son Springett and, part of the way, by John Whiting, a prolific Quaker writer, he set out from Bristol in November 1694. Penn moved south to Chew Magna, then west to Claverham, and finally to Whiting's hometown of Wrington, about a dozen miles southwest of Bristol. From Wrington Penn returned to Bristol, where he spent several weeks attending "very large meetings." Departing Bristol again, Penn headed south and west, through Dorsetshire and Devonshire, holding Meetings "in most of the great towns" of these counties. Turning north and arriving in the cathedral city of Wells, Penn reunited with Whiting, and by late December they had returned to Wrington. They held a large Meeting in the town hall there on the night that Queen Mary died.[3]

During these travels, Penn visited Meetings and preached in public halls, Meetinghouses, and even on one occasion, when a large enough hall could not be secured, in a field, outside Somerton. Whiting and Penn parted at Barrow, with Whiting returning home and Penn proceeding on to the Bristol Monthly Meeting, in late December 1694. All along the way, Whiting reported, Penn's reputation preceded him, and crowds turned out for "great meeting[s] in the town hall[s] . . . in most places, which the mayors general consented to, for the respect they had to him." London Friend Henry Gouldney wrote that "Bristol was scarcely ever so visited and [Penn] never better received. . . . Twas supposed that several times they had about 4000 at a meeting there, and persons of great account generally satisfied."[4]

A year later, Penn once again made his way to the west, where he again drew large and enthusiastic crowds. Before setting out, he had written to the Duke of Shrewsbury, the Secretary of State, requesting a letter attesting that he had been cleared of all charges against him, "that I am fair with government and under the protection of it." Penn was particularly concerned about the potential for trouble since he would be traveling and preaching during an election season, when political tensions might be heightened. The duke reassured Penn that if anyone interfered with him "upon a mistaken zeal to serve the government," Shrewsbury would "not fail to do everything in my power" to rectify the situation. As it turned out, Penn did in fact encounter some election-related hostility, and was nearly imprisoned at Wells in mid-November 1695. His brief account of the episode, in which he referred to "that dark city of Wells, where a meeting never was to that day" is recounted in a letter to Aaron Atkinson, a Bristol Friend who would later journey to Pennsylvania, but Whiting's *Persecution exposed* provides more detail about what happened there.[5]

According to Whiting, a group of Friends, including Richard Vickris (whom Penn had spared a death sentence, by obtaining him a pardon in 1684), had secured use of the Wells market house for a Meeting. But others in town, "having been drinking Colonel Berkeley's election ale," persuaded the clerk of the market to refuse them access. Fortunately, the Quakers secured space at the Crown Inn just down the street, where they were able to reserve "a large room, and balcony, facing the market place." By the time William Penn stepped onto the balcony to speak to the gathered crowd, several thousand people had assembled. Unbeknownst to Penn and the Friends with him, Mayor Matthew Baron had issued a warrant for the arrest of "William Penn and several other Quakers," who were allegedly "now riotously and unlawfully assembled and gathered together in this city, and . . . preaching or teaching in a house not licensed according to the late Act of Parliament." Penn was apprehended while preaching and taken before the mayor. With William Hughes, the chancellor of Wells Cathedral, Mayor Baron questioned Penn, and he was ultimately, as he put it, "dismissed honorably." Following his narrow brush with the law Penn departed with one of the justices of the peace, "who had gladly heard him that day, and was friendly." Penn then left Wells along with Vickris.[6]

* * *

Penn's two western trips had enabled him to reestablish a public profile after years of lying low, but he had other interests as well. At some point during his first tour, Penn had met Hannah Callowhill, the daughter of prominent Bristol merchant and fellow Friend Thomas Callowhill, a button manufacturer and linen draper who had purchased more than five thousand acres of Pennsylvania land from Penn in 1681. He had known the family for some time: Hannah's grandfather, Dennis Hollister, one of the first Quakers in Bristol, had welcomed a young William Penn to lodge into his home in 1669 as the young Quaker was preparing to set out for Ireland.

Penn called his 1695 western tour "a working time as well as a wooing time." Hannah, whom Penn described to Aaron Atkinson as "lovely in the truth, above most of the Daughters of Zion," was less than half Penn's age, and some Friends expressed unease about the swift progression of the widower's affections. The Callowhill family's wealth led some (particularly if they were well acquainted with Penn's financial woes) to wonder about the purity of his intentions, but Penn's family voiced few qualms. Letitia—"Tishe," to friends and family—told Hannah a year later that she had suspected her father's affection "at [his] first coming from Bristol" after his 1694 travels there. "Though I kept it to myself," she wrote, "I perceived which way his inclinations were going" by the frequency with which he talked about her and his effusive praise of her character. (Penn himself claimed to Hannah that she had been "seated . . . upon my spirit, many times, before I ever opened my mouth to man or woman about thee.") Tishe sent a gift of venison as a token of her friendship. Margaret Lowther, Penn's sister, sent her a pot of lobsters in December 1695.[7]

Like many a savvy suitor, William Penn approached Hannah through her parents, sharing a recipe for drying fruit with her mother (also named Hannah) and assuring the elder Hannah in June 1695 that she and her family were "daily fresh in my [memory] upon the best account." His stock of recipes and medications was not limited to the Callowhill recommendations; that same month he offered Derbyshire Quaker John Gratton a recipe for the treatment of jaundice. The treatment involved drinking garlic boiled in milk, or ivory shavings boiled in white wine. Penn seemed to acknowledge what he was asking—"If thou canst" drink garlic boiled in milk, he instructed Gratton—as well as to express some uncertainty about the likelihood of a cure, telling Gratton that "I hope thy jaundice will be cured." When he sent Hannah three gallons of French brandy in January 1696, he insisted that she give one to her mother.[8]

The first surviving piece of correspondence between William Penn and Hannah Callowhill dates from September 10, 1695, and contains a straightforward declaration of the widower's love: "I behold, love, and value thee, and desire, above all other considerations, to be known, received, and esteemed by thee." Hannah was evidently less forthcoming with her affections; William added that he "would persuade myself thou art of the same mind, though it is hard to make thee say so." Following his 1695 tour, Penn returned home to Warminghurst, writing to Hannah that he had arrived "safely home, if I may truly call any place so where thou art not." "I left so much of my heart there [in Bristol]," he told her, "that it is very improperly said that I am here."[9]

The couple announced their intention to marry on November 11, 1695, at the Bristol Monthly Meeting, and reaffirmed those intentions two weeks later. On December 11, he announced his intention to marry to his own Meeting, the Horsham (Sussex) Men's Monthly Meeting. In customary Quaker fashion, the Meeting appointed a committee of Friends to "enquire concerning [Penn's] clearness" regarding marriage. Early the next month the committee reported that "he is very clear in that matter," and ordered a certificate drawn up to that effect and sent to Bristol Friends.[10]

Over the course of the next two months Penn would write to Hannah at a feverish pace—several times a week on average. Unfortunately, no letters from Hannah to William survive from their courtship, and knowing more about the young Friend's attitude toward her suitor would greatly enhance our understanding of this time in her and Penn's life. In mid-January 1696, William was still plying Hannah to be more open about her feelings toward him. "It would exceedingly add to my joy, that I might find renewed testimonies of thy sense . . . in the returns of the same unalterable love, of which I cannot doubt." A month later, he alluded to the fact that she harbored doubts, bolstered no doubt by the murmurings of Friends, about their suitability or compatibility, noting "thy general indifference, if not aversion, [to] my years, and character." Just a day later, he expressed his hopes that "the slowest beginnings are often the most safe and successful."[11]

But if we lack firsthand knowledge of Hannah's state of mind (and heart), the eighteen letters that survive from her suitor between December 1695 and February 1696 provide a great deal of insight into the middle-aged William Penn. They of course contain the customary, and at times effusive, expressions of love: "my love is renewed daily toward thee. . . . Neither distance, nor absence, nor any other thing hath any power to lessen it, or in the least cool or abate of the reality or fervency of it." He described a love "that lives and flows to thee every day, with continual desire for thy felicity in every way" and called himself "the man of the world that most entirely loves and values thee, above every sincere comfort." He expressed delight at her gift of a dove to him and referred to her love—perhaps surprisingly, perhaps not, given how much grief his colony had given him—as "a proprietorship [I value] above that of Pennsylvania."[12]

Much of the correspondence covers prosaic and mundane matters of everyday life. He expressed great concern about her health, chiding her to listen to her doctors and nurses, while at the same time offering his own homegrown remedies, such as heated milk or wine sacks applied to the eyes. He rejoiced when he heard of her recovery from illness. He passed along a recipe for "convulsion water" to be taken "three days before the full and change of the moon, one spoonful . . . as often as oppressed with wind." He provided glimpses of his own health, reporting a recurrent problem with minor nosebleeds and an undisclosed illness that laid him low during January 1696.[13]

He told her about his children; Letitia's role in assisting at childbirths, and Springett's travels to oversee lands in and around Lewes that he had inherited from his mother. He reported on Billy, his namesake, who spent much of January battling influenza, and adds in other domestic details like Billy's getting a haircut. Billy's condition seesawed throughout the month, with his father describing his "drooping condition . . . being sensibly worse, but this evening he is more pert and lively, though not out of danger." William used Hannah's suggested combination of bitter and cordial herbs in an attempt to improve Billy's condition, but the results were inconclusive. A week later Billy was "at best, at a stand," though by early February his father pronounced him "stronger and hungry, and has no fever." Finally, on February 9, 1696, a jubilant William wrote to Hannah that Billy "is much better, and visibly increases in his looks and strength" and even "quarrels us all for victuals 4 or 5 times a day." After the tense, month-long bout of flu that Billy suffered, Springett's "ugly cold and cough" in early February must have seemed rather trivial.[14]

He asked her to write more clearly, so that he did "not lose or miss a word of thine," and more frequently as well, noting at one point that he had written ten letters to her four replies. At times gently, at others more pointedly, he expressed his dissatisfaction with her (relatively) infrequent replies, and urged her to "mend thy pace." Then again, he worried about having upset her with his frequent importuning. It pained him to think, he wrote, "that anything I have writ should make thee uneasy, whom I love & prefer above all the world, & in whose love I seek my own happiness."[15]

And, always, he expressed his impatience to wed—"let nothing protract or delay it"—and to set up their new household. By late January he was telling Hannah that "I intend, as fast as I can, to make thee my most dear wife, and to love, prize, and tender thee above all my worldly comforts." A number of details still remained to be worked out, of course, including which goods to arrange for delivery to the Bristol home that Hannah's parents had located for the newlyweds; which servants to hire, a decision that included the delicate question of whether to keep Gulielma's housekeeper Sarah Hersent with Penn's new family; and practical questions like the color Hannah desired for the interior of the couple's coach. Penn expressed his preference for country- over city-bred servants, decrying "the pride, conceitedness, and gossiping of too many of city education," though he left final decisions about the household largely in Hannah's hands. Penn preferred country over city generally, and though he deferred to Hannah and her family's wishes he clearly did not relish moving into a smaller home in an urban setting. Then again, doing so may have been a condition of obtaining her parents' consent, as Pennsylvania Quaker Thomas Janney reported that "I am told also that he must live in [Bristol] for her parents can not part with her."[16]

Remarriage after the death of a spouse was common in early modern England, considering the high mortality rates women faced, with childbirth just the most obvious and significant risk. That said, some of Penn's London Friends would surely have preferred a slightly longer period of mourning, a slightly extended courtship, or a slightly more appropriate (in their view) object of his affection. The concerns that Friends voiced, many of them sotto voce, reflected perceptions that the chronically indebted Friend might have things other than love on his mind. There was opposition, or at least concern, among many Friends, about what Penn called "my matter." Henry Gouldney wrote to John Rodes that "this affair is not very well relished by many." Others attempted to balance their concern for Penn's plans with more general esteem for the man himself: "I know not how to show dislike at what he doth; he is a man to whom I have given preference in my respect and esteem to any I know, therefore must be excused, if I am sparing of writing against his present proceedings." As with most criticism, Penn took it poorly, and insisted on the validity of his own experience of love: "I know what moved, how it came, how I received it, and in whose sight, and how it has lived in [the Lord's] present, and been an increase of my life and joy." He tried to use the murmuring of Friends as a way of cementing his relationship with Hannah: "What we have met with will but help to sanctify that day to our unspeakable comfort." Penn was insulted by the insinuations that he was simply after Hannah's money or that he was rushing things, and his impending marriage strained Penn's relationships with such Friends as Gratton, who did not attend the wedding, although several months later he wrote expressing his regret for the rift that had opened up between the two men. On Penn's return from Ireland in 1698, Gratton wrote to him once again, evoking their former intimacy: "Dear Friend, is the cords broke that drawed thee formerly to see us; are we not worthy of one visit in all thy life time; canst thou pass us by forever?" (Penn responded the following July, assuring Gratton that "I remember thee often.")[17]

Despite the slow progress of Hannah's affections, the concerns of many Friends, and the pronounced age difference between the two, William Penn and Hannah Callowhill were married on March 5, 1696. The marriage certificate was signed by sixty-eight witnesses, most of whom hailed from Bristol, and five of whom were members of Gulielma's family. While the marriage had alienated Penn from some of his former London associates, many of whom "seem to have made a special point of staying away to signal their disapproval," nonetheless "Bristol Friends . . . warmly welcomed" Penn into their community.[18]

Of course Penn's remarriage was also bound to have an impact on his colony. Janney reported that he was making a lucrative match, with a dowry rumored to be £10,000, but quickly pointed out that, since Penn was obliged to stay near Hannah's family, "I gather that he is in no capacity to come to Pennsylvania at present." All of this should make Pennsylvania Friends consider carefully whether having Penn return for another brief visit was in anyone's best interests.[19]

* * *

Scholars have at times drawn fairly stark contrasts between Penn's two wives, presenting Gulielma as the "true love" of Penn's youth, a beautiful "soul mate" who died tragically young, with "plain" Hannah as the practical helpmeet of a corpulent, middle-aged Penn. (One of Penn's earlier biographers, Harry Emerson Wildes, called Gulielma a "striking beauty" while describing Hannah as "clever, attractive, and possessed of . . . marked serenity," despite the fact that almost no reliable visual images of either woman survive.) To be sure, the women hailed from different social backgrounds, with Gulielma and William sharing class roots among the minor gentry while the Callowhills represented the newly ascendant merchant class. And of course Penn and Gulielma were twenty-eight and twenty-seven respectively when they wed, whereas William and Hannah's ages diverged significantly.[20]

It is possible to push these distinctions too far, however. Alison Duncan Hirsch has persuasively argued that "the two women had much in common: both appear to have been wealthy, intelligent, devout, physically attractive, active in Quaker affairs, and astute in business matters." Each of Penn's wives brought considerable wealth to the marriage, and each of his marriages represented the uniting of a major Quaker figure with an influential Quaker family. In 1672, Penn was a famous young Quaker convert, recently acquitted in a famous trial, bearing the name of a nationally known naval figure, and clearly in the early stages of an illustrious career as a Public Friend. In 1696, he was a colonial proprietor, the controversial confidant of a recently deposed king, and a well-connected public figure who had recently regained access to the halls of power. Penn clearly professed his ardent love for Gulielma in correspondence just prior to his journey to America in 1682, and had filled many letters to Hannah with effusive and ardent declarations of love. Each marriage lasted more than two decades— twenty-two years each, to be exact—and was by all accounts close and loving. The marriages also represent two different periods in the history of English Quakerism—one emerging from its tempestuous origins and another coming to terms with the increasing respectability and prosperity of its members—and thus the differences between the two women and their relationships with Penn may tell us as much about the history and development of Quakerism as they do about the affairs of Penn's heart.[21]

* * *

But Penn's joy in his new marriage to Hannah was destined to be interrupted before long. His eldest son Springett, whom Quaker John Tomkins called "the most beloved of his children," took ill not long after the wedding and died on April 10, 1696. "Last night arrived here," wrote Tomkins on April 16, "the corpse of Springett Penn, in its passage to Buckingham, there to be interred tomorrow at Jordans by his mother. Our dear friend W. P. accompanies the corpse with his wife, his son, and daughter, and father Callowhill . . . This is an occasion of great sorrow to our friend, but it is his portion to have wormwood mingled with his drink."[22]

Penn was devastated. Springett, whom Penn described as "from his childhood manifest[ing] a disposition to goodness" (pointing particularly to his "humility, plainness and truth," and "a tenderness and softness of nature"), had suffered with a cold and cough in January, but it was young William Jr. who had actually received the lion's share of his father's attention as he battled influenza for the better part of that month. In a remembrance published several years later, Penn praised Springett's piety and the way that he faced his demise. Once, "when I went to Meeting, at parting, he said, Remember me, my dear father, before the Lord: Though I cannot go to

Meetings, yet I have many good Meetings; the Lord comes in upon my spirit, I have heavenly Meetings with him by myself." Father and son passed tender moments together in Springett's final days, and the son voiced a desire, if he recovered, to accompany his father on future preaching tours. In telling the story of Springett's final days, Penn called him "my comfort and hope, and one of the most tender and dutiful, as well as ingenuous and virtuous youths I knew ... My friend and companion, as well as most affectionate and dutiful child."[23]

Springett Penn was buried next to his mother and several of William and Gulielma's other children, at the Jordans Meetinghouse in Buckinghamshire. In his grief, Penn sought the company of Friends. Tomkins wrote, "He intends soon after this to be at Bristol, to be at yearly meeting there, and afterwards to yearly meeting at London."[24]

* * *

One constant in William Penn's life from the mid-1680s through the 1690s was a deep dismay caused by the conflicts that continued to roil Pennsylvania. His most faithful correspondent, Robert Turner, was both a strong supporter and an honest source of often unpleasant truths. Turner wrote on behalf of the Council in late summer 1694, telling Penn that "the people murmur," that Thomas Lloyd "is absent from the country," and that Thomas Holme's eyesight continued to deteriorate—to say nothing of his drinking problem (both fatal flaws in a surveyor). The lack of contact made governing the province extremely challenging and well-nigh impossible, precisely the reason that some Pennsylvania Friends sought to keep him in the dark. "Thou hast given me no answer, nor to many other things of thy own concern." Turner followed this letter with another, a month later, which included details about a brewing legal battle over the Schuylkill River ferry crossing. Penn had granted Philip England, a Quaker originally from Dublin, exclusive rights to maintain a ferry for Schuylkill crossings at High Street, but a Welsh resident had also begun operating one nearby. The Council jailed the Welsh ferrymaster and seized his boat, which set off further unrest. All this was made more complicated, Turner complained, by the fact that Penn "gives not one word of answer to mine sent thee about them." Turner too had a personal stake in some of these disputes. Penn had verbally promised him that a market would be established near his property close to the Delaware dock. The Provincial Council, however, had decreed that it be held only at High and Second Streets. Not surprisingly, development near Turner's property had dwindled in the wake of this decision, and he lamented "the ruins and desolation of houses this way, since the market removed." More than three years later Turner would still be complaining to Penn about the matter.[25]

The Pennsylvania government was shaken that fall, as well, by the death of Thomas Lloyd. Here again, mistrust and dissension prevailed, as a seemingly simple matter—the retrieval of the Great Seal from its deceased keeper's residence—took on an air of political intrigue. Lloyd's widow Patience refused to deliver the seal to the Council, and informed them that Assembly Speaker David Lloyd had already attempted to secure it from her. Ultimately Patience entrusted it to Margaret Cook, the wife of Councilor Arthur Cook, but given the developing rift between Cook and other Councilors, to say nothing of tensions between the Assembly and Council, the official seal of the colony quickly became a potential spoil of political conflict. Attendance at Council meetings was flagging, as some Councilors spent more time at their country estates than on official business in the capital, others focused on their own business dealings, and others, like Holme, dealt with accumulating physical ailments. Penn attempted to reinstate some order in the business of tax and rent collection, commissioning Samuel Jennings as Receiver General in late September, but there was clearly much ground to be made up and, as before, difficulties in communication hobbled his efforts.[26]

In addition to his constant concern with his missing rents and revenues, Penn's unhappiness with Pennsylvania affairs had always been motivated by two related concerns: for the moral and spiritual health of the community, as he had envisioned it during the early 1680s and, in his more hopeful moments, still aspired for it to be; and for the harm that reports making their way back to England could do to his colony. "As to the present condition of the province," he wrote in November 1694, "pray be careful that the charter be strictly observed and all vice and impiety diligently suppressed." Two years later, Penn complained to Turner that "I hear vice reigns, to the reproach of the province"; he urged Turner to have Markham "suppress it with a high hand." On this issue, Penn and Turner were in complete agreement. Turner lamented the colony's "growing debauchery" the following spring, and five months after that Penn again repeated his injunctions against vice and immorality, citing reports reaching him that "there is no place more overrun with wickedness, sins so very scandalous, openly committed in defiance of law and virtue." Turner wrote back to Penn that "wickedness grows and vice remains . . . to the sorrow and reproach of God's people." This connection between "vice" and "reproach" clearly indicates Penn's two related concerns: not only would observance of the charter and the suppression of vice guard Pennsylvanians' civil liberties and ensure a sober and prosperous polity, it would frustrate the efforts of Penn's enemies to undermine his newly regained proprietorship by defaming the colony and its leaders.[27]

* * *

Chief among those aspersions was the accusation that Pennsylvania's government was shirking its responsibility to its own defense as well as that of the colonies more generally. Although he no longer controlled Pennsylvania's government, Benjamin Fletcher still coordinated colonial defenses in his capacity as

Governor of New York, and he reported to the Lords of Trade that Pennsylvania was continuing to neglect its assigned quota of men or money. Penn had agreed to rectify this situation as a condition of regaining his proprietorship, and struggled to justify his government's continued recalcitrance, particularly when, as he pointed out to leading Pennsylvania Quakers, Friends in England paid taxes that supported the war against France. "Here we pay to carry on a vigorous war against France . . . Friends here admire at the difficulty of the people there to pay, saying it seems to contradict us here." Surely, he went on, such payments could be defined in such a way to assuage Quakers' consciences, either through paying a third party to make the arrangements or levying an assessment "for mixed services."[28]

Penn was clearly worried that continued reports about Pennsylvania's recalcitrance with regard to militia affairs "may overset the government again." A 1696 petition from Pennsylvania's Anglicans complained about the lack of a militia, which the colony's Quaker governors "not only refuse to settle . . . but give all the discouragement they can," and about the government's failure to follow requirements of the charter in the management of elections and court sessions. And indeed, the Board of Trade returned to the quota issue on several occasions, noting Pennsylvania's continued flouting of its obligations in February 1697 and directing Penn to ensure the contribution of "either . . . men or money for the general security of [the] colonies on the continent of America." Given the colony's relative youth compared to its neighbors to the north and south, Penn argued, Pennsylvania's quota was unduly excessive: "We are but 14 years old [and] have never seen the repeated returns [that] New York, Maryland, and Virginia, etc. have enjoyed." In this Penn echoed objections made by the Assembly in November 1696, protesting that neighboring provinces, "having been long settled and had greater advantages of time and trade," ought to provide more than Pennsylvania. But his objections were to no avail. Penn had hoped that his appointment of the Anglican Markham as his Deputy Governor would calm royal concerns, and that Markham "having the military power, answers their [the Lords of Trade's] intentions." But Markham could not order the Assembly to act, and the stalemate continued.[29]

The militia issue was just one of a number of attacks on the Quaker administration of Pennsylvania. The colony's legal system, with its prohibition on oaths, offended the consciences of many non-Quakers, for whom the absence of swearing in the courtroom raised the specter of rampant untruthfulness and anarchy. (Quaker defenses—that they punished untruthful witnesses as if they had violated a sworn oath—rang hollow to such critics.) In short, the Anglicans argued, we "are openly exposed to ruin by daily and woeful experiences" as a result of their living under "the Quakers [who] are prejudiced and partial to all persons that are not of their persuasion," to say nothing of their "principles, doctrine, and public preaching," which "do most blasphemously deny our blessed Lord and Saviour Jesus Christ." "How then can we expect honesty and justice from such men?" They petitioned the king to appoint a royal governor, perhaps Francis Nicholson, a staunch Anglican, military man, and defender of royal authority in America then serving as governor of Maryland. Nicholson had cut his teeth as Lieutenant Governor to Edmund Andros in Massachusetts, and was no fan of Quakers.[30]

But Quakers did not take these charges lying down, and submitted their own counter-petition in May 1696, denying the charges and denouncing their critics as little more than participants in "night revels and other licentious practices." They knew, though, that the militia argument had the potential to fatally undermine their authority, particularly since Penn had offered guarantees in 1694 when appealing for the return of his authority. Offering what the editors of Penn's *Papers* call a "disingenuous argument," Pennsylvania Friends insisted that "there is as much of a militia here now as ever in Governor Fletcher's time." Fletcher had been unable to get the Assembly to vote funds for the militia before, so they were technically correct. Even more circuitously, they claimed that "we know none that are denied to bear arms that place their security in them." In other words, anyone who wants to defend the colony with arms can do so. Hardly encouraging to Anglicans, one imagines. The Quaker petition concluded with a defense of Friends' principles and an insistence on their faith in Christ.[31]

In polemics and rhetorical maneuvers designed to contest attacks from England, the colony's ruling elite minimized the distance between themselves and the proprietor. They pointed out that "for the sake of our friend and governor were many of us induced to adventure with him and expose ourselves . . . to the hazard and inconveniencies of such an undertaking." When dealing with him directly, of course, they had long charted their own course, often in direct opposition to the interests of the absentee landlord who had now been in England for more than a decade.[32]

* * *

But of all the contention in Penn's American affairs during these years—tensions between Pennsylvania and the Lower Counties, dueling petitions to the Crown, debates over the militia—the most momentous development came with the adoption, totally unbeknownst to Penn, of a new Frame of Government in November 1696. This issue, like so many others, was intertwined with the militia controversy. The Assembly pressured Markham into accepting the new Frame by making passage of a bill providing money for colonial defense contingent on his approval of it. (Markham had responded to a similar move a year earlier by dissolving the Assembly, but by 1696 he could delay no longer.) Markham's acquiescence may have been responsible for the "good understanding between the Governor and the Assembly" that Samuel Carpenter described to

Penn in a letter later that month. He also informed Penn that David Lloyd had
been sent to New York to make the payment, though the Council described the
payment as "for the supply and relief of those Indians . . . that are in friendship
with the English," and to be used for "necessaries of food and raiment."[33]

The new Frame of Government was the culmination of a nearly fifteen-year
struggle by the Assembly to gain legislative initiative. The Assembly had made
"nearly unstoppable . . . progress toward complete control of the government."
But far from settling matters, the new Frame ushered in another period of political conflict. Declaring that the original Frame was "not deemed in all respects
suitably accommodated to our present circumstances," the new constitution
provided that "the representatives of the freemen, when met in Assembly, shall
have power to prepare and propose to the Governor and Council all such bills as
the major part of them, shall see needful to be passed into laws." It also reduced
the number of members in the Council and Assembly, and inserted a franchise
and officeholding requirement (twenty-one years of age and fifty acres of land).
Although the Assembly described the new Frame as "as near to our charter of
privileges as we could, considering thy absence and the present circumstances
of affairs," it was clearly a major reconfiguration of political power in the colony,
and one that departed sharply from the proprietor's founding vision. Not surprisingly, its introduction immediately polarized an already divided society;
more ominously for Penn, it also reflected the rising influence of Assembly
Speaker David Lloyd.[34]

On its face, the adoption of a new Frame of Government was blatantly illegal, since the Frame adopted by the General Assembly in April 1683 contained
specific language laying out procedures for its own amendment. According to
Section 24 of the 1683 Frame, changes to the charter required "the consent of the
Proprietary and Governor, his heirs or assigns, and six parts of seven of the said
freemen in provincial Council and Assembly met," a requirement that had clearly
not been obtained. Divisions came to a head during the March 1697 elections,
at which voters in Philadelphia insisted on following the electoral procedures
laid out in the 1683 Frame. Thus, while the surrounding counties were electing
two Council representatives and four Assemblymen, Philadelphians insisted
on electing three and six, respectively. That same month, more than a hundred
Pennsylvanians presented a petition to Governor Markham objecting to the new
governing document. When Penn regained his proprietorship after Fletcher's administration, the petitioners argued, the original Frame of Government should
have, by rights, been reinstated. A number of the signers of this petition were
longstanding allies of Penn, but others were part of a broad coalition, including
the growing number of Anglicans in the colony, who opposed the new Frame's
"conscious tightening of the reins of power by the most affluent and powerful
segment of provincial society."[35]

Others wrote to the proprietor directly, urging Penn to reject this "new pretended Frame" with its "innovations made on our ancient approved laws and constitutions," which had resulted in the "razing of our very constitution." Turner elaborated on these objections, explaining that Friends in the colony would only elect Friends to the government, which "gives occasion of muttering and discontent," exacerbating tensions between Quakers and non-Quakers and risking further appeals to England. Surprisingly, given his willingness to direct detailed complaints at his subordinates in Pennsylvania, Penn's only direct reference to the 1696 Frame simply reiterated that the form of government was his own particular prerogative as colonial proprietor, and that departing too starkly from practice in other colonies could bring them unwanted attention: "It may awaken an objection on us that we cannot so easily answer, but furnish our enemies with a weapon to wound us."[36]

Then again, there are two sides to every dispute, and Penn also heard from supporters of the new Frame. David Lloyd and several others wrote to Penn about the disaffection of some Philadelphians, "prompted on by Robert Turner" and others, who made "great disturbances amongst the people under pretense of standing up for the people's liberties and the old charter, as they termed it." Proponents of the new system charged their opponents with playing into the hands of Quakers' enemies in England, who wanted to take the government away from Friends once again. "It is suspected that Colonel [Robert] Quary is now coming over into England," working in tandem with Maryland's Governor Nicholson to spread damaging information as part of Maryland's ongoing efforts to undermine Pennsylvania's claim to the Lower Counties. (Quary, judge of the newly-established Vice-Admiralty Court for the colony, would return the following summer, but the concern was already real.) The upshot of this letter was to implore Penn once again, "the great need . . . of thy coming to us and that with all speed. . . . We entreat thee, make no delay but hasten hasten to us." Carpenter too had earlier implored Penn that "nothing less [than] thy coming over will remedy these things in my opinion." As to the complaints about the exclusion of non-Friends from office, the Council and Assembly offered a straightforward, if dubious, justification: since Friends outnumbered non-Friends in the colony, and since Friends had invested more than non-Friends in the founding and settlement of the province, it was only right that "as representatives of the people Friends far exceed [non-Friends] in number."[37]

Letters from Pennsylvania's leadership attempted to justify their constitutional innovation by emphasizing the uncertainty they faced in their attempts to rule the colony at such a distance from the proprietor, who (on paper at least) held final say over their affairs. Carpenter gently reminded Penn that "thou left us in the beginning and infancy of those things much if not altogether unsettled and unexperienced," and further argued that the surveyors and secretaries of the province had progressively distanced themselves from the people. Along with continuing uncertainty brought on by the lack of a Surveyor General— the position had been left unfilled after Thomas Holme's death in 1695— adjustments to the structure of government were needed in order to govern the colony in ways that safeguarded the people's liberties and interests.[38]

As a result of the ongoing uncertainty caused by "want of thy presence," the Council and Assembly wrote, inhabitants of the colony found it increasingly difficult to sell or buy land with confidence. And indeed, Penn continued to receive complaints from settlers who had purchased land in the colony's early days and continued to be disappointed (at best) or bitter and venomous (at worst). Pennsylvanian Joseph Richard complained about "the trouble and cost that I have been put to . . . for my being so long as fifteen years and upwards detained of sixty acres of land." In February 1699 Thomas Fitzwater, a prominent Philadelphia Quaker, wrote to Penn of his fears of being turned out of his land "by sinister-ended men." Seeing no hope of relief from anyone in Pennsylvania when his land was resurveyed by Thomas Fairman, he appealed to the proprietor: "I apply myself to thee."[39]

Not that these concerns prevented the proprietor from continuing to sell land: he wrote in December 1697 that 150 or 160 Friends would be accompanying John Rodes from Darbyshire, and he wrote to the Welsh Quaker Hugh Roberts about "thy purpose of going with a large company for America." With Roberts more specifically, Penn seemed to have multiple motives, as he asked the Friend to "watch the motions of the discontented and inform me of it in London."[40]

* * *

The adoption of a new Frame of Government, then, grew out of Pennsylvania's unique circumstances, including an absent proprietor; Quakers and non-Quakers living in close proximity, often in mistrust or rivalry; and government attempts to navigate between English law and conditions on the ground in America. Recall that the Anglican petition of 1695 had cited the prohibition on oaths as a major grievance of the colony's non-Quakers; the issue continued to provide a key area of contention for Friends in England as well. By spring 1696, the Toleration Act had been in effect in England for seven years, and conditions for Dissenters had improved immeasurably, yet Friends still faced challenges to living conscientiously. Although gathering for worship no longer incurred legal or financial penalties, nor (for the most part) threatened believers' physical well-being, the Test Acts remained in effect, freezing many Dissenters out of government service and university posts.

Perhaps the most significant hurdle to Friends' entry into English society lay in the Quaker prohibition on swearing oaths. As John Spurr has observed, life in seventeenth-century England was "littered with oaths: oaths of religion, oaths about tax assessment. . . . Officeholders . . . from parish constables and churchwardens to the King himself, were bound by oath to perform their functions truly." As a result, the campaign for the right to offer affirmations in lieu of oaths, a long-held goal of Friends, assumed increasing importance as the 1690s proceeded. These efforts came to a head in the middle of the decade, when Friends' increasingly important role in the imperial economy, particularly among the ranks of urban merchants and tradesmen, provided them with a more visible platform from which to advocate for their concerns.[41]

These debates did not take place in a vacuum. In February 1696, as legislation permitting affirmations in place of oaths was under consideration in Parliament, a plot to assassinate King William came to light. Parliament immediately enacted an "association" endorsing William's "rightful and lawful" rule, which members of both Houses of Parliament swore, and which then was sent to local officials and even to private citizens all over England for them to subscribe as well. Not surprisingly, such pledges raised concerns for Friends. Fortunately for Quakers, the king, who had been personally lobbied by George Whitehead a year earlier, saw the affirmation cause as an opportunity to consolidate his support. Or, put differently, King William preferred an attested affirmation of loyalty over a refused oath, and embraced the legislation as a way of securing his subjects' allegiance.[42]

The passage of the Affirmation Act in April 1696 represented both the achievement of a long-sought goal and a new challenge, as the particular wording of the proposed attestation brought about yet another dilemma for Friends. Having so long defined themselves as opposed to something, Quakers now had to face the question of what, precisely, they were *for*; in other words, to define more clearly exactly what constituted an oath. Over the course of the 1690s, Quarterly and Yearly Meetings had discussed the various options and their suitability. Many Quakers found the language in the Affirmation Act, by which individuals were to "declare in the presence of Almighty God, the witness of the truth of what I say," deeply problematic. Leading Friends like Whitehead, who were in touch with political realities in Parliament, argued that unless the affirmation mentioned God in some form, Parliament would never pass the bill. But some Friends found the language of the affirmation contained in the law to be indistinguishable, or insufficiently distinguishable, from an oath. After all, Friends were still required to "declare in the presence of Almighty God," and for some members of the group, which had grounded its opposition to swearing upon Christ's injunction to "let your yay be yay, your nay be nay," it looked like a distinction without a difference.[43]

What should have been an occasion for celebration, then, turned into an intra-Quaker debate over the specific wording of the affirmation. Penn was dragged into the debate, largely against his will. In the wake of the Act's passage, the Meeting for Sufferings issued an epistle aimed at clarifying, for those who remained uncertain, "what solemn words Friends might use, or admit of, and not vary from our known principle, Swear not at all." The epistle collected the testimonies of prominent Friends—from Fox, Burroughs, Howgill, and Barclay to Penington, Whitehead, and Penn—and clearly pronounced the new legislation adequate to address the objections that Friends had advanced for years. "Let none therefore," the epistle concluded, "call this a subjecting our testimony to the will of man." But Penn worried about the potential harm of broadcasting divisions within the Society so publicly. "To tell abroad that there is differing sentiments among us," he cautioned the Meeting, "will be of ill consequence to the reputation of Truth, and separates [e.g., Keith and his supporters] will make their use of it to our disadvantage." He worried about the ultimate consequences that a heavy-handed emphasis on taking the affirmation would produce: "Brother will be set against brother, and one Friend's testimony against another." Furthermore, and practically speaking, too emphatic an acceptance of the legislation could well preclude efforts to loosen the wording in the future, by suggesting that the issue was settled, when in fact some Friends continued to find it impossible to conscientiously affirm as required by the Act.[44]

* * *

If there was an organizing thread that linked William Penn's activities after 1696, it was the defense of his colony, and the American colonies more generally, from ever-closer royal oversight and control. While Penn was settling into his new marriage and mourning for his son, and while the Affirmation Act was making its way through Parliament, other developments with important implications for American affairs were also under way. In March 1696, Parliament passed a new Navigation Act, and two months later the king created a new Board of Trade, staffed not by the Privy Councilors with whom Penn had developed longstanding personal relationships, but by professional administrators (including, for one, John Locke).[45]

The board asked Edward Randolph, the king's Surveyor General of Customs for the North American colonies, to look into colonial compliance with the Trade and Navigation Acts. Randolph had long experience in the colonies: he had played an important role in revoking the Massachusetts Bay Colony's charter in 1684 and remained a staunch supporter of royal control over colonial affairs. Randolph presented the results of his investigations to the House of Lords on February 20, 1697, in a paper that listed each colony and enumerated violations of the Trade and Navigation Acts currently occurring within each one's borders. The colonies, he alleged, at best failed to enforce the Acts and at worst actively colluded with pirates and smugglers to undermine enforcement of the acts and thus enrich colonial leaders at the expense of the Crown. Randolph proposed that the Crown set up Admiralty Courts, headed by a King's Attorney General, that would follow English civil procedures and whose verdicts would be rendered by royally appointed judges, not local juries. The proposal grew out of a sense that colonial courts were either unable or unwilling to prosecute violators of the Navigation Act, or that colonial officials were hopelessly compromised in their ability to enforce the law within their own borders. (In Pennsylvania, as in many other colonies, such cases were prosecuted through the common law courts, and thus individuals accused of violating the Navigation Acts were guaranteed jury trials. Not surprisingly, given that the juries were populated by colonists, such trials often ended in acquittals.) Nicholson had also complained to the Board of Trade about this problem, writing that he found it exceedingly difficult to get "a ship or vessel condemned for any breach of the Acts of Trade and Navigation . . . where they are tried by juries."[46]

Randolph accused the Attorneys General of Virginia, Maryland, Pennsylvania, and Massachusetts of a variety of offenses, ranging from incompetence to failing to prosecute illegal trade. About Pennsylvania he was particularly scathing, and Markham came in for particularly harsh criticism. "The Acts of Trade are not observed in this province. The judges in the Courts of Judicature are not legally qualified. . . . The governor is a favourer of the pirates. . . . Pennsylvania lies in the centre between Maryland and New York, most commodiously for the illegal trade. It will soon become a staple of Scotch and Holland goods." Of the Lower Counties, Randolph wrote, "Pirates are harboured there, and purchase their provisions of bread, beer, &c. at Philadelphia." He proposed that the Lower Counties be annexed to Maryland and placed under Governor Nicholson's control.[47]

But Pennsylvania officials did not take Randolph's criticism lying down. In addition to denying all charges, Markham used a time-tested strategy and blamed someone else, implicating his predecessor Fletcher, who (Markham claimed) had protected pirates, accepting "a purse of gold" from one group and selling a seized pirate vessel for his own benefit, netting £800 in the process. Markham's abhorrence of Randolph only grew as time went on. I "called him to account," Markham wrote to Penn in the spring of 1697, making Randolph "as humble as any spaniel dog." No sooner had he left Philadelphia, though, than Randolph "fell to abusing and reviling me." Markham was no Quaker, and was hardly bound by any peace testimony. He was, though, bound by gout. He assured Penn that "Had I not been so lame at the time, I would have . . . made him know what wood my cudgel was made of." But Markham also realized the damage that Randolph's reports could, and did, do to Penn's view of his deputy. "I perceive . . . you are very much displeased with me . . . you charge me with avarice and I cannot take it to be less than a doubt or suspicion of my honesty." "I have served you faithfully," he insisted, "but desire not to be a burden."[48]

The Pennsylvania government also denied Randolph's allegations, pointing out that they were in fact currently holding several accused privateers "in close prison," though their prosecution was complicated by the fact that the alleged crimes had been committed on the high seas, and by uncertainties about the respective jurisdictions of the admiralty courts vis-à-vis the Pennsylvania court system. Unfortunately (for colonial authorities, not the pirates), the pirates escaped from Philadelphia prison, which hardly inspired the English government's confidence in the colonists' commitment to enforcing the Trade and Navigation Acts. Then again, the Navigation Act was not well-enforced in any of the American colonies: one scholar calls the Act "not totally ineffective" and its history as evidence of "the inability of authorities to make their influence felt in a distant and expansive landscape."[49]

If these challenges threatened Penn's (and Pennsylvania's) autonomy, however, it was also true that Penn was playing an increasingly prominent role in rallying opposition to Randolph's proposals, and petitioned the king and House of Lords to allow proprietors and colonial agents a chance to reply in their own defense. The editors of Penn's *Papers* describe him as "the de facto leader of the proprietors and agents of the nonroyal colonies," calling Penn "the only proprietor with the necessary interest, energy, and influence to do battle with the Board of Trade." Penn's correspondence with Fitz-John Winthrop, grandson of the famed founder of Massachusetts Bay, who was then serving as a London agent for the Connecticut colony, makes clear that others in London looked to him for leadership and guidance as to the best way to preserve their colonies' autonomy. Early in 1697, Winthrop told Penn that "we are flushed with success under your conduct in our general affair," and expressed the group's desire that Penn return to London in person to spearhead the resistance to Randolph. The Earl of Arran went so far as to muse about "when you come to have the government of that continent [America]," a suggestion that would be important and noteworthy if it were not so laughable. The prospect of the English government placing Penn in charge of anything larger than his own territories, given his past performance, political track record, and the rumors reaching England about Pennsylvania affairs, seems rather near zero.[50]

Yet notwithstanding his rising profile among colonial agents in London, Penn faced lingering suspicion and hostility from many at Court, not least from the king himself. William pointed out to Penn that if—as Penn himself so frequently claimed in his defense—a colony's trade and prosperity ought to incur royal favor, then surely failure of colonial officials to enforce laws placed a colony's government in danger of replacement. "It is manifest," the king wrote to Penn in late April 1697, "that very great abuses have been and continue still to be practiced" in Pennsylvania.[51]

* * *

For proprietors, who considered their colonies quite literally their property, Randolph's proposals for Admiralty Courts struck at the heart of their authority. Having two distinct powers, one directly appointed by the Crown and one emanating from the proprietor, would not only violate Penn's charter (which granted him the right to appoint officers, set up ports, and collect customs), he claimed, but would also "alarm . . . the people and planters, that they will halt both their trade and improvement and ruin me." In defending his interests, Penn called on a range of influential allies, including Secretary of State for the Northern Department Sir William Trumbull; Richard Coote, the Earl of Bellomont, whom the king named governor of Massachusetts, New York, and New Hampshire, and Captain General of the colonies all the way south to the Jerseys, in 1697; the Earl of Arran; and his old friend Sunderland. Also important in this effort was William Blathwayt, the acting Secretary of State who had been named to the Board of Trade as well, and who has been described as "the chief technician of an adolescent empire." Penn had, of course, longstanding acquaintances with Arran, whose father he had known, and Sunderland, and developed a cordial alliance with Bellomont. (To Trumbull, he belittled Randolph as "a little officer.")[52]

But while colonial authorities attempted to defend their interests against Randolph's schemes, tensions between individual proprietors remained. Nicholson sent a long report from Maryland, accusing Pennsylvania's government of turning a blind eye to smuggling and piracy, violating the Navigation Act, and harboring deserters from royal ships. The longstanding disputes between Pennsylvania and Maryland over their respective borders dragged on as well. Despite Penn's victory in 1685, an official line of division between the two colonies had not yet been drawn, and in the summer of 1697 the Board of Trade ordered Nicholson to do so "at the first convenient season." Late that year, the Assembly informed Penn that Nicholson had entered Sussex County, and had been discouraging settlers there from paying taxes to Pennsylvania. This incursion was part of a pattern of behavior on Nicholson's part; two years earlier, he had entered Pennsylvania, querying residents about unjust actions committed by their government and attempting to alienate them from their rulers. Then again, Penn was not above surreptitiously gathering information about Nicholson. Markham kept Penn informed of Nicholson's encroachments on the Lower Counties and the stratagems Nicholson employed to turn inhabitants of the Lower Counties against Pennsylvania. One Marylander wrote that Nicholson was "the greatest monster in nature as ever was heard of in these parts." Whereas once Penn had done battle with Baltimore over the borders between their two colonies, and with Dongan over Indian purchases, Susquehanna lands, and the fur trade, he now faced new rivals. Nicholson's actions represented yet another round in the battles that Maryland and Pennsylvania had been fighting for nearly fifteen years, and figures like Randolph and Quary continued to vex Penn's attempt to convince the Crown of his good behavior.[53]

Maryland officials, furthermore, consistently attempted to discourage Pennsylvania's trade, placing a 10 percent duty on all English goods destined for Pennsylvania that passed through Maryland, and imposing steep duties on beer imported to Maryland from Pennsylvania. In a report to William Popple at the Board of Trade, Penn called these laws "churlish and destroying a good correspondence between the King's subjects in both provinces," and he submitted a formal complaint about them to the Board of Trade in February 1697. A blistering letter to Nicholson in November 1697, in which Penn rehashed years of accumulated slights and provocations (from rumormongering and false accusations against Markham to armed incursions into Pennsylvania and the Lower Counties), showed just how raw the Maryland dispute remained, a decade after its "resolution," with Penn using terms like "villainous" and "foul" and denouncing Nicholson for working behind his back to undermine Pennsylvania's reputation. In Penn's view, Nicholson and Randolph were aiming at nothing less than the complete severing of the Lower Counties from Pennsylvania and placing them under Maryland's jurisdiction. (About this, Penn was right.) He accused Randolph of raising his complaints about Pennsylvania "only to dispossess us."[54]

But Penn also came into conflict with other proprietors. He appeared before the Board of Trade in December 1696, objecting to New York Governor Fletcher's collection of customs duties from ships heading to East Jersey, and submitted an extensive list of complaints about Fletcher, which had been gathered by New York merchant Peter De la Noy in 1695. The proprietors of both East and West Jersey continued to complain about these practices throughout the spring and summer of 1697, though the Board of Trade showed little enthusiasm for their appeal. The proprietors attempted to pursue the matter before Treasury officials in September, but they were fighting an uphill battle, and by summer 1698 the Board of Trade had confirmed the primacy of the port of New York over that of Perth Amboy and East Jersey, citing longstanding practice and the expenses that New York incurred through its role in colonial defense.[55]

Then again, not all Penn's relationships were so strained. In January 1697, he did, at long last, obtain title to the Susquehanna lands from Thomas Dongan, about which the two had fallen out during Penn's first trip to Pennsylvania.[56]

* * *

Regardless of how much opposition to Randolph's proposals Penn stoked, his intentions were never entirely negative and self-interested. He also had ideas about ways to unite the colonies around their common interests and allegiance, and to enhance their common prosperity. He laid out some of these ideas in *A brief and plain scheam*, his attempt to find common ground between royal officials who wanted to exert control over colonial affairs and proprietors' and settlers' aspirations for autonomy. The *Scheam* aimed to make the colonies, in Penn's words, "more useful to the Crown, and one another's peace and safety." It called for annual assemblies of colonial representatives during wartime (and biennial assemblies during peacetime) to coordinate defensive preparations and foster intercolonial cooperation, with a Diet not so different from the one Penn had proposed for European powers in his essay on European peace four years earlier. Chaired by the governor of New York, the colonial assembly would settle disputes between provinces relating to trade, debts, criminal justice, and defense. Penn's *Scheam* stood little chance of success; as Owen Stanwood puts it, "Every design for colonial reorganization had to navigate the thicket of court politics, in which various factions tried to scuttle any proposals that did not advance their particular political agendas." Although it was not accepted by the Lords of Trade, it was discussed carefully in the context of the Lords' continuing concern with the defense of the American colonies. Then again, looking forward fifty years or so, we might see Penn's plan as a precursor to Benjamin Franklin's Albany Plan of 1754, which proposed a system of intercolonial cooperation and governance to combat the French threat and facilitate relations with Indian tribes.[57]

In a submission to the House of Lords at around this same time, Penn turned his attention more specifically to trade, insisting that all that was required for the American trade to flourish were three things: "hands . . . time . . . [and] a better discipline." In other words—hardly a surprising claim from a proprietor who invited "sober people of all sorts" to his colony—Penn argued that the provisions of the Navigation Act restricting the sale of American lands to English nationals discouraged foreigners from settling in the colonies, reducing the number of "hands" to build up the colonies' prosperity. "The French refugees," he pointed out, "are most skillful in silk, wine, fruit, and if sufficiently encouraged," would contribute to the prosperity of the colonies. "Time," in the form of a reprieve from custom duties, would also benefit the building up of American trade. Finally, with regard to "discipline," Penn exhorted both governments and people to a concern for the common good, condemning both the "study of private gain in officers, and the too great indulgence of licentiousness in the people."[58]

* * *

Penn's return to public prominence masked his continuing financial instability. The late 1690s brought no slowing in the growth of Penn's debts and no slackening in his willingness to complain to Pennsylvanians about it. "I have not seen sixpence these twice six years," he lamented at the end of 1696, adding that Pennsbury was in dire condition while "everyone mind[s] his own things" without a care for the proprietor whose vision and resources had gotten the entire undertaking off the ground. Early the next year he told Sir William Trumbull that he had "spent and lost above 30,000 pounds [on Pennsylvania] already." His Irish properties, which should have yielded up to £1,500 per year, were providing nothing, thanks to an unstable political situation and the military occupation that continued in the long aftermath of the Glorious Revolution. As before, Penn's complaints about his precarious finances fell largely on deaf ears, particularly since a number of leading Pennsylvanians were facing their own financial difficulties. Samuel Carpenter, for example, wrote to Penn during the summer of 1697 and confessed that "I cannot at present see how I can pay what I owe in England," to say nothing of the £10,000 Penn had proposed as a loan from his colonists to finance his own return to America, to say nothing of the £500 or £600 the proprietor continued to insist that the colonists had promised him more than a decade earlier.[59]

Complaints about his financial condition were nothing new for Penn, of course, and his situation continued to deteriorate even after the infusion of funds brought about by his marriage in 1696. (At one point, Penn's finances nearly led him back into suspicion of treason. Penn had borrowed £500 from Sir John Friend, one of the chief conspirators in the Assassination Plot uncovered in early 1696. Not long after Friend's execution on April 3, 1696, Penn received a summons from Secretary of the Treasury William Lowndes in July, asking him to explain his indebtedness to a known conspirator.) Since having signed Pennsylvania over to Philip Ford in 1682 and entered into additional financial agreements with Ford in 1690, Penn had, in effect, been leasing his own colony back from Ford, at roughly £600 per year, in the hopes of eventually buying it back, a transaction that Ford valued at the intriguingly precise amount of £12,714. But the prospect of him finding more than £12,000 was, to say the least, highly unlikely. Worse yet, Penn was mortified to learn that several leading Pennsylvania Quakers had refused to honor bills he had transferred to Ford to cover a portion of his annual payment the following spring. This turn of events occasioned a bitter outburst to his Commissioners of Property, in which Penn recounted his relinquishing of customs duties during the colony's first year, his expenses in prosecuting the dispute with Baltimore and frustrating Randolph's pretensions, and the failure of his colonists to remit any quitrents for more than a dozen years. "Are not these credit enough to give a governor and proprietor . . . honor at least for 300 and odd pounds, but in my own country to suffer that disgrace upon me?" In a private letter to Carpenter he called the refusal of his bills "the greatest injury to my credit, I ever sustained." Carpenter expressed his sympathy, but protested that it was "not for want of love and good will" toward Penn, but that he himself owed "a great deal of money at interest and [am] worse in my estate by 3000 pounds than I was three years ago." Ultimately the bills were honored, but it was a sign of further things to come.[60]

* * *

Pennsylvania continued to vex Penn's finances, but it also cast a long shadow in other ways. The Keithian schism remained in the public eye even after Keith was disowned by the London Yearly Meeting in May 1695. Writing to Turner and Holme in Pennsylvania, Penn had described Keith as "as before, most passionate rude, and outrageous. Licks up the very vomit of T. Hicks and J. Faldo," thus equating Keith with two of the Friends' most vociferous and energetic nemeses of the 1670s. Then again, he noted, in terms of actual adherents, Keith was no Story or Wilkinson—"never did one go from us that carried fewer with him"— and the ejection of Keith, he insisted, had little negative effect on the Society generally.[61]

Keith, however, continued to assail Friends, denouncing them in *Gross error and hypocrisy detected*, which he published shortly after the Yearly Meeting disowned him. Keith expressed particular animus toward Whitehead and Penn, gathering passages out of their writings to advance his charges and assailing them for denying basic tenets of Christian belief. A host of prominent Friends converged in defense of the Yearly Meeting, Penn, Whitehead, and Quakers more generally. A year earlier, Samuel Jennings had published *The state of the case*, which defended Pennsylvania Quakers in their prosecution of Keith and his allies. Thomas Ellwood had published *An epistle to Friends* shortly after the Yearly Meeting's judgment, arguing that "the separation lay at [Keith's] door . . . [and] hath been of great disservice to the Truth, and given great occasion of offense and stumbling to many." John Penington attacked Keith in *An apostate exposed* in 1695.[62]

But perhaps not surprisingly, given his leading role in both English and American Quakerism, Penn came in for the lion's share of Keith's invective. "I, of all men, he runs at, and has most unworthily used," Penn wrote in late 1696. That same year, he published *More work for George Keith*, which pointed out how vigorously Keith had defended Quakers during their earlier disputes with London Baptists, and contrasted that performance with his more recent denunciations. "But what is astonishing, and incredible as transubstantiation," Penn wrote, "Keith . . . will have it that he is by no means altered." Never one to shy from an argument, Keith responded in detail to each of these attacks, and between 1694 and 1697 alone no fewer than three dozen pamphlets appeared on either side of the dispute. And still the controversy simmered: in *The deism of William Penn and his brethren destructive of the Christian Religion*, Keith claimed that Quakers—led by Penn—had left the Christian fold entirely.[63]

Keith repeatedly attempted to arrange a debate between himself and London Quakers, preferably Penn and Whitehead, at Turner's Hall in London, where he and his followers held their Meetings. The Friends declined to attend, instead attempting to arrange a smaller, more private affair with Keith and a few of his supporters. London Friend Thomas Story was left to publicly declare the reasons for refusing to engage with Keith, including his "very passionate and abusive behavior"; the likelihood that such a public meeting would be "attended with heats, levity, and confusion, and answer not the end desired by sober and enquiring men"; and the danger of civil unrest due to Keith's "weak and unbridled temper." Keith, who would take holy orders as an Anglican priest in 1700, continued to publicly denounce Friends, allying himself with the Irish Anglican controversialist Charles Leslie, who in *Snake in the grass*, much to Penn's embarrassment, published a letter Penn had written to Turner early on in the schism, in which he had written sympathetically about Keith.[64]

Keith's attacks on Quakers were not merely theological jousting. The passage of a Blasphemy Act in 1697 made denial of the Trinity grounds for exclusion from public office, or even prison. (No convictions as a result of this bill were ever recorded, but it remained on the books into the nineteenth century.) Although much of the concern about blasphemy derived from the publication of John Toland's *Christianity not mysterious* in 1695, rather than from Quaker separatists, Quakers were always at risk of being swept up in the anti-Trinitarian net. Penn published two brief pieces in 1697 criticizing the bill and pointing out that the doctrine of the Trinity does not appear in the plain words of Scripture (arguments he had made nearly thirty years earlier in *The Sandy foundation shaken*), and expressing concern about the broad uses to which such legislation had been put in the past.[65]

All the while, Penn kept up his work in defense of Quakerism. In "A Visitation to the Jews," published as an appendix to John Tomkins's *Harmony of the Old and New Testament*, Penn appealed to Jews to heed the Light Within and accept Jesus as the Messiah. He presented yet another exposition of Quaker principles in *Primitive Christianity revived*, which once again attempted to present topics like the Inner Light, the Quaker Meeting, Friends' views on oaths, tithes, peace, and so on, in a clear and accessible manner. In late 1696, Penn attempted to arrange a debate with Joseph Stennett, a Baptist pastor twenty years his junior, though it is not clear whether the confrontation ever took place. He signed a letter to the young Czar Peter the Great when the czar visited London in early 1698, and accompanied Whitehead and several others to present the young emperor with some Quaker literature. The czar even attended a Quaker Meeting in London in April 1698. Unfortunately Penn did not receive a personal meeting with Peter, but he wrote a note to emphasizing Friends' "piety and charity," which he called "the two legs Christian religion stands upon."[66]

Penn also found himself working with other Friends to improve the educational opportunities available to Quaker youth. At some point during this time, a group of Bristol Friends, perhaps at Penn's urging, extended an invitation to his old Dutch friend William Sewel to take up the post of schoolmaster at a Quaker school there. Though praising Penn profusely, and reiterating his high esteem for Penn and English Friends more generally, Sewel declined the offer, citing his unwillingness to leave his homeland and resettle in a new country. In addition, Sewel voiced a certain obligation to the embattled Dutch Quaker community. "The number of our people as thou knowest is scanty," he wrote to Penn in August 1696, and his departure might further weaken the community. Besides, he added, "God has put me in this country a witness for his name and truth."[67]

Schooling was also a concern in Pennsylvania. From 1684 to 1689 Quakers had operated a school, but by the late 1690s they hoped to endow it more permanently under the auspices of the Philadelphia Monthly Meeting. A number of leading Quakers petitioned Penn to incorporate a school for the purposes of educating "all children and servants, male and female" whose parents wished them to attend, to instruct "the rich at reasonable rates, and the poor . . . for nothing." Unfortunately, although Penn would comply with their request in 1701, efforts to create a school connected to the Philadelphia Meeting became entangled with the zero-sum nature of relations between the colony's Quakers and Anglicans, who wanted to establish a school of their own.[68]

* * *

During the spring and summer of 1697, much of the mutual bitterness and acrimony that had been building, not only between Penn and his colonists but among the various factions in Pennsylvania, burst once again into the open. In the wake of the contested elections of March 1697, Robert Turner, Penn's "staunchest ally in the colony," wrote the proprietor a blistering letter denouncing the "faction" that had, either with Penn's approval or, at least, without his objection, overturned the Frame of Government and monopolized the levers of power. He quoted Penn's own writings back to him and all but accused Penn of abandoning Pennsylvania to David Lloyd, at the expense of his longstanding allies. "Thou hast left us too much to ourselves," Turner wrote, and as a result of the "late arbitrary proceedings" setting aside the Frame of Government, "spoil and havoc is made of the poor people under thy government." The people need "surveyors and commissioners to settle them in their purchases, for want of which can neither buy nor sell but are perplexed with unwarrantable surveyors crossing their . . . lines and dividing their lands as they please for money," Turner reported, adding a few lines about the dismal state of Penn's manor at Pennsbury. As the year went on Turner again wrote to Penn denouncing the government's imposition of unjust taxes, its exercise of power beyond what the proprietor had granted, and even the declining physical condition of Governor Markham, whom Turner described as "infirm and much distempered."[69]

Penn had already lashed out at Markham and the Council in a letter earlier in the year, a letter lacking the customary effusive greetings of love and esteem. "Friends," Penn had written, "The accusations . . . that come for England against your government not only tend to our ruin but our disgrace. That you wink at a Scotch trade, and a Dutch one too . . . against law and the English interest . . . and also that you do not only wink at but embrace pirates, ships, and men." He closed with a series of injunctions, which reiterated previous demands like legislating against vice and licentiousness, controlling the issuance of any more licenses for pubs and inns, and administering justice impartially. How effective such injunctions could really be, from such a distance, remained an open question.[70]

Yet, notwithstanding his harsh words for Markham and the Council, Penn knew better than to broadcast his concerns to outside audiences. He always defended his deputy publicly, and reminded English critics like Randolph that "the Queen desired that he might be my deputy . . . while the war lasted." Since Markham was not a Quaker, the argument went, he would be more forthcoming with men and material for the colonial defense effort. He routinely appealed to the Board of Trade to allow Markham the opportunity to respond formally to Randolph's charges. He grasped at any evidence of Markham's probity that he could find, including an exculpatory letter from Francis Jones, a prominent Philadelphia Anglican merchant, that "in my judgment there can be no fitter person for the King's interest and the interest of the province" than Markham. Jones criticized the behavior of the Maryland government toward Pennsylvania and—addressing one of Randolph's most serious charges, that Markham had conducted business with the pirate John Day—informed Penn that the reason Markham had done so was to safeguard shipping to and from the colony, as a result of "our having three sloops taken by the French off the coast just before." That said, Penn also expressed his willingness to replace Markham should the Board of Trade insist: "If Colonel Markham hath done ill, it will be fit to turn him out, and I shall do it heartily."[71]

In all these communications Penn attempted to speak frankly with his colonists while maintaining a united front to outsiders. He cultivated Randolph's acquaintance while the Surveyor General was in England, seeking to ensure more favorable reports when he returned to America. He complained to Pennsylvania Friends that "the piracy has pushed us hard," and that Markham's commission to the pirate Day showed, if not collusion on his deputy's part, then at least "some reflection on [Markham] for not guarding the jail." (Then again, Penn no doubt considered it better to be thought careless than to be thought corrupt.)[72]

* * *

Not all was gloom and doom, however. Despite some friction over the lack of their countrymen being elected to the Assembly or Council, the colony's Swedes sent Penn an address of thanks for his role in facilitating the arrival of new ministers, devotional materials, and theological books from their home country. These Lutherans had been relying on lay leaders since the deaths of their two priests several years earlier. In response to their plea, King Charles XI of Sweden sent three clergymen and a supply of books, which Penn approved and sent along in 1697.[73]

And he had an ally in Lord Bellomont, who arrived in America in April 1698. The two men shared an antipathy toward Fletcher, and Bellomont kept Penn informed of the doings of royal officials, often in colorful prose. "I never in my life had such a surfeit of flattery and lies" as during my first conversation with Fletcher, he wrote to Penn in June 1698. Of Jeremiah Bass, who briefly served as Deputy Governor of both Jerseys, "I never was so sick of a man's company since I was born." Calling Bass a "cormorant in eating and drinking" and a "great lover of his belly," he described the governor "cramming so large a breakfast of salt pork or beef . . . and with it so large a dose of Bristol double beer impregnated with a good quantity of brandy sugar and spice." Before Bellomont was even out of bed in the morning, Bass "would be so flustered in the face and his eyes staring . . . that with me he passed for drunk [and] so heated his brain that he had two fits of frenzy." To top it all off, Bass "pretend[s] to the greatest sanctity of life that could be, and would feign have been preaching to us on ship board." Then again, alliances notwithstanding, Bellomont carried out the Board of Trade's injunction to suppress the ports at Perth Amboy and privilege the port of New York.[74]

* * *

If American affairs caused the lion's share of Penn's distress, his Irish concerns did not help much either. He had long complained about the "ruined" state of his Irish lands, estimating the amount of his loss there at more than £9,000, or, in a remarkably exact reckoning offered in late 1698, £9,706. Penn had not set foot in Ireland for nearly thirty years. Finally, in May 1698, bearing a certificate from the Horsham Monthly Meeting attesting to his good standing, Penn set out for Ireland with his son William and Thomas Everett, a Friend from Norfolk. They were joined by Thomas Story, a London Friend, originally from Cumberland, whom Penn had met earlier in the decade and with whom he had become quite close. (Twenty years later, Story would be the first person Hannah Penn would write with news of her husband's death.) Penn had several goals in making the trip, in addition to attempting to get his estates in order. He had been indicted for treason in 1691 and desperately wanted to clear his name. He also hoped, of course, to visit Friends along the way.[75]

The company arrived in Dublin on May 6, 1698, and attended the half-year General Meeting of Irish Friends there two days later. Story reported that "we were greatly comforted, not only in the enjoyment of the blessed presence of the Lord, but also in observing the unity, mildness, and order which appeared among Friends." The Meeting was attended by "people of all ranks, qualities, and professions . . . chiefly on account of our Friend William Penn; who was ever furnished by the Truth with matter fully to answer their expectations."[76]

Dealing with the treason indictment turned out to be far easier than Penn had expected or feared. He had called upon the Earl of Arran to vouch for his whereabouts in February 1689, when, according to Robert Fuller, the informer in the case, Penn was in Ireland, knee-deep in Jacobite plotting and subverting the government. In fact, Penn claimed, he was in London the entire time, and those like Arran who had been with him could prove it. As it turned out, he did not need Arran's letters, and wrote to the earl a week later that "I have got as well off my ugly business as was possible."[77]

Although Friends continued to encounter hostility from various corners, the sorts of persecution that Penn had witnessed on his previous travels in Ireland were a distant memory. He and his companions set out from Dublin on May 27, and traveled south to Wexford, where a local Justice of the Peace dined with them after a "very large and open" Meeting. They wrote to the London Yearly Meeting, reporting "many large and blessed opportunities in several parts, Meetings being crowded by people of all ranks and persuasions." But trouble could arise at any time. On June 3, as they set out from New Ross on their way to Waterford, soldiers accosted the company, citing a law against papists possessing horses. As an indication of just how much things had changed since 1670, however, the Friends received an apologetic letter from the Lords Justices of Ireland themselves, expressing their dissatisfaction with "the ill treatment you met with at Ross," and assuring them that "in the meantime orders are sent . . . for putting the said two officers in arrest." The charges were eventually dropped since Penn was, in Story's words, "not a man of revenge, but of justice and mercy."[78]

Finally, on June 7, the company entered the barony of Imokilly and arrived at Penn's estate at Shanagarry, which he had not seen since 1670. A few days later they continued on to Cork, the site of Penn's convincement more than thirty years earlier. After more than a month spent in and around Cork, including several days spent viewing Penn's lands in Ibaune and Barrymore, the three travelers spent another month ranging as far west as Limerick, and as far north as Armagh. They visited William Edmundson, "our ancient and honorable Friend," then living at Roseanallis, about a hundred miles west of Dublin, and Story reported large and vibrant Meetings everywhere they went. In Cashel, County Tipperary, the bishop prevailed upon the mayor to break up a Quaker Meeting, but Friends insisted on their rights under the Toleration Act and Penn went to see the bishop himself. (Attempting to save face, the bishop later alleged that Friends had gathered armed papists at their meeting, but Penn assured the Lords Justices that there was no truth to this charge.)[79]

As in his previous visits, Penn mixed the business of a landowner with the business of Friends. The trip also saw Penn the controversialist on full display. Story's journal recounts a pamphlet debate between Penn and a "journeyman woolcomber," the Baptist John Plimpton. Penn and Plimpton had sparred in

Melksham, England, during Penn's second western preaching tour several years earlier, and Plimpton had been denouncing Quakers in general, and Penn in particular, ever since. He may even have traveled to Dublin in 1698 with the express purpose of goading Penn into a public debate. About a week after his arrival, Penn and three other Friends, including Story and leading Irish Quaker Anthony Sharp, published *Gospel truths*, a brief eleven-point pamphlet laying out the essential principles of Quaker teaching. The work was animated by a "coarse and scurrilous" attack on Friends by Plimpton. Plimpton replied with the self-explanatory *A Quaker no Christian*, to which Penn, Story, and Everett responded—predictably—with *A Quaker a Christian*, defending Friends' teachings on the Trinity, the Light Within, and the divinity of Christ.[80]

But Plimpton the renegade Baptist was not the only critic Penn confronted during his time in Ireland. He also faced off, in writing, against Edward Wetenhall, the Bishop of Cork and Ross. Wetenhall responded to *Gospel Truths* in early July by telling Penn and his colleagues that "you cannot be accounted Christians," and presenting Friends' principles as containing "not one word of the Church, because you are resolved . . . to make and maintain a schism or party forever." He professed unease about the precise meaning of the "Light Within," calling Quakers "confused" about "the very fundamental principle . . . you profess." Attempting to be merciful on Quakers, apparently, Wetenhall called them "a harmless well-meaning people, but under strong delusions." Their correspondence continued after Penn returned to England, when Wetenhall replied more fully to him in print, and noted that having read more of Penn's work "I see . . . you come nearer to us and the Truth. I pray God unite you to us and all of us to him."[81]

Not all his Irish activities related to Friends' business or his own personal affairs. Penn also took advantage of the opportunity to present the Lords Justices with his views on improving the Irish economy. In taking this step, Penn was entering into a thorny political debate that touched on a number of interconnected issues: the long history of England's (social, political, religious, and economic) domination of Ireland, the competing economic interests of the nations' wool and linen trades, and the relative roles played by the East India Company and Irish actors in the broader British economy. In his *Discourse on Trade*, which one economic historian has described as "launch[ing] the attack upon the woolen industry of Ireland," John Cary had described Ireland as "of all the plantations settled by the English . . . most injurious to the trade of this kingdom," and argued for asserting English supremacy over Ireland's economy. The goal, in Cary's view, should be to "make Ireland profitable to England, and in some measure recompense the vast charges we have been at for its reduction and delivery out of the hands of foreign powers and popish cut-throats" over the past half-century at least. (In other words, make the Irish finance their own occupation.) Penn advocated a different route, calling for removing the duty on wool exported from Ireland to England and for easing the conditions under which Irish sheep could be imported to England, as well as a number of other measures that he thought would bolster Irish prosperity and more closely cement the interests of the Irish with that of England. (His views broadly agreed with proposals advanced by John Locke.) He also pointed out that, nearly a decade after James II used Ireland as the point of entry for his attempt to retake his throne, the ongoing practice of quartering English troops in Irish homes served little purpose but to antagonize the population.[82]

Penn returned to England by late summer. The company set sail from Cork on August 19 and landed at Minehead two days later, in time for further news from Pennsylvania to motivate Penn to, at last, begin making concrete plans to return to America. His presence, it turned out, was sorely needed.

* * *

That news was announced in the first sentence of a letter from Philadelphia: "Colonel Quary is lately arrived." Quary and Penn had not always been opponents; a year earlier, Quary had provided information that put Markham's dealings with the purported pirate Captain Day in a positive light. According to Robert Snead, a Philadelphian who provided information to the colony's detractors in Maryland as well as in England, by May 1698 Penn had "found a way to make [Quary] his friend."[83]

But Penn's relationship with Quary would soon turn frosty, as the colonel became merely the latest, in Penn's mind, to seek the ruin of Pennsylvania and his ouster from his proprietorship. Upon his arrival in Pennsylvania, Quary immediately raised an objection to Pennsylvania legislation regarding juries, insisting that the Vice-Admiralty Courts were to be presided over by a judge—in this case, Quary himself. In December, Penn informed the Board of Trade that he had exercised his veto over the objectionable law, and asked the Board to consider the Pennsylvania government "not so disobedient as mistaken and ignorant," admitting that "the law in itself is . . . darkly, and if I may say so, inconsistently worded."[84]

Over the next six months Quary wrote repeatedly, in great detail, from Pennsylvania to the Board of Trade, and his accounts of affairs there were uniformly scathing. Colonial officials seized the goods of suspected pirates for their own purposes, "openly affront[ing] the King's authority" by persistence in "their beloved profitable darling, illegal trade." Quary claimed to have accepted his commission as judge with mixed feelings, "knowing them to be a perverse, obstinate, and turbulent people who will submit to no laws but their own." He offered damning accounts of miscarriages of justice and corruption and taking particular aim at Markham and David Lloyd, who mocked the Admiralty Court's commission and called those who supported its operations "greater enemies to the rights and liberties of the people than those who promoted ship-money in the time of King Charles I." To make matters worse, David Lloyd, who ostensibly filled the office of the King's Attorney-General, refused to file suits on the King's behalf. In March 1699, Quary informed the Board of Trade that the government "threatened and discouraged me and the rest of the officers" from fulfilling our duties, "affronted his Sacred Majesty in open court," and attempted to dissuade individuals from filing suits in the Vice-Admiralty Courts. To Quary's great chagrin, his letters went unanswered until summer 1699. Penn had powerful allies in London, he complained, and "it is the general discourse of this place that Mr. Penn hath greater interest at Court now than ever he had in King James's reign." No doubt Quary interpreted the lack of response to his missives as further evidence of that influence. Without the board's active involvement to bring the Pennsylvanians to heel, Quary insisted, "the King's interest must sink here."[85]

* * *

Though he no longer burned with the zeal of the newly convinced or the utopian aspirations that fired his early plans for Pennsylvania, William Penn reentered public life during the second half of the 1690s as an energetic defender of Quakers against their critics. This reentry was not without controversy, given the unfavorable publicity that Penn's actions under James II and since the Revolution had brought upon him. Some Friends, including his former co-defendant William Mead and his fellow controversialist George Whitehead, worried that Penn's newly regained access to the halls of power could once again bring Quakers unfavorable attention. When the Morning Meeting had taken up the publication of a second edition of George Fox's journal in 1694, Mead objected to the inclusion of a preface written by Penn. The Morning Meeting's minutes reported that Mead "refuses to hear it read, being resolved it shall not be printed with the Journal if he can help it," and Penn's preface to the journal was omitted when the second edition appeared in 1694. (Penn published it separately as *A brief account of the rise and progress of the people called Quakers*.)[86]

During these years, Penn was trying to do a number of different things simultaneously. From afar, and with very imperfect information, he attempted to mediate between the colony's various factions in their ongoing disputes over the form of Pennsylvania's government, and to find some way to safeguard his own interests. He also attempted to rally proprietors and other figures in colonial affairs around opposition to royal policy and the personnel advancing and implementing it. And of course he advocated for his own interests against those of other proprietors.

Penn had great faith in his powers of persuasion, and thus his dilemma became clear: Could he better safeguard his interests and work for the good of Pennsylvania in England, where he had been able to frustrate attempts to once again strip him of his proprietorship, or should he return to America? He continued to believe that, if he could just engage face to face with the inhabitants of his colony, much of the enmity of the past decade would dissipate, and they could reach moderate compromises that would benefit all parties. Such an outcome could only be achieved by his returning in person, as he and all the parties to the dispute repeatedly claimed to want. At times he seemed to cast his mind back to early days: "Dear Friends," he wrote in late 1697, "I remember you, and that in great love, excusing all hard thoughts of any about me, and hardly one day passes me that my soul is not poured out to the Lord for you."[87]

* * *

Finally, early in 1699, he began making concrete plans to return at long last to Pennsylvania, after fifteen years away. On July 14, the Horsham Monthly Meeting issued a certificate addressed to "the Church of Christ in Philadelphia," regarding William Penn's "intended voyage into his province of Pennsylvania." The certificate testified to Penn's

> service in the church of Christ; wherein he hath been a worthy and blessed instrument in the hand of the Lord, both in his ministry and conversation; and has always sought the prosperity of the blessed truth, peace and concord, in the church of Christ; and hath walked among us in all humility, godly sincerity and brotherly love, to our great refreshment and comfort; who hath with much labour and travail on all occasions, endeavoured the defence of truth against its opposers, and the preservation of true unity and good order in the church of Christ.

A month later he preached a "farewell sermon" at the Friends Meeting in Westminster. In early September, he wrote to Friends from the Isle of Wight, "I must leave you, but I can never forget you."[88]

12

Pirates, Penn, and the Pennsylvanians

The Penn family—William, Hannah, and twenty-year-old Letitia—set sail from the Isle of Wight on board the *Canterbury*, bound for Philadelphia, on September 3, 1699. William Jr., who had married in January 1699, remained in England at Warminghurst. Hannah was five months pregnant. Penn carried something else with him as well: explicit instructions from the Board of Trade, communicated before his departure and soon to be followed in writing, directing him to remove Markham, Attorney General David Lloyd, and Philadelphia Justice of the Peace Anthony Morris, from public office. These orders further complicated the delicate balancing act he had been attempting—with varying degrees of success— for the past fifteen years.[1] Also accompanying the Penns on this journey was James Logan, a former schoolmaster and linen merchant originally from Ireland, whom Penn had met in Bristol and hired as his secretary. Logan, who turned twenty-five on the journey, would spend the rest of his life in Pennsylvania except for several journeys to England, and would toil on the Penn family's behalf for more than four decades. He would try—with decidedly mixed results—to represent Penn's (and later, Hannah's, and later still, her sons') interests even while many Pennsylvanians' hostility to the proprietors grew.[2]

The ocean crossing was "a long and sometimes a rude passage," with the company spending thirteen weeks at sea, Penn recounted in a surprisingly cordial letter to Francis Nicholson, his former nemesis as governor of Maryland now serving as governor of Virginia. The silver lining to this long and difficult ocean passage: it enabled the Penns and their shipmates to avoid the worst of the yellow fever epidemic that had descended on the colony, and particularly on Philadelphia, during the summer of 1699.[3]

* * *

Spread by the bite of the *Aedis aegypti* mosquito and exacerbated by the colony's trade with the Caribbean and West Indies, yellow fever "sowed death and panic throughout Philadelphia and its environs." It would continue to do so periodically through the late eighteenth century, including one particularly devastating outbreak in 1793, when Philadelphia was both the new nation's capital and its largest city. Isaac Norris called it "the Barbadoes distemper," and described its effect on its victims without embellishment: "They void and vomit blood . . . very few recover." Thomas Story, who had arrived in America earlier that year, reported that "in this distemper had died six, seven, and sometimes eight a-day, for several weeks together." The situation was so dire that Friends considered postponing the 1699 Yearly Meeting. After prayer and consideration, they decided to hold the Meeting as scheduled, and Story marveled that "though the distemper was very raging and prevalent all the week before, yet there was not one taken ill during the whole time of the Meeting, either of those who came there on that account, or of the people of the town." In all, more than two hundred people died over the course of two or three months, before seasonal northwest winds picked up, dispersing the pestilence.[4]

The ebbing of the epidemic was especially welcome to the proprietor and his wife, as Hannah was nearing her "lying in" time. On the afternoon of January 28, 1700, eight weeks after her arrival in America and just three days into the General Assembly session, which was keeping her husband quite busy, Hannah Penn gave birth to her son John in the "Slate Roof House," the governor's residence on Second Street in Philadelphia. The only one of Penn's children to be born in America, John was afterwards referred to as "the American." It was an auspicious beginning to Penn's second visit to his province.[5]

* * *

The proprietor set out with great energy to bring his colony's affairs to order, chairing a session of the Provincial Council for the first time in more than fifteen years on December 21, 1699. Finally, after years of issuing proclamations and complaining about the dilatoriness or outright insubordination of colonial authorities, he was in a position to deal with problems directly and not through hectoring correspondence that took weeks or months to reach its intended audience. At the meeting, he took great pains to emphasize "the resentment of our superiors in England, of the countenance said to be given here to piracy and illegal trade." Attempting to ingratiate himself with royal officials, he even invited Quary, as Judge of the Admiralty Court, to attend the next Council meeting.[6]

The English authorities were expecting results. By the time he departed England, the Board of Trade had nullified the colony's law against fraud and illegal trade, which had guaranteed that those accused of illegal trade would be tried in Pennsylvania courts, where they would be assured a jury trial, rather than in the admiralty court, which offered no such guarantees. An order from the Board instructed Penn to remove David Lloyd, Markham, and Morris. Like Lloyd, Morris wielded a great deal of influence in the colony, and would be elected Mayor of Philadelphia in 1703. Penn did as instructed, though such steps were bound to cast him in an unpopular light just as he was trying to build bridges with a community from which he had been absent for more than a decade. Penn attempted to defend Markham to royal officials, pointing to his "impotency . . . having been so rudely handled with the gout, that he has not the use of his legs, and but little of his hands, so that he can not only not go, but not ride and is a prisoner to his chamber, a very disagreeable condition to the business of a governor." But he removed him from office, nonetheless. To many of his colonists, Penn was little more than an absentee landlord—fond of making demands and issuing directives but woefully uninformed about conditions on the ground; an instrument of distant Crown officials rather than an advocate for his own Friends. In removing Lloyd, especially, Penn alienated one of only two trained lawyers in the entire colony, along with many of his supporters in the Assembly.[7]

From the moment he arrived, Penn became intimately familiar with the various factions that had made Pennsylvania's politics so contentious over the years: a Philadelphia Quaker elite, a growing and increasingly assertive Anglican minority, and a largely non-Quaker population in the Lower Counties. Seven months into his return visit, he told the Duke of Hamilton, whom he had known since James's reign during the 1680s, that he had encountered "a good deal of kindness and respect, yet some faction and uneasiness." Later that year, Penn offered Charlwood Lawton, one of his attorneys, a somewhat more dour account. Since arriving back in his colony, Penn wrote, he had encountered "faction in government and almost indissoluble knots in property."[8]

The "knots in property" were particularly vexing to Pennsylvanians, as the colony had been without a Surveyor General since the death of Thomas Holme in 1695. Disputes and contention over land continued to roil the colony; not even Thomas Fairman, who had served as Holme's deputy, was immune. Fairman found himself involved in a nasty dispute—with Penn himself—over his possession and use of Petty's Island in the Delaware River. Penn attempted to stem the chaos by appointing Edward Penington, Gulielma's half-brother, as the colony's Surveyor General in May 1700, and commissioning Logan to settle land titles in the colony and collect debts. He also began appointing courts of inquiry, commissioning officers to inquire into land titles and claims, summon individuals to produce records of their holdings, and make determinations about (paid and unpaid) quitrents. Such commissions, of course, hardly endeared Penn to his colonists.[9]

In addition to these competing interests and disputes over land and property, political contention remained. Shortly after his arrival, Robert Turner, Griffith Jones, and several others urged Penn to hold elections as specified in the 1683 Frame instead of the newer and unauthorized 1696 version. Although Penn sympathized with their arguments, he was more interested in acting speedily to mollify the Board of Trade, and decided to summon the 1699 Assembly back for an additional session with the express purpose of passing laws against piracy and fraudulent trade before holding new elections. (He did so despite the fact that, as he told the Secretary of State James Vernon, "the season has been very rude for the members to travel, especially from the capes [and] the winter was so severe.")[10]

The General Assembly promptly passed the two laws Penn desired. He reported these measures to Crown officials as evidence of his good faith efforts to curtail piracy, and excused the previous inadequacies of Pennsylvania legislation as the result of "inexpert clerkship" and inexperience rather than corruption or mendacity. The Assembly echoed his view and ascribed their shortcomings to "inadvertency or want of judgment." It was not a completely disingenuous claim, as there were very few trained lawyers in the colony, which often contributed to confusion in legal affairs and, indeed, had made Penn so reluctant to turn David Lloyd out of office. (He commissioned Quary's protégé, Anglican John Moore, as Attorney General in spring 1701).[11]

While the Assembly was dealing with the important issues of piracy and trade, some colonists attempted to raise broader concerns with the proprietor. Benjamin Chambers, who had taken over as president of the Free Society and was currently the colony's acting Receiver General, presented Penn with a detailed list of urgent concerns in early February 1700. They ranged from the valuation of money to the urgent need for impartial, properly trained surveyors and an Office of Property, which would enable colonists to attain secure titles to their lands and facilitate the collection of rents. John Jones, a master carpenter, submitted a detailed assessment of the funds required to set up a public house for Philadelphia. Noting that "houses of entertainment . . . often prove the nurseries of debauchery, profaneness, and wickedness," yet if reasonably regulated, "they would be an honor and credit to the place where they are erected and countenanced," Jones and his wife estimated that an investment of £500 could set up a respectable and well-appointed facility for the city.[12]

While cooperating with the Board of Trade's clear directions legislation on piracy and trade, Penn nonetheless bitterly complained to correspondents in England about the overreaching of Admiralty officials, who had eagerly expanded their powers to include "every private cause and action that relates to any vessel, be it . . . wages, bread, beer, sails, smith-work, carpenter's work done at the key or in dock." Quary even held up Penn's nomination of a water bailiff, on the argument that Admiralty Courts held jurisdiction over all maritime matters. Although the Admiralty Courts were established solely to prosecute alleged violations of the Navigation Acts, he complained, their officials claimed to "have all the power even in creeks not [over] 20 foot," concluding that "I hope to live 7 years to see those that give away men's estates without a jury punished." The proprietor's affairs would further be aided, Penn wrote, if Lawton would "hinder Randolph, our enemy, a knave, from returning." Penn also appealed to the Lords of Admiralty to assist in settling these disputes by "distinguishing the just boundaries of the civil and maritime powers, where they border one upon another." Surely it "cannot be conceived," reasoned Penn,

> that the Courts of Admiralty, erected in these plantations chiefly for trial of offences against the Acts of Trade and piracy, were ever designed to extend so far as that nothing should be done afoot of the shore in any creek or river but by its powers, and that all actions of bakers, butchers, and victuallers, smiths, cordwainers etc. suing for provisions furnished to or work done for vessels . . . should be tried in the Admiralty only and without a jury.

Juries were central to the fundamental rights of Englishmen, he insisted, pointing out that Pennsylvanians "came hither to have more not less freedom than at home." This issue continued to vex him and other colonists, and he took it up with Robert Harley, an increasingly influential Member of Parliament, asking what could be done about Admiralty officials who "pretend not only to try causes that relate to . . . unlawful trade, or piracy, but whatever is done in the river or creeks . . . or anything relating to the building of any small craft."[13]

In addition to legislative matters, the Assembly appealed to Penn to use his influence to rectify another festering grievance: Anglican John Bewley, the royal customs collector in Philadelphia, refused to allow Quaker ship owners to register their vessels by making attestation or solemn affirmations, as was the case in England as well as in other American colonies. Rather, he insisted on a sworn oath, which he knew was anathema to Friends. Whether this decision came at Bewley's own initiative or (as Penn suspected) at the instigation of Randolph is unclear, but the disadvantage it put Friends under was not. Penn repeatedly raised the issue in correspondence with the Board of Trade as well as the Commissioners of Custom, since requiring oaths "destroys trade and discourages shipping," but had still not received any satisfactory answer well into the following year.[14]

In the brief span of time that he had been back in Pennsylvania—just over two months—Penn had carried out the orders of the Board of Trade with efficiency and dispatch. He was under no illusion, however, about the costs of these accomplishments for his relationship with his colonists. Ejecting Lloyd and Morris from office, "one that is their only lawyer . . . and the [other their] most active Justice of the Peace," had poisoned relations with many in the upper counties, "that consist mostly of our Friends." The law against fraudulent trade, on the other hand, had targeted the practice, widespread in the Lower Counties, of underestimating the weight of hogsheads of tobacco in order to evade the penny-per-pound duty on tobacco and shortchange royal customs collections.

Shippers of tobacco, countenanced by "my one-eyed friend Randolph," had long assumed a uniform weight of four hundred pounds per hogshead, when in fact many weighed half again, or even twice, that much. Penn had told the Commissioners of Customs that by virtue of repacking tobacco many were able to fit eight hundred or nine hundred pounds into a hogshead. "The King has lost within these 12 years about 8000 pounds" in customs duties, he claimed. Then again, by putting an end to that practice, the Pennsylvania law "has disobliged the lower counties that make tobacco" and "angered our tobacconists." (Nor was this ruse the only shenanigan employed by planters in the Lower Counties: from his post as governor of Maryland, Nicholson had long complained that Delaware farmers "cunningly convey[ed] their tobacco in casks with flour or bread at each end.")[15]

* * *

While in England, Penn had attempted to bring together representatives of the colonies to advance their interests vis-à-vis the Crown and fend off encroachments on their affairs. In America he similarly attempted to rally colonial officials to speak with one voice about their common concerns. "I desire with all sincerity a good understanding among the governors of the provinces . . . and the prosperity of the respective provinces," he wrote to Nicholson just a week after arriving. A day later, to Nicholson's successor in Maryland, Nathaniel Blakiston, he professed his desire to pursue friendly relations with his neighbors, "to be dutiful to the Crown, careful of its revenues and the good of the mother country." After all, the colonies, "though independent of one another, are all subject to the Crown of England." He expressed similar sentiments to Sir William Beeston, Lieutenant Governor and soon to be Captain-General of Jamaica, in early February 1700, of his desire for "a friendly correspondence, for the service of the Crown . . . and to maintain a friendly commerce between both colonies." He also reached out to Ralph Grey, the Governor of Barbados; Christopher Codrington, Captain General of the Leeward Islands; and Governor Fitz-John Winthrop of Connecticut, with whom he had worked in London during the 1690s. (To Winthrop, Penn confessed that despite the arrival of three ships with no news from England, he was pleased, "for then we hear of no wars.")[16]

Early in October 1700, Penn traveled to New York for a governors' conference with Nicholson, Blakiston, and Bellomont. Unfortunately Blakiston was taken ill at Burlington, West Jersey, on the way to New York, and forced to turn back. Nicholson, too, became ill, and although he was able to attend Penn later reported that he "hardly got to New York for extreme weakness which . . . rendered our conferences not so effectual as was wished." Penn described Nicholson as "knocked down that night" and "very low indeed."[17]

But the governors did, on the heels of their meeting, come to agreement on a number of issues, and drafted a statement to the Board of Trade, making a series of proposals to improve conditions in the colonies. The governors

advocated "one standard for coin, and money . . . through all the colonies,"
the establishment of a mint in New York, the enactment of duties on foreign
timber coming into England to encourage the export of American timber, and
a relaxation of the prohibition on exporting wool from one colony to another.
The governors also encouraged the Board of Trade to work with the French to
settle the northern (Canadian) borders, which would ease trade with the Indians
and help smooth land disputes among settlers. On a number of related issues—
"runaways, rovers, and fraudulent debtors" as well as immigrants from other
European countries—the governors asked for standardization of law and practice across the colonies so as to prevent individuals "coming from one province
to another for shelter." They also requested that individuals naturalized in the
colonies be granted "the rights and privileges of English subjects, except being
masters or commanders of vessels and ships of trade." Other proposals, such as
limiting the appeals colonists could make to England, incentivizing the apprehension of pirates by awarding "a proportion of the prey" (i.e., booty or plunder)
to those who assisted in their capture, and improving postal services, aimed to
strengthen colonial institutions. The Board of Trade responded with customary
vagueness, thanking the governors for their useful proposals and pledging to
take their views under consideration. It is not clear that it ever did.[18]

Of particular concern to the governors was the issue of marriages, a topic
that included servants marrying without their employers' knowledge, as well as
instances of outright bigamy and desertion. They agreed that the issue affected all
of their jurisdictions, and proposed "that some effectual method be taken for prevention of bigamy and clandestine marriages too frequent in these colonies." Penn
told Bellomont that he was particularly committed to working "for the prevention
of clandestine [marriages] and hindering double ones," a situation that "grows
scandalous especially in my southern neighborhood [i.e., the Lower Counties]."
He offered further recommendations and proposals to the Board of Trade in early
December as well.[19]

Overall, the aim of these efforts was to unify colonial authorities so they
might better fight for their own interests. Penn bemoaned that "unamerican
understandings . . . and misintelligence should prevail," and feared that the colonies would "dwindle to nothing." In spring 1701, he lamented that "we see so
little of an American understanding among those whose business it is to super-
intend it"; and to Lawton, he insisted that "an American understanding is necessary to judge well of what is best here." He recommended that former governors
who had served well ought to be brought into the Crown's oversight processes,
and that only individuals of "good morals, and character at home" be appointed
as officers in colonial administrations.[20]

* * *

Elections in March 1700 proceeded according to the procedures laid out in the 1683 Frame of Government, and the General Assembly gathered on April 1. Penn informed the Council in his opening speech that "we have much to do to establish [Pennsylvania's] constitution and courts of justice." He exhorted them to unity and the common good: "Away with all parties, and look on yourselves and what is good for all as a body politic . . . Study peace and be at unity, eye the good of all." The chief "party" division in Pennsylvania, of course, was religion, and Penn lamented reports that religious differences among the populace had seeped into the political process. "At the late election at Philadelphia, I was grieved to hear some make it a matter of religion." (In those March 1700 elections, not a single non-Quaker Councilor or Assemblyman had been elected from Philadelphia, the heart of the Quaker elite.) "No," Penn went on, government is "human and moral relating to trade, traffic, and public good consisting in virtue and justice; where these are maintained, there is government indeed." Here Penn harkened back to his emphasis on civil interest—the notion that government works best when it attends to matters of peace and prosperity and does not use the power of the state to favor one religious group over another. It was a message he had been preaching since his convincement in Cork more than three decades earlier.[21]

The proceedings were not without drama. The freemen of Chester County elected David Lloyd to the Council as one of their representatives, ensuring him a continued platform for his defenses of the Assembly's role in the colony's governance and his opposition to Quary, Randolph, and the admiralty courts (and, of course, to Penn himself, who had removed him from office the previous December). But Lloyd's position was not unassailable. Quary appeared before the Council in mid-May, charging Lloyd with "unparalleled misdemeanors and affronts against His Majesty." A day later, the Council suspended Lloyd pending the outcome of a trial on those charges. (The trial never happened.)[22]

Pennsylvania's land titles remained in dire need of systematization and confirmation, the colony's code of laws was muddled, and its constitutional framework—the Frame of Government, of which two different versions attracted support from various factions—rested on uncertain foundations. In response to a question from a member of the Council, Penn agreed to study the charter and Frame(s) of Government, and to "keep what's good in either, to lay aside what's inconvenient and burdensome, and to add to both what may best suit the common good." At the same time, he reiterated his view, codified in the 1683 Frame, that the Assembly did not possess the right to initiate legislation; the Council was "to prepare laws, and the Assembly to consent to them; we are two bodies yet but one power, the one prepares, the other consents."[23]

* * *

With the conclusion of the General Assembly session in early June, the Penn family relocated to Pennsbury, up the Delaware River and outside the city, with about a half-dozen servants and a small handful of slaves. The move to Pennsbury marked the beginning of an intense correspondence with Logan, who for the most part remained in Philadelphia. The Pennsbury estate was overseen by Penn's steward John Sotcher, but it required a steady supply of goods and workers from Philadelphia and the surrounding towns. Both William and Hannah wrote frequently to Logan with a range of requests and instructions about official and unofficial business. Indeed, the term "secretary" hardly begins to describe the broad range of tasks that Logan was expected to perform, from drafting proclamations to negotiating with the natives, from arranging for supplies to be sent up the river to dealing with recalcitrant disputants in property conflicts. In the space of one month during the summer of 1700, for example, William and Hannah requested bricks, boards, lime, bacon, chocolate, flour, coffee, pans, a saddle, linens, turpentine, paper, furs, foxes (a gift for London merchant John Askew), pewter or brass buttons, a stew-pan, a soup dish, and candle wicks. They were also in dire need of a plumber, they told Logan, "for the house suffers in great rains." Some of these goods were to be delivered directly to the estate, while others could be delivered to Burlington, New Jersey, about ten miles downriver.[24]

Penn traveled to Philadelphia by barge if necessary, although he preferred to have business and visitors come to him when he was in residence at Pennsbury. During 1700 the situation was made more difficult due to an unspecified illness that he suffered in June, which continued to plague him even after the summer was over. Issues with his leg made it difficult for him to travel in the barge and forced him to "write part of [this letter] upon the bed"; whether or not they were connected to Penn's need for a diuretic ("I took sal mirabile [sulfate of soda] today and yesterday") is not clear. In late July, Hannah asked Logan to send "a little more oil . . . for my husband's leg." By September Penn pronounced his leg "well advanced," though that very month Hannah reported to Logan that he "has been for some time, especially the two days past, much indisposed with a feverish cold."[25]

Hannah was settling into her role, and although she wrote to a friend in England that "I have had my health much better than in England," in a letter from spring 1701 she referred to Pennsylvania as "this desolate land." (Seventeenth-century meanings of the word "desolate" included both "uninhabited," which is somewhat neutral, or the more customary "bereft of joy or comfort." Neither one makes Hannah sound all that thrilled about her new abode.) Her son John, now fourteen months old, "grows bravely . . . very pleasant and lively, much like his father." (The fact that he "has five teeth" might have contributed to her stated plans to "think of weaning him in a little time.") She described her husband as "exceedingly pressed in business," and followed this description by attributing his frenetic pace to "his too long stay in England, which will I fear occasion his stay here to be too long also." Given how frequently Penn voiced his desire to remain in Pennsylvania for a lengthy period, if not for the rest of this life, one wonders whether or not Hannah had come to Pennsylvania assuming their stay would be a short one.[26]

The Penn–Logan correspondence provides glimpses of the domestic situation at Pennsbury, including the slaves who worked on the estate. Hannah reported to Logan in late July 1700 that Jack and Parthenia, a married slave couple, were about to be separated, having received "news that . . . Parthenia is sold to Barbados." (The passive voice here obscures the agency behind, and conditions of, the sale: Who initiated it? Who owned Parthenia?) Not surprisingly, Jack expressed a desire to return to Philadelphia to see his wife, but Hannah told Logan that she was "loath to let him go because our washing approaches." Then again, "if I were fully satisfied of her honesty, I should be willing to have her come up by boat, to help about the washing." Hannah hesitated, though, because she suspected Parthenia of stealing linens from their Philadelphia house.[27]

* * *

One of the best ways for colonial authorities to prove their effectiveness to Crown officials, Penn believed, was to take decisive action against pirates and to vigorously prosecute violations of the Navigation Acts. He issued a proclamation calling for swift action against pirates even before the Assembly met, and the legislation passed by the Assembly in its first meeting after his return represented the next step in that process. But there was always more to be done.[28]

The history of Pennsylvania and the history of piracy intertwine in significant ways during these years. The notorious Captain Kidd, for example, began his career plundering French ships in the service of Governor Codrington of the Leeward Islands around 1689. After losing his own ship to a mutiny, he settled in New York before, in 1696, taking on a privateering mission sponsored by English and American authorities, including Penn's friend and fellow colonial governor Lord Bellomont, who had earlier (in the words of Daniel Defoe) recommended Kidd "as a person very fit to be entrusted with the command of a government ship, and to be employed in cruising upon the pirates." Kidd's fortunes took a downward turn when he attacked an East India Company vessel; he was eventually seized by his old accomplice Bellomont and sent to England for trial, where he was convicted and executed in May 1701. When William Penn arrived in Pennsylvania in 1699, he imprisoned Robert Bradenham, who had served as Kidd's surgeon before defecting to a rival pirate crew on Saint Marie. Penn and Quary together examined Bradenham, whom Penn described as "an ingenious fellow." Bradenham would eventually offer testimony in the trial that resulted in Kidd's conviction.[29]

Further complicating the prosecution of pirates—and relations between the colony's Quakers and Anglicans—was Penn's discovery that "Bradenham's gold was by him left in the hands of the Church of England minister, one Edward Portlock," for safekeeping. By the time Penn uncovered this information in late 1700, Portlock had already left for Maryland. As Penn put it, "our black-bird is fled with the gold in his pocket," and he appealed to Secretary of State Vernon, and to Governors Blakiston and Nicholson, for assistance in locating and apprehending Portlock. Penn could not resist pointing out, too, the brazen hypocrisy of Portlock, who "inveigh[ed] against the Quakers for their being too tame and easy to pirates," all the while "in the pulpit . . . he himself . . . stood possessed of a pirate's treasure got by the worst of ways."[30]

Henry Every, or Avery as Daniel Defoe called him in his *General history of the pyrates*, "was represented in Europe, as one that had raised himself to the dignity of a King" with the lucrative nature of his pirating exploits rivaled only by their brevity—his career lasted only about two years—and by the mystery of his disappearance. As first mate on the *Charles II*, Every orchestrated a May 1694 mutiny. Sixteen months later, the renamed *Fancy* encountered a convoy of ships from the Mughal empire and emerged from an exceedingly violent confrontation with an astounding haul of jewels and precious metals. After pillaging the *Ganj-i-Sawai*, Every's crew dispersed throughout the West Indies and North America, and although six were captured and tried at London, Every himself was never apprehended, nor was his treasure ever located. By 1700 two alleged members of Every's crew, James Brown and one Evans, were being held in Pennsylvania jails. Evans claimed to have been acquitted in London, and Brown (with apparent support from a number of witnesses) insisted that he had paid passage on Every's ship without knowing its pirating background and had not participated in any illegal activities. Penn felt compelled to send them both to New York, but seemed especially vexed about Brown, whom he judged to be "more unhappy than culpable." If Bellomont saw fit to accept Brown's explanation and forgo prosecution, Penn suggested, "it will not be very disagreeable to many discreet people, the fellow being an industrious planter" who seemed to have gotten himself in the wrong place at the wrong time and was currently supporting a wife and child.[31]

Combating piracy involved far more, of course, than simply passing laws against it. The logistics of transporting suspected pirates occupied a great deal of Penn's time, especially during his early months in America, and kept him in contact with Lieutenant Governor John Nanfan of New York, and John Tatham, Judge of Burlington County court. (Tatham's own daughter Dorothy had recently run off with a pirate, and been married in a Quaker-run tavern in Burlington in February 1700. It is not clear which infuriated Tatham more, his daughter's marriage to a pirate or her association with Quakers. In any event, he revoked the tavern's license when Burlington Quakers refused to hand over the pirate.) Penn also remained busy seeking affidavits from inhabitants who might have information about pirates or may have accepted goods from them, and announced the construction of a new "prison . . . with a strong wall, grates, rings and chains, and an officer to attend," while pointing out that no revenues had been provided by the Crown for the construction or maintenance of this vital public expense.[32]

In an extensive report to the Board of Trade in late April 1700, Penn related all the steps he had taken to suppress piracy, but he also found himself conflicted about some of these dealings with pirates, suspected pirates, and former pirates. He wrote to Bellomont asking for advice about some former pirates who had been connected with Kidd and were now living quietly in Pennsylvania. "In old Fletcher's time," Penn told Bellomont, taking aim at a period when the colony had been taken from Penn's control, "those very men had permits to settle and almost everybody has at one time or other had dealings with them." These individuals had not only been protected by Fletcher but had, in the intervening years, "married, built, and planted." They were "poor and married men, and have children," and Penn wanted to be certain that the Crown demanded their apprehension before disrupting their lives and subjecting them to prosecution.[33]

Penn's concerns here were both humanitarian and financial. On the one hand, "My difficulty is in sending persons married and settled these 7 or 8 years and whose substance is small and I am confident not meant by the King in his secretary's letter." Setting aside questions about degrees of guilt, furthermore, "To be at the charge of transporting them and of supporting their wives and children, if they miscarry, is a hardship upon the province." He worried that if the expenses of capturing pirates, securing their treasure, and transporting them to England fell entirely on the colonies, Americans would see little incentive for vigilance in their efforts against piracy. Indeed, early in April Penn received a bill for £29 in costs associated with transporting the two accused pirates. Logan paid it and marked the bill "to be charged to the Queen." Whether Penn was ever reimbursed is not known.[34]

By late summer Penn's efforts appear to have paid dividends, as the Board of Trade acknowledged "the reformation you have made since your arrival, by displacing officers who have been complained against for irregular conduct, by seizing pirates and endeavoring in general to suppress and discountenance all illegal and undue practices."[35] He continued to proclaim his fidelity to the Crown and his eagerness to take action against pirates while also repeating, often, just how thankless a task it all was. "I am intently doing the King's business at my own charges, and not one penny of money from the people neither before a late law of custom on rum and wine that will not defray half my housekeeping," he wrote to the embattled Lord Chancellor and President of the Royal Society, John Somers. Early in 1701, Bellomont determined that accused pirates should be sent to Boston to await transportation to England, which only added to the expenses incurred by

the Pennsylvania government. Penn called it "extremely hard upon this government to be obliged to conduct [pirates] to governments beyond their own."[36]

* * *

As the number of Anglicans in Pennsylvania continued to grow, Penn knew that
he had to handle them with a deft touch to avoid trouble with the English government. Assuring Crown officials that "churchmen not only have their liberty
but may and actually have a share in the government," he attributed much of
the anti-Quaker animus to envy. He attempted to maintain good relations with
the colony's Anglicans whenever possible, and praised Evan Evans, the newly
arrived Anglican rector of Christ Church in Philadelphia, as "a man sober and
of a mild disposition." "While he behaves himself with candor and ingenuity, he
shall want no goodwill from me," Penn wrote.[37]

Before long, however, Pennsylvania's long-simmering Quaker–Anglican discord
boiled over once again. In November 1700 Pennsylvania passed a law requiring
parents (or masters, in the case of servants) to consent to any marriage, and providing clear procedures for publicizing proposed marriages. The law's purpose was
to minimize the risk of what Penn had called "clandestine" or "double" marriages.
Evans, who arrived in Philadelphia to take up the rectorship of Christ Church in
1700, told Penn that the law violated his canonical oath as a priest of the Anglican
church, which had its own procedures for marriages. The church, Evans insisted,
required only that a proposed couple be not nearer than first cousins and that their
proposed union be "three times published in his congregation." The Pennsylvania
law required that proposed marriages be published three times in a *public* place. Penn
attempted to convince Governor Nicholson, a staunch defender of the Anglican interest in America, to intervene and convince Evans that nothing in the law infringed
on either his conscience or his canonical obligations, but it was a difficult case to
make given the longstanding tensions between the two religious communities.[38]

On the one hand, such tensions are to be expected when two hostile
communities live side by side. But the growing and increasingly bold Anglican
presence in Pennsylvania, Penn understood, threatened the very character of the
province he and Friends had worked so hard to build. Colonel Quary, Governor
Nicholson, the Bishop of London, and George Keith—who was ordained as
an Anglican priest in 1700, and returned to America in 1702—all aimed to
strengthen Anglican influence and thereby weaken and undermine Friends.
"The church is their cry, and to disturb us, their merit, whose labors have made
the place. They misrepresent all we do and would make us dissenters in our own
country": or, even more seriously, "dissenters, and worse than that in our own
country." Penn denounced "the heat of a few church-men, who . . . under the protection of the Bishop of London . . . make it their business to inveigh against us,

and our government," and pronounced the behavior of many of the province's Anglicans "very impertinent and provoking."[39]

* * *

Lord Bellomont's death in March 1701 deprived Penn of both a friend and an important political ally among the Crown's personnel in America, just as efforts to enhance the cooperation between the colonies were beginning to make headway. Penn and Bellomont had forged a close and cordial working relationship in England, and they had continued that relationship in America. The governors' conference in October 1700 might have represented the beginning of an alliance that would advocate effectively to the Crown on behalf of colonial interests. After all, Penn never tired of complaining about the baleful influence of "un-American understandings" among those charged with making decisions about colonial affairs. Bellomont's health had been failing for years, and gout had rendered him unable to visit Pennsylvania following Penn's arrival. As Penn put it to Bellomont's widow (perhaps less than tactfully), "He has had many fits that have alarmed thee for this great change, so that the latter part of his life had been a preparative for your parting." To the New York Council, he wrote that "You have lost a governor, but I a friend and an honorable and friendly neighbor."[40]

Looking to the future, Penn did not expect that New England and New York would again be placed under one command, due to both the thanklessness and the magnitude of the task: "Few lords caring for the honor of being his successor, and it may be too big for a commoner." Colonial defense continued to prove a sticking point, even between the governor and his own Assembly. Early in 1701 the king directed Pennsylvania to provide £350 for the building of "fortifications on the frontiers of New York" and, in the event of an actual invasion, eighty men or its equivalent. In early August 1701, the Assembly flatly declined the king's request, though different groups declined for different reasons. Representatives from Pennsylvania claimed poverty and an already high level of taxation, though they also announced their readiness to fulfill royal commands "so far as our religious persuasions shall permit." Assembly members from the Lower Counties pointed to their own "weak and naked condition," and further stressed that they were "the frontiers of [Pennsylvania], and daily threatened with an approaching war, [yet] having neither standing militia nor persons empowered to command the people in case of invasion" and objected to providing for the defense of others when their own had not been secured. Then again, Pennsylvania was not alone in its recalcitrance; New York Governor Nanfan informed the Board of Trade that the call for support had been rebuffed by the governor of Virginia (Nicholson) as well.[41]

* * *

Despite having his hands full with Pennsylvania, Penn remained intensely interested in developments in the broader region. During 1700 and into 1701,
increasing unrest over land titles and rising anti-proprietor sentiment plagued
East Jersey. Penn wrote to New Jersey Governor Andrew Hamilton in the spring
of 1701, encouraging him to deal firmly with rioters. But far more worrisome to
him was the potential surrender of the East Jersey government to the Crown.
The colony's proprietors had been discussing such an option for several years,
though with twenty-four proprietors no decision was a simple one. Penn was
quite concerned about these discussions, particularly in light of the fact that the
proprietors had just secured a victory in their long-running battle to have the
port at Perth Amboy recognized as a free port (one open to all traders), despite
previous rulings from the Board of Trade and the English government favoring
New York. In May 1700 a London jury had ruled in favor of Perth Amboy, and
thus Penn was even more surprised to hear the proprietors talk of surrendering
their government to the Crown after achieving such a potentially lucrative and
long-held goal. He urged Lawton to attempt to dissuade them from doing so.⁴²

Nor had he ever entirely let go of the notion of developing the Susquehanna
Valley, which he continued to hope, despite numerous disappointments,
offered a lucrative economic opportunity. Success in this undertaking would
require maintaining good relations not only with New York, but also with the
tribes like the Susquehannocks and Shawnees who lived in the area. Although
Pennsylvanians had maintained fairly cordial relations with the local tribes,
tensions always lurked just below the surface. In May 1700 several Indians, apparently having been employed by English masters in either New York or the
Lower Counties (they might have been slaves; the sources are unclear), escaped
and sought refuge with tribes in the Susquehanna Valley. The resulting confrontation, in which whites forcibly recaptured the runaways and shot several of the
Indians' dogs, elicited an appeal to Penn from two of the sachems, asking for
"an equal share of [Penn's] favor and protection . . . as the rest of our brethren."⁴³

The culmination of Penn's efforts came between September 1700, when
the Susquehannocks confirmed his purchase of lands from Governor Dongan,
and late April 1701, when some forty natives along with the chiefs of the
Susquehannock, Shawnee, Piscataway, and Iroquois tribes met with Penn in
Philadelphia and signed a treaty of friendship and alliance. The treaty signed on
April 23 expressed the hopes of the parties that "they shall forever hereafter be
as one head and one heart and live in true friendship and amity as one people."
It laid out procedures for settling differences and cemented the alliance between
the tribes and Penn (and, more broadly, the English), confirmed Penn's owner-
ship of lands in the Susquehanna Valley, and granted Penn a monopoly on the
Indian fur trade. Each of these three aspects of the treaty represented a vital piece
of Penn's aspirations for expansion, which he had nurtured since the early 1680s.
As a sign of the significance with which Penn invested this alliance, he traveled in

June to Conestoga, the Susquehannocks' chief village, to pay a visit and perhaps engage in some surveying. Penn's Susquehanna Valley enterprise seemed, at long last, within reach.[44]

As part of his ongoing efforts to maintain these achievements, Penn sought ways to minimize conflict between tribes, attempting to convince them to submit differences to the colonial authorities and not fight each other: "It were to be wished," he wrote to the Council of New York just a few weeks after the signing of the treaty in Philadelphia, "we could oblige all the Indians that live amongst us or in amity with us to submit their differences to the respective governments they live under that by their authority they might be ended and not by military attempts of their own." Such an outcome would, of course, foster peace, but it would also ensure English dominance of native affairs. He wrote more bluntly to Governor Nanfan that it was "better that [the tribes] depended on each respective [English] government they were under than that they were a confederacy of themselves for that might teach them to be more formidable to us than yet they are to the common enemy."[45]

* * *

Despite the important legal and political tasks before him—reviewing the colony's laws, taking on pirates, codifying property titles, negotiating with natives—Penn also faced no shortage of mundane tasks like dealing with conflicts over street layout and maintenance, which led to the appointment of commissioners charged specifically with street work. Having laid out particular tracts for specific groups during Pennsylvania's infancy, Penn faced resentment over Germantown's exemption from Philadelphia county taxes, while Germantown residents requested Penn to confirm the location of their weekly market, which they hoped to locate "in the road or high way where the cross street of Germantown goes down towards the Schuylkill." The growth and continuing development of Philadelphia led to an increased demand for river docks and landings, and Samuel Carpenter offered to fund a public landing at the south end of town. And there was still no line drawn between Maryland and Pennsylvania, more than fifteen years later, despite Penn's victory over Baltimore in 1685: he wrote to Governor Blakiston about "the business of a line between the provinces when a proper season presents."[46]

Legal and financial disputes remained endemic in Penn's dealings with the Lower Counties. In March 1701, the Commissioners of the Treasury reminded him of the conditions upon which he had been granted the Lower Counties by the then Duke of York. He had agreed to establish an office for registering land titles and collecting rents, and forward half of those rents to the duke. Those rents had never been received, the commissioners informed him, nor had they seen any evidence that Penn had even attempted to establish an office for their collection. They asked for an accounting, though never followed through on the implicit threats to take back the counties from Penn's control.[47]

The paucity of trained lawyers in Pennsylvania had long vexed the proprietor; it was one of the reasons he was so reluctant to remove David Lloyd from office. Having incurred Lloyd's enmity, he found himself, as the process of revising the colony's laws got under way, in search of qualified legal advice, or at least input from individuals with experience in legal matters. In September 1700, while Penn suffered with a fever, Hannah passed along his request to Logan, that he "tell Thomas Story to read over the laws carefully and observe their shortness or other defects." He also sought the input of John Guest, a member of the New York Supreme Court, later appointing him a Justice of the Peace for Philadelphia, as well as a member of the Provincial Council and eventually Chief Justice of the Pennsylvania Supreme Court. Three months later he admitted to Bellomont that "I long to hear your lawyers are come" so that they might assist Pennsylvanians in arguing against the Admiralty Courts and establishing the centrality of jury trials.[48]

* * *

William Penn had begun to feel at home in America. (About Hannah's views we can only speculate, though her description of Pennsylvania as "desolate" does not inspire much confidence.) He wrote to Sir John Lowther that "it would not displease me to lay my bones where I have laid my labor, money, and solicitation in Pennsylvania." But he became increasingly concerned with developments in England that threatened the proprietary colonies. In April 1701 a Reunification Bill, which would have stripped the rights of government from proprietors, was introduced in the House of Lords. Though it did not advance, the bill's introduction indicated that the environment was becoming increasingly hostile, despite Penn's attempts to assuage the Board of Trade's concerns, and that a return to royal control remained possible.[49]

During the summer of 1701, Penn received information from numerous sources about the seriousness of the threat. In the space of two days (August 26 and 27) he dashed off nearly a dozen letters to influential figures in the English government as well as to the Board of Trade itself. Penn worked multiple angles in defense of his colony, both public advocacy and private persuasion. He provided Lawton, and his own son William, with talking points to use in his defense. These points defended Penn's honor, and emphasized the profits that proprietary colonies provided for the Crown, the significant risks that the proprietors shouldered in underwriting settlements, and the fact that the Crown already possessed veto power over colonial laws and the appointments of governors and deputies. Publicly, Penn authored (or had his surrogates author) *The case of William Penn, Esq.*, emphasizing the same points that he and his surrogates were making in private: that proprietors had been granted governing power when they were granted their territories, and that they thus had a property right in the exercise of political power in their colonies; that proprietary governments, as opposed to appointed governors who only served limited amounts of time, benefited the Crown because they developed a long-term interest in the prosperity of the colony; and that the king already possessed a great deal of power over the colonies.[50]

Penn's justifications of his own colonial undertaking also tended toward the self-pitying; he emphasized that he had relinquished a significant debt to his father in taking on the proprietorship of Pennsylvania, and had sunk vast sums into the colonial enterprise over the past two decades: "I received it in consideration of a debt of [£16,000] owing to my father in [16]80, and ... I have expended above 20,000 [pounds] upon it," he wrote to one correspondent, telling another that "the loss of the government defeats me of the means and hopes of being reimbursed." (Elsewhere, he claimed that the figure was £30,000.) The defense of proprietary colonies, furthermore, was not simply about his own finances; it was related to the sanctity of property rights, and thus this issue "might justly engage the thoughts of all Englishmen to whom property is sacred." If royal grants could be withdrawn at will, who could say where the limits of the government's power lay? "By no argument but that a Parliament can do anything can our grants be vacated"; and he reflected back on his foundational commitments, from the very early days of his career, that Parliament was subject to fundamental law.[51]

Penn pointed to Randolph, Bass, and Quary—the first "as arbitrary a villain as lives," the second "more a fool and as willing to be as much a knave"—as instigators of the most recent threatening proposals, chief villains "joined . . . against proprietary governments." Bass, "in a letter to a member of Parliament last sessions induced the vacating of all charter proprietary," founded on (in Penn's view) the specious distinction between governing power, which he aimed to withdraw from proprietors, and property rights, which he claimed not to touch. It was precisely for the opportunity to set up a government of their own that Friends had undertaken the arduous and expensive journey to America and "made an improved property out of a savage and wilderness one."[52]

Over the course of the summer of 1701, Penn became increasingly worried about threats to his charter. Although on August 16 he had written to Sir John Lowther that he expected to "pass away a year or two at least" in Pennsylvania, just a week later he had decided that he would have to return once again to London and advocate for himself and the colonies in person. He instructed Logan to tell Pennsylvanians that "my inclinations run strongly to a country and proprietary life," and that Hannah had promised to return to America with him upon completion of the business in London, though whether or not he believed the claim is unclear. But he clearly viewed his presence in person to be essential. "No man living can defend us or bargain for us better than myself," he wrote to

Logan. He told the Assembly on September 15 that although he "cannot think of such a voyage without great reluctancy of mind, having promised myself the quietness of the wilderness," nonetheless he had "reason to believe I can at this time best serve you and myself on that side of the water."[53]

But of course returning to England was not simply a matter of packing a bag and setting sail. As always, Penn needed money, and charged Logan with selling parcels of land. It was a particularly opportune moment, as property values were increasing: "While land is high and valuable, I am willing to dispose of many good patches that else I should have chosen to have kept." He also realized how vital it was to come to some agreements with the Assembly on property regulation and a Frame of Government. Thus he advised the Assembly that "what you do, do it quickly, remembering that the Parliament sits at the end of the next month, and that the sooner I am there the safer."[54]

* * *

The Charter of Privileges—signed by Penn in late October 1701—represented the best agreement Penn could make with the Assembly amidst his urgent preparations for returning to England. The Assembly took an assertive stance toward the proprietor, submitting a petition containing no fewer than twenty-one specific demands just a week after he announced his plans to sail for England. The petition mirrored almost exactly a petition, drafted by Lloyd, that Philadelphia residents submitted to the Assembly. Isaac Norris, writing from Philadelphia, observed that the Assembly "are now worse than ever believing themselves cock-sure of the government change," and that the proprietor "is much grieved at this parting carriage of the people, and highly resents" the Assembly's petition. With Penn's control of Pennsylvania threatened by forces in England, and his position in Pennsylvania increasingly under attack from David Lloyd and the Assembly, the proprietor had little choice but to accede to the Charter of Privileges, which Jane Calvert has accurately described as a "peaceful coup d'état." For all intents and purposes, William Penn had been eclipsed in his own colony, three decades after its founding.[55]

The Charter, signed by Penn on October 28, 1701, contained no theoretical preamble about the goals of government or human nature, but instead offered a skeletal historical narrative laying out the basic elements of Pennsylvania's history as a proprietary colony. It referred to the Frame ratified in 1683, which had been "found in some parts of it, not so suitable to the present circumstances of the inhabitants," and indicated that Penn was providing "another, better adapted to answer the present circumstances and conditions of the said inhabitants." The first head of the Charter enshrined liberty of conscience for all who confessed belief in God and pledged to "live quietly under the civil government." It restricted officeholding to Christians, and provided for an "Assembly yearly chosen," which was responsible for "prepar[ing] bills in order to pass into laws," determine its own adjournment, and "impeach criminals, and redress grievances." This was perhaps the most significant concession Penn made during his entire proprietorship of Pennsylvania. Six-sevenths of the Assembly members could petition the governor for changes to the government, allowing Penn to maintain at least the semblance of an orderly political and constitutional process in the colony. But in an implicit nod to his failed 1688 search for a "new Magna Charta" for liberty of conscience in England, Penn insisted in the Charter:

> Because the happiness of mankind depends so much upon the enjoying of liberty of their consciences as aforesaid . . . the first article of this charter relating to liberty of conscience . . . according to the true intent and meaning of, shall be kept and remain, without any alteration, inviolably for ever.

The final sections of the Charter provided for the separation of the Upper and Lower Counties if their deputies chose not to meet together. And indeed, the formal separation of Delaware from Pennsylvania took place just a few years later.[56]

* * *

Although Penn had performed almost all the tasks that the Board of Trade had demanded during his nearly two-year stay in America, his actions had exacted a heavy price. In carrying out the board's demands, Penn had made himself increasingly unpopular with his own colonists and ensured the unremitting hostility of David Lloyd, a skilled lawyer and popular politician. The border dispute with Maryland continued to fester; relations between the Quaker-dominated government and non-Quakers, particularly the colony's Anglicans, remained; and the uncertainty of land titles continued to cause friction between the proprietor and his colonists. He and Hannah had welcomed a son—John, who came to be known as "the American" or, as his father later put it, "my Pennsylvanian"—in late January 1700, and Penn continued to profess his desire and intention to return to America once again after defending his proprietorship in London. But as he had learned during his second stay in America, Penn's colony had matured during his fifteen years away, and he was no longer the fresh-faced young visionary of 1682.[57]

Penn sailed for England uncertain what he would find when he got there, but justifiably concerned about the prospects for proprietary colonies like Pennsylvania.

13

Back in England

Given the inherent uncertainty of early modern ocean crossings, it is not surprising that William Penn wrote out a will before embarking on his return voyage to England in October 1701. (He had done so in 1684 as well, before leaving America for the first time.) In it, he acknowledged that his estates in England, Ireland, and America were "either entailed or encumbered," and instructed that, in the event of his death, "what is saleable" should "be sold for payment of my just debts." To his eldest surviving son, William Jr., Penn left the proprietorship of Pennsylvania and the Lower Counties; to his daughter Letitia, 100,000 acres; and to young John, 150,000 acres. In each case, he divided the land grants between the province (Pennsylvania) and the territories (Lower Counties). Reflecting Quaker principles, Penn implored his children "that they never go to law, but if any dispute should arise" they submit their case to the Meeting for Sufferings, if in England, or the Philadelphia Quarterly Meeting, if in America. To the child Hannah was then carrying, he left land as well—though "one hundred thousand acres, if a boy, and seventy thousand acres, if a girl." Hannah was to receive five thousand acres, and Logan one thousand. John and Mary Sotcher, who had served as chief steward and housekeeper at Pennsbury and married shortly before the Penns returned in 1701, received land as well. In addition, "I give ... my blacks their freedom," Penn instructed, with one slave in particular— "old Sam"—receiving a hundred acres.[1]

At the same time as he signed the Charter of Privileges, which dealt with the institutional structures of the colony's government, Penn signed another document, the Charter of Property. The Charter of Property was designed to address the confusion and uncertainty in land titles that had long bedeviled Pennsylvania residents. The Charter established a new institution, the General Court, an elected body with authority to adjudicate property disputes. Penn worried about the implications of the Charter of Property, which was written in haste as he prepared to set sail, and declined to affix the colony's Great Seal to it. To the editors of his papers, "it seems probable that he never actually intended it to go into effect." Given how zealously he protected his proprietary privileges, and how reluctantly he had agreed to the changes in the Charter of Privileges, such suspicions seem plausible. He wrote to Logan before he had even sailed, telling him to "forbear the complete passing of" the Charter until Penn had a firmer grasp of affairs in England and could think through the details of providing the Lower Counties with their own charter as well. Sure enough, just a few months later, Penn wrote to Andrew Hamilton, his newly appointed Lieutenant Governor, and to the Provincial Council, instructing them not to affix the Great Seal to the Charter of Property. The decision was no doubt in Penn's best interest, but it was yet another nail in the coffin of constructive relations with his settlers.[2]

Before leaving, Penn had commissioned Logan as Receiver General of the colony, charged with collecting taxes and rents; and appointed Edward Shippen, Griffith Owen, Thomas Story, and Logan, all trusted confidants, as Commissioners of Property with authority to grant and confirm lands. For Logan, he left a list of instructions, the first item on which was, not surprisingly, "to receive all that is due to me." But there were other assignments that would prove even more onerous to Logan, such as Penn's insistence on completion of two mills—which never proved profitable—and payment of salaries for a variety of colonial officials. He also instructed Logan—as if his responsibilities as secretary, commissioner of property, and Receiver General would not keep him busy enough—to "write me diligently advising me of everything relating to my interest."[3]

Despite "a troublesome and costly journey," Penn confided to Logan that "my coming I do more and more see necessary." For one thing, his son William, who had been assigned to lobby Parliament along with Penn's attorney, Charlwood Lawton, had overspent the allowance his father had granted him for those purposes. And somewhat incredibly, Penn found himself in the same situation as he had nearly twenty years earlier, when he returned to England to prosecute his dispute with Baltimore: lacking important papers that had been left behind in Pennsylvania. He implored Logan to "fail not to send what I so much need, and was so indiscreetly disregarded . . . all requisite certificates and affidavits . . . as to our conduct, and our foolish knavish enemies also." But given the vagaries of transatlantic communications, this task was easier commanded than performed. Six months later Penn still had not received the materials he needed, and pronounced it "to my inexpressible trouble, and I fear my irreparable disappointment." "I will not fall into resentment by too long dwelling on this unpleasant subject," he wrote, "but I must tell thee I am very unhappy."[4]

* * *

Logan's first letter to Penn following the proprietor's departure assured him that "all things have gone very smooth and easy since thy departure without the least obstruction or emotion," yet it also contained reports of continuing tensions with the colony's Anglicans; the departure of Colonel Quary for England with a number of reports sure to criticize the conduct of Pennsylvania's government; ongoing difficulties in collecting taxes, spurred on by the opposition of David Lloyd; and the last gasp of the Susquehanna project. An additional communication from the Commissioners of Property, no doubt intended to help the proprietor navigate through his increasingly ominous financial situation, estimated that Penn had "at least twenty thousand pounds money . . . [that] may certainly be raised." Then again, the value of Pennsylvania currency was only about two-thirds that of English pounds sterling, and the chronic difficulties in collecting rents and taxes made Penn's chances of ever seeing such an amount exceedingly remote.[5]

The Commissioners of Property set about their business with vigor, despite daunting prospects. If Penn had been unable to collect rents and taxes effectively while he was in America, how successful were his agents likely to be when he was three thousand miles away? Owen told the proprietor that they were hard at work: "We have as much business as we can compass or go through." The progress of many of these transactions was further slowed by the death, from smallpox, of Surveyor General Edward Penington in January 1702. Penington's proposed replacement as Surveyor General, Jacob Taylor, "also had the same distemper . . . which has been a second hindrance," Logan wrote. Much of Penn's correspondence with the commissioners over the course of 1703 was taken up with detailed descriptions of individuals who had appealed to him in England after perceived ill treatment by Pennsylvania officials, or directions about matters pertaining to his or his family's own significant landholdings in the colony. Many of the claimants made arguments about what was due to them based on verbal assurances that Penn had allegedly offered in years past, which complicated the commissioners' tasks immeasurably.[6]

Pennsylvania continued to be awash in political uncertainty. Penn had nominated Andrew Hamilton as Lieutenant Governor shortly before his departure in 1701, but Hamilton had yet to receive the royal approval to hold that office. But there was an even more pressing problem: an acute dearth of currency in the colony. "The scarcity of money lays us all under the greatest difficulties." This situation was not unprecedented, and affected many of the American colonies, but the situation in Pennsylvania seems to have worsened considerably after Penn's departure, arousing suspicion of the now-distant proprietor. "The quantity was lessening all the time thou wast here," Logan wrote, "but since the decay appears so very great that we know not to what reason to ascribe it, but gives many occasion to believe and say thou hast carried great sums out with thee." Late in May 1702, Logan wrote once again of "the sudden extraordinary scarcity of money amongst us." And in late July, he placed money woes within a broader litany about the difficulties facing the colony: "The great scarcity of money, and the decay of trade this summer, with that and the small-pox, has been very discouraging, and makes business very difficult."[7]

Despite the commissioners' best efforts, Owen was forced to report to Penn in the spring of 1702 that "there are many that have not as yet paid their tax," though Logan "is very diligent and laborious." Thomas Fairman, the surveyor, described Logan to Penn as "sharp and true to thy interest." In June 1702 Logan admitted, "The rents are behind still"; later that summer, complaining of over-work, he confessed that "I shall scarce get anything by rents, not having time to collect them myself." Six months later, Logan was still hard at work, attempting to create "an exact rent-roll for the city" on his own, a herculean task that involved "measur[ing] every foot of it with my own hands, as I go along." And despite personally spending two days in Chester during May 1703, Logan had received "only 50 shillings, such is the scarcity of money in the country that I . . . must take the country product for pay." (Logan eventually spent nearly two weeks there, collecting only about £20, and later maintained that money "seems almost to have taken its leave of this continent.")[8]

Of course larger political and economic forces lay behind this currency shortage, and economies throughout the empire were affected. Penn continued to maintain a keen interest in the disparity between the value of currency in England compared to the colonies, though he confessed that the technicalities of currency valuation were beyond his comprehension. "I wish all were at a par," he told the Board of Trade in the spring of 1703, "that an ounce of silver should be an ounce of silver in all the Dominions of the Crown." He suggested that currency be valued according to its weight, while acknowledging that this solution would be "troublesome, unless the Queen will allow us a Mint."[9]

* * *

Compared to their perilous and extended Atlantic crossing during 1699—which took nearly thirteen weeks—the Penns' return voyage in late 1701 took just a month. The captain was "very civil," he wrote, and "Tish and Johnny after the first 5 days, hearty and well, and Johnny exceeding cheerful all the way." Shortly after their arrival in England, Hannah and young John, along with her father, Thomas Callowhill, departed for Bristol, where on March 9, 1702, she gave birth to another son, named Thomas for her father. William and Letitia went to London, where he quickly got to work renewing old acquaintances and opposing the Reunification Bill.[10]

In that work, almost immediately upon his return to England, Penn was thrust right back into the very same disputes that had occupied so much of his time during the late 1690s, often with the very same cast of characters: the Board of Trade, Colonel Quary, Anglican officials, and Edward Randolph. The proposed Reunification Bill, which the board had urged Parliament to adopt, was set aside due to other, more immediate, concerns, including the death of King William on March 8, 1702, and the looming threat of war (again) with France and Spain. But even with the bill's failure, the political atmosphere was hardly promising for proprietary governments. The East and West Jersey proprietors, in Penn's words, "weakly made haste to surrender" their charter to the Crown, a surrender that was formalized by mid-April 1702.[11]

At some point Penn seems to have decided, as he did during the late 1690s as well, that if he could not prevent the consolidation of royal authority over the colonies, he could at least attempt to influence the manner in which it took place. Penn renewed his acquaintance with Robert Harley, who had risen to the post of Speaker of the House of Commons, as well as with Charles Montagu, Lord Manchester, then serving as Secretary of State as well as a commissioner on the Board of Trade. He continued formulating his own ideas about colonial affairs, seeking a way to preserve the rights of proprietors while addressing the concerns of Crown officials about colonial defense, trade, and the administration of justice. Penn's proposals involved separating the military from civil governments in the colonies, and having the Crown appoint military governors while the "civil authority and administration" remained with the proprietors. A royally appointed "Commander in Chief" would exercise authority over customs and revenue matters. Manchester asked Penn to forward him those proposals: "There is no time to be lost," he wrote in mid-February 1702, although unfortunately for Penn his suggestions were rejected by the board as in "no ways fit." On the other hand, fortunately for Penn, when Parliament set the Reunification Bill aside in the spring of 1702, the threat to colonial governments passed—for a time.[12]

* * *

As was so often the case, war loomed on the horizon and shaped the contexts within which Penn and his contemporaries operated. William III had spent much of his reign (indeed, much of his life) engaged in an extended campaign against France, and the king's death in March 1702, from injuries sustained in a horseback riding accident in London's Hyde Park a month earlier, and the accession of Mary's sister Anne, did not fundamentally alter the longstanding rivalry between the two powers. The 1697 Treaty of Ryswick, which had concluded William's previous war with France, had sidestepped large issues surrounding the fate of the Spanish empire, leaving a tenuous peace easily thrown into turmoil when, in the words of historian Julian Hoppit, "on 1 November 1700, Charles [II, King of Spain], showing no respect for the calculation of foreign powers, died." The War of Spanish Succession grew out of Charles II's grant of his throne to the Duke of Anjou, grandson of Louis XIV, then on the throne of France. Later that year the British, Dutch, and Austrians revived their Grand Alliance. The king had been favoring John Churchill, Lord Marlborough, in the months leading up to his death, naming him ambassador to The Hague, commander of English

forces, and chief negotiator of the new alliance. In May 1702 Anne, having elevated Marlborough to Captain General, declared war on France, and the battle
was joined. The war would stretch on for more than a decade before the Treaty
of Utrecht brought it to an end in the spring of 1713.[13]

For Pennsylvanians, the war remained a relatively distant reality, as most of
the North American action in what became known as Queen Anne's War took
place to the north or south of them. In New England, settlers engaged in combat
with French and Indians in Quebec and the New French colony of Acadia, trying
without success to capture Quebec City and suffering the horrific Deerfield raid
in early 1704, in which French and Indian forces killed nearly fifty settlers and
carried more than a hundred away to Canada. English settlers to the south engaged
in skirmishes with the Spanish in Florida, with particularly cruel consequences
for southern tribes like the Apalachee, who bore the brunt of the carnage; more
than a thousand men, women, and children were massacred, and four thousand
sent into slavery, in 1704 alone. Although the militia issue had long proved to be
a source of deep division between Quakers and non-Quakers in Pennsylvania,
the main consequences for Pennsylvania and its neighbors lay in the war's sharp
disruption of trade, shipping, and communication. And the disruption was significant, with more than five hundred allied ships, on average, taken each year.[14]

* * *

Penn's first year back in England was a year of deaths, births, and marriage.
His dear friend Phineas Pemberton had been in failing health when he left
Pennsylvania, and Logan wrote in May 1702 with news of Pemberton's death.
Penn mourned Pemberton, a founding member of Bucks County Quakerism
and neighbor at Pennsbury, calling him "the ablest as well as one of the best men
in the province." He "was a true friend to thee and the government," said Samuel
Carpenter, and Logan referred to him as a "pillar of Bucks County." (Pemberton
was laid to rest at Pennsbury, and to this day Pennsbury Manor's "Living History
Theater" offers reenactments of his funeral, complete with readings of his will.)[15]

The death that held the most significant consequences for Penn, and whose
ramifications would bring despair and heartbreak down on his head over the
next decade, was that of his longtime agent and business manager Philip Ford.
Penn had employed Ford almost continuously ever since his 1669 trip to Ireland.
Over the course of that relationship, he had signed a number of documents that
offered Pennsylvania as collateral for loans Ford extended to Penn. Penn appears
to have read few of these legal papers closely, and several were signed in the rush
of business as he prepared to sail for America in 1682. Regardless, although
Penn's poor financial situation was no secret, none of these details were public
knowledge, and Ford's death on January 8, 1702, threatened to bring Penn
and Pennsylvania into severe disrepute at a highly sensitive political moment.

Ford's will offered Penn the opportunity to regain his proprietorship in exchange for a payment of just over £11,000. Penn had, to put it mildly, nowhere near that amount of money, and the publication of these details would profoundly embarrass him. He thus began a concerted effort to convince Bridget Ford, Philip's widow, not to probate the will, but rather to work out a scheme of private payments. Managing the Ford business would increasingly weigh on Penn's mind, and would ultimately break forth in a protracted and bitter legal struggle that cast a long shadow over his final years.[16]

The year 1702 was also one of births, with William and Hannah welcoming young Thomas in March. William Jr.'s wife Mary was also pregnant, and would deliver another William Penn the following year, bringing the number of Penn grandchildren (along with Gulielma, born in November 1699, and Springett, born fifteen months later in February 1701) to three. Penn wrote Logan with the news of the baby's birth, reporting his new grandchild, "a fine boy . . . called William, so that now we are major, minor, and minimus." Little John, in his second year, suffered an "extreme illness" but had recovered by late June, when Penn reported him to be "perpetually busy in building or play" except when eating or sleeping. By fall he was cutting some new teeth.[17]

Separated for much of 1702 due to Penn's business in London and Hannah's childbirth at Bristol (Penn remarking ruefully that he had not been with his family "but seventeen days these five months"), the family came together in August for Letitia's marriage to William Aubrey, a London merchant of Welsh heritage. These preparations were not without controversy, as Letitia had (perhaps) been "under some particular engagement" to one William Masters in Philadelphia before her return to England. William Penn Jr. reported to Logan that the marriage had been cleared by Friends Meetings, with both Letitia and Masters present, and that Masters "could prove no engagement." "Masters," he wrote, "made a mighty noise here, but it lasted not long." (Indeed, the Philadelphia Women's Meeting had granted Letitia a certificate of good behavior upon her departure in 1701, which certified, according to Pennsylvania historian John Watson, who claimed to have seen the certificate, that "she was under no marriage engagements to the best of their knowledge and belief.") But there was evidently some drama within the community of Friends, and Penn noted that "S. Penington's, if not S. Harwood's, striving for William Masters against faith, truth, righteousness . . . will not be easily forgotten." Nonetheless, "things came honorably off," with Masters' "father's friends nobly testifying against the actions of both."[18]

Penn's worsening financial condition made it difficult to provide for the young couple. A notoriously cash-poor father of the bride, he was forced to borrow the funds for his own daughter's marriage settlement—from his future son-in-law. In a complicated financial arrangement, Penn borrowed £3,000 from Aubrey— some of it, perhaps, to keep the Fords at bay—and gave Aubrey a mortgage on lands in Ireland valued at £5,000. (Letitia already had more than five thousand acres in Pennsylvania, and the couple also received lands in England.) Not surprisingly, given the indebtedness and obligation present from the outset, to say nothing of Aubrey's argumentative character and Penn's hypersensitivity to perceived slights, Aubrey's relationship with his in-laws was a tense one. Calling Aubrey a "muck worm" (an early modern epithet meaning miser), Hannah lamented that he "esteems our friendship so little" as to decline to advance them money to pay some of their bills. Penn himself had no better view of Aubrey. More than three years later, Penn implored Logan to help him settle his accounts with Aubrey, "of whom I would be clear of all men; he has a bitter tongue, and I wish I had nothing to do with him in money matters."[19]

Letitia instructed Logan to sell her Pennsylvania lots, inaugurating a contentious years-long relationship in which Logan was the frequent object of the couple's complaint and invective. Charged with making the best deal possible for her land, but acutely aware of the scarcity of currency and the difficulties inherent in such property transactions (and well aware of her father's dire financial situation), Logan did, in his mind, as best he could. He wrote to Letitia just before her marriage that he hoped "in one year to be able to raise thee a good portion from which is already settled on thee in this Province," but also informed her that many of these sales would not yield ready cash. "Though I mention money," he explained, "I receive no such thing but by discounts and transfers." To make matters worse, Logan also loaned Samuel Carpenter £200 of the first £300 he received from selling Letitia's lots in Philadelphia, money that Carpenter surely could not repay, as his own financial situation continued to deteriorate. Carpenter was deeply indebted, and Logan described him to Penn as "much depressed of late in his spirits, about his encumbrances, which are heavy." By 1705 Carpenter was offering almost all of his holdings in Pennsylvania and the Jerseys to any interested buyer.[20]

The frequent and extended separations of Penn and his wife were decidedly not to Hannah's liking. "I can not with any satisfaction endure thy absence much longer," she wrote from Bristol in the fall of 1703, detailing the strain placed on her by the necessity of caring for her aging parents as well as the infant Hannah Margarita, who had been born in late August. The family was together at Warminghurst in early January 1704, with Hannah reminding her husband before he set out from London to bring butter, breeches for John, and a coat for the baby.[21]

* * *

Even in the absence of parliamentary action, the Board of Trade, encouraged by Quary's allegations, continued to pressure Penn about the conduct of his colonial government. "Here has been villainous work against us," he wrote to the Council in January 1702. "Such fallacy, malice, and tricking, tis contemptible as

well as wicked; but I do not despond." Quary appeared before the Board in late
March 1702, presenting detailed complaints from the colony's Anglicans and
inhabitants of the Lower Counties. Penn had long suspected that Quary and his
allies, particularly John Moore, who had served in a number of official capacities
in the Admiralty Courts and was a vigorous supporter of both the Anglican interest and royal centralization, were not merely out to undermine his standing
with the Crown and Board of Trade, but in fact wanted to take control of
Pennsylvania themselves. (Logan once described Moore as Quary's "viceregent
in mischief.") These suspicions were further strengthened by a letter Penn received from Jacques le Tort, a French Huguenot who had fled persecution in
France. "At his last trip to London [Quary] could not resist saying that he would
have you deprived of your government and take it himself," le Tort wrote. Aside
from offering his view that Quary "is very ill informed or rather very malicious"
in the allegations he lodged against Penn's government, le Tort added a veritable
encomium to life in the colony:

> I can truthfully say that in all the time I lived there I always saw justice,
> peace, and friendship practiced between the peoples, and religions were
> always professed there with complete calmness and good sense until
> Mr. Quary and Mr. John Moore his son-in-law came there, who have
> always made as much trouble as they could, which hasn't corresponded
> to the kindness and courtesy with which you have treated them.

The letter must have been extraordinarily welcome news to Penn, who was just
then preparing to contest Quary's allegations before the Board.[22]

As March turned to April, Penn's relationship with the Board of Trade continued to deteriorate. The Board summoned him in early April to respond to
Quary's charges, which it described as "divers complaints relating to the laws,
to the administration of justice, the militia and defense of those provinces, to
piracy encouraged and illegal trade practiced there, and other irregularities." It
requested the "speedy attendance of [Penn] or an agent" but assured the proprietor, if tersely, that "they are unwilling to [report to the queen] without first
hearing from you." Penn sent Lawton, whom the Board provided with copies
of Quary's accusations for the proprietor to review. Penn stressed his health
woes—"I was too infirm to stand an hour or two with legs as feeble as mine
are well known to have been"—as well as pressing family commitments, with a
sick son (John) in one place and a wife recovering from childbirth in another
(Bristol).[23]

The explosive confrontation before the Board of Trade took place in April
1702, when Penn attended several meetings in person to hear and respond to
Quary's allegations. Very little of this was new, but the political environment had

turned increasingly hostile to colonial governments, and Penn clearly felt as if he was (again) fighting for his political life.

Quary, who had by now replaced Randolph as leader of the charge against proprietary governments, presented the Board of Trade with a number of sweeping claims: "illegal trade is carried on there more than ever," "acts passed . . . to prevent illegal trade are not put in execution," and the country was "left defenseless and exposed to all hazards both by land and sea." (He also added some particularly explosive charges about the administration of justice in the colony, alleging that "a man committed for bestiality with a mare" was not prosecuted, and "the son of an eminent Quaker committed for a rape . . . got off without a trial.") Quary's reports painted a damning portrait of a settlement under the grip of a faction that prevented royal officials from carrying out their duties, shielded their own members from prosecution, and failed to perform the most basic functions of governance: protecting the people from external attack. Quary pointed out that Anthony Morris, whom Penn had removed from office on the board's orders in 1699, had been returned to office "and made . . . one of [Penn's] chief magistrates." He also cited Penn's commissioning of water bailiffs as an infringement on the work of the Admiralty Courts, and noted that the proprietor had "prevailed upon the Assembly . . . to make a present to him of 2000 pounds" while refusing to make the required payment toward Pennsylvania's share for the defense of New York.[24]

Penn offered a range of responses to Quary's charges. He denied some of them outright. "I never, to my knowledge, invited or entertained one French Indian in my life"; "[Quary] never complained to me, that I can remember, of such neglect"; "This . . . I positively disown." He made insinuations about Quary's motives. "I wonder, if it be true, that Col. Quary . . . never told me so before"; "I had long ago Col. Quarry's licence to re-employ [Anthony Morris], after a thorough examination of him"; "Col. Quarry is the chief agent . . . [of] the Indian trade." He also claimed that Quary was resurrecting discredited old claims like the militia issue, insisting that Pennsylvania and the Lower Counties were "[no] more defenceless than Maryland or Virginia" and repeating, rather disingenuously, Pennsylvania Quakers' earlier defenses that "there's as much [a militia] as there was in Col. Fletcher's time."[25]

The dispute got even uglier with a series of increasingly bitter and personal attacks conducted by Penn and Quary through dueling correspondence with the board. The back-and-forth becomes difficult to track at times, with documents bearing titles like "[Penn's] Rejoinder to Col. Quary's reply to my second answer to his second Memorial of Complaints." In late June Penn accused Quary of ignorance of the law, conflict of interest, corruption, and exceeding his commission by "extending . . . his admiralty jurisdiction to cases . . . proper to common law courts." He scoffed at Quary's "proofs" and the "clamours" he made against

Pennsylvania. Quary fired back by referring to the Pennsylvanians as "a people that had so long practiced illegal trade and found the sweet of it," and denouncing Penn's earlier "promises that both he and those in his Government should be aiding and assisting me, no part of which promises was ever performed, but, on the contrary, all the discouragement and opposition given me." But Quary was just getting warmed up. Penn, he claimed, "pretend[s] to be a Minister or Preacher" who "thinks that he hath a privilege to abuse all that dare speak truth of him." "How far this squares with the character of a gentleman, or is consistent with pretensions to religion and infallibility," he opined, "let the world judge." In private correspondence, Penn was equally unsparing in his description of Quary, calling him "an artful knave" who has advanced "horrid prevarications and most audacious untruths and denials of truths." (By the end of 1703 Penn told Logan that, in his view, "a worse man than Quary does not live.")[26]

The disputes before the board continued well into the summer months. Penn reported to Logan that on June 26 he and the board "had a long and warm debate . . . about Col. Quary." In the meantime he continued to press Logan to recruit any colonists who could attest to the falsity of Quary's charges. Ultimately, though, Penn considered the Board of Trade to be prejudiced against his case. He criticized its "misapprehension and partiality" in mid-August 1702, and denounced "the partiality of those gentlemen . . . in favor of the common enemy of our poor country." He successfully appealed to have his case considered by the Privy Council's Committee of Ministers, which was charged with oversight of the colonies. Lord Nottingham, then serving as Secretary of State and a member of the Privy Council, was an ally of Penn's, and his support greatly increased the likelihood of a favorable outcome.[27]

* * *

The increasingly acrimonious relationship between Penn and the Board of Trade was obviously shaped by the Quary allegations, but a host of familiar issues— tension with Pennsylvania's Anglicans, the continued uncertainty surrounding Penn's claims to the Lower Counties—also served to poison it.

Although Penn and Bishop of London Henry Compton—who was himself appointed to the Board of Trade as an ex officio member in late June 1702— came to some agreement resolving Anglican objections to the colony's 1701 marriage law, relations between Quakers and Anglicans in the colony continued to be tense, especially after the arrival of staunch Anglican Edward Hyde, Viscount Cornbury, as the replacement for Penn's friend Lord Bellomont. Cornbury was named Governor of New York in September 1701, shortly before Penn departed for England, and Governor of New Jersey in December 1702. Penn knew of Cornbury's Anglican commitments, of course, but had initially hoped for good relations, telling Logan that Cornbury "comes upon the church's favor, but [with] Whig principles as people talk."[28]

Cornbury visited Philadelphia and Pennsbury in mid-June 1702, where he was hosted by the government and, according to Logan, received a good impression of the colony and its leaders. (Logan's gifts of Pennsylvania wine and beer surely did not hurt their efforts.) But before much longer, Cornbury's favoritism toward the colony's Anglicans became apparent, and Pennsylvania Quakers found themselves facing yet another hostile royal official who encouraged Anglican criticisms of Quaker rule, and refused to do anything that might give Pennsylvania the appearance of being well ordered and competently governed. Cornbury's commission as Governor of New Jersey in December 1702, after the proprietors of that colony surrendered their government to the Crown, further expanded his influence and emboldened Quary and others who had long aimed to undermine Penn's authority. The two officials formed a close alliance, with Quary inviting Cornbury to lodge at his home in New York. Cornbury visited Philadelphia again the following summer, where he worshipped with the Anglicans and dined at John Moore's home. To Logan, his intentions were clear: "He designs to have this government, if to be effected, annexed to his; and no doubt his backing Quary's representations will be a great strength to the design." After "Lord Cornbury's . . . visit to this place" in the summer of 1703, Logan expected "that it will be difficult to engage any of the churchmen to serve [in the Council]." In fact, Quary went so far as to propose that Cornbury petition the Queen for the governorship of Pennsylvania in addition to that of New York and the Jerseys, a request that Penn considered outrageous and shameful meddling. For his part, Cornbury wisely declined to make such a request to the Crown, though he did say that he stood ready to obey the queen's commands, whatever they might be.[29]

In his ongoing efforts to smooth the turmoil between Anglicans and Quakers and ease political tensions, Penn in early 1703 named Roger Mompesson, an Admiralty judge whom he described as a "moderate churchman . . . thought by the judicious here to be very able," as his Attorney General. Logan suggested making Mompesson President of the Council, "with a considerable power vested in him alone," after Hamilton's death and later even proposed him for Lieutenant Governor, claiming, "He is on the spot, and doubtless would accept."[30]

The question of oaths also concerned the board, as it not only served as an indicator of tension between Quakers and Anglicans but also undermined the administration of justice and the perceived legitimacy of officeholders. In May 1702, it requested clarification from Penn as to whether all public officers in Pennsylvania and the Lower Counties swore the requisite oaths or the affirmation permitted to Quakers, and whether all persons who desired to swear oaths in public proceedings were permitted to do so. (Swearing an oath required someone to administer the oath as well, and thus courts or other public bodies dominated by Friends posed a difficulty for those who insisted on swearing oaths in their own proceedings.) The board became increasingly impatient for Penn's response to these queries, writing him a month later that they were "yet in expectation of your answer[s]" and that furthermore—illustrating the intertwined nature of the various forces arrayed against Penn and the problems he faced—"they do also expect that you do inform them of your title to the soil and Government of the three Lower Counties." Penn did not formally answer the board until the end of November, a delay that held up the Crown's approval of Hamilton as his Lieutenant Governor and further exasperated the board, which clearly felt it had bent over backward to allow Penn sufficient time to respond to its queries.[31]

Quary had long accused the Pennsylvania government of refusing to ensure that all jury members either swore or affirmed. He made particular reference to the case of London merchant Thomas Byfield, who claimed that the jury in his suit against Pennsylvania ship captain John King had neither sworn nor taken the affirmation. (The case was eventually settled by arbitration.) Further allegations of this sort made their way to Cornbury in New York, and thence to the Board of Trade, which directed Penn to put a stop to such proceedings. Oaths and affirmations for Council members and other public office holders also became enmeshed in this issue, which continued to pit Anglicans against Quakers in a variety of public settings.[32]

Finally, Penn was forced to deal with resurgent challenges to his claim to the Lower Counties. Despite his victory over Baltimore in 1685, Penn had never been able to settle the boundary issue definitively. (Historian John Oldmixon, writing in 1708, declared that "the line of partition between Pennsylvania and Maryland is imaginary.") Conflict had continued through the 1690s and well into the new century. When the Board of Trade instructed Penn to have his government proclaim the accession of Queen Anne to the people of his colony in March 1702, proclamations that were always accompanied by declarations of loyalty; its instructions addressed him only as proprietor and governor of "the province of Pennsylvania" and made no mention of the Lower Counties ("nor so much as an etc," Penn groused). Given this omission, he claimed to Popple, "I know not how to order her to be proclaimed in the three Lower Counties," and returned the proclamation to the board for further instructions. While such an insistence on the recognition of his authority over the Lower Counties was clearly important to Penn, those in his colony were left wondering why their neighbors in Virginia, Maryland, Massachusetts, New York, and the Jerseys had all received orders to proclaim the queen while they heard nothing from their proprietor. "We much admire," Logan wrote, that "we cannot now hear from thee, nor have orders to proclaim the queen, it being done everywhere around us." Three weeks later, having still not heard anything from the proprietor, Logan wrote that "tis imagined, by the friends of the government, that the orders have been delivered to thee, and some way omitted to be despatched, but others would render it a contrary way. 'Tis a great reflection upon us, whatever the cause be."[33]

This particular instance of one commission's wording—leaving off the Lower Counties in Penn's instructions to proclaim the queen—provides a window into the difficulties Penn continued to encounter with regard to his southern border. William Blathwayt, longtime member of the Board of Trade and advocate of re-exerting centralized royal authority over the colonies, raised the issue of Penn's failure to remit quitrents from the Lower Counties to the Crown. Penn's old nemesis Edward Randolph reappeared on the scene, calling Penn the "pretended governor of the three lower Counties on the Delaware Bay" and questioning his claim to the Lower Counties. (Michael G. Hall, Randolph's biographer, has noted the vituperative hostility between the two men: "Very few men could bring this sophisticated and kindly Quaker to the edge of profanity, but Randolph was one of them.") To those challenging his authority and conduct with regard to the Lower Counties, Penn laid out in no uncertain terms, and with a clear exasperation, a brief historical narrative of the past two decades:

I had a grant from H.R.H. James Duke of York . . . in '82, and had possession solemnly given by President Moll and Ephraim Hermon, the Duke's Commissioners in the same year, all which is upon record at the Castle of New York, and that is all the satisfaction [Quary] and his employers shall have from me. And till the law has determined otherwise, I shall expect obedience from those that are under my government, at their own peril; the late king having already given sanction to many laws made by the Upper and Lower Counties conjointly.

Needless to say, Penn's declaration here did not satisfy the board, which had requested to see Penn's title to the soil and government of the counties.[34]

Not only did such challenges undermine his own authority, Penn claimed, but they encouraged lawbreakers in the colonies: "I hope none who seek the Queen's Peace and the colonies' prosperity will give the least shadow of encouragement and slacken people's obedience unto settled authorities." In late January 1703 the Board of Trade, having been informed by Quary of the political contention between the Upper and Lower Counties, requested that Penn provide copies of "the several grand charters [i.e., the Charter of Privileges and the Charter of Property] . . . granted by you in Pennsylvania." And upon returning home from Philadelphia in September 1703, William Clarke, a longstanding Council member and local officeholder from the Lower Counties, found an ejection notice and a summons to defend his claim to land on which he had been living for years (land whose titles had been issued by Penn). These provocations were part of a larger pattern, he told Penn, whereby Maryland officials sought to throw doubt on land titles in the Lower Counties, and claim that "they have Maryland rights for a great part of the best tracts of land in the three lower counties." Such efforts had direct and adverse effects on important matters like tax and rent collection, which had slowed to a crawl. "Not only in the County of Sussex the people do refuse to pay their quitrents but also in the County of Kent, for the chief there lately as I came down from Philadelphia told me that they . . . would pay no more till they see a better authority from the Crown of England for it."[35]

In all of these situations, the Council claimed, Quary had one goal: "to have the whole government represented to . . . be in confusion and . . . necessary to be taken into the Queen's more immediate care," and in pursuit of this end "they magnify every small occurrence where they can have the least grounds." Contention and division were fomented not only by Quary but also by Pennsylvania Quakers' old nemesis Francis Nicholson, now governor of Virginia, who continued to stir up tensions, encouraging Anglicans to build a church on the New Castle town green.[36]

* * *

One final point of conflict with the Board of Trade lay with its resistance to Penn's appointment of Andrew Hamilton, a Scottish merchant who had served previously as the governor of East and West Jersey, as his Lieutenant Governor. Hamilton had been removed from office in the Jerseys in favor of Jeremiah Basse in 1697, under the claim—later overturned—that only natural-born Englishmen could serve as colonial governors, and returned to office in 1699. Randolph's claims that, as governor, Hamilton had countenanced illegal trade, sparked the board's hesitation. Hamilton protested his innocence of all the charges, asking for a hearing before Lord Cornbury so that he might prove that "every part of it is fiction and malice." He condemned Quary as "an incendiary in the Jerseys and a fomenter of prejudices between the Queen's subjects of England and Scotland," and more generally lamented his inability to respond to attacks on his character from such a distance: "No man . . . will be safe in America if the oaths of such scoundrels be received in England to condemn him." Hamilton pronounced it "very hard to be thrown out of the Queen's favor upon the scandalous oaths and false suggestions of some and sly insinuations of others," and insisted that had he been in England the rogues would never have dared level the accusations against him. Penn did record a small victory when the board agreed to allow those accused of misconduct in America to answer such accusations "upon the spot . . . that nobody may be murdered in the dark."[37]

The board's refusal to recommend Hamilton's approval as Penn's Deputy Governor had undermined Hamilton's already uncertain political authority, and prevented him from taking firm and decisive action on colonial defense. The militia question, and the perceived susceptibility of Pennsylvania and the Lower

Counties to attacks by the French and their allies among the native tribes, continued to pose difficulties for Friends as war spread from Europe to America. Upon taking up his office as deputy, Hamilton had "put the people in expectation of a militia . . . but held his hand till he might hear of his approbation"—but as time went by and that approbation remained ungranted, Hamilton's political influence progressively weakened. Hamilton urged the proprietor to secure his approval by the Crown, for "without an approbation it will be impossible for me to form such a militia as will be sufficient to protect the inhabitants and can but precariously preserve the decencies of government among the licentious part of them." With the outbreak of war, Hamilton, who was not a Quaker, sought to take defensive measures, including raising a militia, but the precarious nature of his authority made effective action impossible. Notwithstanding the fact that Hamilton took "all possible care to act inoffensively," his hands were tied. With the surrender of the East Jersey charter by the proprietors in 1702, the ongoing uncertainty about the status of Hamilton's authority had the effect of, as Logan put it, making "this government too precarious to be called one . . . our circumstances are uneasy and require a speedy redress."[38]

Penn knew that, after the outbreak of war in 1702, the militia and defense issues were only going to become more problematic for Pennsylvania Quakers. Even after he had successfully weathered Quary's allegations, he confided to Logan that the defense issue was the only real concern of substance: "Militia is all they have to hit us with." But if militia was "all" that "they" had, it was still an important and potentially fatal issue for Friends. In late July Logan reported to Penn that

> the governor . . . recommended the people to think of putting themselves in a posture of defence; and since that, has issued commissions for one company of militia. . . . Those of the hot Church party oppose it to their utmost, because they would have nothing done that may look with a good countenance at home. They have done all they can to dissuade all from touching with it.

"Nobody can imagine," Hamilton lamented, "what ungentlemanlike practices are set afoot by those who . . . call themselves churchmen to discourage those who have enlisted themselves to continue." For example, in 1702, Governor Hamilton commissioned one George Lowther to form a militia company in the capital. Lowther quickly discovered that despite their complaints about the lack of a militia in the province, Pennsylvania Anglicans had little interest in supporting one, assuming that "for them to form themselves into a militia now would be the readiest method to secure the Quakers government, (the want of one being the greatest objection against it)."[39]

Logan saw quite clearly the danger that such a situation posed for Pennsylvania Friends, and how hollow the Quaker peace testimony rang to those concerned with their own safety. Though he offered a clear defense to critics of the Quaker peace testimony, that "we were a peaceable people, had wholly renounced war, and the spirit of it; that we were willing to commit ourselves to the protection of God alone," Logan plainly understood that "this will not answer in English government." After all, officials like Quary and Cornbury had little regard for the lives of Quakers—if Friends "should . . . lose our lives only, it would be little to the crown," he admitted—"but others are involved with us, and should the enemy make themselves master of the country it would too sensibly touch England in the rest of her colonies."[40]

From the Crown's perspective, the militia issue represented just one piece of a larger and interconnected set of concerns raised by the Quaker peace testimony. The colony's quota of £350, payable to the governor of New York, had still, in May 1703, not been paid. The Board passed along the Queen's insistence that Penn "give strict charge to your Deputy Governor in that Province, that he use his utmost endeavors with the Council and Assembly there, to induce them to an effectual compliance with the said directions."[41]

The Board eventually dropped its objections to Hamilton so long as Penn agreed—which he did, extremely reluctantly—to acknowledge the queen's claim to the Lower Counties. This acknowledgment, with its implication that his authority over the Lower Counties was on less than solid ground, pained Penn deeply, and still the approval of Hamilton languished: it was not until January 21, 1703, after Penn had produced a copy of the colony's laws and agreed to provide £2,000 as security for Hamilton's performance and enforcement of the Navigation Acts, that the Queen acted on the Board's recommendation. In a final, cruel irony, Hamilton died three months later, on April 16, after having "lay sick of a putrid and hectic fever for about nine weeks." If Hamilton, while living, had been weakened by his lack of Crown approval, which made oversight of the government as well as collection of taxes and rents difficult, after death the situation became even more dire. "His loss will prove exceeding fatal to all the revenues of government," Logan wrote shortly after Hamilton's passing, "which were at a stand before in expectation of his approbation." Penn long believed that had Hamilton lived, he would have prevented the alliance of Quary and Cornbury and dealt effectively with the Crown's concerns over the colony's defense.[42]

Although he initially had proposed to the Board of Trade to return his old lieutenant William Markham to office, or to appoint John Finney, Philadelphia sheriff and a member of the Council, as Hamilton's replacement, Penn soon changed his mind and submitted the name of "the son of an old friend of mine," twenty-six-year-old political neophyte John Evans, an Anglican of Welsh background. Evidently Penn hoped that what Evans, who had been recommended to him by Lawton, his attorney, lacked in experience—he had none, except having had "a liberal education, been abroad and knows the world very well, is sober, discreet, and of a good understanding"—he would make up in energy and initiative. He clearly hoped, too, that Evans would get along with Evan Evans (no relation), the Welsh Anglican priest of Christ Church in Philadelphia, and smooth relations with Anglicans more generally. Unlike his predecessor, Evans received swift approval from the Crown. Even though things moved quickly in England, given the vagaries of transatlantic correspondence Pennsylvanians did not hear about Hamilton's replacement for months. Penn's instructions, sent to Evans from Bristol in early August, included a recommendation to rely closely on Logan's knowledge of the situation on the ground in Pennsylvania: "He knows the factious, the friendly, the sincere, the hollow, the bold, the timid, the able, and the weak." He also provided a list of "the chief of our enemies" and counseled Evans not to compel Friends to support a militia. "All I can agree to is a law that those that are desirous that a militia . . . may be raised . . . may be gratified; but none that profess a conscientious tenderness therein compelled in person or purse, or the worse used because thereof." And of course he impressed on Evans "the absolute necessity of establishing a revenue forthwith."[43]

* * *

A large portion of the increasing friction between Penn and the Pennsylvania authorities boiled down to the mutual and implacable hostility between the proprietor and David Lloyd. Lloyd apparently succeeded in preventing the Bucks County Court from meeting for much of its 1702 session, much to Hamilton's chagrin, and made common cause with his former rival John Moore to obstruct court proceedings wherever possible. In 1702 Moore appointed Lloyd—whom, recall, the Crown had insisted that Penn remove from office in 1699 for undermining the Admiralty Courts—as a Deputy Judge of the Admiralty Courts. Lloyd and Moore "both join in endeavoring to stop the courts, and procrastinate acts of justice," Logan wrote Penn late in 1702, and the confusion in the colony's courts resulted largely from "an intrigue of [David Lloyd's and John Moore's] to confuse all our courts and their proceedings."[44]

As had been the case in previous episodes of conflict, Penn's grasp of the realities of the political situation for Pennsylvania Quakers tended toward the unrealistic. In Penn's absence, Pennsylvania Quakers occupied a precarious position, with royal officials looking for any irregularities in legal proceedings, legislation, or other procedures, and the Lower Counties eager to take umbrage at Friends' dominance of colonial government. And yet Penn showed little sympathy for their predicament. "I admire at your weakness in not keeping to law," he wrote in late 1703, telling Logan and other Friends to "pluck up that English and Christian courage to not suffer yourselves to be thus treated and put upon." It was easy for him to say, from the relative comfort of London, or Warminghurst, or Bristol.[45]

* * *

In late July 1702 Logan had told Penn that, in his view, "thy presence in the country would mend all much." Later that year Logan once again urged on Penn that "thy affairs . . . deserve thy . . . immediate presence." But between health concerns, his growing family, and his increasing indebtedness, a return to America was not in the cards. Although his health was generally good, the steady accumulation of afflictions was beginning to take its toll. He experienced persistent trouble in early 1702 with "my sore leg and toe" and told Robert Harley, speaker of the House of Commons, that he had not been able to descend his stairs for three or four weeks. By late 1703, he was complaining of "the beginning of the gout," which often made it difficult for him to write.[46]

Penn did, however, begin preparations for sending his son William Jr. to Pennsylvania to represent his interest and assist Logan in his duties. William Jr. intended his journey, according to his father, to "see how he likes [America], and so to stay, or return to fetch his wife, or settle [in England]." Caution and concern are evident when Penn speaks about his son, and he clearly hoped that time among Friends in America might reform some of young William's wayward tendencies: "No rambling to New York," he had told Logan earlier, "he has wit [and] must be handled with much love, and much wisdom."[47]

These plans were put on hold when word of a smallpox infestation in the colony reached England. Although Griffith Owen, a physician originally from Lancashire, frequent officeholder, and one of Penn's supporters, described the outbreak as "not . . . very mortal," Hamilton later claimed that it was "far more terrible than that sickness which happened at Philadelphia" before Penn's arrival in 1699. The sickness claimed the lives of Edward Penington, the Surveyor General, and his wife. New York and Boston were also afflicted, and Logan's description of his own experience captures the severity of the smallpox as well as the fever that followed it in many cases. One fit "held me almost speechless and besides my senses twelve hours on a stretch . . . it lies much in my head and makes me incapable of all business." A month later Logan still reported feeling "the dregs of the distemper." The pox and fever took the life of Colonel Gabriel Minviele, Mayor of New York, as well as of Matthew Clarkson, secretary to the New York Council, and two of Penn's servants at Pennsbury. They persisted into the winter of 1702–1703, affecting the Lower Counties of Sussex and Kent: "more fatal, 'tis affirmed, than that of York last year, or of Philadelphia in 1699; it reigned most of the winter, but is now happily over."[48]

By 1703 the worst of the sickness had passed, and plans for William Jr.'s visit were revived. Penn was under no illusions about his son's character, though he held himself at least partially responsible, given the long absences during William's childhood that the colony and its business had required of him. Penn hoped that Logan (who was, after all, just five years older than William Jr.) would be able to help William Jr. understand the nature of the proprietary interest, and to get to know the colony, its people, and its laws. Penn also instructed Logan to "weigh down his levities, temper his resentments, and inform his understandings," to "watch him, outwit, and honestly overreach him—for his good." Tellingly, he added, "Suffer him not to be in any public house after the allowed hours" nor to "quarre[l] with our enemies." Knowing that William Jr.'s Quaker witness left something to be desired, his father nonetheless encouraged Friends to show kindness to his son "that they may . . . gain him, at least civilly if not religiously."[49]

Whether he knew his father's descriptions of him or not, the younger Penn surely knew that reports of his behavior and character were reaching Pennsylvania. He urged Logan to vouch for him to Pennsylvanians "that I might have an opportunity of vindicating myself . . . you will be assured I am far different from what I am represented to be," and when "I make my personal appearance among you . . . I will show you I have been villainously treated."[50]

* * *

Despite his extensive commitments in London, Penn remained active as a leading Quaker, in the capital as well as Sussex, where he retained his home at Warminghurst, and in Bristol. In August 1702, Penn circulated a general epistle to Friends, exhorting them to unity and warning them about slackening their pursuit of truth, their love for each other, or their commitment to the Light. And when Queen Anne dissolved Parliament in late May 1702, the London Yearly Meeting appointed Penn, Whitehead, and Bristol Quaker Benjamin Coole to draft an address to present to Her Majesty. The queen, whom Penn had known when she was Princess Anne during his days as a close advisor to her father, James II, had announced that despite her fervent affection for the Church of England, she would be "very careful to preserve and maintain the Act of Toleration," a guarantee for which Friends wished to express their gratitude. A week later, Penn and a company of Friends met the Queen at Windsor Castle to render "humble and hearty acknowledgements" of thanks for her words, and to "assur[e] her (on behalf of all our Friends) of our sincere affection and Christian obedience." According to Nicholas Gates, a Quaker from Kent, the queen replied, "Mr. Penn, I am well pleased that what I have done is to your satisfaction, that you and your Friends may be assured of my protection."[51]

This desire to maintain royal goodwill was not merely a formality. Of course conditions for Quakers, indeed for Dissenters in general, had been radically improved by the passage of the Toleration Act in 1689 and the Affirmation Act seven years later. But the Anglican hierarchy had never fully made its peace with the new order, and religious tensions regularly seeped into the political process.

Early in Anne's reign, Anglicans in Parliament introduced a bill to address the phenomenon of "occasional conformity," whereby Dissenters attended Anglican services occasionally in order to maintain their eligibility to hold public office, while more regularly frequenting their own congregations. The proposed legislation would make such practices grounds for fines and dismissal from office. Although the bill died in the House of Lords, there was considerable support for it in the Commons, and Penn weighed in on the issue in a brief pamphlet entitled *Considerations on the bill*, published in 1703. He denounced the bill as divisive, reopening old wounds by describing Dissenting meetings as "conventicles," terminology that had provided the pretense for the persecutions of the 1660s, 1670s, and 1680s. Finally, although Quakers had consistently declined to serve in government, and thus were unlikely to be affected by the legislation, they recognized the broader principle at stake in this debate: "As it is our Christian Principle to suffer for conscience, so the same makes us plead for the liberty of it, to all whose morals and obedience to the government cannot justly be questioned." Where such sanctions exist on the exercise of conscience, the tract concluded, "we cannot think . . . toleration secure."[52]

The occasional conformity debate also provided Penn the opportunity to seek leniency in the case of Daniel Defoe, the noted London Dissenter, merchant, and sometime Crown operative. Defoe's best-known writings were still ahead of him: *Robinson Crusoe* would be published in 1719, *Moll Flanders* three years after that. But his 1702 satire *The Shortest-way with the Dissenters* had landed Defoe in Newgate Prison, convicted of seditious libel. *The Shortest-way* had purported to argue for the harshest of terms against Dissenters who practiced occasional conformity. What the nation needed to deal with Dissenters' nefarious influence, Defoe (satirically) argued, was not fines but harsh punishment:

> The light foolish handling of them by mulcts, fines, [etc.] 'tis their glory and their advantage! If the gallows instead of the counter, and the galleys instead of the fines; were the reward of going to a conventicle . . . there would not be so many sufferers! . . . If one severe law were . . . punctually executed, that Whoever was found at a Conventicle should be banished the nation, and the Preacher be hanged; we should soon see an end of the tale! They would all come to church again, and one age would make us all one again!

Defoe's *Shortest-way*—like a later satire, Jonathan Swift's *Modest proposal*—mocked advocates of severity against Dissenters and sought to attain its desired effect by shocking its audience with its apparently serious "proposal."[53]

Defoe was sentenced to stand in the pillory for three days at the end of July 1703. Two weeks before his sentence was carried out, Defoe wrote to thank

Penn for the "extraordinary kindness" he had shown, especially since they were not personally acquainted, and insisted that despite his admission of having written the tract, and much to the chagrin of his jailors, "I have no accomplices" and thus could not name them to prosecutors. On the day of his appointed punishment, instead of being the target of rotten fruit and other projectiles, Defoe encountered an outpouring of public support, and was eventually released thanks to Penn's ally Robert Harley.[54]

But Penn's longstanding prominence in the Quaker community also gave rise to tensions with Pennsylvania Friends. In 1703, for example, a dispute burst out over 1,250 acres of Pennsylvania land that Penn had bestowed as a gift upon George Fox. Although the lot had never been surveyed, Fox had left it to the Philadelphia Monthly Meeting, and Philadelphia Friends had unsuccessfully argued for the grant before the Commissioners of Property. Leading Friends (Samuel Carpenter, David Lloyd, and Anthony Morris) in turn attempted to recruit Thomas Lower, Fox's son-in-law, to intervene with Penn to assist their cause. Although Penn agreed to provide land for Friends' purposes, he insisted that such a grant occupy "no part of the city ground," since doing so at this point, two decades into the settlement of Pennsylvania, would involve "a perfect overthrow of the model of the city."[55]

Nor was Penn ever quite free from his old friend and more recent nemesis George Keith, who had, after attacking Penn in print (and in person) during the 1690s, formed an alliance with Anglican divine Thomas Bray, founder of the Society for the Promotion of Christian Knowledge. The Society supported Keith's return to America in 1702, where he attempted to debate Quakers as well as New England Puritans. Keith's return to Pennsylvania in early 1703, in which he attempted to bait Friends into public disputes, was largely ignored, and Logan reported to Penn that his own former followers, "those called Keithians here . . . are his great opponents, and in short in this place his execution has been exceeding small." As his contribution to combating any residual sympathy for Keith in the colony, Penn sent "2 or 300 books against [Keith]" to Pennsylvania in April 1703.[56]

* * *

Penn's return to England in late 1701 had brought his many creditors back to his doorstep, and his correspondence with Logan and Pennsylvania Friends took on an increased urgency, if that was possible, on matters of money. "Fail not to send me . . . the value of rents due, supply . . . lands saleable, [etc.] that I may make a judgment to myself, and a good argument to others as occasion offers." "Get in all debts due to me." "Hasten in my rents and debts and transmit them with all possible speed as fast as thou canst, for I expect a war."[57]

His financial woes steadily worsened as time passed. Samuel Jennings, Penn's Receiver General, responsible for collecting money due the proprietor, left

Pennsylvania and settled in West Jersey without remitting him any sums. As before, Penn complained about ungrateful colonists taking advantage of his generosity. "God forgive those wretched people who have misused me so, and preserve my spirit over it." Nor was he above attempting to shame his colonists into assisting him, instructing Logan to tell Friends there that "I am distressed for want of supply; that I am forced to borrow money and add debt to debt instead of paying them off," having incurred enormous costs by necessity of "attendances, draughts of answers, conferences, counsels' opinions, hearings, &c., with the charge that follows them." As a result, he faced "melting expenses," and begged Logan to "make returns with all speed, or I am undone." By early 1703, Penn's description of his financial situation, never lacking in melodrama or despair, reached new heights (or, perhaps, new lows): "I never was so low and reduced."[58]

As Penn continued to face financial challenges in England, Logan continued to attempt, with little success, to represent his interests in Pennsylvania. Given the war's impact on shipping and trade, even basic communication posed enormous difficulties, with Logan detailing for Penn (in correspondence, no less) a litany of lost letters, documents, and packets, by date and description, to absolve himself of Penn's charges of neglect. His lonely task was made more difficulty by the increasingly bold anti-proprietary party, which had coalesced around Lloyd and Moore. The two former rivals had joined forces in 1702, brought together by their shared opposition to Penn. Logan frequently despaired about effectively serving the proprietor in such a hostile environment. "None in Pennsylvania undergoes the trouble I do," he lamented in August 1702, casting himself as a true friend to Penn surrounded by others more concerned with their own gain. "Many are full of talking friendship, but whatever has to be done lies wholly on me. . . . I could never have thought that some in thy absence would pay all their professions of service, they so liberally made, so slightly as with wind only." Logan admitted that the situation "makes things sometimes heavier than I can bear. . . . I much want some further support here, someday I may fall by." Nor did representing the proprietor endear Logan to his neighbors. "I am universally found fault with by the common vogue of the country," he wrote, and described defending Penn's interests as akin to "sail[ing] against wind and tide." At the end of one of his plaintive reports, Logan entreated Penn for "a pound of good tea of which I am grown a great drinker"; he even offered to pay for it himself.[59]

Penn, on the other hand, was well practiced at self-pity and was a demanding taskmaster. He asked Logan repeatedly about Pennsbury: the condition of the grounds, the buildings, the crops, and the servants. He continued to express concern about the estate's condition. He even asked Logan to explore the possibility of having a house built on one of his lots, "for Pennsbury will hardly accommodate my son's family and mine, unless enlarged." He attempted to reassure Logan of his confidence in him—"I know thy ability, doubt not thy integrity, [and] I wish I could make [thy station] lighter"—even while he frequently castigated him for failing to keep him fully informed of goings-on in the colony. Increasingly desperate for funds and increasingly disconnected from the realities of Pennsylvania life, Penn peppered Logan with increasingly petulant and improbable demands, such as "send me all the silver thou canst get anywhere or of anything . . . rather than leave me destitute." If he could not collect Penn's rents and debts in sterling, Penn wrote, he would "much rather [have] furs and skins, than tobacco." He criticized Logan for not doing more to develop the colony's fur trade and advised him to be sure that no one was cutting wood on Penn's lands. Were he to be granted a monopoly on the colony's fur trade, Penn insisted, even if only for seven or eleven years, he could free himself entirely from debt. (Logan shot this idea down as painfully out of touch: "the merchants will never bear it.")[60]

Trade of all sorts, particularly to the Caribbean, continued to be hampered by the smallpox epidemic and the war, as well as pirates off Martinique and Guadeloupe, whom Logan described as "exceedingly mischievous." Trade woes contributed to the near impossibility of collecting rents; the price of wheat collapsed, and in the absence of a peace, access to Spanish trade continued to be blocked. In the spring of 1703, when collecting Penn's rents, Logan found people, as he put it, "willing to pay . . . but have it not," and as a result they offer to pay in wheat, "but that will not do," as there was no market for it. The lone bright spot for Pennsylvania's tobacco trade came in the form of a violent storm in late 1703 that decimated the Maryland and Virginia tobacco yields.[61]

* * *

Even after the threat of parliamentary action seemed to have passed, Penn's weariness with his proprietary situation had clearly taken its toll. "I believe this Parliament will not meddle with our grants," he wrote to Logan in late July 1702, "but I am willing to settle things." Penn had previously, if only in the depths of exasperation, raised the possibility of surrendering his government back to the Crown, if an acceptable financial settlement could be reached. With the surrender of the New Jersey proprietorship in April 1702, it is not surprising that rumors about Pennsylvania's fate swirled as well. "It is generally believed here," Logan wrote in May 1702, that Parliament will pass the Reunification Bill, and that the war would provide additional arguments for centralized control. Such a prospect was not viewed negatively by all in Pennsylvania, however, he insisted, "provided thou canst make good terms for thyself and them; for they seem both weary and careless of government."[62]

By the spring of 1703 Penn's sense of desperation about the situation in Pennsylvania, his ongoing struggles with the Board of Trade, and his worsening financial affairs led him to take a step he had hinted at privately but never yet taken. On May 11, he wrote to the Board of Trade offering, "upon a reasonable satisfaction," to "resign to the Crown, the government" of his American territories. What exactly Penn intended by "resign" or "surrender" to the Crown is not entirely clear, since his initial proposed terms—a payment of £30,000, continued authority to nominate colonial governors, confirmation of his claims to both the colony and the Lower Counties, and preservation of the constitution and laws including liberty of conscience and affirmations by Friends—seemed decidedly one-sided in his own favor. Put another way, he would be surrendering all of the uncertainty and frustration, but retaining political control and the potential to benefit from the province's prosperity. Or, put another way, he would surrender the risk but retain the reward. The Board of Trade considered Penn's terms "very unreasonable," and the proposal would languish for years. But Penn had made, without a doubt, a radical proposal, an explicit repudiation of the high hopes with which he had, as a young Dissenter, invested his colony's status as a "holy experiment" for liberty of conscience.[63]

Throughout the long and protracted negotiations over Penn's proposed surrender, he continued to profess his love for Friends there and even insisted (how believably, we can only speculate) that "after I have done with the government, and called upon Ireland, if the Lord give me life, I purpose to fly to you as fast as I can." But as rumors about Penn's offer to surrender his government to the Crown made their way across the Atlantic, they only added to the chaotic political scene on the ground. Former Jersey governor Basse, returning to New Jersey as the colony's secretary under Cornbury in 1703, spread word that Penn had demanded £10,000 for his government. John Usher, Lieutenant Governor of New Hampshire, claimed that the sum was £15,000. Logan expressed his concern about the security of Penn's interests in the case of a surrender, and pointed to the Jerseys as a cautionary tale: "To fall under such a commission as is over our river, would startle any man who ever had entertained a notion of freedom."[64]

* * *

William Penn Jr. and the new Deputy Governor, Evans, finally set sail for America in October 1703, and arrived in Pennsylvania in February 1704. They had been at sea for more than four months, "sixteen weeks out of sight of land . . . a long and tedious passage and full of violent storms." But the real storms, as both William Penns would soon find out, were only just beginning.[65]

14

William Jr.

The year 1704 dawned with William Penn enjoying a brief respite from the despair and discouragement with which his American affairs had so often afflicted him. His newly appointed Lieutenant Governor, John Evans, had received swift approval from the Crown. Evans and Penn's own son, William Jr., had departed for Pennsylvania, a journey that Penn hoped would both set his government on a firm footing and begin the process of grooming young William to take his place as proprietor when the time came. He remained one of the best-known Friends in England, and enjoyed a European reputation. Penn exhorted Irish Friends to remain steadfast in the faith and greeted "my ancient and worthy Friend and brother, William Edmundson." (Edmundson would live on, until the age of eighty-five, passing away in 1712 just a few months before the fatal stroke that marked the beginning of the end of Penn's public career.) Relatively free of major health problems, he and Hannah had welcomed two new children in the previous two years, and by spring Hannah would be pregnant again.[1]

Across the Atlantic, however, tension with the colonial government continued. A further sign of generational transition, and a milestone in the colony's history, came with the death of William Markham in June 1704. Markham had played a singular role in Pennsylvania's history from the very beginning, arriving in the colony even before Penn himself. He had overseen the first steps in the development of Philadelphia, initiated negotiations with Lord Baltimore and the native tribes, and served as Penn's deputy and representative in numerous capacities. His tenure had been controversial, to be sure. Markham served in Fletcher's controversial administration during 1692–94 and was responsible for agreeing to the 1696 Frame of Government, which caused the proprietor no shortage of trouble. He was frequently accused, particularly by Randolph and Quary, of corruption, turning a blind eye to (if not actively encouraging) illegal trade, and colluding with pirates. Nonetheless Penn consistently, if not always enthusiastically or convincingly, defended Markham, who was after all his cousin. As with so many other matters, James Logan was left to make sense of Markham's effects, and he lamented the disordered state of his papers

and the claims that Markham's widow made about money the proprietor purportedly owed her late husband.[2]

* * *

"I have been at Pennsbury and like it well," William Penn Jr. wrote to his father in
February 1704, not long after his arrival in Pennsylvania. "If thee wouldst allow
me a good gardener, I could make it one of the pleasantest places in the world."
(He also requested "some more hounds" as well as the horse "thee promised to
get for me.") William Jr.'s stay began auspiciously, and Logan wrote that he had
been "very well received," hoping that in America young William would find an
escape from the temptations that had, in England, "led him out into his youthful
sallies." He was made a member of the Provincial Council, although he was
never the most faithful attender. Shortly thereafter, young William accompanied
Logan and Attorney General Roger Mompesson to a Pennsbury meeting with a
delegation of natives ("100 Indians . . . of which 9 were kings").[3]

Before long, however, William's relationship with Logan began to deteriorate. "The directions given me can by no means satisfy him," Logan confessed to
Penn, and the young Penn refused to confine his spending to the rather modest
allowance his father had granted him. Relations with other leading figures in the
colony soon followed suit. In September, William Jr. was involved in a "fray" at
Enoch Story's tavern in Philadelphia. After a night of drinking, a number of the
colony's "young gentry" (including William Jr.) brawled with the city watch,
which had attempted to bring their gathering to order. In the process, William Jr.
received some blows, but the wounds to his pride and sense of self-importance
were likely even more severe. A grand jury considered indicting those involved in
the affair, but Lieutenant Governor Evans intervened to quash the proceedings.[4]

These events accelerated the younger Penn's break with Pennsylvania Friends,
as well as his increasingly close relationship with Lord and Lady Cornbury,
whom he soon entertained at Pennsbury. They also hastened his decision to
bring his brief, turbulent, and unhappy stay in Pennsylvania to an end, to sell
his Pennsylvania lands, and to wash his hands of America once and for all. He
sold his seven-thousand-acre manor, Williamstadt (current-day Norristown,
Pennsylvania), to Isaac Norris and William Trent, for £850. By early October he
was on board the Jersey and heading home. His return was not only a personal
disappointment for his father but also, given the debts that his son had run up
during his stay, represented a real financial burden.[5]

Writing to the proprietor in the wake of his son's departure, Logan counseled
tenderness and understanding, telling Penn that his son "has much good nature . . . but is unhappy chiefly by indiscretion." It was too bad, Logan continued,
that young William's wife had not accompanied him, as her presence might have
prevented some of his carousing. But at the root of William Jr.'s behavior, Logan

thought, was "the belief that thou has a greater regard to thy second children than thy first, and an emulation between his own and thy younger rivets him in it." Penn partly blamed himself and the demands that Pennsylvania had placed on him during William's youth. Commenting on the "melancholy scene" in the wake of his son's departure, he observed that "Pennsylvania began it by my absence here and there it is accomplished, with expense, disappointment, ingratitude, and poverty." But for all those who might have considered the young Penn to have gotten away with breaking the law, at least one observer—his father—saw William as the victim in the matter, and refused to let the matter drop. In the aftermath of the event, Penn condemned "bad Friends treatment" of his son, which had "stumbled him from the blessed truth." And years later, Penn continued to implore Logan to pursue the matter, to "let my son have justice against the authors of that barbarous affront committed upon him." (Not only was he Penn's son, Penn pointed out, but he was also a leading member of the Council, and thus not under the authority of the night watch.)[6]

His exit from the Pennsylvania scene was only the beginning of William Penn Jr.'s frustrations with his lot in life. Although his father wrote to Evans in September 1705 that William Jr. was "well, and grown great at Court," a string of disappointments followed. He unsuccessfully stood for election to Parliament, a defeat that his father hoped would temper his aspirations and make him more amenable to private pursuits. He also unsuccessfully sought a position in the army or navy. By late 1705 William Jr. had "[gone] off from truth's way," in his father's words, and renounced Quakerism, which wounded Penn deeply. A year later, he attempted to secure a position in Ireland, and the suggestion that he be made "captain of a foot company" insulted his father, who told Harley that William would "go dig potatoes first." Penn asked Harley to help secure his son a post in the civil administration in Ireland, while speculating about the connection between his son's renunciation of Quakerism and his difficulty advancing in a worldly career: "My poor son may have this just reflection, and I the satisfaction, of seeing his conformity to the world to be his ruin, instead of his advancement."[7]

Although he admitted to Logan, from time to time, his feelings of guilt and responsibility for his role in William Jr.'s failures, he was also capable of scornful condemnation of his son when the mood struck him. "He has been of no use, but much expense and grief to me, many ways and years too," he confided to Logan in 1707, "being not of that service and benefit to me that some sons are, and tis well known I was to my father before I married." This last comment—with its selective amnesia about the grief he had brought to his own father—provides a remarkable illustration of Penn's capacity for self-pity.[8]

* * *

In Pennsylvania, Logan continued his uphill battle to represent the proprietor's interests, though he frequently grew despondent over "the difficulties I am oppressed with here." Friends who had promised to help defray Penn's expenses for returning to England to defend the colony simply refused, citing lack of resources. Logan insisted that matters were largely out of his hands, having to do more with the ongoing war with France and Spain than with his own lack of effort. He also pointed out that he was only one individual, in a hostile political environment, and that he and colonial officials had received very few letters from Penn, which only increased his discouragement. Correspondence had surely been affected by the European hostilities. For example, the *Cornbury*, on which Logan had placed letters to Penn, was taken by the French in 1703, and "the captain ... threw all his letters and therefore some dangerous packets of mine overboard." To truly secure his interests, Logan suggested, would require Penn's return to Pennsylvania once again. Nonetheless, Penn complained about the lack of news reaching him from the colony: "Since thine of [December 5, 1703]," Penn wrote in mid-July 1704, "not one scrip of paper has come from thee to me." Penn also expected Logan to represent his interest in New Jersey, where he still held land. But Logan's task on this front was made more difficult by the fact that he lacked copies of Penn's deeds to those lands, without which nothing of substance could be done.[9]

By early 1705, to the thankless task of continuing to serve as Penn's secretary was added disappointment in love, as Philadelphian Ann Shippen spurned Logan for Thomas Story, whom she would marry the following year. Ann's father Edward Shippen had arrived in Philadelphia from Boston in 1694, initiating a prosperous and influential public career that would see him serve as Mayor of Philadelphia, Council member, Commissioner of Property, and acting Lieutenant Governor after Hamilton's death. Logan's and Story's rivalry for Ann's affections no doubt had something to do with the rift that had developed between the two men sometime in 1703, although by the time of Thomas and Ann's wedding the two had apparently reconciled. "Thomas Story carries very well since his marriage," Logan wrote to William Penn Jr. "He and I are very great friends, for I think the whole business is not now worth a quarrel." (That said, Logan's name does not appear on the couple's marriage certificate.)[10]

Never the most understanding of employers, Penn continued to press Logan on a number of fronts, peppering him with long lists of requests: "pray be very mindful of my Jersey lands ... I will have no more [Philadelphia] bank lots disposed of ... without my special and fresh leave"; "use thy utmost wits to get intelligence of the motions of our enemies." In one letter alone, he implored his secretary to do a better job of collecting his revenues ("I live but from hand to mouth, and hardly that"), to send him furs, to have a house built for him in Philadelphia, and to stop Pennsylvanians from cutting timber on his lands. While expressing his sympathy for Logan's "unhappy love," he immediately mentioned that "some say ... that thy amours have so altered or influenced thee, that thou art grown touchy and apt to give short and rough answers, which many call

haughty." Indeed, whether due to disappointments in love or simply his person-
ality characteristics, Logan's personal manner did not always advance his efforts
to look after Penn's affairs. Although Griffith Owen described Logan as "true to
thy interest and I know not where thou might have another so capable to manage
thy business," he admitted that Logan "has not a pleasing way to gain the love of
the people," pointing to his "slighting and provoking way of expression" as "the
reason that so few speaks well of him."[11]

Logan continued to face the proprietor's hectoring demands and personal
criticism, which were exacerbated by Penn's unhappiness with the lack of information about his properties. "I can neither sell, or borrow, until I know what
I have . . let it not be said that after five years time I know not what I have to
sell or mortgage," he implored Logan, exhorting him to complete the rent roll
he had begun and to update him on the process of resurveying Pennsylvania
lands. "I am unspeakably disappointed in not knowing how my interest lies, as
to bonds, rent rolls, etc; what received, and what paid." Logan described the rent
roll project as "a mighty work . . . and will make many quires of paper." He could
not promise when he would be able to complete it, and denied that he had ever
implied it was completed and ready for Penn's inspection.[12]

Penn was not the only member of his family who expressed criticisms of
Logan. His son-in-law William Aubrey wrote in early 1704 expressing "great dissatisfaction" at Logan's handling of his and Letitia's affairs, and accused Logan of
converting money owed him to the proprietor's use. Letitia had also written Logan
a letter he described as "exceeding sharp." Logan was clearly unhappy with the criticism he received from Letitia and William Aubrey, and offered to resign in favor
of an agent more to their liking. He continued to experience difficulty collecting
the funds owed to the Aubreys, but defended himself as doing the best job possible
given scarce currency and economic hardships in the colony.[13]

Nor were Logan and Penn the only two actors who often felt themselves
out of touch with distant events. Isaac Norris spoke for many Pennsylvanians
when he opined in early 1705 that it would be helpful "if we could hear what
was become of our laws on that side [of the Atlantic]." Then again, Norris might
have wished to remain in the dark, since a year later the queen, acting on the
recommendations of her Attorney-General and the Board of Trade, rejected
nearly half of the 105 laws that the colonial government had submitted.[14]

* * *

Lingering tensions between Quakers and Anglicans in the colony—reflected
and encouraged by Quary and Cornbury—continued to worry Penn, and he
conducted a spirited campaign to protect Pennsylvania's Quaker character,
complaining to Robert Harley about "officious and turbulent persons" who
aimed to make Friends "dissenters in our own country." What Anglicans really

wanted in Pennsylvania, he insisted, was not merely the liberty to worship in their own manner, but to "have the government, that they may be lords of our labors." Their efforts undermined effective government, harmed the economy, and divided the people. Penn exhorted Evans to do what he could to mitigate such contention and to conduct himself with "temper and prudence," and praised him for "keeping a good decorum" and for making "so great a part of the best of the church people sensible of their base and unreasonable designs" against the proprietor. By the end of 1705, Evans had set up a "well appointed and regular" militia in the Lower Counties and had even managed to assemble a few companies of non-Quakers in Pennsylvania as well.[15]

Over the course of 1706, however, relations between Penn and his Lieutenant Governor cooled considerably. Logan cited increasing popular disaffection toward Evans, whom he described as increasingly imperious and embracing a "private way of management." Evans had prosecuted William Biles, a prominent Bucks County Friend and member of the Assembly, for calling Evans "but a boy ... not fit to be our governor" and insisting that "we'll kick him out." Although Biles's remarks were not made in any official capacity, Evans's actions aroused the Assembly's opposition out of concern for its members' privileges. (David Lloyd served as Biles's attorney, further polarizing matters.) A year later, despite claiming that he was willing to forgive Biles, Evans threw him in jail, refusing to listen to leading Friends who had counseled him to show moderation.[16]

But the major bone of contention between Evans and the Friends—and between Evans and the proprietor—had to do with the militia issue, and Evans's unwillingness to defend Friends' exemption from militia service. Although Penn had pointedly directed Evans that "I am sure thou wouldst not impose any thing upon them that is contrary to their professed principles," differences remained. Continuing tensions with the French and Indians, and an expansion of the French fleet in the Caribbean, revived debates over militias that had complicated Penn's relations with the English government for years. French ships sacked St. Christopher and Nevis in early 1706. Evans used rumors about an impending move against New York by the French fleet to raise a general alarm, and—in Logan's words—"published a proclamation requiring all persons without fail to furnish themselves with arms and ammunition." Shortly thereafter, the level of fear in the area was raised still further when officers from the Lower Counties arrived with reports that "6 French vessels were in the river and 4 of them had actually passed [New Castle]."[17]

Brandishing a letter purportedly written by the Sussex County sheriff that "Lewes is burnt"—a letter that turned out to be a rank forgery perpetrated by Evans himself—the Lieutenant Governor summoned Philadelphia residents who were willing to bear arms, throwing "the whole town and great part of the country [into] the deepest confusion." Logan had the presence of mind to "haste[n] a little way down the river with a light boat," discovered the hoax, and was thus able to "undeceive[e] the people, who were in as miserable a consternation and confusion as if an enemy had really been in the midst of them." And the people had indeed been thrown into confusion and turmoil. "The people threw their goods into wells and all manner of holes, greatly to their damage," Logan wrote. "Women were taken ill, and the distress very great." Logan denounced Evans's actions as "most mischievous boyish trick," which had "given many hearty well-wishers to the Government occasion to remember Wm. Biles' words with much more charity."[18]

The good news was that Pennsylvania was not in fact under attack by the French. But Logan accurately understood the ramifications of what had just happened, and warned Penn that agitation for a militia would only increase in the wake of this provocation. Indeed, a few days after the false alarm, "the members of the Council who are not Friends made it evidently appear how naked and defenseless the place would be in the case of a real attack by an enemy," and renewed their push for the establishment of a militia and the raising of money to build a fort. If the Assembly would not act, they threatened, they would make a direct appeal to the queen. Non-Friends claimed to honor Quakers' refusal to fight—"they knew well the Quakers would not fight themselves, nor did they desire it of them, only that all others that can fight should be compelled to it and that all persons should contribute to the public charge." If "contribute to the public charge" meant supporting a militia with public funds, however, there was little chance that the Assembly would comply. In Logan's assessment, Evans "really thinks he is discharging his duty" as governor, and if Friends looked on Evans as an enemy "they really wrong him." But he expected that the Assembly would refuse to acquiesce to Evans's request for funding a militia—which it did, when summoned later that spring—and held that an appeal to the queen could be fatal to Friends' interests in Pennsylvania.[19]

All of these events served to incense Penn against Evans, in whom he had previously lodged such trust. He chastised his deputy for fomenting the rumors of a French attack "by thy knowledge, if not contrivance, when at the same time, thou knewst there was no reality" in the rumors. He sharply criticized Evans for the Militia Act, passed in 1705 by the Assembly for the Lower Counties, at a session attended by Evans and Quary. Under the Act, Quakers in the Lower Counties faced fines and seizure of goods for refusing to serve in the militia. Penn was direct and unsparing in his criticism of Evans: Friends' suffering for not bearing arms "touches my conscience as well as honor." Refusal to bear arms, after all, was "our very characteristic," and to be punished for those principles "is a violation of our constitution and custom too." (Penn objected to the substance of the Act as well as the implied claim that the Lower Counties Assembly possessed the right to legislate for the Lower Counties alone.) The Militia Act also provided David Lloyd with more ammunition for his criticism of Penn's proprietorship: in a vitriolic letter of July 1705, he wrote with unbridled animosity that "here is a militia authorized by thy lieutenant under thy seal and thy own coat of arms."[20]

Also complicating Penn's relationship with his colonists was the ongoing issue of affirmations and oaths. Although the Affirmation Act of 1696 had resolved many of these questions in England, Pennsylvania Quakers continued to face hostility from royal officials on these matters, and the uncertainty affected a wide range of public functions. In January 1706 the Assembly passed a law permitting jurors and public officeholders to affirm rather than swear during public proceedings, and wrote to Penn asking him to support the law when it came for review before the Board of Trade. In late 1706 London attorney George Wilcox, representing the colony's Anglicans, entered a series of objections against the Pennsylvania law to the Board, claiming that the act aimed to "establish Quakerism in the . . . province," and that it undermined the confidence of the people in the government and judicial system. Penn defended the colonial law the next year, denouncing the Anglican move as an attempt to "unqualify us for shares in our own government" and to make Friends "dissenters in our own country," despite the fact that Pennsylvania was "a province or colony of their own making, at the known hazard of their lives and fortunes and a vast expense and labor for 26 years past." He pointed out the severe consequences for the administration of justice if Friends were excluded from participation, and reiterated that, for Friends, "the security of an affirmation . . . is certainly as valid as that of an oath with those that are free to take it." (Penn had gotten some advice on his replies from Isaac Norris, who was then visiting England; Norris interpreted the objections to the law as evidence that "tis plain nothing less than blowing us out of all is aimed at or will satisfy [the Anglicans]."[21]

Finally, Penn criticized what he considered Evans's extravagant lifestyle. Logan had arranged for Evans and William Penn Jr. to lodge in several houses after their arrival in 1704, and had attempted to obtain reimbursement for those costs out of the public treasury, requesting that Evans "give me an order to the treasurer to pay off and reimburse past charges." Evans refused to do so, insisting that he be paid a salary from the government in addition to the £200 Penn promised him when offering him the position of Lieutenant Governor in 1703. Logan, after all, was under constant pressure from Penn to contain the proprietor's expenses, and Evans and Logan got into a heated disagreement over this matter. Penn erupted at Evans, in a letter to Logan: "If he must [entertain] like Lord Cornbury or Colonel Seymour, he had need of great supplies; but then let the country give them, I can't; nor does so small a colony and infant too, require such expense." Adding insult to injury, Evans refused to pay Logan for William

Penn Jr.'s lodging costs, leaving Logan to petition, reluctantly, to the proprietor for those funds.[22]

* * *

The idea of surrendering his government to the Crown continued to appeal to Penn, not least because of the opportunity it offered to regain control of his desperate finances and retire some of his mounting debts. Compared to other colonial founders, Penn claimed, he had emerged in particularly poor financial health as a result of his colonial undertaking, and he called the prospect of a royal takeover without the preservation of Pennsylvania's guarantees of liberty of conscience or an adequate financial arrangement for the founder "a perfect ruin to me and my family as well as an irreparable disappointment of the people that made it a country." (Penn confided to Harley that, though he had asked for £30,000, he would accept £20,000.)[23]

That said, he sought to maintain maximum flexibility by keeping his ultimate intentions to himself. Penn told Evans in early 1704 that "I am much more likely to keep my government than to sell or lose it," and he assured his Lieutenant Governor that, even in the event of a surrender to the Crown, he would ensure continuation of Evans's appointment. In large part, this change in Penn's plans seemed to result from his recent success in convincing the Board of Trade of Quary's misbehavior. In mid-March 1704, Penn submitted a memorial to the board elaborating Quary's undermining of his government—his exaggerations of Pennsylvania's political turmoil, his attempts to sow discord between the Upper and Lower Counties, his open call for the queen to grant Pennsylvania's government to Cornbury—and claimed to Logan that the board had "at last come to dislike his busy and turbulent proceedings" and would be sending a letter rebuking him. "His being an officer shall not exempt him from correction, or support him in his seditious and factious practices with impunity." In early May the board did write to Quary, but its instructions were rather gentler than Penn had implied they would be: the board merely exhorted Quary to work to mend relations with Pennsylvanians. Still, it was something.[24]

Despite the prospect of a handsome payoff, and being advised by many to "sell all to the Crown, and let them take their own course," Penn hesitated. His hesitation was grounded in his understanding of the significance of the goals to which he had aspired in the founding of Pennsylvania: "For God was with me in seeking, getting, and settling of it, and there some that have not forsaken their first love to truth and me, whom I would live and die with." If he could be sure of continued harmony, perhaps he would hold off on the surrender negotiations; but he was not confident of such an outcome, given his past and recent experiences.[25]

As the person most familiar with Penn's financial situation, Logan offered his frank assessment of the proprietor's predicament. He stressed how important it was that Penn free himself from debt, both for his own reputation and that of his family: "I take the discharging of these debts to be the first of all worldly things to be laboured. Justice indispensably requires it; besides that, 'tis impossible for thee and thine to be easy in the enjoyment of anything till this be done." In the best of all circumstances—a settled peace freeing up trade routes, Penn personally on hand in America to assist collection of money owed to him—he might expect to raise £25,000 within a few years, but then again money in the colonies was worth less than money in London, and peace would surely not arrive overnight. Penn's reluctance to sell the government to the Crown, considering his enormous debts, struck Logan as "most unaccountable," and he warned that if Penn were going to sell he should do so very soon, before his opponents in Pennsylvania had the opportunity to cast aspersions before the Board of Trade.[26]

Furthermore, by 1705 Penn's always precarious financial outlook had turned positively dire. His continuing efforts to placate the Fords were going nowhere, and he feared that they would file the will and bring his debts into public view. Family matters, including his son William's disastrous and expensive journey to Pennsylvania and his own continuing indebtedness to his vexatious son-in-law Aubrey, were also taking their toll. Logan wrote in late 1704 that he could see no prospect for restoring harmony to the country without a surrender to the Crown, blaming colonists' use of the charter offered by Penn in 1701 against him. And so in early 1705, he revived negotiations with the Crown.[27]

Although the amount remained uncertain, Penn insisted on maintaining the inhabitants' "entire liberty of conscience," which he later explained to mean "not only that relating to worship, but education, or schools, a coercive ministerial maintenance [i.e., tithes], the militia." After all, as he explained to the board later that year, "The Act of Toleration does not reach all the particulars requisite to secure the liberty of that people in religious matters." Penn later clarified that in addition to "faith, worship, and discipline and by public and private meetings related thereunto," he considered Friends entitled to erect their own schools, marry according to Quaker procedures, and be exempted from militia service and forced payments to any clergy or religious body. Penn continued to assure Friends in America that he would not abandon them and would insist on protections for Quakers in any agreement with the Crown.[28]

Then again, the political situation in Pennsylvania was fluid, to say the least, and by mid-1705 Logan was actually counseling Penn to slow down the negotiations, as he detected a slight improvement in the proprietor's fortunes. That improvement, in Logan's view, was driven by popular unhappiness with the factious behavior of Lloyd and the Assembly and a fall election that produced an Assembly composed of "honest" members committed to providing the province with good government. He also praised Griffith Jones, the newly elected Mayor of Philadelphia, who, despite past tensions, was likely "the best magistrate Philadelphia ever had in my time, of any kind, and fully made good all his promises to thee at thy departure in paying, at least accounting for . . . all his quit-rents, tax, &c., most punctually." (Jones, proprietor of the Blue Anchor tavern in Philadelphia, had earlier been a Keithian supporter, and often allied with David Lloyd in opposition to the proprietor.)[29]

* * *

A Pennsylvania resident who paid his quitrents and taxes "most punctually," even one who had behaved as antagonistically toward Penn in the past as Griffith Jones had, was a rare and treasured commodity. Even three thousand miles away, Penn was never free from the politics of Pennsylvania land distribution, much of which involved overlapping claims and grants erroneously made by Penn himself. More than two decades into the settlement, for example, lands that Penn had promised to eminent Quakers like Benjamin Furly and "my old worthy friend, Thomas Ellwood" continued to require his attention. Some of these disputes originated in promises Penn had made, often verbal or offhand, to individuals or groups. Writing about one such incident, Logan noted that "in one of thy letters thou [told] me that they had agreed to it, which agreement, I suppose, was only verbally," and Logan insisted to Penn that he "get a release under hand and seal" in order for such agreements to be considered binding and legitimate.[30]

In other cases, Penn's increasingly serious financial woes threatened his holdings in Pennsylvania, and he showed only an intermittent realization of this fact. He admitted to Logan that if the Fords' case went against him he would be forced to sell "part of my manors and what else I can" to raise funds. Yet in the same letter, he instructed Logan to "buy some pretty tracts of plantations" for "the provision of my younger children." In August 1706, Logan finally sent Penn the rent roll on which he had been working for so long, but it was not yet complete, and payment of rents would require an aggressive collection effort.[31]

The boundary with Maryland, whose officials continued to harass settlers in the Lower Counties and discourage them from allegiance to Penn, proved no end of worry for Penn. Rumors continued to fly regarding how Penn's surrender negotiations would affect settlers in the Lower Counties, with one rumor claiming that the Lower Counties would be granted to Cornbury. In summer 1705, Thomas Fairman reported that land troubles persisted in the Lower Counties, where "Lord Baltimore's . . . commissioners continue to grant lands in our province." (Fairman was not the most reliable source, however, as he claimed that the colony still held at least 100,000 acres available for the proprietor to sell. Logan harbored grave doubts about Fairman's abilities, later telling Penn that "there's little more than wind in him.") The proprietor continued to voice concern about Baltimore's conduct to the Board of Trade. He claimed that Baltimore had "by little bribes got the new maps altered," but Penn insisted that he possessed copies of "the old maps, at and before my grant," which would vindicate his claims. Penn's suggestion that he should be present when the line between the two colonies was run—"I had rather it be done while I was on the spot"—promised to delay an already long-delayed exercise.[32]

* * *

In Logan's first letter to Penn after his son's arrival, the secretary had observed (perhaps a bit optimistically) that "the only difficulty we now labor under is the separation of the province and territories." He blamed "that unhappy Charter of Privileges," which had sketched out procedures for the separation of the two governments and which "will, most certainly, utterly separate the province and the territories." Logan also reported that Evans was "exceedingly troubled that he understood nothing of this difference between the Upper and Lower Counties before he left England." The initial enthusiasm for the new deputy's arrival, however, convinced Pennsylvania's and the Lower Counties' representatives to continue negotiations about maintaining their union. But by mid-May 1704, Logan was writing to Penn with stark news: "upper and lower counties entirely disunited," which alarmed Penn, who had spent a great deal of effort in asserting his authority in the Lower Counties against the Board's queries. "What will the Queen think after all my memorials to preserve the government without a seam, to find . . . it is torn in two." Penn told Evans that he "lament[ed] the separation of the province and counties; and I affirm I never intended so, but upon condition I lost my government," a creative reading of the fairly plain language of the Charter of Privileges.[33]

While acknowledging the baleful implications of separate legislatures for Penn's interests with the Crown, Logan insisted that any other course of action would have led to a complete and likely irrevocable rupture between the two. The following year Logan told Penn that "we have two assemblies sitting at once." A further blow to Penn's influence in the Lower Counties came with the death of his longtime friend, Council member, and faithful supporter William Clarke, who "sickened, as he thought, of a surfeit of cherries" and died in 1705. (Small consolation, perhaps, that Clarke did not live to see his son's fiancée, Rebecca Curtis, become pregnant with the child of her own brother-in-law to-be.)[34]

* * *

If Penn had thought that his son and Evans might restore political harmony to the colony, such hopes were dashed before the year was out. Notwithstanding the positive reception Evans received—Logan had written appreciatively, early on, that Evans "acquits himself beyond what could possibly be expected from his years: is master of his temper to a great degree"—the Assembly's continuing pressure for real political power continued to vex its proprietor. Logan denounced the Assembly repeatedly, comparing them to the Parliament of 1641, which, as everyone knew, had precipitated a civil war and ultimately beheaded King Charles I.

The slight improvement in harmonious political relations during the 1705 Assembly sessions was quickly scuttled with the next year's returns, which Logan called "the worst that ever I knew in the province."[35]

David Lloyd's rising influence just a few years after Penn had removed him from office at the Board of Trade's insistence was a bitter blow to the proprietor, who blamed Lloyd for almost singlehandedly alienating the people from him. The Assembly wrote to Penn in late May 1704, objecting to the terms of the commission he had granted to Evans, which reserved to Penn final approval of all bills passed by the Pennsylvania government and granted Evans authority to adjourn the Assembly, which it insisted was in violation of the Charter of Privileges.[36] The departure of Roger Mompesson for New York, where he had been appointed chief justice, deprived the colony of a skilled politician and legal mind at just the time that tensions between Assembly and proprietor, to say nothing of Pennsylvania and the Lower Counties, were once again on the rise.

But a tense situation was about to turn positively explosive. Facing sharp tensions with Evans (and ultimately, really, with Penn, who had commissioned him), the Assembly adjourned on August 25, 1704, and assigned a committee to draft a petition to the proprietor. The resulting address, signed "by order of the House" but clearly written by Lloyd, condemned Penn's conduct, accusing him of making promises of "divers large privileges" to encourage settlers to embark with him to Pennsylvania and then, once in America, laying aside the Frame of Government "by subtle contrivance and artifice." Union with the Lower Counties, which Penn considered one of his defining acts as proprietor, was denounced in no uncertain terms, with the Assembly further claiming that "we cannot find that thou had any such grant" to the government of the Lower Counties. They condemned Penn's absenteeism—"thy stay here at first coming was not above two years"—after which Penn left to prosecute the dispute with Baltimore, "and did not return [until] 1699 . . . whilst the interest of this province was sinking." His return found Penn "full of resentment, and many of our applications and addresses . . . answered by recriminations or bitter invectives"; Penn had clearly believed the false insinuations of Quary and their adversaries rather than "thy honest Friends." Upon returning to England again in 1701, Penn had granted a Charter of Property but refused to affix the seal to it, and in direct contradiction to the second article of the Charter of Privileges, granted his Lieutenant Governor the power to prorogue or dissolve the Assembly. The Assembly charged Logan and the province's surveyors with "very great abuses . . . and extortions" and—in a final parting shot—urged Penn to suppress vice in the colony, "which, to our great trouble we have to acquaint thee is more rife and common amongst us, since the arrival of thy deputy and son." The Assembly denounced the rumors of Penn's negotiations with the Crown regarding a surrender of the government, which they told him "we shall deem no less than a betraying us."[37]

Details of the remonstrance's drafting and passage were rather unclear. Logan claimed that Lloyd signed the remonstrance in the Assembly's name without showing it to members, and falsified Assembly minutes to cover up what he had done. Isaac Norris—himself a member of the Assembly—plainly declared that the remonstrance had been drafted by Lloyd based on the Assembly's general directions, but that the Assembly had certainly not approved its content. Nonetheless, its damaging impact on Penn's reputation was not diminished, especially since Lloyd also sent a copy of the remonstrance to eminent London Friends Whitehead, Mead, and Lower. In an accompanying letter, Lloyd excoriated Penn as "remiss in performing his promises and engagements towards us," and pointed to the "revels and disorders which young William Penn and his gang of loose fellows" had let loose on the colony. Lloyd's injection of internal Pennsylvania political disputes into the world of English Quakerism infuriated and embarrassed Penn. How much the English Friends knew about Pennsylvania affairs is not entirely clear, nor how much they knew personally of the individuals who were appealing to them (Jones, for example, was a former Keithian supporter).[38]

Penn urged Logan and Evans to find a way to prosecute Lloyd for falsifying Assembly records, and even harkened back to Lloyd's outbursts against Quary in 1698, which had precipitated his removal from office in 1699: "If [it] can yet be prosecuted, then let it be done with all expedition." For years after the August 1704 remonstrance, Penn displayed a laser-like focus on exacting revenge for the affront. "I expect that Friends and the Assembly will do my justice upon DL," he wrote in January 1705. If prosecution was not possible, Penn instructed Logan to "make that ungrateful hypocrite DL as uneasy as can be. . . . I would have [Evans] snub and discourage him all he can." In September of that year, he wrote to Logan that "I will have that mischievous man, David Lloyd, brought on his knees"; and that same month, to the Lieutenant Governor, "what can be made appear against D.L. fail not to use effectually, for he is the greatest of villains." Three years later, Penn was still fixated on Lloyd's actions, telling Logan to "Get [Evans] and the best of my Friends . . . to bestir themselves and browbeat that villainous fellow DL."[39]

Yet Logan insisted to Penn that many in the colony opposed Lloyd's faction and were not irreparably alienated from the proprietor. He gently chided Penn, noting that many settlers had indeed risked their lives and fortunes in coming to Pennsylvania, and that the proprietor had offered a range of inducements for people to join him in the grand undertaking. Not all their requests were unreasonable, he insisted, and many—ungrateful for his long service though they might seem—were only seeking confirmation of pledges made to them. In this sense, Penn granting their requests ought "not so much to be accounted acts of grace as performances of a covenant." In late July 1706, Logan insisted to Penn that, despite his implacable animosity toward Lloyd, the man was a skilled legislator. "There are many excellent . . . laws, which, it must be owned, are chiefly owing to David Lloyd. Were it not for that man's baseness, and vindictive spirit against thee, he might have been exceedingly useful." He even held out the possibility of bringing Lloyd back into the proprietor's service: given different circumstances, "I doubt he is irreconcilable to thy interest."[40]

* * *

But even more troubles were on the horizon. On July 10, 1705, Penn's Commissioners of Property were summoned to meet with David Lloyd, Isaac Norris, and John Moore "upon a business they had to communicate with us." The business turned out to be a letter that Philip Ford Jr. had sent to those three Friends, laying out details of the Fords' claim against Penn (which would soon become public, but at this point had not yet been divulged). The letter was clear and straightforward, claiming that Philip Ford (Sr.) had purchased Pennsylvania and the Lower Counties from Penn in 1697 and that shortly thereafter he leased them back to Penn, who had "paid . . . rent but very dully." "In the meantime," Ford requested that the Friends would "give notice to the inhabitants not to pay [Penn's] agents any quitrents." In relating this unwelcome news to Penn, Logan added that David Lloyd was obviously "not displeased," whereas Penn's supporters were "extremely grieved." Norris reached out to the Fords, acknowledging the justice of their desire for payment but asking them to pursue their case against Penn in the Friends' way, "with as much temper and respect to him, as well as regard to the quiet of the whole country, as the thing will bear, remembering that thy father was his friend from the beginning." By December 1705, the Fords had provided Lloyd and Moore with power of attorney to represent their interests in Pennsylvania, and were—according to Logan, at least, who noted that Lloyd remained "very insolent"—working in conjunction with Quary to undermine Penn.[41]

The disclosure of the Ford business was the first step in what quickly became an open and poisonous rupture between Penn and Lloyd. Later in July 1705, Lloyd wrote Penn a blistering letter, denouncing his personal and proprietary conduct. Lloyd's missive—essentially a continuation of what he had issued in the Assembly's name the previous year—began by taking aim at one of Penn's favorite talking points, the copious sums he had invested in the province and the way that Pennsylvania had impoverished him. Lloyd begged Penn "not to . . . insinuate as if thou hast not had suitable returns and compensations from the people here for all thy pains, hazards, expenses, and employment of thy interest and the best part of thy life which thou sayst Pennsylvania has cost thee." What, in point of fact, had Penn really done for the colony? Penn's promotional acumen and promises to procure liberties for his settlers "were great motives to induce [settlers] to adventure upon the settlement of this colony and give thee such great rates for land." Despite his claims to advocate for Friends and ensure royal approval of the colony's laws on his most recent return to England, Lloyd continued, "I did not believe that thou couldst be an extraordinary agent for the people in these times, since thou neglected in the reign of King James when it lay in thy power to do them some good." While admitting that most of the people "would rather thou should continue governor in chief and come to live amongst us rather than . . . sell or surrender the government," he also denounced "thy lieutenant and Assembly of the three lower Counties" for forming a militia and punishing those who refused to fight.[42]

Despite Penn's constant complaints about the failure of Pennsylvanians to provide him with revenue, Lloyd insisted that "the people are ready to support thy government though thou has given no true demonstration yet that thou wilt support the constitutions by which they act." The broadside continued with bracing personal attacks: "How canst thou pretend to be a man of peace and truth when thou acts so contrary thereunto[?]" As he moved toward his conclusion, Lloyd claimed—in words that surely would have left Penn laughing, had he been the laughing sort—that what he wrote did not "procee[d] from any malice or revenge for I can sincerely say that I bear thee none," signing off as "thy abused, though real, Friend."[43]

Ironically, perhaps, the circumstances surrounding Lloyd's remonstrance and his increasingly public campaign against Penn sparked a backlash of sorts, a resurgence of support for the proprietor. Lloyd and his supporters made the Ford letter public, seeking, in the words of Griffith Owen, to "dra[w] the people's affections from thee." But Owen, Story, and Logan circulated a letter expressing support for Penn and apparently gathered several hundred signatures. The ensuing October 1705 elections were marked, he told Penn, by "much striving and shouting . . . as was never before here," and Lloyd was only barely elected to the Assembly from the city of Philadelphia. Notwithstanding the controversy and tumult, however, Owen interpreted the results of the election as favorable to the proprietor's interest, and reported that the Assembly was hard at work amending the laws that the Crown had rejected. And in an aside that Penn surely appreciated, Owen denounced "the prejudice and malice" of men like Lloyd, who "have increased their estates considerably in this country." "It seems as if nothing would satisfy them but to have thee out of the government."[44]

* * *

All of this political strife took place against an economic backdrop that continued to worsen Penn's prospects. One of the chief difficulties continued to be the dearth of currency: in mid-February 1706 Logan noted "the incredible scarcity of money," which made the collection of taxes nearly impossible, and a month later he was even more direct: "The country has no money, [and] I know not whether to receive thy dues or not, seeing they can by no means be had in money." The "great decay of trade and poverty of the planters, from whom chiefly we receive our pay, makes my life so uncomfortable, that it is not worth the living: I am ground on all sides. I know it is impossible to satisfy thee thus," yet "the condition of our affairs will not enable me to do better." A succession of poor harvests worsened the situation, and Samuel Carpenter was forced to report in the summer of 1706 that "we have not money, nor corn and other product to answer public debts and supply private necessities . . . our last two crops having failed exceedingly." Many would have liked to pay, and expressed their affection for the proprietor and their willingness to fulfil their obligations, but the fact was that "money [is] scarce, trading dead, and people poor."[45]

The opening of trade with the Spanish West Indies in June 1704, despite the ongoing War of Spanish Succession, promised to improve the situation, but it was only a beginning, and future prospects depended on the further course of the war. Marlborough's victory at Blenheim in August 1704 represented another promising development, and Penn hoped that "this next campaign will make an end of the war." Penn seemed to expect the queen's lifting of the prohibition on trade with Spain to have swift and dramatic effects on Pennsylvania's economy. Despite this prospect, Logan still recommended that Penn proceed with surrender negotiations, since "it's present money thou wants, without any delay." Furthermore, French privateers based on Martinique continued to vex efforts to bolster trade with the Caribbean, and a number of ships were taken. By late 1707 Logan was forced to report to Penn that, though he had recently sent over £500 for the proprietor, "remittances are exceeding difficult." Residents often "generally agree to pay, but can get very little—they are exceedingly poor."[46]

Challenges to the Pennsylvania economy were rooted closer to home, as well, since Maryland continued to levy import taxes on liquor from Pennsylvania, and to ban imports of flour, bread, horses, and tobacco entirely. Penn considered such actions blatantly illegal, and attempted to intervene by writing to Nathaniel Blakiston, the former governor of Maryland now serving as the colony's London agent, and to the Board of Trade. Penn's attempt to operate mills had collapsed, too. No millers would stay with the undertaking since the prospects for profit were so meager, and four had already left by 1707. "I wish she were sold for she is a lasting charge and no profit," Logan wrote bluntly to Penn in June 1707.[47]

* * *

Logan continued in an unenviable position, attempting to represent, to the best of his abilities, Penn's interests in Pennsylvania. It was a lonely task. In September 1706 he wrote to Penn that he had "never experienced so great a depression of spirits as I have this last summer." Logan's responsibilities included not only his many obligations in Pennsylvania but also serving as Penn's representative for New Jersey, where Penn's landholdings were mired in uncertainty. (Many of

Penn's holdings in the Jerseys were the result of his role mediating the Fenwick–
Byllinge dispute, and thus originated in arrangements and understandings
dating back to the 1670s.) After years spent attempting to untangle the complicated and often overlapping—and, occasionally, contradictory—paper trail of
surveys, deeds, conveyances, and titles, Logan wrote Penn a lengthy account of
his Jersey property, the gist of which was that Penn's tenants were increasingly
uneasy about paying rents to someone whose title to the land was uncertain,
and that many inhabitants of the Jerseys (especially Cornbury and his Anglican
allies) were hostile to Friends generally and Penn specifically.[48]

The news of the Ford case and Penn's distance from the scene only made
Logan's job more difficult. As rumors about the case's progress through the
English courts made their way to Pennsylvania, Logan became increasingly
desperate for reliable news about the proceedings. "Thy silence especially in
so arduous a conjuncture gives me very great uneasiness, being altogether in
the dark what measures in any case are proper to take." Logan complained
about Evans, whom he described as living "now very retired," and thus "thy interest as far as it depends on the government, particularly as to fines and taxes,
is very much neglected." Attempts by members of the Assembly to impeach
Logan surely did not improve his mood, either. Logan knew, however, that
he and Evans needed to remain allied if Penn were to have any representation
whatsoever, and acknowledged that "I must not break with the [Lieutenant]
Governor for it might do much more mischief and . . . no good at all." Logan
toyed with the idea of going to England himself, to offer Penn his expertise
about the colony's affairs in his struggles with the Fords. The proprietor, however, wanted him to remain in America, so that he could provide Penn with
reliable information about conditions on the ground and with an ally in the
province to oppose the Lloydians. "Think not of coming," he insisted, "for tis
there I want thee most."[49]

Amid all of the recrimination and bitterness, Penn constantly professed
his desire to return to Pennsylvania. "I am broken and divided," he wrote to
supporters in Pennsylvania late in 1705, lamenting his troubles in both England
and America. If his debts were cleared, he would immediately return. He told
Logan that he was considering a "surprise" return to Pennsylvania, "for when
I come I will endeavour not to be expected," though precisely how he would
have managed such a feat, Penn did not say. He even went so far as to request—
in yet another clear indicator of the yawning disconnect between proprietor and
people—that Pennsylvania Quakers provide him with £10,000 to finance his
return, with him promising to "repa[y] the principal as fast as land can be sold."
In August 1706, Logan assured him point blank that the funds would not be
forthcoming: "There are no buyers of land." By June 1707 Penn had reduced
the desired amount, promising to come to Pennsylvania and live for the rest
of his life "if Friends there will come in, though but for 5000 sterling." It likely

never occurred to him that the prospect of Penn spending the rest of his life in Pennsylvania might not appeal to Pennsylvanians.[50]

* * *

After so many disagreements and so much animosity, the two William Penns, father and son, finally found something they could agree on: it was time to sell Warminghurst Place. William and Gulielma had bought the estate—which included a sizable house and roughly three hundred acres of land—in the spring of 1676, and over the intervening years it had served as the family's primary residence as well as a gathering place for Sussex Friends. (Drafts of Pennsylvania's founding documents were likely composed, at least in part, at Warminghurst.) William Jr. and Mary Penn had been living there since 1699. With Penn's increasing debts, and the shift of his center of gravity toward Bristol and Hannah's family, Warminghurst was a continual strain on Penn's already strained finances. But not even the prospect of selling off the property could hide Penn's bitterness toward his son and daughter-in-law, particularly Mary, whom he wished "had brought more wisdom since she brought so little money to help the family." William Jr. had "cost me more money than [Mary] brought by her unreasonable, and . . . imprudent obstinacy for dwelling [at Warminghurst]," to which, he observed, she had no claim except for "being my son's impetuous inclination."[51]

Although the sale of Warminghurst in November 1707 brought Penn more than £8,000 and represented "a significant step . . . toward the retirement of his burdensome debts," it did not directly help with the dispute with the Fords, since funds from the Warminghurst sale were needed to satisfy other debts. Sir James Butler, who represented Arundel (about ten miles to the southwest of Warminghurst) in Parliament, purchased the estate. Butler soon demolished the house and built a new one on its location, and at least some accounts attribute his actions to a desire to "remove all trace of the old Quaker."[52]

* * *

After years of ultimately unsuccessful behind-the-scenes negotiations, the Fords entered their case against Penn in the Court of Chancery on October 31, 1705. To the personal shame this threw on Penn was added the embarrassment of an intra-Quaker dispute being taken into the law courts. In fact Penn complained to the Fords' Meeting (Devonshire House, in London) about their actions, and by late December 1705 the Devonshire House Monthly Meeting had condemned the Fords for, in Penn's words, "refusing to refer our difference to Friends to be equally chosen between us . . . in a most insolent manner, after monthly repeated meetings [and] advice . . . to induce them."[53]

The Fords' claim was relatively straightforward: Philip Ford had lent Penn a significant amount of money over the course of their long partnership. "Mr. Penn did, about twenty-three years since, upon his first entrance upon [Pennsylvania and the

Lower Counties] prevail with the said Philip Ford to lend him 3000 pounds ... upon a mortgage of some part of the said premises." In subsequent years Ford provided "further helps and credits with other great sums of money," totaling roughly £6,900, and in 1690 Penn agreed to convey Pennsylvania to Ford when he was unable to repay what he owed. After 1697, Ford had agreed to allow Penn to rent Pennsylvania at an annual rent of £630, yet Penn had not made regular payments.[54]

But Penn was an experienced adversary. After securing a much-needed delay in order to examine his records and prepare his response, Penn and his lawyers filed a counter-complaint of their own against the Ford family and their trustees in late February 1706. In his cross-complaint, Penn presented himself as the wronged party. He had, he alleged, employed Ford since 1669, paying him a regular salary with which Ford "seemed very well contented and satisfied." He had trusted Ford's integrity, "entirely relying upon his good name and honesty [and] committed the whole of his affairs to him." Penn admitted to carelessness and to structuring the language of his agreements with Ford to help his longtime agent evade the tax payments that would have accrued on an interest-bearing loan, but accused the Fords of questionable accounting practices, refusing to correct errors in the sums owed, excessive interest charges, trickery, and extortion. For example, he claimed that in August 1682 the Fords, knowing he was busily organizing a major voyage to America, "took that opportunity of imposing upon and of ... surprising [him]," who, "crediting the integrity of ... Philip Ford and being then in a great hurry and confusion," signed the account "without perusal or having any copy thereof."[55]

In addition to multiple objections to specific sums—Penn placed his indebtedness at roughly £4,500 rather than the £14,000 claimed by the Fords—he also cited his longstanding relationship with his agent in his defense. He claimed that the Fords "did consult and contrive how they might ... defraud him," and insisted that he had trusted both Fords and their promise to rectify any errors that would subsequently come to light. Penn also attempted to delay and draw out the proceedings, requesting that Bridget Ford be compelled to provide "the books, papers, accounts, memorandums, bills of parcel, invoices, receipts, and papers" relevant to the case for him "to peruse and examine." Since part of the Fords' claim involved sums related to the Free Society of Traders, Penn wrote to Pennsylvania, requesting that Edward Shippen

> send over the bond ... that Philip Ford gave the old Society of Free Traders ... also, get ... the governing party of the old Pennsylvania Company or Society, to meet together and ... to ask for, demand, procure, and obtain of and from Bridget Ford ... all such books of accounts, writings, and sums of money as are in her custody, belonging to the said Society.

Not surprisingly, Bridget Ford replied to Penn's complaint, in early June 1706, and simply reiterated that Penn had signed various papers agreeing to pay the Fords rent to retain possession of Pennsylvania. (While excoriating Ford in terms that likely resonated with Penn's sense of outrage, Logan also noted Penn's "too great confidence in another's honesty.") And so the case proceeded.[56]

* * *

As he entered his seventh decade, William Penn was the father of a growing family. He and Hannah had welcomed three children between 1704 and 1707: Margaret, named for Penn's mother and sister, in November 1704; Richard, who "fills up my brother Richard Penn's vacancy," in January 1706; and, just over a year later, Dennis (for Hannah's grandfather), in February 1707. Despite having noted the beginnings of gout late in 1703, Penn did not suffer any major health incidents during these years, though he did mention what was likely a stroke, in early 1705, describing it as an "indisposition" that "left my head uncapable of allowing me to write." Elsewhere he called it a "stroke of illness that . . . much affected my head" and that had produced "weakness of my head and eyes" and "a troublesome swimming in my head." But he and his family, by and large, avoided extended illnesses during these years.[57]

In the fall of 1705, with the Fords' claim having been filed, Penn drafted another will. He acknowledged that "it is my unhappiness and sorrow to be indebted," but justified himself by attributing his financial woes not to extravagance or profligacy, but rather to "liberality to the needy, supporting Pennsylvania [in England and America] without grateful and sufficient supplies," helping Friends, and—perhaps most bitterly, in a pointed rebuke to the Fords—"the extortious treatment I have had by some I entirely trusted." No doubt thinking of William Jr.'s perception of his father's favoritism toward his younger children, he charged "all my children to live with fear towards God and love towards one another," and offered young William two-thirds of his Pennsylvania estates, and the proprietorship, if he would grant the Penn estates in County Cork to his younger siblings. If he would not do so, then the will provided for the younger children to receive two-thirds of Pennsylvania rents and lands, with young John receiving a double share and William Jr. receiving just one-third. A codicil to this will, dated August 6, 1707, provided for Letitia, attempting to ensure her an equal share and also providing that she receive a piece of gold jewelry that Penn's mother had given to Gulielma; and directed an almshouse to be built near Bristol for poor ship captains in memory of Penn's father, the admiral.[58]

Although his time and energy were increasingly taken up by his defenses against the Fords and by his growing clan, Penn remained an active Quaker and one of the most visible Friends in England. He attempted to secure the release of Samuel Bownas, a traveling Public Friend who had been imprisoned by Lord Cornbury in New York in the fall of 1702. In mid-1704, under the

impression that Bownas was still imprisoned (he had in fact been released in
the previous September, though he did not return to England until 1706),
Penn secured a letter to Cornbury from his father, the Earl of Clarendon,
hoping to obtain Bownas's release.[59]

Penn also maintained a cordial correspondence with the Dickinson brothers,
Jonathan and Caleb, prosperous (and slaveholding) Friends from Jamaica who
had visited Philadelphia in the late 1690s after surviving a harrowing shipwreck
and an arduous journey from Florida to Philadelphia. (Jonathan would return to settle in Philadelphia and serve two terms as mayor.) Penn and a group
of investors had secured a patent for exploring for shipwrecks in the waters
surrounding Jamaica, and although Penn had offered to contribute £300 toward
an expedition, nothing ever came of the idea. Penn continued to maintain a
warm personal relationship with the Dickinsons, reporting from the 1706 Yearly
Meeting that Friends had remembered them in their prayers, and passing on his
greetings from Hannah, who "desires her Philadelphian love to you and kind
and honest Mary." In June 1707 he had the unfortunate task of informing the
brothers of the death of their uncle. "Your old uncle Dickinson," he wrote, "has
at last gone to his long home 84 and rich."[60]

His old friend, the Dutch Quaker Benjamin Furly, wrote asking him for his
"recipe against the dropsy" (edema). It involved mixing Rhenish wine and cream
of tartar, though Furly did not recall the amounts or proportions. He also used
the occasion of this medical inquiry to ask Penn about the five thousand acres
he had obtained for Burgomaster Adrian Vroesen, of Rotterdam. Penn was able
to provide better service with the medicine than with the land, which apparently
had not yet been laid out. Furly reported that the patient "has found great relief,
inso much that . . . I found her dropsy half abated, and she came down the stairs,
which I was very glad to see." Whether or not Penn's recipe came from a family
source is not known, but the wine/tartar combination was a widely circulated
treatment for dropsy.[61]

***

By 1706, with the Ford case weighing on his mind, Penn was clearly wearying of
Logan's waffling. "Thou hast shifted thy judgment about selling the government,
one time with all speed, and another time keep it; one time sell all . . . another
time government only." Despite his confidence in Logan's ability and the quality
of his service, Penn confessed that Logan's various recommendations made him
"stagger under diversity of directions." He intended to keep his government, "if
it be practicable," but clearly much depended on how the Ford case turned out.
Still, Logan sometimes vacillated in his advice to Penn about the surrender. "A
surrender is the only thing that can make thee easy," he wrote in April 1707,
while just a month later he opined that the recently completed union of Great

Britain and Scotland could double land values in America and that "I should be very cautious at this time of selling."[62]

Penn's criticisms were not always fair to his secretary. Logan had consistently advocated Penn surrendering to the government if he could secure good terms. Logan knew as well as anyone that Penn's debts were just too great, and prospects for their repayment from his Pennsylvania revenue too dubious. After discussing the matter with Samuel Carpenter, whose judgment Logan considered among "the best of any man's in the province," Penn's secretary offered his private conviction that "if thou canst get anything for it from the Crown, and good terms for the people with it, 'tis the only thing advisable at this juncture, for this Province cannot now raise anything, they have it not." A month later Logan again recommended surrender, this time suggesting a direct appeal to the Queen:

> Procure a fair audience of the Queen herself, to throw thyself on her favour, telling her thy whole circumstances ... and so make her a tender of the government, in case she will grant thee for a consideration sufficient to clear thee of the incumbrances only, what thy making this colony and thereby enlarging her dominions, has cost thee.

If this appeal was successful, Logan went on, Penn should then "come as speedily as possible to a positive agreement." After a tumultuous meeting of the Assemblies (for Pennsylvania and the Lower Counties) in fall 1706, Logan once again advised Penn to "proceed vigorously in the surrender, treating, if possible, at once with the Queen and the Lord Treasurer, thy friend, and let the formalities after be managed by the Lords Commissioners."[63]

And so, after pursuing the negotiations for surrender in fits and starts for the better part of four years, and with the Ford case hanging over his head, Penn revived the matter once again with an inquiry to the Board of Trade in January 1707. Despite his past difficulties with the Board, it proved receptive to Penn's proposal and offered praise of his stewardship of the colony. In its recommendation to Lord Sunderland, the board pointed to the

> great expense, many risks and dangers, both to his person and fortune, with continued pains and industry [accomplishing] a very difficult undertaking, by cultivating and improving what before was a desolate wilderness, into a well peopled colony, which ... does yearly add a considerable revenue to her majesty.

It further noted that Penn's "public work ... has much impaired and diminished his own private fortune," although it proposed that any surrender should include

both Pennsylvania and the Lower Counties, and should be "absolute and unconditional." Still, there was no word about the amount to be paid in the transaction. Penn asked Isaac Norris for details of Pennsylvania's economic production,
revenues, and chief exports so that he could present a defensible account of the
current state of affairs. By July, Penn's asking price had dropped from £30,000 to
£20,000.[64]

The Board of Trade gave its conditional approval to the surrender in February
1707, but many details remained to be settled, and the Ford litigation promised
to complicate any proposed settlement.[65]

While Penn negotiated with the Crown and attempted to stave off the
Fords' charges, the rupture between Pennsylvania and the Lower Counties
had become virtually complete. Earlier, Penn had used a reference to the
judgment of Solomon to describe the separation of the two territories: "This
cutting the child in two may one day fall heavy on the authors of it." Two separate Assemblies met in November 1706, one in Philadelphia and the other
in New Castle, with the latter approving construction of a fort to raise funds
for colonial defense by demanding payment from all ships heading north up
the Delaware River toward Philadelphia. Such a step was sure to increase the
tensions between the two territories, since neither the Crown nor the proprietor had given permission for such a scheme. Logan feared the prospect
of "a perfect war between Philadelphia and New Castle." Sure enough, it was
not long before Philadelphia merchants began raising vocal and sustained opposition to the New Castle fort. In spring 1707, ship captain Richard Hill
refused to pay the tax and was fired upon, at which point he took the fort's
commander prisoner and proceeded to Salem, New Jersey, depositing the
commander with Cornbury, who reprimanded both the commander and
Evans. More than two hundred Philadelphians, many of them merchants,
signed a remonstrance against the act that had required the payments and
funded the fort's construction.[66]

Penn's eagerness to sell his government back to the Crown had much to do
with his increasingly despondent assessment of the political environment in
the colony and the colonists' increasingly implacable hostility to his interests.
Late in 1706, for example, Logan had informed Penn that the members of the
Pennsylvania Assembly "are bent upon putting a stop to the surrender." Among
the leaders of this effort were Lloyd, "thy inveterate revengeful enemy," Griffith
Jones, whom he now described as "out of unity [with Friends] and . . . of a
scandalous character," and Joseph Wilcox, "the chief of the Keithians." The
1706 Assembly sessions featured a great deal of contention between the
Assembly and Evans, and hostility toward Logan as well. Logan described
the Pennsylvania Assembly's opposition to the proprietor as nearly total; the
New Castle gathering, by contrast, he called "not at all well affected to thee or

thy administration. Yet they are men of honour when compared to those vile vipers [the Pennsylvania Assembly] who . . . would wound thee equally deep in thy temporal and religious character." Before it adjourned, the Philadelphia Assembly drafted an address to Penn and sent it—again—to English Friends, calling for the dismissal of both Evans and Logan. Penn declined to replace his lieutenant and secretary, but he did reprimand Evans for his laxity in punishing vice, for spreading the false alarm about the French attack, and for acquiescing in the Lower Counties militia bill. The Assembly adopted another address in June 1707, again sending a copy to Whitehead, Mead, and Lower, complaining of "arbitrary practices," which had "become an intolerable burden and oppression to the inhabitants of this province." Subsequent Assembly sessions included an acrimonious dispute between Evans and Lloyd in early 1707—the speaker refused to rise when addressing the governor, which Evans took as rank insubordination—and multiple attempts to impeach Logan, spurred on by David Lloyd.[67]

* * *

Penn continued to try to staff his colonial administration with supporters and to neutralize the Admiralty Courts and royal officials. Roger Mompesson, who, as one of Penn's attorneys in England, had argued in favor of jury trials in colonial Admiralty proceedings, had himself been appointed Judge of the Admiralty Courts for New England, New York, New Jersey, and Pennsylvania in 1703. In March of that year Penn described him as also willing to take up the position of Pennsylvania Attorney General, and to "rectify matters in law, and to put you into better methods." In October 1704, Cornbury appointed him Chief Justice of the New York Supreme Court, and over the next few years Mompesson added the same position in New Jersey as well as a seat on the Council in both places (while surrendering some of his admiralty jurisdictions). In April 1706 Mompesson assumed the position of Chief Justice of Pennsylvania, but the Assembly proved reluctant to provide him a salary, and it is not clear whether he actually took up the position.[68]

Colonel Quary continued to vex Penn as he had in years past. Although Evans and Quary had gotten along smoothly during Evans's early days in the colony—with the Colonel even inviting the young governor to dinner at his house—Penn continued to view Quary with unremitting hostility, and Quary continued to exert an enormous influence over Pennsylvania and the Lower Counties. Evans mistrusted Quary as well, particularly after Quary summarily installed his ally John Moore as collector for the port of Philadelphia without consulting the governor.[69]

But surprisingly, Quary and Penn would have something of a rapprochement after 1706. Logan was initially skeptical of Penn's newfound generosity toward

Quary. "Can the leopard change his skin?" Logan asked incredulously. "I cannot understand the policy of admitting a professed enemy within our walls because he changes his face." But the thaw in relations between Penn and Quary continued, and the colonel returned to Pennsylvania, Penn reported, "highly disposed to favor our affairs" and "promis[ing] great moderation." Quary rebuffed requests by Lloyd and the Assembly for assistance with their address complaining against Penn, Evans, and Logan, and early in 1707 Logan wrote Penn that "I frequently visit and dine with him."[70]

Quary eventually settled in Pennsylvania and expressed interest in leasing Pennsbury, which no doubt appealed to Penn for a number of reasons, not least his longstanding concern about reports of Pennsbury's "declining condition, notwithstanding the money I laid out, when there." Penn had consistently made clear to Logan his unhappiness about the charge of keeping up his estate. "Let me not be put to more charge there," he told Logan, "but only to keep it in re-pair. "I have spent too much there already," he wrote to John and Mary Sotcher, his chief servants at Pennsbury, and voiced his willingness to lease the estate "to one that would not misuse it." As Penn's relationship with Quary grew in-creasingly amiable, he instructed Logan to "let him have Pennsbury upon pretty good terms, and for what time he will." Logan and Quary agreed to an annual rent of £40, but rumors about the Ford verdicts stalled the final execution of the agreement.[71]

* * *

While Penn had many things to be worried about, the Ford case was the most potentially damaging to his financial, social, and legal well-being. Even after a preliminary ruling that seemed to go in the Fords' favor, the case was far from over. Penn withdrew his original complaint and filed a second one on December 23, 1706, arguing many of the same points. His editors explain that "By putting in a new bill [of complaint], Penn was apparently hoping that he could out-last the Fords' willingness to accumulate high legal costs." Unfortunately for Penn, the Fords answered Penn's second complaint in relatively short order, to which Penn, again, replied, three weeks later, before Sir William Cowper, who had recently been elevated from Lord Keeper of the Great Seal to Lord High Chancellor of Great Britain, the union with Scotland having taken effect that month. Having little success before Cowper, Penn and his lawyers spent much of the summer of 1707 preparing to appeal their case to the House of Lords, where, Penn told Logan, "I have great hopes to have the accounts reduced to at least a [half]."[72]

Yet the case would never make it to the House of Lords, because the Fords took another legal tack and in late June 1707 filed a civil suit for nonpayment of rent against Penn in the Court of Common Pleas. They claimed that Penn owed £3,150 in back rent (five years at £630 per year), and also asked for £100 in damages. The jury decided against Penn, and recommended a slightly lower award (just over £2,900), which the judge approved in late November 1707. Isaac Norris, then in England, reported that Penn was already considering refusing to pay and entering debtor's prison instead, that "it has been his friends' as well as his own opinion that he ought to do it rather than pay the money . . . and thereby bear his testimony as honourably against the extortion and fraud of that account . . . and bear it as a persecution."[73] Ultimately he decided not to pay, and it was for this amount—just under £3,000—that Penn was confined in the Fleet, London's prison for debtors, on January 7, 1708.

15

"Prison" and After

"Governor Penn was last fourth-day arrested at Gracechurch Street Meeting, by order of Philip Ford, on an execution on the special verdict for about 3,000 [pounds] rent. He has, by the advice of all his best friends, turned himself over to the Fleet." So wrote Isaac Norris to Richard Hill, a Philadelphia Friend and ship captain, on January 10, 1708, just a few days after Penn had been apprehended outside one of the main Quaker Meetinghouses in London.[1]

It would be a bit misleading, however, to speak of Penn as "confined to" debtors' prison. In fact, although the prison itself stood just north of London's Fleet Bridge and Ludgate Hill, Penn had been granted the option of lodging at the nearby Old Bailey (on the next street, about a block to the east). He had some liberty of movement, though he was not averse to using his confinement as a reason to avoid unpleasant tasks, like a summons from the Board of Trade to discuss the seemingly interminable issue of the Maryland boundary line. He entertained visitors, held Meetings with Friends, and even replaced his Lieutenant Governor—all from his lodgings at the Fleet. In other words, as Norris put it, Penn lived "comfortably enough for the circumstance." Then again, a number of important decisions were put on hold during his nine-month confinement, including examination of Pennsylvania's laws before Crown officials, further discussions of the Maryland boundary, and the surrender of his government to the Crown. His negotiating position was, to say the least, rather weaker than it had been earlier.[2]

* * *

Having won a jury's judgment against Penn and secured his confinement at the Fleet, the Fords appealed to the Queen for a judgment granting them possession of Pennsylvania. As they (correctly) argued, so long as Penn remained in debtors' prison, and so long as their chancery case languished, they had little prospect of receiving either the money Penn owed them or control of Pennsylvania. And as long as Penn remained proprietor and could appoint colonial officers, it would be difficult for them to collect any revenues. But Penn had, at that point, only been convicted of failure to pay back rent. The question of the proprietorship was a separate matter; that case was still pending. The Fords had jumped the gun and made a tactical error. William Cowper, the Lord Chancellor, dismissed their petition, according to Penn, as "improper and unreasonable." A week later, Cowper officially reported to the Queen that "since [the possession of Pennsylvania] being a question yet depending and undecided in the Court of Chancery . . . it would be inconvenient to your Majesty's subjects in those parts that the possession should be so often shifted." In other words, the Fords had approached the Crown "too soon."[3]

Despite this somewhat Pyrrhic victory, Penn's legal situation remained dire, and his ongoing confinement reflected poorly on him and on Friends more generally. And so he entered into negotiations with the Fords, mediated by leading Friends eager for the dispute to be resolved quickly and quietly. Members of the Meeting for Sufferings in London facilitated these negotiations, which also involved Penn's father-in-law, Thomas Callowhill. Penn continued to attempt, whenever possible, to undermine the Fords' accounting of what he owed—the Fords, recall, had originally claimed that Penn owed them nearly £14,000—identifying specific examples of "exorbitant interest and considerations." By late summer, negotiations were nearing completion, and the Fords had agreed to accept a payment of £7,600 to satisfy all their claims. The agreement was concluded in late September, and Penn was restored to his liberty. Then again, of the £7,600 he paid the Fords, all but £1,000 of it was borrowed from a group of over three dozen Friends who, as Penn put it rather delicately, "help me in this affair." Nine of those Friends became trustees of Pennsylvania, providing Penn with a friendlier set of creditors but not a fundamentally improved financial picture. He still faced the loss of Pennsylvania if he could not come up with £6,600 in two years, a prospect, given Penn's past performance, just this side of impossible.[4]

* * *

One obligation that Penn was likely only too happy to evade during his time at the Fleet was a summons to appear before the Board of Trade. More than twenty years after his victory over Baltimore, the matter of the border with Maryland continued to plague him. In late March, Penn excused himself as "under restraint" and unable to discuss the dispute. He insisted that he had tried to settle the dispute during his most recent stay in America, but to no avail. "In 1700, I went to Maryland . . . to settle the matter, in pursuance of the order of the Board . . . believing the Lord Baltimore had sent his agents to join with me in finishing it; but Colonel Darnell [Lord Baltimore's agent] assured me he had no such direction from his Lord, and refused to enter upon it." As it turned out, neither Penn nor Baltimore made themselves available to the Board as requested, and several face-to-face meetings with each other during the fall produced no resolution. Penn did, in early 1709, submit a detailed narrative to the Board, outlining the history of the Lower Counties from their discovery by Henry Hudson in 1609 to King Charles II's grant of the territory to James, Duke of York, in the 1670s. Baltimore continued to press the issue, attempting to have the 1685 decision set aside and the case reopened. Penn, of course, argued for the integrity of the original order, and enlisted the aid of allies like Lord Somers, president of the Privy Council. Ultimately, Baltimore was rebuffed, not once but twice: in January 1709, and again in June, after he had filed a second appeal. The Queen's Order in Council of June 23, 1709, instructed that "the Lord Baltimore's petition be dismissed this Board; and . . . the . . . Order of Council of the 13th of November 1685, be ratified and confirmed in all its points, and be put in execution without any further delay." Penn even arranged for the public reprinting of the decision in a broadside entitled *The case of William Penn . . . against the Lord Baltimore's pretensions*. Still, the dispute would linger another sixty years, until King George III approved the Mason–Dixon line.[5]

* * *

Though Penn had plenty to worry about in England, he continued to monitor developments in Pennsylvania as best he could. His dissatisfaction with the administration of Lieutenant Governor John Evans had been on the rise for some time. Tensions were exacerbated when Whitehead, Lower, and Mead paid a visit to the Fleet. These three leading Friends had received several letters from David Lloyd and the Pennsylvania Assembly laying out their grievances against Penn, Evans, and Logan. Although he succeeded in exposing Lloyd's hyperbole about conditions in Pennsylvania, and in vindicating Logan's conduct against the Assembly's impeachment charges, Penn did decide to replace Evans with a new Lieutenant Governor.

The decision was rooted in a number of factors. There were, of course, political grievances, including Evans's role in spreading the false alarm alleging a French invasion in 1706, the ongoing uncertainty in the colony's court system, and the discord that had been sown by "the New Castle law to pay toll going from and coming to Philadelphia." All these episodes offered Penn evidence of Evans's increasing inability or unwillingness to rule with a firm hand in the proprietor's interest and to maintain social harmony. But there were other, more troubling developments of a more personal nature, which Penn's austere sense of virtue could not abide. Evans had gotten a young Quaker woman, Susannah Harwood, pregnant, and then ordered her mother, who had been imprisoned for debt, released, turning a blind eye when she escaped the colony. He undertook "a lewd voyage to Susquehanna," where he engaged in unspecified, but clearly shocking, "vilest . . . practices with the wives and daughters of the [native] people at Conestoga." To all these other offenses, "last, if not worst of all, his pardon of the blackest crime [sodomy] in Griffith Jones's . . . son"—an apparent bribe to overlook offenses committed by the son of a powerful Philadelphian—seems to have been the last straw. Simply put, Penn wrote to Logan, "my soul mourns under these things."[6]

Penn quickly settled on forty-six-year-old Charles Gookin as Evans's replacement. An Anglican, like Evans, who hailed from a family with a long history of involvement in English colonization, Gookin came with "a recommending character from persons of great rank" and "assures me," Penn wrote to Logan, that "he intends to . . . end his days" in Pennsylvania (a resolution Gookin would quickly reconsider). Perhaps most importantly, Penn claimed, Gookin would comport himself "by sobriety and thriftiness rather than luxury or rapaciousness." Queen Anne offered her approval of Gookin in mid-July, after Penn once again pledged the required £2,000 security for his lieutenant's observance of the Acts of Trade, and (grudgingly) repeated the declaration acknowledging the queen's claim to the Lower Counties.[7]

Gookin prepared to set out for Pennsylvania while the proprietor paved the way for his arrival by describing him to Friends there as "I hope sober and friendly to us, and . . . just to all and merciful to such as deserve it." To the Council, Penn referred to Gookin as "of years and experience, of a quiet and easy temper, that will give offense to none." The contrast between Evans, who received Penn's appointment while in his mid-twenties, and the forty-six-year-old Gookin could hardly have been more striking. "He is sober," Penn continued, "understands to command and obey; moderate in his temper, and of what they call a good family. . . . He is not voluptuous, so he will be an example of thriftiness."[8]

He may not have been voluptuous, luxurious, or rapacious, but Gookin certainly was ambitious. Logan reported that, not long after his arrival, Gookin was "apprehensive that he has changed for the worse"; in other words, that giving up his military commission for the lieutenant governorship of Penn's colony may have dealt a blow to his prospects for advancement. Gookin also realized, as he traveled through Virginia and Maryland on his way to assume his new post, that he was being paid much less than the governors of those colonies, and expressed concern that "his whole allowance will scarce be a subsistence." Logan told Penn that Gookin "believes himself a loser" in having accepted Penn's offer of the lieutenant governorship.[9]

Not surprisingly, Evans was displeased at being set aside, although Logan suggested that his main worry, at least initially, was how the loss of his office would affect his wooing of John Moore's daughter. (He needn't have worried; the two were married in April 1709.) The disputes over money that had divided Logan and Evans continued, with Evans claiming that he was due £400, Penn agreeing only to £300, and Logan caught firmly in the middle. The Assembly for the Lower Counties seems to have dangled its governorship before Evans in an attempt to enlist his support for their efforts at separation from Pennsylvania. Despite his unhappiness with Penn, Evans declined, remaining in Pennsylvania as part of a scheme to develop mines but sidestepping political controversy after his exit from office.[10]

Evans was not the only Lieutenant Governor to demand Logan's attention. Even from beyond the grave, Markham continued to bedevil Logan and Penn. The late Lieutenant Governor's estate, which presented itself in a disorganized and nearly incoherent set of papers, continued to tax even Logan's considerable acumen in legal matters, to say nothing of basic accounting. Markham's widow Joanna claimed that Penn owed her money for her late husband's services collecting his quitrents, money that Penn steadfastly refused to pay. She and her daughter further claimed that Penn had granted Markham five thousand acres, but they lacked any deed, title, or other documents confirming this promise.[11]

* * *

Despite his bitterness at Lloyd and the Assembly, and his constant insistence that his impoverishment stemmed largely from Pennsylvanians' unwillingness to pay him what they owed, Penn continued to profess a strong desire to return to America and spend the rest of his days there. While still confined at the Fleet he envisioned having his debts paid, then "visit[ing] Friends . . . in each county," seeing family in Bristol, inspecting his properties in Ireland, and then settling in Pennsylvania once and for all. "I hope next spring if not next fall to set forth," he wrote. Most importantly, perhaps, Penn insisted to Pennsylvania Friends that he would "come honorably to you" with debts cleared, and suggested that they might assist in that endeavor: "If honest Friends [in Pennsylvania] will help to discharge some of this debt . . . I shall take it kindly." In mid-September 1708, as the final touches were being put on the agreement with the Fords, Penn wrote to Samuel and Hannah Carpenter, his old and dear Friends in Philadelphia, that he hoped "with my wife and children [to] be with you" by the end of 1709. He also voiced this desire to the Provincial Council: "I long to be with you, and if the Lord bring me and mine there, I hope not to return, on almost any terms." Even as 1709 arrived and he remained in England, Penn wrote to Logan that "I do assure thee that if the country would settle upon me 600 pounds [per year] . . . I would hasten over this following summer." Anticipating this proposed journey, he instructed Logan to prepare a place "for me and my family by the first day of next [June 1710] if the Lord permit, or sooner," and to be sure that "Pennsbury [is] in inhabitable order, with the gardens, that we may subsist in good measure upon it." He had earlier referred to Pennsbury in correspondence with John and Mary Sotcher as "beloved of us all," adding that "I like [Pennsbury] for a place better than any I have ever lived at."[12]

His persistent hope that Pennsylvanians would contribute toward the relief of his debts illustrated once again Penn's lack of knowledge, or rather his re-fusal to acknowledge, that he was viewed by many in Pennsylvania as a distant and demanding figure whose presence was not particularly desired. The prospect that they would open their purses to finance his return was highly unlikely. Then again, Penn was not the only Friend who harbored unrealistic expectations about what was possible in America: Whitehead, Lower, and Mead exhorted Pennsylvania Friends to comport themselves in a manner worthy of Quakers and resolve their differences, leading Samuel Carpenter to state flat out that "There can be no such thing as they have supposed, that we can prevail with the Assembly or others in a Friendly way."[13]

Whenever Penn's thoughts turned to Pennsylvania, they quickly moved on to the possibility of evening the score with David Lloyd. He continued to demand his prosecution for the 1704 remonstrance, complaining about "quack lawyers" and Lloyd's "numbskulls," and pointing to the correspondence between Lloyd and the Fords as evidence of "conspiracy against me." Norris implied that Lloyd had spread rumors that the agreement with the Fords had fallen through, which further unsettled colonial affairs and made successful collection of rents increasingly improbable. But Logan, who had a far better sense of political realities in the colony, pointedly remarked that, like it or not, Lloyd commanded a very strong political faction in the Assembly and could not simply be prosecuted for past offenses without bringing on "the greatest convulsions." In March 1709 he told Penn that "David Lloyd's party is, for number . . . much the strongest, and therefore will always be able to oppose thee in Assemblies, till other methods are taken." Although he agreed with Penn that Lloyd "ought by all means to be prosecuted . . . for that remonstrance sent in 1704," Logan insisted that without "the original papers under his hand" a conviction was likely impossible. Instead, Logan recommended that Penn write a letter to Friends laying out Lloyd's actions and the way in which he had made "his private revenge with a pretense of asserting only the people's right."[14]

* * *

But it was not only Pennsylvania Friends who vexed Penn as he emerged from the Fleet and prepared to return to public life. The year 1709 saw the colony's Anglicans petition the Crown yet again, over a host of familiar and long-running grievances: the lack of a militia, the ban on oaths, and the procedures for electing Assembly and Council members. The petition accused the government of illegally altering the Supreme Court and of leaving the Lower Counties without a functioning government. And as a final parting shot, it denounced Quakers as a group "who in their principles, doctrine, and public preaching do most blasphemously deny our blessed Lord and Savior Jesus Christ. How then can we expect honesty and justice from such men?"[15]

Even some Friends were becoming concerned about the conflict between Quakerism and politics. The ongoing war (both in Europe, and with French and

Indian forces in North America) and the persistent worry about the militia issue—
the tension, if not the downright incompatibility, between embracing Friends' principles and occupying positions of authority in the colonial government—weighed
on many of them. The continuing presence of French warships and privateers off
their coasts and in the Delaware Bay during the summer of 1708, Logan confessed,
"has brought Friends to a pretty general confession that a due administration of
government (especially in a time of war) under an English constitution, is irreconcilable with our principles." In public, though, Logan attempted to combat Anglican
disaffection. With regard to the assertion that the Lower Counties were exposed to
dangers and left without a militia, Logan wrote, "All these counties are in as good
a posture of defence as any of the neighboring Colonies immediately under the
Queen's Government, there being scarce a man [except Quakers] but . . . serves as
regularly as any militia whatever, and are now generally well furnished with arms,
drums, and colours, by an Act of Assembly of their own making."

Severely complicating Penn's position was a raid by French forces on Lewes, in
Sussex County, in the spring of 1709. The episode—in which eighty men from a
captured English warship plundered the town, took four hostages and ransomed
them for produce and livestock, and killed a ship captain—shook the inhabitants
of both Pennsylvania and the Lower Counties. Not only did it cause a great fear
of potential invasion in Philadelphia, which sat just over a hundred miles up the
Delaware River, but it inflamed already existing tensions between Friends and non-
Friends. Logan reported on the nature of the disputes in a May letter to Penn:

> Those who differ from us in persuasion . . . are full of
> complaints. . . . [T]heir arguments to shew the absurdity of pretending
> to government, without applying force . . . where necessary to defend
> the subject, in their lives and property, cannot possibly be answered to
> their satisfaction. That a private murderer or robber should be taken
> and hanged, and yet public ones should be suffered to proceed without
> any resistance, is made the subject of so much banter and scorn, that
> 'tis very uneasy to those concerned . . . to tell them that they are free
> to fight themselves if they please. . . . [T]hey plead the unreasonable-
> ness of their being, both at all hazard and expense, in defending what
> others are at least as deeply concerned in. They want . . . a law for a
> militia, which shall oblige all to serve that can, and those that cannot
> to contribute a due proportion of the expense. . . . for my own part,
> I cannot but freely join in sentiments with those of the best thought
> here, among thy friends, that it would be much better for us to be en-
> tirely eased from the burthen, upon any reasonable terms.

Between Baltimore's renewed assault on the Lower Counties and the raid on
Lewes, Logan feared the worst for Pennsylvania Friends.[16]

In March 1709 the queen demanded militia support for an invasion of
Canada. Gookin estimated the cost of providing those soldiers at approximately £4,000. The Pennsylvania Assembly voted just £500 "to be employed as
she shall think fit," and even delayed payment of that sum. Logan reported that
Pennsylvania and New Jersey were the only two colonies not to have complied
with the queen's orders, and he feared the ramifications. As had happened before, an Anglican Lieutenant Governor of Pennsylvania found himself wedged
between fears of French and Indian attacks, royal demands to provide for the
colony's defense, and an Assembly dominated by Friends who refused to provide support for fulfilling those demands (and a distant and demanding proprietor to boot). Thus the Assembly's relationship with Gookin came to resemble
its earlier rocky relationship with Evans and, at times, Markham. "Our governor
meets with great discouragements from the Assembly," Norris wrote to Penn in
December 1709, describing them as "wits and critics upon everything that is said
and done" and confiding that "I see no room to expect much effectual business."
As the militia debate continued in Pennsylvania and the Lower Counties, and as
peace negotiations at The Hague foundered, Penn sought another way to ensure
the safety of his colony and to salvage trade to and from America. He appealed
to Lord Sunderland, the son of his old friend, for additional warships to protect New York and Pennsylvania, which he called "the granaries of the English
dominions in America." But he had little hope of convincing an already skeptical
Crown to defend a colony that had, so far, refused to defend itself.[17]

* * *

Resolving the status of the Lower Counties—which had bedeviled him for
nearly three decades now—was essential to the continued viability of Penn's
colony, and Logan understood that the Lower Counties lay at the heart of a legal,
political, and cultural minefield that threatened to destroy Penn's government.
If Penn really did wish "to spend the remaining part of thy life here, it will be
absolutely necessary . . . to get all matters relative to the Lower Counties fully
settled." Hopes for a reunification of the Lower Counties with Pennsylvania,
Logan insisted, were simply not realistic, and the best that Penn could hope
for was amiable relations between the two. Logan knew that such an outcome
deeply grieved the proprietor, given the high hopes with which he had invested
the union of the Lower Counties with Pennsylvania in 1682, but he pointedly
told Penn that "thou knows, by thy last being here, that these people are widely
different from what thou left them in 1684, and since 1701 they are not at all
mended."[18]

Word that the Assembly for the Lower Counties was preparing an address
to the queen, denouncing Penn's government and either requesting their own
governor or a union with a neighboring colony (New York, New Jersey, or
Maryland), further worried Logan. He clearly thought it best for Penn to accept

the division between Pennsylvania and the Lower Counties and to think about ways to ensure the smooth functioning of government in both places. Besides, he asked, "why shouldst thou contend for those who so little regard thee?" The best that could be hoped for, he thought, was to frustrate the mission of John Coutts, a New Castle merchant and speaker of the Assembly for the Lower Counties, who had set out for England to petition the Queen for a separation from Penn's control—perhaps through the offices of Coutts's old friend William Penn Jr. When Logan learned that Coutts's real aim was to gain the governorship for himself, that "he resolves . . . to get a commission for the government of those counties to himself, so much has his ambition and most arrogant spirit blinded him," the situation only got more complicated.[19]

* * *

Of much more immediate concern to Penn, of course, were his ongoing financial difficulties. His settlement with the Fords placed Pennsylvania, and his own personal prospects, in far more sympathetic hands, and the sale of Warminghurst had eliminated an enormous drain on his resources, but his financial position remained shaky. For a time, he nourished hopes that the discovery of silver mines in Pennsylvania would right his financial ship. Francois Luis Mitchell, a Swiss adventurer and former soldier in the French army, had undertaken some explorations in the colony, and although Penn was disappointed that initial samples brought over by Isaac Norris had turned out to be "no better than iron," he remained hopeful that mines held the potential to "quickly end my misfortunes, and enable me to do wonders for that poor country after all the ingratitude as well as injustice of some perverse tempers in it." By early 1709, however, the promise of the mines remained unfulfilled, and both Logan and Penn were viewing Mitchell with increasing suspicion. "I fear Mitchell has tricked us all," Logan wrote in early 1709. "He is subtle, and scarce to be trusted." Mitchell traveled to England seeking a patent for land on the Potomac, and while there, he visited Penn and suggested that had Logan and Evans not quarreled, the mines project might have turned a profit. Logan later dismissed this claim, along with the entire mines scheme, as "a very fiction," and it certainly turned out to be so in Pennsylvania. For his part, Mitchell convinced the proprietors of Carolina to grant him 2,500 acres there as part of an ongoing project of settling Palatine refugees (Swiss Protestants, many of them Mennonites) in the British colonies in America, and he settled in New Bern, along the Neuse River in coastal North Carolina. Although Penn wrote to Gookin in June 1710 that he had "made a contract with . . . Mitchell" and Christoph von Graffenreid, a Swiss nobleman with a penchant for adventures, "for the discovering, opening, and working certain mines"—possibly with natives doing the work—no copy of the purported contract has been found.[20]

Ultimately, the silver mines were yet one more initiative that had captured Penn's imagination but would fail to yield concrete benefits. Yet he remained eager to explore new undertakings that might provide him with much-needed revenue. He made an unsuccessful proposal to the Earl of Godolphin, seeking to secure a contract to provision English warships in the West Indies. Although he had suggested that supplying English ships from Pennsylvania would provide fresher and cheaper foodstuffs than sending them from Europe, the commissioners for victualing the navy observed that Pennsylvania's "prices on examination appear to be higher than what have been generally paid by our agent at Jamaica," and recommended that "it will not be for Her Majesty's service to contract with them in the manner they propose." With the collapse of wheat prices in Portugal, the prospects for selling grain at a profit and bringing in additional revenue remained remote. Despite Penn's persistent hopes, Pennsylvania simply never produced the revenue Penn needed to dig himself out of debt.[21]

* * *

As he had been doing since he entered Penn's employ, Logan continued to represent Penn amid hostility from Evans and the Assembly, as well as rising tension with Colonel Quary. Logan and Evans had clashed over the latter's excessive expenses and his unwillingness to account for them, a conflict that continued during the settling of accounts following Evans's dismissal. Logan was not confident in a positive outcome to this exercise, particularly as Evans had received many sums of which he, Logan, was only dimly aware (e.g., unrecorded fines and the £80 bribe paid by Griffith Jones for Evans to pardon his son). Adding to these uncertainties was the fact that Thomas Grey, clerk of the Provincial Council, had left for Maryland or Virginia and taken the account books with him. Logan also continued to face the implacable hostility of the Assembly, which had initiated impeachment proceedings against him in 1707.

In Logan's ongoing efforts to collect Penn's rents, absolutely nothing had changed. He told Penn that since news of his confinement at the Fleet had reached America, collection of quitrents had become nearly impossible: "I can scarce receive anything." Even many who were sympathetic to and supportive of Penn were reluctant to pay what they owed until the situation with the Fords was resolved. And when it was resolved, and a new mortgage made to a new set of trustees, the uncertainty remained, as Penn still faced the potential loss of Pennsylvania, if he failed to pay the trustees on schedule. Penn had merely replaced his indebtedness to the Fords with indebtedness to a group of leading Friends, and his ownership of Pennsylvania remained as precarious as ever. Yet Penn, as always, continued to make a host of demands of Logan. "Forget not my East and West Jersey interests"; "Hast thou done nothing yet with Biddle about Beaumont's 300 acres upon Rancocas Creek?"; "Let not poor Pennsbury be forgotten or neglected"—and all this in just one letter from September 1708.[22]

Although Penn and Quary had mended fences to some degree after their bitter contests before the Board of Trade, Penn continued, despite Logan's assurances, to mistrust the colonel. While Penn frequently denounced Quary—"Colonel Quary [sic] has broke his word, by vile letters he sent against us"—and Quary continued to feud with Evan Evans, the rector of Christ Church in Philadelphia, Logan consistently attempted to maintain harmonious relations. Even as late as the summer of 1712, he told Penn that "I must for my own part frankly own, that I never found [Quary] since his last arrival here from England in 1706, otherwise than very civil and obliging."[23]

By 1711, however, Penn had received detailed information from John French, sheriff of New Castle, accusing Quary and Moore of using their positions to profit from the seizure of ships engaged in illegal trading. French claimed that Quary had offered him £300 to grant Quary possession of two ships seized in Delaware Bay, and wrote an aggrieved letter to the proprietor proclaiming his integrity. French even traveled to England to defend his reputation before the Lord High Treasurer, where he was successful thanks in part to Penn's assistance. Unfortunately for French, it would prove to be a hollow victory: while he was in England, Gookin seized the ships' cargo, nearly five hundred hogsheads of sugar, and sold it, depriving Penn and the Queen of their rightful shares.[24]

* * *

In the midst of all the legal contestation, conflict over Pennsylvania, and Penn's imprisonment and eventual release, family life went on. In a letter to Samuel and Hannah Carpenter shortly before his release from the Fleet, Penn took stock of his family after the recent birth of "a second Hannah" earlier that month, on September 5, 1708. They were still grieving the death of their first Hannah, daughter Hannah Margarita, whom her father described as "our dear sweet Hannah ... the wittiest and womanliest creature that her age could show" and "our ... remarkable one." (Penn's wife Hannah was herself a "second" Hannah, so named after a sister of that name who was born in 1664 but died in childhood.) William and Hannah's little flock comprised "four boys, John, Thomas, Richard, and Dennis, and two girls, Margaret and Hannah." Their joy over their newborn daughter, this second Hannah, would be short-lived; the child survived just five months, dying on January 24, 1709, in London. "I have lost my last sweet nursery," Penn wrote to Logan from Reading, in late February.[25]

Following his release from the Fleet, Penn divided his time between Bristol, where his family remained based, and London, where business frequently demanded his attention. While in London during June and July 1709, he stayed with his daughter Letitia and her husband William Aubrey, and also visited his sister Margaret Lowther. He sent Hannah and the children gifts of coffee, chocolate, and medicinal wines as well as venison from a deer granted by the Duchess of Marlborough from one of her estates. Business in London and the search for a house to rent kept him from rejoining the family until late July 1709. He consistently expressed his desire to be with them but was slowed by an illness of some sort, which required bleeding in London. "Considering what blood I have lost," he wrote to Hannah, "20 ounces, it is as fast as is fit." (He was "blooded" again in January 1710, "12 ounces.") By July 22 he had arrived in Newbury, about halfway between London and Bristol, hoping to be home soon, and even lodging a supper request for his return: "tripe and ox muggets [entrails, or intestines] with some parsley guts [sweetbreads]."[26]

Later that year, while again away from home, he sent sturgeon, brawn (a meat product), tea (which, on another occasion, he recommended she not spoil by adding milk, but "drink it upon its own merit"), and a penknife. He also sent back raisins, almonds, figs, macaroons, sugar, orange root (a medicinal plant), gingerbread, and a book for each of his children. A month later, it was oranges, lemons, chestnuts, and gingerbread. He expressed both his eagerness for Hannah and the children to join him in London, and concern about the poor quality of the London air and its potential implications for his family's health, though as 1709 turned to 1710 his eagerness for his family seemed to overpower his caution: "Thou . . . should have come up with me, or at least sooner, yet I say again, stay if thou art pleased . . . or leave them and Sarah and come with John and Peggy and the maids."[27]

Given the perennial strife over money, and the ways in which his family ties were intertwined with his financial troubles, Penn's London visits with the Aubreys must have been anything but dull. In October 1709, he described William Aubrey as being "in so great a rage" against Logan over money owed him and Letitia from Pennsylvania land sales. Worse yet, Penn wrote to Logan, "he says thou tellest his attorneys, I have ordered thee to pay him nothing." Several years later Penn still described Letitia and her husband as "under the greatest uneasiness for their money," which they blamed Logan for failing to provide. Penn remained deeply indebted to his father-in-law Thomas Callowhill, who had incurred significant financial risk of his own in order to help Penn settle his debts and obtain his release from the Fleet.[28]

His letters to his family during these years are tender and loving: "I embrace thee and my dear lambs, beyond words," and, to son John, "I cannot love you better than I do." "I am pretty well," he wrote to Hannah, "but I have not my dearest nearest Friend and my dearly beloved children with me." He confessed to her in late 1709 that "our distance grows very uncomfortable to me," and that he hoped "that we shall never be so long asunder again, fourteen days is enough." "My head often makes me a little thoughtful, and wish for thee, more than formerly," he wrote in early 1710. He was solicitous about her health, and consulted with acquaintances in London who provided a number of recommendations, including drinking "strong port white wine and hot well water . . . and not to use malt liquors," and to make her chocolate and tea with hot well water. Having consulted a "Dr. Philips" in London regarding a health issue Hannah was facing, for example, Penn reported the doctor's view that Hannah's condition was likely "wind and not [kidney] stone"—and that she was likely suffering "hysteric vapors in those lower parts." The doctor recommended Peruvian bark, a widely used medicinal herb, and a few months later Penn was describing Hannah as "hearty . . . now."[29]

William and Hannah's older children—John, then eight years old, and Thomas, aged six—attended a Quaker boarding school run by Joseph Nicholson, a Yorkshire Friend who had settled in Reading, about forty miles west of London. Penn's letters to his children are filled with encouragement. He told the boys "to follow your book two hours in the forenoon [morning], and two hours in the afternoon, and do readily what you are bid." In addition to their reading, he added, they should "write an hour in the afternoon." Given the deaths of so many around him—from infants born to both Gulielma and Hannah, as well as his brother Richard and his son Springett—it is not surprising that he urged Hannah to exercise great care for their health, and to hold them out of school if there was any sign of "fever in your lane or near it." He also imparted important practical information to his boys—"Don't overdo the poor little horse" to Thomas; and to John, "Take care of thy little horse daily and don't ride alone." "Pray let not Johnny ride on horseback in deep, dirty, or in windy places," he implored Hannah. A growing young boy, John was looking for a larger horse by 1710, to which his father agreed while noting ruefully that his current horse was "free of all faults but littleness." He playfully teased young John—"my little American"—about Margaret Taylor, daughter of London Friends James and Elizabeth Taylor, "thy little wife" who followed him around "call[ing] me father" during one of his visits.[30]

Hannah's slow recovery from childbirth in late 1708 and early 1709 was not the only illness that afflicted the Penn family during these years. In addition to the loss of their daughter, William and Hannah's other children endured health scares as well. In early 1711, Dennis suffered "three or four fits of a fever." Young John, whose bout with rheumatic fever as an infant had left him susceptible to infection, suffered a "severe illness" in August 1712. In September 1709, Penn referred to his "lame leg" in asking to delay an appearance before the Board of Trade. That said, he seemed rather proud just a few months later to tell Hannah that a number of people had recently told him that "they see no difference from twenty years ago," which meant, "that I am upon equal terms with thee, it seems" (not exactly: he was sixty-five to her thirty-eight). Perhaps he spoke too soon: just four days later, he wrote again, telling Hannah that he had been feverish, and was hoping not to have to be bled. Apparently he hoped in vain, and a few weeks later, he could merely say: "I am not worse." He suffered his first stroke sometime in April 1712, and it clearly affected his body as well as his mind. He excused his penmanship to a correspondent in early May: "Forgive my [scrawl].... This is one of my first letters since my severe illness."[31]

* * *

For someone who had once been among the most visible Friends in England—to say nothing of Europe and America—William Penn was clearly slowing down as he moved through his seventh decade. He held Meetings while confined at the Old Bailey, signed a certificate attesting the clearness of a London Quaker couple for marriage, and provided Pennsylvania Friends with their long-requested school charter. In fall 1709 and early 1710 he combined a trip through Berkshire, where he was looking for houses to rent, with a preaching tour in Kent. The search for a suitable house continued into January 1710, with William sending Hannah details of a number of possible homes and pointing out the benefits and drawbacks of each. (They eventually settled on Ruscombe, in Berkshire, about a third of the way between London and Bristol on the main road connecting the two cities.) He wrote to the Bristol Yearly Meeting in April 1711, expressing his regret at his inability to join them and assuring them of his continuing love toward Friends.[32]

Generational turnover continued in the Society of Friends. Penn was devastated to learn of the death of his dear friend, sometime lawyer, and trustee for Pennsylvania, Irish Friend Thomas Cuppage, in January 1709: "I have lost a great friend and the church a great member; his parts, though plain were masculine and strong, his integrity incorruptible, his friendship firm and his zeal and love for truth always fresh and tender. May I wish to find so able and so compassionate a Friend in England, Ireland, or America," and worried that Cuppage's work on behalf of his settlement with the Fords had somehow hastened his death.[33]

Penn's spell in debtors' prison was deeply embarrassing to him, but it did not prevent him from maintaining his close association with elites in English government and society. Some of these interactions were more personal in nature. Charles Mordaunt, Lord Peterborough, whom Penn had recruited to assist him in opposing the Reunification Bill during the early years of the eighteenth century, wrote to Penn in the spring of 1709 hoping to see him during a trip to Bath to take the waters. Others were more relevant to Friends' business. Penn sent a copy of his 1693 *Essay toward the peace of Europe* to the Duke of Marlborough, who had risen from a page during the Stuart monarchy to become one of the most powerful figures at Court, and was just then setting out for (eventually unsuccessful) peace negotiations at The Hague. By late 1711, Penn's political influence was waning along with his health. He could do nothing to prevent the passage of an Occasional Conformity Bill in 1711, which barred persons attending Nonconformist churches from holding office in England or Wales.

His letter to Harley, now Earl of Oxford, has a plaintive and pathetic tone: "I am heartily sorry I am now good for nothing. Twas otherways in former days." In early 1712, Penn attempted to facilitate a meeting between Oxford and a group of Quakers (including his old friends Ellwood and Whitehead) who were petitioning for a revised affirmation bill. Thanks to solid opposition from the Church of England, however, their efforts were unsuccessful, failing in the Commons in February 1712.[34]

* * *

Penn's slow but steady retreat from public life went hand in hand with his revival of negotiations about the surrender of his government to the Crown. He wrote a lengthy and bitter letter to Friends in Pennsylvania in June 1710, recounting his high hopes during the early days of colonization and lamenting that "while [Pennsylvania] has proved a land of freedom and flourishing it should become for me, by whose means it was principally made a country the cause of grief, trouble, and poverty." Far from merely differences in opinion about the best interests of the country, Penn pointed to "attacks on my reputation," "secret insinuations against my justice," and "the violence . . . shown against my secretary" (Logan remained under threat of impeachment even though Gookin had temporarily put a stop to the proceedings).[35]

But Penn was not only concerned about his own stake in these matters. He admonished Pennsylvanians to think more broadly, since "the peoples of many nations in Europe look on that country as a land of ease and quiet . . . the world [has] their eyes upon you." And it was not only the world, but God himself: "I fear the kind hand of providence that has so long favored and protected you, will . . . be at length provoked [and] reduce those that have been so clamorous and causelessly discontented." He told them, in closing, that he would "consider more closely of my own private and sinking circumstances in relation to that province"; in other words, that he intended to revive the negotiations over his surrender. Indeed, just a month later he renewed his application to the Queen, stating that despite his noble motives and indefatigable efforts, because of the ingratitude and disorderliness of the inhabitants "his fatigues and expense have become unsupportable to him."[36]

News of promising October 1710 Pennsylvania election returns—the entire Assembly was replaced with new members, and the new Assembly promised to be far more sympathetic to Penn's interests—could not dissuade him from his newfound resolution to sell back the government to the Crown. Some observers, like Sussex County Quaker Samuel Preston, even dared to hope for a reunion with the Lower Counties, telling Penn that "the Lower Counties . . . renewed and pressed again . . . [for] a union with the province, and are hearty in their inclinations to thy government." (How realistic this hope was remains unclear.)

Preston also praised Gookin's administration and expressed his hope that the "overthrow and change of the old members of the Assembly . . . gives me confidence to say the posture of affairs in Pennsylvania looks with a good face." Norris, too, voiced his opinion that the outcome of the 1710 elections was the best Penn could have hoped for. But Penn had, by this point, made up his mind, and even if the Pennsylvania Assembly's February 28, 1711, address—with its conciliatory tone, its report of amending laws as directed by the Crown, and its voting of a revenue for the government—had reached him sooner, he had likely passed a point of no return with his Americans.[37]

The renewal of surrender negotiations initiated another round of correspondence, queries, and meetings with the Board of Trade, which irritated Penn, who felt he had answered all of these questions already in years past. He repeated his request for a payment of £20,000, though he now offered to allow the payment to be spread over seven years. In a more extensive document submitted to the board, Penn once again recounted the bitter experiences that had brought him to this pass:

> When that government was first granted me, I could not easily imagine I should ever be obliged to treat thus of a surrender. I had then good reason to hope that if by my industry and vast expenses I should make a settled colony of it, and add such an improvement to the dominions of the Crown, I might without interruption peaceably enjoy the advantages of it . . . yet so it proved, that soon after its first settlement the easy ear the ministry from time to time lent to the unjust complaints of some designing and prejudiced men, has rendered my possession of it a perpetual uneasiness.

Each of his visits to the colony had been cut short by the necessity of returning to England to fend off assaults on his proprietorship, which made it impossible for him to reap the benefits of colonization. As for estimating the revenues that the colony generated—one of the requests the board had made of him, as a way of arriving at a fair price as well as evaluating the benefits that would accrue to the Crown in reclaiming the government—Penn pointed out both the prosperity that had been created and its continuation into the future:

> [L]ess than 30 years ago, the whole was a wilderness, out of which is now raised a thriving well settled colony, able and willing to support itself. . . . The trade of the place . . . has augmented the Queen's Revenue by a great many thousands, the improvements are even surprising to those who have viewed them and consider the infancy of the settlement. . . . 'tis obvious, that it is not the present value only that is to

be estimated, but what it is continually growing and improving to in futurity.

Finally, Penn noted the specifically Quaker dimension of the settlement and urged that special consideration be given in any surrender "both to the people that went over [with] me in respect to their religious perswasions and to myself and family that may be settled there." (He had earlier requested that the board bestow "some particular mark of respect" on him and his family, "distinguishing them above the rank of those who have planted under him.")[38]

By February 1711, the Board of Trade had recommended to the Queen that "revesting the government of Pennsylvania in your Majesty will be a benefit to the trade of this kingdom," as well as to the administration of justice in the province and enforcement of the Navigation Acts. The board did not, however, render any judgment on Penn's asking price nor on the question of indulgence for the particularly Quaker features of the colonial government. Penn asked Gookin to work with the Assembly and Council to inform him "what is fit for them in modesty to ask (of the Crown as well as me)" before any change of administration. He also insisted that the costs of government be adequately funded, and that Gookin and Penn himself be provided for by the Assembly.[39]

Reaction to news of the surrender negotiations was mixed. Isaac Norris admitted that "it a little damps us, but as things are it may be for the better." Joseph Growden, one of the most prosperous First Purchasers and frequent member of the Assembly and Council, expressed disappointment with the way that Penn had been treated by his own province's government, denouncing "a churlish disposition and a continual raking and scraping after money" by many colonial officials. Growden insisted that "thy government of Pennsylvania is an honorable and very worthy thing," adding that although "the charges of keeping it up hitherto . . . have been great and hard to be borne," nonetheless "it is another thing now; the incidental perquisites of profit are growing yearly." Though Growden had been in Pennsylvania for three decades, he might have been overly optimistic in his reading of the situation on the ground. After all, he went on to say that he wished William Penn Jr. would return to Pennsylvania: "I doubt not he would be most cheerfully welcomed and honorably treated by the people in general."[40]

But by late May 1711, Friends in Pennsylvania, facing the ongoing implacable hostility of Anglicans and the vague rumors about Penn's surrender, had decided to weigh in. They reminded Penn—as if he needed reminding—of the Quaker roots of the enterprise, how "the hearts of many Friends . . . by the good will of God inclined to come into this country." And not Friends only: "other conscientious people of other persuasions" dearly hoped that their children would continue to enjoy the liberties they had enjoyed in Pennsylvania. They worried that a surrender would result in increased taxes and "many sufferings and inconveniences" for Friends, and that it would also reflect poorly on Penn himself: "Will not a voluntary surrender give occasion for some people to reflect upon thee for so doing, especially thy enemies?" Then again, they acknowledged that Penn had endured nearly three decades of criticism, personal attacks, and condemnation, and had invested enormous sums for little return. Even more critically (and self-servingly), they admitted that the unremitting hostility of Anglicans, whose "frequent attempts to wrest the government out of thy hands" and to deprive Friends of the benefits of the Affirmation Act aimed "to make thee and Friends dissenters under thy own government."[41] If Penn did pursue a surrender, they urged him "to make the best terms thou canst for us and other dissenters," paying particular attention to liberty of conscience and the colony's Affirmation Acts, for without such protections "Friends will be laid by as useless members of the government and exposed to sufferings." They noted the obstinacy of the Lower Counties, and asked Penn not to grant their requests for equal representation, since Pennsylvania was so much more populous.[42]

Notwithstanding the promising developments in the 1710 election and the recent thaw in relations between the Assembly and the proprietor, Penn noted that "from what I have already undergone, I have been so far reduced to a necessity of taking these measures which were entered on a considerable time ago, that I still think it advisable to pursue them." He pledged to try to wrap up unfinished business like the marking of the boundary line with Maryland, which was directly related to the security of land sales and hence to producing revenue to pay off Penn's trustees. As they awaited the Board of Trade's judgment, Logan reiterated the importance of settling the line, writing to Penn in May 1712 that "we all grow very uneasy about the division line . . . If we sell and take money for land that shall be adjudged to Maryland . . . how shall we be justified?" Logan's concerns were magnified by the fact that Penn's trustees had written to the colony's Commissioners of Property that they had yet to receive enough funds to cover even the interest on the principal lent to Penn. Logan also observed that if the affirmation law was repealed, "we are reduced to a real slavery for if in all points of such a government as this none but churchmen are to judge us, thou fully knows the consequences." Penn did attempt to reward Logan for his long service, instructing the commissioners to pay him "1000 pounds of Pennsylvania money" and a regular salary in the future. (Then again, promises of money in Pennsylvania were generally hollow ones, since, as Logan had repeatedly informed Penn, "money is so extremely scarce that we cannot as yet get any in.")[43]

By early 1712, Attorney General Northey had drafted papers effecting the surrender, though Penn's continuing health concerns intruded on further progress. He wrote to his old friend Harley, now Earl of Oxford and Lord High Treasurer, at the end of February about his "present weakness," which made him unable to personally attend proceedings since he was "wearing a nightgown still, which makes . . . an odd figure at the Treasury." By late spring Logan reported hearing unsubstantiated rumors that the surrender had been completed, which "alarms the people more than could be expected after the fair warning they have repeatedly had from thy letters last year." But it was not until July 17, 1712, that the Lord High Treasurer, after discussions with the Board of Trade and Penn himself, "resolve[d] to move Her Majesty to accept the said surrender and conveyance." The amount was reduced to £16,000 over seven years; Penn ultimately agreed to accept only £12,000 if it were paid in four years. Although he claimed to have "taken effectual care that all the laws and privileges I have granted to [Friends] shall be observed by the Queen's governors," he did not actually receive any specific guarantees to that effect. Finally, on September 9, 1712, the queen ordered the Treasury to pay Penn "1000 pounds as an advance . . . as part of the said sum of 12,000 pounds agreed" for the surrender of the government of Pennsylvania to the Crown.[44]

Even as he pursued the surrender of his government, and a return to Pennsylvania became increasingly unlikely given his advancing age and accumulating health worries, Penn continued to profess a desire to see his colony again. "Nothing but our eternal felicity is more our prayer to the Lord than that we may live if not die among you and yours." Even after his first stroke in April 1712, Penn wrote to Logan that "If I can get away by the seventh month I come, else must stay till next spring." He told Friends in Pennsylvania in summer 1712 that he hoped "to see you if God give me life this fall, but I grow old and infirm, yet would gladly see you once more before I die."[45]

* * *

Even while negotiations for the surrender were still in process, Pennsylvania Friends continued to rely on the proprietor to represent their interests against the constant and unremitting opposition of the colony's Anglicans. The Assembly submitted an address directly to the Queen in early 1711, protesting Anglican efforts to insist on oaths in legal settings. But two could play the game of appealing to London. The vestry of Christ Church in Philadelphia petitioned the Bishop of London, asking his protection against the Church of England's "restless enemies, the Quakers" and requesting that he petition the Queen on their behalf. The grievances were nothing new—the naked and defenseless condition of the colony, and an affirmation law that Anglicans considered prejudicial to the administration of justice—but the issues were raised with renewed vigor, sensing a weakened proprietary interest.[46]

The Crown did repeal the colony's Affirmation Act in 1711, but the following year the Assembly had passed another one, as well as a law enabling religious societies to buy and receive lands. Both of these pieces of legislation were anathema to the colony's Anglicans. (Logan described opposition as inspired by "nothing but a tyrannical spirit of prelacy and injustice.") Once again, Anglicans drafted addresses to England, this time to the Queen, the Bishop of London, and the Earl of Clarendon. As Logan described the situation, the addresses "treat Friends as . . . little better than rebels . . . with other constructions equally unjust and malicious." Even more challenging was the fact that Pennsylvania Quakers did not always know when appeals were sent to the Queen or the Bishop of London, since they were often drafted in secret and sent by Anglicans from other places, like Burlington, New Jersey.[47]

* * *

But Penn had other things on his mind by 1712. On or about April 6 of that year, he rewrote his last will and testament. It departed sharply from the one he had signed in 1705 and executed before witnesses in August 1707. (Of course, much had happened in his financial affairs as well as his personal life since that time, not least his deep disappointment in William Jr.) In this will William Penn Jr. fared rather badly. Penn froze his eldest son out of the inheritance of Pennsylvania and the Lower Counties entirely, describing William Jr. as "being well provided for by . . . his mother's estate and my father's estate." As he was then in the midst of negotiations regarding the surrender of his government, which he hoped to see completed as quickly as possible, he left his Pennsylvania government to two members of the Queen's cabinet and longtime friends, the Earls of Oxford (Harley) and Poulett, directing them to "dispose thereof to the Queen or any other person to the best advantage and profit they can." He left his lands in America to an assorted group of Friends and relatives (including Hannah, her father, and his sister Margaret) and instructed that "they shall sell and dispose of so much thereof as shall be sufficient to pay all my just debts," after which William Jr.'s three children, Gulielma Maria, Springett, and William III, were to receive 10,000 acres apiece. (It is not clear whether this provision was ever fulfilled, though he also left 10,000 acres to Letitia, who sold hers.) Beyond that, Penn left all of his American lands to his children by Hannah, leaving his wife to determine the amounts to be received by each. Finally, in a codicil, Penn left Hannah £300 per year, out of his American rents, for the education of their children, with the closing wish that "I desire they may settle at least in good part in America."[48]

Although he insisted that he made this will "with a clear understanding of what I did then," to remove any doubt as to his intentions or his state of mind he again signed the will a month later, on May 27, at his house in Ruscombe in the presence of seven witnesses. Given the way the relationship between Hannah and William Jr. would deteriorate after Penn's death, it was a well-advised, but ultimately futile, step.[49]

* * *

On October 4, 1712, while in Bristol, where he had been staying since the August death of Hannah's father (which took place just eight weeks after the death of her mother), Penn began a letter to Logan. The topics covered in that letter were routine, issues about which the two men had corresponded for years: the surrender negotiations, Pennsylvania Friends' continued unwillingness to help Penn with his financial difficulties, clashes with Aubrey over money. Penn wrote that his son John had been devastated by his grandfather's death, and "almost followed his grandfather through an excess of sorrow at his death and burial."[50]

Just a few lines further down the page, after speculating about the prospects for European peace, admonishing Logan to humility and discretion, and mentioning the visit of Sybilla Masters, a New Jersey Friend who later received a patent for a corn mill, Penn began a new sentence. "She . . ."

Just then he was hit with another, far more serious, stroke.

* * *

From this point on, a biography of William Penn becomes, simultaneously, a biography of Hannah Penn. Legally speaking, her position was precarious, since although Penn was incapacitated after his October 1712 stroke, and although he had named Hannah as executrix of his most recent will and had settled the proprietorship on their children, he was still alive and thus his will was largely beside the point. Much Pennsylvania business required his attention or, at the least, his signature on official documents, and thus Hannah faced the challenging task of getting her enfeebled spouse to sign papers regarding Pennsylvania. She also faced the unremitting hostility of William Jr., who considered himself unjustly shut out of the proprietorship.[51]

A week after the stroke that struck down her husband, Hannah sat down to finish writing the letter he had begun, telling Logan that, while writing, Penn "was taken with a second fit of lethargic illness." His doctors implored her "to keep all business from him until he is stronger." Penn was strong enough to jot a few lines to Logan several weeks later—really just briefly completing the letter he had begun—pronouncing himself "through the Lord's mercy pretty well." This brief postscript, however, did not make reference to any substantive or detailed points of business, and though his editors point out that in this letter "his hand is still strong," they also observe that "he repeats himself, and his language is confused." Meanwhile, in Pennsylvania, Logan, having not yet heard of Penn's latest spell, was composing a defensive and tetchy letter to Penn, vindicating his conduct on a number of fronts against the proprietor's criticisms.[52]

In addition to her worry about her husband's health and her grief over her own parents' recent deaths, Hannah Penn also found herself, after October

1712, thrust into the complex world of Penn's American affairs and his many other business dealings. She surely could not have been pleased to receive Logan's letter to Penn of late February 1713, which not only related that Pennsylvanians had been subjected to "repeated accounts of thy decease," but also showed just how out of touch her husband had been in many aspects of colonial affairs. Logan informed Penn that his recent instructions about Letitia's lands in Pennsylvania were impossible to fulfill, as the patents he had drawn up for his daughter's manors, "being done in a hurry" during his last visit to America, turned out to infringe on lands owned by others, whose claims had been confirmed several years earlier on Penn's explicit directions. In other words, "the whole business is long ago settled under hand and seal, and . . . can be altered in no other way." Despite suffering "a most afflicting sciatica and rheumatism," Logan continued, he was attempting to gather in money due to Penn and the Aubreys, but he repeated his earlier assertions that money continued to be "extremely scarce with us." He pressed Penn to arrange for the boundary line with Maryland to be drawn, since it affected "thousands of pounds due for lands already sold and for quitrents." Continuing rumors about the terms of Penn's surrender undermined the likelihood of gathering in money owed, but Logan planned to redouble his efforts, and even to visit Penn's New Jersey properties within the coming months.[53]

Hannah relied on Logan's experience in dealing with American affairs since, as she put it, her husband "is recovered to a degree of health and strength, yet has never attained his wonted strength in expression, nor is he able to engage in business as formerly." She consulted with Penn's lawyers about whether the surrender might be confirmed, and on matters like the boundary with Maryland, and told Logan that she would welcome him to visit her in England to offer advice on the management of Pennsylvania and the Lower Counties. Despite an appeal from Hannah and the trustees in 1714, which gained the support of the Privy Council in March 1714, the surrender never came to pass, due in large part to Queen Anne's death in August 1714 and the changes at Court that followed. The Earl of Oxford was impeached and sent to the Tower of London, and Charles Spencer, son of Penn's old friend the Earl of Sunderland, was sent to Ireland as Lord-Lieutenant.[54]

As time went by, Penn's physical and mental condition fluctuated wildly, and Hannah took on an increasing amount of responsibility for managing his affairs. She told Logan in early 1714 that Penn was "not well enough to digest and answer the particulars" of his inquiries about Pennsylvania, but that he was "a little better within these few weeks than for many months before," an outcome she attributed to "the present course of medicine that we think has been hitherto blessed to him." Not only was he unable to work through the various issues at hand, Hannah said, but informing him about them "will be to no purpose and but increase his cares." Hannah herself often suffered with "pains in my head." Penn was well enough to attend the Reading Meeting in early 1714, though the next year his wife referred to "two or three little returns of his paralytic disorder" while adding that "he is now in pretty good health, not worse in his speech than for some months past." In September 1715 she described him as "pretty hearty," though by early the next year he was "troubled with lameness and swelling in his legs," which Hannah was relieved to discover was gout, and not palsy.[55]

In several of her letters, Hannah provided a tender glimpse of her husband in his twilight years. Although scholars have often pronounced his final six years unworthy of examination—describing the post-stroke Penn as, for example, a "sweet, gentle, invalid with a vacant smile on his face"—it seems clear that he had periods of lucidity even while he remained impaired in his ability to attend to his worldly affairs. Her accounts have a poignancy to them and offer a window into the private world into which Penn had withdrawn after his stroke. "When I keep the thoughts of business out of his head," she wrote in January 1715, "he is very sweet, comfortable, and easy, and is cheerfully resigned to the Lord's will, takes delight in his children, his friends and family comforts as formerly." Later that year, she wrote to Logan that "he walks about the garden and common here daily and has been several times at Meeting, at Reading." Despite his misfortunes, she described him in the spring of 1716 as "blessed under his misfortunes with a sweet and comfortable serenity of mind," despite "a return of his fits."[56]

She excused her lack of attention to the details about which Logan had pressed her by explaining that "my poor husband's weakness continues and he is scarce ever easy . . . unless I am at his elbow and to write in his sight . . . renew[s] his cares and the thoughts of what he was wont to do himself." Congratulating Logan on his marriage, she told him that William also sent his best wishes, "and has will enough to write to thee . . . but his writing is as imperfect as his speech, and I therefore avoid it." Around the same time, Thomas Story, having visited the family at Ruscombe, commented that Penn's "memory was almost quite lost and the use of his understanding suspended."[57]

Hannah was more than just a caregiver, though. She worked with Herbert Springett, Penn's chief lawyer, to deal with disputes over his Irish lands in County Cork, and to address the claims of Thomas Fairman Jr., the son of Penn's late surveyor, who sought resolution of his father's landholdings in Pennsylvania. In 1718, she defended Penn's claims to the Lower Counties against John Gordon, the Earl of Sutherland, who attempted to convince King George I to grant him the Lower Counties in lieu of repayment of a debt the Crown owed him. (The request was denied.) She took over the role of intermediary between Logan and the continually disgruntled Aubrey. And she attempted, unsuccessfully, to secure additional payments toward the surrender of the government that her husband had concluded shortly before his affliction.[58]

By late 1715, relations between the Pennsylvania government and Gookin had reached a breaking point. The Lieutenant Governor's behavior had grown increasingly erratic and arbitrary. Hannah and the trustees, working with Logan, decided to replace him. After considering several candidates, they settled in September 1716 on William Keith, who had replaced Quary as Surveyor-General in America two years earlier. Keith would serve as Lieutenant Governor until 1726, crossing paths with a young transplant from Massachusetts named Benjamin Franklin.[59]

Hannah also oversaw the family at Ruscombe, an obligation made more demanding by William Jr.'s abandonment of his wife and children, which added to both her financial and emotional burdens. She thanked Thomas Story for his gift of wine, citron water (a distilled beverage made of citron juice and sugar soaked in brandy, which Hannah described as "of all cordials, [Penn's] favorite one"), and nuts during his trip to England in early 1715. Penn "as well as he can, returns thee his hearty acknowledgment." Later that year, Hannah took William to Bath, where she wrote to her son Thomas that he "drinks about a quart of the Bath water, and has a good stomach after it." William Jr., she told Logan, had not been to see his father in eighteen months.[60]

* * *

By the summer of 1718, William Penn's health had been in a precarious state for nearly six years. Story, who had been in England since 1714 traveling in the Quaker ministry, had visited with the family on a number of occasions, most recently in late July of that year. Just a day after his departure, Hannah began a letter to Story, telling him that her husband's condition had taken a turn. "He altered much," she wrote, and "was taken with shivering and lowness of spirit, and divers symptoms like a sudden change." "My poor husband is this day grown so much worse," she continued, "that I can't expect his continuance till this time tomorrow." And then, on July 30, an addendum to the letter broke the news: "My poor dearest's last breath was fetched this morning between 2 and 3 o'clock."[61]

Epilogue

He was a man of great abilities, of an excellent sweetness of disposition, quick of thought and ready utterance . . . And though in old age by reason of some shocks of a violent distemper his intellects were much impaired, yet his sweetness and loving disposition surmounted its utmost efforts and remained when reason almost failed.

William Penn's portrait is now likely to find its way into many homes remote from the . . . Society of Friends, but—as a trade mark! Quakerism is one thing, Quaker Rolled White Oats are another.[1]

When he received Hannah's letter announcing her husband's death, Thomas Story wrote, "I was much broken in my Spirit." Story promptly set out with Penn's son John to be with the family at Ruscombe. Their reunion, he reported, "occasioned a fresh remembrance of the deceased, and also a renewed flood of many tears from all eyes." On August 5, Story accompanied the family on the twenty-mile journey northeast to Jordans, where William Penn was laid to rest at Jordans Meetinghouse, alongside Gulielma, his son Springett, and five of his other children. The records of Jordans Meeting refer to nearly thirty Public Friends and a numerous company "of Friends and others" who were in attendance. Story described it as "a large Meeting of Friends, and others, from many places," which was "well spoken of by strangers afterwards." He stayed with the Penn family for several days while Penn's will was read, and advised Hannah on a range of issues. He returned once again a few days later, having been asked by Hannah for "some further advice concerning their affairs, being of great moment, and accompanied with many and considerable difficulties."[2]

What these "many and considerable difficulties" were, Story does not say. Penn's finances had been in disarray for years, and his debts remained formidable, though this would hardly have been news to Hannah. The more likely culprit was William Jr., whose relationship with Hannah deteriorated quickly after the reading of his father's will. The younger Penn had always felt that his father favored Hannah and her children over him and his siblings (Penn's children with Gulielma). Although his father's 1701 will had left the proprietorship

356

of Pennsylvania to William Jr., by 1712, when he drafted his final will, Penn had changed his mind definitively, and left his eldest surviving son only Gulielma's and Sir William's estates. By that time, the son had largely forsaken his wife and children as well as the Society of Friends, and following his father's stroke he mostly disappeared from Penn's life. In 1714, Hannah confided to a correspondent that "I have not seen [William Jr.] this half year, nor has he seen his father these eighteen months." Her financial records show that she supported Mary and the children to the tune of £300 between 1713 and 1718.[3]

Just five weeks after Penn's death Hannah wrote to Story that William Jr. "seems to think himself, or nobody, entitled to the government." By January 1719, attempts to settle disputes between the two had broken down entirely, and the son had challenged his father's will in court. William Jr. particularly protested the codicil that granted Hannah an annual income of £300. Objecting as well to the will's separation of the government of Pennsylvania (which Penn had left in the hands of two of his old friends, the Earl of Oxford, Robert Harley, and John Poulett) from ownership of the land (left to Hannah and trustees), William Jr. insisted that he should inherit both. But even more provocations were on the way. On January 14, 1719, with no legal basis whatsoever, William Jr. claimed the proprietorship for himself and issued a commission instructing Lieutenant Governor Keith to "make known my accession to the government" of Pennsylvania and the Lower Counties. It was a bold but ill-advised attempt to assert control in clear violation of his father's last wishes. When the Assembly received the commission, it demurred. The Board of Trade later clarified that William Penn Jr.'s claims to the proprietorship were invalid, though the case would drag on for years before eventually being decided in Hannah's (and her children's) favor, shortly before her death in December 1726. By then William Penn Jr. had been dead for years, having passed away in France, apparently of consumption, in 1720.[4]

In the meantime, however, Hannah Penn, whom Logan described as "blessed with a strong judgement and excellent good sense to a degree uncommon to her sex," emerged as a fierce defender of her husband's memory. She did not forget those who had caused him difficulty, referring to David Lloyd as "a troublesome ill-tempered man who has always showed himself to be an inveterate enemy of my poor husband." Her son Thomas remained in London as an apprentice, and frequently was called upon by his mother for his assistance in family or business matters (collecting money, paying creditors, obtaining supplies). By the end of 1719, John and Margaret seem to have joined Thomas in London, while the youngest two boys, Richard and Dennis, attended school. Hannah soon realized that it was not feasible to maintain her residence at Ruscombe, and set about downsizing her living situation and her retinue of servants. "It would be my greatest pleasure," she wrote to her cousin, "to find myself in a capacity to pay my dear husband's debts."[5]

From 1718 down to the American Revolution, the proprietorship of Pennsylvania was divided between the founder's sons and grandsons. John, "the American," held a 50 percent share, while his brothers Thomas and Richard split the other half. Thomas arrived in Pennsylvania in August 1732, intending, as his father once had, to set the colony's land titles in order and ensure payments due to the proprietor's family. As his father before him had also discovered, such a task was easier said than done, and the relationship between the Pennsylvanians and William Penn's children and grandchildren became increasingly strained with the passage of time. It was Thomas Penn, after all, who along with Logan orchestrated the infamous and underhanded "Walking Purchase," which in 1737 defrauded the Lenapes out of more than a million acres based on specious claims about a treaty the natives had signed with his father.[6]

John, never in the best of health, died in 1746, and Thomas, as the eldest surviving son, inherited his share and became chief proprietor. Readers of Benjamin Franklin's *Autobiography* will be familiar with Thomas Penn, who traveled with Franklin to discuss colonial defense at the Albany Conference in 1754. Franklin's relationship with Penn cooled considerably over time, however, as the Penn family consistently attempted to prevent the Assembly from taxing its property for the purposes of colonial defense (or, for that matter, almost any purpose). As the Assembly's representative, Franklin clashed repeatedly with Thomas Penn.[7] Thomas appointed his nephew, Richard's son John, as governor in 1763, just in time for an outbreak of violence, in which the murder of settlers in western Pennsylvania sparked reprisals against natives in Conestoga and the surrounding area by Scots-Irish frontiersmen known as the Paxton Boys. The Paxton Boys ultimately marched on the government in Philadelphia. Only a meeting organized by Franklin, at which the Paxton Boys aired their grievances, defused the situation.[8]

After Thomas's death in 1775, the proprietorship passed to his son John—often called John Penn of Stoke, to distinguish him from John Penn the American—whose term as proprietor would be cut short by the American Revolution. He lived in Philadelphia for five years during the 1780s before returning to England once and for all, eventually serving in Parliament. His Philadelphia home, The Solitude, which he designed himself, still stands on the grounds of the Philadelphia Zoo.[9]

But if relations with William Penn's sons and grandsons remained rocky, the passing of time enshrined the founder himself ever more firmly in the colony's founding mythology, smoothing over the bitter disagreements between the colony and its proprietor. A heroic apostle of religious dissent who brought forth a land that served as a beacon for oppressed believers, and who treated the natives with kindness and respect: this is the portrait of William Penn passed down to generations of Pennsylvanians. Among the crafters of this founding mythology, perhaps the most important were Benjamin West, "Parson" Mason

Locke Weems, and Edward Hicks. Thomas Penn commissioned West to paint his father signing his purported 1682 treaty with the natives at Shackamaxon. The resulting painting, *Penn's Treaty with the Indians*, presents a portly Penn with outstretched hands, greeting the natives against an incongruous backdrop of multistory brick buildings. The painting clearly aims to revive an image of benevolent paternalism in the person of the founder, and to divert attention from more recent, and far more troubling, relations between the two communities, epitomized by the Walking Purchase and the Paxton Boys. Weems—the popular author who gave us George Washington chopping down the cherry tree—published a biography of the founder in 1836, downplaying his subject's religious radicalism and holding Penn up as a model of virtuous moral rectitude. In other words, Weems's Penn was "first and foremost a talented and virtuous colonial leader, a pious family man [who] laid the groundwork for the successful colony that would bear his name." And in the mid-1830s, Edward Hicks, a painter and Quaker minister from Bucks County, Pennsylvania, produced a number of variations on West's original, insisting in a caption accompanying one of them that the treaty was "made without an oath and never broken." Whether or not the treaty ever actually took place—there is no solid record—it surely was not made in 1681, as Hicks claimed, since Penn did not arrive in America until the following year.[10]

* * *

As Penn's colony prepared to mark the two-hundredth anniversary of its founder's arrival on American shores, its General Assembly voted unanimously to seek the repatriation of Penn's remains from their rural resting place in England to a grand crypt built to house them in Center City Philadelphia. And so in 1881 Philadelphia lawyer George Harrison crossed the Atlantic to England on a mission on behalf of Henry Hoyt, the governor of Pennsylvania. In Harrison's (and the legislature's) view, there was no reason why Penn should rest in the remote English countryside when "it is for his labors on behalf of this country . . . that his name is celebrated in the annals of mankind." What better place to lay the founder to rest, once and for all, than in the heart of the city he had brought into being on the banks of the Delaware?[11]

After accepting the assignment, Harrison began to get an inkling that the task might be more challenging than he had been led to believe. Although he insisted that the plan to relocate Penn's remains had gained the approval of "eminent Friends in England" and numerous American luminaries and Penn descendants— and despite bearing credentials from Governor Hoyt, the city of Philadelphia, and the United States State Department—Harrison discovered upon arriving in England that the Jordans Meeting, which controlled the burial ground, had not been consulted. Worse yet, as word of Harrison's mission spread, Friends across England began to coalesce in opposition to it. Having read of Harrison's arrival in *The Times of London*, Leeds Friend George Tatham wrote to Richard Littleboy, a prominent member of the Jordans Meeting, to express his hope that "friends of thy meeting will have something to say on the above proposal. I hope you will see that it is <u>not</u> carried out." Dozens of similar communications arrived in Jordans, including one from Philadelphia Friend Thomas Scattergood, which denounced the proposal as "hastily and in my opinion <u>foolishly</u> acceded to by the authorities of the state of Pennsylvania and the city of Philadelphia."[12]

Littleboy and the Jordans Friends insisted that Penn himself had selected Jordans as his resting place, and that he chose that "quiet and retired spot" to rest with his wives and children, to say nothing of his dear friends the Ellwoods. The "pomp and circumstance" that would surely be involved in transporting his remains across the Atlantic, and the customary military parade that so often accompanied such undertakings, were "utterly repugnant to his known character and sentiments." After an unprofitable meeting between Harrison and the Littleboy brothers (Richard and John, who was Clerk of Jordans Meeting) on July 18, the two sides traded arguments and rebuttals in the pages of the London *Times*.[13]

Harrison doubted that the Jordans Friends really held legal control over the burial ground, and he disputed their claim that, due to earlier removal of the Penn headstones, no one knew exactly where Penn was buried. (Harrison insisted that "everyone knew" that Penn had been buried in a leaden coffin.) He compared Penn's current resting place—"in the lowliest hollow . . . in an unfrequented neighborhood, whose very existence is comparatively unknown"—with the prospect of laying the founder to rest "in a tomb in the midst of his own square, laid out by himself in the center of the city of Philadelphia, where now are under construction its great public buildings, through whose avenues thousands must daily pass." Harrison referred, surely, to the ongoing construction of Philadelphia City Hall, although scholars have uncovered no obvious candidate for such a space in the building's blueprints. Although Harrison made an impassioned case, Littleboy's final response, written on behalf of the Jordans trustees on August 13, fired back that "the voice of William Penn speaks just as loudly from beneath the green turf at Jordans, as it could do from under the shadow of a stately dome in the city of Philadelphia."[14]

By August 15, having spent six weeks in London, Harrison received the final refusal and prepared to return to America. And so William Penn remains to this day, with Gulielma, Hannah and five of his young children, and with Thomas and Mary Ellwood, (somewhere) in the burial ground outside Jordans Meetinghouse in Buckinghamshire.

* * *

Those who sought to house Penn's remains in a grand tomb in the city he built were clearly aiming to secure his legacy. What is that legacy? What might we say about the rich, complex, and paradoxical life of William Penn as it has been traced in these pages? Penn's life and career brings home, of course, the inseparability of religion and politics in the early modern world. Although it is true that Penn used terms like "church" and "state," and that he insisted on a conceptual and institutional separation of the two in terms similar to those famously articulated later by John Locke, he did not adopt the kinds of dichotomies that twenty-first-century audiences, and least of all twenty-first-century *American* audiences, take for granted. For example, Penn's conversion to Quakerism—which modern readers might consider an obviously "religious" component of his identity—was simultaneously a *political* act. It took aim at established structures of power and privilege in English society, marked Penn as an outsider, barred him from a host of social and political opportunities, and opened him to a variety of political sanctions and repercussions. At the same time, Penn clearly considered "political" activism—his agitation for imprisoned and persecuted Dissenters, his colonizing venture in America, and his campaign for James's tolerationist agenda—a *religious* duty, part of his overriding responsibility to the Inner Light and to the Society of Friends. Although the Quaker Meeting and the corridors of governmental power were distinct institutions, and Penn's activities in one were not always popular among members of the other, religion and politics were inseparable for him. Failing to appreciate the ways in which the two were fused in Penn's outlook and, indeed, in his life yields a truncated understanding of the significance of his accomplishments both in England and in America. I have attempted, in this book, to offer neither a "political" nor a "religious" life of Penn, but rather one that sees the two terms as different ways of describing the dynamics that influenced Penn's life and career.

Similarly, we should not draw a sharp distinction between Penn the Englishman and Penn the American. On the one hand, despite laying the groundwork for an American colony and working closely with other proprietors for nearly forty years, Penn's intellectual, religious, social, and political center of gravity always remained in England. He was deeply and profoundly shaped by the political and religious conflicts of the mid-seventeenth century. Viewing Penn simply as an "American founder" underplays his extended absences from Pennsylvania and his continued preoccupations with events in England. Despite his suggestion in 1683 that he was "like to be an adopted American," no such adoption ever really took place. On the other hand, Penn was no ordinary Restoration Dissenter. He was proprietor and governor of a major American colony and a Fellow of the Royal Society deeply committed to the project of imperial expansion. I have attempted to offer a broader, Atlantic perspective on Penn's life in these pages, one that refuses to divide the "English" from the "American" Penn, suggesting that in Penn's case English and American perspectives shared borders as fluid as the ocean that separated and connected them.

* * *

Although Penn was hardly the only theorist of toleration in seventeenth-century England, and Pennsylvania was hardly the only place to guarantee rights of conscience to its settlers, Penn's life and career illustrate both the promise and the paradoxes of toleration in theory and practice, as it emerged in the early modern world. Penn envisioned a society that enshrined liberty of conscience as its fundamental principle, to the degree that he pronounced it unalterable in the Charter of Privileges in 1701 even as he backed away from almost all the institutional arrangements he had embraced in his original founding documents. Penn also took pains to ensure the existence of representative political institutions, which embodied the people's consent, though he surely took no pleasure in the fact that those institutions' ideas about how Pennsylvania society should be governed turned out to differ markedly from his own. In the heady days of 1681 and 1682, he surely never imagined—or if he did, he quickly put it out of his mind—that his colonists' views could diverge so sharply from his own intentions for Pennsylvania.

But what were those intentions? Penn's ambivalence regarding Pennsylvania and scholars' subsequent attempts to assess the colony's developments often embrace Penn's description of his colony as a "holy experiment." Pennsylvania historian Edwin Bronner once wrote that "the founding of colonial Pennsylvania was a great success," and that as a colonizing venture, "the founding of Pennsylvania was a triumph for William Penn and those who joined with him in the undertaking." He continued, however, by claiming that "the 'holy experiment,' as Penn himself understood the term, was a failure." "The holy experiment, which Penn had held up to the world to examine in 1682," he wrote, "[seemed] shopworn and tawdry" just a decade later.[15]

But what might Penn have meant by using the enticing image of an experiment, holy or otherwise? In what sense did he consider his colony to be an "experiment"? The longstanding view is influenced by a certain notion of science, and the importance of testing theories or hypotheses by observation of phenomena. (Penn was, of course, made a Fellow of the Royal Society just before he left for America, so there is something to this idea.) On this view, the idea of an experiment involves "a carefully designed procedure, verification . . . repetition and independent replication, followed rapidly by dissemination. The experiment was intended to answer a [particular] question." Seen this way, Pennsylvania would "answer the question" of whether people of different faiths could live together in (relative) harmony and build a society where all worked together for the common good in support of their shared civil interest. In other words, the "holy experiment" was meant to test a theory: the theory that religious diversity was compatible with political security, that toleration would lead not to a rekindling of civil war but rather to a pacific, godly, and prosperous society. In this understanding of a holy experiment, the theory that Penn had been articulating for more than a decade in England would be vindicated—or not—by the ensuing history of his colony.[16]

But this understanding may not at all be what Penn had in mind. J. William Frost has argued that there were multiple senses of the term "experiment" in circulation during Penn's time, and that he may well have used the term not in its scientific sense but as a synonym for "experience." For example, when recounting his conversion experience in the pages of his *Journal*, George Fox wrote that he came to know God's design "experimentally," or by experience. And Penn described himself as "not without some knowledge experimental of what I say" in justifying Quakerism's doctrines early in his career as a controversialist. On this understanding of what an experiment means, Penn saw his colony as a "holy place," or a place where holiness could be experienced, and not necessarily a controlled procedure to validate a hypothesis.[17]

It seems unlikely that we will ever know precisely what Penn meant when he used this famous phrase. But it is also worth noting that the term "holy experiment" occurs just one time, in a piece of private correspondence. Had Penn intended to hold up the notion of a "holy experiment" before the wider world, we might expect him to have repeated the term, or to invoke it in public contexts, but he didn't. In addition, notwithstanding Penn's reliance on networks of Quakers to entice settlers to his province, the public face of Penn's promotional efforts often downplayed its Quaker dimensions. The English version of *Some account* nowhere mentions a "holy experiment" for the cause of religious liberty. Jean Soderlund attributes the omission of any mention of Penn's religious intentions for the colony to the fact that he was already widely known as a Quaker; this explanation is likely true, but the silence is still worth noting.[18]

In fact, it may be the case that continuing to think of Pennsylvania as a "holy experiment" makes it almost impossible to assess what actually *did* occur over the colony's first few decades. Experiments, after all, lend themselves almost automatically to the language of "failure" and "success." Such an orientation then leads us to ask why such an experiment failed and who or what was responsible for its failure, and to engage in a kind of highly politicized blame game: Penn's inattentiveness or demanding nature, quarrelsome Pennsylvania Quaker elites, David Lloyd, Randolph and Quary, Crown officials all.

In fact, most of the promising recent scholarship on Pennsylvania's early history has largely eschewed questions about "holy experiments" and looked more carefully at the actual, complex development of the place. Jessica Roney has identified colonial Philadelphia as a seedbed of American civic life and voluntary association, emphasizing the concrete ways in which Pennsylvania's people, who arrived in the colony for any number of reasons, navigated the challenges of their common lives. Elizabeth Milroy has focused on the city's layout and the way in which it both drew on and departed from previous city plans (either Paris's broad avenues, or the various plans for rebuilding London after the fire of 1666) and seventeenth-century formal gardens like London's St. James Park. John Smolenski has advanced an interpretation that views Pennsylvania as producing a "creole Quakerism" in which Old World practices were transformed by American realities. Jean Soderlund has brought to life the complex native world that predated Penn's colony and the ways in which dynamics from that preexistent social reality provided the context within which Penn and the Pennsylvanians operated. Jane Calvert views Penn's colony as part of a larger phenomenon, "Quaker constitutionalism," that stretched down to the Revolution and continues to animate political and legal discourse to this day. Evan Haefeli has pointed out that Pennsylvania was hardly the only place to guarantee rights of conscience to its settlers, and that profitable comparisons can be drawn to a range of other places, from American colonies like Rhode Island and Carolina to more far-flung settlements such as Jamaica and Barbados. Patrick Erben has explored the ways in which Pennsylvanians bridged linguistic and cultural divides in an attempt to create an inclusive community in a situation where diversity predominated. And these are only a few examples of a vibrant and growing body of scholarship.[19]

These interpretations of early Pennsylvania tend to downplay the notion of a singular "holy experiment"—whatever that might have meant—and instead show the vibrant, disputatious, utopian society that was set in motion as its ambitious young founder and the thousands of Europeans who took up his invitation interacted with the native and hybrid worlds that were already well established on the ground in America. Born out of a unique constellation of political events in England, nurtured by the founder's largely unsuccessful decade-long campaign for religious toleration in his home country, and shaped by Penn's earlier experiences in Ireland, France, Germany, Holland, and West Jersey, Pennsylvania's founding embodied the high hopes of a young activist for liberty of conscience. Like so many other utopians, Penn was deeply disappointed with the results. But there are surely many reasons to think that "holy experiment" does not exhaust the profitable ways of understanding Pennsylvania. The aspirations to godliness, unity, harmony, and Quaker consensus were surely part of what Penn had in mind when he set out to create "Penn's woods." But his holy experiment had political, economic, civic, cultural, and architectural dimensions as well, dimensions that we would do well to remember when attempting to come to grips with its complex origins and development, and the complex legacy it shares with its founder.

* * *

Three hundred years after his death, William Penn remains a vibrant image in American culture, although, as I have noted elsewhere, he is "a figure whom many know a little, but few know well." Some of the more noteworthy images, of course, include the pastoral scenes offered by West and Hicks, not to mention Alexander Milne Calder's thirty-seven-foot-tall bronze statue of Penn that looms over Philadelphia from atop City Hall. Readers of this account of Penn's life who venture to Pennsylvania or New Jersey will notice familiar names: Logan Square and Callowhill Street in Philadelphia; Norristown and Springettsbury, Pennsylvania; and Pennington (with an added "n"), New Jersey, to name just a few. And of course the image of Quakers in America has long been associated with the food company that bears their name, and the legend that Penn is "the man on the Quaker Oats box" persists, despite evidence to the contrary: company officials insist that his name is Larry.[20]

In the end, perhaps there is something appropriate about the honorary American citizenship granted to William and Hannah Penn in 1984 by President Ronald Reagan. Just six other individuals, including Winston Churchill, Mother Teresa, and the Marquis de Lafayette, have been so honored, and Hannah Penn was the first woman. That the country did not even exist for fifty years after Hannah's death, and sixty years after William's, appears to have been no obstacle to a nation eager to claim them as its own. And in fact it may be quite fitting, since Penn did, after all, express his hope that God would make his Pennsylvania "the seed of a nation." The notion of Pennsylvania as the origin of a nation sits uneasily, of course, alongside the fact that Penn was a latecomer to the enterprise of American colonization, and that his colony was shoehorned in between the preexisting settlements of New York to the north, New Jersey to the east, and Maryland to the south. And it must also share conceptual space in the American founding myth with claims that predated it, like John Winthrop's evocation of Massachusetts Bay as "a city on a hill." But it does suggest a more capacious and constructive understanding of the relationship between his settlement and the others that had already been planted there, and the common American concerns that those colonies came to see themselves as sharing over the next century, than the more insular notion of a Quaker "holy experiment."[21]

And so it was that when representatives from those colonies gathered in 1776, to "assume among the powers of the earth, the separate and equal station to which the Laws of Nature and of Nature's God entitle them," they did so in the capital city of Penn's "seed of a nation," which would later go on, briefly, to serve as that nation's capital. And a dozen years later, when another body of representatives gathered, this time to craft a governing document to organize the common affairs of those states under a more robust central government empowered to carry out the basic tasks of governance, Philadelphia, not surprisingly, once again played host. Surely the idea of an American political future separate from England hardly crossed Penn's mind, but he no doubt would note that the very first amendment later appended to that governing document forbade the legislative branch from making any "law respecting an establishment of religion, or prohibiting the free exercise thereof; or abridging the freedom of speech, or of the press; or the right of the people peaceably to assemble, and to petition the Government for a redress of grievances." He himself had invoked that family of rights—worship, speech, press, assembly, petitioning—many times in the course of his long career, and he considered them essential to living a life of conscientious integrity in a diverse world.[22]

Over the intervening years, of course—three hundred since Penn's death, more than two hundred since the ratification of the First Amendment—debates over the meaning, extent, and ramifications of religious liberty remain unsettled, its foundations widely agreed upon in the abstract while remaining deeply contentious in practice. Basic freedom of worship, such as was sought by tolerationists in Penn's generation, no longer represents the most serious obstacle to liberty of conscience in many contemporary societies. That said, even in the country that likes to claim religious freedom as its signal contribution to modern political life, not all religious communities are created equal. The same religious liberty that gave rise to the extraordinary American religious marketplace served to marginalize and exclude Catholics, Jews, and a host of other religious communities, and creative interpretations of zoning and public safety regulations are still employed to prevent the building of mosques in some American communities. But without question, the right to worship with like-minded believers, itself, hardly arouses the sort of opposition faced by Penn and his tolerationist contemporaries.

But these debates will never, of course, be fully settled, and the achievements remain precarious and contested, since religious values contribute in complex and subtle ways to personal and collective identity, and to the ways in which individuals and groups navigate their world. After all, as we have seen, Quakers continued to argue against oaths and military service long after they had achieved the liberty to worship. Likewise, members of contemporary religious communities continue to advocate for constitutional protection of practices that flow from their most fundamental commitments. Questions of gender, sexuality, and reproductive choice illustrate the powerful contemporary ways in which conscience to intertwine with the exercise of social and political power. Debates over the meaning, extent, and limitations of claims of conscience continue to unsettle political discourse in the United States and around the world. Perhaps it is in the persistence of these debates, rather than in the purported success or failure of any particular "holy experiment," that William Penn's legacy will prove most enduring.

MAPS

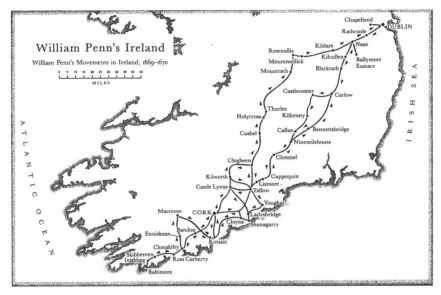

1. William Penn's Ireland: William Penn's movements in Ireland, 1669–1670. From *The Papers of William Penn, Volume 1: 1644–1679*, ed. Mary Maples Dunn and Richard S. Dunn (Philadelphia: University of Pennsylvania Press, 1981), p. 104. Reprinted with permission of the University of Pennsylvania Press.

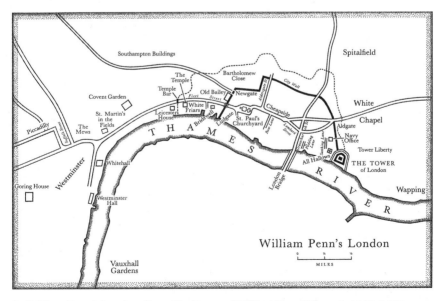

2. William Penn's London. From *The Papers of William Penn, Volume 1: 1644–1679*, ed. Mary Maples Dunn and Richard S. Dunn (Philadelphia: University of Pennsylvania Press, 1981), p. 178. Reprinted with permission of the University of Pennsylvania Press.

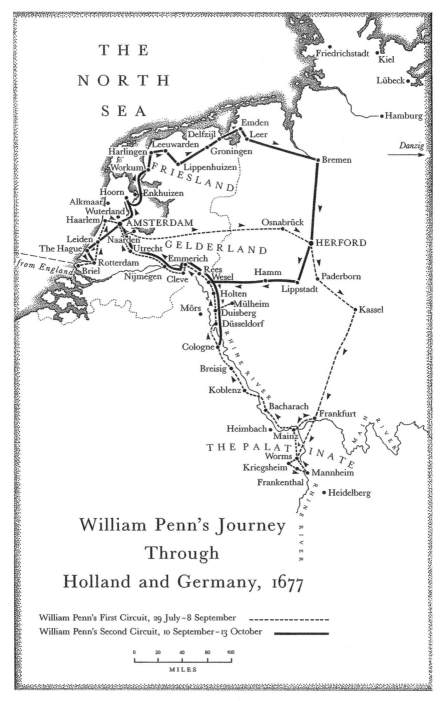

THE

NORTH

SEA

Friedrichstadt • • Kiel

Lübeck •

• Hamburg

Danzig

Emden
Delfzijl • Leer
Leeuwarden
Harlingen • Groningen
Workum • Lippenhuizen
F R I E S L A N D
Hoorn • Enkhuizen
Alkmaar •
Wuterland
Haarlem • • AMSTERDAM
Leiden • Naarden
The Hague • Utrecht G E L D E R L A N D
from England • Rotterdam Emmerich
• Briel Nijmegen Cleve Rées
Wesel

Bremen

Osnabrück

HERFORD

Paderborn

Hamm
Lippstadt

Holten
Mörs • • Mülheim
• Duisberg
• Düsseldorf

Kassel

Cologne •

R H I N E   R I V E R

Breisig •

Koblenz •

Bacharach
Frankfurt

Heimbach •
Mainz
THE PALAT I N A T E
Worms
Kriegsheim • • Mannheim
Frankenthal
• Heidelberg

M A I N   R I V E R

R H I N E   R I V E R

William Penn's Journey

Through

Holland and Germany, 1677

William Penn's First Circuit, 29 July – 8 September – – – – – – – –
William Penn's Second Circuit, 10 September – 13 October ————

0   20   40   80   100

MILES

3. William Penn's journey through Holland and Germany, 1677. From *The Papers of William Penn, Volume 1: 1644–1679*, ed. Mary Maples Dunn and Richard S. Dunn (Philadelphia: University of Pennsylvania Press, 1981), p. 429. Reprinted with permission of the University of Pennsylvania Press.

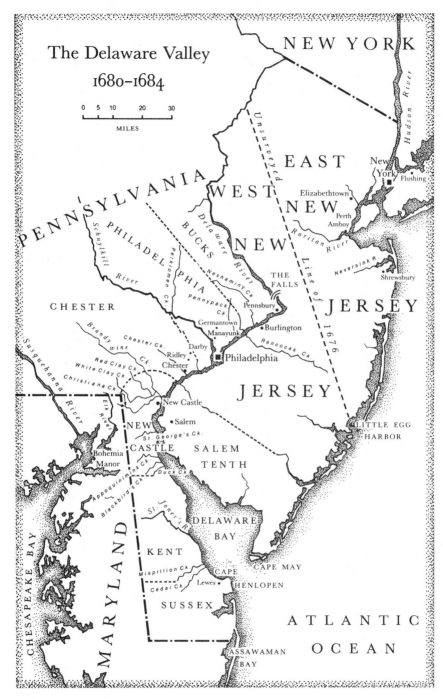

4. The Delaware Valley, 1680–1684. From *The Papers of William Penn, Volume 2: 1680–1684*, ed. Mary Maples Dunn and Richard S. Dunn (Philadelphia: University of Pennsylvania Press, 1981), p. 307. Reprinted with permission of the University of Pennsylvania Press.

NOTES

Prologue

1. Prynne, *Histrio-mastix*; Lilburne, *A work of the beast*, 31. For the history of the Fleet from its earliest days until its eventual demolition in 1846, see Brown, *A History of the Fleet Prison*; and Thornbury, "The Fleet Prison."
2. Newton, "Clandestine Marriage in Early Modern London," 159, 174; see, more generally, Brown, "The Rise and Fall of the Fleet Marriages," and Burn, *The Fleet Registers*.
3. *A brief collection*; Lilburne, *Liberty vindicated against slavery*; Pitt, *Cry of the oppressed*, Preface.
4. Dunn, "William Penn and the Selling of Pennsylvania," 328.
5. Isaac Norris to James Logan, March 6, 1708, *Penn-Logan* II: 262.
6. The phrase "sober people of all sorts" is from the Fundamental Constitutions of Pennsylvania, summer 1681, *PWP* II: 143.

Chapter 1

1. For the full text of the epitaph, see Penn, *Memorials*, II: 580. Additional images may be found at http://www.stmaryredcliffe.co.uk/st-mary-redcliffe-and-the-penn-family.html.
2. Will of Sir William Penn, January 20, 1670, *PWP* I: 149.
3. Conner, *Sir William Penn*; Jenkins, *Family of William Penn*, 2, 151–152; on the Penn grandchildren buried at Holy Trinity Penn, see http://holytrinityandstmargarets.co.uk/about/.
4. Grant, *Quaker and Courtier*, 3–4. Sybil Penn, also known as the "Grey Lady of Hampton Court," has apparently haunted the palace since her tomb was disturbed in 1829; see http://www.dailymail.co.uk/news/article-2967734/Is-spooky-apparition-Grey-Lady-Hampton-Court-Schoolgirls-claim-captured-ghost-servant-died-small-pox-nursing-Elizabeth-palace.html.
5. For various accounts of William Penn of Minety, see *Quakeriana* 1: 6–7, 154–155; Grant, *Quaker and Courtier*, 4; Jenkins, *Family of William Penn*, 7. Lea, *Genealogical Gleanings*, claims that the Glastonbury monk was actually David, William of Minety's father (3). John Aubrey wrote that "At Mintie is an abundance of wild mint, from whence the village is denominated": see Aubrey, *Natural history of Wiltshire*, 49. The will of William Penn of Minety is in Lea, *Genealogical Gleanings*, 9; it is also reprinted, along with a variety of related wills and family memoranda, in Coleman, *A Pedigree and Genealogical Notes*.
6. Jenkins, *Family*, 5; Watson, *Annals*, I: 119; "I chose New Wales," To Robert Turner, March 5, 1681, *PWP* II: 83.
7. Jordan, *Colonial and Revolutionary Families*, I: 2–3; Lea, *Genealogical Gleanings*, 327–328.
8. Penn, *Memorials*, I: 1–2; quotations from Sacks, *The Widening Gate*, 19, 12, 52–53, 54.

9. Penn, *Memorials*, I: 1, 3. For the events in Giles's life recounted in this paragraph see the following entries in *CSP Domestic, Charles I*: October 24, 1630, #78 (Tetuan); Undated 1631, #86 (hawks); December 1636, #51 (voyage for Sallee), January 7, 1637, #45 (slow progress of preparations); January 14, 1637, #86 ("knowledge of the people"); Undated 1637, #108 ("expected"); November 30, 1637, #88 ("a man").

10. George Penn's "humble remonstrance" is reprinted in Penn, *Memorials*, I: 552–553.

11. Pepys, *Diary*, entry for September 29, 1661; Penn, *Memorials*, II: 555–556. On Pepys, see Tomalin, *Samuel Pepys*.

12. "educated," Penn, *Memorials*, I: 2–3, "If God ever," I: 94.

13. Penn, *Memorials*, I: 52.

14. "the daughter," Penn, *Memorials*, II: 572; "well-looked," Pepys; *Diary*, entry for August 19, 1664; "unworldly," Harrison, *Remains*, 15. Details about the marriage and the lands that Margaret (van der Schuren) Penn inherited from her first husband are scanty, but an intriguing document at the Clare County (Ireland) library does provide important information: see Lynch, "Burkes and Jasper's Pound."

15. Church records indicate the marriage of widow Margaret van der Schuren with then Captain Penn: "1643. June 6th. William Penne and Margaret van der Schuren, by Dr Dyke, Lecturer . . . witness Mr Roach, churchwarden then." If accurate, Pepys's account would suggest that the wedding took place on January 6, 1644, rather than June 6, 1643. Not only would I suggest that, when forced to choose between Pepys and a church register, we should probably go with the church register, but the June 6 date has been confirmed as well by the Rt. Rev. Dr. Stephen Platten, Chaplain to St. Martin-within-Ludgate (personal correspondence, January 9, 2018).

16. "Description of house on Tower Hill."

17. Ship's journal reprinted in Penn, *Memorials*, I: 104.

18. "Twas upon a Monday," Aubrey, *Brief lives*, 238. For broader background on the world into which Penn was born, see, among the many histories of London, Porter, *London: A Social History*, esp. chs. 3–6; and *London: A Social and Cultural History*.

19. Baptism, October 23, 1644, *PWP* I: 30. For the history of All Hallows, see *All Hallows by the Tower*, and Grummet, *All Hallows*. I owe further thanks to Adey Grummet at All Hallows for helpful information about the rectors (personal correspondence, October 2016).

20. Brailsford, *Making of William Penn*, chs. 2 and 3; Penn, *Memorials*, vol. I.

21. Penn, *Memorials*, I: 254–255, ch. 3; Knighton, "Penn, Sir William."

22. "disease-ridden," Moretta, *William Penn*, 4; George Fox defended Penn's wig-wearing in a letter to Henry Sidon, May 25, 1677, *PWP* I: 376–377.

23. For the size of the town, see Powell, *History of the County of Essex*, 317–318. For Chigwell and Wanstead more generally see Lysons, *The Environs of London*, IV: 111–129 and 231–244, respectively. Scholars are divided on whether the family lived in Chigwell, where Penn attended school, or Wanstead, seven miles to the south. Moretta (*William Penn*, 10) claims that Margaret relocated to Wanstead, as do Peare (*William Penn*, 14) and Janney (*Life of William Penn*, 22). Myers sides with Chigwell (*William Penn's Early Life in Brief*, 24), as does Brailsford (*Making of William Penn*, ch. 4). In today's urban geography, both Wanstead and Chigwell have Underground stops on the Hainault loop of the Central Line.

    The timing of the move has also puzzled biographers, some of whom suggest that Margaret Penn took her son from London shortly after his baptism. Others maintain that the move came several years later, before which time Margaret and young William had lived in the house on Tower Hill. Those suggesting an earlier departure from London include Stoughton (*William Penn*, 3) and Jenkins (*Family*, 31). Moretta mentions an August 1645 recall to London and ensuing visit to his wife and two-year-old son (the son born in October 1644). Moretta seems to be referring to Admiral Penn's 1646 recall to London, which was not an arrest but rather for repairs to his ship. Moretta recounts, a bit breathlessly, that "When [Admiral Penn] stepped into his London home [in 1645], he found a frightened wife who had endured over a year of civil war without her husband and had nursed her son through smallpox" (*William Penn*, 4); the wording here and at other places in Moretta's account of Penn's younger years closely parallels Peare's.

24. "a demanding regime," Coffey and Lim, "Introduction," in *Cambridge Companion to Puritanism*, 4.

25. "particularly godly," Spurr, *English Puritanism*, 192; "steeped in Puritanism," Stoughton, *William Penn*, 6; "the most life," Hampden quoted in Spurr, *English Puritanism*, 193. See also Webster, *Godly Clergy*, 16, 36. East Anglia is one of the pathways explored in Fisher, *Albion's Seed*.

26. Stoughton, *William Penn*, 5–6. The petition was printed as a broadside and published in London; see *To the right honourable the knights, citizens, and burgesses of the Commons House of Parliament*; and also Davids, *Annals of Evangelical Nonconformity in the County of Essex*, 220–224.

27. Age 9 claim from Chigwell School website on Penn House: https://www.chigwell-school.org/forms-houses/. I owe a debt of gratitude to Ms. Gillian Punt, the Chigwell School's Development Office Manager, for showing me around the school, including the Penn window itself, during summer 2016. "All Chigwellians," Swallow, *Chigwell Register*, 14. This tradition is certainly well established: a dozen pages on, the *Register* reports that Penn's early boyhood was spent in nearby Wanstead, with the boy "going daily to Chigwell School" (*Chigwell Register*, 26).

28. Moretta, *William Penn*, 7, 8. Moretta's claims that young Penn was "at the top of his class in all of his subjects," and that the teachers at Chigwell were "pedantic, stuffy, and somewhat effeminate personalities," seem hard to credit, since we do not know who those teachers were, nor who else attended the school, nor how Penn's contemporaries performed in their studies. On the school and the archbishop, see Carlisle, *A Concise Description*, I: 415–423; Page and Round, *Victoria History*, II: 544; and Cranfield, "Harsnett, Samuel."

29. For the archbishop's instructions, see *Chigwell Register*, 18–19; they called for a schoolmaster skilled not only in math and figures but in teaching penmanship, including the widely used secretary hand (which noted penman Martin Billingsley called the "usuall hand of England"; see *The pen's excellencie*, 10). The standard texts were Cleonard's *Greek Grammar* and Lily's *Short introduction of grammar*; see Page and Round, *Victoria History*, II: 544–545.

30. Aubrey, *Brief lives*, 238; list of masters of Chigwell in Stott, "Early History of Chigwell School," 6–8. How the Chigwell curriculum played out in the life of the Founder is difficult to know. Peare refers to "the orthodox influence of Chigwell" on the young Penn (*William Penn*, 15), but hard evidence is scanty. Brailsford finds the origins of Penn's aversion to swearing, lying, and cursing in his experience at Chigwell, whose founding ordinances singled out these vices for "severe chastisement" (Page and Round, *Victoria History*, II: 545); and the democratic impulses in Penn's 1682 Frame of Government to the "mingling of castes" at Chigwell thirty-odd years earlier (Brailsford, *Making of William Penn*, 28–29; also Hull, *William Penn*, 68–69).

31. "mighty lively," Aubrey, *Brief lives*, 239. Aubrey was an Original Fellow of the Royal Society, elected in 1663; Penn was elected in November 1681, eight months after he received his colonial charter. For the letter in question, see To John Aubrey, June 13, 1683, *PWP* II: 395–396. More generally, on Aubrey, see Scurr, *John Aubrey*. Royal Society details from the Society's website, at https://docs.google.com/spreadsheets/d/1RVVZY00MZNrK2YCTTzVrbTFH2t3RxoAZah128gQR-NM/pubhtml#.

32. "solitary and spiritual," To Mary Pennyman, November 22, 1673, *PWP* I: 265; "delighted in retirement" and "first sense," Aubrey, *Brief lives*, 238; "visited my soul," To the Countess, September 3, 1677, *PWP* I: 460; "the Lord first appeared," Travels in Holland and Germany, September 13, 1677, *PWP* I: 476.

33. Pestana, *English Conquest of Jamaica*, 7; also Brailsford, *Making of William Penn*, ch. 6.

34. Pestana, *English Conquest of Jamaica*, chs. 1–5.

35. See Worden, "Oliver Cromwell and the Sin of Achan." Also Penn, *Memorials*, II: ch. 5. Family details from Jordan, *Family*, 4; *PWP* I: 151n3; and Brailsford, *Making of William Penn*, 59.

36. Ring, *Macroom Through the Mists of Time*, ch. 2; Brailsford, *Making of William Penn*, ch. 7.

37. See Canny, "Ideology of English Colonization."

38. Canny, *Making Ireland British*, 572.

39. "not the product," Canny, *Making Ireland British*, 577; Spenser, *A view of the present state of Ireland*. On the Nine Years' War, see Morgan, *Tyrone's Rebellion*. The literature on Spenser and Ireland is extensive: see, for just a sampling, Maley, "A View of the Present State of Ireland," and, on the broader import of Spenser in Irish cultural memory, Frawley, "Edmund Spenser and Transhistorical Memory in Ireland."

40. Canny, *Making Ireland British*, 547.

41. Ring, *Macroom Through the Mists of Time*, 87–89.

42. "Convincement of William Penn," 22.
43. To William Burroughs, c. 1675, *PWP* I: 303.

Chapter 2

1. "The grandest," Beddard, "Restoration Oxford," 822; "Those who," Porter, "University and Society," 25.
2. "it was only," Curthoys, *Cardinal's College*, 46, 48; "powerhouse," Tyacke, "Introduction," 6; Porter, "University and Society," 41.
3. "a golden age," Tyacke, "Introduction," 2; see also Taylor, "The Royal Visit to Oxford"; Elliott and Buttrey, "The Royal Plays at Christ Church"; Curthoys, *Cardinal's College*, 102, 108; Roy and Reinhart, "Oxford and the Civil Wars," 694–695.
4. "a remarkable dean," Curthoys, *Cardinal's College*, 111; Worden notes Owen's "institutional caution" ("Cromwellian Oxford," 753). Penn recounts the treatment of Quakers in Oxford in Penn and Whitehead, *Serious Apology*, 184; "fellow sufferers," Angell, "William Penn's Debts," 167. On Owen more generally, whom Worden describes Owen as "direct[ing] the dissenting faction of the college" ("Cromwellian Oxford," 849), see Toon, *God's Statesman*. On the tolerationist alliance during the late 1660s, and Penn's and Owen's roles in it, see Murphy, *Liberty, Conscience, and Toleration*, ch. 2; De Krey, *London and the Restoration*; and De Krey, "Rethinking the Restoration."
5. Alumni Aedis Christi (Christ Church admissions register), October 26, 1660; Foster, *Alumni Oxonsiensis*, 1141; Oxford University matriculation register 1648–1662, p. 22. Thanks to Anna Petre of the Oxford University Archives for providing me with an image of these pages and for the Bodleian staff for allowing me to view the originals. As shown by the Christ Church records (Christ Church Cautions Book 1657–1675), the caution money was received on July 29, 1660 (p. 89), and paid back to his tutor, John Vincent, on Penn's behalf, on May 31, 1662 (p. 101). Oxford University register of subscription at matriculation, 1660–1693, p. 5; "sons of the social elite," Porter, "University and Society," 36; Bill, *Education at Christ Church*, 175.
6. "intransigent episcopalian," Beddard, "Restoration Oxford," 829; "linchpin," Worden, "Cromwellian Oxford," 847–850; "became," Beddard, "Restoration Oxford," 853.
7. "the acquisition," Feingold, "The Humanities," 215. The choice of a tutor was "of almost paramount importance," since in addition to overseeing academic pursuits the tutor acted *in loco parentis* for the student; see Porter, "University and Society," 64. See also Tyacke, "Introduction," 8–9; Bill, *Education at Christ Church*; Feingold, "The Humanities," 305.

   That an individual who would go on to such fame spent two years at one of the world's most prominent institutions of higher learning and left so sparse a record has driven many of Penn's biographers to fanciful speculation. We simply don't know, for example, whether Penn "began to bond with [a] small group of nonconformist lads," as one biographer has put it (Moretta, *William Penn*, 23). Another implied that Penn and John Locke were "comrades" (Janney, *Life of William Penn*, 23), an assertion for which no evidence exists. And there is certainly no evidence that Penn was already a Quaker sympathizer by the time he left Oxford in 1662, as Rupert Holland has suggested (*William Penn*, 7–8). For the verses, see "Verses on the Death of Henry, Duke of Gloucester," November 1660, *PWP* I: 30–31.
8. Pepys, *Diary*, entry for April 22, 1661. On Pepys's connection with Sir William Penn, see Knighton, *Pepys and the Navy*, 18–24.
9. "a great sufferer," To Mary Pennyman, November 22, 1673, *PWP* I: 264; "my persecution," *PWP* I: 476; Pepys, *Diary*, entries for January 22 and 25, 1662.
10. "expelled," "Convincement," 22; "banished," *PWP* I: 476; "many of you," *Quakerism, a new nickname*, 233–234.
11. Harris, "Sexual and Religious Libertinism"; Endy, *William Penn*, 95–97; Pepys, *Diary*, entries for March 16, 1662, and April 28, 1662.
12. "sociable and hospitable," Tomalin, *Samuel Pepys*, 123; for the increased tensions see Tomalin, *Samuel Pepys*, 139–141; Brailsford, *Making of William Penn*, 109–110.
13. Brailsford, *Making of William Penn*, ch. 13.
14. Black, *The British and the Grand Tour*, 5–6; "a fully established," Chaney, *Evolution of the Grand Tour*, 58.

15. "great opportunity," Black, *The British and the Grand Tour*, 109; see also Brailsford, *Making of William Penn*, chs. 13 and 14.
16. See Kenyon, *Robert Spencer*; and Speck, "Spencer, Robert."
17. "without contest," Armstrong, *Calvinism and the Amyraut Heresy*, xviii; Hagglund, "Guest editor's introduction." See also Fillet, "Les Relations."
18. Armstrong, *Calvinism and the Amyraut Heresy*, chs. 1, 2; Endy, *William Penn*, esp. ch. 5, at 228–256; Tolles and Alderfer, "Introduction," xxv. Both Amyraut and Penn were influenced by Lord Herbert of Cherbury's articulation, in his 1624 *De veritate* (translated to English in 1633), of the common elements of all religions.
19. "God wanted," Brockliss, *French Higher Education*, 248; "What Amyraut found," Angell, "William Penn's Debts," 164; "J. Calvin's," Penn, *England's present interest*, 41.
20. Details of curriculum from Hagglund, "Guest editor's introduction," 152–153; "heard," unknown author to Sir William Penn, April 24, 1664, *PWP* I: 31–32; Fillet, "Les relations," 125–126.
21. Pepys, *Diary*, entry for August 30, 1664; regarding William's attentions to Elizabeth, see *PWP* I: 33n1; "from thirteen years of age," To William Burroughs, c. 1675, *PWP* I: 303; "Ah Tyrant Lust," c. 1664, *PWP* I: 32; Kenyon, *Robert Spencer*, 6–7.
22. Penn, *No cross, no crown*, 2nd ed., 148–149; Ruff, *Violence in Early Modern Europe*, 91–92, 128–130.
23. "the third university," Holdsworth, *A Portrait of Lincoln's Inn*, 13; "a valuable foundation," Geiter, "Penn, William." Given Penn's short stay at the Inn, it seems unlikely that he actually "gained considerable knowledge of the law" at Lincoln's Inn (Myers, *Early Life in Brief*, 31).
24. "son and heir," *Records of the Honorable Society of Lincoln's Inn*, 295. On manucaptors, see Peacey, "Led by the Hand." The manucaptors signed the admissions register but are not reproduced in the print volume. I thank Frances Bellis, Assistant Librarian at Lincoln's Inn, for allowing me to consult the original registers. On Lincoln's Inn more generally, see Holdsworth, *A Portrait*.
25. On the chapel, see Spilsbury, *Lincoln's Inn*, 49–75.
26. "gangrenous inflammation," Mullet, *The Bubonic Plague in England*, 14.
27. Mullet, *The Bubonic Plague in England*, 48, 67–68, ch. 6; "the excuse," Shrewsbury, *A History of Bubonic Plague*, 484.
28. "rife among the seamen,"; Penn and Pett letter, *CSP Domestic, Charles II, 1665–1666*, October 25, 1665, #75; "notwithstanding," Defoe, *Journal*, 208; Shrewsbury, *History of the Bubonic Plague*, 485, 464; Moote and Moote, *The Great Plague*, esp. chs. 1, 2; On Milton and Ellwood, see Shorter, *Highways and Byways of Buckinghamshire*, ch. 15. Milton and Penn are intriguing figures to consider in tandem: Elizabeth Sauer brilliantly draws out some of these connections in "New Worlds and Holy Experiments."
29. Defoe, *Journal*, 212; Shrewsbury, *History*, 480–481; also Moote and Moote, *The Great Plague*, ch. 13.
30. Penn, *Memorials*, II: 296; Knighton, "Penn, Sir William."
31. To Sir William Penn, April 23, 1665, *PWP* I: 33–34.
32. To Sir William Penn, May 6, 1665, *PWP* I: 34–35.
33. To Sir William Penn, May 6, 1665, *PWP* I: 35.
34. "two theological giants," Angell, "William Penn's Debts," 168.

Chapter 3

1. "Mrs. Wallis," To Sir William Penn, May 6, 1665, *PWP* I: 34. More generally, see Wallis, "Who Was Colonel Wallis?"
2. Sir William Penn to Sir George Lane, February 8, 1666, *PWP* I: 39–40. See, more generally, Morgan, "The Cromwellian Conquest of Ireland"; and Horning, "The Irish Worlds of William Penn."
3. Wallis, "Who Was Colonel Wallis?," 12; "afford . . . all the Irish favor," From Sir William Penn, May 5, 1666, *PWP* I: 40; "my frame of mind," From Sir William Penn, February 2, 1667, *PWP* I: 43; "you know well," From Sir William Penn, June 1666, in Penn, *Memorials*, II: 234.

4. "serpent," Brailsford, *Making of William Penn*, 158; From Sir William Penn, February 2, 1667, *PWP* I: 43; Wallis, "Who Was Colonel Wallis?"

5. Details from Lynch, *Roger Boyle: First Earl of Orrery*, 53–56, 103.

6. "unpaid for months," Beckett, *The Making of Modern Ireland*, 128; Carte, *The Life of James, Duke of Ormond*, IV: 251–256.

7. "to his no small reputation," Captain Richard Rooth to Sir William Penn, July 19, 1666, in Penn, *Memorials*, II: 430; "youthful desires," From Sir William Penn, July 17, 1666, *PWP* I: 42; "God sending," Sir William Penn to the Duke of Ormond, August 7, 1666, in Penn, *Memorials*, II: 432–433.

8. "a shattered fleet," From Sir William Penn, June 1666, in Penn, *Memorials*, II: 397.

9. Quotation from Rege Sincera, *Observations*, 34.

10. For the purported (and likely apocryphal) comments by Bludworth, see Tinniswood, *By Permission of Heaven*, 44; Evelyn, *Diary*, entry for September 3, 1666, II: 21; Pepys, *Diary*, entries for September 4 and September 5, 1666. On Pepys and Sir William during the Fire, see Tomalin, *Samuel Pepys*, 224–226.

11. "even laboring in person," Evelyn, *Diary*, entry for September 6, 1666, II: 23.

12. "The negligence," Rege Sincera, *Obervations*, 27; "the heavy hand," *Observations*, 4.

13. "went again," Evelyn, *Diary*, entry for September 10, 1666, II: 26; "London was," Evelyn, *Diary*, entry for September 3, 1666, II: 21; "presented His Majesty," Evelyn, *Diary*, entry for September 13, 1666, II: 26; see also Downes, "Wren, Christopher." For the rebuilding process see Reddaway, *The Rebuilding of London*. On the lessons of rebuilding and the ways they might have informed Penn's thinking during the early 1680s, see Milroy, *The Grid and the River*, 15–17.

14. Pepys, *Diary*, entry for February 16, 1667; From Sir William Penn, May 21, 1667, *PWP* I: 46.

15. From Sir William Penn, in Penn, *Memorials*, II: 241.

16. "I have reason," From Sir William Penn, April 6, 1667, *PWP* I: 44; "I think," From Sir William Penn, April 9, 1667, *PWP* I: 45; "I know not," From Sir William Penn, May 21, 1667, *PWP* I: 46. Copies of the letters patent—both an abstract, and the letters in their entirety—are held in the Cork City and County Archives. See "Abstract from Patent" and "Patent to Sir William Penn."

17. "the rock," McCormick, *William Petty and the Ambitions of Political Arithmetic*, 117, also 99–103; see also Canny, "The Irish Background to Penn's Experiment," and Gallo, "William Penn, William Petty, and Surveying." See also Petty's own account of the Down Survey, published posthumously after its discovery in 1834: *The history of the survey of Ireland*.

18. From Sir William Penn, October 12, 1667, *PWP* I: 50; "repair to me," From Sir William Penn, October 22, 1667, *PWP* I: 50.

19. "new and heavenly-minded," Penn, Preface to Fox, *Journal*, n.p.; "there was none," Fox, *Journal*, 8.

20. See Benson, "That of God in Every Man."

21. This section draws on several of the definitive histories of Quakerism, including Moore, *Light in Their Consciences*; Braithwaite, *Beginnings*; and Ingle, *First Among Friends*. For an overview of Quakerism more generally, the best sources include *The Oxford Handbook of Quaker Studies*, and Dandelion, *The Quakers: A Very Short Introduction* on the role of women in the Society of Friends, see Mack, *Visionary Women*; and Weimer, "Elizabeth Hooton."

22. "creative moment," Braithwaite, *Beginnings*, 86; Moore, *Light*, 35; "was more than usually," Kunze, *Margaret Fell*, pp. 15, 32.

23. "the most brilliant," Braithwaite, *Beginnings*, 241; on Margaret Fell's role see Mack, *Visionary Women*, 216–219, 245–246; and Kunze, *Margaret Fell*. On convincement, see Tousley, "Sin, Convincement, Purity, and Perfection." "Convincement" also provides a way to distinguish those who become Quakers as a result of spiritual seeking and repentance from "Quakers by birth," who are born into the Society of Friends to Quaker parents.

24. Bowden, *History of the Society of Friends*, I: 121–122; Mack, *Visionary Women*, 256–260; Levy, "Puritanism in the Southern Colonies," 154; Weeks, *Southern Quakers and Slavery*, 7, 16–19; Haefeli, *New Netherland*, ch. 6; Murphy and Weimer, "Colonial Quakerism."

25. For the history of Quakerism in Ireland, written by early modern Irish Friends themselves, see Wight and Rutty, *History*; Holme and Fuller, *A brief relation*; and Edmundson, *Journal*. See also Greaves, *God's Other Children*, esp. 28–35, chs. 7 and 8; Douglas, *Beginnings of Quakerism in Ireland*; and for Cork more specifically, Harrison, *Cork City Quakers*. See also "Record of Friends Travelling in Ireland." Both of Penn's visits—in 1669 and 1698—are included in that document.

26. On Nayler, see Moore, *Light in Their Consciences*, ch. 3; Damrosch, *Sorrows of the Quaker Jesus*; Ingle, *First Among Friends*, esp. ch. 10. The gendered dynamics of the Nayler episode are explored in Mack, *Visionary Women*, 197–206.

27. "Convincement," 22.

28. "in a," From Lord Shannon, August 20, 1667, *PWP* I: 48–49; "the malice of," From Lord Shannon, October 14, 1667, *PWP* 1: 052.

29. See the two letters from Sir William Penn, October 12 and 22, 1667, *PWP* I: 50; quotations from *Ulmorum acherons*, 1, 2, 5, 6.

30. Carroll, "Thomas Loe"; "if he knew," "Convincement," 23.

31. "Convincement," 23; for the Quaker peace testimony see *A declaration from the harmless and innocent people of God, called Quakers*; also available online at http://www.quaker.org/peaceweb/pdecla07.html.

32. "Convincement," 23.

33. To the Earl of Orrery, November 4, 1667, *PWP* I: 51–52.

34. Ibid. Although only Penn's letter has survived, another letter was written on behalf of the group, with Penn as one signatory among many; see *PWP* I: 54n3.

35. From the Earl of Orrery, November 5, 1667, *PWP* I: 53.

36. "strengthening himself," "Convincement," 24; Bishop, *New England judged*; George Bishop to Sir William Penn, November 30, 1667, *PWP* I: 50.

37. "the gloomy and dark day," Penn's eulogy of Coale in *Books and divers epistles*, 15; "kept his temper," "Convincement," 24. Coale's writings are collected in Coale, *The books and divers epistles of the faithful servant of the Lord Josiah Coale*. Years later, Lodowick Muggleton would claim to have hastened Coale's death by putting a curse on him, a claim that drew a scathing rebuke from William Penn.

38. "Convincement," 24. Just a year later, he would elaborate more than a dozen specific reasons for this Quaker practice in the first edition of *No cross, no crown*.

39. "Convincement," 24.

40. Ibid., 24–25.

41. Ibid., 25.

42. Ibid., 25–26.

43. Besse, in Penn, *A Collection of the Works*, I: 4; Pepys, *Diary*, entry from December 29, 1667. Pepys's dismissive remarks about Penn's Quakerism did not prevent him from leaving the admiral's son a small gift in his will upon his death in 1703. See Tomalin, *Samuel Pepys*, 371.

44. "who at that time," The Two Kingdoms, 1668, *PWP* I: 60; "I [have] been made," Two Kingdoms, 1668, *PWP* I: 67.

45. "rushed into the scrimmage," Barbour, "The Young Controversialist," 16.

46. Quotations from To Isaac Penington, October 17, 1667, *PWP* I: 70–71. Penn gave Gulielma an abbreviated account of Loe's death in a letter of October 7, 1667, *PWP* I: 68. On Penn's developing relationship with Whitehead see Brailsford, *Making of William Penn*, ch. 26.

47. Quotations from Clapham, *A guide to the true religion*, 62, 63–64, 18; Clapham, *Full discovery*, ch. 12. Clapham was hardly the only one denouncing Quakers as blasphemers: see Manning, "Accusations of Blasphemy in English Anti-Quaker Polemic." The narrative in the following pages draws on Barbour, "The Young Controversialist."

48. Penn, *The guide mistaken*, 4, 54.

49. Ibid., 62–63.

50. Danson had participated in a public dispute with Quakers Whitehead, Richard Hubberthorne, and Samuel Fischer in the spring of 1659—later published as Danson, *The Quakers' folly*—in which he referred to Quakerism as "a deformed monster" [To the reader].

51. Penn's narrative as related in the next few paragraphs is taken from the preface, "To the Unprejudiced Reader," in *The sandy foundation shaken*. "Prove all things" refers to 1 Thessalonians 5:21.

52. Vincent, *Foundation*, 9.

53. "zealous endeavor," ibid., 10. Milton, "On the New Forcers of Conscience Under the Long Parliament."

54. Barbour, "Young Controversialist," 19. Vincent tells the story somewhat differently in *Foundation*; and the private communications between Penn and Vincent are reprinted in *PWP* I: 73–80.

55. Danson, *Synopsis of Quakerism*; Whitehead, *The divinity of Christ*.

56. Pepys, *Diary*, entry for February 12, 1669.

57. Penn, *Sandy foundation*. The Privy Council's order directing Penn and Darby to be imprisoned (December 16, 1668) is reprinted in *PWP* I: 82–83; for Stillingfleet's permission to visit, see Lord Arlington to the Lieutenant of the Tower, January 4, 1699, *PWP* I: 86; Penn's later recollections of Stillingfleet are found in his "Account of my life since my Convincement," *PWP* III: 337. For the threats of the Bishop of London, see To Gulielma Springett, December 1668, *PWP* I: 85.

58. To Gulielma Springett, December 1668, *PWP* I: 85; To London Friends, December 1668, *PWP* I: 83; Sir William Penn's petition is found in "Minutes of the Proceedings of the Privy Council."

59. To Lord Arlington, June 19, 1669, *PWP* I: 89–95.

60. To Lord Arlington, *PWP* I: 91–92.

61. To Lodowick Muggleton, February 11, 1669, *PWP* I: 87; see also Greene, "Muggletonians and Quakers," 118; and Bailey, "Muggletonian-Quaker Debates."

62. Penn, *No cross, no crown*.

63. "the favor of an access," To Lord Arlington, June 19, 1669, *PWP* I: 95; "sensible of the impiety" (97); Penn, *Innocency with her open face*. For Stillingfleet's assessment, see "Release from the Tower," July 28, 1669, *PWP* I: 97. On Penn's time in the Tower see Brailsford, *Making of William Penn*, chs. 27–29.

Chapter 4

1. From Sir William Penn, October 6, 1669, in Penn, *Memorials*, II: 571–572.

2. Irish Journal, *PWP* I: 103.

3. The wrath of Ellwood's father is recounted in Ellwood, *History*, 82–87.

4. "a dynastic union," Ingle, *First Among Friends*, 225–226; "had expected," Kunze, *Margaret Fell*, 56–57, 170–171.

5. See Penn, "William Penn's testimony regarding the marriage of Margaret Fell and George Fox." Thanks to Tabitha Driver, Printed Books Librarian at Friends House Library, London, for providing me with an image of Penn's testimony.

6. "their mutual aim," Kunze, *Margaret Fell*, 57; "being with child," From Elizabeth Bowman, July 16, 1670, *PWP* I: 158; "menopausal miscarriage," Kunze, *Margaret Fell*, 56. On the Fell/Fox marriage, see also Mack, *Visionary Women*, 226–228, 302–304.

7. Quotations from *PWP* I: 101.

8. "but to no purpose," Irish Journal, *PWP* I: 105.

9. Quotations from ibid., 105.

10. Ibid., 108.

11. To Mayor Louis Desmynieres, November 5, 1669, *PWP* I: 147; Greaves, *God's Other Children*, 278.

12. "one of his key contacts," Greaves, *Dublin's Merchant-Quaker*, 103. The definitive work is Greaves, *Dublin's Merchant-Quaker*, esp. 96–103. For a list of the West Jersey proprietors see http://www.archstreetfriends.org/exhibit/archives/100shares.html.

13. "with all civility" and "the Address was not read," Irish Journal, *PWP* I: 107; "Nothing was done," Irish Journal, *PWP* I: 109.

14. "the estate being neglected," Irish Journal, *PWP* I: 108. Exactly which lands Gulielma held is not clear, but "Note on Irish Land held by Guli Springett" indicates a holding of roughly forty-three acres in County Meath.

15. "ill of a stoppage," Irish Journal, *PWP* I: 117.

16. On "improvement," see Canny, *Making Ireland British*, 281ff; "by which it may," Irish Journal, *PWP* I: 112; "well improved," Irish Journal, *PWP* I: 110; "I abated," Irish Journal, *PWP* I: 115; "could not agree," Irish Journal, *PWP* I: 113, 119; "Captain Richard Smith's wife," Irish Journal, *PWP* I: 116.

17. Davenport, *An explanation of Roman-Catholick belief*; Penn, *A seasonable caveat*, esp. ch. 9; "it is not our purpose," *Seasonable caveat*, 36.

18. *Seasonable caveat*, 36; Penn, *Great case*.

19. "the mayor himself," Irish Journal, *PWP* I: 120; "a precious Meeting" and "many of the dirtiest," Irish Journal, *PWP* I: 119; "I spoke much," Irish Journal, *PWP* I: 117.

20. Quotations from *PWP* I: 120, 121.

21. "I set about," Irish Journal, *PWP* I: 121. Penn, *Great case*, title page, and "To the King." For the broader context in which *Great case* appeared, see Murphy, *Liberty, Conscience, and Toleration*, ch. 2. The discussion here is adapted from my "The Roads to and from Cork."

22. "proceeded and almost finished" and "sent one sheet," Irish Journal, *PWP* I: 122.

23. "he abused me" and "they missed me," Irish Journal, *PWP* I: 127; "I shall never," From Lord O'Brien, May 18, 1670, *PWP* I: 154; "I cannot agree," From Lord O'Brien, May 18, 1670, *PWP* I: 155. Further complicating these titles and names: both Orrerys were named Roger Boyle.

24. "for I find myself," From Sir William Penn, April 29, 1670, *PWP* I: 152.

25. "For all his obvious and sincere piety," "William Penn's Links with Ireland," 5; "a great bargain," Irish Journal, *PWP* I: 122.

26. "a popish colonel" and "papists," Irish Journal, *PWP* I: 130; "the moral religion," Irish Journal, *PWP* I: 106; "haughty, insinuating fellow," Irish Journal, *PWP* I: 137n142.

27. "my father's business," Irish Journal, *PWP* I: 129.

28. "caused my hair," Irish Journal, *PWP* I: 108; "shaved my head," Irish Journal, *PWP* I: 117; George Fox to Henry Sidon, May 25, 1677, *PWP* I: 376–377. See also Kunze, *Margaret Fell*, 175–176. Wigs would remain an issue within the Society of Friends; Richard Vann cites a 1714 communication from the London Yearly Meeting that "if any Friend wants hair, they should acquaint the Men's Meeting they belong to, and have their approbation and consent, before they get any" (*Social Development*, 192).

29. *Persecution appearing with its own open face*, in William Armorer (London, 1667); "but yourselves" and "we would rather," From Gulielma Springett and Mary Penington, July 16, 1670, *PWP* I: 156–157; "had been cruelly used," From John Gay, July 23, 1670, *PWP* I: 162.

30. From John Gay, July 23, 1670, *PWP* I: 160–161; Penn, *A letter of love to the uoung convinced*, 5.

31. From John Gay, July 23, 1670, *PWP* I: 161.

32. "we were," Penn, *The peoples ancient and just liberties, asserted*, 18; "unlawfully," Starling, *An answer to a seditious and scandalous pamphlet*, 10.

33. I have placed quotation marks around the term "transcript" here, since these are not transcripts in the sense that twenty-first-century audiences understand the term. *The peoples ancient and just liberties* presents Penn and Mead in a clearly stylized and heroic construction, as railroaded by a persecuting state-church system. See Murphy, *Liberty, Conscience, and Toleration*, ch. 3.

34. To Sir William Penn, August 15, 1670, *PWP* I: 173.

35. "that he would see me whipped" and "I told him," To Sir William Penn, August 15, 1670, *PWP* I: 173; on the accusations, see Penn, *Memorials*, II: chs. 7, 8.

36. De Krey, "First Restoration Crisis"; on Penn's early imprisonments more generally see Murphy, "From Practice to Theory to Practice."

37. *Peoples*, 6.

38. Ibid., 7–8.

39. Phillips and Thompson, "Jurors v. Judges," 213; "I saw Mr. Penn speaking," *Peoples*, 8–9; "There was such a great noise," "Mr. Penn I suppose," and "Observe this evidence," *Peoples*, 9.

40. "elevat[ed] a misdemeanor accusation," Horle, *Quakers and the English Legal System*, 116; "If it be common," *Peoples*, 10.

41. "I have asked," *Peoples*, 11; "this ensuing trial," *Peoples*, 3; "the question is not," *Peoples*, 11.

42. "You are a troublesome fellow," *Peoples*, 11; "you deserve" and "at least ten or twelve," *Peoples*, 14.

43. On the importance of juries and the dynamics of the seventeenth-century courtroom, see Archer, *Questions and Answers in the English Courtroom (1640–1760)*, 85–90; Horle, *The Quakers and the English Legal System*, 107–113; Brooks, *Law, Politics, and Society*; and *Twelve Good Men and True*.

44. "guilty of speaking," *Peoples*, 16; "We the jurors" and "you shall not," *Peoples*, 17; "The freedom of jurors," De Krey, "The First Restoration Crisis," 573.

45. "I will have," *Peoples*, 19.

46. "distemper," To Sir William Penn, September 5, 1670, *PWP* I: 177; other quotations from Penn's letter to Sir William Penn, September 7, 1670, *PWP* I: 180.

47. Penn, *No cross, no crown*, 2nd ed., 571–572.
48. Will of Sir William Penn, January 20, 1670, *PWP* I: 149.
49. To Peter Mews, December 10, 1670, *PWP* I: 182.
50. On the map, see To the Commissioners of the Navy, December 2, 1670, *PWP* I: 183; To the Commissioners of the Navy, December 31, 1670, *PWP* 1: 283; "God's Controversy Proclaimed," 1670, *PWP* I: 184–191.
51. Quotations from Ellwood, *History*, 281–282. Tension between Ives and Friends was longstanding, dating back at least to 1668, when Quaker Solomon Eccles denounced Ives by insisting that "Jeremy['s] faith is false, and so is thy doctrine, and thy profession is rotten, and thy god is thy belly" (Eccles, *The Quakers challenge*, 4).
52. "the sergeant came," Injustice Detected, February 1671, *PWP* I: 196; "scrupling any oath," Injustice Detected, *PWP* I: 198; "your father was my friend" and "you stir the people up," Injustice Detected, *PWP* I: 200.
53. "Twas then," Injustice Detected, February 1671, *PWP* I: 200; "thy religion," Injustice Detected, *PWP* I: 201.
54. The unpublished transcript, Injustice Detected, is in *PWP* I: 194–204; the verses, "An Holy Tryumph," 1671, *PWP* I: 205; Petition to Parliament, April 1671, *PWP* I: 205–208. Fox urged Penn to complete his reply to Jenner in his letter of May 24, 1671, *PWP* I: 208–209; "spreading gangrene," Jenner, *Quakerism anatomized*, "To the Reader"; Penn and Whitehead, *A serious apology*; Penn, *Truth rescued*; actually March 1671; To the Sheriffs of London, June 3, 1671, *PWP* I: 211–212.
55. *The great case of liberty of conscience*, 2nd ed.; Parker, *A discourse of ecclesiastical politie*. For the broader contours of the antitolerationist position, see Murphy, *Liberty, Conscience, and Toleration*, 36–47; and Murphy, *Conscience and Community*, 151–155.
56. "That plain English," *Great case*, 4; "By liberty of conscience," *Great case*, 11–12.
57. *Great case*, 15, 21–22. For the broader context in which Penn published *Great case*, see Murphy, *Liberty, Conscience, and Toleration*, chs. 2, 3.
58. "directly invade," *Great case*, 12, 13; Scriptural examples, *Great case*, ch. 3; "story . . . as old as the Reformation," *Great case*, 32.
59. *Great case*, 16, 19, 20, 22.
60. "an external order," *Great case*, 23; "the superstructure," *Great case*, 29, 30; "the question," *Peoples*, 11.
61. "are so far," *Great case*, 27; on Holland, *Great case*, 41; also *Great case*, ch. 6.
62. "yet the infliction," *Great case*, 24.

Chapter 5

1. Ingle, *First Among Friends*, 273; Baxter, *Practical Works*, I: 91.
2. Rudyard, *The second part*.
3. See Sachse, "Benjamin Furly, An English Merchant at Rotterdam," and Hull, *Benjamin Furly and Quakerism in Rotterdam*. Despite this close connection, there is no evidence to support the longstanding claim that Locke and Penn were close. To the contrary, Locke distrusted Penn's embrace of James II. Yet scholars continue to perpetuate the idea that Penn sought a pardon for Locke during the 1680s. This claim is made most recently by Miller in *The Religious Roots of the First Amendment*. But Miller is only the most recent in a long line promoting this mistaken idea, including Tolles and Alderfer, who pronounce Locke Penn's "faithful and trustworthy friend" ("Introduction," xiii), and Brailsford, who mentions Penn's "old friend, John Locke" (*Making of William Penn*, 348).
4. Penn, A Trumpet Sounded, September 9, 1671, *PWP* 1: 351.
5. "I have cleared," A Trumpet Sounded, September 9, 1671, *PWP* 1: 351; "glory, pride" and "sweep the streets," To Dutch Friends, June 14, 1672, *PWP* 1: 389; To Friends in Holland or Germany, September 1, 1673, *PWP* 1:532; To the little flock and family of God, December 4, 1673, *PWP* 1: 545.
6. To John de Labadie's Company, October 8, 1671, *PWP* I: 216–217.
7. *CSP Domestic, Charles II, 1671*, October 26, 1671, #175.
8. "Quakers might," Spurr, " 'The Strongest Bond of Conscience,' " 159; "the ground of one," On Litigation against Oaths, November 15, 1671, *PWP* I: 221. The scene with Robinson,

discussed in Chapter 4 above, is related in Injustice Detected, *PWP* I: 193–208. On oaths in early modern England more generally, see Condren, *Argument and Authority in Early Modern England*.

9. Penn, *A treatise of oaths*; Hull, *William Penn*, 205; Peare, *William Penn*, 167; Endy, *William Penn and Early Quakerism*; *PWP* V: 201–205.

10. All quotations from Narrative of the Sufferings of Quakers in the Isle of Ely, November 1671, *PWP* I: 222–230: "think they" (223); "the Devil's offspring" (225); "ancient constitution" (225); "moral impossibility" (224).

11. Ibid., 228–230.

12. Miller, "A Suffering People," 86; see also Fletcher, "The Enforcement of the Conventicle Acts 1664–1679;" "civil uniformity," To Daniel Fleming, 1673, *PWP* I: 268.

13. On the king's efforts to aid Dissenters, see Rose, *Godly Kingship*, 98–104, 171–180. For the text of the Declaration of Indulgence, see Kenyon, *The Stuart Constitution*, 382 (doc. 113); see also Bate, *The Declaration of Indulgence, 1672*, ch. 5.

14. Although the documentary evidence is sparse, see Hodgkin, *Gulielma, Wife of William Penn*.

15. Quotations from Ellwood, *History*: "in all respects" (226); "expressed" (229); "sparklings of desire" (228); "openly and secretly" and "till at length" (226).

16. *Minute Book of the Monthly Meeting…for the Upperside of Buckinghamshire*, 12, 13. As Hirsch has argued ("A Tale of Two Wives,"), scholars have perpetuated the notion of Gulielma as Penn's "true love" and his second marriage as one of practicality and convenience. Her argument lays out the complex reasons for such interpretations, including developments within Quakerism and contemporary ideas about love and marriage. William and Gulielma's courtship has been rendered into verse—see Baker, *Penn the Statesman and Gulielma*, a verse biography of Penn in which the name "Hannah" appears only three times in more than 250 pages—and dramatized in Huckel, *Dreamer of Dreams*, a fictionalized diary of Gulielma's. No such celebratory accounts exist about Penn's second courtship and marriage, to the best of my knowledge.

17. The marriage certificate, April 4, 1672, is in *PWP* I: 238–239.

18. *PWP* I: 232; "who seemed drawn," Vann, *Social Development of English Quakerism*, 187; "arise purely and simply," Right Marriage, 1671, *PWP* I: 234; "appear before the justice," Kunze, *Margaret Fell*, 158. See also Lloyd, *Quaker Social History*, ch. 4; Davies, *The Quakers in English Society*, ch. 2; Mack, *Visionary Women*, 285–293.

19. "as by," Penn, "William Penn's testimony regarding the marriage of Margaret Fell and George Fox"; "which gives to every man," Right Marriage, 1671, *PWP* I: 233.

20. *PWP* I: 241. See also Dunn, "Penny Wise and Pound Foolish," 39, 40.

21. "large, living, and open," On Truth's Account: Journey through Kent, Sussex, and Surrey, 1672, *PWP* I: 242; "with all sorts" and the story of the young ruffian, *PWP* I: 243.

22. "convincing," On Truth's Account: Journey through Kent, Sussex, and Surrey, *PWP* I: 243; "the parlor, kitchen" and "many confessed," On Truth's Account, *PWP* I: 244.

23. *PWP* I: 259.

24. On the issuance and withdrawal of the Declaration, see Bate, *Declaration of Indulgence*, chs. 5 and 6; Rose, *Godly Kingship*, 98–104, 171–184. For the Test Act, see Kenyon, *Stuart Constituton*, 2nd ed., 351–353; "for pure conscience," Petition to the House of Commons, March 1673, *PWP* I: 260; "promise, verify," *PWP* I: 261.

25. "We have been plundered," To Squire Bowles, 1674, *PWP* I: 276; To JH and companion, March 31, 1674, *PWP* I: 281; "some gentle caution," To JH and companion, *PWP* I: 278; "you have work enough," *PWP* I: 279.

26. See Angell, "God, Christ, and the Light," Benson, " 'That of God in Every Man' "; "pretended an immediate mission," Jenner, *Quakerism anatomized*, 23. See also Danson, *Synopsis of Quakerism*, chs. 6, 7; Faldo, *Quakerism no Christianity*, chs. 3–5.

27. "the universality" and "predestination," To Edward Terry, January 29, 1673, *PWP* 1:501; "an excellent transcript," To W.B., 1674, *PWP* 1: 571; "the Scriptures and the spirit," To J. Keetch, 1674, *PWP* 1: 578; "popish school-personality," To John Collinges, January 22, 1674, *PWP* I: 270.

28. Hallywell, *An account of Familism*, "the refuse of the world" (124); "not only destructive" (Epistle Dedicatory, 1–2). Penn, *Wisdom justified*, "ignorance and calumny" (title page); "a friend to all men" (134).

29. Penn, *Urim and Thummin*, 5; Parker, *A testimony of the light within*. For context of the dispute with Grevill see *PWP* V: 170–171.

30. Cheyney, *A skirmish made upon Quakerism*; Penn, *The skirmisher defeated.*

31. On More, see Lichtenstein, *Henry More.* From Henry More, May 22, 1675, *PWP* I: 304–326; "wit and seriousness" (304); "several excellent passages," "two such able," and "the Quakers have emerged" (305); "there is no ground" (322).

32. Penn, *Sandy foundation*; Vincent, *Foundation of God*, 6; Hedworth, *The spirit of the Quakers tried*, 4, 39. On Socinianism and Unitarianism, see Wilbur, *History of Unitarianism*; and Mortimer, "Early Modern Socinianism and Unitarianism."

33. Penn, *The spirit of truth vindicated* (1672), "Why . . . does the man" (5); "universal" (74).

34. Penn, *Plain-dealing with a traducing Anabaptist*; "error and blasphemy" (5); "a strange use" (3).

35. "O barbarous cruelty!" *Plain-dealing*, 11; "un-Christian," *Plain-dealing*, 19; To John Morse, February 2, 1673, *PWP* 1: 503.

36. "a false god," Faldo, *Quakerism no Christianity*, ch. 17; "false, anti-Christian" (61); "great shoals," "know[ing] no God" (Preface); "no more call themselves" (final pg., unnumb.). Ellwood mentions Hicks and the disputes with Quakers in his *History*, ch. 7.

37. Penn, *Quakerism a new nick-name*; "proofs" (76, 91); "No adversary" (206); "wretched scribbler" (228).

38. Hicks, *A dialogue between a Christian and a Quaker*, 78; Penn and Whitehead, *The Christian-Quaker*; Description of a True Quaker, c. 1673, *PWP* 1: 476.

39. Hicks, *A continuation of the dialogue between a Christian and a Quaker*; Penn, *Reason against railing*; To Neighbors, c. 1674, *PWP* 1: 585.

40. Penn, *The counterfeit Christian detected; and the real Quaker justified*; "till they might," Rudyard, *The Barbican cheat detected*, 9.

41. "how furiously," To John Faldo, October 3, 1674, *PWP* 1: 647. Accounts of the Quaker–Baptist debates came from both sides: see Mead, *A brief narrative of the second meeting*; *The Quakers appeal answered*; Plant, *A contest for Christianity*, to which Ellwood replied in *Forgery no Christianity.*

42. "Caviling Baptists," Ellwood, *History*, 214; Faldo, *XXI Divines*, "which when opened" (96), "industriously avoided" (5); Penn, *A just rebuke.*

43. "are for casting us" and "hath preached up," To Richard Baxter, October 8, 1675, *PWP* I: 345.

44. "Let [Penn]," Baxter's account of debate with William Penn, October 1675, *PWP* 2: 182; "tedious harangues," To Richard Baxter, October 6, 1675, *PWP* I: 339; "designing, persecuting spirit," From Richard Baxter, October 6, 1675, *PWP* I: 340; "while he himself," *PWP* I: 342; "neither a good man," To Richard Baxter, October 8, 1675, *PWP* I: 348. For the timing of these two debates and the Penn–Baxter correspondence, see Thomas, "Letters of William Penn and Richard Baxter."

45. To Henry Clark, April 4, 1674, *PWP* 1: 619; see also Pestana, "The conventionality of the notorious John Perrot"; Martin, "Tradition and Innovation," 8–11; Murphy and Weimer, "Colonial Quakerism."

46. "endeavour to heal," To William Mucklow, October 18, 1672, *PWP* I: 250; "we pull off," 252–253; "the trivialness," 255; "conceited," 254; "thereby strengthening" and "one in the ground," To Mary Pennyman, November 22, 1673, *PWP* I: 263.

47. "come in, come home," To William Mucklow, October 18, 1672, *PWP* I: 256; Mucklow, *The spirit of the hat*, 38; Penn, *The spirit of Alexander the coppersmith lately revived*, 6. Penn's title refers to Alexander, whose opposition to the Apostle Paul is mentioned briefly in Paul's second letter to Timothy.

48. Mucklow, *Tyranny and hypocrisy detected*, 8; Penn, *Judas against the Jews combined against Christ and his followers.*

49. "a nation-wide system," Lloyd, *Quaker Social History*, 8. On the introduction of the meetings, the way that they fostered a broader transatlantic Quaker community, and the resistance they sparked, see Landes, *London Quakers*; and Mack, *Visionary Women*, 283–285.

50. Mack, *Visionary Women*, 288 (and see, more generally, ch. 8); "the greatest source," Martin, "Tradition Versus Innovation," 13–14. On the Box Meeting see Landes, *London Quakers*, 33–34. Mack further observes that "the separate women's meeting was good for women; indeed, it may be said to have been a cradle not only of modern feminism but of the movements of abolitionism, women's suffrage, and peace activism" (349). On men's and women's meetings see Epistle from the London Yearly Meeting, May 3, 1675, *PWP* I: 329–330; on the Penn/Fox/ Fell alliance against the dissenters, see Kunze, *Margaret Fell*, 173–175; and Ingle, *First Among Friends*, ch. 16.

51. Braithwaite, *Second Period of Quakerism,* 278; Knights, *Politics and Opinion.*
52. Morning Meeting, September 15, 1673, Morning Meeting Minutes (1673–1692), 1; Braithwaite, *Second Period,* 281; Martin, "Tradition Versus Innovation," 13. See also Landes, *London Quakers,* 24–29, 38–39.
53. Fox's imprisonment during 1674 and 1675 brought to the fore internal Quaker disagreements about the proper posture toward the legal system. His unwillingness to request a pardon no doubt reflected a reluctance to game the system or to admit guilt. Fox did, though, allow errors in the indictment to be used to secure his release. For the October 18, 1675, Morning Meeting, see Morning Meeting Minutes (1673–1692), 7–8; "and not decline," Epistle from the London Yearly Meeting, May 3, 1675, *PWP* I: 331.
54. "pragmatists," Horle, "Changing Quaker Attitudes," 18; "the Meeting," "Meeting for Sufferings: The Initial Remit," Meeting for Sufferings, Minutes, 1.
55. "the business," Meeting for Sufferings, Minutes, 39. See also Landes, *London Quakers,* 29–32, 66–67, 69; Greaves, *God's Other Children,* 359.
56. "The charismatic," Moore, *Light,* 228, and more generally, Part IV; Ingle, *First Among Friends,* 255–257. For the controversy surrounding the Second Day's Morning Meeting see Mack, *Visionary Women,* ch. 8; David J. Hall, "The Fiery Trial of Their Infallible Examination."
57. "and not," Penn, *The spirit of truth vindicated,* 5.
58. Berg, *The Arrest of George Fox*; Kunze, *Margaret Fell,* 172–173.
59. "weakly and sick," From George Fox and Thomas Lower, August 28, 1674, *PWP* I: 289; "dear George," To Friends and Brethren, March 10, 1675, *PWP* 2: 026.
60. Penn, "Fragments," 241; To George Fox, November 21, 1674, *PWP* 1: 660; reprinted in Janney, *Life,* 111; From George Fox and Margaret Fox, November 25, 1674, *PWP* 1: 665.
61. "If thou canst," From George Fox and Thomas Lower, October 10, 1674, *PWP* I: 295; To George Fox, December 1, 1674, *PWP* I: 297; "Fox's principled refusal," Horle, "Changing Quaker Attitudes," 35.
62. "what I can say," From George Fox, January 11, 1675, *PWP* I: 299; To Margaret Fox, March 16, 1675, *PWP* 2: 041.
63. "indicated the necessity," Horle, "Changing Quaker Attitudes," 35.
64. From George Fox and Thomas Lower, August 28, 1674, *PWP* I: 288; "we think to challenge," To George Fox, September 5, 1674, *PWP* I: 292.
65. William Penn and Upperside Monthly Meeting to Friends at Missenden and elsewhere, June 5, 1672, *PWP* 1: 385; *Minute Book of the Monthly Meeting,* 14, 17 (Ford and Goshell), 25 (Gigger); "continue and cherish," A Marriage Discipline, June 4, 1673, *PWP* I: 261.
66. To Charles II, 1674, *PWP* I: 283–284.
67. *PWP* I: 383.

Chapter 6

1. Penn famously claimed that Pennsylvania was "a name the King would give it in honour to my father"; To Robert Turner, March 5, 1681, *PWP* II: 83; "opening of joy," To Robert Turner, Anthony Sharp, and Roger Roberts, April 12, 1681, *PWP* II: 89; "there is no evidence," *PWP* I: 38. Much of this chapter's account of New Jersey colonization is taken from Pomfret's three classic histories—*Colonial New Jersey, The Province of East Jersey,* and *The Province of West Jersey* and more recent work by Lurie ("New Jersey: The Unique Proprietary" and "Colonial Period"). Penn's correspondence with Fenwick is printed in *PWP* I: 384–387.
2. Lurie, "Colonial Period," 33.
3. "Concession and Agreement," available online at http://avalon.law.yale.edu/17th_century/ nj02.asp. Quitrents were imported from the English system, but ended up causing a great deal of difficulty due to the distances between landlord and tenant. See Bond, "The Quit-Rent System in the American Colonies."
4. All quotations from Penn's letter to John Fenwick, January 11, 1674, *PWP* I: 384.
5. "I am sorry," To John Fenwick, February 13, 1674, *PWP* I: 386.
6. "consumed by," Pomfret, *New Jersey,* 38–39; see also Shourds, *History and Genealogy of Fenwick's Colony,* 4–12; Lurie, "New Jersey," 41–42. Lurie points out that Philip Carteret was also imprisoned by Andros (44), who later deescalated tensions by appointing West Jersey

commissioners as magistrates, subordinate to his authority, for governing in New Jersey, a more auspicious beginning than Fenwick's (Pomfret, *New Jersey*, 43; *West Jersey*, 103–104).

7. See Knights, *Politics and Opinion in Crisis, 1678–1681.*

8. The Mason–Dixon line, surveyed during the 1760s, finally settled a Pennsylvania–Maryland dispute that dated back to the 1680s; the Rhode Island–Massachusetts border was not settled until 1838, and it took a US Supreme Court decision (*Rhode Island v. Massachusetts*, 37 US 657 [1838]).

9. The West New Jersey Concessions, August 1676, *PWP* I: 388–408.

10. "we lay a foundation," To Richard Hartshorne, August 26, 1676, *PWP* I: 416; trial by jury, West New Jersey Concessions ch. 17; "it shall be lawful," ch. 38; "That no men," ch. 16; "have full power," ch. 21.

11. "one of the most innovative," *PWP* I: 387; "easily the most radical," Black, *The West Jersey Concessions and Agreements of 1676/77: A Roundtable of Historians.*

12. "let the country know," To the West New Jersey Commissioners, August 18, 1676, *PWP* I: 412–413; "ours is called" and "being as such," To Richard Hartshorne, August 26, 1676, *PWP* I: 416; "it being in the minds," *PWP* I: 417.

13. "in real tenderness," To Prospective Settlers in West New Jersey, August 26, 1676, *PWP* I: 420; "lest any of them," *PWP* I: 419.

14. Calvert, *Quaker Constitutionalism*, esp. chs. 1, 2.

15. "wholesome air," From William Clark, April 20, 1678, *PWP* 2: 666; From George Hutchinson, June 7, 1678, *PWP* I: 542–543; *The case of New Jersey stated*, c. 1680, *PWP* 2: 752; reprinted in Smith, *History*, 117ff; Pomfret, *West New Jersey*, 110–112.

16. "much blame," To George Fox, September 9, 1675, *PWP* 2: 117; Penn's entreaties to Fox are in his letter to Fox, March 4, 1676, *PWP* I: 359–360; on the aftermath of the Draw-well meeting see Braithwaite, *Second Period*, 304–308.

17. William Penn and Friends to Friends and Brethren, May 8, 1676, *PWP* 2: 331; "The Lord stop you," To John Raunce and Charles Harris, September 11, 1676, *PWP* I: 370; "loose and libertine" (371); "blood will lie" (372); "your mourning Friend" (373).

18. "of those that first," London Yearly Meeting to Friends, May 18, 1676, *PWP* 2: 341; Penn, *The continued cry*; Penn, *The second part of The continued cry.*

19. William Penn et al. to Friends at Uxbridge, Kingston, February 1, 1676, *PWP* 2: 326; Minute of Sussex Quarterly Meeting at William Penn's house, March 19, 1677, *PWP* 2: 431.

20. "larger and far costlier establishment," *PWP* I: 574; see also *PWP* I: 574–576.

21. To Margaret Fox, August 14, 1682, *PWP* II: 227–228; To Margaret Fox, October 29, 1684, *PWP* II: 605–607; Kunze, *Margaret Fell*, 176. The tension with Mead dated to the 1680s, when Mead expressed opposition to Penn's close relationship with King James II; see Ingle, *First Among Friends*, 279.

22. "thy dear wife," From Margaret Fox, October 1677, *PWP* I: 513; "was a mother superior," Kunze, *Margaret Fell*, 177.

23. "the first systematic," *PWP* I: 275n1; Barclay, *Theologaie verae Christianae apologia*. On Barclay more generally, see Trueblood, *Robert Barclay.*

24. "could make a step," From Robert Barclay, September 5, 1676, *PWP* I: 369; Fox and Burnyeat, *A New England firebrand quenched*; Williams, *George Fox digged out of his burrows*. This trip would mark the beginning of a long and fruitful relationship between Penn and German Pietists; see Erben, "William Penn: German Pietist(?)."

25. "where the Lord," An Account of My Journey into Holland and Germany, 1677, *PWP* I: 430; "a great company of people" (430); "all things ended" (431).

26. "let [controversies]," An Account, 1677, *PWP* I: 434; "For we marry none" (434); "to the end" (435). In the words of William Hull, "The form of society and rules of discipline which had been adopted in England were successfully transplanted to the Netherlands." Hull, *William Penn and the Dutch Quaker Migration*, 73.

27. "we cannot join," An Account, 1677, *PWP* I: 437; Penn, *The great case*, 43.

28. See Gummere, "Letter from William Penn to Elizabeth . . . with an introduction," 84; "Her meekness and humility," Penn, *No cross, no crown*, 2nd ed., 566; "to favor," An Account, 1677, *PWP* I: 440; "the same blessed power" and "an account" (443); "they heard me" (447).

29. "who was worthy," An Account, 1677, *PWP* I: 447; "a dark popish town" and "ancient, grave, and serious" (446).

30. "all people," An Account, 1677, *PWP* I: 452; "what encouragement" and "very excellent" (452–453).

31. "a great popish city," An Account, 1677, *PWP* I: 456; "a strict hand" (457); "the Graf called us" (458); "he commanded" (459).

32. "because of that suffering," An Account, 1677, *PWP* I: 459; "my parents" (462); "And as for" (464).

33. "a serious, plain people," An Account, 1677, *PWP* I: 474; "the Lord first appeared" (476); "the Lord visited me" (477).

34. "where Friends," An Account, 1677, *PWP* I: 482–483; "reported to have been" (483).

35. "the truth had passage," An Account, 1677, *PWP* I: 486; "of my retreat" (487).

36. "We rid," An Account, 1677, *PWP* I: 488; "My soul," Gummere, "Letter," 90; "what a persecution" (90); "thou canst not hear" (91); "Christianly" (94).

37. "a zeal" and all subsequent quotations regarding Neander, An Account, 1677, *PWP* I: 490; "were extremely affected" (492); "the most virulent" and "the lust" (499).

38. "Nor sea nor land," To Friends in Holland and Germany, October 24, 1677, *PWP* 2: 566; "My soul has been made sad," To Pieter Hendricks, November 19, 1677, *PWP* I: 517.

39. "endeavour to" and "allay their heat," To the Earl of Middlesex and Dorset, November 17, 1677, *PWP* I: 515.

40. "that our word," To the Commons of England, in *Works*, I: 117; "a sort of," "we have good will," and "I am far from," Two Speeches to a Committee of Parliament, March 22, 1678, *PWP* I: 534; Two Toleration Bills, 1678, *PWP* I: 537–540.

41. "will hardly suffer" and "moved to go amongst them," From Margaret Fox, October 1677, *PWP* I: 513; William Penn et al. to Friends in Sussex and Hampshire, November 5, 1677, *PWP* 2: 572; The Dissatisfactions of William Rogers and others, February 1, 1678, *PWP* I: 520–533.

42. "We are not satisfied," The Dissatisfactions of William Rogers and Others, February 1, 1678, *PWP* I: 521; "How comes it to pass" (526); on marriage, and Fox's marriage (529); "confess that it was not well done of me," John Story's Apology, October 20, 1679, *PWP* I: 556.

43. "whenever I had any business," Penn, "Fragments," 242. For more detailed historical information on the Plot, see Kenyon, *The Popish Plot*; and Hinds, *"The Horrid Popish Plot,"* 71–81.

44. *Journal of the House of Commons*, November 1, 1678.

45. "they say," From John Gratton, December 19, 1678, *PWP* I: 545. Penn had to make a special appeal to the Privy Council for the release of papers in Langhorne's possession: see Release of Papers from Richard Langhorne's Custody, April 16, 1679, *PWP* I: 550.

46. "My soul," William Penn's Epistle to the Children of Light, November 4, 1678, in *Works*, I: 223–226; "all this work," From George Fox, January 13, 1679, *PWP* 2: 702; reprinted in *Journal of the Friends Historical Society* 11 (1914), 19–21.

47. On Sidney see Houston, *Algernon Sidney and the Republican Heritage,* and Scott, *Algernon Sidney and the Restoration Crisis.* For general background on early modern elections, see Thrush, "Elections"; and Lipson, "Elections to the Exclusion Parliaments, 1679–1681"; "for to me," To Algernon Sidney, March 1, 1679, *PWP* I: 547.

48. "the discovery," To Pieter Hendricks and Jan Claus, November 27, 1679, *PWP* I: 557–558. Kenyon describes the trials as "not an attempt to ascertain the truth or administer justice . . . [but rather] a morality play, staged as a demonstration of government power, an affirmation of kingly authority, and a warning to the unwary" (*Popish Plot*, 116). For contemporary narratives of the plot, see Oates, *The discovery of the Popish Plot*; and Bedloe, *A narrative and impartial discovery.* On the processions, see Williams, "The Pope-Burning Processions."

49. From Sir John Pelham, July 25, 1679, *PWP* I: 553–554; To Algernon Sidney, July 29, 1679, *PWP* I: 554–555.

50. Hinds, *"Horrid Popish Plot,"* 12.

51. For Penn's testimony before Parliament, see Two Speeches to a Committee of Parliament, March 22, 1678, *PWP* I: 533–536; on Penn's anti-Catholicism compared to contemporaries, see Endy, *William Penn,* 139–140; "two acts of Parliament" and "many of us," in *To the King, Lords and Commons,* Dedication, 59 (see also "A General Abridgment of our Sufferings," in *To the King, Lords, and Commons,* 67–70; for Penn's possible authorship of this piece, see *PWP* V: 253); Whitehead, *An account.*

52. Penn, *England's great interest*, 4.
53. "reputed Reformed world," *An address to Protestants* (61); "our great declension" (140); "is a restoring" (190); "we have the better religion" (191); "drunkenness" (7).
54. Penn, *An address*, 33.
55. "church evils," *An address* (61); "to love justice" (194–195; see also 116–120); "thieves, murderers" (195).
56. "manifesto," Scott, *Algernon Sidney*, 135; Penn, *England's great interest*, 2.
57. the foundation," Penn, *One project for the good of England*, 1–2; "All English Protestants," Penn, *One project*, 3; on religion, see *One project*, 1 (also Penn, *An address*, 81, 99ff). Thus, Penn became one of the key figures in the movement that Scott Sowerby calls "anti-anti-popery" ("Opposition to Anti-Popery," 42–43); see also Lake, "Anti-popery."
58. "a phantasie," *A seasonable corrective to the one project for the good of England*, 2; "Government," *A seasonable corrective*, 2. See, more generally, *A seasonable corrective*, 4, 6, 7; and Goldie, "The Theory of Religious Intolerance."
59. See Penn, "Fragments," 240–242.

Chapter 7

1. "along with," News of William Penn's Departure, in *William Penn and the Foundinig of Pennsylvania*, 178; "love that many waters," *William Penn's last farewell*, 2; To Stephen Crisp, August 30, 1682, *PWP* 3: 595. See also Balderston, "The Real 'Welcome' Passengers."
2. To Thomas Janney, August 21, 1682, *PWP* II: 106. A credible reconstruction of the petition has been offered by the editors of Penn's *Papers*; see *PWP* II: 32-33.
3. "part of the territory," Minute of the Committee of Trade, June 25, 1680, *PWP* II: 39; "he had not seen," From Robert Barclay, January 11, 1680, *PWP* II: 24; "very willing," Sir John Werden to William Blathwayt, October 16, 1680, *PWP* II: 44.
4. "precise location," *PWP* II: 256; "description by lines of longitude," "under what meridian," and "it were most," Sir John Werden to William Blathwayt, November 20, 1680, *PWP* II: 48. Sally Schwartz gently suggests that "Penn's knowledge of the land and people he acquired in 1681 and 1682 seems to have been limited" (Schwartz, "William Penn and Toleration," 295).
5. Minute of the Committee of Trade, January 22, 1681, *PWP* II: 57.
6. All quotations from To Robert Turner, March 5, 1681, *PWP* II: 83. On Turner, see Balderston, "Robert Turner."
7. "not only to provide," Janney, *Life of William Penn*, 163. For more recent and nuanced versions of the Quaker interpretation, see Hamm, *The Quakers in America*, 27; Calvert, *Quaker Constitutionalism*, 105; *William Penn and the Founding of Pennsylvania*, 114; and Tully, *Forming American Politics*, 257–258.
8. Geiter, "The Restoration Crisis," and her *William Penn*.
9. Mary Maples, "William Penn, Classical Republican"; Mood, "William Penn and English Politics." Calvert also mentions in passing the political affinities between Whigs and Quakers, though her focus is on the religious differences that undergirded these issues (*Quaker Constitutionalism*, 82–83). "you shall be governed," To the inhabitants of Pennsylvania, April 8, 1681, *PWP* II: 84. Later that year, he promised the inhabitants of the Lower Counties that "you shall find me and my government easy, free, and just"; see To Planters in Maryland, September 16, 1681, *PWP* II: 112. "Any government," Frame of Government, May 1682, *PWP* II: 213.
10. "one of," Richard S. Dunn, "William Penn and the Selling of Pennsylvania," 323; "I desire to," Penn to — [unknown], July 1681, cited in Taylor, *American Colonies*, 266; "The service of God," To William Blathwayt and Francis Guin, November 21, 1682, *PWP* II: 311.
11. For details on the purported debt owed to Sir William, see *PWP* II: 30–31; "bringing back," From William Markham, March 27, 1684, *PWP* II: 536; "personal connections," *PWP* II: 22.
12. To Robert Turner, March 5, 1681, *PWP* II: 83; "Founding a successful proprietary colony," *PWP* II: 81; Minutes of the London Meeting for Sufferings, April 29, 1681, *PWP* II: 94; Petition to Parliament, November 1680, *PWP* II: 50–56.
13. "being planted," Sir John Werden to William Blathwayt, June 23, 1680, *PWP* II: 37; "till I myself," Commission to William Markham, April 10, 1681, *PWP* II: 86; To Lord Baltimore,

April 10, 1681, II: 87; "as my understanding," To Robert Turner, Anthony Sharp, and Roger Roberts, April 12, 1681, *PWP* II: 89; From Robert Barclay, June 25, 1681, *PWP* II: 95–96; "Thou has land," From Robert Barclay, November 19, 1681, *PWP* II: 132; "several sober persons," From Robert Barclay, December 17, 1681, *PWP* II: 133.

14. Penn, *Some account*, 62. "Ireland and our plantations," Coke, *A discourse*, 43–44; "seeds of nations," *Some Account*, 59; Coke emphasized the fact that, unlike Spain, England depletes itself through colonization (*A discourse*, 12–13). On the different character of Spanish and English settlement, see, among others, J. H. Elliott, *Empires of the Atlantic World*, esp. Part 2. "The people and governor," *Some account*, 5; "most fitted," *Some account*, 63. For Furly's involvement, see Kane, "Notes on Early Pennsylvania Promotional Literature," 162–163; and on *Some account* as a broader contribution to an emerging imperial vision, see Wanibuchi, "William Penn's Imperial Landscape."

15. "that it hath pleased the Lord," To Friends in the countries, March 1681(?), *PWP* 3: 139; Penn, *Some account*, 58–59; Tully, *Forming American Politics*, 29–30; Smolenski, *Friends and Strangers*, 61. For the relationship between *Some Account* and *A Brief account*, see Kane, "Notes," 150–168.

16. To James Harrison, August 25, 1681, *PWP* II: 108.

17. From Robert Barclay, August 19, 1681, *PWP* II: 104–105; From Robert Barclay, September 23, 1681, *PWP* II: 115–117. On the early history of Delaware, see Munroe, *Colonial Delaware: A History*, chs. 1–3; also Munroe, *A History of Delaware*, chs. 1 and 2.

18. For more on this aspect of settlement, see Taylor, *American Colonies*, ch. 12. On Maryland in particular, see especially Sutto, *Loyal Protestants and Dangerous Papists*.

19. "during the mid-seventeenth century," Taylor, *American Colonies*, 206; see also 210, 212.

20. Ingle, *First Among Friends*, 238.

21. Soderlund, *Quakers and Slavery*, 3–4; Gragg, *Quaker Community on Barbados*, 38–39, 44; Edmundson, *Journal*, 54–55, 73; Ingle, *First Among Friends*, 233 ; Braithwaite, *Beginnings of Quakerism*, 402.

22. See "that we...teach," Fox's Letter to Governor of Barbados, 1671; see Angell, "An Early Version of George Fox's 'Letter to the Governor of Barbados,'" 288.

23. "particularly confused," *PWP* II: 111; To Planters in Maryland, September 16, 1681, *PWP* II: 112; "a thing not kindly taken," Lord Baltimore to William Markham, June 5, 1682, *PWP* II: 259.

24. Richter, *Facing East from Indian Country*, 2–3; Jean Soderlund, *Lenape Country*, esp. Introduction. See also *Friends and Enemies*, and *Beyond the Covenant Chain*.

25. "a polyglot society," Soderlund, *Lenape Country*, 9; "only the latest," Merrell, Afterword, in *Friends and Enemies*, 263. The emergence and development of that society prior to Penn's arrival are the focus of Soderlund, *Lenape Country*, chs. 1–6. On Markham's arrival, see Soderlund, *Lenape Country*, 149–156.

26. See Hsueh, *Hybrid Constitutions*, 100; Smolenski, *Friends and Strangers*, 123; Pencak and Richter, "Introduction," in *Friends and Enemies*; Soderlund, *Lenape Country*; Goode, "*Racontyn Marenit*."

27. To the Kings of the Indians, *PWP* II: 128–129; To the Emperor of Canada, June 21, 1682, *PWP* II: 261; Soderlund, *Lenape Country*, 169–170.

28. Sugrue, "Peopling and Depeopling;" Goode, "Native American—Pennsylvanian Relations 1681–1753"; Roach, "The Planting of Philadelphia: I," 42–43; Nash, "City Planning"; Spady, "Colonialism and the Discursive Antecedents of *Penn's Treaty with the Indians*"; Newman, "Treaty of Shackamaxon"; and more generally Newman, *On Records*, ch. 3; Greer, "Dispossession in a Commercial Idiom."

29. On the sale of lands in Pennsylvania, see *PWP* II: 632; Conditions or Concessions to the First Purchasers, July 11, 1681, *PWP* II: 98; "an unstable and fractious mix," Taylor, *American Colonies*, 131; "sober and industrious," To the inhabitants of Pennsylvania, April 8, 1681, *PWP* II: 84.

30. "till altered," Conditions or Concessions to the First Purchasers, *PWP* II: 100.

31. "recruited," *PWP* II: 632; see also Pomfret, "The First Purchasers of Pennsylvania"; Vann, "Quakerism: Made in America?"; Dunn, "Penny Wise and Pound Foolish," 45. See also Roach, "The Planting of Philadelphia: II," 159–160, and *PWP* II: Appendix.

32. "a great town," Initial Plans for Philadelphia/Instructions given to . . . William Crispin, John Bezar, and Nathaniel Allen . . ., September 30, 1681, *PWP* II: 119; "Conscious of the destruction," Milroy, *The Grid and the River*, 13; "a green country town," Initial Plans, *PWP* II: 121; "I do call," Additional instructions to William Markham, October 28, 1681, *PWP* II: 129.

33. Roach, "The Planting of Philadelphia: I," 20; Crispin, "Captain William Crispin"; "a crowd of people," Roach, "Planting of Philadelphia: I," 26. On Holme, who would play an increasingly vital role in Pennsylvania affairs, see Corcoran, *Thomas Holme*.

34. Penn, Fundamental Constitutions, summer 1681, *PWP* II: 142.

35. "the free possession," Fundamental Constitutions, summer 1681, *PWP* II: 143; "that they may" (145); "that we may" (149–150); "nor any playhouses" (151).

36. See John Darnall's comments on Pennsylvania's government, *PWP* II: 156–162; Thomas Rudyard's commentary on the Frame of Government, *PWP* II: 184–189; Benjamin Furly's commentary and critique, *PWP* II: 228–237. Rudyard's comments are elaborated by Ned C. Landsman, " 'Of the Grand Assembly or Parliament.' "

37. "any government," The Frame of Government and Laws Agreed Upon in England, 1682, *PWP* II: 213; "great end of all government" (214).

38. "That all persons," The Frame of Government and Laws Agreed Upon in England, 1682, *PWP* II: 225; "possess faith in Jesus Christ" (224).

39. "a good country," To Algernon Sidney, October 13, 1681, *PWP* II: 124–125; "far preferred," Benjamin Furly's Criticism of The Frame of Government, post May 1682, *PWP* II: 235; Gary Nash has suggested an answer to Furly's question. "Penn's circle of backers caused him to deviate markedly from his own ideas on government in favor of a system more to their liking and advantage." Nash, "The Framing of Government in Pennsylvania," esp. at 184, 191.

40. *The articles, settlement, and offices of the Free Society of Traders*, i.

41. To Robert Turner, August 25, 1681, *PWP* II: 110; "lessons of," Gary Nash, "The Free Society of Traders," 148; Charter of the Free Society of Traders, March 24, 1682, *PWP* II: 246–256.

42. "all such offenses," Frame of Government and Laws Agreed Upon in England, 1682, *PWP* II: 225; Locke, *Second Treatise*, sec. 6.

43. "Pennsylvania prospers," To James Harrison, January 19, 1682, *PWP* II: 244; "be cool, and patient," To Elizabeth Woodhouse, March 8, 1682, *PWP* II: 245; "I purpose," To Dr. Woodhouse, March 29, 1682, *PWP* 3: 436m; "the daily bearing," *No cross, no crown*, 2nd ed., title pg.

44. All quotations from To Gulielma Penn and Children, August 4, 1682, *PWP* II: 269–275.

45. To Margaret Fox, August 14, 1682, *PWP* II: 277; From Sir William Petty, August 14, 1682, *PWP* II: 278–280; Deed for New Castle, August 24, 1682, *PWP* II: 281–284; "by the end," Pomfret, *New Jersey*, 50; Pomfret, *East New Jersey*, 134.

46. To Springett Penn, Letitia Penn, and William Penn, Jr., August 19, 1682, *PWP* II: 280–281.

47. *PWP* II: 290; for the documents Penn signed, see Business Agreements with Philip Ford, August 1682, *PWP* II: 290–295. On Penn's financial difficulties at this point, see Dunn, "William Penn and the Selling of Pennsylvania," 327. For a primary source, see From Joseph Harris, May 19, 1683, *William Penn and the Founding of Pennsylvania*, 218–220.

48. Pomfret, "The First Purchasers," 161; Balderston, "The Real *Welcome* Passengers," 35.

Chapter 8

1. Balderston, "The Real *Welcome* Passengers"; John Moll's account of the surrender of the Three Lower Counties to William Penn, 1682, *PWP* II: 305–308; "assuring them" and "liberty of conscience," *William Penn and the Founding of Pennsylvania*, 188; "impatient to secure," Ryerson, "William Penn's Gentry Commonwealth," 409. For the writs, dated November 8, 1682, see *PWP* II: 309–311.

   For overviews of religious liberty in early Pennsylvania, see Frost, *A Perfect Freedom*; Bronner, *William Penn's Holy Experiment*; and Schwartz, *A Mixed Multitude*.

2. Chester Assembly details from *William Penn and the Founding of Pennsylvania*, 225; Ryerson, "Penn's Gentry Commonwealth," 410; Commonwealth, *Charter to William Penn*, 474; *Votes and Proceedings*, 2–3; "that as one" and "mak[ing] them as free," *Votes and Proceedings*, 3; Naturalization of Swedish Inhabitants, January 11, 1683, *PWP* II: 337. For more on the Chester Assembly, see Johannsen, "The Conflict Between the Three Lower Counties on the

Delaware and the Province of Pennsylvania," 98–101. The phrase "sober people of all sorts" is from the first Fundamental Constitution, summer 1681, *PWP* II: 143.

3. Great Law, chapter 1. For Locke's criticisms, see "Pennsylvania Laws," 182; on the connection between liberty of conscience and restrictions on speech, see Bejan, *The Bonds of Civility*.

4. On More, see Assembly Minutes, in *William Penn and the Founding of Pennsylvania*, 231–232. Nash calls More "aristocratic, unstable, and by nature condescending" ("Free Society of Traders," 161; see also Hoffer and Hull, "The First American Impeachments"); "perverse and stubborn," From James Claypoole, April 1, 1683, *PWP* I: 371; "extensive feudal privileges," Roach, "Planting of Philadelphia: I," 43; "we are like to suffer," From James Claypoole, April 1, 1683, *PWP* II: 370–371; "all but defunct," Nash, "The Free Society of Traders," 173.

5. On these developments, and the laying out of city lots, see Roach, "Planting of Philadelphia: I."

6. "Look[ing] with misgivings," Corcoran, *Thomas Holme*, 93; "had oversold," Roach, "Planting of Philadelphia: I," 27; From Thomas Holme, November 9, 1683, *PWP* II: 501. Jack P. Greene notes that "Pennsylvania was begun with a massive migration of families that brought eight thousand people to the colony in just five years": see Greene, *Pursuits of Happiness*, 47. Pomfret estimates that by 1686 more than six thousand Quakers had emigrated to Pennsylvania, and 1,500 to West Jersey (*East New Jersey*, 131).

7. On surveying, see From William Clarke, January 13, 1683, *PWP* II: 343; "well approved of," Letter of Thomas Paschall, 1683, in *Narratives of Early Pennsylvania*, 250; "The Governor's own," Ryerson, "Penn's Gentry Commonwealth," 414.

8. "Colonists," *PWP* II: 483; names and occupations from Roach, "Planting of Philadelphia: II"; "we are resolved," From Jacob Vandewalle, August 24, 1684, *PWP* II: 595.

9. From Philip Ford, September 19, 1682, *PWP* II: 303; From George Hutcheson, February 17, 1683, *PWP* 4: 067; Ford, *A vindication of William Penn*; "whatever men may say," To John Alloway, November 29, 1683, *PWP* II: 503; "I never wished," From Thomas Paschall, 1683, *Narratives of Early Pennsylvania*, 251.

10. Penn's claims about progress in settlement, arrivals, and buildings: To John Alloway, November 29, 1683, *PWP* II: 504; To the Earl of Rochester, June 14, 1683, PWP II: 397–398; To Lord North, July 24, 1683, *PWP* II: 414; To the Earl of Sunderland, July 28, 1683, *PWP* II: 416; "I like the land," To William Blathwayt and Francis Gwyn, November 21, 1682, *PWP* II: 311; "the air proveth sweet and good," To Lord North (415); "all send forth," "I have had better venison," and "are savage to us," To the Earl of Sunderland (417); see also To the Earl of Arran, January 9, 1683, *PWP* II: 512.

11. Minute of the Philadelphia Monthly Meeting, January 9, 1683, *PWP* II: 333–334; "we . . . are as flesh," To Friends in Great Britain, March 17, 1683, *PWP* II: 528. On the early meetings, see Janney, *Life of William Penn*, 234; and Pomfret, *West New Jersey*, 222–223; "blessings flow amongst us," To John Blaykling and others, April 16, 1683, *PWP* II: 376 (see also To John Alloway, November 29, 1683, *PWP* II: 503–505). On the proposed Barbadian settlement, see From Elizabeth Gretton, March 20, 1684, *PWP* II: 533; To Ralph Fretwell, April 3, 1684, *PWP* II: 546–547.

12. "We should look selfish," To Jasper Batt, February 5, 1683, *PWP* II: 348; "meddling, intruding" (348). For Batt's reply to Penn, August 1683, see *PWP* II: 462–466. "I have had a great exercise," From Stephen Crisp, May 4, 1684, *PWP* 4: 854; "I know it is always best," From James Claypoole, April 1, 1683, *PWP* II: 370.

13. Rudyard had earlier suggested a two-stage governance structure, pre- and post-1690, for some of these very reasons; see Thomas Rudyard's commentary on the Frame of Government, January 13, 1682, *PWP* II: 184–189. Ryerson argues that "Penn's constitution provided a government that was simply too large for the rude young colony" ("Penn's Gentry Commonwealth," 410); "we have chosen," Petition from New Castle County, February 20, 1683, *PWP* II: 621–622; "it may do best," To William Clarke, February 1683, *PWP* II: 344. (Virtually identical documents from freeholders of Chester, Kent, and Sussex Counties, also during February 1683, *PWP* II: 620–624.)

14. "a good number at present," To William Markham, February 12, 1683, *PWP* II: 353; "the fewness of people," Act of Settlement, March 19, 1683, *PWP* II: 364. Pennsylvania was not unique in this regard. Similar difficulties had arisen in Carolina; see Hsueh, *Hybrid*

Constitutions, 65. "the popular assembly," Calvert, *Quaker Constitutionalism*, 103; "passed 83 laws," To John Blakling, Thomas Cam, et al., April 16, 1683, *PWP* II: 376; "assumed a civic identity," Smolenski, *Friends and Strangers*, 90. For Assembly records, see *Votes and Proceedings*,18.

15. Act of Settlement, March 19, 1683, *PWP* II: 362–366; Second Frame of Government, April 1683, in *William Penn and the Founding of Pennsylvania*, 265-275; "All in all," Ryerson, "Penn's Gentry Commonwealth," 412; Tully, *Forming American Politics*, 31, 258–260.

16. Balderston, "The Mystery of William Penn," 82. On Petty's enduring importance in both scientific and economic circles, see Hoppit, *A Land of Liberty?*, 190–192.

17. "The air, heat, and cold" and "fish in these parts," To John Aubrey, June 13, 1683, *PWP* II: 395; Tavern Regulations, March 23, 1683, *PWP* II: 367–368. "I am still alive," *A letter . . . to the Committee of the Free Society of Traders*, 1; "dry, cold, piercing, and hungry" (1); "elk, as big" (4), "In liberality," "if they are," and "under a dark night" (6). For more on Penn's use of maps see Mann, "Beyond the Bounds,"; and on Penn's letters in the context of the Royal Society, see Wanibuchi, "William Penn's Imperial Landscape."

18. From Philip Ford, September 19, 1682, *PWP* II: 303; From John Tucker, January 8, 1683, *PWP* II: 331; From Anthony Lowther, August 4, 1683, *PWP* II: 425–426; From Captain John Purvis, April 28, 1684, *PWP* 4: 850.

19. From Philip Ford, September 19, 1682, *PWP* II: 303; From James Claypoole, April 1, 1683, *PWP* II: 370; "it was near dead," Gulielma Penn to Margaret Fox, August 21, 1683, *PWP* II: 460; "I am altogether unfit," From Anthony Lowther, August 5, 1683, *PWP* II: 427. On the relationship between Gulielma Penn and Margaret Fox, see Kunze, *Margaret Fell*, 178–179.

20. To Lord Culpeper, February 5, 1683, *PWP* II: 350.

21. There was always more to the Penn–Baltimore dispute than vague measurements in America meted out from Whitehall. See Sutto, "William Penn, Charles Calvert, and the Limits of Royal Authority," 295, 296. On the Maryland–Virginia dispute, see From John Purvis, May 21, 1684, *PWP* II: 556n2.

22. "a little time," To Augustine Herrman, November 2, 1682, *PWP* II: 309; "Penn wanted ocean access," Sutto, "William Penn, Charles Calvert," 295; "in winter time," From George Heathcote, December 7, 1682, *PWP* II: 320; "extremely desirous" (357–358); "not often deceived," To Lord Baltimore, April 23, 1683, *PWP* II: 384; "upon serious thoughts," To Lord Baltimore, May 30, 1683, *PWP* II: 388; "you know well," From Sir William Penn, June 1666, in Penn, *Memorials*, II: 234.

23. From Lord Baltimore, June 24, 1683, *PWP* II: 405–409; for the depositions, see Deposition of Harmon Cornielson, May 5, 1683, *PWP* 4: 184; Deposition of Helmanus Wiltbanck, May 5, 1683, *PWP* 4: 186; From William Clarke, June 21, 1683, *PWP* II: 400–401; Instructions to commissioners, July 2, 1683, *PWP* II: 410–411; To William Markham, September 1, 1683, *PWP* II: 472; To the Earl of Sunderland, July 28, 1683, *PWP* II: 417. By March of the following year Markham was writing to express his hope that Penn would come in person to be present when the case was argued: From William Markham, March 27, 1684, *PWP* II: 534–539. To the Committee of Trade, August 14, 1683, *PWP* II: 431–437; for accounts of Baltimore's harassment, see From James Walliam and John White, September 8, 1683, *PWP* II: 485–486. More generally, see Munroe, *Colonial Delaware*, ch. 4.

24. For the New Castle fort, see From William Welch, April 5, 1684, *PWP* II: 547; From Thomas Dongan, May 1, 1684, *PWP* II: 554–555; To the Duke of York, February 2, 1684, *PWP* II: 518–520; To the Duke of York, June 8, 1684, *PWP* II: 560–561; From Thomas Dongan, May 1, 1684, *PWP* II: 555.

25. "we might not seize," From William Welch, February 18, 1684, *PWP* II: 522. For the affidavits, see From Nicholas Bayard, December 23, 1683, *PWP* 4: 633; From Nicholas Bayard, April 16, 1684, *PWP* II: 549–550; Deposition of Peter Laurensen, February 24, 1683, *PWP* 4: 081; Deposition of Peter Cock, Peter Rambo, and Hans Mansson, June 25, 1684, *PWP* 4: 907; Deposition of the ancient Swedes, January 11, 1684, *PWP* 4: 708. For more information on these depositions, see Dunlap and Weslager, "More Missing Evidence: Two Depositions by Early Swedish Settlers"; and Wainwright, "The Missing Evidence: Penn v. Baltimore."

26. From Thomas Rudyard, January 13, 1683, *PWP* II: 340.

27. From Thomas Rudyard, March 13, 1683, *PWP* 4: 099; To the Proprietors of East New Jersey, July 11, 1683, *PWP* II: 412–413; "[Penn] tried to act," *PWP* II: 339; William Penn and

proprietors of East New Jersey commission to Robert Barclay as Governor, July 17, 1683, *PWP* 4: 302; Robert Barclay commission to Gawen Lawrie as Deputy-Governor, July 27, 1683, *PWP* 4: 332.

28. Luke Watson's sale to William Penn of right and title to East Jersey, July 5, 1683, *PWP* 4: 285; "seems not to be well pleased," From Thomas Dongan, October 22, 1683, *PWP* II: 493; From George Heathcote, November 4, 1683, *PWP* 4: 598; William Penn's answer to Thomas Rudyard, June 26, 1684, *PWP* 4: 913.

29. *PWP* II: 300; From John Darnall, September 14, 1682, *PWP* II: 300–301; "Some said" and "wouldst rather," From James Nevill, March 3, 1683, *PWP* II: 355; "I do foresee" (356); John Fenwick deed to William Penn, March 30, 1683, *PWP* 4: 142.

30. "great and . . . irreparable injuries" and "England is filled," To the Governor and Council of West New Jersey, June 11, 1683, *PWP* II: 391; "it is hard for me," To the Governor and Council of West New Jersey, June 20, 1683, *PWP* II: 399; "untrue and unkind reflections," To Robert Turner, March 31, 1684, *PWP* II: 540. See also Pomfret, *East New Jersey*, 134.

31. To Thomas Lloyd, October 7, 1684, *PWP* II: 604.

32. "not only watered," Nash, "The Quest for the Susquehanna Valley," 3; Commission and Instructions to James Graham and William Haige, August 2, 1683, *PWP* II: 423–424; To Worthy Friend, July 30, 1683, *PWP* 4: 363.

33. "a slight opinion," From William Haige, August 29 1683, *PWP* II: 469; "find they cannot," From Thomas Dongan, October 10, 1683, *PWP* II: 488–489. Dongan was acting at the behest Sir John Werden, the Duke of York's secretary (Pomfret, *East New Jersey*, 254–255).

34. "If Penn purchased," Nash, "Quest for the Susquehanna," 8; "when I have anything to say," From Thomas Dongan, March 17, 1684, *PWP* II: 532.

35. "as for your affair," From Thomas Dongan, October 10, 1683, *PWP* II: 489; "I have always written," From Thomas Dongan, March 17, 1684, *PWP* II: 532. Dongan's governorship was later surrendered back to Andros when James II placed New York under the Dominion of New England in 1688.

36. "encountered little overt criticism," *PWP* II: 569; Petition from Philadelphia Merchants, May 30, 1684, *PWP* II: 558–559. Release of Customs Duty, July 2, 1683, *PWP* II: 411–412; "I receive neither custom," To tenants in New Castle, Chester, Philadelphia, and Bucks Counties, November 9, 1683, *PWP* II: 501.

37. Remonstrance from the Inhabitants of Philadelphia, July 1684, *PWP* II: 571. This remonstrance is apparently a different document than the objections submitted to them by Anthony Weston in February 1684, for which Weston was sentenced to be whipped in the Philadelphia marketplace. See *Minutes of the Provincial Council*, I: 92; and Smolenski, *Friends and Strangers*, 146–148. "I have made the most purchases," The Proprietor's Reply, July 1684, *PWP* II: 574–576.

38. "guilty of," *Minutes of Provincial Council* I: 96. Jean Soderlund convincingly situates the Mattson trial in the broader context of tensions between Pennsylvania Quakers (*Lenape Country*, 156–167).

39. On Pennsbury, see *PWP* II: 568–569; "great and unsufferable," From James Harrison, *PWP* II: 525; To Friends in Great Britain, March 17, 1684, *PWP* II: 529; Gardening Directions for Ralph Smyth, August 1684, *PWP* II: 584–585.

40. Roach, "Planting of Philadelphia: II," 193. The full range of the Council's attentions is recounted in *Minutes of the Provincial Council*, I: 57–119.

41. "the greatest mistake," Ryerson, "Penn's Gentry Commonwealth," 415; "What had begun," Roach, "Planting of Philadelphia: I," 5.

42. Commission to President Thomas Lloyd and the Provincial Council, August 6, 1684, *PWP* II: 583.

43. Prayer for Philadelphia, August 12, 1684, *WilliamPenn and the Founding of Pennsylvania*, 396.

Chapter 9

1. To James Harrison, October 7, 1684, *PWP* II: 601; "to me" (602).

2. To Thomas Lloyd, October 7, 1684, *PWP* II: 604; To Thomas Lloyd and the Provincial Council, Authority to commission William Markham Secretary of the Province and Territories, and my Secretary as Proprietary, March 18, 1685, *PWP* 5: 133.

3. From Robert Turner, October 31, 1685, *PWP* 5: 325; To Thomas Lloyd, October 2, 1685: "I received [your letter] but sorry to see the date from New York, though I am sensible of thy true love and care for Pennsylvania," *PWP* 5: 286; To Thomas Lloyd, September 21, 1686, *PWP* III: 117.
4. To Margaret Fox, October 29, 1684, *PWP* II: 606. Penn recounts the Vickris incident in A History of My Life from 1684, 1691-1692, *PWP* III: 342.
5. Soderlund, *William Penn and the Founding of Pennsylvania*, 299.
6. From Philip Theodore Lehnmann, September 23, 1684, *PWP* II: 599; "be sold for as much," To James Harrison, October 7, 1684, *PWP* II: 602; East meets West, *PWP* II: 600n10.
7. Memorandum concerning the conviction of WP, January 26, 1685, *PWP* 5: 086; Pardon by James II, March 9, 1686, *PWP* III: 83-84; To James Harrison, April 24, 1686, *PWP* III: 91.
8. To Thomas Lloyd, March 16, 1685, *PWP* III: 31; see also Nagy, *Popular Medicine in Seventeenth-Century England*, 44-45, which references hot frying pans being held near the head of a stroke victim, as well as leeches applied to the rectum, as staples of early modern treatment.
9. "he desired not," To Thomas Lloyd, March 16, 1685, *PWP* III: 32; To Thomas Lloyd and the Provincial Council, March 17, 1685, *PWP* 5: 133.
10. "I shall make it," James quoted in Miller, *James II*, 120.
11. For details of the rebellions, as well as their repercussions and aftermath, see Pincus, *1688*, chs. 2, 3; J. R. Jones, *The Revolution of 1688 in England*, 57-66; Miller, *James II*, ch. 10.
12. "great preaching here," To Stephen Crisp, February 28, 1685, *PWP* III: 30; "I will keep my word," James, quoted in Miller, *James II*, 136.
13. Penn denounced Louis in a letter to Robert Turner, April 24, 1686, *PWP* 5: 424; for the context of the Revocation, see Jones, *Revolution*, ch. 7. The claim that James aimed at French-style absolutism is advanced by Pincus, *1688*, ch. 5, 126-127, 176-177. On Louis and his religious policy more generally, see Wilkinson, *Louis XIV*.
14. "In France," To James Harrison, October 25, 1685, *PWP* III: 65; "the two letters," Penn, *Fiction Found out*, 1; "I am no Roman Catholic," To John Tillotson, January 29, 1686, *PWP* III: 80.
15. "taken orders at Rome," Popple, *A letter to Mr. Penn*, 5 (see also *A letter, containing some reflections*); "No toleration," cited in Sowerby, *Making Toleration*, 172. The Penn–Popple friendship is elaborated in Robbins, "Absolute Liberty," 190-223. See also Sachse, "The Mob and the Revolution of 1688."
16. For skeptical interpretations of James's motives, see Pincus, *1688*; the editors of Penn's *Papers* claim that James "only really wanted toleration for Catholics" (*PWP* III: 26). For a different perspective, see Murphy, *Liberty, Conscience, and Toleration*, ch. 6; and Sowerby, "William Penn and James II."
17. "well and quiet," From Samuel Carpenter, December 25, 1684, *PWP* II: 612, 613. On the early history of the Philadelphia Yearly Meeting see Mekeel, "The Founding Years, 1681-1789," 14-55. "there is here much robbery," From Nicholas More, December 1, 1684, *PWP* II: 608. On Lloyd, see *PWP* III: 86n2; for Penn's later denunciation of the Assembly, see To the Commissioners of State, February 1, 1687, *PWP* III: 145. More informed Penn of the events surrounding Rousby's murder in his letter of December 1, 1684, *PWP* II: 608.
18. "somebody be deputed," To Ralph Fretwell, April 3, 1684, *PWP* II: 546; for Fretwell's complaints, see "wants abilities," From Ralph Fretwell, October 1684, *PWP* 5: 005; "absence at New York," From Ralph Fretwell, December 1684, *PWP* 5: 023. On the meeting's location, see Roney, *Governed by a Spirit of Opposition*, ch. 1; "as to Ralph," From Robert Turner, October 31, 1685, *PWP* 5: 325. See also Corcoran, *Thomas Holme*, 203-209.
19. "I am heartily sorry," From Samuel Carpenter, December 25, 1684, *PWP* II: 613; "the Society," From James Graham, December 20, 1685, *PWP* 5: 049.
20. "we have had no account," Petition from the Free Society of Traders, June 15, 1685, *PWP* III: 58; "try what is possible," To Thomas Lloyd, June 6, 1687, *PWP* 5: 792; "a great reproach," To the Provincial Council, c. June 1686, *PWP* III: 95; Markham detailed the lawsuit in his letter to Penn, August 22, 1686, *PWP* III: 103-104; also From James Harrison, Arthur Cook, and John Simcock, October 3, 1686, *PWP* III: 124-126.
21. Nash, *Quakers and Politics*, 104. See also Nash, "The Free Society."
22. Petition to James II, c. August 18, 1685, and Report of the Lords of Trade, September 2, 1685, *PWP* III: 59-61; on royal disaffection with Calvert, see Sutto, "William Penn,

Charles Calvert, and the Limits of Royal Authority," and Pincus, *1688*, 141; "that the land," Order in Privy Council, November 13, 1685, *PWP* III: 69. See also Minute of the Lords of Trade, October 8, 1685, *PWP* 5: 296; To the President and Provincial Council, October 21, 1685, *PWP* 5: 308. More generally on the history of Maryland see Sutto, *Loyal Protestants*.

23. "a collection of," Penn, *A further account*, 65; "wheat, barley" (69); "Next summer" (15).

24. "I hasten to you," To the President and Provincial Council, October 21, 1685, *PWP* 5: 308; "packet upon packet" and "Americanizing my family," To Thomas Lloyd, September 21, 1686, *PWP* III: 117. See also To James Harrison, September 23, 1686, *PWP* III: 123, where Penn writes that "my wife is give up," which the editors of *PWP* interpret to mean she had consented to return to Pennsylvania with him.

25. "willingly sucked into," Tully, *Forming American Politics*, 33; "my old post and province," A History of my Life from 1684, c. 1691–1692, *PWP* III: 342; Earl of Sunderland to Sir Robert Sawyer, June 6, 1686, *PWP* III: 97; "My being here," To Thomas Lloyd, September 21, 1686, *PWP* III: 117.

26. "I have been an instrument," To Thomas Lloyd, September 21, 1686, *PWP* III: 117; "open, large, and sweet" (119).

27. Penn rebutted each of these charges in a letter to Stephen Crisp, February 28, 1685, *PWP* III: 29.

28. "sufficiently watched," To the Provincial Council, c. June 1686, *PWP* III: 93–94; see also To Thomas Lloyd, September 21, 1686, *PWP* III: 119–120; "Cannot more friendly," To Thomas Lloyd and others, August 15, 1685, *PWP* III: 50; see also To the Provincial Council, August 19, 1685, *PWP* 5: 264.

29. "remember that your station," To the Provincial Council, June 1686, *PWP* III: 94; "many eyes are upon you," To the Provincial Council, April 24, 1686, *PWP* III: 88; "Be you peacemakers," To the Provincial Council, September 25, 1686, *PWP* 5: 536; "I am extremely sorry," To Thomas Lloyd, November 17, 1686, *PWP* III: 128; "we have much ado," To the Provincial Council, June 6, 1687, *PWP* 5: 786.

30. For these various estimates, see: £3,000, To Thomas Lloyd, March 16, 1685, *PWP* III: 33; £1,500, To Thomas Lloyd and others, August 1685, *PWP* III: 48; £6,000, To Thomas Lloyd, September 21, 1686, *PWP* III: 118; £5,000, To James Harrison, September 23, 1686, *PWP* III: 122.

31. From William Markham, August 22, 1686, *PWP* III: 101; "no other notice" (102); "cold entertainment," From Thomas Holme, November 25, 1686, *PWP* III: 132. On his inability to return without funds, see To James Harrison, January 28, 1687, *PWP* III: 137.

32. "my new rents," To the Commissioners of Property, February 1, 1687, *PWP* III: 143; Penn mentions Carpenter's rent inventory somewhat uncertainly in his letter to Harrison of January 28, 1687 ("Samuel Carpenter made an inventory I think of my rents"), but it has never been found (*PWP* III: 138, 141n34); "the province will," From David Lloyd, October 2, 1686, *PWP* 5: 552; "I could have been glad," To James Harrison, November 20, 1686, *PWP* 5: 604. Wanibuchi discusses Penn's aspirations for Pennsylvania's winemaking in "William Penn's Imperial Landscape."

33. "that vile C.A.," From Thomas Holme, May 24, 1687, *PWP* III: 157. Penn raised the issue in his letter to the Commissioners of Property, February 1, 1687, *PWP* III: 142. See also Corcoran, *Thomas Holme*, chs. 13, 15, 16. On the broader history of the Welsh in Pennsylvania, and its impact not only on American affairs but on Quakerism in Wales, see Allen, "In Search of a New Jerusalem"; and Rees, *A History of Quakers*.

34. Welsh tract petition to the Commissioners of Property, April 23, 1688, *PWP* 6: 008; "the most railing," From Phineas Pemberton, January 27, 1687, *PWP* 5: 648; "To knock one in the head," From Joseph Growden, March 1688, *PWP* 5: 951.

35. "move slowly," To Thomas Lloyd and others, May 18, 1685, *PWP* III: 44; "He is a man I love" (44); "speak earnestly" and "drinking collations," To Thomas Lloyd, May 19, 1685, *PWP* 5: 158; "the great oak," To the Commissioners of Property, February 1, 1687, *PWP* III: 142. See also Corcoran, *Thomas Holme*, ch. 13.

36. "I should have been glad," To James Harrison, September 23, 1686, *PWP* III: 122. In October 1685, he wrote that he had not heard from Harrison for five months (October 4, 1685, *PWP* 5: 290); "Let me hear all," To James Harrison, September 8, 1687, *PWP* III: 162.

37. Ship contents, "Invoice of Goods shipped from London," December 9, 1685, *PWP* 5: 349, reprinted in *Pennsylvania Magazine of History and Biography* 37 (1913): 380; "I would have a kitchen," To James Harrison, March 18, 1685, *PWP* III: 39; poplars and the barge into dry dock, To James Harrison, May 19, 1685, *PWP* III: 56; bannister, To James Harrison, January 28, 1687, *PWP* III: 137, spacing of fence rails (138); shingling of roof, From William Markham, July 21, 1688, *PWP* III: 199. "my family," To James Harrison, September–October 1686, *PWP* 5: 542; "Pray don't," To James Harrison, February 1687, *PWP* 5: 669.

38. Harrison's letter of October 3, 1686, in *A letter from Doctor More*, 8; From James Reid, May 14, 1686, *PWP* 5: 442.

39. James Claypoole to Edward Claypoole, December 2, 1683, quoted in Wax, "Quaker Merchants," 146–147; "bother and expense," Wax, "Quaker Merchants," 156.

40. Brown, "Pennsylvania's Antislavery Pioneers," 59–60. *An exhortation and caution to Friends*; "intended to," Cadbury, "Another Early Quaker Anti-Slavery Document," 211; Brown, "Pennsylvania's Antislavery Pioneers."

41. On Penn's slaveholding, see *PWP* III: 67n8; and Ingle, *First Among Friends*, 232. For the longer history of Quakers and slavery, see Soderlund, *Quakers and Slavery*, and more generally, Hoppit, *A Land of Liberty?*, 265–269; "It were better," To James Harrison, October 25, 1685, *PWP* III: 66; "as good as bought," To James Harrison, December 4, 1685, *PWP* 5: 344; "my black," To Phineas Pemberton, February 8, 1687, *PWP* 5: 701.

42. "Even Quakers," Landes, *London Quakers*, 168; 1712 epistle, Landes, *London Quakers*, 73.

43. "I should think," To Gulielma Penn, August 6, 1684, *PWP* III: 587; "I was very weak," Gulielma Penn to Margaret Fox, August 21, 1683, *PWP* III: 460.

44. "I wonder I have not," To the Provincial Council, April 13, 1686, *PWP* 5: 409; "I have writ to you several times," To Thomas Lloyd, Thomas Holme, and Robert Turner, April 22, 1686, *PWP* 5: 409; To the Commissioners of State, December 27, 1687, *PWP* III: 170.

45. To the Commissioners of State, December 21, 1687, *PWP* III: 168–169.

46. To Thomas Lloyd, November 17, 1686, *PWP* III: 129.

47. "so slightly regarded" and "by proclamations," To James Harrison, January 28, 1687, *PWP* III: 136–137; Proclamation About Caves in Philadelphia, January 24, 1687, *PWP* III: 134; To the Commissioners of Property, February 1, 1687, *PWP* III: 142–144; To the Commissioners of State, February 1, 1687, *PWP* III: 144–146; To the Commissioners of State, December 21, 1687, *PWP* III: 168–169.

48. "There are grudges" and "many disorders," From Thomas Holme, November 25, 1686, *PWP* III: 131; "No hope," From Thomas Holme, May 24, 1687, *PWP* III: 160.

49. "sober and ingenious," To the Provincial Council, April 24, 1686, *PWP* III: 88–89; "more a colonist," Lokken, *David Lloyd*, 24–25.

50. See Orders of the Proprietors of East Jersey, July 3, 1685.

51. To Sir Daniel Fleming, November 6, 1686, *PWP* III: 127–128; "Meetings never larger," To Robert Turner, spring 1687, *PWP* 5: 734; "I never doubted," From William Sewel, December 20, 1689, *PWP* 6: 380, reprinted in *William Sewel of Amsterdam*, 90; "suppress or refute," From William Sewel, August 7, 1690, *PWP* 6: 471, reprinted in Hull, *William Sewel of Amsterdam*, 93. See also from William Sewel, August 30, 1686, *PWP* III: 115; From William Sewel, November 26, 1686, *PWP* 5: 734; From William Sewel, September 12, 1687, *PWP* III: 166–167.

52. Penn's funeral sermon for Rebecca Travers is reprinted, and analyzed, in Graves, "Travelers Here in this Vale of Tears."

53. Buckingham, *A short discourse*; To the Duke of Buckingham, February 16, 1686, *PWP* III: 147–148. For Buckingham's side of the exchange, see From Buckingham, February 22, 1687, *PWP* 5: 723; and From Buckingham, March 4, 1687, *PWP* 5: 726.

54. "pays twenty pounds," Penn, *Defence of the Duke of Buckingham's book*, 27–28; "There's not one word," Penn, *Annimadversions*, 1–2.

55. "free and open profession," Penn, *Perswasive*, 1; "I always premise," Penn, *Perswasive*, 1–2. For the rhetorical nature of claims to moderation, see Shagan, *The Rule of Moderation*, 287, 306.

56. "the down-right toleration," Penn, *Perswasive*, 15; "Interest will not lie," Penn, *Perswasive*, 2nd ed., 25, and *Perswasive to Moderation*, 2nd ed., Preface. For the broader history of the phrase, see Gunn, "'Interest Will Not Lie'"; "no man suffers," *Perswasive*, 20; "as men," *Perswasive*, 33.

57. Penn, *Perswasive*, "severity" (Preface), "the interest" (Preface), "be ruined" (36), "to be loved" (27).

58. For the scriptural arguments see *Perswasive*, 38–39; "admitted of all" (46); sheep and goats (44).

59. "That the Church," Penn, *Perswasive*, 42–43; "We have other laws enough" (45). Penn's role in articulating the tolerationist position in support of James's efforts is outlined in Rose, *Godly Kingship*, 188–194.

60. From Henry Sidney, September 17, 1687, *PWP* III: 164. On William's life and career, see Claydon, *William III*, chs. 1 and 2.

61. Henry Care, *A vindication*; "Those who defended," Rose, *Godly Kingship*, 264. See also Pincus, *1688*, ch. 6; Jones, *Revolution*, 59–66; Speck, *Reluctant Revolutionaries*; and Kenyon, "The Commission for Ecclesiastical Causes."

62. "the resolution," Care, *Animadversions*, 37. On *Godden v. Hales*, see Dixon, "Godden v Hales Revisited," but compare Speck, *Reluctant Revolutionaries*. See also Rose, *Godly Kingship*, 89–115, 184–202; John Miller, *James II*, esp. 155–158, 165; and Carolyn A. Edie, "Revolution and the Rule of Law."

63. Mark Knights has argued that the addresses of thanks to the king were of dubious value, since "[v]ery few came unsolicited or without remodeling of corporations or livery companies, making them questionable representations of public opinion" (*Representation and Misrepresentation*, 123). See Sowerby, *Making Toleration*, for another view. For the Quaker address of May 1687, see *PWP* III: 155–156; "Friends unwilling," To Robert Turner, spring 1687, *PWP* 5: 734. James's pardon of Quakers in March 1686 is in *CSP Domestic, James II*, March 15, 1686, #274.

64. "You are . . . to be hugged," Halifax, *Letter to a Dissenter*, 3; "the benefit of the end" (10), "all the former haughtiness" (11). See Pincus, *1688*, ch. 7. For an alternate view, see Goldie, "John Locke's Circle."

65. Penn, *Letter; Second letter; Third letter;* "we cannot agree," Penn, *Good advice*, 58; "hav[ing] a few offices," Penn, *Second letter*, 16.

66. "Let each tub" and "the government should stand," *Second letter*, 5; "if we could not," Penn, in Popple, *A letter to Mr. Penn*, 16; "Should a man's being," Penn, *Third letter*, 14.

67. "quit those," Penn, *Good advice*, 44; see also Penn, *Second letter*, 17; Penn, *Letter*, 2.

68. "intellectual architect," Sowerby, "Of Different Complexions," 41. See also Sowerby, *Making Toleration*, 140, which refers to Penn's letter regarding the regulation of Huntingdon (for details of which see *PWP* III: 175–177).

69. "settle," The King's Answer, May 24, 1687, *PWP* III: 156; "have . . . constraint," *Good advice*, 45; "another Great Charter," *Second letter*, 18; [establish] liberty of conscience," Care, *Animadversions*, 10; "Magna Charta," Penn, *The great and popular objection*, 8; "we hope here," To the Commissioners of State, October 21, 1687, *PWP* 5: 840.

70. [Thomas Comber], *Three considerations*, 1; and *Some queries*, 8; "James and the repealers," Sowerby, *Making Toleration*, 94.

71. Sowerby, "Of Different Complexions" 41–42; Sowerby, *Making Toleration*, 40–41; on James's parliamentary campaign, see From Thomas Marriett, c. 1688, *PWP* III: 172–175; To Richard Jobson, January 19, 1688, *PWP* III: 175–176. See also Goldie, "John Locke's Circle"; Jones, *Revolution*, 234; Pincus, *1688*, 204, and ch. 7. On Petty, see Sowerby, *Making Toleration*, 258.

72. Miller, *James II*, 181–182; Geiter, *William Penn*, 57–58; Kenyon, *Robert Spencer*, 197–198.

73. Pincus, *1688*, ch. 6; Jones, *Revolution*, ch. 6; Miller, *James II*, 171. For Penn's communication with the Magdalen Fellows, see Letter to Dr. Bayly, September 26, 1687, *PWP* 5: 823; Jones, *Revolution*, 120.

74. "such just and equal," James II, reprinted in Browning, *English Historical Documents*, 400. The bishops' reply is reprinted in Kenyon, *Stuart Constitution*, 407; for the order for reading James's Declaration, see James II, Order in Council. On the reaction, see Bennett, "The Seven Bishops"; Miller, "James II and Toleration"; and Rose, *Godly Kingship*, ch. 6.

75. "To the Commissioners of State," September 18, 1688, *PWP* III: 209.

76. To Thomas Lloyd, March 28, 1688, *PWP* III: 183–184; "let him see," To the Commissioners of State, September 18, 1688, *PWP* III: 209. Lokken titles his chapter on Blackwell "The Lloyds Revolt" (*David Lloyd*, ch. 4).

77. "much dissatisfaction," From William Markham, July 21, 1688, *PWP* III: 195; "belief" (197); "they must proceed" (198).
78. "your sole continuance," John Blackwell to President Lloyd, November 11, 1688, reprinted in *Pennsylvania Archives*, I: 107; "a great number of boys" and "found the place," From John Blackwell, April 1689, *PWP* III: 219.
79. Wainwright, "Governor John Blackwell," 462.

Chapter 10

1. Details from Miller, *James II*, 208–209. For overviews of the period covered in this chapter see Hoppit, *A Land of Liberty?*; Rose, *England in the 1690s*; Pincus, *1688*; Kishlansky, *A Monarchy Transformed*, chs. 10–13; Miller, *The Glorious Revolution*; and *The Revolution of 1688–89: Changing Perspectives*.
2. Penn, *Some Fruits of Solitude*; Penn, *An essay toward the present and future peace of Europe*.
3. See Pincus, *1688*, 404; Claydon, *William III*, esp. 166–170.
4. See Pincus, *1688*, 285–286; "some ease," preamble to Toleration Act, in Browning, *English Historical Documents*, 400–403; Hoppit puts it succinctly: "The exclusive relationship between citizenship and Anglicanism was severed" (*A Land of Liberty?*, 33); Locke, quoted in Hoppit, *A Land of Liberty?*, 33.
5. Claydon, *William III*, 42–46, 179–187; Hoppit, *A Land of Liberty?*, 89–110; Rose, *England in the 1690s*, ch. 4. This war should not be confused with the other "Nine Years' War" mentioned earlier in reference to Ireland (1593–1603).
6. "I do profess," To the Earl of Shrewsbury, March 7, 1689, *PWP* III: 236; Braithwaite, *Second Period*, 151–152.
7. "make strict," The Earl of Nottingham to William Sharpe, June 22, 1689, *PWP* III: 251; "I am no fighter," To the Marquis of Halifax, June 28, 1689, *PWP* III: 252. On the arrest see *PWP* III: 251n.
8. Epistle to the Quakers, [late 1689?], *PWP* III: 269; Penn's May 1691 letter to the London Yearly Meeting is reprinted in *Works*, I: 140.
9. For the details of these proclamations see *PWP* III: 283n3; "I am well," To the Provincial Council, September 15, 1690, *PWP* III: 284; "follow him," *PWP* III: 278.
10. There has been significant debate over what these documents establish. Compare Geiter, "William Penn and Jacobitism," with Braithwaite, *Second Period*, 163–165. "Mr. Penn," *CSP Domestic, William III, 1690–1691*, January 20, 1691; "he was a true," Viscount Sidney to William III, February 27, 1691, *PWP* III: 293; "justice and goodness," To the Lord Romney, April 22, 1691, *PWP* 6: 571, reprinted in Penn, "Inedited Letters," 192; "I know of no invasions," To the Lord Romney, n.d. 1691, *PWP* 6: 525, reprinted in "Inedited Letters," 194; "when I speak," From Viscount Sidney, November 7, 1691, *PWP* III: 332.
11. "that night," To Thomas Lloyd, June 14, 1691, *PWP* III: 327 (this is the letter headed "England"); "speak to the King," To Archbishop Tillotson, October 31, 1691, *PWP* III: 331; "I shall never misuse," To Lord Nottingham, June 12, 1692, *PWP* 6: 653; "Let him go," To the Earl of Nottingham, November 21, 1692, *PWP* III: 353; "been above," To —, n.d. (1692), *PWP* 6: 703, reprinted in "Inedited Letters," 198.
12. "a bill found," To —, n.d. (1692), *PWP* 6: 703, reprinted in "Inedited Letters," 199; "whatever are my faults," To the Earl of Rochester, c. 1692, *PWP* III: 352.
13. "my estate in Ireland," To —, n.d. (1692), *PWP* 6: 703, reprinted in "Inedited Letters," 199; see also Simms, *Jacobite Ireland*.
14. "I was going," *PWP* III: 351; he claimed the same to the Earl of Rochester, *PWP* III: 352 and to Thomas Lloyd, June 14, 1691, *PWP* III: 326; *Some proposals for a second settlement*; "I have begun" and "to go for America," To Friends in Ireland, January 8, 1691, *PWP* III: 292; "a way for me," To Thomas Holme, n.d. (1690), *PWP* 6: 405.
15. Nash, "Quest for Susquehannah," 18; "one of the most active," Zimmerman, "Daniel Coxe and the New Mediterranean Sea Company," 86, also 88–89; and Pomfret, *West New Jersey*, ch. 9.
16. "to throw all," To the Provincial Council, August 12, 1689, *PWP* III: 253; "wound," From Phineas Pemberton and others, c. April 1689, *PWP* III: 247.

NOTES TO PAGES 208–215   397

17. "it is hard to imagine," Calvert, *Quaker Constitutionalism*, 117; "he hath lived" and "to be overwhelmed," From Phineas Pemberton and others, April 1689, *PWP* III: 247; "want of true love," From John Simcock and other Provincial Councilors, April 9, 1689, *PWP* III: 237; "unsuitable," From John Blackwell, May 1, 1689, *PWP* III: 243; see also From John Blackwell, June 24, 1689, *PWP* 6: 319. This narrative of Blackwell's tenure draws on Nicholas Wainwright, "Governor John Blackwell." See also Calvert, *Quaker Constitutionalism*, 116–120; Nash, *Quakers and Politics*, ch. 3; Horsefield, "The Origin of Blackwell's Model."
    As Calvert puts it, "With Friends' persecution at the hands of Massachusetts Puritans only a few years behind them, and their disavowal of all things military, the decision was disastrous to [Penn's] relationship with them" (*Quaker Constitutionalism*, 117).
18. Nash, *Quakers and Politics*, 117; "I can get," From John Blackwell, May 1, 1689, *PWP* III: 245; Wainwright, "Governor John Blackwell," 464; From John Simcock and other Provincial Councilors, April 9, 1689, *PWP* III: 237; "harsh, unkind, and arbitrary," From Phineas Pemberton and others, c. April 1689, *PWP* III: 248; From Phineas Pemberton, April 8, 1689, *PWP* 6: 277.
19. "a faction" and "he knows no superiors," From John Blackwell, May 1, 1689, *PWP* III: 245; remaining quotations from From John Blackwell, June 24, 1689, *PWP* 6: 319.
20. From John Blackwell, June 24, 1689, *PWP* 6: 319; "succeeded only," Nash, *Quakers and Politics*, 126.
21. "call all persons," Instructions to John Blackwell, September 25, 1689, *PWP* III: 259–261; "such a people," From John Blackwell, January 13, 1690, *PWP* 6: 414; "the wild beasts," John Blackwell to To Thomas Hartley, quoted in Nuttall, "Governor John Blackwell," 141.
22. "Taking up," From John Blackwell, January 13, 1690, *PWP* 6: 414; Bronner, *William Penn's Holy Experiment*, 73.
23. "a loser," From John Blackwell, May 15, 1690, *PWP* III: 281.
24. *PWP* III: 283n9; Nash, *Quakers and Politics*, 118; *PWP* III: 240n; Munroe, *Colonial Delaware: A History*, 98–99.
25. To Thomas Lloyd and others, December 30, 1689, *PWP* 6: 404.
26. "I have not," To the Provincial Council, September 15, 1690, *PWP* III: 284; "I hoped," To the Provincial Council, November 11, 1690, *PWP* III: 285; "I know not," To the Provincial Council, November 13, 1690, *PWP* III: 288; To the Provincial Council, November 11, 1690, *PWP* III: 285–288; also To the Commissioners of Property, November 17, 1690, *PWP* 6: 514; Commission to Jennings and Commissioners of Property, November 14, 1690, *PWP* 6: 510, 511.
27. "most disagreeable," Declaration, April 1, 1691, in Proud, *History*, I: 355; *PWP* III: 299; Declaration of the Council of the Lower Counties, April 6, 1691, *PWP* 6: 548; "laboring," From Robert Turner, May 23, 1691, *PWP* III: 323; "some of us," From the Council of the Lower Counties, April 6, 1691, *PWP* III: 296; "we are in," From Turner, May 23, 1691, *PWP* III: 320.
28. "loose clubs," From the Provincial Council, April 11, 1691, *PWP* III: 304–305; "not been so kind," From Joseph Growden, *PWP* III: 309; "we are forsaken," From the Provincial Council and Assembly, May 18, 1691, *PWP* III: 316, 317; text reads "principals." For broader background on the growing rift between Pennsylvania and the Lower Counties see Johannsen, "Conflict," 101–109.
29. "for whose sake," From the Provincial Council, April 11, 1691, *PWP* III: 303; "fidelity to thee," From the Provincial Council and Assembly, May 18, 1691, *PWP* III: 317; "all the hardships," From John Simcock and other Councilors, April 9, 1689, *PWP* III: 238; "we have labored," From Phineas Pemberton and others, April 1689, *PWP* III: 247.
30. "unwilling that," From Joseph Growden, April 29, 1691, *PWP* III: 307.
31. To the deposed members of the Provincial Council, September 15, 1693, *PWP* III: 376; "I am not," From Thomas Lloyd, December 21, 1693, *PWP* III: 385; "I have not," To Thomas Lloyd's Supporters, April 24, 1694, *PWP* III: 390; "we know him better," From Thomas Lloyd's Supporters, January 18, 1694, *PWP* III: 386.
32. "an absolute overthrowing," To the Provincial Council, November 11, 1690, *PWP* III: 286, 287; "Surely," To the Provincial Council, November 11, 1690, *PWP* III: 287. See Nash, *Quakers and Politics*, 112, 121; Calvert, *Quaker Constitutionalism*, 120.
33. "Your division," To the Provincial Council, September 11, 1691, *PWP* III: 328; "You of the lower counties," September 11, 1691, *PWP* III: 329; "to act," From the Provincial Council, April 6, 1692, *PWP* III: 349.

34. See Tully, *Forming American Politics*, 416–419; To a Weighty Friend in England, June 29, 1692, *PWP* III: 350.

35. "My concerns," To the Earl of Rochester, 1692, *PWP* III: 352; "you can not imagine," To the Provincial Council, September 11, 1691, *PWP* III: 328.

36. "to give thee," To Governor Fletcher, December 5, 1692, *PWP* III: 358; "deliver your representations," Extract of a letter from William Penn to a person in Pennsylvania, December 1692, *CSP Colonial, 1689–1692*, #2668; Minute of Lords of Trade and Plantations, February 2, 1694, *CSP Colonial, 1693–1696*, #860; *An address.* The Fletcher regime is described in Nash, *Quakers and Politics*, 181–187; and Johanssen, "Conflict," 109–112.

37. For the disputes with New England Puritans, see Keith, *The Presbyterian and Independent visible churches in New-England*, and Mather, *The principles of the Protestant religion*. Keith responded to Mather in *The pretended antidote proved poison* and *A serious appeal to all the more sober, impartial & judicious people in New-England*, and defended Rhode Island Quakers in *The Christian faith of the people of God, called in scorn, Quakers.*

   For more on Keith, and a more extended narrative of events, see Kirby, *George Keith*; *The Keithian Schism in Early Pennsylvania*; Murphy, *Conscience and Community*, ch. 5; Murphy, "Persecuting Quakers?"; Pomfret, *West New Jersey*, ch. 13; and Smolenski, *Friends and Strangers*, ch. 4.

38. Keith, *Some reasons and causes*, 7–9. See also Martin, "Tradition and Innovation," 15–18.

39. Keith, *An appeal from the twenty eight judges*, 1–2, 6, 7, 8.

40. Keith, *New-England's spirit of persecution*; for the anti-Quaker polemics, see, e.g., Leeds, *News of a trumpet*.

41. To Robert Turner, November 29, 1692, *PWP* III: 354–355. Smolenski emphasizes the radical nature of Keith's belief in the transmigration of souls (*Friends and Strangers*, 171–172).

42. From Hugh Roberts, early 1693, *PWP* III: 359–360. Landes argues that Penn's hesitation to condemn Keith mirrored that of London Friends, who were "slower to react to [Keith's] challenge and held the hope of reconciliation for longer than Pennsylvania Quakers" (*London Quakers*, 58). Once they did act, however, Landes argues that their epistles were quite effective in undermining Keith's movement in the colonies (62–63).

43. To Friends in Pennsylvania, December 11, 1693, *PWP* III: 383.

44. "may be fairly," Keith, *Anti-Christs and Sadducees detected*, 3. Butler addresses some of the schism's aftereffects on Pennsylvania society in "Into Pennsylvania's Spiritual Abyss."

45. "A whole stratum," Nash, *Quakers and Politics*, 160; also 154. Tolles calls Lloyd "the patriarch and progenitor of the Philadelphia Quaker aristocracy" (*Meeting House and Counting House*, 120).

46. See also Landes, *London Quakers*, which describes the controversy as "a symptom of Quaker Atlantic activity, where one man's expectations were influenced by his colonial experience" (168).

47. *Some letters and an abstract of letters from Pennsylvania*, "found the government" (11); "The bank" (12); "your hearts" (3).

48. Penn, *A key opening the way*, title page.

49. "chiefly concerned," Penn, *Just measures*; "exercise their gifts" (8).

50. Penn, *Some fruits of solitude.*

51. Steve Pincus has argued that James was "a great and outspoken admirer of the modern absolutist state created by Louis XIV," while most of his subjects "desperately wanted their kings to put a halt to the overweening power of France." See Pincus, *1688*, 317, 305, 337. See also James Walker, "The English Exiles."

52. Pincus, *1688*, ch. 12; Rose, *England in the 1690s*, ch. 4.

53. "bloody tragedies," Penn, *An essay toward the present and future peace of Europe*, 1; "Peace preserves" (3).

54. "to avoid," Penn, *Essay*, 19; "an estimate" (16); "the Empire" (17–18); "in the sight of" (28). On the Venetian system, see McLellan, *The Oligarchy of Venice*, 159–160. For example, the Duke of Sully's 1638 "Grand Design" viewed Europe as distinctly Christian. See Sully, *Memoirs of the Duke of Sully*, IV: Bk. 30; see also H. D. Schmidt, "The Establishment of 'Europe' as a Political Expression"; Dorpalen, "The European Polity," and Kuehl, *Seeking World Order*, ch. 1.

55. "as free as ever," To Friends in Pennsylvania, December 11, 1693, *PWP* III: 383; "I am glad," From John Gratton, January 2, 1694, *PWP* 6: 798.

56. To the Provincial Council, September 15, 1690, *PWP* III: 285; "almost ruined," To the Earl of Rochester, 1692, *PWP* III: 352; "a loss," To Hugh Roberts, December 6, 1689, *PWP* III: 265; To Thomas Lloyd, June 4, 1691, *PWP* III: 326; To the Inhabitants of Pennsylvania, February 4, 1693, *PWP* III: 374–375.

57. To the Earl of Nottingham, July 31, 1690, *PWP* III: 283; To the Earl of Nottingham, November 21, 1692, *PWP* III: 353–354; To Sir John Rodes, October 1693, *PWP* III: 380; "delight and diversion," To Hugh Roberts, December 6, 1689, *PWP* III: 265.

58. "a choice and seasoned," Burnyeat, *The truth exalted*, 12; "fixed and bright" (14); "bold and able," Barclay, *Truth triumphant*, Testimony.

59. "I am to be," To Margaret Fox, January 13, 1691, *PWP* 6: 532; "He earnestly recommended," To Thomas Lloyd, June 14, 1691, *PWP* III: 327; "plainness, zeal," *Journal*, Preface. Details of Fox's death from Ingle, *First Among Friends*, ch. 17 and Epilogue.

60. "dangerously relapsed," To the Earl of Nottingham, November 21, 1692, *PWP* III: 353; "heard," From John Gratton, November 9, 1693, *PWP* 6: 787; "has run," To Robert Barclay, Jr., October 31, 1693, *PWP* 6: 785; "extreme great affliction," To Robert Turner, February 27, 1694, *PWP* III: 388.

61. "she was an excelling," *An account of the blessed end*, 7; "one of the most," To Thomas Lloyd's Supporters, April 24, 1694, *PWP* III: 389.

62. "in the center," Breviate of Petition to Queen Mary and the Privy Council, July 4, 1694, *PWP* III: 395, 396; Report of the Lords of Trade, August 1 and 3, 1694, *PWP* III: 397–402.

63. "has given us," Proclamation reprinted in Proud, *History*, I: 404; "the supplying," Report of the Lords of Trade, August 1 and 3, 1694, *PWP* III: 397, 398; "we must creep," To the Provincial Council, November 24, 1694, *PWP* III: 405.

64. Pincus, *1688*, 264.

Chapter 11

1. "helped to boost," Rose, *England in the 1690s*, 134; "unhappily taken," To the Provincial Council, November 24, 1694, *PWP* III: 406; "no amount," Rose, *England in the 1690s*, 143.

2. On this child, see Henry J. Cadbury, "Hannah Callowhill and Penn's Second Marriage," 78–79.

3. Details of the tour in Whiting, *Persecution exposed*, 237.

4. "great meeting[s]," Whiting, *Persecution exposed*, 237; "Bristol was scarcely," Henry Gouldney to Sir John Rodes, November 6, 1694, in *A Quaker Post-bag*, 60.

5. "that I am fair," To the Duke of Shrewsbury, October 5, 1695, *PWP* III: 414; "upon a mistaken zeal," From the Duke of Shrewsbury, October 6, 1695, *PWP* III: 415; "that dark city," To Aaron Atkinson, November 22, 1695, *PWP* III: 420.

6. "having been drinking" and "a large room," Whiting, *Persecution exposed*, 240; "William Penn and some other Quakers," *Works* I: 142; "dismissed honorably," To Aaron Atkinson, November 22, 1695, *PWP* III: 421; "who had gladly heard him," Whiting, *Persecution exposed*, 242.

7. "a working time," To John Gratton, December 12, 1695, *PWP* III: 423; "lovely in the truth," To Aaron Atkinson, November 22, 1695, *PWP* III: 421; Letitia Penn to Hannah Callowhill, December 12, 1695, *PWP* III: 424; "was seated," To Hannah Callowhill, January 28, 1696, *PWP* III: 425. On Margaret Lowther's gift of lobsters, see *PWP* III: 434n19. The best sources on Hannah are Drinker, *Hannah and the Proprietorship of Pennsylvania*; and Hirsch, "A Tale of Two Wives."

8. "daily fresh," To Hannah Callowhill, Sr., June 28, 1695, *PWP* III: 411; To John Gratton, August 21, 1695, *PWP* 6: 975; To Hannah Callowhill, January 17, 1696, *PWP* 7: 042.

9. To Hannah Callowhill: "I behold" and "would persuade myself," September 10, 1695, *PWP* III: 413; "safely home," December 7, 1695, *PWP* 6: 997.

10. Announcement and reaffirmation to Bristol Meeting, *PWP* III: 413–414n1; "enquire concerning" and "he is very clear," William Penn's declarations concerning marriage, December 11, 1695, and January 8, 1696, *PWP* 6: 999.

11. To Hannah Callowhill: "It would exceedingly add," January 17, 1696, *PWP* 7: 042; "thy general indifference," February 5, 1696, *PWP* III: 428 (the text is lined through but legible); "the slowest beginnings," February 6, 1696, *PWP* 7: 104.

12. To Hannah Callowhill: "my love is renewed," December 17, 1695, *PWP* 6: 1006; "that lives and flows," February 1, 1696, *PWP* 7: 087; "the man of the world," February 11, 1696, *PWP* 7: 114; gift of dove and "a proprietorship," February 5, 1696, *PWP* III: 430.

13. To Hannah Callowhill: December 17, 1695, *PWP* 6: 1006; January 2, 1696, *PWP* 7: 014; January 21, 1696, *PWP* 7: 055; "convulsion water," January 28, 1696, *PWP* III: 425; December 7, 1695, *PWP* 6: 997.

14. To Hannah Callowhill: January 28, 1696, *PWP* III: 425; January 14, 1696, *PWP* 7: 037; January 17, 1696, *PWP* 7: 042; "drooping condition," January 23, 1696, *PWP* 7: 065; January 21, 1696, *PWP* 7: 055; "at best, at a stand," January 30, 1696, *PWP* 7: 075; "stronger and hungry," February 5, 1696, *PWP* III: 428; "quarrels us all," February 9, 1696, *PWP* III: 431; Springett's "ugly cold and cough," February 14, 1696, *PWP* 7: 123.

15. To Hannah Callowhill: "not lose or miss a word," January 2, 1696, *PWP* 7: 014; "mend thy pace," January 21, 1696, *PWP* 7: 055; "that anything I have writ," January 19, 1696, *PWP* 7: 049.

16. "let nothing," To Hannah Callowhill, January 4, 1696, *PWP* 7: 019; "I intend," to Hannah Callowhill, January 23, 1696, *PWP* 7: 065; To Hannah Callowhill, January 28, 1696, *PWP* III: 426, and February 9, 1696, *PWP* III: 432; "the pride," February 1, 1696, *PWP* 7: 087; "I am told," Thomas Janney to Phineas Pemberton, November 17, 1695, *PWP* III: 419.

17. "my matter," To John Gratton, December 12, 1695, *PWP* III: 422; "this affair," Henry Gouldney to John Rodes, November 12, 1695, *A Quaker Post-bag*, 62; "I know not," John Tomkins to John Rodes, October 22, 1695, *A Quaker Post-bag*, 127; "I know what moved," To John Gratton, December 12, 1695, *PWP* III: 422; "what we have met with," To Hannah Callowhill, January 4, 1696, *PWP* 7: 019; "Dear Friend," From John Gratton, October 1, 1698, *PWP* 7: 750; "I remember thee often," To John Gratton, July 1699, *A Quaker Post-bag*, 12. See also Cadbury, "Hannah Callowhill," 82.

18. "seem to have," *PWP* III: 394. The marriage certificate is reprinted in *PWP* III: 435.

19. Thomas Janney to Phineas Pemberton, November 17, 1695, *PWP* III: 419.

20. Wildes, *William Penn*, 279.

21. Hirsch, "A Tale of Two Wives," 430.

22. John Tomkins to John Rodes, April 16, 1696, *A Quaker Post-bag*, 130.

23. Penn, *An account of the blessed end*; the work is paginated 1–10 with the account of Gulielma's passing, and then begins again at p. 1 for Springett's account; "from his childhood" (1–2); "humility, plainness" and "a tenderness" (2); "when I went to meeting" (4–5); "my comfort and hope" (17–18).

24. Tomkins to Rodes, April 16, 1696, *A Quaker Post-bag*, 130.

25. "the people murmur," "is absent," and "Thou hast," From Robert Turner, August 13, 1694, *PWP* 6: 900; "gives not one word" and "the ruins and desolation," From Robert Turner, September 17, 1694, *PWP* III: 403; From Robert Turner, December 9, 1697, *PWP* III: 532–534.

26. Lloyd died on either September 10 or 11, 1694. On the controversy over the Great Seal, see From Robert Turner, September 17, 1694, *PWP* III: 402–403; Penn's commission to Jennings, September 28, 1694, as receiver-general is in *PWP* 6: 915.

27. "As to the present condition," To the Provincial Council, November 24, 1694, *PWP* III: 406; "I hear vice reigns," To Robert Turner, December 25, 1696, *PWP* III: 472; "growing debauchery," From Robert Turner, April 15, 1697, *PWP* III: 511; "there is no place more overrun," To William Markham and the Council, September 5, 1697, *PWP* III: 518; "wickedness grows," From Robert Turner, December 9, 1697, *PWP* III: 533.

28. "Here we pay" and "for mixed services," To Arthur Cook and others, November 5, 1695, *PWP* III: 416.

29. "overset the government," To Arthur Cook and others, November 5, 1695, *PWP* III: 416; "not only refuse," The Anglican Petition, c. 1695–1696, *PWP* III: 444; "either . . . men or money," From the Board of Trade, February 9, 1697, *PWP* 7: 345; "we are but 14 years old," Memorial to the Board of Trade, February 12, 1697, *PWP* III: 485; "having been long settled," From the Pennsylvania Assembly, November 7, 1696, *PWP* 7: 242; "having the military power," Philip Ford to William Blathwayt, December 14, 1694, *PWP* 6: 929.

30. The Anglican Petition, c. 1695–1696, *PWP* III: 443–445; on Nicholson, see Webb, "The Strange Career of Francis Nicholson."

31. All quotations from The Quaker petition, May 20, 1696, *PWP* III: 445–447; "disingenuous argument," 449n18.

32. The Quaker petition, May 20, 1696, *PWP* III: 447.

33. "good understanding," From Samuel Carpenter, November 17, 1696, *PWP* III: 466; "for the supply and relief," *PWP* III: 468n9. Details of the Frame's passage are laid out in Nash, *Quakers and Politics*, 201–207; and Lokken, *David Lloyd*, ch. 7.

34. "nearly unstoppable," Calvert, *Quaker Constitutionalism*, 127; "not deemed," Draft of The Frame of Government of 1696, November 7, 1696, *PWP* III: 458; "the representatives" (462); "as near to our charter," From the Pennsylvania Assembly, November 7, 1696, *PWP* 7: 242. See also Lokken, *David Lloyd*, ch. 7.

35. "the consent," Second Frame of Government, April 2, 1683, in *William Penn and the Founding of Pennsylvania*, 272; "conscious tightening," Nash, *Quakers and Politics*, 205. The petition to Markham (Remonstrance of Philadelphia Inhabitants), March 12, 1697, is in *PWP* III: 499–502.

36. "new pretended Frame," From Robert Turner and others, April 9, 1697, *PWP* III: 508; "innovations" (507); "gives occasion," From Robert Turner, April 15, 1697, *PWP* III: 510; "It may awaken," To Samuel Carpenter and others, December 1, 1697, *PWP* III: 531.

37. "prompted on," "great disturbances," and "it is suspected," From Anthony Morris and others, March 22, 1697, *PWP* III: 503; "the great need" (504); "Nothing less," From Samuel Carpenter, November 17, 1696, *PWP* III: 468; "as representatives," From the Provincial Council and Assembly, May 25, 1697, *PWP* III: 515.

38. "thou left us," From Samuel Carpenter, November 17, 1697, *PWP* III: 467.

39. "want of thy presence," From the Provincial Council and Assembly, May 25, 1697, *PWP* III: 515; "the trouble and cost," From Joseph Richards, July 11, 1698, *PWP* 7: 736; "by sinister-ended men" and "I apply," From Thomas Fitzwater, February 20, 1699, *PWP* 8: 033.

40. On the Darbyshire group, see To Samuel Carpenter and others, December 1, 1697, *PWP* III: 530; "thy purpose" and "watch the motions," To Hugh Roberts, February 17, 1698, *PWP* III: 539.

41. Spurr, "Perjury, Profanity, and Politics," 30.

42. Geiter, "Affirmation, Assassination, and Association." For a detailed narrative of the plot itself, see Garrett, *The Triumphs of Providence*.

43. "declare in the presence," *PWP* III: 451n2; Whitehead, *Christian progress*, 645–655; for the scriptural passage, see Matthew 5:37.

44. "what solemn words," Meeting for Sufferings, *An epistle*, 3; "Let none" (14); "to tell abroad" and "brother will be set," To the Meeting for Sufferings, May 7, 1696, *PWP* III: 450; On the Act and the context surrounding it, see Braithwaite, *Second Period*, 183–188; Geiter, "Affirmation, Assassination, and Association," and Frost, "The Affirmation Controversy and Religious Liberty."

45. See Hoppit, *Land of Liberty?*, 190–194, 246–248.

46. Randolph's reports are mentioned by the Board of Trade in its letter to Penn on February 9, 1697, *PWP* 7: 345; also Randolph's reports to the Board, which appear throughout August 1696 in the *CSP Colonial*: see especially August 17, 1696, #149. The February 20 report is included in *Manuscripts of the House of Lords*, II: 440–444; "a ship or vessel," Extract from a letter from Colonel Nicholson to the Board of Trade, July 13, 1697, *PWP* 7: 509. The best source on Randolph's life and career is Michael Hall, *Edward Randolph and the American Colonies*; see also Johanssen, "Conflict," 122–123.

47. "The Acts of Trade," Randolph, *Manuscripts of the House of Lords*, II: 442; "pirates are harboured there," 441. See also Hall, *Edward Randolph*, 173–175.

48. "a purse of gold," "called him to account," "as humble," "fell to abusing," and "Had I not," From William Markham, April 24, 1697, *PWP* III: 512–513; "I perceive," From William Markham, May 1, 1697, *PWP* 7: 476.

49. "in close prison," From the Provincial Council and Assembly, May 25, 1697, *PWP* III: 516; the pirates' escape was relayed to Penn in a letter from Samuel Carpenter, July 30, 1607, *PWP* 7: 518; "not totally," Hart, "'Naturally cut out . . . for unlawful trade,'" 226, 241.

50. See petition from proprietors, *CSP Colonial*: November 5, 1696, #365; "the de facto leader," *PWP* III: 470; "we are flushed with success," From John Winthrop, January 4, 1697, *PWP* III: 475; "when you come to have," From the Earl of Arran, September 4, 1696, *PWP* III: 455.

51. From King William, April 22, 1697, *PWP* 7: 468.

52. "alarm . . . the people," To Sir William Trumbull, January 4, 1697, *PWP* III: 476; From Lord Bellomont, February 1697, *PWP* III: 481; "the chief technician," Webb, "William Blathwayt,

Imperial Fixer: From Popish Plot to Glorious Revolution," 4; and "William Blathwayt, Imperial Fixer: Muddling Through to Empire, 1689-1717"; "a little officer," To Trumbull, January 4, 1697, *PWP* III: 476.

53. For Nicholson's letter of March 27, 1697, see *PWP* III: 491n3; "at the first convenient season," To William Markham, September 1, 1697, *PWP* 7: 533; From the Pennsylvania Assembly, November 7, 1696, *PWP* 7: 242; From William Markham, March 1, 1697, *PWP* III: 490; From William Markham, February 22, 1697, *PWP* 7: 374; "the greatest monster," From Gerard Slye, June 27, 1698, *PWP* 7: 708. More generally, see Webb, "The Strange Career," and Nash, "Maryland's Economic War with Pennsylvania."

54. "churlish," To William Popple, December 9, 1696, *PWP* 7: 288; formal complaint, Memorial to the Board of Trade objecting to two Maryland laws, February 12, 1697, *PWP* 7: 355; "villainous" and "foul," To Francis Nicholson, November 22, 1697, *PWP* III: 528; "only to dispossess us," To Edward Randolph, October 16, 1697, *PWP* III: 520.

55. De la Noy's complaints about Fletcher are reprinted in Broadhead, *Documents relative to the colonial history of the state of New-York . . .*, IV: 221-224. For correspondence pertaining to the proprietors' complaints about Fletcher and customs, see Mr. Penn's Observations on the Proceedings of Governor Fletcher, December 11, 1696, *Documents relative to . . .*, IV: 246; Petition of East and West Jersey Proprietors to the Treasury Commissioners, March 1, 1697, *PWP* 7: 382; Customs Officers to the Board of Trade, August 31, 1697, *PWP* 7: 528; William Popple to Mr. Lowndes, September 14, 1697, *PWP* 7: 541; Petition of East Jersey proprietors to Commissioners of the Treasury, September 21, 1697, *PWP* 7: 547; From the Earl of Bellomont, June 21,1698, *PWP* III: 547.

56. Lease from Thomas Dongan, January 12, 1697, *PWP* III: 477-478.

57. "more useful," Draft of *A Briefe and Plaine Scheam*, February 8, 1697, *PWP* III: 482; "Every design," Stanwood, *The Empire Reformed*, 182; 1754 Albany Plan of Union, online at http://www.constitution.org/bcp/albany.htm.

58. Proposal for the advancement of trade in America, March 4, 1697, *PWP* III: 493.

59. "I have not seen sixpence," To Robert Turner, December 25, 1696, *PWP* III: 472; "spent and lost," To Sir William Trumbull, January 4, 1697, *PWP* III: 476; "I cannot," From Samuel Carpenter, July 30, 1697, *PWP* 7: 518.

60. On the Assassination Plot, see Pincus, *1688*, ch. 14; and Garrett, *The Triumphs of Providence*. For the inquiry regarding Sir John Friend, see From William Lowndes, July 31, 1696, *PWP* 7: 198. On the arrangements with Ford, see *PWP* III: 542; for Ford's calculation, see Philip Ford's agreement with William Penn, April 10, 1697, *PWP* 7: 454; "Are not these," To the Commissioners of Propriety, May 2, 1698, *PWP* III: 542-543; "the greatest injury," To Samuel Carpenter, April 27, 1698, *PWP* 7: 672; "not for want of love," From Samuel Carpenter, November 19, 1698, *PWP* III: 559-560.

61. To Robert Turner and Thomas Holme, June 20, 1695, *PWP* III: 409.

62. Keith, *Gross error and hypocrisy detected*; Jennings, *The state of the case*; "the separation," Ellwood, *An epistle to Friends*, 10; Penington, *An apostate exposed*.

63. "I, of all men," To Robert Turner, December 25, 1696, *PWP* III: 471; "But what is astonishing," Penn, *More work for George Keith*, Preface; Keith, *The deism of William Penn*.

64. "very passionate," Story, *Reasons why*, 1; Leslie, *The Snake in the grass*. Penn lamented, in a letter to Turner in early 1699, that "part of my letter to thee is printed in a most wicked book" (To Robert Turner, February 16, 1999, *PWP* III: 569). On Leslie's attack on Quakers, see Gill, "William Penn as Preface Writer, Historian, and Controversialist.".

65. Penn, *Some considerations upon the bill*; Penn, *Caution humbly offered*. On Deism in England, see Lucci, *Scripture and Deism*; idem., "Deism, Freethinking, and Toleration."

66. Tomkins, *Harmony of the Old and New Testaments*, 123-146; Penn, *Primitive Christianity Revived*; To Joseph Stennett, November 3 and November 4, 1696, *PWP* 7: 236, 238. For the story of the Friends visiting Peter, see Whitehead, *Christian progress*, 669-672; "piety and charity," To the Czar of Muscovy, April 18, 1698, *PWP* III: 541.

67. From William Sewel, August 2, 1696, in Hull, *William Sewel of Amsterdam*, 150.

68. Petition for a Free Public School, February 10, 1698, *PWP* III: 536-537.

69. "staunchest ally," *PWP* III: 498; "Thou hast left us," From Robert Turner, June 26, 1697, *PWP* 7: 490; "infirm," From Robert Turner, December 9, 1697, *PWP* III: 534.

70. "Friends," To William Markham and the Council, September 5, 1697, *PWP* III: 517–518.
71. "the queen desired," To William Popple, October 15, 1697, *PWP* III: 519; "in my judgment," From Francis Jones, November 13, 1697, *PWP* III: 524; "our having three sloops" (526); "If Colonel Markham hath done ill," To William Popple, October 15, 1697, *PWP* III: 519. See Burgess, *Politics of Piracy*.
72. "the piracy," To Samuel Carpenter and others, December 1, 1697, *PWP* III: 530–531.
73. From the Swedish inhabitants, October 30, 1697, *PWP* III: 521–523.
74. From the Earl of Bellomont, June 21, 1698, *PWP* II: 547.
75. To Samuel Carpenter and others, November 9, 1698, *PWP* III: 557; Horsham Monthly Meeting re: William Penn's visit to Ireland, January 12, 1698, *PWP* 7: 636. Much of this chronology of Penn's trip to Ireland is taken from Forbes, "A 'Lost' Quaker-Baptist Pamphlet Debate," and Story, *Journal*, 127–146. On Ireland during this period, see Rose, *England in the 1690s*, ch. 7; Hoppit, *Land of Liberty?*, 258.
76. Story, *Journal*, 128.
77. To the Earl of Arran, May 7, 1698, *PWP* III: 544; To the Earl of Arran, May 13, 1698, *PWP* III: 545.
78. "very large and open," Story, *Journal*, 129; "many large and blessed opportunities," An Epistle to the Yearly Meeting in London, June 2, 1698, *Works*, I: 235; "the ill treatment," From the Marquis of Winchester and Lord Gallway, June 11, 1698, *PWP* 7: 698; "not a man of revenge," Story, *Journal*, 132.
79. "our ancient and honourable Friend," Story, *Journal*, 136.
80. "journeyman woolcomber," Story, *Journal*, 128; Penn, Story, and Sharp, *Gospel Truths*; Plimpton, *A Quaker no Christian*; Penn, Story, and Everett, *A Quaker a Christian*. On Plimpton more generally, see Forbes, "A 'Lost' Quaker-Baptist Pamphlet Debate."
81. "you cannot," "The Testimony of the Bishop of Cork," in Penn, *A defence of a paper, entitled, Gospel-truths*, 8; "not one word" (9–10); "Light within" (12); "a harmless well-meaning people" (17); "I see," From the Bishop of Cork and Ross, August 26, 1698, *PWP* III: 556.
82. "launch[ing] the attack," Kearney, "The Political Background to English Mercantilism," 484; "of all the plantations," Cary, *An essay on the state of England*, 89; "make Ireland profitable" (98). To the Lord's Justices of Ireland, July 1, 1698, *PWP* III: 548–551; on Locke's views, see *PWP* III: 551n5.
83. "Colonel Quary," From Samuel Carpenter, July 4, 1698, *PWP* III: 552; "found a way," Robert Snead to Francis Nicholson, May 6, 1698, *PWP* 7: 682.
84. From Samuel Carpenter and others, July 4, 1698, *PWP* III: 553; "the law in itself," To the Board of Trade, December 19, 1698, *PWP* III: 561.
85. "openly affronting," "knowing them," Quary to Board of Trade, September 6, 1698, *CSP Colonial,William and Mary*, #796; "greater enemies" and "threatened and discouraged," Colonel Quary to the Board of Trade, March 1, 1699, *CSP Colonial*: #138; "it is the general discourse," Robert Quary to the Board of Trade, May 18, 1699, *PWP* III: 571; "the King's interest" (572). See also Lokken, *David Lloyd*, ch. 8.
86. "refuses," Minutes from January and March 1694, Morning Meeting minutes (1692–1700), 34; Penn, *A brief account of the rise*; Catie Gill places the controversy over Penn's authorship of the Preface in the broader context of Quakerism in the mid-1690s: see "William Penn as Preface Writer and Controversialist."
87. "Dear Friends," To Samuel Carpenter and others, December 1, 1697, *PWP* III: 530.
88. The certificate is reproduced in Buck, *William Penn in America*, 220–222; "I must leave you," in *Works* I: 238.

Chapter 12

1. The directive from the board is From the Board of Trade, September 12, 1699, *PWP* III: 576–677.
2. Logan becomes an increasingly central character in the story from this point on. General sources on Logan include E. Gordon Alderfer, "James Logan," and Tolles, *James Logan and the Culture of Provincial America*.

3. "long and sometimes rude," To Francis Nicholson, December 12, 1699, *PWP* III: 578.
4. "sowed death and panic," Simon Finger, "Yellow Fever; "the Barbadoes distemper," Isaac Norris to Jonathan Dickinson, in *Penn–Logan* I: lviii; "in this distemper" and "though the distemper," Story, *Journal*, 223–224; Penn reported to Secretary Vernon (February 26, 1700, *PWP* 8: 277) that 215 people had died. Most of the secondary literature on yellow fever in America focuses on several particularly noteworthy outbreaks, compared to which the 1699 Philadelphia episode pales: Philadelphia 1793, Memphis 1898. See Finger, *The Contagious City*; Crosby, *The American Plague*.
5. Birth certificate, *PWP* 8: 247.
6. Council Minutes, December 21, 22, 1699, *Minutes* I: 565–566.
7. From the Board of Trade, *PWP* III: 577; "impotency," To the Commissioners of Customs, May 7, 1700, *PWP* 8: 444; Calvert, *Quaker Constitutionalism*, 131. For a rosier, though unconvincing, portrait of the Penn–Lloyd relationship, see Konkle, "David Lloyd, Penn's Great Lawmaker." More accurate is Lokken, *David Lloyd*. For Penn's letter informing Board of Trade of his having removed Lloyd, Markham, and Morris from office, see To the Board of Trade, February 27, 1700, *PWP* III: 587.
8. "a good deal," To the Duke of Hamilton, July 5, 1700, *PWP* III: 605; "faction in government," To Charlwood Lawton, December 10, 1700, *PWP* III: 624.
9. From Thomas Fairman, August 7, 1700, *PWP* III: 611; Commission to Edward Penington, May 4, 1700, *PWP* 8: 436; Commission to James Logan, May 26, 1701, *PWP* 9: 243; Commission to Phineas Pemberton, William Biles, and Richard Hough, December 19, 1700, *PWP* 8: 699.
10. From Robert Turner and others, January 5, 1700, *PWP* III: 580–581; "the season," To Secretary Vernon, February 26, 1700, *PWP* 8: 277.
11. "inexpert clerkship," To the Board of Trade, February 27, 1700, *PWP* III: 587; "inadvertency," From the General Assembly, February 9, 1700, *PWP* III: 585; Commission to John Moore as Attorney-General, May 31, 1701, *PWP* 9: 254.
12. From Benjamin Chambers, February 1, 1700, *PWP* 8: 235; "houses of entertainment," From John Jones, January 4, 1700, *PWP* 8: 190.
13. "every private cause," To the Board of Trade, April 28, 1700, *PWP* III: 595; "have all the power," To Charlwood Lawton, December 10, 1700, *PWP* III: 625; "hinder Randolph" (626); "distinguishing the just boundaries," To the Lords of Admiralty, December 10, 1700, *PWP* 8: 672; "came hither," To the Board of Trade, April 28, 1700, *PWP* III: 593; "pretend not only," To Robert Harley, c. April 1701, *PWP* IV: 44. See also To Commissioners of Custom, March 6, 1701, *PWP* IV: 33–35.
14. For the Bewley affair, see From the General Assembly, February 9, 1700, *PWP* III: 585, and To the Board of Trade, February 27, 1700, *PWP* III: 589. On the issue more broadly, see To the Commissioners of Custom, February 28, 1700, *PWP* 8: 305; To the Board of Trade, April 28, 1700, *PWP* III: 597; To the Commissioners of Custom, March 6, 1701, *PWP* IV: 34. The disputes over affirmations would continue; nearly a dozen years later the Philadelphia Yearly Meeting would write to Friends in London reporting their "uneasiness about the affirmation, and desiring Friends [there] would use their endeavours with the Parliament to get relief therein." See London Yearly Meeting, Minutes, IV: 174–175.
15. "one that is," "my one-eyed friend Randolph," and "The King has lost," To the Commissioners of Custom, May 7, 1700, *PWP* 8: 444; "has disobliged," To Baron Somers, October 22, 1700, *PWP* III: 620; "angered," To Robert Harley, c. April 1701, *PWP* IV: 44; "cunningly convey," Nicholson quoted in Munroe, *Colonial Delaware*, 104.
16. "I desire," To Francis Nicholson, December 12, 1699, *PWP* III: 578; "to be dutiful," To Nathaniel Blakiston, December 13, 1699, *PWP* III: 579; "though independent," To Nathaniel Blakiston, January 13, 1700, *PWP* 8: 215; "a friendly correspondence," To Sir Thomas Beeston, General of Jamaica, February 2, 1700, *PWP* 8: 243; To Governor Ralph Grey of Barbados, February 2, 1700, *PWP* 8: 245; To Colonel Codrington, March 15, 1700, *PWP* 8: 318; To Governor Winthrop, May 13, 1700, *PWP* 8: 467.
17. "hardly got to New York," To Baron Somers, October 22, 1700, *PWP* III: 621–622; "knocked down," To Governor Blakiston, October 10, 1700, *PWP* 8: 589.

18. All quotations from To the Board of Trade, c. October 1700, *PWP* III: 618; for the Board's response see From the Board of Trade, April 15, 1701, *PWP* 9: 201.

19. "that some effectual method," To the Board of Trade, c. October 1700, *PWP* III: 619; "for the prevention," To Lord Bellomont, October 10, 1700, *PWP* 8: 583; To the Board of Trade, December 8, 1700, *PWP* 8: 647a.

20. "unamerican understandings," To the Duke of Hamilton, July 5, 1700, *PWP* III: 606; "we see so little," To Robert Harley, c. April 1701, *PWP* IV: 42–43; "an American understanding," to Charlwood Lawton, July 2, 1701, *PWP* IV: 57.

21. Speech to Council, April 1, 1700, *Minutes* I: 596.

22. "unparalleled misdemeanors," Council Minutes, May 14, 1700, *Minutes* I: 603; see also *PWP* III: 598n5.

23. Speech to Council, April 1, 1700, *Minutes* I: 596, 597.

24. Lists: To James Logan, August 31, 1700, *Penn–Logan* I: 12; To James Logan, August 7, 1700, *PWP* III: 613–614; for the plumber, see To James Logan, September 3, 1700, *Penn–Logan* I: 14. See also to Edward Hunloke, c. 1701, *PWP* 9: 015.

25. To the Earl of Bellomont, July 4, 1700, *PWP* III: 603–604; "write part" and "I took," To James Logan, July 23, 1700, *PWP* III: 609; "a little more oil," Hannah Penn to James Logan, post July 23, 1700, *PWP* III: 610; "well advanced," To James Logan, September 7, 1700, *Penn–Logan* I: 15; "has been," Hannah Penn to James Logan, c. September 1700, *PWP* III: 617.

26. Hannah Penn to Elizabeth Taylor, March 6, 1701, *PWP* IV: 35–36.

27. Hannah Penn to James Logan, post July 23, 1700, *PWP* III: 610.

28. Proclamation dated December 23, 1699, *PWP* 8: 175; published as *By the proprietary of the province of Pennsylvania, and counties annexed.*

29. "as a person," Defoe, *A general history of the pyrates*, 440; "an ingenious fellow," To Lord Bellomont, February 27, 1700, *PWP* 8: 300. See Ritchie, *Captain Kidd*; see also Sherry, *Raiders and Rebels*; and Hanna, *Pirate Nests.*

30. "Bradenham's gold," To Charlwood Lawton, December 21, 1700, *PWP* III: 631; "our blackbird," To Lawton (*PWP* III: 631); "inveigh[ed]" and "in the pulpit," To Secretary Vernon, December 30, 1700, *PWP* 8: 738. See also To the Board of Trade, December 31, 1700, *PWP* 8: 755; To Governor Blakiston, January 20, 1701, *PWP* 9: 030.

31. "was represented," Defoe, *General History*, 49; "more unhappy," To Lord Bellomont, April 18, 1700, *PWP* 8: 367; "it will not be very disagreeable," To Lord Bellomont, April 23, 1700, *PWP* 8: 387.

32. For details of the incident with Tatham's daughter, see Hanna, *Pirate Nests*, 278–279; To John Tatham, March 21, 1700, *PWP* 8: 324; To Luke Watson, April 15, 1700, *PWP* 8: 357; To Nehemiah Field and Jonathon Baily, April 15, 1700, *PWP* 8: 359; and To John Donaldson, Robert French, and Cornelius Empson, April 15, 1700, *PWP* 8: 362; "prison," To Secretary Vernon, February 26, 1700, *PWP* 8: 277.

33. "In old Fletcher's time," To Lord Bellomont, April 23, 1700, *PWP* 8: 387; "married," To Lord Bellomont, February 27, 1700, *PWP* 8: 300.

34. "My difficulty," To Lord Bellomont, n.d. (1700), *PWP* 8: 308; To Colonel Codrington, March 15, 1700, *PWP* 8: 318; "to be charged," Henry Mallow: Bill to William Penn, April 3, 1700, *PWP* 8: 335.

35. "the reformation," From the Board of Trade, August 23, 1700, *PWP* 8: 526.

36. "I am intently," To Baron Somers, October 22, 1700, *PWP* III: 620; "extremely hard," To Governor Nanfan, February 12, 1701, *PWP* 9: 044.

37. "churchmen," To Baron Somers, October 22, 1700, *PWP* III: 621; To the Duke of Hamilton, July 5, 1700, *PWP* III: 606; "a man sober," To Robert Assheton, November 9, 1700, *PWP* III: 623.

38. "three times published," To Charlwood Lawton, December 21 [more likely 31], 1700, *PWP* III: 629–630; To Governor Nicholson, December 31, 1700, *PWP* 8: 743.

39. "The church," To Charlwood Lawton, December 10, 1700, *PWP* III: 626; "dissenters, and worse," To Robert Harley, c. April 1701, *PWP* IV: 45; "the heat" and "very impertinent" (45).

40. To Robert Harley, c. April 1701, *PWP* IV: 42; To the Duke of Hamilton, July 5, 1700, *PWP* III: 606; To Charlwood Lawton, July 2, 1701, *PWP* IV: 57; To the Earl of Bellomont, January

30, 1700, *PWP* III: 583; "He has had," To the Countess of Bellomont, March 17, 1701, *PWP* IV: 37–38; "You have lost," To the Council of New York, March 17, 1701, *PWP* 9: 126.

41. "Few lords," To General Codrington, March 31, 1701, *PWP* 9: 151; "fortifications," From William III, January 19, 1701, *PWP* 9: 024; "so far as," From the Pennsylvania Assembly, August 6, 1701, *PWP* IV: 62; "weak and naked," Council meeting, August 6, 1701, *Minutes* II: 31; From Governor Nanfan, October 18, 1701, *PWP* 9: 619.

42. To Andrew Hamilton, April 3, 1701, *PWP* IV: 47–48; To Charlwood Lawton, December 10, 1700, *PWP* III: 626.

43. From Connoodaghtoh and Meealloua, May 1, 1700, *PWP* III: 601.

44. "they shall forever," Articles of Agreement with the Susquehanna Indians, April 23, 1701, *PWP* IV: 51; see also Jennings, *The Ambiguous Iroquois Empire*, 235–240; and Jennings, "Brother Miquon: Good Lord!"

45. "It were to be wished," To the Council of New York, May 17, 1701, *PWP* 9: 234; "better that," To Governor Nanfan, July 2, 1701, *PWP* 9: 306.

46. Petition from Philadelphia citizens, February 1701, *PWP* IV: 30–31; To Francis Cook and others, June 2, 1701, *PWP* 9: 259; Petition of the inhabitants of Darby, September 3, 1701, *PWP* 9: 488; From Francis Daniel Pastorius, February 17, 1701, *PWP* IV: 32–33; "in the road," Petition of Francis Daniel Pastorius, June 28, 1701, *PWP* 9: 284; From Samuel Carpenter, March 5, 1701, *PWP* 9: 083; "the business," To Governor Blackiston, March 6, 1701, *PWP* 9: 086.

47. From the Commissioners of the Treasury, March 27, 1701, *PWP* IV: 38–39.

48. "tell Thomas Story," Hannah Penn to James Logan, c. September 1700, *PWP* III: 617; on Guest, see *PWP* III: 618n3; "I long to hear," To the Earl of Bellomont, December 30, 1700, *PWP* III: 637.

49. To Sir John Lowther, August 16, 1701, *PWP* IV: 66. On the bill more generally see Hall, *Edward Randolph*, 208–213.

50. To William Penn Jr., January 2, 1701, *PWP* IV: 27–28; To Charlwood Lawton, December 21 [likely 31], 1700, *PWP* III: 629–634; *The case of William Penn, Esq.* For more on these developments see Olson, "William Penn, Parliament, and Proprietary Government." For related correspondence see To Robert Harley, c. April 1701, *PWP* IV: 42–49; To Charlwood Lawton, July 2, 1701, *PWP* IV: 57–59; To Sir John Lowther, August 16, 1701, *PWP* IV: 65–66.

51. "I received it," To the Earl of Romney, September 6, 1701, *PWP* IV: 80; "the loss," To Charlwood Lawton, August 18, 1701, *PWP* IV: 69; for the £30,000 figure see To Robert Harley, c. April 1701, *PWP* IV: 44, and To Charlwood Lawton, July 2, 1701, *PWP* IV: 58; "might justly," To the Board of Trade, August 26, 1701, *PWP* IV: 78; "By no argument," to Lawton, August 18, 1701, *PWP* IV: 68.

52. "as arbitrary" and "more a fool," To Charlwood Lawton, December 12, 1700, *PWP* III: 632; "in a letter" (632); "made an improved property" (633).

53. "pass away," To Sir John Lowther, August 16, 1701, *PWP* IV: 65–66; "my inclinations," To James Logan, September 8, 1701, *Penn–Logan* I: 55; "No man" (56); "cannot think," Governor's Speech to the Assembly, September 15, 1701, *Minutes* II: 35.

54. "while land," To James Logan, September 8, 1701, *PWP* IV: 87; "what you do," Governor's speech to Assembly, September 15, 1701, *Minutes* II: 35.

55. From the Pennsylvania Assembly, September 20, 1701, *PWP* IV: 91–92; Inhabitants of Philadelphia to the Pennsylvania Assembly, September 17, 1701, *PWP* 9: 536; "are now worse," Norris to Daniel Zachary, October 3, 1701, *Penn–Logan* I: 57; "peaceful coup d'état," Calvert, *Quaker Constitutionalism*, 133.

56. "found in some parts," Charter of Privileges, October 28, 1701, *PWP* IV: 105–109. On the separation, see Johanssen, "Conflict," esp. 128–132.

57. "my Pennsylvanian," Last Will and Testament, October 20, 1705, *PWP* IV: 396.

Chapter 13

1. Last Will and Testament, October 30, 1701, *PWP* IV: 112–115.

2. For the text of the Charter, see Edwin B. Bronner, "Penn's Charter of Property of 1701"; "it seems probable," *PWP* IV: 115; Declaration about the Charter of Property, October 31, 1701,

PWP IV: 115–116; To Andrew Hamilton, January 8, 1702, *PWP* 10: 033; To the Provincial Council, January 10, 1702, *PWP* IV: 151–152. See also Lokken, *David Lloyd*, ch. 9.

3. To the Commissioners of Property, November 1, 1701, *PWP* IV: 117–118; "to receive all," To James Logan, November 3, 1701, *PWP* IV: 119; "write me" (120). For Logan's report of the failing mill enterprise, see From James Logan, October 2, 1702, *PWP* IV: 192–193.

4. "a troublesome and costly journey," To James Logan, January 4, 1702, *PWP* IV: 141; "fail not" (142); "to my inexpressible trouble," To James Logan, June 21, 1702, *Penn–Logan* I:111.

5. "all things," From James Logan, December 2, 1702, *PWP* IV: 125; "at least," From the Commissioners of Property, December 3, 1701, *PWP* IV: 131.

6. "we have as much," From Griffith Owen, May 8, 1702, *PWP* IV: 168; Penington's death reported by Owen (169); "also had the same distemper," From James Logan, May 7, 1702, *Penn–Logan* I: 94; To Edward Shippen et al., January 10, 1703, *Penn–Logan* I:160–163.

7. "The scarcity" and "the quantity," From James Logan, May 7, 1702, *Penn–Logan* I: 94; "the sudden," From James Logan, May 28, 1702, *Penn–Logan* I: 105; "The great scarcity," From James Logan, July 29, 1702, *Penn–Logan* I: 126.

8. "there are many," From Griffith Owen, May 8, 1702, *PWP* IV: 169; "sharp and true," From Thomas Fairman, May 12, 1702, *PWP* 10: 205; "The rents," From James Logan, June 18, 1702, *Penn–Logan* I: 108; "I shall scarce," From James Logan, August 13, 1702, *Penn–Logan* I: 127; "an exact rent-roll," From James Logan, March 3, 1703, *Penn–Logan* I: 173; "only fifty shillings," From James Logan, May 6, 1703, *PWP* 10: 948; "seems almost," From James Logan, June 14, 1703, *Penn–Logan* I: 192.

9. To Board of Trade, April 21, 1703, *PWP* 10: 903, reprinted in *CSP Colonial, 1702–1703,* #604.

10. "very civil," To James Logan, January 4, 1702, *PWP* 10: 008.

11. "weakly made haste," To the Provincial Council, January 10, 1702, *PWP* IV: 152; see also Pomfret, *East New Jersey*, 360; Pomfret, *West New Jersey*, 213.

12. "there is no time," From Lord Manchester, February 16, 1702, *PWP* 10: 048; "in no ways fit," Proposal to reunite proprietary colonies to the Crown, c. February 17, 1702, *PWP* IV: 153.

13. "on 1 November," Hoppit, *A Land of Liberty?*, 109; see more generally Hoppit, *A Land of Liberty?*, 106–123 on William's wars, and ch. 9 on Anne's reign; and Jones, *War and Economy*.

14. On Queen Anne's War, see McLay, "Queen Anne's War"; Hoppit, *A Land of Liberty?*, 112. For the Apalachee, see John Hann, *The Apalachee*.

15. "the ablest," To James Logan, June 21, 1702, *Penn–Logan* I: 116; "a true friend," From Samuel Carpenter, May 10, 1702, *PWP* 10: 192; "a pillar," From James Logan, May 7, 1702, *Penn–Logan* I: 94.

16. For these details see *PWP* IV: 399.

17. "a fine boy," To James Logan, March 28, 1703, *PWP* IV: 212; "extreme illness," To James Logan, June 27, 1702, *PWP* 10: 329; "perpetually busy," To James Logan, June 21, 1702, *Penn–Logan* I: 116; To John and Mary Sotcher, September 8, 1702, *PWP* 10: 485; To James Logan, July 7, 1702, *PWP* 10: 354.

18. "but seventeen days," To James Logan, June 21, 1702, *Penn–Logan* I: 116; "under some," From James Logan, May 28, 1702, *Penn–Logan* I: 105; "could prove no engagement," William Penn Jr. to James Logan, August 18, 1702, *Penn–Logan* I: 130; "made a mighty noise" (*Penn–Logan* I: 136n); Watson, *Annals of Philadelphia*, I: 117. Jenkins (*Family of William Penn*, 63) suggests that Penn disapproved of the relationship with Masters, insisted on an end to it, and arranged the match with Aubrey himself upon their return to London; "S. Penington's," To James Logan, September 6, 1702, *Penn–Logan* I: 134.

19. Articles of Agreement between William Penn and William Aubrey, August 6, 1702, *PWP* 10: 407; "muck worm," From Hannah Penn, December 27, 1703, *PWP* IV: 252; "of whom," To James Logan, June 10, 1707, *PWP* IV: 578–579.

20. "in one year," Logan to Letitia Penn, August 14, 1702, *Penn–Logan* I: 129; *PWP* IV: 266n25; "much depressed," From James Logan, September 2, 1703, *Penn–Logan* I: 232; Samuel Carpenter to Jonathan Dickinson, c. 1705, *Penn–Logan* I: 232n2.

21. "I can not," From Hannah Penn, October 13, 1703, *PWP* IV: 245; From Hannah Penn, December 27, 1703, *PWP* IV: 251–252.

22. "Here has been," To the Provincial Council, January 10, 1702, *PWP* IV: 152; "viceregent," From James Logan, September 11, 1703, *Penn–Logan* I: 238; From Jacques Le Tort, March 4, 1702, *PWP* IV: 156.

23. "divers complaints," From William Popple, April 4, 1702, *PWP* 10: 079; "I was too infirm," To the Board of Trade, April 7, 1702, *PWP* IV: 158–159.

24. "illegal trade," Abstract of Robert Quary's complaint, c. April 16, 1702, *PWP* IV: 160; "a man committed" (161); "prevailed upon" (160); "and made," Quary to the Lords of Trade, April 20, 1702, *PWP* 10: 091, in *CSP Colonial, 1702*, #356. Critics of Quakerism collected testimony alleging the maladministration of justice in the colony, including a richly detailed narrative referring to Quakers as "a pestiferous people" and "wolves in sheep's clothing" whose judges refused to convict fellow Friends. "It is well for these partial judges that they never take oaths to do equal justice," an observer reported: see "A true narrative of several remarkable passages."

     With regard to the water bailiffs specifically, Penn's view was upheld by Attorney-General Sir Edward Northey, who registered his opinion in early July that the water bailiff's jurisdiction reached only "within the rivers which is within the jurisdiction of the common law courts" (Northey to the Board of Trade, c. July 1702, *PWP* IV: 177). This was a major victory for Penn in his running dispute with Quary. See Hall, *Edward Randolph*, 211–217.

25. "I never," "[Quary] never," "This," "I wonder," and "there's as much," William Penn's Reply, c. April 28, 1702, *PWP* IV: 161–164; "I had long ago," "Colonel Quary is," and "[no] more defenceless," To the Lords of Trade, April 29, 1702, *PWP* 10, 162.

26. "Rejoinder," June 22, 1702, *PWP* 10: 293; "extending," Complaints against Col. Robert Quary, *Penn–Logan* I: 35; "proofs" and "clamours," Memorial to the Lords of Trade, *PWP* 10: 293; "a people," Copy of Colonel Quary's Answer to Mr. Penn's complaints against him, June 23, 1702, *PWP* 10: 297; also in *CSP Colonial 1702*, #648; "an artful knave," To James Logan, July 28, 1702, *PWP* IV: 178, "horrid prevarications" (180); "a worse man," December 4, 1703, *Penn–Logan* I: 249.

27. "had a long," To James Logan, June 27, 1702, *PWP* 10: 329; To James Logan, June 21, 1702, *Penn–Logan* I: 111; "misapprehension," August 12, 1702, *PWP* 10: 431; "the partiality," To the Earl of Nottingham, August 22, 1702, *PWP* IV: 185.

28. *PWP* IV: 183n49; "comes upon," January 4, 1702, *PWP* IV: 146.

29. From James Logan, June 23, 1702, *Penn–Logan* I: 109–111; *PWP* IV: 151n90; "he designs," From James Logan, September 2, 1703, *Penn–Logan* I: 225; "Lord Cornbury's . . . visit" (221); From James Logan, September 7, 1703, *Penn–Logan* I: 223.

30. "moderate churchman," To James Logan, March 28, 1703, *PWP* IV: 211–212; "with a considerable," From James Logan, July 9, 1703, *Penn–Logan* I: 200; To James Logan, September 7, 1703, *Penn–Logan* I: 236; "He is on the spot," From James Logan, September 8, 1703, *Penn–Logan* I: 238.

31. From William Popple, May 19, 1702, *PWP* 10: 213; "yet in expectation," From Popple, June 23, 1702, *PWP* 10: 314; To the Board of Trade, c. November 30, 1702, *PWP* IV: 196–197.

32. On Byfield, see *PWP* IV: 166n16.

33. "The line of partition," Oldmixon, *British Empire in America*, I: 79; "nor so much," "I know not," To William Popple, March 28, 1702, *PWP* IV: 157; "We much admire," From James Logan, June 18, 1702, *Penn–Logan* I: 111; "Tis imagined," From James Logan, July 9, 1702, *Penn–Logan* I: 117.

34. William Blathwayt memorial to the Commissioners of the Treasury, c. 1702, *PWP* 10: 084; "pretended governor," Edward Randolph to the Board of Trade June 16, 1702, *PWP* 10: 237; "Very few men," Hall, *Edward Randolph*, 214–215; "I had a grant," To the Council of Trade and Plantations, June 22, 1702, *PWP* 10: 293, in *CSP Colonial, 1702*, #638ii.

35. "I hope none," To the Council of Trade and Plantations, June 22, 1702, *PWP* 10: 293, also in *CSP Colonial, 1702*, #638ii; "the several," From William Popple, January 28, 1703, *PWP* IV: 217; "they have Maryland rights," From William Clarke, September 6, 1703, *PWP* 11: 018.

36. "to have," From the Provincial Council, August 26, 1703, *PWP* IV: 236; From James Logan, June 14, 1703, *Penn–Logan* I: 192.

37. Whitehead, *East Jersey under the proprietary governments*, 137–138; To James Logan, September 23, 1702, *Penn–Logan* I: 136–137; "every part" and "an incendiary," From Andrew Hamilton, October 21, 1702, *PWP* 10: 544; "No man" and "very hard," From Andrew

Hamilton, December 11, 1702, *PWP* 10: 697; "upon the spot," To James Logan, February 23, 1703, *PWP* IV: 210.

38. "put the people," From James Logan, May 2, 1702, *Penn–Logan* I: 88; "without an approbation," From Andrew Hamilton, May 7, 1702, *PWP* 10:169; "all possible care," From James Logan, July 9, 1702, *Penn–Logan* I: 118; "this government" (121).

39. "Militia," To James Logan, July 28, 1702, *PWP* IV: 179; "the governor," From James Logan, July 29, 1702, *Penn–Logan* I: 124; "Nobody," From Andrew Hamilton, September 19, 1702, *PWP* IV: 186; "for them," From James Logan, December 1, 1702, *Penn–Logan* I: 152.

40. From James Logan, September 2, 1703, *Penn–Logan* I: 228.

41. From the Council of Trade, May 21, 1703, *PWP* 10: 964, also in *CSP Colonial, 1702–1703*, #718.

42. The grudging nature of Penn's agreement is evident in the three separate versions of the "Declaration on the Crown's Claim of Right to the Lower Counties," December 1702, *PWP* IV: 198–200; Order of Queen in Council, January 21, 1703, *PWP* 10: 728, also in *CSP Colonial 1702–1703*, #219; "lay sick," From James Logan, April 29, 1703, *Penn–Logan* I: 186; "His loss," From James Logan, June 14, 1703, *Penn–Logan* I: 191; To James Logan, December 4, 1703, *Penn–Logan* I: 248.

43. "the son," To James Logan, August 27, 1703, *PWP* IV: 240; "has had," To the Board of Trade, July 8, 1703, *PWP* IV: 227; Commission to John Evans, August 2, 1703, *PWP* 10: 1069; "he knows," To John Evans, August 9, 1703, *PWP* IV: 231–232.

44. From Andrew Hamilton, September 19, 1702, *PWP* IV: 186; "both join," From James Logan, December 1, 1702, *Penn–Logan* I: 148; "an intrigue," From James Logan, October 2, 1702, *PWP* IV: 190.

45. To James Logan, December 4, 1703, *Penn–Logan* I: 248.

46. "thy presence," From James Logan, July 29, 1702, *Penn–Logan* I: 126; "thy affairs," October 2, 1702, *PWP* IV: 191; "my sore leg," To the Provincial Council, January 10, 1702, *PWP* IV: 151; To Robert Harley, January 31, 1702, *PWP* 10: 043; "the beginning," To James Logan, December 31, 1703, *Penn–Logan* I: 262.

47. "see how," To James Logan, August 27, 1703, *PWP* IV: 241; "no rambling," To James Logan, January 4, 1702, *PWP* IV: 146.

48. "not . . . very mortal," From Griffith Owen, May 8, 1702, *PWP* IV: 169; "far more terrible," From Andrew Hamilton, September 19, 1702, *PWP* IV: 187; "held me," From James Logan, September 11, 1702, *Penn–Logan* I: 135; "the dregs," From James Logan, October 2, 1702, *PWP* IV: 188; "more fatal," From James Logan, March 3, 1703, *Penn–Logan* I: 173.

49. "weigh down," To James Logan, January 24, 1703, *PWP* IV: 208; "suffer him not," To James Logan, August 27, 1683, *PWP* IV: 243; "that they may," To James Logan, January 24, 1703, *PWP* IV: 208.

50. William Penn Jr., to James Logan, August 18, 1702, *Penn–Logan* I: 130.

51. Epistle to Friends, August 9, 1702, *PWP* 10: 416; "very careful," *PWP* IV: 174n2; "humble and hearty," Address to the Queen, c. June 3, 1702, *PWP* IV: 173; "Mr. Penn," Nicholas Gates's report, June 3, 1702, *PWP* IV: 173.

52. *Considerations on the bill*, 3; see also Hoppit, *A Land of Liberty?*, 289–291.

53. Defoe, *The shortest-way with the Dissenters*; see also Cook, "Defoe and Swift: Contrasts in Satire."

54. From Daniel Defoe, July 12, 1703, *PWP* IV: 228–229.

55. Thomas Lower to Samuel Carpenter et al., March 31, 1703, *PWP* 10: 823.

56. "those called Keithians," From James Logan, March 3, 1703, *Penn–Logan* I: 179; "2 or 300," To James Logan, April 1, 1703, *PWP* IV: 220. See also Allen and McClure, *Two Hundred Years*; and Clarke, *A History of the SPCK*.

57. "Do not fail" and "Get in," To James Logan, January 4, 1702, *PWP* IV: 142; "Hasten in," To James Logan, January 4, 1702, *PWP* 10: 008.

58. On Jennings, see *PWP* IV: 147n19; "God forgive," To James Logan, January 4, 1702, *PWP* IV: 146; "I am distressed," To James Logan, June 21, 1702, *Penn–Logan* I: 112–113; "I never was," To James Logan, February 24, 1703, *Penn–Logan* I: 166–167.

59. From James Logan, December 5, 1703, *Penn–Logan* I: 253; "None in Pennsylvania," From James Logan, August 13, 1702, *Penn–Logan* I: 127; "I am universally," From James Logan, October 2, 1702, *PWP* IV: 191; "a pound," September 2, 1703, *Penn–Logan* I: 236.

60. "for Pennsbury," To James Logan, April 1, 1703, *PWP* IV: 219; "I know," To James Logan, January 24, 1703, *PWP* IV: 206; "send me" (205); "much rather," To James Logan, June 6, 1703, *PWP* IV: 222; To James Logan, February 23, 1703, *PWP* IV: 209–210; "the merchants," From James Logan, July 9, 1703, *Penn–Logan* I: 202.

61. "exceedingly mischievous," From James Logan, September 11, 1703, *Penn–Logan* I: 240; From James Logan, December 1, 1702, *Penn–Logan* I: 147; "willing to pay," From James Logan, May 13, 1703, *Penn–Logan* I: 187; From James Logan, December 5, 1703, *Penn–Logan* I: 254.

62. "I believe," To James Logan, July 28, 1702, *PWP* IV: 178; To Thomas Lloyd, November 17, 1686, *PWP* III: 129; "It is generally believed," From James Logan, May 2, 1702, *Penn–Logan* I: 87.

63. "upon a reasonable satisfaction," To the Board of Trade, May 11, 1702, *PWP* IV: 221; Proposals for surrender of the government of Pennsylvania, June 18, 1703, *PWP* IV: 224–226; "very unreasonable," *PWP* IV: 221.

64. "after I have done," To James Logan, June 6, 1703, *PWP* IV: 222; From James Logan, September 2, 1703, *Penn–Logan* I: 226; From James Logan, December 5, 1703, *PWP* IV: 246; "to fall under," From James Logan, September 29, 1703, *Penn–Logan* I: 245.

65. From William Penn Jr., February 15, 1704, *PWP* IV: 261.

Chapter 14

1. To the Half-Yearly Meeting in Dublin, April 26, 1704, *PWP* IV: 278.

2. For that correspondence see Logan to Widow Markham, May 12, 1705, *Penn–Logan* II: 23; James Logan to Johannah Markham, September 13, 1705, *Penn–Logan* II: 63–64.

3. "I have been," From William Penn Jr., February 15, 1704, *PWP* IV: 261; "very well received," From James Logan, February 15, 1704, *PWP* IV: 263; "100 Indians," From James Logan, March 14, 1704, *PWP* IV: 276.

4. "The directions," From James Logan, July 14, 1704, *PWP* IV: 289; Logan described the incident in his letter to Penn, September 28, 1704, *Penn–Logan* I: 317–320. On Story's tavern see Shields, "The Demonization of the Tavern," and Shields, *Civil Tongues*, 63. Enoch Story was the son of Robert Story, whose widow Patience had married Thomas Lloyd.

5. From James Logan, September 28, 1704, *Penn–Logan*, I: 318–320; *PWP* IV: 532n27; To James Logan, November 2, 1704, *Penn–Logan* I: 341.

6. "has much good nature," From James Logan, November 22, 1704, *PWP* IV: 311; "melancholy scene," To James Logan, January 16, 1705, *PWP* IV: 322; "bad Friends treatment," January 16, 1705, *PWP* IV: 323; "let my son," To James Logan, February 9, 1706, *PWP* IV: 531.

7. "well," To John Evans, September 22, 1705, *PWP* IV: 394; To James Logan, April 30/May 10, 1705, *PWP* IV: 346–348; "had [gone] off," To Samuel Carpenter and others, November 18, 1705, *PWP* IV: 515; "captain of a foot company" and "my poor son," To Robert Harley, July 14, 1706, *PWP* 12: 792.

8. "He has been," To James Logan, June 10, 1707, *PWP* IV: 580.

9. "the difficulties," From James Logan, May 26, 1704, *Penn–Logan* I: 288; Copy of the Subscription obtained by Mr. Penn for money from the Inhabitants of Pennsylvania, May 30, 1704, *PWP* 11: 265; in *CSP Colonial, 1704*, #354; "the captain," From James Logan, February 15, 1704, *PWP* IV: 262; From James Logan, February 11, 1705, *PWP* IV: 331; "since thine," To James Logan, July 11, 1704, *PWP* IV: 280. On the lack of records see the following letters from James Logan: November 22, 1704, *PWP* IV: 312; February 11, 1705, *PWP* IV: 331; April 5, 1705, *Penn–Logan* II: 3–4.

10. "Thomas Story," Logan to William Penn, Jr, August 12, 1706, *Penn–Logan* II: 158.

11. "pray," March 10/April 8, 1704, *PWP* IV: 271–272; "I live," To James Logan, July 11, 1704, *PWP* IV: 281; "unhappy love," To James Logan, January 16, 1705, *PWP* IV: 326; "true to thy interest," From Griffith Owen, November 9, 1705, *PWP* IV: 514.

12. On the rent-roll, see To James Logan, July 11, 1704, *PWP* IV: 281; "I can neither," To James Logan, January 16, 1705, *PWP* IV: 323; "I am" (326); "a mighty work," From James Logan, February 11, 1705, *PWP* IV: 333; for Logan's demurral, see From James Logan, April 5, 1705, *Penn–Logan* II: 13.

13. "great dissatisfaction," Logan to William Aubrey, May 30, 1705, *Penn–Logan* II: 29; "exceeding sharp" (30); From James Logan, July 4, 1705, *PWP* IV: 364–365; From James Logan, November 8, 1705, *Penn–Logan* II: 88.

14. "if we could hear," From Isaac Norris, February 13, 1705, *PWP* 11: 504; On the Laws of Pennsylvania, July 26, 1705, *PWP* IV: 387–391.

15. "dissenters," To Robert Harley, February 9, 1704, *PWP* IV: 259; "temper and prudence," To John Evans, February 26, 1705, *PWP* IV: 343; "so great," To John Evans, September 30, 1705, *PWP* 12: 251; "well appointed," John Evans to the Board of Trade, November 9, 1705, *PWP* 12: 377.

16. From James Logan, May 28, 1706, *PWP* IV: 536; "private way," June 12, 1706, *Penn–Logan* II: 135; "but a boy," From James Logan, July 4, 1705, *PWP* IV: 362; From James Logan, June 12, 1706, *Penn–Logan* II: 131–133.

17. "I am sure," To John Evans, February 16, 1706, *PWP* 12: 531; "published a proclamation," From James Logan, May 28, 1706, *PWP* IV: 534.

18. On the forgery, see *PWP* IV: 540n21; "the whole town," From James Logan, May 28, 1706, *PWP* IV: 535–536; "The people," From James Logan, June 12, 1706, *Penn–Logan* II: 134–135.

19. "the members," From James Logan, May 28, 1706, *Penn–Logan* II: 124–126.

20. "by thy knowledge," To John Evans, May 15, 1707, *PWP* IV: 575; on the Militia Act, see *PWP* IV:577n4; "here is," From David Lloyd, July 19, 1705, *PWP* IV: 377–378.

21. From the Pennsylvania Assembly, January 12, 1706, *PWP* 12: 494, reprinted in *Pennsylvania Archives*, 8th ser., I: 561; "establish Quakerism," George Wilcox's Memorial, November 6, 1706, *PWP* IV: 586; "unqualify us," The Proprietor's Reply, August 14, 1707, *PWP* IV: 588–590; "tis plain," From Isaac Norris, July 30, 1707, *PWP* 12: 250.

22. "give me," From James Logan, May 28, 1706, *PWP* IV: 537; "If he," To James Logan, February 9, 1706, *PWP* IV: 529.

23. "a perfect ruin," To Robert Harley, February 9, 1704, *PWP* IV: 260.

24. "I am," To John Evans, March 5, 1704, *PWP* 11: 172, reprinted in *New England Historical and Genealogical Register* 26 (1872), 425; Penn had also voiced his support for Evans and assured him he would look after his interest in the event he surrendered the government in letters from November 6, 1704, *PWP* IV: 307; and To James Logan, February 9, 1706, *PWP* IV: 529; "at last," to James Logan, March 10, 1704, *PWP* IV:267–268; Board of Trade to Col. Quary, May 11, 1704, *CSP Colonial, 1704–1705,* #312.

25. To James Logan, September 16, 1704, *PWP* 11: 355, reprinted in *Pennsylvania Magazine of History and Biography* 7 (1883): 229; see also To James Logan, September 14, 1705, *Penn–Logan* II: 64.

26. "I take," To James Logan, August 22, 1705, *Penn–Logan* II: 41; £25,000 figure (46); "most unaccountable" (48).

27. From James Logan, November 22, 1704, *PWP* IV: 309.

28. "entire," To the Board of Trade, November 22, 1704, *PWP* IV: 309; "not only," To the Board of Trade, January 11, 1705, *PWP* IV: 321; "The Act," To the Board of Trade, June 6, 1705, *PWP* IV: 359; "faith, worship," Requests to Queen Anne, September 1, 1705, *PWP* IV: 392; on the school/hospital, see From the Philadelphia Monthly Meeting, August 7, 1706, *PWP* 12: 806; and *PWP* IV: 557n1; To Samuel Carpenter and others, November 18, 1705, *PWP* IV: 516.

29. From James Logan, July 4, 1706, *PWP* IV: 361; "honest," From James Logan, October 24, 1705, *PWP* 12: 272; "the best magistrate," From James Logan, August 22, 1705, *Penn–Logan* II: 57.

30. On Furly, see To James Logan, March 10, 1704, *PWP* IV: 270; on Ellwood, see To the Commissioners of Property, March 20, 1704, *Penn–Logan* I: 280–281; "In one," From James Logan, August 22, 1705, *Penn–Logan* II: 55.

31. "part of my manors," To James Logan, February 7, 1706, *PWP* IV: 526; August 10, 1706, *Penn–Logan* II: 150–151.

32. From James Logan, September 28, 1704, *Penn–Logan* I: 319; "Lord Baltimore's … commissioners," From Thomas Fairman, August 27, 1705, *PWP* IV: 386; "there's little," From James Logan, January 5, 1708, *Penn–Logan* II: 253; "by little bribes," To James Logan, September 14, 1705, *Penn–Logan* II: 66; "I had rather," To James Logan, February 7, 1706, *PWP* IV: 526.

33. "the only difficulty," From James Logan, February 15, 1704, *PWP* IV: 263; "exceedingly troubled" (264); "will, most certainly," From James Logan, April 3, 1704, *Penn–Logan* I: 282; "upper and lower," From James Logan, May 16, 1704, *PWP* 11: 236; "What will," To James Logan, July 22, 1704, *PWP* IV: 284; "lamente[d]," To Evans, September 30, 1705, *PWP* 12: 251, reprinted in *New England Historical and Genealogical Register* 36 (1882): 426.

34. From James Logan, November 22, 1704, *PWP* IV: 310; "we have," From James Logan, October 24, 1705, *PWP* 12: 272; "sickened," From James Logan, July 4, 1705, *PWP* IV: 363–364. See also Lokken, *David Lloyd*, ch. 11.

35. "acquits himself," From James Logan, May 25, 1704, *Penn–Logan* I: 285; From James Logan, November 22, 1704, *PWP* IV: 309; "the worst," October 6, 1706, *Penn–Logan* II: 171.

36. From the Pennsylvania Assembly, May 26, 1704, *PWP* 11: 258. In late 1705, Attorney General Northey ruled that bills passed by the Assembly and confirmed by Penn's Deputy Governor "are absolute, unless repealed by H.M., and [Penn's] saving of the final assent to himself . . . is absolutely void and contrary to the Charter" (Attorney General to the Board of Trade, October 19, 1705, *PWP* 12: 256, in *CSP Colonial 1704–1705*, #1383).

37. From the Pennsylvania Assembly, August 25, 1704, *PWP* IV: 295–303.

38. From James Logan, October 27, 1704, *Penn–Logan* I: 338; Isaac Norris to Samuel Carpenter, November 6, 1707, *Penn–Logan* II: 248–249; "remiss," David Lloyd to George Whitehead, William Mead, and Thomas Lower, October 3, 1704, *PWP* IV: 304; "revels" (306); From James Logan, August 10, 1706, *Penn–Logan* II: 147; From James Logan, December 20, 1706, *Penn–Logan* II: 189–190. See also Lokken, *David Lloyd*, ch. 12.

39. "if," To John Evans, February 26, 1705, *PWP* IV: 342; "I expect," To James Logan, January 16, 1705, *PWP* IV: 326; "make that," To James Logan, April 30, 1705, *PWP* IV: 347; "I will have," To James Logan, September 14, 1705, *Penn–Logan*, II: 71; "what can," To John Evans, September 22, 1705, *PWP* IV: 393; "Get," To James Logan, June 10, 1707, *PWP* IV: 578.

40. "are not," From James Logan, April 5, 1705, *Penn–Logan* II: 11; "There are," From James Logan, July 27, 1706, *Penn–Logan* II: 142.

41. "upon a business," From James Logan, July 13, 1705, *PWP* IV: 370–371; "with as much," Isaac Norris to Philip Ford, August 29, 1705, *Penn–Logan* II: 61–62; "very insolent," From James Logan, December 12, 1705, *Penn–Logan* II: 94.

42. From David Lloyd, July 19, 1705, *PWP* IV: 373–383.

43. Ibid., 380–382.

44. From Griffith Owen, November 9, 1705, *PWP* IV: 513–514. See also From James Logan, December 12, 1705, *Penn–Logan* II: 93.

45. "the incredible scarcity," From James Logan, February 15, 1704, *PWP* IV: 264; "The country," From James Logan, March 14, 1704, *PWP* IV: 276; "great decay," From James Logan, May 26, 1704, *Penn–Logan* I: 288; "we have not money," From Samuel Carpenter, August 18, 1706, *PWP* IV: 554–555. See also From James Logan, March 3, 1707: "Our crops have failed last year as well as the preceding, and we are reduced exceeding low" (*Penn–Logan* II: 196).

46. On trade with the Spanish West Indies, see *PWP* IV: 287n32, and From James Logan, July 14, 1704, *PWP* IV: 289; "this next campaign," To John Evans, February 26, 1705, *PWP* IV: 343; To James Logan, September 14, 1705, *Penn–Logan* II: 70; "it's present money," September 15, 1706, *Penn-Logan* II: 169; "remittances are," From James Logan, January 5, 1708, *Penn–Logan* II: 253.

47. From Isaac Norris, February 13, 1705, *PWP* 11: 504; To Richard Hill, July 22, 1707, *PWP* IV: 585; "I wish," From James Logan, June 6, 1707, *PWP* 13: 210. More generally, see Nash, "Maryland's Economic War with Pennsylvania."

48. "never experienced," From James Logan, September 15, 1706, *Penn–Logan* II: 167; From James Logan, summer 1707 (sent January 5, 1708), *PWP* 13: 362.

49. "Thy silence," From James Logan, late 1707, *PWP* 13: 343; "Think not," To James Logan, July 8, 1707, *PWP* IV: 579.

50. "I am broken," To Samuel Carpenter and others, November 18, 1705, *PWP* IV: 516; "for when," To James Logan, September 14, 1705, *Penn–Logan* II: 69; "repay the principal," To Samuel Carpenter and others, February 3, 1706, *PWP* IV: 518; "There are," From James Logan, August 14, 1706, *Penn–Logan* II: 157; "if Friends," To James Logan, June 10, 1707, *PWP* IV: 579.

51. To James Logan, June 10, 1707, *PWP* IV: 587.

52. For the £,8000 figure, see *PWP* IV: 596n1; "a significant step," *PWP* IV: 767; "remove all trace," https://www.visitchurches.org.uk/visit/church-listing/holy-sepulchre-warminghurst.html.

53. "refusing," To Samuel Carpenter and others, February 3, 1706, *PWP* IV: 517; also To James Logan, December 28, 1705, *PWP* IV: 522; and Devonshire House Friends, December 26, 1705, cited in *Penn–Logan* II: 94–95.

54. The Fords' Bill of Complaint, October 31, 1705, *PWP* IV: 402.

55. "seemed," Cross Bill of Complaint against the Fords and others, February 23, 1706, *PWP* IV: 417; "entirely relying," Statement of Accounts with Philip Ford, c. June 1706, *PWP* IV: 453; "took that opportunity" (IV: 419).

56. Alleged overcharges in the Ford accounts, c. April 1706, *PWP* IV: 500–506; "did consult," Cross Bill of Complaint, February 23, 1706, *PWP* IV: 425; "to peruse" (447); "send over," To James Logan, February 16, 1706, *Penn–Logan* II: 108; "too great," From James Logan, August 10, 1706, *Penn–Logan* II: 149.

57. "fills up," To James Logan, March 2, 1706, *Penn–Logan* II: 110; "indisposition," To Roger Mompesson, February 17, 1705, *PWP* IV: 337; "stroke of illness," To Edward Southwell, February 20, 1705, *PWP* 11: 520; "weakness," To Friends in Pennsylvania, February 26, 1705, *PWP* IV: 338; "a troublesome swimming," To John Evans, February 26, 1705, *PWP* IV: 341.

58. Last Will and Testament, October 20, 1705, *PWP* IV: 394–396.

59. To James Logan, July 22, 1704, *PWP* IV: 285. More generally, see Bownas, *Account of the life, travels . . . of Samuel Bownas*, 100–152.

60. To Jonathan and Caleb Dickinson, March 6, 1706, *Penn–Logan* II: 111–112; "desires," To Jonathan and Caleb Dickinson, May 30, 1706, *PWP* 12: 688; "Your old uncle," To Jonathan and Caleb Dickinson, June 17, 1707, *PWP* 13: 230.

61. "recipe," From Benjamin Furly, August 10, 1706, *PWP* 12: 811; "has found," From Furly, December 18, 1706, *PWP* 13: 025. See A. B., *The sick-mans rare jewel*, esp. ch. 19; also Culpeper, *Culpeper's English physician*, 163–165.

62. "Thou hast," To James Logan, February 9, 1706, *PWP* IV: 529; "if it be practicable," To James Logan, March 2, 1706, *Penn–Logan* II: 110; "A surrender," From James Logan, April 12, 1707, *Penn–Logan* II: 208; "I should be," From James Logan, May 20, 1707, *Penn–Logan* II: 227.

63. "of the best," From James Logan, August 14, 1706, *Penn–Logan* II: 156; "procure," From James Logan, September 15, 1706, *Penn–Logan* II: 167; and again in a letter of November 26, 1706, *PWP* IV: 562; "proceed vigorously," From James Logan, December 20, 1706, *Penn–Logan* II: 190.

64. To the Council of Trade, January 29, 1707, *PWP* 13: 086; "great expense," Board of Trade to the Earl of Sunderland, February 5, 1707, *PWP* IV: 572; Norris reponds to Penn's inquiries in From Isaac Norris, April 3, 1707, *PWP* 13: 130; see also Queries Concerning the Surrender of Pennsylvania, May 12, 1707, IV: 583; To William Popple, Jr., July 2, 1707, *PWP* IV: 584.

65. Board of Trade to the Earl of Sunderland, February 5, 1707, *PWP* IV: 571–572.

66. "This cutting," To James Logan, September 14, 1705, *Penn–Logan* II: 66; "a perfect war," From James Logan, November 26, 1706, *PWP* IV: 561; for the remonstrance, see Watson, *Annals*, III: 72.

67. "are bent," " From James Logan, December 5, 1706, *PWP* 13: 021; more generally, Logan described the 1706 Assembly as dominated by former Keithians (December 20, 1706, *Penn–Logan* II: 186–187); "not at all," From James Logan, December 20, 1706, *Penn–Logan* II: 189; Penn's reprimand to Evans is in a letter of May 15, 1707, *PWP* IV: 575–577; see also To Samuel Carpenter and others, October 7, 1707, *PWP* IV: 591–592; Remonstrance from Pennsylvania Assembly, June 10, 1707, *PWP* 13: 223, reprinted in *Pennsylvania Archives*, 8th ser., I: 768–772; "arbitrary practices," Pennsylvania Assembly to George Whitehead, William Mead, and Thomas Lower, June 10, 1707, *PWP* 13: 223; reprinted in *Pennsylvania Archives*, 8th ser., I: 772; on the tension between Evans and Lloyd, see From James Logan, April 1, 1707, *Penn–Logan* II: 194–195. More generally on these disputes see Lokken, *David Lloyd*, ch. 16.

68. "rectify matters," To James Logan, March 28, 1703, *PWP* IV: 211; *PWP* IV: 338n9; From James Logan, November 26, 1706, *PWP* IV: 561.

69. From James Logan, May 17, 1705, *Penn–Logan* II: 26.

70. "Can the leopard," From James Logan, August 10, 1706, *Penn–Logan* II: 153–154; "highly disposed," To John Evans, February 7, 1706, *PWP* 12: 505, reprinted in *New England Historical and Genealogical Register* 26 (1872): 429; "I frequently visit," March 3, 1707, *Penn–Logan* II: 196.

71. *PWP* 577n14; "declining condition," To James Logan, March 10, 1704, *PWP* IV: 269; "Let me not," To James Logan, July 11, 1704, *PWP* IV: 282; "I have spent," To John and Mary Sotcher, October 12, 1705, *PWP* 12: 255; "let him," To James Logan, July 8, 1707, *PWP* IV: 580; From James Logan, June 28, 1707, *Penn–Logan* II: 231.

72. "By putting," *PWP* IV: 469; "I have great hopes," June 10, 1707, *PWP* IV: 578.

73. *PWP* IV: 489; "It has been," Isaac Norris to Richard Hill, November 29, 1707, *Penn–Logan* II: 251.

Chapter 15

1. Isaac Norris to Richard Hill, January 10, 1708, *Penn–Logan* II: 255.

2. "comfortably enough," Isaac Norris to James Logan, March 6, 1708, *Penn–Logan* II: 262; To James Logan, September 29, 1708, *PWP* IV: 620.

3. "improper," To Henry Cane, February 28, 1708, *PWP* IV: 596; "since," Lord Chancellor Cowper's Report, March 9, 1708, *PWP* IV: 500.

4. "exorbitant," To Nicholas Gates, July 19, 1708, *PWP* 13: 505; *PWP* IV: 611, 625n26; "help me," To James Logan, September 29, 1708, *PWP* IV: 619.

5. "under restraint," To William Popple, Jr., c. March 29, 1708, *PWP* 13: 418; "In 1700," To William Popple, Jr., March 3, 1708, *PWP* 13: 401; From William Popple, Jr., December 18, 1708, *PWP* 13: 612; Case Against Lord Baltimore, c. January 12, 1709, *PWP* 13: 652; To Lord Somers, March 31, 1709, *PWP* 13: 738; To James Logan, February 27, 1709, *PWP* IV: 635–636; Order in Privy Council, June 23, 1709, *PWP* IV: 651; Penn, *Case of William Penn … against the Lord Baltimore's pretensions.*

6. "the New Castle law," "a lewd voyage," and "my soul": To James Logan, May 3, 1708, *PWP* IV: 597; "last," To James Logan, September 29, 1708, *PWP* IV: 618.

7. "a recommending character," To James Logan, May 3, 1708, *PWP* IV: 597; IV: 607–608; Queen Anne's approval of Governor Charles Gookin, July 18, 1708, *PWP* IV: 607–608. The Gookin family's longer-term involvement in English colonization in Ireland and America is worth noting in the context of Pennsylvania; for that broader background, see Pecoraro, *"Mr. Gookin out of Ireland, entirely on his own adventure."*

8. "I hope," To Samuel and Hannah Carpenter, September 16, 1708, *PWP* IV: 615; "of years," To Samuel Carpenter and others, September 28, 1708, *PWP* IV: 616; "he is sober" (617).

9. "apprehensive," From James Logan, February 3, 1709, *PWP* IV: 630; "his whole allowance" (631); "believes himself," From James Logan, May 12, 1709, *Penn–Logan* II: 345.

10. From James Logan, September 1, 1708, *Penn–Logan* II: 284; From James Logan, February 24, 1709, *Penn–Logan* II: 319.

11. To James Logan, September 29, 1708, *PWP* IV: 621; From James Logan, March 6, 1709, *Penn–Logan* II: 335.

12. "visit[ing] Friends," To James Logan, May 18, 1708, *PWP* IV: 602; "if honest Friends" (603); "come honorably," To Samuel and Hannah Carpenter, September 16, 1708, *PWP* IV: 614; "I do assure thee," To James Logan, March 3, 1709, *PWP* IV: 638; "with my wife," To Samuel and Hannah Carpenter, September 16, 1708, *PWP* IV: 614; "I long," To Samuel Carpenter and others, September 28, 1708, *PWP* IV: 617; "for me and my family," To James Logan, June 26, 1709, *Penn–Logan* II: 354–355; "beloved," To John and Mary Sotcher, May 18, 1708, *PWP* 13: 430, reprinted in *Publications of the Genealogical Society of Pennsylvania* 4 (1910): 267.

    In fall 1709, Penn reported hearing unflattering rumors about Logan's and John Sotcher's lax pace of clearing land at Pennsbury (to James Logan, October 14, 1709, *PWP* IV: 662). Nonetheless, he consistently praised the Sotchers for their dedicated service to Pennsbury.

13. From Samuel Carpenter, October 1, 1709, *PWP* 14: 035.

14. "quack lawyers," To James Logan, October 14, 1709, *PWP* IV: 661; "numbskulls" (660); "conspiracy," To James Logan, May 18, 1708, *PWP* IV: 602; From Isaac Norris, September 6, 1708, *Penn–Logan* II: 288; "the greatest convulsions," From James Logan, July 19, 1708, *PWP*

13: 507, reprinted in *Journal of the Friends' Historical Society* 9 (1912): 88; "David Lloyd's party," From James Logan, March 6, 1709, *Penn–Logan* II: 336; "ought by all means," From James Logan, February 3, 1709, *PWP* IV: 631; "his private revenge" (632).

Rumors like those spread by Lloyd, as well as hearsay and gossip of various kinds about Penn's situation in England, were particularly widespread during 1708 due to the effects of a particularly difficult winter, which rendered correspondence even less reliable than usual. In fact, correspondence had become downright deadly: "We have not been able, that I can find, to convey one letter thither all this winter, because of the rigour of the season. The bearer of one pacquet was froze to death, and an express sent in the 11th-month, by land, we fear, has also lost his life, not being arrived there a month after" (From James Logan, March 12, 1708, *Penn–Logan* II: 266).

15. Petition against Penn's government, n.d. (1708–1709), *PWP* 13: 640.

16. "has brought," From James Logan, July 19, 1708, *PWP* 13: 507; reprinted in *Journal of the Friends' Historical Society* 9 (1912), 89; "all these counties," From James Logan, March 5, 1709, *Penn–Logan* II: 331; "Those who differ," From James Logan, May 11, 1709, *Penn–Logan* II: 345; From James Logan, June 14, 1709, *Penn–Logan* II: 350.

17. *PWP* IV: 650n4; "as she shall think fit," From James Logan, June 4, 1709, *Penn–Logan* II: 349 (see also From James Logan, August 29, 1709, *Penn–Logan* II: 357); "Our governor," From Isaac Norris, December 2, 1709, *PWP* IV: 665; Memorial to Lord Sunderland, March 27, 1710, *PWP* 14: 111, reprinted in "Inedited Letters": 206.

18. "to spend the remaining part," From James Logan, November 22, 1708, *Penn–Logan* II: 303; "thou knows," January 17, 1709, *Penn–Logan* II: 310.

19. "why shouldst," June 14, 1709, *PWP* IV: 648; From James Logan, March 6, 1709, *Penn–Logan* II: 334; Logan to William Penn, Jr., March 10, 1709, *PWP* 13: 729; "he resolves," From James Logan, April 7, 1709, *PWP* IV: 640. For the broader background to Coutts's journey, see Munroe, *Colonial Delaware*, ch. 6; idem., *History of Delaware*, ch. 3.

20. "no better," To James Logan, May 3, 1708, *PWP* IV: 600; "quickly end," To John Evans, September 7, 1708, *PWP* 13: 530; "I fear," From James Logan, February 3, 1709, *PWP* IV: 632; "He is subtle," From James Logan, February 24, 1709, *Penn–Logan* II: 319; for Mitchell's charges about Evans and Logan, see To James Logan, March 3, 1709, *PWP* IV: 639; "a very fiction," From James Logan, June 14, 1709, *PWP* IV: 649; on Mitchell's appeal to the Carolina proprietors, see To James Logan, October 14, 1709, *PWP* IV: 661; "made a contract," To Charles Gookin, June 14, 1710, *PWP* IV: 674. For more details on the mining enterprise, see Wust, "From Carolina to Connecticut."

21. To the Earl of Godolphin, May 2, 1709, *PWP* IV: 642; "prices," Commissioners for Victualling the Navy: Report on William Penn's Memorial, July 23, 1709, *PWP* 14: 019; To James Logan, August 15, 1712, *PWP* IV: 725n5.

22. "I can scarce," From James Logan, March 12, 1708, *Penn–Logan* II: 265; see also From James Logan, July 19, 1708, *PWP* 13: 507, reprinted in *Journal of the Friends' Historical Society* 9 (1912): 87–88; From James Logan, February 3, 1709, *PWP* IV: 632; From James Logan, June 14, 1709, *PWP* IV: 648–649; "Forget not," To James Logan, September 29. 1708, *PWP* IV: 621, 622.

23. "Colonel Quarry [sic]," September 11, 1708, *Penn–Logan* II: 289; "I must," From James Logan, July 4, 1712, *PWP* 14: 418; *PWP* IV: 714n11.

24. From John French, April 21, 1711, *PWP* 14: 258; Petition of William Penn and John French to the Lord High Treasurer, April 11, 1712, *PWP* 14: 381; From John French, November 18, 1712, *PWP* 14: 456.

25. "our dear sweet Hannah," To John and Mary Sotcher, May 18, 1708, *PWP* 13: 430, reprinted in *Publications of Genealogical Society of Pennsylvania* 4 (1910): 267; "our . . . remarkable one," To Samuel and Hannah Carpenter, September 16, 1708, *PWP* IV: 615; "four boys" (615); "I have lost," To James Logan, February 27, 1709, *PWP* IV: 636. On Hannah Callowhill Penn as a "second Hannah," see Cadbury, "Hannah Callowhill," 76–78.

The Carpenters would soon have health concerns of their own, as Samuel would fall gravely ill during 1709, suffering fever, jaundice, distemper, and colic, which "brought me near to my grave." Even though "I recover daily," he wrote to Penn, "I go not abroad for fear of a relapse, being very poor in body and . . . spirits" [From Samuel Carpenter, October 1,

1709, *PWP* 14: 035). This physical illness came on the heels of Samuel's repeated brushes with bankruptcy.

26. To Hannah Penn, July 9, 1709, *PWP* IV: 658; "Considering," To Hannah Penn, July 20, 1709, *PWP* IV: 659; "tripe" (659); "12 ounces," To John Penn, January 7, 1710, *PWP* 14: 079.

27. "drink it," To Hannah Penn, December 20, 1709, *PWP* IV: 668; penknife (669); To Hannah Penn, January 19, 1710, *PWP* IV: 671; "Thou," To Hannah Penn, February 7, 1710, *PWP* 14: 103.

28. "in so great a rage," To James Logan, October 14, 1709, *PWP* IV: 661; "under the greatest," To James Logan, October 4, 1712, *PWP* IV: 727; From Thomas Callowhill, February 16, 1711, *PWP* IV: 692–693.

29. "I embrace thee," To Hannah Penn, June 25, 1709, *PWP* IV: 657; "I cannot," To John Penn, January 7, 1710, *PWP* 14: 079; "I am pretty well" and "our distance," To Hannah Penn, December 20, 1709, *PWP* IV: 669; "strong port white wine" (668); "that we shall," To Hannah Penn, January 17, 1710, *PWP* 14: 083; "My head," To Hannah Penn, February 7, 1710, *PWP* 14: 103; "wind and not stone," To Hannah Penn, July 1, 1709, *PWP* 14: 005; "hearty," To James Logan, October 14, 1709, *PWP* IV: 662.

30. *PWP* IV: 615n4; "to follow your book" and "don't overdo," To Thomas Penn, October 22, 1709, *PWP* IV: 664; "write an hour," To Hannah Penn, December 20, 1709, *PWP* IV: 668; "fever" (669); "Take care," To John Penn, December 15, 1709, *PWP* IV: 667; "Pray let not," To Hannah Penn, February 7, 1710, *PWP* 14: 103; "free of all faults," To Hannah Penn, January 19, 1710, *PWP* IV: 671; "my little American," To Hannah Penn, January 17, 1710, *PWP* 14: 083; "thy little wife," To John Penn, January 7, 1710, *PWP* 14: 079.

31. "three or four," To Friends in Pennsylvania, February 10, 1711, *PWP* IV: 688; "severe illness," To James Logan, August 15, 1712, *PWP* IV: 724; "lame leg," To William Popple, September 12, 1709, *PWP* 14: 029; "they see no difference," To Hannah Penn, December 20, 1709, *PWP* IV: 669; To Hannah Penn, December 24, 1709, *PWP* 14: 074; "I am not worse," To Hannah Penn, January 19, 1710, *PWP* IV: 671; "Forgive," to Widow Thornton, May 15, 1712, *PWP* 14: 388.

32. To Friends at Horsleydown Quarterly Meeting, September 14, 1708, *PWP* 13: 534; To Samuel Carpenter and others, September 28, 1708, *PWP* IV: 617; To Thomas Penn, October 22, 1709, *PWP* IV: 664; To Hannah Penn, January 19, 1710, *PWP* IV: 672; To the Yearly Meeting at Bristol, April 28, 1711, *PWP* 14: 268.

33. To Amos Strettle, January 8, 1709, *PWP* IV: 627–628.

34. From the Earl of Peterborough, c. May–June 1709, *PWP* IV: 646; To the Duke of Marlborough, May 6, 1709, *PWP* IV: 644; "I am heartily sorry," To the Earl of Oxford, December 6, 1711, *PWP* IV: 710; To the Earl of Oxford, January or February 1712, *PWP* IV: 711; To James Logan, March 7, 1712, *PWP* IV: 713. For details on these issues, see Braithwaite, *Second Period*, 191–204; and Frost, "The Affirmation Controversy and Religious Liberty."

35. To Friends in Pennsylvania, June 29, 1710, *PWP* IV: 676–678.

36. "The peoples," To Friends in Pennsylvania, June 29, 1710, *PWP* IV: 678; "the world" (680); "I fear" (679); "his fatigues," To Queen Anne, July 31, 1710, *PWP* IV: 682. Penn's letter to Friends employs language reminiscent of John Winthrop's "Model of Christian Charity," with its emphatic identification of the Massachusetts Bay Colony as "a city on hill ... the eyes of all people are upon us," though Penn would not have known about Winthrop's "Model" specifically. On Winthrop and Penn more generally, see Mazzaferro, "William Penn and Colonial Political Science"; and Dunn, "An Odd Couple."

37. "the Lower Counties," From Samuel Preston, November 28, 1710, *PWP* 14: 177; From Isaac Norris, November 23, 1710, *PWP* 14: 172; From the Pennsylvania Assembly, February 28 1711, *PWP* 14: 234.

38. Queries Concerning the Surrender of Pennsylvania, November–December 1710, *PWP* IV: 683–686; Memorial to the Council of Trade and Plantations, February 2, 1711, *PWP* 14: 209, in *CSP Colonial 1710–1711*, #633; "some particular mark," To Queen Anne, July 31, 1710, *PWP* IV: 683.

39. "revesting," Board of Trade to Queen Anne, February 13, 1711, *PWP* IV: 690; "what is fit," To Charles Gookin, March 14, 1711, *PWP* IV: 694.

40. "it a little," From Isaac Norris, May 3, 1711, *PWP* IV: 699; "a churlish disposition," From Joseph Growden, May 3, 1711, *PWP* 14: 270.

41. From Edward Shippen and others, May 23, 1711, *PWP* IV: 700–702; see also From Griffith Owen, June 24, 1711, *PWP* 14: 284.

42. From Edward Shippen and others, May 23, 1711, *PWP* IV: 700–704.

43. "from what," To Charles Gookin, March 14, 1711, *PWP* IV: 694; "we all grow" and "we are reduced," From James Logan, May 25, 1712, *PWP* 14: 390; Trustees of Pennsylvania to the Commissioners of Property, November 30, 1711, *PWP* IV: 709; "1000 pounds," To the Commissioners of Property, December 8, 1711, *PWP* 14: 341; "Money," From James Logan, June 12, 1712, *PWP* IV: 720.

44. "present weakness," To the Lord High Treasurer, February 28, 1712, *PWP* 14: 371; "alarms the people," From James Logan, June 12, 1712, *PWP* IV: 720; "resolve[d] to," Minutes of the Treasury re: William Penn's surrender of the government, July 17, 1712, *PWP* 14: 423; To James Logan, July 24, 1712, *PWP* IV: 722; "taken effectual care," To Friends in Pennsylvania, July 24, 1712, *PWP* IV: 723; "1000 pounds," Queen Anne's order to the Treasury, September 9, 1712, *PWP* IV: 726.

45. "Nothing," To Friends in Pennsylvania, February 10, 1711, *PWP* IV: 687; "If I can get away," To James Logan, July 24, 1712, *PWP* IV: 722; "to see you," To Friends in Pennsylvania, July 24, 1712, *PWP* IV: 723–724.

46. From the Pennsylvania Assembly, February 28, 1711, *PWP* 14: 234; Pennsylvania Assembly to Queen Anne, February 28, 1711, *PWP* 14: 237; "restless enemies," Copy of the Vestry's letter to the Bishop of London, April 10, 1711, *PWP* IV: 698.

47. "nothing but," From James Logan, July 4, 1712, *PWP* 14: 418; "treat Friends," From James Logan, June 29, 1712, *PWP* 14: 414.

48. Last Will and Testament, April 6, 1712, *PWP* IV: 716–717.

49. Ibid., 717.

50. To James Logan, October 8, 1712, *PWP* IV: 729.

51. Drinker, *Hannah Penn*, 34–37.

52. "was taken" and "through the Lord's mercy," Hannah Penn to James Logan, October 13, 1712, *PWP* IV: 729; "his hand," *PWP* IV: 730n21; From James Logan, November 24, 1712, *PWP* 14: 460;

53. From James Logan, February 26, 1713, *PWP* IV: 734–738.

54. "is recovered," Hannah Penn to James Logan, October 17, 1713, *PWP* IV: 740–741; Drinker, *Hannah Penn*, 57, 75–79.

55. "a little better" and "will be to no purpose," Hannah Penn to James Logan, February 16, 1714, in Drinker, *Hannah Penn*, 52; "pains" (54); "two or three," Hannah Penn to James Logan, January 22, 1715, in Drinker, *Hannah Penn*, 62; "pretty hearty," Hannah Penn to James Logan, September 10, 1715, in Drinker, *Hannah Penn*, 84; "troubled," Hannah Penn to Thomas Story, January 29, 1716, in Drinker, *Hannah Penn*, 87.

56. "sweet, gentle," Tolles and Alderfer, "Introduction," xvi; "When I keep," Hannah Penn to James Logan, January 22, 1715, in Drinker, *Hannah Penn*, 62–63; "he walks," Hannah Penn to James Logan, September 19, 1715, in Drinker, *Hannah Penn*, 84; "blessed," Hannah Penn to the Provincial Council, April 6, 1716, in Drinker, *Hannah Penn*, 94.

57. "my poor husband's weakness," February 24, 1715, Hannah Penn to James Logan, in Drinker, *Hannah Penn*, 65; "and has will enough" (65); "memory," Thomas Story, quoted in Drinker, *Hannah Penn*, 68.

58. Controversy with Ralph Freke, July 18, 1714, *PWP* IV: 743–744; From Thomas Fairman, Jr., August 20, 1717, *PWP* 14: 588; Hannah Penn to the Earl of Sunderland, March 27, 1718, *PWP* IV: 747; Drinker, *Hannah Penn*, 72–73. On the attempt to collect from the Treasury see "Petition of Hannah, wife of William Penn."

59. Drinker, *Hannah Penn*, 85–86; Hannah Penn to James Logan, October 17, 1713, *PWP* IV: 742–744.

60. "of all cordials," Hannah Penn to Thomas Story, February 27, 1715, 14: 525; "drinks about a quart," Hannah Penn to Thomas Penn, May 11, 1715, *PWP* IV: 745.

61. Hannah Penn to Thomas Story, July 28 and 30, 1718, *PWP* IV: 748.

Epilogue

1. Quotations, respectively, Reading Quarterly Meeting to London Yearly Meeting, April 21, 1719, *PWP* IV: 753; *Quakeriana*, I: 26.
2. "I was much broken," Story, *Journal*, 607; see also Grant, "In England's Pennsylvania," 560.
3. "I have not," Jenkins, *Family*, 89; financial records from *PWP* IV: 752n3.
4. "seems to think," Hannah Penn to Thomas Story, September 4, 1718, in Drinker, *Hannah Penn*, 119; Drinker, *Hannah Penn*, 185; "make known," William Penn, Jr., to William Keith, January 14, 1719, in Jenkins, *Family*, 124. More generally on these developments, see Jenkins, *Family*, 120–126.
5. "blessed," in Drinker, *Hannah Penn*, 118; "a troublesome," Hannah Penn to James Logan, January 5, 1719, in Drinker, *Hannah Penn*, 132; "it would be," quoted in Drinker, *Hannah Penn*, 124.
6. On the Walking Purchase, see Harper, *Promised Land*; Treese, *The Storm Gathering*.
7. Franklin *Autobiography*, chs. 12, 15, 19.
8. Kenny, *Peaceable Kingdom Lost*.
9. On Thomas Penn, see Jenkins, *Family*, 145; Treese, *The Storm Gathering*.
10. Greer, "Dispossession in a Commercial Idiom"; "first and foremost," Ryan, *Imaginary Friends*, 136.
11. "it is for his labors," Harrison, *Remains of William Penn*, 21.
12. For Tatham's and Scattergood's letters, as well as many others, see Littleboy Papers, Friends Library London.
13. "quiet and retired spot," Harrison, *Remains*, 42.
14. "in the lowliest hollow," Harrison, *Remains*, 50; "in a tomb" (49); "the voice" (63). See also Milroy, "The Elusive Body."
15. "The founding of colonial Pennsylvania," Bronner, "The Failure of the Holy Experiment in Pennsylvania," 93; "the 'holy experiment'," 94; "shopworn and tawdry," 105.
16. "a carefully designed procedure," Wootton, *The Invention of Science*, 311.
17. Frost. "William Penn's Experiment in the Wilderness."
18. *William Penn and the Founding of Pennsylvania*, 58.
19. Roney, *Governed by a Spirit of Opposition*; Milroy, *The Grid and the River*; Smolenski, *Friends and Strangers*; Soderlund, *Lenape Country*; Calvert, *Quaker Constitutionalism*; Haefeli, "Pennsylvania's Religious Freedom in Comparative Colonial Context"; Erben, *A Harmony of the Spirits*.
20. "a figure," Murphy, *Liberty, Conscience, and Toleration*, ix; on "Larry" the "Quaker Oats man," see https://www.huffingtonpost.com/2012/03/29/quaker-oats-man_n_1389414.html.
21. "seed of a nation," To Robert Turner, March 1681, *PWP* II: 83; on the Penn statue, see Milroy, "The Elusive Body."
22. The literature on the history of religious liberty in early America is immense, but especially worthwhile treatments include Beneke, *Beyond Toleration*; and Miller, *Religious Roots of the First Amendment*.

BIBLIOGRAPHY

Primary

ARCHIVAL

Abstract from Patent from King Charles II to Sir William Penn, Knight. 1667. Cork City and County Archives, U229/143/1a.

Alumni Aedis Christi. Christ Church admissions register. Christ Church College Archives, DP i.a.2.

Christ Church Cautions Book 1657–1675. Christ Church College Archives, xiii.b.4.

Description of house on Tower Hill occupied by William Penn in 1650. Friends Library, London, MS Box 12/18.

Littleboy, Richard. Papers of Richard Littleboy. Friends Library London, MS Box V 1/5.

London Yearly Meeting, Minutes. Volume 4: 1709–1713. Friends Library London, YM/M.

Meeting for Sufferings, Minutes. Friends Library London, MfS/M1.

Morning Meeting, Minutes. Friends Library London, YM/MfS/MOR/M (1673–1692), (1692–1700).

Note on lands held by Guli Springett. Friends Historical Library, Quaker House, Dublin, 53/40.

Oxford University matriculation register, 1648–1662. Oxford University Archives, SP 37.

Oxford University register of subscription at matriculation, 1660–1694. Oxford University Archives, SP 41.

Patent to Sir William Penn of lands at Shanagarry et al. Roll of Chancery Ireland, 1667. Cork City and County Archives, U229/164/1Bundle.

Penn, William. William Penn's testimony regarding the marriage of Margaret Fell and George Fox. October 1669. Friends Library London, Port. 10.53.

Petition of Hannah, wife of William Penn, and creditors of the same to George I for the completion of an agreement for an allowance to him of £12000 upon a surrender of the government of Pennsylvania [circa 1715]. British Library, Egerton MS 2168, f. 5.

Record of Friends Travelling in Ireland. Cork City and County Archives, IE CCCA/U622; reprinted in *Journal of the Friends' Historical Society* 10 (1916): 157–180.

A true narrative of several remarkable passages relating to the Quakers government . . . from the year 94 to the year 1701. Bodleian Library, Ms. Clarendon 102 f.24.

"William Penn's Links with Ireland." *Ireland: A Weekly Bulletin of the Department of External Affairs* (1960). Friends Historical Library, Quaker House, Dublin, MSS B53.

The distinction between primary and secondary sources is not always a clean one. Generally speaking, I include works by Penn and his contemporaries, or in the broader early modern period, as "primary," and all other works as secondary.

PUBLISHED

A. B., *The sick-mans rare jewel*. London, 1674.

An address of some of the peaceable and well affected freeholders and inhabitants of the town and county of Philadelphia. New York, 1693.

Angell, Stephen W. "An Early Version of George Fox's 'Letter to the Governor of Barbados.'" *Quaker Studies* 19 (2015): 277–294.

The articles, settlement, and offices of the Free Society of Traders in Pennsylvania. London, 1682.

Aubrey, John. *The natural history of Wiltshire . . . written between 1656 and 1691*. London: J. B. Nichols and Son, 1847.

———. *Brief lives*, ed. John Buchanan-Brown. New York: Penguin, 2000.

Barclay, Robert. *Theologaie verae Christianae apologia*. Amsterdam, 1676.

———. *An Apology for the true Christian divinity*. London, 1678.

———. *Truth triumphant through the spiritual warfare, Christian labours, and writings of that able and faithful servant of Jesus Christ, Robert Barclay*. London, 1692.

Baxter, Richard. *The Practical Works of the Rev. Richard Baxter*. Vol. I. London: Duncan, 1830.

Bedloe, William. *A narrative and impartial discovery of the horrid Popish plot*. London, 1679.

Billingsley, Martin. *The pen's excellencie, or the secretaries delight*. London, 1618.

Bishop, George. *New England judged, not by man's, but the spirit of the Lord*. London, 1661.

Bownas, Samuel. *An account of the life, travels, and Christian experiences in the work of the ministry of Samuel Bownas*. Philadelphia: Dunlap, 1759.

A brief collection of some part of the exactions, extortions, oppressions, tyrannies, and excesses . . . done by Alexander Harris, warden of the Fleet. London, 1621.

Brodhead, John Romeyn. *Documents relative to the colonial history of the state of New-York . . .*, ed. E. B. O'Callaghan. Vol. IV. Albany: Weed, Parsons, and Company, 1854.

Browning, Andrew, ed. *English Historical Documents 1660–1714*. Vol. VIII. London, 1953.

Buckingham, George Villiers, Duke of. *A short discourse on the reasonableness of men's having a religion*. London, 1687.

Burnyeat, John. *The truth exalted in the writings of that eminent and faithful servant of Christ, John Burnyeat*. London, 1691.

By the proprietary of the province of Pennsylvania, and counties annexed, with the advice of the Council: A Proclamation. Philadelphia, 1699.

Cadbury, Henry. "Another Early Quaker Anti-Slavery Document." *Journal of Negro History* 27 (1942): 210–215.

Calendar of State Papers, Colonial Series. America and West Indies. Volumes from 1689–1711. London: Her Majesty's Stationery Office, 1901–1928. Online at http://www.british-history. ac.uk/search/series/cal-state-papers--colonial--america-west-indies.

Calendar of State Papers, Domestic, Charles I. London: Her Majesty's Stationery Office, 1858–1897. Online at http://www.british-history.ac.uk/search/series/cal-state-papers--domestic--chas1.

Calendar of State Papers, Domestic, Charles II. London: Her Majesty's Stationery Office, 1860–1939. Online at http://www.british-history.ac.uk/search/series/cal-state-papers--domestic--chas2.

Calendar of State Papers, Domestic, James II. London: Her Majesty's Stationery Office, 1960-1972. Online at http://www.british-history.ac.uk/search/series/cal-state-papers--domestic--jas2.

Calendar of State Papers, Domestic, William and Mary. London: Her Majesty's Stationery Office, 1895–1908. Online at https://www.british-history.ac.uk/search/series/cal-state-papers--domestic--will-mary.

Care, Henry. *Animadversions on a late paper, entituled, A letter to a Dissenter upon occasion of His Majesties late gracious declaration of indulgence*. London, 1687.

———. *A vindication of the proceedings of His Majesties ecclesiastical commissioners*. London, 1688.

Cary, John. *An essay on the state of England in relation to its trade*. London, 1695.

Cheyney, John. *A skirmish made upon Quakerism*. London, 1676.

Clapham, Jonathan. *A full discovery and confutation of the wicked and damnable doctrines of the Quakers*. London, 1656.

——A guide to the true religion, or, A discourse directing to make a wise choice of that religion men venture their salvation upon. London, 1668.

Coale, Josiah. The books and divers epistles of the faithful servant of the Lord Josiah Coale collected and published, as it was desired by him the day of his departure out of this life. London, 1671.

Coke, Roger. A discourse of trade. London, 1670.

[Comber, Thomas]. Three considerations proposed to Mr. William Penn, concerning the validity and security of his new magna charta for liberty of conscience. London, 1688.

Commonwealth of Pennsylvania. Charter to William Penn and Laws of the Province of Pennsylvania, 1682–1700, comp. and ed. Staughton George, Benjamin M. Nead, and Thomas McCamant. Harrisburg: Lane S. Hart, 1879.

"The Concession and Agreement of the Lords Proprietors of the Province of . . . New Jersey." 1664. Available online at http://avalon.law.yale.edu/17th_century/nj02.asp

"The Convincement of William Penn." Journal of the Friends' Historical Society 32 (1935): 22–26.

Correspondence Between William Penn and James Logan, ed. Deborah Logan and Edward Armstrong. 2 vols. Philadelphia: Lippincott, 1870–1872.

Culpeper, Nicholas. Culpeper's English physician and complete herbal. London, 1794.

Danson, Thomas. The Quakers folly made manifest to all men. London, 1659.

——. A synopsis of Quakerism. London, 1668.

Davenport, Christopher. An explanation of Roman-Catholick belief. 4th ed. S.n., 1670.

A declaration from the harmless and innocent people of God, called Quakers. London, 1660.

Defoe, Daniel. The shortest-way with the Dissenters. London, 1702.

——. A general history of the pyrates, ed. Manuel Schonhorn. Mineola, NY: Dover, 1999.

——. Journal of the plague year. New York: Oxford University Press, 2010.

Dunlap, A. R., and C. A. Weslager. "More Missing Evidence: Two Depositions by Early Swedish Settlers." Pennsylvania Magazine of History and Biography 91 (1967): 35–45.

Eccles, Solomon. The Quakers challenge. London, 1668.

Edmundson, William. A journal of the life, travels, sufferings, and labour of love in the work of the ministry, of William Edmundson. Dublin: Samuel Fairbrother, 1715.

Ellwood, Thomas. Forgery no Christianity. London, 1674.

——. An epistle to Friends. London, 1694.

——. The history of the life of Thomas Ellwood. London, 1714.

Evelyn, John. Diary of John Evelyn, ed William Bray. 2 vols. New York and London: Walter Dunne, 1901.

An exhortation and caution to Friends, concerning buying or keeping of Negroes. New York, 1693.

Faldo, John. Quakerism no Christianity. London, 1673.

——. XXI Divines . . . cleared of the unjust criminations of Will. Penn. London, 1675.

Ford, Philip. A vindication of William Penn . . . from the aspersions spread abroad. London, 1683.

Fox, George. A journal, or historical account . . . of that ancient . . . servant of Jesus Christ, George Fox. London, 1694.

Fox, George, and John Burnyeat. A New England firebrand quenched. London, 1678.

Franklin, Benjamin. Autobiography of Benjamin Franklin. New York: Henry Holt and Company, 1916.

Great Law of Pennsylvania. 1682. Online at http://www.phmc.state.pa.us/portal/communities/documents/1681-1776/great-law.html.

Gummere, Amelia M. "Letter from William Penn to Elizabeth, Princess Palatine, Abbess of the Protestant Convent of Hereford, 1677, with an introduction." Bulletin of Friends' Historical Society of Philadelphia 4 (1912): 82–97.

Halifax, George Savile, Marquis of. A letter to a Dissenter. London, 1687.

Hallywell, Henry. An account of Familism as it is revived and propagated by the Quakers. London, 1673.

Hedworth, Henry. The spirit of the Quakers tried. London, 1672.

Herbert, Edward, Lord Cherbury. De veritate. Paris, 1624 [published in English as On Truth, London, 1633].

Hicks, Thomas. *A continuation of the dialogue between a Christian and a Quaker*. London, 1673.

———. *A dialogue between a Christian and a Quaker*. London, 1673.

Holme, Thomas, and Abraham Fuller. *A brief relation of . . . the sufferings of . . . Quakers in Ireland.* Dublin, 1672.

James II. Order in Council, May 4, 1688. *The London Gazette*. Online at https://www.thegazette. co.uk/London/issue/2344/page/1. *Journal of the House of Commons*. Vol. 9, 1667–1687.

Jenner, Thomas. *Quakerism anatomized and confuted*. Dublin, 1670.

Jennings, Samuel. *The state of the case*. London, 1694.

Keith, George. *The Presbyterian and Independent visible churches in New-England . . . brought to the test*. Philadelphia, 1689.

———. *The pretended antidote proved poison*. London, 1690.

———. *An appeal from the twenty eight judges to the spirit of truth and true judgment*. Philadelphia, 1692.

———. *The Christian faith of the people of God, called in scorn, Quakers in Rhode Island.* Philadelphia, 1692.

———. *A serious appeal to all the more sober, impartial & judicious people in New-England.* Philadelphia, 1692.

———. *Some reasons and causes of the late seperation [sic] that hath come to pass at Philadelphia*, 1692.

———. *New-England's spirit of persecution transmitted to Pennsilvania [sic]*. New York, 1693.

———. *Gross error and hypocrisy detected*. London, 1695.

———. *The Anti-Christs and Sadducees detected*. London, 1696.

———. *The deism of William Penn*. London, 1699.

———. *The Keithian Controversy in Early Pennsylvania*, ed. J. William Frost. Norwood, PA, 1980.

Kenyon, J. P., ed. *The Stuart Constitution: Documents and Commentary*. 2nd ed. New York: Cambridge University Press, 1986.

Leeds, Daniel. *News of a trumpet sounding in the wilderness*. New York, 1697.

Leslie, Charles. *The snake in the grass, or Satan transform'd into an angel of light*. London, 1696.

A letter, containing some reflections, on a discourse called Good advice to the Church of England. London, 1688.

A letter from Doctor More. London, 1687.

Lilburne, John. *A work of the beast*. London, 1638.

———. *Liberty vindicated against slavery*. London, 1646.

Locke, John. "Pennsylvania Laws." In *A letter concerning toleration and other writings*, ed. Mark Goldie. Indianapolis: Liberty Fund, 2010.

The Manuscripts of the House of Lords, 1695–1697. Vol. II. London, 1903.

Mather, Cotton. *The principles of the Protestant religion*. Boston, 1690.

Mead, William. *A brief narrative of the second meeting between the . . . Quakers and Baptists.* London, 1674.

Meeting for Sufferings. *An epistle from the Meeting for sufferings*. London, 1696.

Milton, John. "On the New Forcers of Conscience Under the Long Parliament." https://www. dartmouth.edu/~milton/reading_room/conscience/text.shtml

The Minute Book of the Monthly Meeting of the Society of Friends for the Upperside of Buckinghamshire, 1669–1690, ed. Beatrice Saxon Snell. High Wycombe: Hague and Gill, 1937.

Minutes of the Provincial Council of Pennsylvania, from the organization to the termination of the Proprietary government. 2 vols. Published by the State. Philadelphia: J. Severns and Co., 1852.

"Minutes of the Proceedings of the Privy Council . . . the 31st March, 1669." *Pennsylvania Magazine of History and Bioigraphy* 19 (1895): 532.

Mucklow, William. *The spirit of the hat*. London, 1673.

———. *Tyranny and hypocrisy detected*. London, 1673.

Narratives of Early Pennsylvania, West New Jersey, and Delaware, ed. Albert Cook Myers. New York: Scribner, 1912.

Oates, Titus. *The discovery of the Popish Plot*. London, 1679.

Orders of the Proprietors of East Jersey, July 3, 1685. In *New Jersey Archives*, 1st series, Vol. I. Newark: Daily Journal, 1880, 492–500.

Parker, Alexander. *A testimony of the light within.* London, 1657.

Parker, Samuel. *A discourse of ecclesiastical politie.* London, 1670.

Penington, John. *An apostate exposed, or George Keith contradicting himself.* London, 1695.

Penn, William. *The guide mistaken, and temporizing rebuked, or, A brief reply to Jonathan Clapham's book.* London, 1668.

———. *The sandy foundation shaken.* London, 1668.

———. *Innocency with her open face presented by way of apology for the book entituled The sandy foundation shaken.* London, 1669.

———. *A letter of love to the young convinced.* London, 1669.

———. *No cross, no crown.* London, 1669.

———. *The peoples ancient and just liberties, asserted.* London, 1670.

———. *A seasonable caveat against popery.* London, 1670.

———. *Truth rescued from imposture.* London, 1670.

———. *The great case of liberty of conscience.* Dublin, 1670.

———. *The great case of liberty of conscience.* 2nd ed. London, 1670.

———. *Plain-dealing with a traducing Anabaptist.* London, 1672.

———. *Quakerism, a new nickname for old Christianity.* London, 1672.

———. *The spirit of truth vindicated.* London, 1672.

———. *Judas against the Jews combined against Christ and his followers.* London, 1673.

———. *Reason against railing.* London, 1673.

———. *The spirit of Alexander the coppersmith lately revived.* London, 1673.

———. *Wisdom justified of her children.* London, 1673.

———. *The counterfeit Christian detected; and the real Quaker justified.* London, 1674.

———. *A just rebuke to one and twenty . . . divines.* London, 1674.

———. *Urim and Thummim, or the doctrines of light and perfection maintained.* London, 1674.

———. *The continued cry of the oppressed for justice.* London, 1675.

———. *England's present interest considered, with honour to the prince and safety to the people.* London, 1675.

———. *The second part of The continued cry of the oppressed for justice.* London, 1676.

———. *The skirmisher defeated.* London, 1676.

———. *An address to Protestants upon the present conjuncture in II [2] parts.* [London], 1679.

———. *England's great interest in the choice of this new Parliament dedicated to all her free-holders and electors.* London, 1679.

———. *One project for the good of England: that is, our civil union is our civil safety.* London, 1679.

———. *Some Account of the province of Pennsilvania in America [sic].* London, 1681. Reprinted in *William Penn and the Founding of Pennsylvania,* ed. Soderlund, 58–66.

———. *A brief account of the province of Pennsilvania in America [sic].* London, 1681.

———. *No cross, no crown.* 2nd ed. London, 1682.

———. *William Penn's last farewel [sic] to England being an epistle containing a salutation to all faithful friends.* London, 1682.

———. *A letter . . . to the Committee of the Free Society of Traders.* London, 1683.

———. *Annimadversions [sic] on the Apology of the Clamorous Squire.* London, 1685.

———. *A Defence of the Duke of Buckinghams book of religion and worship.* London, 1685.

———. *Fiction found out.* London, 1685.

———. *A further account of the province of Pennsylvania.* London, 1685.

———. *A perswasive to moderation to Dissenting Christians in prudence and conscience.* London, 1685.

———. *Good advice to the Church of England, Roman-Catholick, and Protestant Dissenter.* London, 1687.

———. *A letter from a gentleman in the country, to his friends in London, upon the subject of the penal laws and tests.* London, 1687.

———. *A second letter from a gentleman in the country to his friends in London upon the subject of the penal laws and tests.* London, 1687.

——. *A third letter from a gentleman in the country, to his friends in London, upon the subject of the penal laws and tests.* London, 1687.

——. *The great and popular objection against the repeal of the penal laws and tests, briefly stated and considered.* London, 1688.

——. *Some proposals for a second settlement in the province of Pennsylvania.* London, 1690.

——. *Just measures, in an epistle of peace and love.* London, 1692.

——. *A key opening the way.* London, 1692.

——. *An essay toward the present and future peace of Europe.* London, 1693.

——. *Some fruits of solitude.* London, 1693.

——. *A brief account of the rise and progress of the people called Quakers.* London, 1694.

——. *More work for George Keith.* London, 1696.

——. *Primitive Christianity revived.* London, 1696.

——. *Caution humbly offered about passing the bill against blasphemy.* London, 1697.

——. *Some considerations upon the bill.* London, 1697.

——. *A defence of a paper, entitled, Gospel-truths: against the exceptions of the Bishop of Cork's testimony.* London, 1698.

——. *An account of the blessed end of Gulielma Maria Penn, and of Springet Penn.* London, 1699.

——. *Considerations on the bill.* London, 1703.

——. *The case of William Penn, Esq.* London, 1701.

——. *The case of William Penn ... against the Lord Baltimore's pretensions.* London, 1709.

——. *A Collection of the Works of William Penn.* 2 vols. London, 1726.

——. "Fragments of an Apology for Himself." *Memoirs of the Historical Society of Pennsylvania*, 3, part 2 (1836): 235–242.

——. "Inedited Letters of William Penn." *Memoirs of the Historical Society of Pennsylvania* 4, part 1 (1840): 167–212.

——. *The Papers of William Penn.* 14 reels, microfilm. Philadelphia: Historical Society of Pennsylvania, 1975.

——. *The Papers of William Penn*, ed. Richard S. and Mary Maples Dunn. 5 vols. Philadelphia: University of Pennsylvania Press, 1981–1987.

Penn, William, and George Whitehead. *A serious apology for the principles & practices of the people call'd Quakers.* London, 1671.

——. *The Christian-Quaker.* London, 1673.

Penn, William, and Richard Richardson. *A treatise of oaths.* London, 1675.

Penn, William, Thomas Story, and Thomas Everett. *A Quaker a Christian.* Dublin, 1698.

Penn, William, Thomas Story, and Anthony Sharp. *Gospel truths.* Dublin, 1698.

Pepys, Samuel. *Diary.* Online at https://www.pepysdiary.com/.

Persecution appearing with its own open face, in William Armorer. London, 1667.

Petty, William. *The history of the survey of Ireland*, ed. Thomas Aiskew Larcom. Dublin: Irish Archaeological Society, 1851.

Pitt, Moses. *The cry of the oppressed.* London, 1691.

Plant, Thomas. *A contest for Christianity.* London, 1674.

Plimpton, John. *A Quaker no Christian.* Dublin, 1698.

Popple, William. *A letter to Mr. Penn with his answer.* London, 1688.

Prynne, William. *Histrio-mastix, The players scourge, or actors tragedie.* London, 1633.

A Quaker Post-bag, sel. and ed. Godfrey Locker Lampson. London: Longmans, Green, and Co., 1910.

The Quakers appeal answered. London, 1674.

Records of the Honorable Society of Lincoln's Inn. Vol. 1: Admissions. London: Lincoln's Inn, 1896.

Rege Sincera. *Observations both historical and moral upon the burning of London, September 1666.* London, 1667.

Rudyard, Thomas. *The second part of the peoples antient and just liberties asserted.* London, 1670.

——. *The Barbican cheat detected.* London, 1674.

A seasonable corrective to the one project for the good of England. London, 1680.

Some letters and an abstract of letters from Pennsylvania. London, 1691.

Some queries concerning liberty of conscience, directed to William Penn and Henry Care. London, 1688.

Spenser, Edmund. *A view of the present state of Ireland* [composed c. 1596]. In *The Historie of Ireland*. Dublin, 1633.

Starling, Sir Samuel. *An answer to a seditious and scandalous pamphlet*. London, 1670.

Story, Thomas. *Reasons why those . . . Quakers, challenged by George Keith . . . refuse their appearance*. London, 1696.

——. *A journal of the life of Thomas Story*. London, 1747.

Sully, Maximilien de Bethune. *Memoirs of the Duke of Sully*, ed. Sir Walter Scott. 4 vols. London: George Bell and Sons, 1891.

Thomas, Roger. "Letters of William Penn and Richard Baxter." *Journal of the Friends' Historical Society* 48 (1956): 204–207.

To the king, lords and commons . . . the case of the people called Quakers. London, 1680.

To the right honourable the knights, citizens, and burgesses of the Commons House of Parliament. The humble petition of some of the parishioners of the parish of Chigwell in the county of Essex, and divers others. London, 1641.

Tomkins, John. *The harmony of the Old and New Testaments*. London, 1697.

Ulmorum acherons; or the history of William Pen's conversion from a gentleman to a Quaker. London, 1682.

Vincent, Thomas. *The foundation of God standeth sure*. London, 1668.

Votes and Proceedings of the House of Representatives of the Province of Pennsylvania, ed. B. Franklin. Vol. I. Philadelphia, 1752.

Wainwright, Nicholas B. "The Missing Evidence: Penn v. Baltimore." *Pennsylvania Magazine of History and Biography* 80 (1956): 227–235.

Watson, John F. [Enlarged . . . by Willis P. Hazard.] *Annals of Philadelphia and Pennsylvania, in the Olden Time*. 3 vols. Philadelphia, 1884.

West New Jersey Concessions. 1677. http://westjersey.org/ca77.htm

Whitehead, George. *The divinity of Christ and the unity of the three*. London, 1669.

——. *An account of some of the late and present sufferings of the people called Quakers*. London, 1680.

——. *The Christian progress of that ancient servant and minister of Jesus Christ, George Whitehead*. London, 1725.

Whiting, John. *Persecution expos'd in some memoirs relating to the sufferings of John Whiting, and many others of the people called Quakers*. London, 1715.

Wight, Thomas, and John Rutty. *A history of the rise and progress of the people called Quakers in Ireland, from . . . 1653 to 1700*. Dublin: I. Jackson, 1751.

William Penn and the Founding of Pennsylvania: A Documentary History, ed. Jean Soderlund. Philadelphia: University of Pennsylvania Press, 1983.

Williams, Roger. *George Fox digged out of his burrows*. Boston, 1676.

Secondary

Alderfer, E. Gordon. "James Logan: The Political Career of a Colonial Scholar." *Pennsylvania History* 24 (1957): 34–54.

All Hallows by the Tower. Eastleigh: Pitkin Pictorials, 1977.

Allen, Richard C. "In Search of a New Jerusalem: A Preliminary Investigation into the Causes and Impact of Welsh Quaker Emigration to Pennsylvania, c. 1660–1750." *Quaker Studies* 9 (2004): 31–53.

Allen, William, and Edmund McClure. *Two Hundred Years: The History of the Society for Promoting Christian Knowledge, 1698–1898*. London, 1898.

Angell, Stephen W. "William Penn's Debts to John Owen and Moses Amyraut on Questions of Truth, Grace, and Religious Toleration." *Quaker Studies* 16 (2012): 157–173.

——. "God, Christ, and the Light." In *The Oxford Handbook of Quaker Studies*, ed. Stephen W. Angell and Pink Dandelion. Oxford: Oxford University Press, 2013, 158–171.

Archer, Dawn. *Questions and Answers in the English Courtroom (1640–1760): A Sociopragmatic Analysis.* Amsterdam and Philadelphia: Johns Benjamins, 2005.

Armstrong, Brian G. *Calvinism and the Amyraut Heresy.* Madison, Milwaukee, and London: University of Wisconsin Press, 1969.

Bailey, Richard. "Muggletonian-Quaker Debates." *Quaker Studies* 16 (2011): 74–84.

Baker, William King. *Penn the Statesman and Gulielma: A Quaker Idyll.* Edinburgh: Oliphants, n.d.

Balderston, Marion. "The Real 'Welcome' Passengers." *Huntington Library Quarterly* 26 (1962): 31–56.

———. "Robert Turner, Merchant of Philadelphia." *Quaker History* 53 (1964): 6–11.

———. "The Mystery of William Penn, the Royal Society, and the First Map of Pennsylvania." *Quaker History* 55 (1966): 79–87.

Barbour, Hugh. "The Young Controversialist." In *The World of William Penn*, ed. Richard S. and Mary Maples Dunn. Philadelphia: University of Pennsylvania Press, 1986, 15–36.

Bate, Frank. *The Declaration of Indulgence, 1672: A Study in the Rise of Organised Dissent.* Liverpool: University of Liverpool Press, 1908.

Beckett, J. C. *The Making of Modern Ireland 1603–1923.* New York: Knopf, 1966.

Beddard, R. A. "Restoration Oxford and the Remaking of the Protestant Establishment." In *The History of the University of Oxford: Volume IV: Seventeenth-Century Oxford*, ed. Nicholas Tyacke. Oxford: Clarendon Press, 1997, 803–862.

Bejan, Teresa M. *Mere Civility: Disagreement and the Limits of Toleration.* Cambridge, MA: Harvard University Press, 2017.

Beneke, Chris. *Beyond Toleration: The Religious Origins of American Pluralism.* New York: Oxford University Press, 2006.

Bennett, G. V. "The Seven Bishops: A Reconsideration." In *Religious Motivation: Biographical and Sociological Problems for the Church Historian*, ed. Derek Baker. Oxford: Blackwell, 1978, 267–287.

Benson, Lewis. "That of God in Every Man: What Did George Fox Mean?" *Quaker Religious Thought* 24 (1970): 2–25.

Berg, Emil P. *The Arrest of George Fox at Armscote Manor.* Ashford: Headley Brothers, 1913.

Beyond the Covenant Chain: The Iroquois and Their Neighbors in Indian North America, 1600–1800, ed. Daniel K. Richter and James H. Merrell. University Park: Penn State University Press, 2003.

Bill, E. G. W. *Education at Christ Church, Oxford, 1660–1800.* Oxford: Oxford University Press, 1988.

Black, Jeremy. *The British and the Grand Tour.* London: Croon Helm, 1985.

Black, Frederick R. In *The West Jersey Concessions and Agreements of 1676/77: A Roundtable of Historians.* Occasional Papers: New Jersey Historical Commission, no. 1, 1979.

Bond, Beverly W. "The Quit-Rent System in the American Colonies." *American Historical Review* 17 (1912): 496–516.

Bowden, James. *The History of the Society of Friends in America.* Vol. 1. London: Charles Gilpin, 1850.

Brailsford, Mabel. *The Making of William Penn.* London and New York: Longmans, Green, and Co., 1930.

Braithwaite, William C. *The Beginnings of Quakerism.* London: Macmillan and Co., 1912.

———. *The Second Period of Quakerism.* London: Macmillan and Co., 1919.

Brockliss, L. W. B. *French Higher Education in the 17th and 18th Centuries.* Oxford: Clarendon Press, 1987.

Bronner, Edwin B. "The Failure of the Holy Experiment in Pennsylvania, 1684–1699." *Pennsylvania History* 21 (1954): 93–108.

———. "Penn's Charter of Property of 1701." *PH* 24 (1957): 267–292.

———. *William Penn's Holy Experiment: The Founding of Pennsylvania, 1681–1701.* New York: Temple University Publications; distributed by Columbia University Press, 1962.

Brooks, Christopher W. *Law, Politics, and Society in Early Modern England*. New York: Cambridge University Press, 2008.

Brown, Ira V. "Pennsylvania's Antislavery Pioneers, 1688-1776." *Pennsylvania History* 55 (1988): 59–77.

Brown, Roger Lee. "The Rise and Fall of the Fleet Marriages." In *Marriage and Society: Studies in the Social History of Marriage*, ed. R. B. Outhwaite. London: Europa, 1981, 117–136.

———. *A History of the Fleet Prison, London: The Anatomy of the Fleet*. Lewiston, NY: Edwin Mellen Press, 1996.

Buck, William Joseph. *William Penn in America*. Philadelphia: Friends' Book Association, 1888.

Burgess, Douglas R. *The Politics of Piracy: Crime and Civil Disobedience in Colonial America*. Lebanon, NH: ForeEdge, 2014.

Burn, John Southerden. *The Fleet Registers, comprising the history of Fleet marriages*. London: Rivington's, 1833.

Butler, Jon. "Into Pennsylvania's Spiritual Abyss: The Rise and Fall of the Later Keithians, 1693–1703." *Pennsylvania Magazine of History and Biography* 101 (1977): 151–170.

Cadbury, Henry J. "Hannah Callowhill and Penn's Second Marriage." *Pennsylvania Magazine of History and Biography* 81 (1957): 76–82.

Calvert, Jane E. *Quaker Constitutionalism and the Political Thought of John Dickinson*. Cambridge, UK: Cambridge University Press, 2009.

Canny, Nicholas. "The Ideology of English Colonization: From Ireland to America." *William and Mary Quarterly* 30 (1973): 575–598.

———. "The Irish Background to Penn's Experiment." In *The World of William Penn*, ed. Richard S. and Mary Maples Dunn. Philadelphia: University of Pennsylvania Press, 1986, 139–156.

———. *Making Ireland British 1580–1650*. Oxford: Oxford University Press, 2001.

Carlisle, Nicholas. *A Concise Description of the Endowed Grammar Schools of England and Wales*. Vol. I. London: Baldwin, Cradock, and Joy, 1818.

Carroll, Kenneth L. "Thomas Loe, Friend of William Penn and Apostle to Ireland." In *Seeking the Light: Essays in Quaker History in Honor of Edwin B. Bronner*, ed. J. William Frost and John M. Moore. Lancaster, PA: Wickersham, 1986, 61-70.

Carte, Thomas. *The Life of James, Duke of Ormond*. Vol. 4. Oxford: Oxford University Press, 1851.

Chaney, Edward. *The Evolution of the Grand Tour: Anglo-Italian Cultural Relations Since the Renaissance*. London: Frank Cass, 1998.

Clarke, W. K. Lowther. *A History of the SPCK*. London: SPCK, 1959.

Claydon, Tony. *William III: Profiles in Power*. New York: Longman, 2002.

Coffey, John, and Paul C. H. Lim. "Introduction." In *The Cambridge Companion to Puritanism*, ed. by John Coffey and Paul C. H. Lim. Cambridge, UK: Cambridge University Press, 2008, 1-18.

Coleman, James M. *A Pedigree and Genealogical Notes . . . of the Highly Distinguished Family of Penn*. London: James Coleman, 1871.

Condren, Conal. *Argument and Authority in Early Modern England: The Presupposition of Oaths and Offices*. Cambridge, UK: Cambridge University Press, 2006.

Conner, Philip Syng Physick. *Sir William Penn, Knight*. Albany: J. Munsell, 1876.

Cook, Richard I. "Defoe and Swift: Contrasts in Satire." *Dalhousie Review* 43 (1963): 28–39.

Corcoran, Irma. *Thomas Holme, 1624–1695: Surveyor General of Pennsylvania*. Philadelphia: American Philosophical Society Memoirs, 1992.

Cranfield, Nicholas W. S. "Harsnett, Samuel." *Oxford Dictionary of National Biography*.

Crispin, M. Jackson. "Captain William Crispin." *Pennsylvania Magazine of History and Biography* 53 (1929): 97–131, and 193–202.

Crosby, Molly Caldwell. *The American Plague: The Untold Story of Yellow Fever, the Epidemic That Shaped Our History*. Berkley: University of California Press, 2006.

Curthoys, Judith. *The Cardinal's College: Christ Church, Chapter and Verse*. London: Profile, 2012.

Damrosch, Leopold. *Sorrows of the Quaker Jesus: James Nayler and the Puritan Crackdown on the Free Spirit*. Cambridge, MA: Harvard University Press, 1996.

Dandelion, Pink. *The Quakers: A Very Short Introduction*. Oxford: Oxford University Press, 2008.

Davids. T. W. *Annals of Evangelical Nonconformity in the County of Essex*. London: Jackson, Walford, and Hodder, 1863.

Davies, Adrian. *The Quakers in English Society, 1655–1725*. Oxford: Clarendon Press, 2000.

De Krey, Gary S. "The First Restoration Crisis: Conscience and Coercion in London, 1667–73." *Albion* 25 (1993): 565–580.

———. "Rethinking the Restoration: Dissenting Cases of Conscience, 1667–1672." *Historical Journal* 38 (1995): 53–83.

———. *London and the Restoration, 1659–1683*. Cambridge, UK: Cambridge University Press, 2005.

Dixon, Dennis. "*Godden v Hales* Revisited: James II and the Dispensing Power." *Journal of Legal History* 27 (2006): 129–152.

Dorpalen, Andreas. "The European Polity: Biography of an Idea." *Journal of Politics* 10 (1948): 712–733.

Douglas, John. *Beginnings of Quakerism in Ireland*. Dublin: Religious Society of Friends of Ireland, 2004.

Downes, Kerry. "Wren, Sir Christopher." *Oxford Dictionary of National Biography*.

Drinker, Sophie Hutchinson. *Hannah Penn and the Proprietorship of Pennsylvania*. Philadelphia: National Society of the Colonial Dames of America in the Commonwealth of Pennsylvania, 1958.

Dunn, Richard S. "William Penn and the Selling of Pennsylvania, 1681–1685." *Proceedings of the American Philosophical Society* 127 (1983): 322–329.

———. "Penny Wise and Pound Foolish: Penn as Businessman." In *The World of William Penn*, ed. Richard S. and Mary Maples Dunn. Philadelphia: University of Pennsylvania Press, 1986, 37–54.

———. "An Odd Couple: John Winthrop and William Penn." *Proceedings of the Massachusetts Historical Society*, 3rd series, 99 (1987): 1–24.

Edie, Carolyn A. "Revolution and the Rule of Law." *Eighteenth-Century Studies* 4 (1977): 434–450.

Elliott, J. H. *Empires of the Atlantic World: Britain and Spain in America, 1492–1830*. New Haven, CT: Yale University Press, 2006.

Elliott, John R. Jr., and John Buttrey. "The Royal Plays at Christ Church in 1636: A New Document." *Theatre Research International* 10 (1985): 93–106.

Endy, Melvin B. Jr. *William Penn and Early Quakerism*. Princeton, NJ: Princeton University Press, 1973.

Erben, Patrick. *A Harmony of the Spirits: Translation and the Language of Community in Early Pennsylvania*. Chapel Hill: University of North Carolina Press, 2012.

Erben, Patrick. "William Penn: German Pietist(?)" In *The Worlds of William Penn*, ed. Andrew R. Murphy and John Smolenski. Forthcoming: Rutgers University Press, 2018.

Feingold, Mordechai. "The Humanities." In *The History of the University of Oxford. Volume IV: Seventeenth-Century Oxford*, ed. Nicholas Tyacke. Oxford: Clarendon Press, 1997, 211–358.

Fillet, Rene. "Les Relations entre la Touraine et la Pennsylvanie au XVIIe Siecle." *XVII–XVIII. Revue de la Société d'études anglo-américaines des XVIIe et XVIIIe siècles* 37 (1993): 121–140.

Finger, Simon. *The Contagious City: The Politics of Public Health in Early Philadelphia*. Ithaca: Cornell University Press, 2012.

———. "Yellow Fever," *Encyclopedia of Greater Philadelphia*. http://philadelphiaencyclopedia.org/archive/yellow-fever/

Fischer, David Hackett. *Albion's Seed: Four British Folkways in America*. New York: Oxford University Press, 1989.

Fletcher, Anthony. "The Enforcement of the Conventicle Acts 1664–1679." In *Persecution and Toleration* (Studies in Church History 21), ed. W. J. Sheils. Padstow, UK: Basil Blackwell, 1984, 235–246.

Forbes, Suzanne. "A 'Lost' Quaker-Baptist Pamphlet Debate Between William Penn and John Plimpton." *Eighteenth-Century Ireland* 32 (2017), 44–64.

Foster, Joseph. *Alumni Oxonsiensis, The Members of the University of Oxford, 1500–1714.* Vol. 3. Oxford: Parker and Co., 1891.

Frawley, Oona. "Edmund Spenser and Transhistorical Memory in Ireland." *Irish University Review* 47 (2017): 32–47.

Friends and Enemies in Penn's Woods: Indians, Colonists, and the Racial Construction of Pennsylvania, ed. by William Pencak and Daniel Richter. University Park: Penn State University Press, 2004.

Frost, J. William. "William Penn's Experiment in the Wilderness: Promise and Legend." *Pennsylvania Magazine of History and Biography* 107 (1983): 577–605.

———. "The Affirmation Controversy and Religious Liberty." In *The World of William Penn,* ed. Richard S. and Mary Maples Dunn. Philadelphia: University of Pennsylvania Press, 1986, 303–322.

———. *A Perfect Freedom: Religious Liberty in Pennsylvania.* New York: Cambridge University Press, 1990.

Gallo, Marcus. "William Penn, William Petty, and Surveying." In *The Worlds of William Penn,* ed. Andrew R. Murphy and John Smolenski. Forthcoming: Rutgers University Press, 2018.

Garrett, Jane. *The Triumphs of Providence: The Assassination Plot, 1696.* Cambridge, UK: Cambridge University Press, 1980.

Geiter, Mary. "Affirmation, Assassination, and Association: The Quakers, Parliament, and the Court in 1696." *Parliamentary History* 16 (1997): 277–288.

———. "The Restoration Crisis and the Launching of Pennsylvania, 1679–1681." *English Historical Review* 112 (1997): 300–318.

———. *William Penn.* New York: Longman, 2000.

———. "William Penn and Jacobitism: A Smoking Gun?" *Historical Research* 73 (2000): 213–218.

———. "Penn, William." *Oxford Dictionary of National Biography.*

Gill, Catie. "William Penn as Preface Writer and Controversialist." In *The Worlds of William Penn,* ed. Andrew R. Murphy and John Smolenski. Forthcoming: Rutgers University Press, 2018.

Goldie, Mark. "The Theory of Religious Intolerance in Restoration England." In *From Persecution to Toleration: The Glorious Revolution and Religion in England,* ed. Ole Peter Grell, Jonathan I. Israel, and Nicholas Tyacke. New York: Oxford University Press, 1991, 331–368.

———. "John Locke's Circle and James II." *Historical Journal* 35 (1992): 557–586.

Goode, Michael. "Native American-Pennsylvanian Relations 1681–1753." *Encyclopedia of Philadelphia.* http://philadelphiaencyclopedia.org/archive/native-american-pennsylvania-relations-1681-1753/

———. "*Racontyn Marenit.*" In *The Worlds of William Penn,* ed. Andrew R. Murphy and John Smolenski. Forthcoming: Rutgers University Press, 2018.

Gragg, Larry. *The Quaker Community on Barbados: Challenging the Culture of the Planter Class.* New York: Columbia University Press, 2009.

Grant, Arthur. "In England's Pennsylvania." *Atlantic Monthly* 102 (October 1908): 556–563.

Grant, Colquhoun, Mrs. *Quaker and Courtier: The Life and Work of William Penn.* New York: E. P. Dutton, 1907.

Graves, Michael. "Travelers Here in This Vale of Tears: William Penn Preaches a Funeral Sermon." *Quaker Studies* 12: 1 (2007): 7–25.

Greaves, Richard L. *God's Other Children: Protestant Nonconformists and the Emergence of Denominational Churches in Ireland, 1660–1700.* Stanford, CA: Stanford University Press, 1997.

———. *Dublin's Merchant-Quaker: Anthony Sharp and the Community of Friends, 1643–1707.* Stanford, CA: Stanford University Press, 1998.

Greene, Douglas G. "Muggletonians and Quakers: A Study in the Interaction of Seventeenth-Century Dissent." *Albion* 15 (1983): 102–122.

Greene, Jack P. *Pursuits of Happiness: The Social Development of Early Modern British Colonies and the Formation of American Culture.* Chapel Hill and London: University of North Carolina Press, 1988.

Greer, Allan. "Dispossession in a Commercial Idiom: From Indian Deeds to Land Cession Treaties." In *Contested Spaces in Early America,* ed. Juliana Barr and Edward Countryman. Philadelphia: University of Pennsylvania Press, 2014, 69–93.

Grummet, Adey. *All Hallows by the Tower.* London: Scala, 2015.

Gunn, J. A. W. "'Interest Will Not Lie': A Seventeenth-Century Political Maxim." *Journal of the History of Ideas* 29 (1968): 551–564.

Haefeli, Evan. *New Netherland and the Dutch Origins of American Religious Liberty.* Philadelphia: University of Pennsylvania Press, 2012.

Haefeli, Evan. "Pennsylvania's Religious Freedom in Comparative Colonial Context." In *The Worlds of William Penn,* ed. Andrew R. Murphy and John Smolenski. Forthcoming: Rutgers University Press, 2018.

Hagglund, Betty. "Guest Editor's Introduction." *Quaker Studies* 16 (2012): 147–156.

Hall, David J. "The Fiery Trial of Their Infallible Examination." In *Censorship and Control of Print in England and France 1600–1910,* ed. Robin Myers and Michael Harris. Winchester: St. Paul's Bibliographies, 1992, 59–86.

Hall, Michael. *Edward Randolph and the American Colonies, 1676–1703.* Chapel Hill: University of North Carolina Press, 1960.

Hamm, Thomas. *The Quakers in America.* New York: Columbia University Press, 2003.

Hann, John H. *The Apalachee: The Land Between the Rivers.* Gainesville: University of Florida Press, 1988.

Hanna, Mark G. *Pirate Nests and the Rise of the British Empire, 1570–1740.* Chapel Hill: University of North Carolina Press, 2015.

Harper, Steven Craig. *Promised Land: Penn's Holy Experiment, the Walking Purchase, and the Dispossession of the Delawares, 1660–1763.* Bethlehem, PA: Lehigh University Press, 2006.

Harris, Tim. "Sexual and Religious Libertinism in Restoration England." In *Lord Rochester in the Restoration World,* ed. Matthew C. Augustine and Steven N. Zwicker. Cambridge, UK: Cambridge University Press, 2015, 162–183.

Harrison, George L. *The Remains of William Penn.* Philadelphia: Globe Printing House, 1882.

Harrison, Richard L. *Cork City Quakers: A Brief History, 1655–1939.* Bantry: published by the author, 1991.

Hart, Emma. "'Naturally Cut Out … for Unlawful Trade': Economic Culture and the Enforcement of the 1696 Navigation Act in the Mainland Colonies." In *Governing the Sea in the Early Modern Era: Essays in Honor of Robert C. Ritchie,* ed. Peter C. Mancall and Carole Shammas. San Marino, CA: Huntington Library Press, 2015, 223–250.

Hinds, Peter. *"The Horrid Popish Plot": Roger L'Estrange and the Circulation of Political Discourse in Late Seventeenth-Century London.* Oxford: British Academy/Oxford University Press, 2010.

Hirsch, Alison Duncan. "A Tale of Two Wives: Mythmaking and the Lives of Gulielma and Hannah Penn." *Pennsylvania History* 61 (1994): 429–456.

Hodgkin, L. V. *Gulielma, Wife of William Penn.* London: Longman, Green, and Company, 1947.

Hoffer, Peter C., and N. E. H. Hull. "The First American Impeachments." *William and Mary Quarterly* 35 (1978): 653–667.

Holdsworth, Angela. *A Portrait of Lincoln's Inn.* London: Third Millennium Publishing, 2007.

Holland, Rupert. *William Penn.* New York: Macmillan, 1915.

Hoppit, Julian. *A Land of Liberty? England, 1689–1727.* Oxford: Clarendon Press, 2000.

Horle, Craig. "Changing Quaker Attitudes Toward Legal Defense: The George Fox Case, 1673–1675, and the Establishment of the Meeting for Sufferings." In *Seeking the Light: Essays in Quaker History in Honor of Edwin B. Bronner,* ed. J. William Frost and John M. Moore. Lancaster, PA: Wickersham, 1986: 17–39.

Horle, Craig W. *The Quakers and the English Legal System 1660–1688.* Philadelphia: University of Pennsylvania Press, 1988.

Horning, Audrey. "The Irish Worlds of William Penn: Culture, Conflict, and Connections." In *The Worlds of William Penn*, ed. Andrew R. Murphy and John Smolenski. Forthcoming: Rutgers University Press, 2018.

Horsefield, J. Keith. "The Origin of Blackwell's Model of a Bank." *William and Mary Quarterly* 23 (1966): 121–135.

Houston, Alan Craig. *Algernon Sidney and the Republican Heritage in England and America.* Princeton, NJ: Princeton University Press, 1991.

Hsueh, Vicki. *Hybrid Constitutions: Challenging Legacies of Law, Privilege, and Culture in Colonial America.* Durham, NC: Duke University Press, 2010.

Huckel, Oliver. *Dreamer of Dreams: Being a New and Intimate Retelling of the Love Story and Life Work of "Will Penn the Quaker."* New York: Crowell, 1916.

Hull, William. *William Sewel of Amsterdam: The First Quaker Historian of Quakerism.* Swarthmore, PA: Swarthmore College, 1933.

———. *William Penn and the Dutch Quaker Migration to Pennsylvania.* Swarthmore, PA: Swarthmore College, 1935.

———. *William Penn: A Topical Biography.* New York: Oxford University Press, 1937.

———. *Benjamin Furly and Quakerism in Rotterdam.* Swarthmore, PA: Swarthmore College, 1941.

Ingle, H. Larry. *First Among Friends: George Fox and the Creation of Quakerism.* New York: Oxford University Press, 1994.

Janney, Samuel M. *The Life of William Penn.* 4th ed. Philadelphia: Friends' Book Association, 1878.

Jenkins, Howard M. *The Family of William Penn, Founder of Pennsylvania.* Philadelphia: Howard M. Jenkins, 1899.

Jennings, Francis. *The Ambiguous Iroquois Empire: The Covenant Chain Confederation of Indian Tribes with English Colonies From its Beginnings to the Lancaster Treaty of 1744.* New York: Norton, 1983.

Jennings, Francis. "Brother Miquon: Good Lord!" In *The World of William Penn*, ed. Richard S. and Mary Maples Dunn. Philadelphia: University of Pennsylvania Press, 1986, 195–214.

Johanssen, Robert W. "The Conflict Between the Three Lower Counties on the Delaware and the Province of Pennsylvania, 1682–1704." *Delaware History* 5 (1952): 96–132.

Jones, D. W. *War and Economy in the Age of William III and Marlborough.* New York: Blackwell, 1988.

Jones, J. R. *The Revolution of 1688 in England.* New York: W. W. Norton, 1972.

Jordan, John W. *Colonial and Revolutionary Families of Pennsylvania.* New York: Lewis Publishing, 1911.

Kane, Hope Frances. "Notes on Early Pennsylvania Promotional Literature." *Pennsylvania Magazine of History and Biography* 63 (1939): 144–168.

Kearney. H. F. "The Political Background to English Mercantilism, 1695–1700." *Economic History Review* 11 (1959): 484–496.

Kenny, Kevin. *Peaceable Kingdom Lost: The Paxton Boys and the Destruction of William Penn's Holy Experiment.* New York: Oxford, 2009.

Kenyon, J. P. *Robert Spencer, Earl of Sunderland, 1641–1702.* New York: Longman, 1958.

———. *The Popish Plot.* London: Heinemann, 1972.

———. "The Commission for Ecclesiastical Causes 1686–1688: A Reconsideration." *The Historical Journal* 34 (1991): 727–736.

Kirby, Ethyn Williams. *George Keith (1638–1716).* New York: D. Appleton, 1942.

Kishlansky, Mark. *A Monarchy Transformed: Britain, 1603–1714.* London: Penguin, 1996.

Knighton, C. S. *Pepys and the Navy.* Phoenix Mill: Sutton, 2003.

Knighton, C. S. "Penn, Sir William (bap. 1621, d. 1670)." *Oxford Dictionary of National Biography.*

Knights, Mark. *Representation and Misrepresentation in Later Stuart Britain: Partisanship and Political Culture.* New York: Oxford University Press, 2005.

Knights, Mark. *Politics and Opinion in the Exclusion Crisis, 1678–1681.* Cambridge, UK: Cambridge University Press, 2006.

Konkle, Burton Alva. "David Lloyd, Penn's Great Lawmaker." *Pennsylvania History* 4 (1937): 153–156.

Kuehl, Warren F. *Seeking World Order: The United States and International Organization to 1920*. Nashville, TN: Vanderbilt University Press, 1969.

Kunze, Bonnelyn Young. *Margaret Fell and the Rise of Quakerism*. Stanford, CA: Stanford University Press, 1994.

Lake, Peter. "Anti-Popery: The Structure of a Prejudice." In *Conflict in Early Stuart England: Studies in Religion and Politics 1603–1642*, ed. Richard Cust and Ann Hughes. London: Longman, 1989, 72–106.

Landes, Jordan. *London Quakers in the Trans-Atlantic World*. Houndmills: Palgrave, 2015.

Landsman, Ned C. "'Of the Grand Assembly or Parliament': Thomas Rudyard's Critique of an Early Draft of the Frame of Government of Pennsylvania." *Pennsylvania Magazine of History and Biography* 105 (1981): 469–482.

Lea, J. Henry. *Genealogical Gleanings, Contributory to a History of the Family of Penn*. Philadelphia: J. B. Lippincott, 1890.

Levy, Babette M. "Early Puritanism in the Southern and Island Colonies." *Proceedings of the American Antiquarian Society* 70 (1960): 73–325.

Lichtenstein, Aharon. *Henry More: The Rational Theology of a Cambridge Platonist*. Cambridge, MA: Harvard University Press, 1962.

Lipson, E. "The Elections to Exclusion Parliaments 1679–1681." *The English Historical Review* 28 (1913): 59–85.

Lloyd, Arnold. *Quaker Social History 1669–1738*. Westport, CT: Greenwood Publishers, 1950.

Lokken, Roy N. *David Lloyd, Colonial Lawmaker*. Seattle: University of Washington Press, 1959.

London: A Social and Cultural History, 1550–1750, ed. Robert O. Bucholz and Joseph P. Ward. Cambridge, UK: Cambridge University Press, 2012.

Lucci, Diego. *Scripture and Deism: The Biblical Criticism of Eighteenth-Century British Deists*. Bern: Peter Lang, 2008.

———. "Deism, Freethinking, and Toleration in Enlightenment England." *History of European Ideas* 43 (2017): 345–358.

Lurie, Maxine N. "New Jersey: The Unique Proprietary." In *A New Jersey Anthology*, ed. Maxine N. Lurie. New Brunswick, NJ: Rutgers University Press, 1994, 37–60.

———. "Colonial Period: The Complex and Contradictory Beginnings of a Mid-Atlantic Province." In *New Jersey: A History of the Garden State*, ed. Maxine N. Lurie and Richard Veit. New Brunswick, NJ, and London: Rutgers University Press, 2012, 33–63.

Lynch, C. "Burkes and Jasper's Pound, Doora, County Clare." http://www.clarelibrary.ie/eolas/coclare/genealogy/don_tran/fam_his/burkes_jaspers_pound.htm.

Lynch, Kathleen M. *Roger Boyle: First Earl of Orrery*. Knoxville: University of Tennessee Press, 1965.

Lysons, Daniel. *The Environs of London*. Vol. 4. London, 1746.

Mack, Phyllis. *Visionary Women: Ecstatic Prophecy in Seventeenth-Century England*. Berkeley and Los Angeles: University of California Press, 1992.

Maley, Willy. "A View of the Present State of Ireland." In *A Critical Companion to Spenser Studies*, ed. Bart Van es. Houndmills: Palgrave, 2006, 210–229.

Mann, Emily. "Beyond the Bounds: William Penn's First Map of Pennsylvania." In *The Worlds of William Penn*, ed. Andrew R. Murphy and John Smolenski. New Brunswick, NJ: Rutgers University Press, 2018.

Manning, David. "Accusations of Blasphemy in English Anti-Quaker Polemic, c. 1660–1701." *Quaker Studies* 14 (2009): 27–56.

Maples, Mary. "William Penn, Classical Republican." *Pennsylvania Magazine of History and Biography* 81 (1957): 138–156.

Martin, Clare J. "Tradition versus Innovation: The Hat, Wilkinson-Story and Keithian Controversies." *Quaker Studies* 8 (2003): 5–22

Mazzaferro, Alexander. "William Penn and Colonial Political Science." In *The Worlds of William Penn*, ed. Andrew R. Murphy and John Smolenski. New Brunswick, NJ: Rutgers University Press, 2018.

McCormick, Ted. *William Petty and the Ambitions of Political Arithmetic*. Oxford: Oxford University Press, 2009.

McLay, K. A. J. "Queen Anne's War." In *The Encyclopedia of War*, ed. Gordon Martel. Oxford: Blackwell, 2011.

McLellan, George B. *The Oligarchy of Venice*. Boston: Houghton Mifflin, 1904.

Mekeel, Arthur J. "The Founding Years, 1681–1789." In *Friends in the Delaware Valley: Philadelphia Yearly Meeting 1681–1981*, ed. John M. Moore. Haverford, PA: Friends Historical Association, 1981:14–55.

Merrell, James. "Afterword." In *Friends and Enemies in Penn's Woods: Indians, Colonists, and the Racial Construction of Pennsylvania*, ed. William Pencak and Daniel Richter. University Park: Penn State University Press, 2004, 259–268.

Miller, John. "James II and Toleration." In *By Force or By Default?*, ed. Eveline Cruickshanks. Edinburgh: J. Donald, 1989, 8–27.

——. *The Glorious Revolution*. 2nd ed. London: Routledge, 1997.

——. *James II*. New Haven, CT, and London: Yale University Press, 2000.

——. "'A Suffering People': English Quakers and Their Neighbours." *Past and Present* 188 (2005): 71–103.

Miller, Nicholas P. *The Religious Roots of the First Amendment: Dissenting Protestants and the Separation of Church and State*. New York: Oxford University Press, 2012.

Milroy, Elizabeth. *The Grid and the River: Philadelphia's Green Spaces, 1682–1876*. University Park: Penn State University Press, 2016.

——. "The Elusive Body of William Penn." In *The Worlds of William Penn*, ed. Andrew R. Murphy and John Smolenski. Forthcoming: Rutgers University Press, 2018.

Mood, Fulmer. "William Penn and English Politics in 1680–81: New Light on the Granting of the Pennsylvania Charter." *Journal of the Friends' Historical Society* 32 (1935): 3–21.

Moore, Rosemary. *The Light in Their Consciences: The Early Quakers in Britain, 1646–1666*. University Park: Penn State University Press, 2000.

Moote, A. Lloyd, and Dorothy C. *The Great Plague: The Story of London's Most Deadly Year*. Baltimore and London: Johns Hopkins University Press, 2004.

Moretta, John A. *William Penn and the Quaker Legacy*. New York: Pearson Longman 2007.

Morgan, Hiram. *Tyrone's Rebellion: The Outbreak of the Nine Years' War in Tudor England*. London: Royal Historical Society, 1993.

Morgan, Rhys. "The Cromwellian Conquest of Ireland (1649–1653)." In *The Encyclopedia of War*, ed. Gordon Martel. Oxford: Blackwell, 2011.

Mortimer, Sarah. "Early Modern Socinianism and Unitarianism." In *The Oxford Handbook of Early Modern Theology, 1600–1800*, ed. Ulrich L. Lehner, Richard A. Muller, and A. G. Roeber. New York: Oxford University Press, 2016, 361–372.

Mullet, Charles F. *The Bubonic Plague in England: An Essay in the History of Preventive Medicine*. Lexington: University of Kentucky Press, 1956.

Munroe, John A. *Colonial Delaware: A History*. Millwood, NY: KTO Press, 1978.

——. *A History of Delaware*. 5th ed. Newark: University of Delaware Press, 2006.

Murphy, Andrew R. *Conscience and Community: Revisiting Toleration and Religious Dissent in Early Modern England and America*. University Park: Penn State University Press, 2001.

——. "Persecuting Quakers? The Politics of Toleration in Early Pennsylvania." In *The First Prejudice: Religious Tolerance and Religious Intolerance in the Making of America*, ed. Christopher Beneke and Chris Grenda. Philadelphia: University of Pennsylvania Press, 2010.

——. *Liberty, Conscience, and Toleration: The Political Thought of William Penn*. New York: Oxford University Press, 2016.

——. "From Practice to Theory to Practice: William Penn from Prison to Pennsylvania." *History of European Ideas* 43, no. 4 (2017): 317–330.

——. "The Roads to and from Cork: Ireland in William Penn's Theory of Religious Toleration." In *The Worlds of William Penn*, ed. Andrew R. Murphy and John Smolenski. New Brunswick, NJ: Rutgers University Press, 2018.

Murphy, Andrew R., and Adrian Chastain Weimer. "Colonial Quakerism." In Volume I, *Beginnings to the Toleration Act*, ed. John Coffey. In *The Oxford History of Protestant Dissenting Traditions*, ed. Mark Noll and Tim Larsen. Forthcoming: Oxford University Press.

Myers, Albert Cook. *William Penn's Early Life in Brief, 1644–1674.* Moylan, PA: Albert Cook Myers, 1937.

Nagy, Doreen Evenden. *Popular Medicine in Seventeenth-Century England.* Madison: University of Wisconsin Press, 1988.

Nash, Gary B. "The Free Society of Traders and the Early Politics of Pennsylvania." *Pennsylvania Magazine of History and Biography* (1965): 147–173.

———. "Maryland's Economic War with Pennsylvania." *Maryland Historical Magazine* 60 (1965): 231–244.

———. "The Framing of Government in Pennsylvania: Ideas in Contact with Reality." *William and Mary Quarterly* (1966): 183–209.

———. "The Quest for the Susquehanna Valley: New York, Pennsylvania, and the Seventeenth-Century Fur Trade." *New York History* 48 (1967): 3–27.

———. *Quakers and Politics: Pennsylvania, 1681–1726.* Princeton: Princeton University Press, 1968.

———. "City Planning and Political Tension in the Seventeenth Century: The Case of Philadelphia." *Proceedings of the American Philosophical Society* 112 (1968): 54–73.

Newman, Andrew. *On Records: Delaware Indians, Colonists, and the Media of History.* Lincoln: University of Nebraska Press, 2012.

———. "Treaty of Shackamaxon." *Encyclopedia of Philadelphia.* http://philadelphiaencyclopedia. org/archive/treaty-of-shackamaxon-2/

Newton, Gill. "Clandestine Marriage in Early Modern London: When, Where, and Why?" *Continuity and Change* 29 (2014): 151–180.

Nuttall, W. L. F. "Governor John Blackwell: His Life in England and America." *Pennsylvania Magazine of History and Biography* 88 (1964): 121-141.

Oldmixon, John. *The British Empire in America containing the history of the discovery, settlement, progress and present state of all the British colonies.* 2 vols. London, 1708.

Olson, Alison Gilbert. "William Penn, Parliament, and Proprietary Government." *William and Mary Quarterly* 18 (1961): 176–195.

The Oxford Handbook of Quaker Studies, ed. Stephen W. Angell and Pink Dandelion. Oxford: Oxford University Press, 2013.

Page, William, and J. Horace Round. *The Victoria History of the County of Essex.* Vol. 2. London: Constable, 1907.

Peacey, J. T. "Led by the Hand: Manucaptors and Patronage at Lincoln's Inn in the Seventeenth Century." *Journal of Legal History* 18 (1997): 26–44.

Peare, Catherine Owens. *William Penn.* Philadelphia and New York: Lippincott, 1957.

Pecoraro, Luke J. *"Mr. Gookin out of Ireland, entirely on his own adventure": An Archaeological Study of Intercolonial and Transatlantic Connections in the Seventeenth Century.* PhD dissertation, Boston University, 2015.

Penn, Granville. *Memorials of the Professional Life and Times of Sir William Penn, Knt.* 2 vols. London: James Duncan, 1833.

Pestana, Carla Gardina. "The Conventionality of the Notorious John Perrot." In *Early Quakers and Their Theological Thought: 1647–1723*, ed. Stephen W. Angell and Pink Dandelion. Cambridge, UK: Cambridge University Press, 2015, 173–189.

———. *The English Conquest of Jamaica: Oliver Cromwell's Bid for Empire.* Cambridge, MA: Harvard University Press, 2017.

Phillips, John A., and Thomas C. Thompson. "Jurors v. Judges in Later Stuart England: The Penn/ Mead Trial and *Bushell's Case*." *Law and Inequality* 4 (1986): 189–229.

Pincus, Steve. *1688: The First Modern Revolution.* New Haven, CT: Yale University Press, 2009.

Pomfret, John Edwin. "The First Purchasers of Pennsylvania 1681–1700." *Pennsylvania Magazine of History and Biography* 75 (1956): 137–163.

————. *The Province of West Jersey, 1609–1702: A Study of the Origins of an American Colony.* Princeton, NJ: Princeton University Press, 1956.

————. *The Province of East Jersey, 1609–1702: The Rebellious Proprietary.* Princeton, NJ: Princeton University Press, 1962.

————. *Colonial New Jersey: A History.* New York: Scribner's, 1973.

Porter, Roy. *London: A Social History.* London: Hamish Hamilton, 1994.

Porter, Stephen. "University and Society." *The History of the University of Oxford. Volume IV: Seventeenth-Century Oxford*, ed. Nicholas Tyacke. Oxford: Clarendon Press, 1997, 25–104.

Powell, W. R., ed. *History of the County of Essex.* London: Oxford University Press, 1973.

Proud, Robert. *The History of Pennsylvania in North America.* Vol. I. Philadelphia: Zachariah Poulson, 1797.

Quakeriana. Vol. I. London, 1894.

Reddaway, Thomas Fiddian. *The Rebuilding of London After the Great Fire.* London: Arnold, 1951.

Rees, T. Mardy. *A History of Quakers in Wales and Their Emigration to North America.* Carmarthen, UK: W. Spurrell and Son, 1925.

The Revolution of 1688–89: Changing Perspectives. Ed. Lois G. Schwoerer. Cambridge, UK: Cambridge University Press, 1992.

Richter, Daniel K. *Facing East from Indian Country: A Native History of Early America.* Cambridge, MA: Harvard University Press, 2001.

Ring, Denis Paul. *Macroom Through the Mists of Time.* Cork: Castle House Publications, 1995.

Ritchie, Robert C. *Captain Kidd and the War Against the Pirates.* Cambridge, MA: Harvard University Press, 1986.

Roach, Hannah Benner. "The Planting of Philadelphia: A Seventeenth-Century Real Estate Development. I." *Pennsylvania Magazine of History and Biography* 92 (1968): 3–47.

————. "The Planting of Philadelphia: A Seventeenth-Century Real Estate Development. II." *Pennsylvania Magazine of History and Biography* 92 (1968): 143–194.

Robbins, Caroline. "Absolute Liberty: The Life and Thought of William Popple." *William and Mary Quarterly* 24 (1967): 190–223.

Roney, Jessica. *Governed by a Spirit of Opposition: The Origins of American Political Practice in Colonial Philadelphia.* Baltimore: Johns Hopkins University Press, 2014.

Rose, Craig. *England in the 1690s: Revolution, Religion, and War.* Oxford: Blackwell, 1999.

Rose, Jacqueline. *Godly Kingship in Restoration England: The Politics of the Royal Supremacy, 1660–1688.* New York: Cambridge University Press, 2011.

Roy, Ian, and Dietrich Reinhart. "Oxford and the Civil Wars." In *The History of the University of Oxford. Volume IV: Seventeenth Century Oxford*, ed. Nicholas Tyacke, 687–732. Oxford: Clarendon Press, 1997.

Ruff, Julius R. *Violence in Early Modern Europe, 1500–1800.* Cambridge, UK: Cambridge University Press, 2001.

Ryan, James Emmett. *Imaginary Friends: Representing Quakers in American Culture, 1650–1950.* Madison: Wisconsin Press, 2009.

Ryerson, Richard Alan. "William Penn's Gentry Commonwealth: An Interpretation of the Constitutional History of Early Pennsylvania, 1681–1701." *Pennsylvania History* 61 (1994): 393–428.

Sachse, Julius P. "Benjamin Furly, An English Merchant at Rotterdam." *Pennsylvania Magazine of History and Biography* 19 (1895): 277–306.

Sachse, William L. "The Mob and the Revolution of 1688." *Journal of British Studies* 4 (1964): 23–40.

Sacks, David Harris. *The Widening Gate: Bristol and the Atlantic Economy, 1450–1700.* Berkeley and Los Angeles: University of California Press, 1991.

Sauer, Elizabeth. "New Worlds and Holy Experiments in the Restoration Literature of Milton, Bunyan, and Penn." In *The Worlds of William Penn*, ed. Andrew R. Murphy and John Smolenski. New Brunswick, NJ: Rutgers University Press, 2018.

Schmidt, H. D. "The Establishment of 'Europe' As a Political Expression." *The Historical Journal*, 172–178.

Schwartz, Sally. "William Penn and Toleration: Foundations of Colonial Pennsylvania." *Pennsylvania History* 50 (1983): 284–312.

——. *A Mixed Multitude: The Struggle for Toleration in Colonial Pennsylvania*. New York: New York University Press, 1988.

Scott, Jonathan. *Algernon Sidney and the Restoration Crisis, 1677–1683*. Cambridge, UK: Cambridge University Press, 1991.

Scurr, Ruth. *John Aubrey, My Own Life*. London: Chatto and Windus, 2015.

Shagan, Ethan. *The Rule of Moderation*. Cambridge, UK: Cambridge University Press, 2011.

Sherry, Frank. *Raiders and Rebels: The Golden Age of Piracy, 1570–1740*. New York: Hearst Marine Books, 1986.

Shields, David S. *Civil Tongues and Polite Letters in British America*. Chapel Hill and London: University of North Carolina Press, 1997.

——. "The Demonization of the Tavern." In *The Serpent in the Cup: Temperance in American Literature*, ed. David S. Reynolds and Debra J. Rosenthal. Amherst: University of Massachusetts Press, 1997, 10–21.

Shorter, Clement King. *Highways and Byways of Buckinghamshire*. London: Macmillan, 1920.

Shourds, Thomas. *History and Genealogy of Fenwick's Colony*. Bridgeton, NJ: George F. Nixon, 1876.

Shrewsbury, J. F. D. *A History of Bubonic Plague in the British Isles*. Cambridge, UK: Cambridge University Press, 2005.

Simms, J. G. *Jacobite Ireland, 1685–91*. London: Routledge and Kegan Paul, 1969.

Smith, Samuel. *History of the Colony of Nova Caesaria, or New Jersey*. Burlington, 1765.

Smolenski, John. *Friends and Strangers: The Making of a Creole Culture in Colonial Pennsylvania*. Philadelphia: University of Pennsylvania Press, 2010.

Soderlund, Jean. *Quakers and Slavery: A Divided Spirit*. Princeton: Princeton University Press, 1985.

——. *Lenape Country: Delaware Valley Society Before William Penn*. Philadelphia: University of Pennsylvania Press, 2014.

Sowerby, Scott. "William Penn and James II." In *The Worlds of William Penn*, ed. Andrew R. Murphy and John Smolenski. New Brunswick, NJ: Rutgers University Press, 2018.

——. "Of Different Complexions: Religious Diversity and National Identity in James II's Toleration Campaigns." *English Historical Review* 124 (2009): 29–52.

——. "Opposition to Anti-Popery in Restoration England." *Journal of British Studies* 51 (2012): 26–49.

——. *Making Toleration: The Repealers and the Glorious Revolution*. Cambridge, MA: Harvard University Press, 2013.

Spady, James O'Neil. "Colonialism and the Discursive Antecedents of *Penn's Treaty with the Indians*." In *Friends and Enemies in Penn's Woods: Indians, Colonists, and the Racial Construction of Pennsylvania*, ed. William Pencak and Daniel Richter. University Park: Penn State University Press, 2004, 18–40.

Speck, William. *Reluctant Revolutionaries: Englishmen and the Revolution of 1688*. New York: Oxford University Press, 1988.

Speck, W. A. "Spencer, Robert, Second Earl of Sunderland" *Oxford Dictionary of National Biography*.

Spilsbury, William Holden. *Lincoln's Inn, its Ancient and Modern Buildings*. London: William Pickering, 1850.

Spurr, John. "Perjury, Profanity, and Politics." *The Seventeenth Century* 8 (1993): 29–50.

——. *English Puritanism, 1603–1689*. New York: St. Martin's Press, 1998.

——. " 'The Strongest Bond of Conscience': Oaths and the Limits of Tolerance in Early Modern England." In *Contexts of Conscience in Early Modern Europe, 1500–1700*, ed. Harold E. Braun and Edward Vallance. Houndsmills: Palgrave, 2004, 151–165.

Stanwood, Owen. *The Empire Reformed: English America in the Age of the Glorious Revolution.* Philadelphia: University of Pennsylvania Press, 2011.

Stott, Godfrey. "Early History of Chigwell School." *The Essex Review* 62 (1953): 4–13.

Stoughton, John. *William Penn, the Founder of Pennsylvania.* London: Hodder and Stoughton, 1882.

Sugrue, Michael. "The Peopling and Depeopling of Early Pennsylvania: Indians and Colonists, 1680–1720." *Pennsylvania Magazine of History and Biography* 116 (1992): 3–31.

Sutto, Antoinette. "William Penn, Charles Calvert, and the Limits of Royal Authority, 1680–1685." *Pennsylvania History* 76 (2009): 276–300.

——. *Loyal Protestants and Dangerous Papists: Maryland and the Politics of Religion in the English Atlantic, 1630–1690.* Charlottesville and London: University of Virginia Press, 2015.

Swallow, Rev. Canon Richard Dawson. *Chigwell Register, Together with a Historical Account of the School,* ed. O. W. Darch and A. S. Tween. Essex: John W. Phelp, 1907.

Taylor, A. J. "The Royal Visit to Oxford In 1636: A Contemporary Narrative." *Oxoniensa* 1 (1936): 151–158.

Taylor, Alan. *American Colonies: The Settling of North America.* New York: Penguin Books, 2001.

Thornbury, Walter. "The Fleet Prison." In *Old and New London: A Narrative of its History, its People, and its Places.* Vol. 2. London: Cassell, Peter, and Galpin, 1873, 404–416.

Thrush, Andrew. "Elections." In *The History of Parliament: The House of Commons 1604–1629,* ed. Andrew Thrush and John P. Ferris. Cambridge, UK: Cambridge University Press, 2010. Online at: http://www.historyofparliamentonline.org/volume/1604-1629/survey/iv-elections.

Tinniswood, Adrian. *By Permission of Heaven: The Story of the Great Fire of London.* London: Riverhead, 2004.

Tolles, Frederick B. *Meeting House and Counting House: The Quaker Merchants of Colonial Philadelphia, 1682–1763.* Chapel Hill: University of North Carolina Press, 1948.

——. *James Logan and the Culture of Provincial America.* Boston: Little Brown, 1957.

Tolles, Frederick B., and E. Gordon Alderfer. "Introduction." In *The Witness of William Penn,* ed. Frederick B. Tolles and E. Gordon Alderfer. New York: Macmillan, 1957, vii–xxvii.

Tomalin, Claire. *Samuel Pepys: The Unrivalled Self.* London: Penguin, 2002.

Toon, Peter. *God's Statesman: The Life and Work of John Owen.* Grand Rapids, MI: Zondervan, 1973.

Tousley, Nikki Coffey. "Sin, Convincement, Purity, and Perfection." In *The Oxford Handbook of Quaker Studies,* ed. Stephen W. Angell and Pink Dandelion. Oxford: Oxford University Press, 2013, 172–186.

Treese, Lorett. *The Storm Gathering: The Penn Family and the American Revolution.* University Park: Penn State University Press, 1992.

Trueblood, D. Elton. *Robert Barclay.* New York: Harper and Row, 1968.

Tully, Alan. *Forming American Politics: Ideals, Interests, and Institutions in Colonial New York and Pennsylvania.* Baltimore: Johns Hopkins University Press, 1994.

Twelve Good Men and True: The Criminal Jury Trial in England, ed. J. S. Cockburn and Thomas A. Green. Princeton: Princeton University Press, 1988.

Tyacke, Nicholas. "Introduction." In *The History of the University of Oxford. Volume IV: Seventeenth-Century Oxford,* ed. Nicholas Tyacke. Oxford: Clarendon Press, 1997, 1–24.

Vann, Richard T. *The Social Development of English Quakerism 1655–1755.* Cambridge, MA: Harvard University Press, 1969.

——. "Quakerism: Made in America?" In *The World of William Penn,* ed. Richard S. and Mary Maples Dunn. Philadelphia: University of Pennsylvania Press, 1986, 157–171.

Wainwright, Nicholas. "Governor John Blackwell." *Pennsylvania Magazine of History and Biography* 74 (1950): 457–472.

Walker, James. "The English Exiles in Holland During the Reigns of Charles II and James II." *Transactions of the Royal Historical Society,* 4th ser., 30 (1948), 111–125.

Wallis, Amy. "Who Was Colonel Wallis?" *Journal of the Friends' Historical Society* 54 (1976): 12–14.

Wanibuchi, Shuichi. "William Penn's Imperial Landscape." In *The Worlds of William Penn*, ed. Andrew R. Murphy and John Smolenski. New Brunswick, NJ: Rutgers University Press, 2018.

Wax, Darold D. "Quaker Merchants and the Slave Trade in Colonial Pennsylvania." *Pennsylvania Magazine of History and Biography* 86 (1962): 143–160.

Webb, Stephen Saunders. "The Strange Career of Francis Nicholson." *William and Mary Quarterly* 23 (1966): 513–548.

————. "William Blathwayt, Imperial Fixer: From Popish Plot to Glorious Revolution," *William and Mary Quarterly* 25 (1968): 3–21.

————. "William Blathwayt, Imperial Fixer: Muddling Through to Empire, 1689–1717." *William and Mary Quarterly* 26 (1969): 373–415.

Webster, Tom. *Godly Clergy in Stuart England: The Caroline Puritan Movement, c. 1620–1643.* Cambridge, UK: Cambridge University Press, 1997.

Weeks, Stephen B. *Southern Quakers and Slavery: A Study in Institutional History.* Baltimore: Johns Hopkins Press, 1896.

Weimer, Adrian C. "Elizabeth Hooton and the Lived Politics of Toleration in Massachusetts Bay." *William and Mary Quarterly* 74 (2017): 43–76.

Whitehead, William A. *East Jersey under the proprietary governments.* [New York]: New Jersey Historical Society, 1846.

Wilbur, Earl Morse. *A History of Unitarianism.* Cambridge, MA: Harvard University Press, 1946.

Wildes, Harry Emerson. *William Penn.* New York: Macmillan, 1974.

Wilkinson, Richard. *Louis XIV.* London and New York: Routledge, 2017.

Williams, Shelia."The Pope-Burning Processions of 1679, 1680, and 1681." *Journal of the Warburg and Courtald Institutes* 21 (1958): 104–118.

Wootton, David. *The Invention of Science: A New History of the Scientific Revolution.* New York: Harper, 2015.

Worden, Blair. "Oliver Cromwell and the Sin of Achan." In *History, Society, and the Churches: Essays in Honour of Owen Chadwick*, ed. Derek Beales and Geoffrey C. Best. Cambridge, UK: Cambridge University Press, 1985, 124–145.

————. "Cromwellian Oxford." In *The History of the University of Oxford. Volume IV: Seventeenth-Century Oxford*, ed. Nicholas Tyacke. Oxford: Clarendon Press, 1997, 733–772.

The World of William Penn, ed. Richard S. and Mary Maples Dunn. Philadelphia: University of Pennsylvania Press, 1986.

The Worlds of William Penn, ed. Andrew R. Murphy and John Smolenski. New Brunswick: Rutgers University Press, 2018.

Wust, Klaus. "From Carolina to Connecticut: Germans and Swiss in Search of Gold and Silver, 1704–1740." *Report of the Society for the History of the Germans in Maryland* 41 (1990): 43–54.

Zimmerman, Albright G. "Daniel Coxe and the New Mediterranean Sea Company." *Pennsylvania Magazine of History and Biography* 76 (1952): 86–96.

INDEX

Note: Page numbers followed by *m* refer to maps; those followed by n refer to notes, with note number. "pl." numbers refer to plates, located after p. 226.